Research and Development in Intelligent Systems XXIV

Max Bramer Frans Coenen Miltos Petridis
Editors

Research and Development in Intelligent Systems XXIV

Proceedings of AI-2007, the Twenty-seventh SGAI International Conference on Innovative Techniques and Applications of Artificial Intelligence

Max Bramer, BSc, PhD, CEng, CITP, FBCS, FIET, FRSA, FHEA
Faculty of Technology
University of Portsmouth, Portsmouth, UK

Frans Coenen, BSc, PhD
Department of Computer Science,
University of Liverpool, Liverpool, UK

Miltos Petridis, DipEng, MBA, PhD, MBCS, AMBA
University of Greenwich, UK

British Library Cataloguing in Publication Data
A catalogue record for this book is available from the British Library

ISBN 978-1-84800-093-3 e-ISBN 978-1-84800-094-0

Printed on acid-free paper

9 8 7 6 5 4 3 2 1

springer.com

TECHNICAL PROGRAMME CHAIR'S INTRODUCTION

M.A.BRAMER
University of Portsmouth, UK

This volume comprises the refereed technical papers presented at AI-2007, the Twenty-seventh SGAI International Conference on Innovative Techniques and Applications of Artificial Intelligence, held in Cambridge in December 2007. The conference was organised by SGAI, the British Computer Society Specialist Group on Artificial Intelligence.

The papers in this volume present new and innovative developments in the field, divided into sections on Constraint Satisfaction, AI Techniques, Data Mining and Machine Learning, Multi-Agent Systems, Data Mining, and Knowledge Acquisition and Management. The volume also includes the text of short papers presented as posters at the conference.

This year's prize for the best refereed technical paper was won by a paper entitled 'An Evolutionary Algorithm-Based Approach to Robust Analog Circuit Design using Constrained Multi-Objective Optimization' by Giuseppe Nicosia, Salvatore Rinaudo and Eva Sciacca. SGAI gratefully acknowledges the long-term sponsorship of Hewlett-Packard Laboratories (Bristol) for this prize, which goes back to the 1980s.

This is the twenty-fourth volume in the *Research and Development* series. The Application Stream papers are published as a companion volume under the title *Applications and Innovations in Intelligent Systems XV*.

On behalf of the conference organising committee I should like to thank all those who contributed to the organisation of this year's technical programme, in particular the programme committee members, the executive programme committee and our administrators Rachel Browning and Bryony Bramer.

Max Bramer
Technical Programme Chair, AI-2007

ACKNOWLEDGEMENTS

AI-2007 CONFERENCE COMMITTEE

Dr. Miltos Petridis University of Greenwich	(Conference Chair and UK CBR Organiser)
Dr. Alun Preece University of Aberdeen	(Deputy Conference Chair, Electronic Services)
Dr Frans Coenen University of Liverpool	(Deputy Conference Chair, Local Arrangements and Deputy Technical Programme Chair)
Prof. Adrian Hopgood De Montfort University	(Workshop Organiser)
Rosemary Gilligan	(Treasurer)
Dr Nirmalie Wiratunga The Robert Gordon University	(Poster Session Organiser)
Professor Max Bramer University of Portsmouth	(Technical Programme Chair)
Richard Ellis Stratum Management Ltd	(Application Programme Chair)
Dr. Tony Allen Nottingham Trent University	(Deputy Application Program Chair)
Alice Kerly University of Birmingham	(Research Student Liaison)
Dr. Maria Fasli University of Essex	(Research Student Liaison)
Rachel Browning BCS	(Conference Administrator)
Bryony Bramer	(Paper Administrator)

TECHNICAL EXECUTIVE PROGRAMME COMMITTEE

Prof. Max Bramer, University of Portsmouth (Chair)

Dr. Frans Coenen, University of Liverpool (Vice-Chair)

Dr. Peter Lucas, University of Nijmegen, The Netherlands

Dr. Miltos Petridis, University of Greenwich

Dr. Nirmalie Wiratunga, The Robert Gordon University, Aberdeen

TECHNICAL PROGRAMME COMMITTEE

Alia Abdelmoty (Cardiff University)

Andreas A Albrecht (University of Hertfordshire)

Roman Belavkin (Middlesex University)

Yaxin Bi (University of Ulster)

Mirko Boettcher (University of Magdeburg, Germany)

Max Bramer (University of Portsmouth)

Krysia Broda (Imperial College, University of London)

Ken Brown (University College Cork)

Frans Coenen (University of Liverpool)

George Coghill (University of Aberdeen)

Ernesto Compatangelo (University of Aberdeen)

Bruno Cremilleux (University of Caen)

Madalina Croitoru (University of Southampton)

Ireneusz Czarnowski (Gdynia Maritime University, Poland)

Richard Dapoigny (University of Savoie)

Marina De Vos (University of Bath)

John Debenham (University of Technology; Sydney)

Stefan Diaconescu (Softwin)
Belen Diaz-Agudo (University Complutense of Madrid)

Nicolas Durand (Universite Louis Pasteur, France)

Anneli Edman (University of Upsala)

Virginia Francisco (Universidad Complutense de Madrid)

Adriana Giret (Universidad Politécnica de Valencia)

Marco Antonio Gomez-Martin (University Conmplutense of Madrid)

Mark Hall (University of Waikato, New Zealand)

Nadim Haque (BT)

Syed Zahid Hassan (Central Queensland University, Australia)

Joana Hois (University of Bremen)

Arjen Hommersom (University of Nijmegen, The Netherlands)

Adrian Hopgood (De Montfort University)

Piotr Jedrzejowicz (Gdynia Maritime University; Poland)

Rasa Jurgelenaite (Radboud University, The Netherlands)

Konstantinos Kotis (University of the Aegean)

Ivan Koychev (Bulgarian Academy of Science)

[illegible] (University of California, Berkeley)

Peter Lucas (University of Nijmegen)

Daniel Manrique Gamo (University of Madrid)

Raphaël Marée (University of Liege, Belgium)

David McSherry (University of Ulster)

Roberto Micalizio (Università di Torino)

Alfonsas Misevicius (Kaunas University of Technology)

David Moffat (University of Strathclyde)

Lars Nolle (Nottingham Trent University)

Tomas Eric Nordlander (University College Cork)

Dan O'Leary (University of Southern California)

Barry O'Sullivan (University College Cork)

Nir Oren (University of Aberdeen)

Filipo Perotto

Alun Preece (University of Aberdeen)

Juan Jose Rodriguez (University of Burgos)

Maria Dolores Rodriguez-Moreno (Universidad de Alcala)

Fernando Saenz Perez (Universidad Complutense de Madrid)

Miguel A. Salido (Universidad Politécnica de Valencia)

[illegible] (University of Rostock, Germany)

[illegible] (Maastricht University, The Netherlands)

Fatih Tasgetiren (Sultan Qaboos University, Oman)

Simon Thompson (BT)

Jon Timmis (University of York)

[illegible] (Università di Torino)

Andrew Tuson (City University)

M.R.C. van Dongen (University College Cork)

Carl Vogel (Trinity College Dublin, Ireland)

Graham Winstanley (University of Brighton)

Nirmalie Wiratunga (Robert Gordon University)

Fei Ling Woon (SDG Consulting UK)

CONTENTS

TECHNICAL KEYNOTE ADDRESS

BEST TECHNICAL PAPER

CONSTRAINT SATISFACTION

AI TECHNIQUES

DATA MINING AND MACHINE LEARNING

MULTI-AGENT SYSTEMS

DATA MINING

TECHNICAL KEYNOTE ADDRESS

Adventures in Personalized Web Search

Barry Smyth
University College Dublin
Dublin, Ireland

Abstract

Even the most conservative estimates of the Web's current size refer to its billions of documents and daily growth rates that are measured in 10's of terabytes. To put this into perspective, in 2000 the entire World-Wide Web consisted of about 20 terabytes of information, now it grows by more than 3 times this every single day. This growth frames the information overload problem that is threatening to stall the information revolution as users find it increasingly difficult to locate the right information at the right time in the right way. Even today's leading search engine technologies are struggling to cope with the sheer quantity of information that is available, a problem that is greatly exacerbated by the apparent inability of Web users to formulate effective search queries that accurately reflect their information needs. This talk will focus on how so-called personalization techniques – which combine ideas from artificial intelligence, user modeling and user interface design – are being used as a practical response to this information overload problem. We will describe the experiences gained, and lessons learned, when it comes to personalizing Web search in the wild, taking special care to consider the issues that are inherent in any approach to personalization in today's privacy conscious world.

Professor Barry Smyth

Barry Smyth received a B.Sc. in computer science from University College Dublin in 1991 and a Ph.D. from Trinity College Dublin in 1996. He is currently the Head of the School of Computer Science and Informatics at University College Dublin where he holds the Digital Chair in Computer Science. He has published over 250 scientific articles in journals and conferences and has received a number of international awards for his research. His research interests include artificial intelligence, case-based reasoning, information retrieval, and user profiling and personalization. In 1999 he co-founded ChangingWorlds Ltd. to commercialise personalization technologies in the mobile sector. Today ChangingWorlds employs more than 100 people and has deployments in more than 40 mobile operators. Barry continues to serve as the company's Chief Scientist.

BEST TECHNICAL PAPER

An Evolutionary Algorithm-Based Approach to Robust Analog Circuit Design using Constrained Multi-Objective Optimization

Giuseppe Nicosia
Department of Mathematics and Computer Science, University of Catania
Catania, Italy

Salvatore Rinaudo
ST Microelectronics, IMS-CAD and Design Group
Catania, Italia

Eva Sciacca
Department of Mathematics and Computer Science, University of Catania
Catania, Italy

Abstract

The increasing complexity of circuit design needs to be managed with appropriate optimization algorithms and accurate statistical descriptions of design models in order to reach the design specifics, thus guaranteeing "*zero defects*". In the *Design for Yield* open problems are the design of effective optimization algorithms and statistical analysis for yield design, which require time consuming techniques. New methods have to balance accuracy, robustness and computational effort. Typical analog integrated circuit optimization problems are computationally hard and require the handling of *multiple, conflicting, and non-commensurate objectives having strong nonlinear interdependence.* This paper tackles the problem by evolutionary algorithms to produce *tradeoff solutions.* In this research work, Integrated Circuit (IC) design has been formulated as a constrained multi-objective optimization problem defined in a mixed integer/discrete/continuous domain. The *RF Low Noise Amplifier, Leapfrog Filter, and Ultra Wideband LNA* real-life circuits were selected as test beds. The proposed algorithm, A-NSGAII, was shown to produce acceptable and robust solutions in the tested applications, where state-of-art algorithms and circuit designers failed. The results show significant improvement in all the chosen IC design problems.

1 Introduction

During the last decade, advances made in fabrication technology and photolithography have fostered the step *from micro- to nano-electronics* allowing circuits to be produced on an ULSI (Ultra Large Scale Integration) basis. This has greatly increased the complexity of state-of-the-art integrated circuits

(ICs) whose design is even more targeted towards system-on-chip or system-in-package solutions [4]. In this context, the role of CAD techniques for circuit analysis and optimization became essential to obtain solutions that satisfy the requested performance with the minimum time effort (i.e., minimizing the *time-to-market*).

Due to the complexity of state-of-the-art analog circuits, global and local optimization algorithms have to be extensively employed to find *a set of feasible solutions* that satisfies all the *objectives* and the *constraints* required by a given application. Typical objective and constraint functions used in the IC design are area, noise, speed, linearity, or power consumption expressed as a function of the *design parameters* such as transistor sizes, resistor/capacitor values, spiral inductor geometry, etc. Very frequently two or more of these *objectives* are *conflicting*, i.e. improving one objective forces another or others to worsen, thus a *suitable tradeoff* has to be accomplished. Traditional single-objective optimization algorithms provide only one solution (sometimes *a set of candidate solutions*) to such problems, which minimizes/maximizes an overall objective function obtained by mixing individual targets through application of properly weighted mathematical operators. As a consequence, such techniques do not allow *multiple competing goals* to be accounted for explicitly. Moreover they do not give circuit designers the freedom to choose among different, *equally feasible* solutions. A big step forward in this direction can be achieved using a multi-objective approach [7]. This technique allows different objectives to be treated *separately and simultaneously* during the optimization process.

The circuit designer is allowed to choose a solution that privileges one objective (considered as primary) with respect to the others or another one that simply provides an acceptable tradeoff among conflicting goals. Another feature that characterizes IC design is that the objectives and the constraints to be optimized are usually defined in a *discrete domain*. Indeed, as far as design for manufacturability is of concern, each optimization variable is related to the physical dimensions of the components placed in the circuit layout, whose resolution is defined by photolithography. Therefore, optimization techniques that cannot manage *mixed continuous/discrete variables* are of limited (if any) applicability in real-life problems. Based on the above considerations, IC design can, in general, be treated as a constrained multi-objective optimization problem (MOP) defined in a mixed continuous/discrete domain.

The paper is structured as follows: Section 2 describes the *nominal design* and the *design for yield* for the analog IC design; Section 3 formally introduces the adopted multi-objective framework; Section 4 presents the multi-objective evolutionary algorithm, A-NSGAII; Sections 5, 6, and 7 detail the three real-world applications faced *RF Low Noise Amplifier, LeapFrog Filter* and *Ultra WideBand Low Noise Amplifier*. For each circuit, the nominal circuits, the design for yield values and the corresponding Pareto Fronts obtained have been reported and the results are compared with those obtained by state-of-art optimization algorithms and designers' circuits. Concluding remarks are presented in Section 8.

2 Nominal Design versus Design for Yield

Analog IC design is a rather complex task that involves two important steps: 1) the definition of a *circuit topology* and 2) *circuit sizing.* The first step requires deep knowledge of microelectronics and *good design experience* because it is essential to verify the overall feasibility of the circuit. The analyses carried out in this step allow the designer to discard solutions that cannot be employed for a given application due to structural incompatibility. The second step consists in defining a set of optimal circuit parameters with the aim to push the performance of the selected topology until all the specifications are met. Iterations might be necessary if the outcome of the second step (*circuit sizing*) does not confirm the feasibility analysis carried out in the first one (*topology definition*). Two types of specifications have to be met in the step of circuit sizing: *1) performance*, i.e., fulfilment of the specifications imposed by a given application, and *2) robustness*, i.e., insensitiveness to parametric and environmental variations. To simplify the design, these two specifications are commonly treated separately. Therefore, the performance is first assessed under the hypotheses that no parametric or environmental variations take place. This task is commonly referred to as *nominal design* because such hypotheses define the so-called nominal (i.e., ideal) operating condition. Nominal design represents a first verification of the feasibility analysis carried out during the topology definition: an unsuccessful outcome mandates circuit topology to be reviewed.

The so-called *nominal operating conditions* are defined a priori and depend on the application for which the IC is being designed. Most commonly they include given values of supply voltage and ambient temperature, and the typical (i.e., mean) fabrication process setup. In these conditions, the nominal design basically consists of determining a set of component parameters (i.e., transistors width and length, resistor or capacitor values, inductor geometry, etc.) of a given circuit topology that satisfy all specifications. If nominal design is successful, then circuit robustness is assessed by verifying that all specifications are satisfied even when *parametric and environmental variations* take place. This is extremely important to ensure that the performance of the IC is still acceptable once it has undergone the fabrication process and it is put in operation in a real-world (as opposed to ideal) environment. This task is referred to as design for robustness or, more commonly, *design for yield.*

The term *yield* in the framework of the microelectronics industry denotes the ratio between the number of chips that have acceptable performance over those that have been manufactured. There are two classes of causes by which the performance of a circuit can be classified as unacceptable: *1) local perturbation* (silicon crystal defects that cause the malfunctioning of a single chip in a wafer) and *2) global perturbations* (process imprecision like mask misalignment, temperature and/or implantation dose variations involving all the chips in a wafer). Since there is a direct correlation between the yield and the production level, yield maximization is a strategic objective of the microelectronics industry [5].

3 IC Design as a Constrained MOP

The research work is motivated by the observation that most circuit design problems involve *multiple, conflicting, and non-commensurate objectives*; hence, it is necessary to use proper algorithms to optimise multiple conflicting objectives while satisfying several constraints. While both integer and discrete variables have a discrete nature, only discrete variables can assume floating-point values (they are often unevenly spaced, by a *step variable*, a designer defined parameter). In general, variables are commonly defined in *a mixed integer discrete continuous domain.* IC design can be defined as a constrained multi-objective optimization problem defined in a mixed integer/discrete/continuous domain. A Multi-objective Optimization Problem (MOP) can be formally defined as follows:

Definition 1 *Find a vector* $\vec{x}^* = [x_1^*, x_2^*, \ldots, x_n^*]^T = [X^{(I)}, X^{(D)}, X^{(C)}]^T$ *which satisfies the variable bounds:*

$$x_i^{(L)} \leq x_i \leq x_i^{(U)} \quad i = 1, 2, \ldots, n \tag{1}$$

satisfies the p equality constraints:

$$h_i(\vec{x}) = 0 \quad i = 1, 2, \ldots, p \tag{2}$$

is subject to the m inequality constraints:

$$g_i(\vec{x}) \geq 0 \quad i = 1, 2, \ldots, m \tag{3}$$

and optimizes the vector function

$$\vec{f}(\vec{x}) = [f_1(\vec{x}), f_2(\vec{x}), \ldots, f_k(\vec{x})]^T \tag{4}$$

where $X^{(I)}, X^{(D)}, X^{(C)}$ *denote feasible subsets of Integer, Discrete and Continuous variables respectively.*

Equations (1), (2) and (3) define the *feasible region*

$$\begin{aligned} \Omega = \{\vec{x} \in \Re^n : x_i^{(L)} \leq x_i \leq x_i^{(U)} \quad & i = 1, 2, \ldots, n; \\ g_i(\vec{x}) \geq 0 \quad & i = 1, 2, \ldots, m; \\ h_i(\vec{x}) = 0 \quad & i = 1, 2, \ldots, p\} \end{aligned} \tag{5}$$

and any point $\vec{x} \in \Omega$ defines a *feasible solution.* The vector function $\vec{f}(\vec{x})$ maps the elements of Ω into a set Λ which represents all possible values of the objective functions:

$$\Lambda = \{\vec{f}(\vec{x}) \in \Re^k : \vec{x} \in \Omega\} \tag{6}$$

The evaluation function of the MOP $f : \Omega \rightarrow \Lambda$, maps decision variables $\vec{x} = (x_1, x_2, \ldots, x_n)$ to vectors $\vec{y} = (y_1, y_2, \ldots, y_k)$.

Definition 2 *A point $\vec{x}^* \in \Omega$ is Pareto optimal if for every $\vec{x} \in \Omega$ and $I = \{1, 2, \dots, k\}$ either,*

$$\forall_{i \in I}(f_i(\vec{x}) = f_i(\vec{x}^*)) \tag{7}$$

or there is at least one $i \in I$ such that

$$f_i(\vec{x}) \geq f_i(\vec{x}^*) \tag{8}$$

A vector $\vec{u} = (u_1, \dots, u_k)$ is said to dominate $\vec{v} = (v_1, \dots, v_k)$, denoted by $\vec{u} \preceq \vec{v}$ if and only if $\vec{u}$ is partially less than $\vec{v}$, i.e., for all $i \in \{1, \dots, k\}$, $u_i \leq v_i \wedge \exists i \in \{1, \dots, k\} : u_i < v_i$. If the vector $\vec{u}$ dominates the vector $\vec{v}$, or mathematically $\vec{u} \preceq \vec{v}$, we also say that $\vec{v}$ is dominated by $\vec{u}$, or $\vec{u}$ is non-dominated by $\vec{v}$.

Definition 3 *For a given MOP $\vec{f}(\vec{x})$, the Pareto optimal set, $\mathcal{P}^*$, is defined as:*

$$\mathcal{P}^* = \{\vec{x} \in \Omega : \neg\exists \vec{x}' \in \Omega \quad \vec{f}(\vec{x}') \preceq \vec{f}(\vec{x})\}. \tag{9}$$

x^* is Pareto optimal if there exists no feasible point x which would decrease some criterion without causing a *simultaneous* increase in at least one other criterion. The notion of *optimum* is changed, we are using the *Edgeworth-Pareto Optimum* notion [6]: the aim is to find good compromises (or trade-offs) rather than a single solution as in global optimization. A Pareto optimal set that truly meets this definition is called a true Pareto optimal set, $\mathcal{P}^*_{true}$. In contrast, a Pareto optimal set that is obtained by means of an optimization method is referred to as an *observed Pareto optimal set*, $\mathcal{P}^*_{obs}$. In reality, an observed Pareto optimal set is an *estimate* of a true Pareto optimal set. Identifying a good estimate $\mathcal{P}^*_{obs}$ is the key factor for the decision maker's selection of a compromise solution, which satisfies the objectives as much as possible. We denote the observed Pareto optimal set at time step t obtained using an optimization method by $\mathcal{P}^{*,t}_{obs}$ (or the current observed Pareto optimal set). Moreover, we have $\mathcal{P}^{*,t}_{obs} = \{\vec{x}^t_1, \dots, \vec{x}^t_\ell\}$ where $\ell = \mid \mathcal{P}^{*,t}_{obs} \mid$ is the total number of observed Pareto solutions at time step t. Obviously, the major problem a decision maker needs to solve, is to find "the best" $\vec{x} \in \mathcal{P}^*_{obs}$.

Definition 4 *For a given MOP $\vec{f}(\vec{x})$ and Pareto optimal set $\mathcal{P}^*$, the Pareto front, $\mathcal{PF}^*$, is defined as:*

$$\mathcal{PF}^* = \{\vec{u} = \vec{f} = (f_1(\vec{x}), \dots, f_k(\vec{x})) \mid \vec{x} \in \mathcal{P}^*\} \tag{10}$$

As for the Pareto optimal set, we can define the *observed Pareto front* [7] at time step t by an optimization method: $\mathcal{PF}^{*,t}_{obs} = \{\vec{u}^t_1, \vec{u}^t_2, \dots, \vec{u}^t_N\}$ where $N = \mid \mathcal{PF}^{*,t}_{obs} \mid$ is the total number of observed Pareto front solutions at time step t. Identifying a good estimate of $\mathcal{PF}^{*,t}_{obs}$ is crucial for the decision maker's selection of a good IC in terms of nominal design and yield value.

Summarizing, for a MOP we can define the following procedures: find the optimal (or the observed) Pareto front; and choose one of the candidate solutions in the Pareto front, using some higher-level information (for instance yield in IC design). In this research work we adopt a simple selection criterion: our selection procedure chooses the non-dominated solution closest to the *ideal point* (for each of the k objectives, there exists one different optimal solution; an objective vector constructed with these individual optimal objective values constitutes the ideal objective vector).

4 The Algorithm

Evolutionary Algorithms (EAs) are a class of stochastic optimization methods that simulate the process of natural evolution [7]. EAs can be defined as *population-based stochastic generate-and-test algorithms.* They operate on a set of candidate solutions, which is subsequently modified by the two basic principles: *selection* and *variation.* While selection mimics the competition for resources among living beings, variation imitates the natural capability of creating new living beings by means of recombination and mutation. Although the underlying mechanisms are simple, these algorithms have proven to be general, robust and powerful search tools [7]. Such approaches do not guarantee that optimal solutions are identified, but try to find a good approximation of suboptimal or optimal solutions. Classical optimization methods use a point-to-point approach, where one solution in each iteration is modified to a different (hopefully better) solution. The outcome is a single optimized solution in a single simulation run. One of the most striking differences to classical optimization algorithms is that EAs, use a *population of candidate solutions* in each iteration instead of a single solution and the outcome is also a population of solutions. An EA can be used to capture multiple optimal solutions in its final population. In evolutionary computing there is *no restriction on the objective function(s)* that can be used.They can be non-differentiable or even discontinuous, there is no need to know the exact form of the objective function and simulations (*runs*) can be used to derive a fitness value. The initial population does not necessarily have to be generated *randomly* but it can also be initialised *ad-hoc* (for instance the designer's circuit). Candidate solutions may be represented by using various codings (binary, integer, real, mixed, etc.). In this paper, a well-known evolutionary algorithm, NSGAII, is used. NSGAII [7] is an elitist evolutionary algorithm with a fast non-dominated sorting procedure and a density estimation of the solutions provided by the crowding distance. In order to tackle the integer/discrete/continuous variables, we designed and implemented a modified version of NSGAII, ADVANCED NSGAII (A-NSGAII). Different kind of mutations could be used, in particular *convex mutation, self-adaptive mutation, Gaussian mutation* and *hybrid Gaussian mutation* [8]. They differ in the procedure used to obtain the mutated value. In detail:

- Self-adaptive mutation is computed by $x_i^{new} = x_i + \sigma_i * N(0,1)$; where $\sigma_i' = \sigma_i * exp((\tau * N(0,1)) + (\tau' * N_i(0,1))$ with $\tau = (\sqrt{2\sqrt{n}})^{-1}$, $\tau' = 1/\sqrt{2n}$, and $\sigma_i^{(t=0)} = ((U_B - L_B)/\sqrt{n}) \times 0.4$
- Hybrid Gaussian Mutation acts according to the following equation:

$x_i^{new} = x_i + \sigma * N(0,1);$

$$\sigma = \begin{cases} \beta * |x_i - x_j|, & x_i \neq x_j, \quad \text{if } x_i * x_j > 0 \\ \beta * |x_i + x_j|, & x_i \neq x_j, \quad \text{if } x_i * x_j < 0 \end{cases}$$

where $\beta \in [0.5, 1.5]$ is a random number obtained with uniform distribution.

- The Gaussian mutation operator instead applies the following equation: $x_i^{new} = x_i + \alpha * N(0,1)$; where $\alpha = (\frac{1}{\beta})e^{(-f)}$ is the mutation potential.

Finally, A-NSGAII uses constrained tournament selection to deal with *unfeasible solutions* during the optimization process. One difficult matter in constrained optimization problems is finding a feasible set. In the first steps it could represent a true challenge. One of the possible reasons is that feasible regions could be a very small subset of the search space. This method uses binary tournament selection, that is, two individuals of the population are chosen and compared and the fittest is copied in the following population. When a problem presents constraints, two solutions can be feasible or unfeasible. Just one of the following cases is possible: (i) both are feasible; (ii) one solution is feasible and the other is not; (iii) both are unfeasible. Case (i) is solved using a dominance relation that takes into account the constraint violation. In case (ii) only the feasible solution is chosen and in case (iii) a penalty function is used (see definition of Ω below). Let $g_j(\mathbf{x}) \geq 0, j = 1 \ldots m$ be the constraints of the normalized problem. The constraints violation is defined as follows:

$$\omega_j = \begin{cases} |g_j(\mathbf{x})|, & \text{if } g_j(\mathbf{x}) < 0; \\ 0, & \text{otherwise.} \end{cases} \tag{11}$$

The overall violation Ω is defined as: $\Omega = \sum_{j=1}^{m} \omega_j(\mathbf{x})$ A solution $\mathbf{x}_i$ is said to "*constrain dominate*" a solution $\mathbf{x}_j$ if one of these conditions is true: (1) Solution $\mathbf{x}_i$ is feasible and $\mathbf{x}_j$ is not. (2) Solutions $\mathbf{x}_i$ and $\mathbf{x}_j$ are infeasible but $\mathbf{x}_i$ has a lesser Ω value. (3) Solutions $\mathbf{x}_i$ and $\mathbf{x}_j$ are both feasible, but $\mathbf{x}_i$ dominates $\mathbf{x}_j$. In constrained tournament selection, the individual having a lower Ω value wins the tournament.

Finally, the optimization process ends when a maximum number of runs is reached or the information gain reaches a final steady state [2].

5 Radio Frequency Low Noise Amplifier

The RF Low Noise Amplifier (LNA) is one of the most critical building blocks in modern integrated radio frequency (RF) transceivers. It is integrated into the receiving chain and is either directly connected to the antenna or placed after the RF pass-band filter [3]. It must enhance input signal levels at gigahertz frequencies whilst preserving the signal-to-noise ratio. Moreover, low DC current consumption is mandatory in all portable hand-held application to

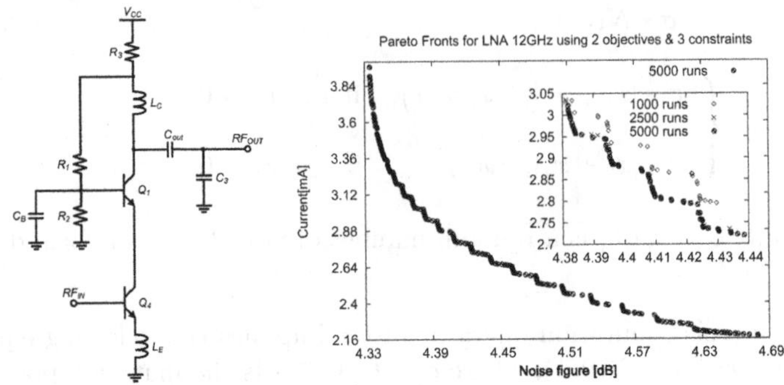

Figure 1: Left plot: Circuit schematic of the RF LNA. Right plot: Pareto Front obtained by A-NSGAII for RF LNA.

allow for long battery life. Other critical performance parameters of LNAs are gain and impedance matching. The circuit schematic of the RF LNA under investigation is shown in Fig. 1 (left plot). It is based on a cascode configuration with integrated emitter degeneration inductor. The cascode topology provides excellent frequency stability at high gain and high isolation between input and output terminals. Moreover, it eliminates Miller amplification of the base collector capacitance making input and output matching almost independent of each other. These advantages are obtained at the cost of negligible drawbacks in comparison with the common-emitter configuration, such as lower output swing and a slight increase in noise figure. The Pareto Front of the RF LNA (obtained after 5000 runs) is sketched in Fig. 1 (right plot). It displays the "*zig-zag*" behaviour that characterizes optimization problems defined in a discrete domain. The algorithm is able to find 664 *distinct non-dominated solutions* that are well distributed and *cover* almost all the trade-off curve. The number, distribution, and coverage of solutions found are all important parameters to assess an algorithm's performance when it is employed in IC design problems. Indeed, they can demonstrate its exploratory capabilities leaving few doubts about the possibility of pushing the performance of the circuit furthermore. The inset plot of Fig. 1 (right plot) shows a zoom of the central part of the Pareto Front where solutions found after 1000 and 2500 runs are also reported. It demonstrates that reducing the computational load by a large amount (up to 5) does not degrade algorithm's performance so much. Indeed, the Pareto Front found after 1000 and 2500 runs still exhibits very good algorithm performance since it includes solutions that differ only slightly from those belonging to the "final" one.

The *nominal performance* of six notable solutions are reported in table 1 together with that of the designer (achieved through "*manual*" sizing). Corresponding values of yield (computed from Montecarlo simulations with 200 samples in the mismatch-only mode), obtained from Montecarlo simulations,

Table 1: Multi-Objective Optimization of RF LNA using 5 objectives with A-NSGAII.

Variable	Min NF	Min I_C	Min S_{11}	Max S_{21}	Min S_{22}	Opt. Nom.	Designer
$Area_1$	2	1	3	1	1	2	2
$Area_4$	3	3	3	3	3	3	3
C_3 (fF)	320	400	440	460	450	400	350
C_{out} (fF)	170	240	150	200	200	170	190
R_1 (Ω)	4k	8.5k	7.3k	5.4k	6.8k	8.2k	6k
R_3 (Ω)	30	80	200	70	10	80	400
V_{BE} (mV)	884	864	887	886	867	877	885
Performance Function							
$\mid S_{11} \mid < -14$ dB	-16.337	-14.884	-19.852	-14.855	-14.603	-16.673	-17.40
$\mid S_{21} \mid > 8$ dB	9.736	8.526	8.378	10.936	8.753	9.402	9.30
$\mid S_{22} \mid < -6$ dB	-21.074	-8.216	-7.374	-21.933	-44.297	-28.223	-10.99
NF < 4.7 dB	4.334	4.670	4.456	4.562	4.606	4.377	4.46
$I_C < 4$ mA	3.985	2.193	3.907	3.981	2.460	3.076	3.70
Yield	64.5%	68%	85.5%	70%	94%	**100%**	99.5%

are also reported. As expected, solutions found (in particular, the optimal nominal solution) using the multi-objective optimization approach *dominate the designer's one* (i.e., the current or noise "nominal" performance is better). However, solutions with minimum noise or minimum current (placed at the edge of the Pareto Front of Fig. 1 (right plot) and thus farthest away from the "ideal" point), exhibit lower values of yield. In fact, statistical fluctuations around the nominal point cause either the current or noise performance to jump out of the feasible set, making the whole circuit faulty. On the other hand, the point selected according to the "optimality" criterion (i.e., placed closest to the "ideal" solution) performs 100% yield (see table 1). In the Pareto Front region closest to the "ideal" point there is a good probability of finding high-yielding circuits before design centering process.

6 LeapFrog Filter

Analog front-end filters are essential components in many electronic equipments ranging from communication systems to medical instruments to signal processors and so on. They provide a narrow pass-band to the signal and attenuate unwanted noise in the stop-band [1]. Fabrication of analog filters in state-of-the-art VLSI technology allows both passive and active components to be integrated in the same silicon die. Although there is a great advantage from the economic point of view, it generally requires wise design because integrated components suffer from higher process tolerances than their discrete counterpart. This feature elects integrated analog filters as excellent candidates to benchmark the performance of circuit optimization tools when yield maximization is of concern. The circuit block employed as test case, i.e. a

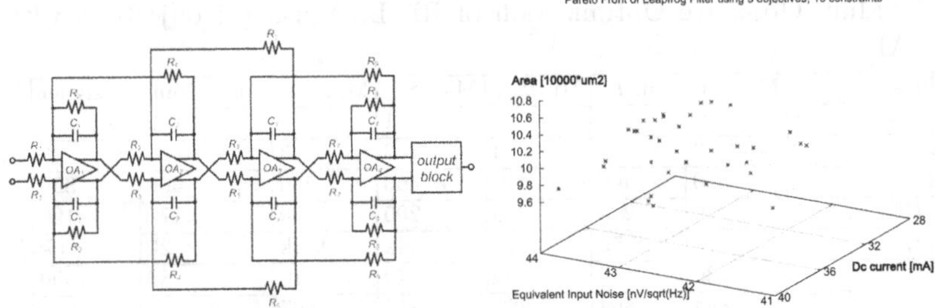

Figure 2: Left Plot: Circuit schematic of the Leapfrog Filter. Right Plot: Pareto Front observed of Leapfrog Filter using 3 objectives and 13 constrains after 30000 runs.

fifth-order leapfrog filter, is depicted in Fig. 2 (left plot). Four leapfrog loops are realized through 4 (equal) differential opamps (OA1-OA4), 18 resistances (two times R1-R9), and 8 capacitances (two times C1-C4). Differential-to-single conversion is performed by the output block, which also implements an additional time constant via a real pole. The filter design was accomplished in two steps: 1) opamps AO1-AO4 were first designed at the transistor level; 2) the passive network of the filter was then optimized using a behavioural model of the opamps. Resistance and capacitance values are calculated on the basis of other quantities that will be treated as input variables of the optimization problem. Expressions relating the resistance and the capacitance values to these quantities are quite complex and will not be reported in the following. The 20 variables used as input of the optimization problem are: k1, k2, k3, k4, m1, m2, m3, m4, Vn1, Vn2, Vn3, Vn4, w0, wrp, Ra, C, C1, L2, C3, L4. The first 4 parameters (k1-k4) influence the output dynamic of each operational amplifier, m1-m4 allow the scaling of the resistances and capacitances leaving the leapfrog time constants unchanged; Vn1-Vn4 impose the equivalent input noise of each operational amplifier; w0 provides a frequency shift of the filter transfer function; wrp is the frequency of the real pole in the output block; Ra through to L4 determine the filter time constants. The set of objective functions and related constraints employed in the formulation of the optimization problem are reported in table 2. Dc gain, pass-band ripples and stop-bands are directly related to the frequency mask of the filter, whereas the network delay is assessed using the group delay (ripple and slope). Other performance metrics are: low-frequency input resistance; output dynamic of each opamp; equivalent input noise, to which both active and passive components contribute; dc current consumption, related to the equivalent opamp input noise in the behavioural model; silicon area. The optimization results obtained by using A-NSGAII are summarized in Table 2, where a comparison with three state-of-the-art deterministic algorithms (Powel's algorithm NEWUOA [12], DIRECT [11], A-CRS [9]) is also reported. None of the investigated algo-

Table 2: LeapFrog Filter results: comparisons among **NEWUOA**[12], **DIRECT**[11], **A-CRS** [9], Designer, and **A-NSGAII**.

Goals	Bounds	newUOA	DIRECT	A-CRS	Designer	A-NSGAII
DC gain	≥ -0.01 dB	-0.003	-0.003	-0.0026	-0.003	-0.0025
Pb ripple 9.1MHz	$\leq 0.8\ dB_{PP}$	**0.95**	**0.86**	**0.85**	**0.806**	0.55
Pb ripple 9.7MHz	$\leq 1.8\ dB_{PP}$	0.97	1.33	1.07	0.97	0.55
Sb 22.5MHz	$\geq 25\ dB_C$	26.60	36.56	31.86	36.64	36.84
Sb 34.2MHz	$\geq 56\ dB_C$	**46.11**	**55.08**	**51.64**	**55.92**	56.23
Gd ripple 9.1MHz	≤ 20 ns	**24.52**	20.7	14.80	19.28	16.17
Gd ripple 9.7MHz	≤ 40 ns	30.55	39.6	16.50	26.36	24.18
Gd slope 6.0MHz	≤ 3 fs/Hz	2.63	1.28	**3.23**	2.10	2.36
Eq. in. resistance	$\geq 12.2\ k\Omega$	**11.82** k	31.54 k	13.42k	**12.18** k	12.24 k
Out. dynamic 1	≤ 2.8 V	**2.88**	2.23	2.72	**2.83**	2.76
Out. dynamic 2	≤ 2.8 V	2.68	1.36	2.20	2.22	2.43
Out. dynamic 3	≤ 2.8 V	**3.17**	2.60	**3.01**	1.71	2.70
Out. dynamic 4	≤ 2.8 V	2.13	1.32	1.43	1.53	1.73
Eq. in. noise	$\leq 44\ nV/Hz^{\frac{1}{2}}$	**47.73**	**139**	**47.41**	**46.44**	42.14
Dc current cons.	$\leq 40mA$	**40.64**	30	**42.17**	39.58	34.47
Silicon area	$\leq 18000\mu m^2$	15964	**29500**	14457	14037	14622
Global Error		85.95%	289.1%	43.9%	7.8%	0
Yield		n.a.	n.a.	n.a.	n.a.	69.5%

rithms is able to find feasible solutions, moreover the best solutions found by such algorithms violate more than one constraint. The *DIRECT* algorithm exhibits the worst performance with huge errors on the equivalent input noise and silicon area. The *NEWUOA* violates 8 out of 16 constraints (in boldface) with moderate errors in each one. The A-CRS performs better than any other investigated algorithm on this test bed, however its best solution is very far from being acceptable because it does not satisfy 6 constraints. It is interesting to note that in most cases such algorithms encountered difficulties in satisfying performance metrics that also have given problems to the designer. Another interpretation is that they are not able to perform better than the designer due to their limited exploration capabilities. On the other hand, A-NSGAII finds feasible solutions also providing a considerable amount of over-achievement in most performance metrics producing high yield values. To further consolidate this concept, Fig. 2 (right plot) shows the Pareto Front of the leapfrog filter obtained after 30000 runs using A-NSGAII. Among the feasible solutions, the algorithm provides 36 non dominated points. Moreover, the degree of coverage and distribution across the objective space is satisfactory.

7 Ultra WideBand Low Noise Amplifier

Ultra wideband (UWB) signalling [14] is the modern art of reusing previously allocated RF bands by hiding signals under the noise floor. UWB systems transmit signals across a much wider frequency than conventional narrowband

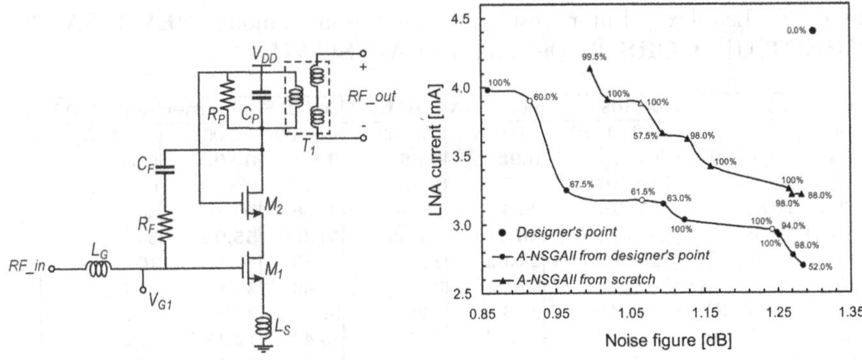

Figure 3: Left Plot: Ultra Wideband Low Noise Amplifier Schematic. Right Plot: Pareto Fronts obtained A-NSGAII. For A-NSGAII the empty triangle and empty circle are *sub-threshold circuits.*

systems do, moreover they are usually very difficult to detect. Government regulators are testing UWB emissions to ensure that adequate protection exists to current users of the communications bands. The amount of spectrum occupied by an UWB signal, i.e. the bandwidth of the UWB signal, is at least 25% of the centre frequency. Thus, an UWB signal centred at 4 GHz would have a minimum bandwidth of 1 GHz. The most common technique for generating an UWB signal is to transmit pulses with durations of less than 1 nanosecond. Recently, the interest in UWB systems for wireless personal area network applications has increased significantly. Due to the extremely low emission levels currently allowed by regulatory agencies, UWB systems tend to be short-range and indoor. The schematic of an UWB Low Noise Amplifier [15] is shown in Fig. 3 (left plot). The UWB LNA adopts a single cascode topology, which allows high input/output isolation to be achieved. The design should be carried out to achieve wideband input matching together with good noise performance. The LS and LG inductors perform the UWB LNA input matching as in the classical narrow-band design, while CF and RF implement an ac resistive feedback to broaden the input matching bandwidth. The value of RF should be chosen as a compromise between the input bandwidth widening and the amount of noise added by the resistor. An RLC shunt resonator represents the load of the LNA. The capacitor CP and the primary winding of the load transformer T1 should be designed to resonate at the frequency of 4 GHz, while the shunt resistance RP was inserted to lower the quality factor of the resonator. Such a shunted resonant load allows an adequate gain spectral flatness to be achieved.

Power consumption is a crucial performance parameter in many fields of electronic design. Indeed, it determines battery life in portable applications such as *mobile phones* or contributes to thermal heating in *VLSI circuits* such as *memories* and *microprocessors*. For these reasons, several efforts have been undertaken to minimize power dissipations in both analog and digital ICs. The *Sub-threshold* operation of MOS transistors has demonstrated to be an effective way to accomplish this task without degrading circuit performance. Besides this, the trend toward sub-threshold operation of MOS transistors has been motivated by the need for reducing the supply voltage in deeply scaled CMOS technologies. In fact, the threshold voltage of nanometre CMOS does not scale down at the same rate as the supply voltage does, moreover it does not scale at all in some cases. The resulting smaller voltage headroom renders the task of IC design even more challenging and makes the sub-threshold operation of MOS devices necessary. The benefits achievable by sub-threshold operations are paid at the price of much higher sensitivity of ICs to variations in supply voltage, temperature and in the fabrication process. This in turn contributes to lower circuit robustness because large deviations from nominal operating conditions are more likely to take place. Therefore, robust design approaches such that described in this paper become essential to avoid faulty operations of MOS-based ICs pushed into the sub-threshold region. Figure 3 (right plot) shows the Pareto Fronts obtained by A-NSGAII. Empty triangles and empty circles indicate the subthreshold circuits discovered by A-NSGAII.

8 Conclusions

The present research work is motivated by the observation that most circuit design problems involve multiple, conflicting, and non-commensurate objectives and several constraints. We formulated IC design as a constrained multi-objective optimization problem defined in a mixed integer/discrete/continuous domain. To face this problem an optimization algorithm, A-NSGAII, for analog circuit sizing has been presented. The proposed algorithm, A-NSGAII, was shown to produce acceptable solutions for RF Low Noise Amplifier, Leapfrog Filter, and Ultra WideBand Low Noise Amplifier where state-of-art techniques and circuit designers failed. The results show significant improvements in both the chosen IC design problems in terms of nominal design and yield values. Furthermore, the results also show that the sizing of robust analog circuits can be achieved at lower computational effort than that required by traditional optimization algorithms minimizing the time-to-market.

Acknowledgment

This research was founded by P.O.N. - Italian Project on "Multi-objective Optimization for the Integrated Circuit Design". The authors would like to express their gratitude to Angelo Marcello Anile, Tonio Biondi, and Santo D'Antona.

References

[1] M. Burns, G. W. Roberts, "**An Introduction to Mixed-Signal IC Test and Measurement**," Oxford University Press, 2001.

[2] V. Cutello, G. Nicosia, M. Pavone, "A hybrid Immune Algorithm with Information Gain for the Graph Coloring Problem," Proc. GECCO'03, LNCS 2723, pp.171-182, 2003.

[3] B. Razavi, "**RF Microelectronics**," Prentice Hall Inc., 1998

[4] P. Magarshack, P.G. Paulin, "System-on-Chip Beyond the Nanometer Wall," 40th DAC, pp. 419-424, 2003.

[5] F. Schenkel, *et al.*, "Mismatch Analysis and Direct Yield Optimization by Spec-Wise Linearization and Feasibility Guided Search," 38th DAC, pp. 858-863, 2001.

[6] W. Stadler, "Fundamentals of multicriteria optimization". In Stadler ed., "**Multicriteria Optimization in Engineering and the Sciences**," pp 1-25, Plenum Press, NY, 1988.

[7] K. Deb, "**Multi-Objective Optimization Using Evolutionary Algorithms**," Wiley, 2001.

[8] V. Cutello, G. Morelli, G. Nicosia, M. Pavone, "Immune Algorithms with Aging Operators for the String Folding Problem and the Protein Folding Problem," Proc. EvoCop'05, LNCS 3448, pp. 80-90, 2005.

[9] L. Cirio, S. Lucidi, F. Parasiliti, M. Villani, "A global optimization approach for the synchronous motors design by finite element analysis," **Int. J. of Applied Electromagnetics and Mechanics**, 16:13-27, 2002.

[10] V. Cutello, G. Narzisi, G. Nicosia, M. Pavone, "Real Coded Clonal Selection Algorithm for Global Numerical Optimization using a new Inversely Proportional Hypermutation Operator," 21st ACM SAC, pp. 950-954, 2006.

[11] J. M. Gablonsky, C. T. Kelley, "A locally-biased form of the DIRECT Algorithm," **J. of Global Optimization**, 21:27-37, 2001.

[12] M.J.D. Powell, "The NEWUOA software for unconstrained optimization without derivatives,", in **Large-Scale Nonlinear Optimization**, eds. G. Di Pillo & M. Roma, Springer (NY), pp. 255-297, 2006.

[13] G. Girlando *et al.*, "Silicon Bipolar LNAs in the X and Ku Bands," **Analog Integrated Circuits and Signal Processing**, 41:119-127, 2004.

[14] B.H. Calhoun, *et al.*, "*Static Noise Margin Variation for Sub-threshold SRAM in 65-nm CMOS*," **IEEE J. of Solid-State Cir.**, 41:1673-1679, 2006.

[15] J. Rabaey, *et al.*, "Ultra-Low-Power Design," **IEEE Circuits and Devices Magazine**, 22(4):23-29, 2006.

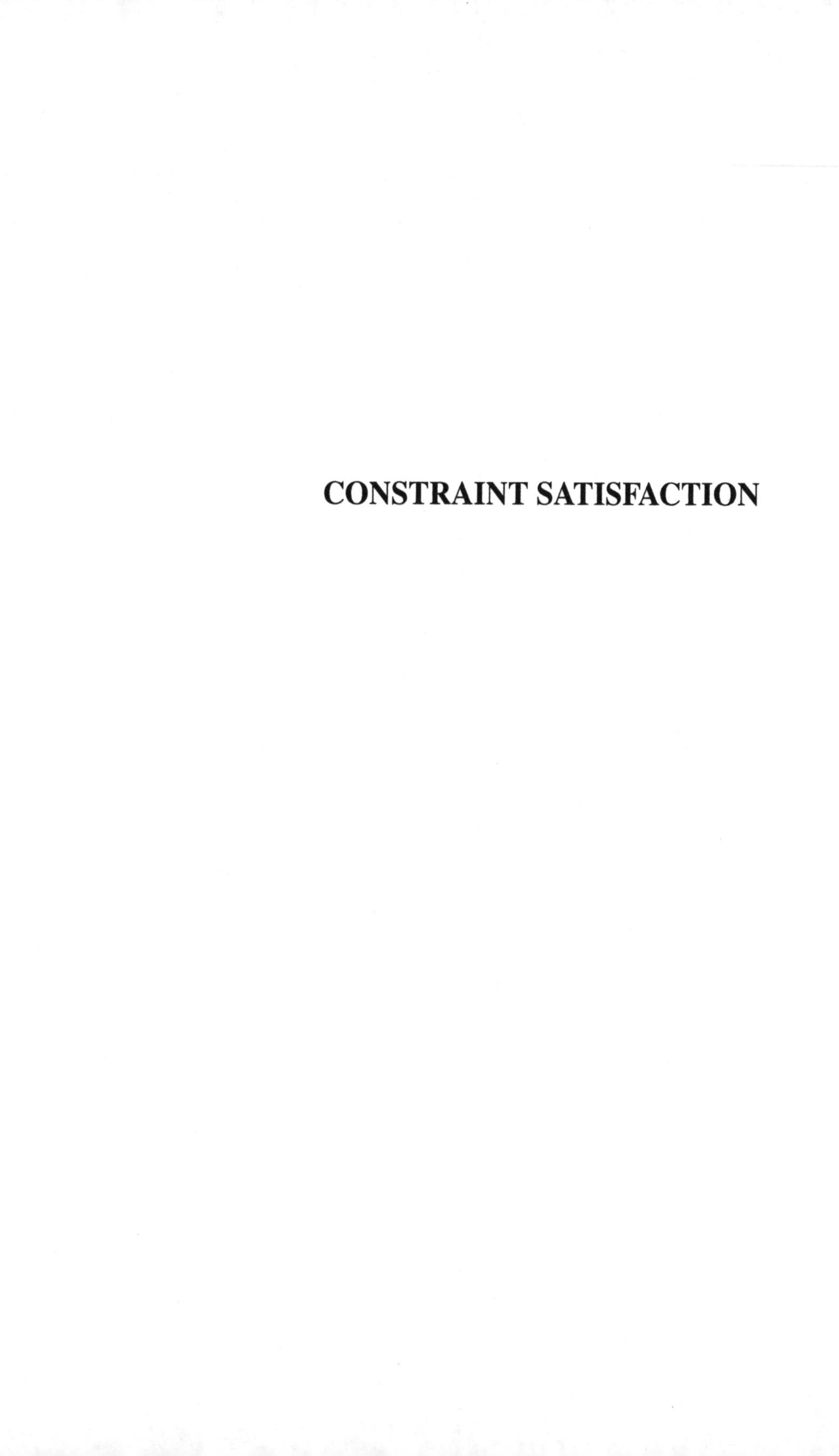

CONSTRAINT SATISFACTION

DisBO-wd: a Distributed Constraint Satisfaction Algorithm for Coarse-Grained Distributed Problems

Muhammed Basharu[1], Inés Arana[2], and Hatem Ahriz[2]

[1] 4C, University College
Cork, Ireland
[2] School of Computing
The Robert Gordon University
Aberdeen, UK
mb@4c.ucc.ie, {ia,ha}@comp.rgu.ac.uk

Abstract. We present a distributed iterative improvement algorithm for solving coarse-grained distributed constraint satisfaction problems (DisCSPs). Our algorithm is inspired by the Distributed Breakout for coarse-grained DisCSPs where we introduce a constraint weight decay and a constraint weight learning mechanism in order to escape local optima. We also introduce some randomisation in order to give the search a better chance of finding the right path to a solution. We show that these mechanisms improve the performance of the algorithm considerably and make it competitive with respect to other algorithms.

1 Introduction

The recent growth of distributed computing has created more opportunities for collaboration between agents (individuals, organisations and computer programs) where there is a shared objective but, at the same time, there is also a competition for resources. Hence, participants make compromises in order to reach agreement - a process which can be automated if the situation is modelled as a Distributed Constraint Satisfaction Problem (DisCSP) [12]. DisCSPs formally describe distributed problems where each participant in the problem is represented by an agent, and the collection of agents have to collaborate in order to reach a satisfactory agreement (or find a solution) for a problem. Research in this emerging field includes problem solving techniques which are classified as constructive search or iterative improvement search. Iterative improvement search is normally able to converge quicker than constructive search on large problems, but it has a propensity to converge to local optima. Previous work on iterative improvement search has considered a variety of techniques for dealing with local optima. Prominent amongst these is the breakout, which attaches weights to constraints which are difficult to satisfy [13].

Distributed iterative improvement algorithms for DisCSPs such as DisPeL[1] and DBA[13] assume that each agent is responsible for one variable only and knows its domain, the constraints which apply to the variable, the agents whose variables are constrained with its variable and the current value for any varible directly related to its own variable. In other words, agents are not allowed to be responsible for whole subproblems, but just a single variable and the problem is said to be *fine-grained.* As a result, there is a very limited amount of computation that agents can perform locally and all the search effort is focused on the distributed collaborative activity which is expensive. In constrast, if agents are allowed to own whole subproblems (i.e. the problem is *coarse-grained*) agents are able to carry out a substantial amount of computation locally.

This paper presents DisBO-wd, an iterative distributed algorithm for solving coarse-grained DisCSPs which uses weights on constraints in order to escape local optima. These weights are continuously decayed throughout the problem solving and increased whenever constraints are not satisfied. Empirical results show that DisBO-wd is effective, solving most problems in reasonable time and at a lower cost than other algorithms.

The remainder of this paper is structured as follows. Section 2 gives some definitions and explains related research. Next, DisBO-wd is introduced in Section 3. Finally, in Section 4, we present the results of empirical evaluations of DisBO-wd along with comparisons with other similar algorithms.

2 Background

A constraint satisfaction problem (CSP) is a triple $< V, D, C >$ where V is a set of variables, D is a set of domains (one per variable) and C is a set of constraints which restrict the values that variables can take simultaneously. Two variables are said to be *neighbours* if they both participate in the same constraint. Some algorithms for solving CSPs attach a *priority* to each variable in order to rank the variables from high to low priority.

A DisCSP is a CSP where the variables, domains and constraints are distributed over a number of agents and whose details cannot be centralised for a number of reasons such as privacy, security and cost. These problems are, therefore, solved by agent-based distributed algorithms which collaborate in order to find a solution. Some algorithms for solving CSPs attach a *priority* to each agent in order to rank the agents from high to low priority, eg. [14].

When DisCSPs are made up of interconnected subproblems which are naturally distinct from other subproblems, each individual subproblem is a CSP with its own set of variables and constraints between those variables, as well as constraints between some variables in the local CSP and variables in other sub-problems (as illustrated in Figure 1). Therefore, rather than representing one variable, each agent in the DisCSP represents a sub-problem, i.e the DisCSP is *coarse-grained.* For example, distributed university timetabling is a coarse grained DisCSP, where agents represent lecturers and each sub-problem is the set of courses taught by an individual. The constraints in the local subproblems (CSPs) include that an individual cannot teach two different courses at the same time (intra-agent constraints), as well as constraints to prevent some clashes with courses taught by other lecturers (inter-agent constraints) either because of student course registrations or resource availability.

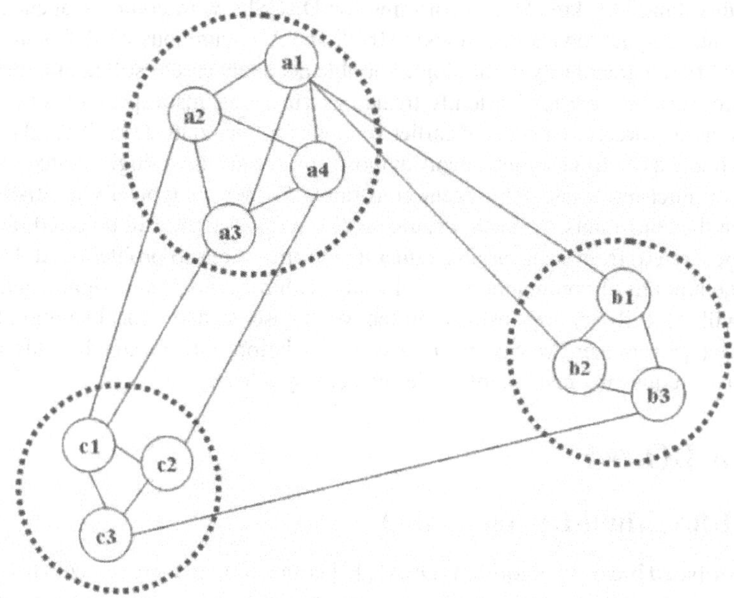

Fig. 1. An illustrative example of a coarse-grained DisCSP, with 3 inter-connected subproblems/agents.

Agents in coarse-grained DisCSPs (with more than one variable per agent) are more complex than fine-grained DisCSP agents (with only one varible per agent since they have much more problem information available and, therefore, can carry out more local inference in the search for a solution. The amount of local computation (and the level of granularity) required by complex agents can vary along two extremes [14], ranging from fine-grained to coarse-grained DisCSPs. If a problem is implemented as a fine-grained DisCSP, each of its subproblems acts as a variable. Therefore, each agent does all its local computation before hand by finding all possible solutions for its subproblem which are taken as the "domain values" of subproblem variable, e.g. [11]. Unfortunately, when local sub-problems are large and complex, it may be impossible or impractical to find all local solutions.

At the other extreme, each variable in a subproblem can be seen as a virtual agent, i.e. a single variable per agent and, therefore, local computation is minimal and all effort is expended on the distributed search. Agents simulate all activities of these virtual agents including communications between them and other real agents. This approach does not take full advantage of local knowledge and, therefore, it is costly since the expense of local computation is significantly lower than that of communications between virtual agents. It appears that an approach where there is a balance between the two extremes could be beneficial, so that agents can enjoy the flexibility of the finest level of granularity and at same time exploit the clustering of local variables to speed up the search.

In distributed backtracking algorithms for DisCSPs with complex agents, most prominently Asynchronous Backtracking [6, 8] and Asynchronous Weak Commitment Search [14], the granularity of the single variable per agent case is still maintained and, therefore, variables are inadvertently treated as virtual agents; especially since these algorithms are direct extensions of earlier versions for fine grained DisCSPs. By taking each variable as a virtual agent, agents in those algorithms use a single strategy to deal with both inter-agent and intra-agent constraints as there is typically no distinction between the constraints. As such, deadlocks (local optima) are still detected (and no-goods generated) from each variable rather than from entire sub-problems. At the same time, the amount of computation done locally within agents is still significant. Each agent will typically try, exhaustively in the worst case, to find a local solution that is consistent with higher priority external variables before either extending the partial solution or requesting revision of earlier choices by other agents.

3 DisBO-wd

3.1 DBA, Multi-DB and DisBO

The distributed breakout algorithm (DBA) [13] is an iterative improvement DisCSP algorithm which uses a single variable per agent. In DBA, agents carry out a distributed steepest descent search by exchanging possible improvements to a candidate solution and implementing the best improvements that do not conflict with each other. Agents act concurrently alternating between the *improve* and *ok?* cycles. In the *improve* cycle, each agent finds the value in its domain that minimises its weighted constraint violations and computes the improvement to its current assignment. These improvements are exchanged between the agents. In the *ok?* cycle the agents with the best improvements are allowed to change their values. Ties are broken with the agents lexicographic IDs in the case that two or more neighbouring agents have the same possible improvement.

In order to escape local optima, DBA attaches a weight to each constraint which is increased whenever the constraint is violated at a quasi-local-optimum, i.e. a state in which a subset of connected agents cannot find any improvements to their local evaluations. Empirical evaluation of DBA showed that it outperformed the Asynchronous Weak Commitment Search on difficult problem instances; DBA solved more problems and it did so in less time [13].

Multi-DB [4, 5] is an extension of DBA for coarse-grained distributed SAT problems. DisBO [2] is another extension for coarse-grained distributed project scheduling and graph colouring. This version was largely based on DBA's framework but differed in its emphasis on increasing weights only at *real* local optima. DisBO differs from Multi-DB in that it has an additional third cycle for global state detection, since weights are only increased when the search is stuck at real local optima and not at quasi-local-optima. Therefore, in addition to the *improve* and *ok?* cycles, there is a *detect-global-state* cycle, which is used to determine that either a solution has been found, that the maximum number of cycles has been reached, or that the search is stuck at a real local optimum. But, the *detect-global-state* cycle is expensive, in terms of messages sent, because it requires agents to continuously exchange state messages until they have determined that all messages have reached all agents in the network. This was needed to get a snapshot of the state of the entire network without resorting to a global broadcast mechanism where each agent is assumed to know every other agent in the network.

DisBO limits the amount of computation done locally within each agent to allow agents to focus on the collaborative aspect of the problem solving activity. In DisBO, each agent's variables are partitioned into two sets, private and public variables. The private variables are those variables that have no inter-agent constraints attached to them. The bulk of the local computation done by agents in DisBO are with these private variables, where in each improvement phase the agents repeatedly select values for these variables that minimise the weighted constraint violations until no further improvements are possible. The public variables, on the other hand, are treated like virtual agents and DBA's coordination heuristic is used to prevent any two public variables (even those within one agent) from changing their values simultaneously unless the concurrent changes do not cause the constraints between them to be violated.

3.2 DisBO-wd

DisBO-wd is our DisCSP algorithm for coarse-grained CSPs based on DisBO where the weight update scheme is replaced with a weight decay scheme inspired on Frank's work on SAT solving with local search [3]. Instead of modifying weights only when a search is stuck at local optima, weights on violated constraints are continuously updated after each move. At the same time, weights are also decayed at a fixed rate during the updates to allow the algorithm focus on recent increments. Frank argues that this strategy allows weights to provide immediate feedback to the variable selection heuristic and hence emphasise those variables in unsatisfied clauses. We modified the update rule further, so that weights on satisfied constraints are continuously decayed as well. Therefore, before computing possible improvements, in DisBO-wd, agents update their constraint weights as follows:

Weights on violated constraints at time t are computed as

$$W_{i,t} = (dr * W_{i,t-1}) + lr$$

Weights on satisfied constraints at time t are decayed as

$$W_{i,t} = max((dr * W_{i,t-1}), 1)$$

where:

dr is the decay rate ($dr < 1$).

lr is the learning rate ($lr > 0$).

From empirical investigations (see section 3.4), we found that DisBO-wd's performance was optimal with the parameters set to $dr = 0.99$ and $lr = 8$. With the new weight update scheme, we were able to reduce the number of DisBO's cycles from three to two, since it was no longer necessary to determine if the search was stuck at real local optima - a big cost saving. We also moved the termination detection mechanism into the *ok?* cycle, as in the original distributed breakout framework. Other modifications such as probabilistic weight resets and probabilistic weight smoothing [7] were considered, but found to be weaker than our new weight decay mechanishm.

In DisBO when two neighbouring variables have the same improvement, the variable with the lower lexicographic ID is deterministically given priority to make its change. We have replaced this coordination heuristic with a random break [10] so in each improvement cycle agents select and communicate random tie-breaking numbers for each variable, and when there is a tie the variable with the lower number is given priority.

3.3 Creating coarse-grained DisCSPs

In order to obtain coarse-grained DisCSPs, publicly available problem instances from CSPLib[1] and SATLib[2], as well as randomly generated problems, were partitioned into evenly sized inter-connected sub-problems using a simple partitioning algorithm which ensured that the cluster of variables within each agent were meaningful, i.e. there are constraints between the variables belonging to an agent. For each agent (a_i) its subproblem was created as follows:

1. A randomly selected variable (x_i) that is not already allocated to another agent is allocated to a_i.
2. A variable constrained with x_i is randomly selected and allocated to a_i.
3. The process of randomly selecting one of the variables already allocated to a_i and selecting a random neighbour of the variable for allocation to a_i is repeated until the number of required variables for a_i have been found.
4. With a small probability (*p*), a randomly selected variable is allocated to a_i, even if it is not connected with any of a_i's existing variables.

3.4 Determining optimal parameter values for DisBO-wd

We have replaced the weight update mechanism of DisBO with the scheme for continuous weight updates proposed in [3]. This new scheme introduces two new parameters into DisBO-wd i.e. the *learning rate (lr)* and the *decay rate (dr)*. The *learning rate* controls how fast weights on violated constraints grow in DisBO-wd, while the *decay rate* biases the search towards the most recent weight increases.

In his work on SAT solving with a modified GSAT [9] algorithm, Frank [3] found that the decay rate was optimal at $dr = 0.999$, more problems were solved within an allotted time than with the value set to 0.95 and 0.99. He also found that the learning rate was optimal at $lr = 1$ compared to runs with the values 8, 16, and 24. However, DisBO-wd differs from GSAT in many respects especially given the amount concurrent changes that take place in distributed search. Therefore, we had to carry out an experiment to determine optimal values for the parameters in the distributed algorithm. We used distributed SAT instances and random DisCSPs, evaluating DisBOs performance on 100 instances in each case, with the parameters set to

[1] www.csplib.org [accessed 26 March 2007].

[2] www.satlib.org [accessed 26 March 2007].

$lr \in \{1,2,3,5,8,10,12,16\}$ and $dr \in \{0.9,0.95,0.98,0.99\}$. In Tables 1 and 2, we summarise the results from this experiment, showing the percentage of problems solved, the average and the median search costs incurred where we limited DisBO-wd to 10,000 iterations on each attempt on the SAT problems and 12,000 iterations on each attempt on the random DisCSPs.

		SAT Problems			Random Problems		
dr	lr	% solved	average cost	median cost	% solved	average cost	median cost
0.9	1	60	85	28	29	1598	462
	2	82	178	90	79	1160	550
	3	84	151	108	95	2298	1458
	5	94	303	141	99	2412	1648
	8	88	273	139	100	2416	1658
	10	92	300	129	96	2472	1876.5
	12	92	233	176	93	2080	1606
	16	88	314	145	94	2260	1286.5
0.95	1	88	208	111	87	1304	663
	2	98	304	144	100	1986	1030.5
	3	100	303	130	100	2226	1414.5
	5	100	329	195	98	1952	1114
	8	100	259	161	93	1922	1238
	10	98	338	181	95	1876	1104
	12	100	314	136	96	2048	1232
	16	100	358	233	100	2050	1182.5

Table 1. Performance of DisBO-wd on Distributed SAT problems and Distributed Random problems for $dr \in \{0.9, 0.95\}$ and variable lr.

The results in Tables 1 and 2 summarise attempts to solve 50-literal SAT instances from the SATLib problem set. As dr increases, DisBO-wd solved more problems but there is no clear relationship between the search costs and the decay rate. Given these results we chose $dr = 0.99$ and $lr = 1$.

Tables 1 and 2 also show the results of 100 runs for random problems with $<$number of variables $n = 60$, number of values in a domain $d = 10$, constraint density $p_1 = 0.1$, constraint tightness $p_2 = 0.5 >$. The search cost is better for high values of dr, suggesting that the search benefits from retaining some information of not too recent weight increases for as long as possible and they are not quickly dominated by newer weight increases. However, it appears that the learning rate lr has a different effect on performance in this domain. The algorithm generally does not fare too well with the smallest and largest values for this parameter. The results, although not clear cut, show that DisBO-wd is optimal with the values 3,8, or 10 (at $dr = 0.99$), where the average search costs are minimal and the percentage of problems solved are significantly high. But, we arbitrarily chose $lr = 8$ and $dr = 0.99$ for the experiments

		SAT Problems			Random Problems		
dr	lr	% solved	average cost	median cost	% solved	average cost	median cost
0.98	1	100	236	119	95	1834	1163
	2	100	375	198	98	1590	1050
	3	100	247	174	96	1568	916
	5	100	263	213	99	1822	1024
	8	100	286	202	99	2114	1038
	10	100	439	176	96	1476	984
	12	100	380	219	100	1752	1082.5
	16	100	386	174	98	2018	1152
0.99	1	100	186	130	97	1668	978
	2	100	252	127	97	1748	1120
	3	100	243	189	97	1506	832
	5	100	235	139	93	1528	826
	8	100	373	235	99	1554	858
	10	100	312	213	100	1682	828.5
	12	100	318	207	96	2152	1432.5
	16	100	269	213	97	2454	1376

Table 2. Performance of DisBO-wd on Distributed SAT problems and Distributed Random problems for $dr \in \{0.98, 0.99\}$ and variable lr.

with the algorithm because it solved slightly more problems than with $lr = 3$ and the search costs were lower than with $lr = 10$.

3.5 DisBO vs. DisBO-wd

A series of experiments were conducted in order to analyse the effect of the various modifications to DisBO. Thus, DisBO and DisBO-wd were compared by evaluating the results of running them on the same problems. Table 3 summarises results from experiments on critically difficult distributed graph colouring problems with 10 variables per agent and $< number\ of\ colours\ k = 3, degree = 4.7 >$ - for an explanation of how these problems were generated see section 3.3. The results show that DisBO-wd solved more problems than DisBO, especially on the larger problems. Furthermore, DisBO-wd required fewer cycles to solve the problems.

Table 4 contains results of experiments on randomly generated problems with $< domain\ size = 10, density\ (p1) = 3n, tightness\ (p2) = 0.5, number\ of\ iterations = 100 * n >$ where n is the number of variables. The results show that, like with graph colouring problems, DisBO-wd solved substantially more problems than DisBO and required fewer cycles.

	% solved		median cost	
num. vars.	DisBO	DisBO-wd	DisBO	DisBO-wd
50	100	100	222	115
60	100	100	366	199
70	98	100	480	249
80	98	100	741	27
90	99	100	1095	536
100	95	100	2121	723
110	92	100	1257	655
120	86	100	2214	1011
130	79	98	2400	1354
140	78	100	3755	1534
150	78	100	4929	2086

Table 3. DisBO vs. DisBO-wd on random distributed graph colouring problems of various sizes. Each point represents attempts on 100 problems.

		% solved		median cost	
num. vars.	num. agents	DisBO	DisBO-wd	DisBO	DisBO-wd
50	5	61	100	474	402
	10	66	100	466	512
100	5	56	100	476	563
	10	58	100	975	569

Table 4. DisBO vs. DisBO-wd on random problems of various sizes. Each point represents attempts on 100 problems.

4 Empirical Evaluation

An experimental evaluation of DisBO-wd was carried out using coarse grained versions of several DisCSPs including boolean satisfiability formulae (SAT) and randomly generated DisCSPs. In each case, the algorithm's performance was compared to the Asynchronous Weak Commitment Search algorithm (Multi-AWCS)[14] and, in the case of SAT problems, to Multi-DB. These two algorithms were selected because they are, to our knowledge, the only distributed local search algorithms which allow more than one variable per agent. Note that Multi-DB was not used with random problems since it was not designed to solve these. The algorithms were compared on the percentage of problems solved within a maximum number of iterations (or cycles)[3]. The number of iterations (cycles) was used as the measure of efficiency - a widely used measure for distributed iterative improvement algorithms since it is machine independent and, in the case of synchronous algorithms, the number of messages exchanged between agents and the number of constraint checks can be inferred or approximated with this metric.

[3] Given its completeness and unlimited time, Multi-AWCS is guaranteed to solve all problems used since they all have solutions. But, in this case we are interested in its performance in bounded time.

Unlike the breakout-based algorithms, Multi-AWCS is a complete algorithm and is not built around the idea of resolving deadlocks by increasing constraint weights. Rather, it combines backtracking and iterative improvement search and deals with local optima through a combination of variable re-ordering and storage of explicit no-goods. Although this algorithm has been shown to outperform other distributed backtracking algorithms [14], it can require an exponential amount of memory to store no-goods.

4.1 Distributed SAT problems

We evaluated the performance of DisBO-wd and the benchmark algorithms on distributed SAT problems. Satisfiable 3-SAT instances from the SATLib dataset made up of formulae with 100, 125 and 150 literals were used for the experiments. These were transformed into coarse-grained DisCSPs with the technique specified in Section 3.3. We did not run any experiments with Multi-DB and Multi-AWCS, rather we used results on experiments with the same instances from [4], published by the algorithms' authors, as benchmarks[4]. Note that the results for Multi-DB are for a version with periodic random restarts, which its authors found solved more problems than the original version [4] and that the version of Multi-AWCS which they used has no no-good learning to keep their comparisons with Multi-DB fair. DisBO-wd was run once on each instance, and was limited to $100n$ iterations (where n is the number of literals in a formulae) before attempts were recorded as unsuccessful. Note that in the experiments reported in [4], Multi-DB and Multi-AWCS were limited to a maximum of $250n$ iterations on their runs and, therefore, we are giving our own algorithm less time to attempt to solve the problem. The results in Tables 5, 6, and 7 show the percentage of problems solved and the average and median search costs for the problems which were successfully solved.

It can be seen from the results that DisBO-wd generally performed substantially better than the other 2 algorithms. Its average and median costs are significantly better than those of Multi-DB and its performance is at least as good with the following two exceptions: (i) SAT problems with 100 literals where the algorithm has only 2 agents - DisBO-wd's cost was higher; (ii) SAT problems with 150 literals where the algorithm has 3 or 5 agents - the percentage of problems solved by DisBO-wd was marginally lower and the median cost with 3 agents was higher. Also note that DisBO-wd has a consistency in its search costs that Multi-DB does not match. For example, average search costs in the 150 literal problems increase by about 350% as the number of agents increase for Multi-DB while DisBO-wd's average search cost remains within a 20% range of the minimum average without a clear degradation in performance as the number of agents increase. While both DisBO-wd and Multi-DB, rely on modifying constraint weights to deal with deadlocks, DisBO-wd is less affected by the distribution of variables to agents.

With respect to Multi-AWCS, DisBO's performance was significantly better in all cases. Multi-AWCS solved the least number of problems and it had the highest search costs.

[4] Variables are randomly distributed amongst agents in [4], so from each agent's perspective the problems may not be exactly the same.

algorithm	agents	% solved	average cost	median cost
Multi-DB	2	99.9	886	346
	4	100	1390	510
	5	100	1640	570
	10	99.6	3230	1150
	20	99.7	3480	1390
Multi-AWCS	2	99.9	1390	436
	4	98.7	4690	1330
	5	97.6	6100	1730
	10	96.8	7630	2270
	20	95.0	8490	2680
DisBO-wd	2	100	923	515
	4	100	948	495
	5	100	984	490
	10	99.9	1003	516
	20	99.8	993	510

Table 5. Performance of DisBO-wd and other algorithms on 1000 random distributed SAT problems with 100 literals distributed evenly amongst different numbers of agents.

algorithm	agents	% solved	average cost	median cost
Multi-DB	5	100	2540	816
	25	100	6300	2330
Multi-AWCS	5	87	19200	9290
	25	80	25500	15800
DisBO-wd	5	100	1727	725
	25	100	1686	921

Table 6. Performance of DisBO-wd and other algorithms on 100 random distributed 125 literal SAT problems.

4.2 Random distributed constraint satisfaction problems

We evaluated the algorithms performance on random DisCSPs. In this experiment Multi-AWCS only produces results in the runs with the smallest sized problems. It is well documented (for example in [8]) that Multi-AWCS can require an exponential amount of memory to store no-goods during an attempt to solve a problem. The number of no-goods generated can increase exponentially on large problems, and since each no-good may be evaluated at least once in each iteration, the length of time to complete each iteration increases dramatically as the search progresses. In our experience with Multi-AWCS, we found that it typically ran out of memory on runs with large problems, especially for DisCSPs with 60 or more variables and the algorithm sometimes required considerable amounts of time to solve even a single instance. We used three groups of problems with varying sizes and 100 problems in each group. The results of these experiments are summarised in Table 8 where we show the percentage

algorithm	agents	% solved	average cost	median cost
Multi-DB	3	100	2180	608
	5	100	3230	1200
	10	96	9030	2090
	15	98	9850	3850
Multi-AWCS	3	81	24300	11100
	5	67	37100	26100
	10	61	39400	36000
	15	61	42300	41700
DisBO-wd	3	99	2078	874
	5	99	2186	910
	10	99	2054	1012
	15	98	1893	898

Table 7. Performance of DisBO-wd and other algorithms on 100 random distributed 150 literal SAT problems.

of problems solved, and the average and the median iterations from successful runs on attempts on 100 instances for each problem size.

Multi-AWCS has lower search costs than DisBO-wd for problems with 50 variables when 5 or 10 agents are employed. It also solves slightly more problems when 5 agents are used. However, Multi-AWCS was unable to return results for problems with 100 and 200 variables, regardless of the number of agents used. DisBO-wd gave results for all problem sizes, although its performance degraded considerably on the largest problems.

algorithm	n	agents	% solved	average cost	median cost.
Multi-AWCS	50	5	100	738	288
		10	98	995	527
	100	5	out	of	memory
		10	out	of	memory
	200	5	out	of	memory
		10	out	of	memory
		20	out	of	memory
DisBO-wd	50	5	94	1927	1336
		10	99	1855	1104
	100	5	83	4996	2922
		10	88	4695	3065
	200	5	62	13454	8060
		10	65	16832	14432
		20	57	13289	9544

Table 8. Performance of algorithms on random DisCSPs ($< n$, domain size $d = 10$, constraint density $p1 \approx 0.1$, constraint tightness $p2 = 0.5 >$).

5 Discussion and conclusions

We have presented DisBO-wd, a distributed iterative improvement algorithm for solving coarse-grained DisCSPs which employs the breakout technique in order to escape local optima. Unlike other similar algorithms, DisBO-wd uses a weight decay and a learning rate in order to control constraint weights. In addition, its agent coordination strategy is non-deterministic, since it contains a stochastic mechanism for tie-breaking when more than one agent offers the best improvement.

DisBO-wd is competitive with respect to Multi-DB, which is the other algorithm that relies on constraint weights to deal with local optima; but unlike DisBO-wd, weights in Multi-DB are allowed to grow unbounded. DisBO-wd's search costs were generally substantially lower than those for Multi-DB in the SAT problems. DisBO-wd was also significantly better than Multi-AWCS in all the experiments with SAT problems. With random problems, Multi-AWCS produced better results for small problems with 50 variables but DisBO-wd was able to return results for large problems (with 100 and 200 problems) which Multi-AWCS was unable to solve due to its memory requirements.

References

1. Muhammed Basharu, Inés Arana, and Hatem Ahriz. Solving DisCSPs with penalty-driven search. In *Proceedings of AAAI 2005 - the Twentieth National Conference of Artificial Intelligence*, pages 47–52. AAAI, 2005.
2. Carlos Eisenberg. *Distributed Constraint Satisfaction For Coordinating And Integrating A Large-Scale, Heterogeneous Enterprise*. PhD thesis, Swiss Federal Institute of Technology (EPFL), Lausanne (Switzerland), September 2003.
3. Jeremy Frank. Learning short-term weights for GSAT. In Martha Pollack, editor, *Proceedings of the 15th International Joint Conference on Artificial Intelligence (IJCAI97)*, pages 384–391, San Francisco, August 1997. Morgan Kaufmann.
4. Katsutoshi Hirayama and Makoto Yokoo. Local search for distributed SAT with complex local problems. In *Proceedings of the first international joint conference on Autonomous agents and multiagent systems*, AAMAS 2002, pages 1199 – 1206, New York, NY, USA, 2002. ACM Press.
5. Katsutoshi Hirayama and Makoto Yokoo. The distributed breakout algorithms. *Artificial Intelligence*, 161(1–2):89–115, January 2005.
6. Katsutoshi Hirayama, Makoto Yokoo, and Kaita Sycara. The phase transition in distributed constraint satisfaction problems: firstresults. In *Proceedings of the International Workshop on Distributed Constraint Satisfaction*, 2000.
7. Frank Hutter, Dave A. D. Tompkins, and Holger H. Hoos. Scaling and probabilistic smoothing: Efficient dynamic local search for SAT. In P. Van Hentenryck, editor, *Proceedings of the 8th International Conference on Principles and Practice of Constraint Programming (CP02)*, volume 2470 of *LNCS*, pages 233–248, London, UK, September 2002. Springer-Verlag.
8. Arnold Maestre and Christian Bessiere. Improving asychronous backtracking for dealing with complex local problems. In Ramon Lpez de Mntaras and Lorenza Saitta, editors, *Proceedings of the 16th Eureopean Conference on Artificial Intelligence (ECAI 2004)*, pages 206–210. IOS Press, August 2004.

9. Bart Selman and Henry A. Kautz. Domain-independent extensions to GSAT: solving large structured satisfiability problems. In Ruzena Bajcsy, editor, *Proceedings of the Thirteenth International Joint Conference on Principles on Artificial Intelligent (IJCAI'93)*, pages 290–294, August 1993.
10. Lars Wittenburg. Distributed constraint solving and optimizing for micro-electro-mechanical systems. Master's thesis, Technical University of Berlin, December 2002.
11. Xiaolong Jin Yi Tang, Jiming Liu. Adaptive compromises in distributed problem solving. In *Proceedings of the 4th International Conference on Intelligent Data Engineeringand Automated Learning IDEAL 2003*, March 2003.
12. Makoto Yokoo, Edmund H. Durfee, Toru Ishida, and Kazuhiro Kuwabara. Distributed constraint satisfaction for formalizing distributed problem solving. In *12th International Conference on Distributed Computing Systems (ICDCS-92)*, pages 614–621, 1992.
13. Makoto Yokoo and Katsutoshi Hirayama. Distributed breakout algorithm for solving distributed constraint satisfaction problems. In *Proceedings of the Second International Conference on Multi-Agent Systems*, pages 401–408. MIT Press, 1996.
14. Makoto Yokoo and Katsutoshi Hirayama. Distributed constraint satisfaction algorithm for complex local problems. In *ICMAS '98: Proceedings of the 3rd International Conference on Multi Agent Systems*, pages 372–379, Washington, DC, USA, July 1998. IEEE Computer Society.

Construction of Heuristics for a Search-Based Approach to Solving Sudoku

S. K. Jones, P. A. Roach, S. Perkins
Department of Computing and Mathematical Sciences, University of Glamorgan, Pontypridd, CF37 1DL, United Kingdom, skjones@glam.ac.uk

Abstract

Sudoku is a logic puzzle, consisting of a 9×9 grid and further subdivided into 'mini-grids' of size 3×3. Each row, column, and 3×3 mini-grid contains the numbers 1 to 9 once, with a true Sudoku grid having a unique solution. Sudoku, along with similar combinatorial structures, has relationships with a range of real-world problems. Much published work on the solution of Sudoku puzzles has acknowledged the link between Sudoku and Latin Squares, thereby recognising the scale of any search space of possible solutions and that the generalization of the puzzle to larger grid sizes is NP-complete. However, most published approaches to the solution of Sudoku puzzles have focussed on the use of constraint satisfaction algorithms that effectively mimic solution by hand, rather than directly exploiting features of the problem domain to reduce the size of the search space and constructing appropriate heuristics for the application of search techniques. This paper highlights important features of the search space to arrive at heuristics employed in a modified steepest ascent hill-climbing algorithm, and proposes a problem initialization and neighbourhood that greatly speed solution through a reduction of problem search space. Results shown demonstrate that this approach is sufficient to solve even the most complex rated puzzles, requiring relatively few moves. An analysis of the nature of the problem search space is offered.

1 Introduction

Sudoku is a number-based logic puzzle, consisting of a 9×9 grid and further subdivided into 'mini-grids' of size 3×3. Each row, column, and 3×3 mini-grid contains the numbers 1 to 9 once, with a true Sudoku grid having a unique solution. Seemingly based primarily on Latin Squares and Magic numbers [1], Sudoku is a puzzle that has achieved great popularity relatively recently. It is attributed to Howard Garns and first published by Dell Magazines in 1979 [2]. Initially, the puzzle was called *Number Place*, but after gaining popularity in Japan it was trademarked by the Nikoli puzzle group under the name Sudoku (*Su* meaning number, and *Doku* meaning single) [2]. The puzzle became internationally successful from about 2005, and has sparked a trend of similar puzzles of different sizes and border constraints. Through its strong relationships with Latin Squares and other combinatorial structures, Sudoku is linked to real-world applications, including conflict free wavelength routing in wide band optical networks, statistical design and error correcting codes [3], as well as timetabling and experimental design [4].

A Sudoku puzzle includes a partial assignment of the values. These assignments are commonly known as *givens* or predefined cells, and are unmovable. Sufficient givens are provided so as to specify a unique solution to the puzzle (*i.e.* the puzzle is *well-formed*). The givens should be chosen so that no given is itself a "logical consequence" [5] of the other givens (*i.e.* no redundant clues are provided). The objective is then to complete the assignment by inserting the missing values in such a way as to satisfy the constraints, by hand using logic or, as is increasingly the trend, by using *automated solutions*. No general means is yet known for determining the minimum number of givens required for a partial assignment that leads to a unique solution [6]. Much experimental work has been conducted in this area, however, and a well-formed puzzle has been constructed with just 17 givens [7]; this is the smallest number achieved to date.

Puzzles are typically categorised in terms of the difficulty in completing them by hand, with the use of four or five rating levels being common. These rating levels are subjective, meaning that the actual ranges and labels can vary greatly. Terms such as 'easy', 'medium' and 'hard' (and even 'tough' and 'diabolical') are commonly used. The time taken by standard constraint based solvers (described below) is sometimes used to categorize the complexity of a published puzzle, whereas some publications use measures of the time taken by groups of human solvers to arrive at the solution. The complexity of a puzzle does not have a simple relationship with the number of givens – the positioning of the givens is a more important determinant of their value as 'hints' than their quantity.

Automated solutions could reasonably be divided into two categories; *constraint based approaches* (some of which effectively mimic the methods that one would use when solving the problem by hand), and *heuristic search optimization algorithms* (which turn some or all problem constraints into aspects of an optimization evaluation function). The latter category is the focus of this paper. Such approaches directly exploit features of the problem domain in order to reduce time spent examining a search space (the space of all possible solutions to a given problem) [8], and are expected to be more generalizable to the solution of puzzles of larger grid sizes, where solution becomes more difficult.

The purpose of this paper is to highlight important features of the search space for Sudoku, to arrive at suitable heuristics for effective solution of a range of Sudoku puzzles. Through the testing of a modified steepest ascent hill-climbing algorithm, an effective problem initialization and neighbourhood definition are described that greatly speed solution by reducing the problem search space. Finally, an analysis of the nature of the problem search space, and of the appropriateness of heuristic search for this problem, is offered.

2 Literature Survey

Many programs for the automatic solution of Sudoku puzzles are currently commercially available. Although generally undocumented, these automatic solvers seem to rely on the types of solving rules used when solving by hand, combined with a certain amount of trial and error [9]. Computer solvers can estimate the difficulty for a human to find the solution, based on the complexity of the solving techniques required.

Several authors have presented Sudoku as a constraint satisfaction problem [5, 10, 11]. In these approaches, rather than attempting to employ an objective function to determine a path through a state space, a solution is viewed as a set of values that can be assigned to a set of variables. Such approaches take advantage of puzzle constraints: given values are fixed; rows, columns and mini-grids are permutations [12]. Some of this interest in constraint satisfaction approaches may stem from the relationship that Sudoku has with Latin Squares and hence with the widely studied *quasi-group completion problem (QCP)* [13]. A Latin Square is an $n \times n$ table of n values, such that no value is repeated in any row and column; through the relationship with Latin Squares, Sudoku has been shown to be NP-Complete for higher dimensions [1]. A Latin Square is also a case of a quasi-group, having clear structure and both easy and hard instances, and as such it has been described as "an ideal testbed" [13] for the application of constraint satisfaction algorithms. QCP has been linked to many real-world problems and its study has revealed properties of search algorithms. A variety of constraint satisfaction approaches have been employed for Sudoku, such as the application of bipartite matching and flow algorithms [5], the use of forward checking and limited discrepancy search algorithms [13], and the application of Conjunctive Normal Form (CNF) in order to produce different encodings of the problem. The latter has been attempted for minimal and extended encodings (*i.e.* with redundant constraints) [10], and an optimised encoding that relies on knowledge of the fixed givens to reduce the number of clauses [11], an approach reported as useful in the solution of larger Sudoku grids.

An Integer Programming approach (the application of Linear Programming to a problem in which all constrained variables are integers) has been used in [6], which considered both puzzle creation and puzzle solution. A branch and bound algorithm was used to determine optimal solutions.

Lastly, an evolutionary approach to the solution of Sudoku puzzles has also been taken through the use of genetic algorithms [12]. In this, the authors designed geometric crossovers that are strongly related to the problem constraints. Much success was achieved with this approach, although genetic algorithms are generally not an ideal approach for the solution of Sudoku, because they do not directly exploit the problems constraints to reduce the examination of the full search space, as the authors acknowledge.

3 The Nature of the Problem

The Sudoku puzzle is deceptively complex. Although not instantly obvious, an empty 9×9 Sudoku puzzle has an extremely large number of goal state solutions: 3,546,146,300,288 in total [14]. Even when givens are in place there is still an extremely large search space.

The approach to Sudoku grid solution taken in this paper is to employ optimization-based search, exploring sections of a search space that represents the possible moves from some initial state of the puzzle to a goal state, *i.e.* a solution to that puzzle. All completed (solved) Sudoku grids are permutations of the numbers 1 to 9 in rows, columns and mini-grids, arranged so as to meet the puzzle constraints. The fixed givens in the initial state of the puzzle already meet the problem constraints. It is known *a priori* which values are missing from the initial grid (*i.e.* how many of each digit), and so these numbers may be placed in the missing spaces, in any order, to form an initial candidate plan, or 'incorrect solution'. Hence, a state in the search space is a structured collection of the correct puzzle objects, placed (with the exception of the givens) in the wrong order. From each state, a change to the state (or move) can be made by swapping any pair of non-given values. If there are n missing values from the initial Sudoku grid, there would be a maximum of $n(n-1)/2$ permutations of those missing values, or moves possible from any state. This indicates how rapidly the state space increases in size with moves from an initial state.

The number of moves possible at each move, and hence the size of the search space, can be reduced however, without affecting whether a goal state can be located. By choosing to place in each mini-grid only those digits which are missing from that mini-grid, one of the problem constraints – that of ensuring that each mini-grid contains all 9 digits – will already be satisfied. In this case, the number of distinct states will be reduced to:

$$\frac{1}{2}\sum_{i=1}^{9}\sum_{j=1}^{9} n_{ij}(n_{ij}-1)$$

where n_{ij} is the number of non-given values in the mini-grid at row i, column j. This represents a reduction of:

$$\frac{1}{2}\sum_{i=1}^{9}\sum_{j=1}^{9} n_{ij}\left(\sum_{a=1}^{9}\sum_{b=1}^{9} n_{ab} - n_{ij}\right)$$

in the number of moves possible from each state.

Further, the number of total possible combinations of non-given values, and therefore the number of distinct states in the search space (another indicator of search space size) is now reduced to the number of permutations of non-given values number within their respective mini-grids, *i.e.*

$$\prod_{i=1}^{9}\prod_{j=1}^{9} n_{ij}!$$

An example Sudoku grid, with 28 givens, is shown in Figure 1. This grid contains 6 mini-grids with 3 givens (and therefore 6 non-given values), 1 mini-grid with 2 givens (and 7 non-given values) and 2 mini-grids with 4 givens (and 5 non-given values). In total, 53 values must be added to form an initial state. Hence, under the scheme proposed above, from each state, 6×6(6-1)/2 + 7(7-1)/2 + 2×5(5-1)/2 = 131 moves (or swaps of pairs of non-given values) are possible – a reduction from 53×(53-1)/2 = 1378. A potential number of 53! combinations, or potential distinct states, has been reduced to 6×6! × 7! × 2×5! distinct states. This reduces the search space enormously, speeding any process of search.

			5	1	2			
						7	6	
9	8	5						3
						4	2	1
		1	9		3	8		
2	5	7						
5						1	9	2
	6	4						
			7	5	8			

Figure 1: An Example Sudoku Grid

4 Modelling the Problem

The Sudoku puzzle is formulated here as a straightforward heuristic state-based search optimization problem, requiring definitions for an optimization technique, state representation, neighbourhood (chosen to reduce the search space), operators, and an objective function that employs information concerning the problem domain.

4.1 Search Technique

The search technique chosen was a modified steepest ascent hill-climbing algorithm, which employs an objective function to ascend the search space making locally optimal decisions on which move to make next, always choosing the highest scoring successor in the entire neighbourhood of the current state [8]. Initially, a best-first search approach was employed, using a priority queue of as-yet unexplored states ordered by objective function score so that the choice of next move was not restricted to the neighbourhood of the current state, but may return to a previously located more promising state and thereby avoid local optima. The highest scored state in such a queue is the state to be expanded next. However, it was found that the queue was not necessary at all in the solution of the easier SuDoku puzzles, as ascent is continuous. In the solution of more difficult puzzles, although the queue was occasionally used to backtrack in the search space, the method became stuck in large plateaus. The queue then became more a means of detecting plateaus than a method contributing to search, and was kept for that purpose (as described further in Section 4.5 below).

The basic algorithm is as follows [8]:

Current-state becomes initial state.
While goal state not found, or complete iteration fails to change Current-state, do:

1. *Let Best-successor be a state.*
2. *For each operator that applies to current state:*
    a. *Apply operator to determine a successor to current state*
    b. *Evaluate successor. If it matches goal state, return with success, else if it is better than Best-successor, change Best-successor to new state.*
3. *If Best-successor is better than Current-state, then Current-state becomes Best-successor.*

A test set of 100 different Sudoku puzzles, which varied in both level of difficulty and number of givens, was constructed. This test set included some puzzles with very hard ratings and a puzzle claimed to be the hardest Sudoku (called AI-Escargot and developed by Arto Inkala [15]).

The need for modifying this method to avoid local maxima and plateaus, and the approach taken to modification, are described in Section 4.5 (below).

4.2 State Representation and Operators

At each stage of the optimization, a current state is transformed by the single application of an operator to a selected successor, or neighbour, in the search space. All successors, or candidate solutions, are evaluated to determine the state with the highest evaluation.

As described in Section 3 (above), the operators are restricted to swaps of pairs of values within a mini-grid (excluding given values from any swap). Hence the neighbourhood is restricted to candidate plans differing only in the positions of two non-given values in a mini-grid. This avoids potential swaps of values between mini-grids that would worsen the solution by breaking one of the puzzle constraints, *i.e.* ensuring that each mini-grid contains all values between 1 and 9.

4.3 The Objective Function

An objective function, f, is required as a measure of the closeness of a given state to a goal state. The function is a weighted sum of n problem domain related factors f_i employing n corresponding weights w_i, the general expression of which is:

$$f = \sum_{i=1}^{n} w_i f_i$$

The factors, or sub-functions, f_i must be chosen as measurable quantities of closeness to goal, such that the function f increases in value the closer a state is to a goal state. These factors embody heuristics for improving states, based on observations on the problem domain.

For the Sudoku puzzle, it is proposed here that the factor f_1 is a count of the number of different digits that appear in each row and column of a current state of the Sudoku grid. States very close to a goal state will typically have few repetitions (or 'clashes') of digits in rows and columns, hence f_1 will score highly. In full, f_1 is defined as:

$$f_1 = \sum_{i=1}^{9} \left| \{x \mid x = a_{ij}, j = 1..9\} \right| + \sum_{j=1}^{9} \left| \{x \mid x = a_{ij}, i = 1..9\} \right|$$

where a_{ij} is the value in the grid at row i, column j. This determines the size of the sets of values found in each row and column, *i.e.* the number of different values in each row and column, and sums them.

When considering the rows and columns of the Sudoku grid, in a given state that is not a goal state, there will be clashes of certain digits in some of those rows and columns. The factor f_1 provides a measure, inversely, of the *overall* number of such clashes. However, clashes involving givens (the pre-defined and fixed values which may not be moved) should be considered to be of greater importance than clashes between two non-given values, as it is known that the position of the non-given value must be incorrect. Therefore, a second factor, or sub-function, f_2 is employed to embody a clearer measure of this consideration. This factor is defined as a count of the number of clashes between any given and non-given digits, and so the factor f_2 will tend to reduce as the grid improves. In full, f_2 is defined as:

$$f_2 = \sum_{g_{pq} \in G} \left| \{i \mid a_{iq} = g_{pq}, i = 1..9, i \neq p\} \cup \{j \mid a_{pj} = g_{pq}, j = 1..9, j \neq q\} \right|$$

where G is set of all givens, g_{pq} at row p, column q.

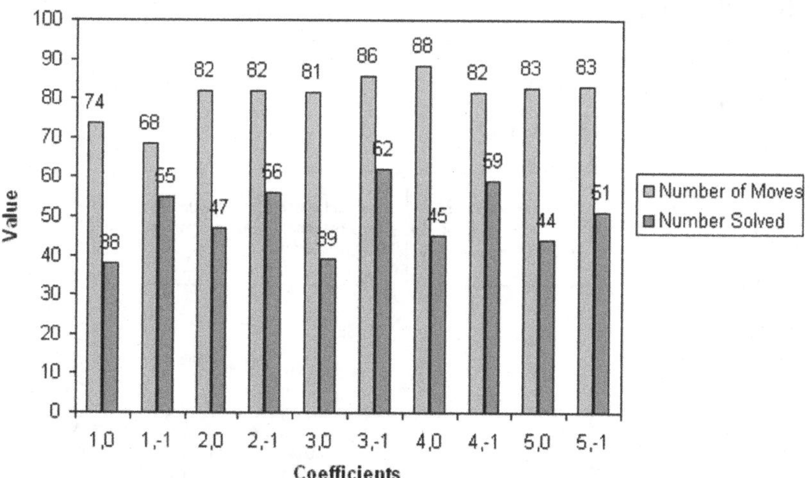

Figure 2 Performance of coefficient pairings

In this implementation of search, trial and error was used to determine appropriate values of the weights w_1 and w_2, with the combination of values that led reliably to solution of a range of puzzles in the least number of iterations (or moves) to be selected. (The number of iterations was chosen as it has a direct link to both the number of total successor states considered, as the number of successors in each state's neighbourhood is constant, and the overall time taken to reach a goal state.) A range of coefficient values were tried for the solution of the test set of 100 Sudoku puzzles (described in Section 4.1), results being shown in Figure 2 for a selection of the tested coefficient pairings. Not all puzzles were solvable using this optimization approach, as search became mired in local optima and plateaus; a cut-off of 200 iterations was found to be a reliable measure of the failure of the method to solve a puzzle. Hence it was deemed necessary to employ a pre-processing stage (Section 4.4 below) and a modification to the algorithm (Section 4.5). The most successful coefficients were then chosen on the basis of reliable and direct ascent in the solution of a broad range of puzzles, with the pairing w_1=1 and w_2=–1 being chosen as, on average, it returned the goal state in the least number of iterations.

4.4 The Initial State

Section 3 defined a state as being a structured collection of the right objects (*i.e.* the missing digits) placed in the empty spaces, such that each mini-grid contains all the digits 1 to 9 (albeit not necessarily in the correct order). These missing digits could be placed in any order so as to construct an initial state for the puzzle. However, a method that provides a good ordering that reduces the amount of search space to be examined, while having itself minimal processing cost, would be of great benefit. It is proposed here that a greedy algorithm approach is employed in the initial placement of the missing digits. A greedy algorithm makes a locally optimum choice at each stage in the solution of a problem, in the hope that a global optimum may be reached [16].

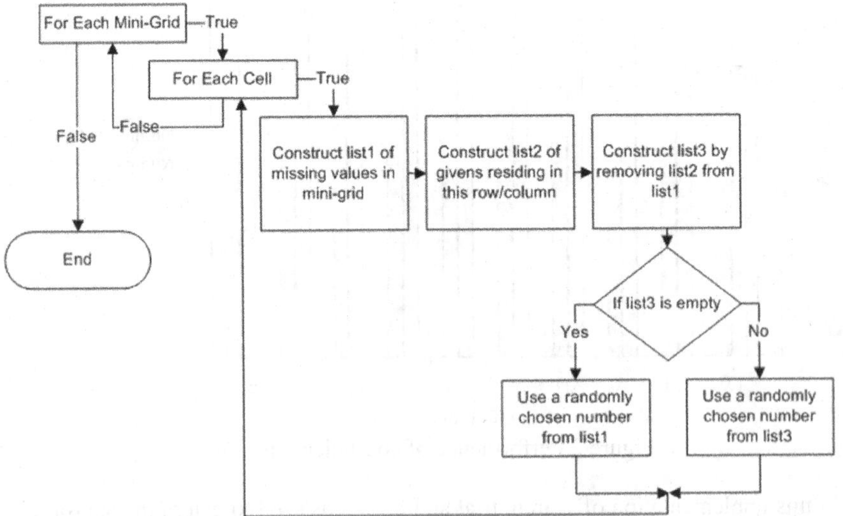

Figure 3 Greedy algorithm for initial placement of missing values

An initial state arrived at through random insertion of the missing digits is likely to contain large numbers of clashes. As a result, any solution to the puzzle is likely to require a large number of swaps. The greedy algorithm proposed here is intended to greatly reduce the number of clashes in the initial state, but not to fully solve the puzzle. The algorithm is detailed in Figure 3. It places the missing numbers in each mini-grid in turn, filling each empty cell with the next available number that produces no clashes with the givens. At some stage within this process, it would be necessary to make placements that do incur clashes, but the overall number of initial clashes is greatly reduced. This employs a greedy algorithm that makes locally optimum choices at each placement, albeit with little realistic hope of finding a global optimum (as the algorithm is not then pursued to make further improvements to the overall placement).

In order to improve this initial placement further, a limited *post-swapping* was performed. All values which clash with a given are swapped with another value in that mini-grid that does not produce a new such clash (selecting other non-given values from the mini-grid, ordered randomly, until a suitable one is found or no more are available, in which case the clash remains). The improvement in performance due to this amendment, measured using those puzzles from the test set that were ultimately solved, is illustrated in Figure 4. This shows averaged measures of the algorithm performance (shown as number of iterations, or moves required to reach a goal), the improvement in the f_1 part of the objective function for the initial state, and the reduction in the number of clashes with givens in the initial state. The cost of performing the initialization is measured in milliseconds. (All tests were performed on a Viglen Intel Pentium 4, 3.40GHz computer, with 1.99GB RAM, using implementations in Java using JDeveloper 10g.) For the low cost in processing time, the greedy algorithm and post-swapping are considered worth performing. It is also worth noting that this improved initialization solved a small number of the easiest puzzles (that have many givens) without the need for subsequent search.

	Greedy algorithm alone	Greedy algorithm and post-swapping
Time to Initialise (ms)	2	5
Number Of Iterations	71	66
f_1 score	164	173
Remaining Clashes	59	26

Figure 4 Difference in performance due to greedy algorithm amendment

4.5 Modification to the Search Algorithm

The success of the hill climbing approach described in this paper is quite strongly related to standard measures of puzzle complexity. For simple Sudoku puzzles, the algorithm is capable of reaching a goal state in relatively few moves. For more difficult puzzles, the approach becomes trapped in local maxima and plateaus, as is common with hill climbing. This leads to an observation concerning the objective function constructed: although the heuristics do ensure, generally, a direct descent through the search space towards a goal, they actually measure relatively little concerning the problem domain. Hence, many states in the space can map to the same objective function value, and for more difficult Sudoku puzzles, it seems common to reach an intermediate state for which many states in its neighbourhood share the same highest objective function score. That is, a plateau is reached, from which the algorithm cannot escape. In initial experimentation, a priority queue was employed to enable backtracking to earlier, more seemingly promising paths. However, this met with limited success, as the same high objective function score might be found in many different parts of the space. Instead, a different approach was taken.

Here, a random-restart hill climbing approach was implemented. The priority queue was used as a means of detecting plateau, such that once the first 10 highest scoring solutions all shared the same score, and none of those solutions had successors with better scores, it was assumed that a plateau had been reached. (Experiments with different cutoffs revealed that 10 was a sufficient number.) At such a point, the queue was cleared and a new initial state was generated (again using the method of Section 4.4). Search recommenced with the new initial state.

All Sudoku puzzles in the test set of 100 puzzles were solved successfully using this modified approach.

5 Evaluation and Conclusions

All tests were performed on a Viglen Intel Pentium 4, 3.40GHz computer, with 1.99GB RAM, using implementations in Java using JDeveloper 10g.

Runs of the algorithm were analyzed as to the time taken (in milliseconds), the number of iterations (moves) which had to be performed to complete each puzzle, and the number of random restarts required. Generally, the number of iterations increased with the rated complexity of the puzzle, as shown in Figure 5 (which shows averaged values for the number of givens, number of iterations, number of restarts and time to solve, for all 100 puzzles in the test set). The hardest of the puzzles required, typically, relatively large numbers of iterations. In all categories, a small number of puzzles required a number of restarts greatly uncharacteristic for that grouping, with all other puzzles completing in similar numbers of iterations. (The median numbers of restarts were 0 for the *Easy* and *Medium* categories, and 3 for the *Hard* and *Hardest* categories.)

Level	Average Number of Givens	Average Number of Iterations	Average Number of Restarts	Average Time to Solve (ms)
Easy	31.12	233.96	0.12	1443996.56
Medium	25.84	392.08	1.08	1256019.20
Hard	23.44	724.60	2.80	3110608.32
Hardest	20.33	3587.58	3.39	34921304.31

Figure 5 Results by Problem Complexity Rating

Similarly, the number of iterations generally decreased with the number of givens (Figure 6). Again, there were exceptions as the relationship between the problem complexity and the number of givens is not entirely straightforward. A small number of puzzles in the category of most givens had already been solved by the initialization (Section 4.4 above). Most puzzles with more than 23 givens required no restarts (with the median numbers of restarts being 0 in all three of those categories, and 3 in the *16-23 Givens* category).

Number of Givens	Average Number of Iterations	Average Number of Restarts	Average Time to Solve (ms)
16-23	1571.652	3.086957	12419636
24-30	548.3182	1.386364	2357723
30-36	64.56522	0.130435	46220.17
37+	1	1.333333	10.33333

Figure 6 Results by Number of Givens

While the objective function was simple, it proved a sufficiently effective measure of closeness to goal state, as demonstrated by the successful solution of all puzzles, and the lack of need for restarts in most of the simpler cases. However, for Sudoku puzzles of greater complexity, the objective function leads to search spaces that have wide plateaus in many regions, preventing the algorithm from reaching a solution from every initialization. Modification of the initialization had a great impact on the ability of the algorithm to reach a goal state, and for all puzzles tested, an appropriate initialization was found from which a direct path to a goal existed without being 'interrupted' by a plateau. (Indeed, initialization was a more important determinant in the speed with which solutions were found than experimentation with the objective function.)

Comparison of the results presented here with constraint satisfaction approaches is made difficult by the segregation of results in those papers according to whether the puzzles considered were solved with or without additional search processing, and no actual timings for solution by any meta-heuristic approach yet appear in the literature; a Linear Programming approach has reported solution of a puzzle with 32 givens in 16 seconds [6], which bears close comparison with results here. However, the purpose of this paper is not to demonstrate the efficiency of the approach described (and indeed, other algorithms could be implemented more efficiently). Rather, the purpose is to show that the puzzle can be solved reliably and in a reasonably small amount of time, using a simple heuristic search approach and straightforward objective function tailored to the problem domain.

The nature of the Sudoku puzzle would indicate that many meta-heuristic approaches (such as genetic algorithms, particle search or ant colony optimization [16]) that employ pools of solutions, and possibly means of mutating solutions to avoid local maxima, might be appropriate. However, this paper demonstrates that such elaborate schemes are probably not justified. The employment of heuristics and problem initialization that directly exploit features of the problem domain are sufficient for the reliable solution of puzzles, regardless of rated complexity and number of givens. Further, it is expected that approach to the construction of heuristics and problem initialization can be generalised to Sudoku grids of greater size.

References

1. Yato T and Seta T. Complexity and Completeness of Finding another Solution and its Application to Puzzles. In: Proceedings of the National Meeting of the Information Processing Society of Japan, IPSJ, Japan, 2002 (SIG Notes IPSJ-2002-AL-87-2)
2. Pegg E. Enumerating Sudoku Variations, available at http://www.maa.org/editorial/mathgames/mathgames_09_05_05.html, 2005
3. Dotu I., del Val A and Cebrian M. Redundant modeling for the quasigroup completion problem. In: Rossi, F. (ed.), Principles and Practice of Constraint Programming (CP 2003), Springer-Verlag, Berlin, 2003, pp 288-302 (Volume 2833 of Lecture Notes in Computer Science)
4. Gomes C and Shmoys D. The Promise of LP to Boost CP Techniques for Combinatorial Problems. In: Jussien N and Laburthe F (eds.), Proceedings of the Fourth International Workshop on Integration of AI and OR techniques in Constraint Programming for Combinatorial Optimisation Problems, CPAIOR, France, 2002, pp 291–305
5. Simonis H. Sudoku as a constraint problem. In: Hnich B, Prosser P and Smith B (eds.) Modelling and Reformulating Constraint Satisfaction Problems, Proceedings of the Fourth International Workshop, CP, 2005, pp 13-27
6. Bartlett AC and Langville AN. An Integer Programming Model for the Sudoku Problem. Preprint, available at http://www.cofc.edu/~langvillea/Sudoku/sudoku2.pdf, 2006
7. Gordon R. Minimum Sudoku. Internal Report. University of Western Australia, 2006
8. Rich E and Knight K. Artificial Intelligence (2nd Edition), McGraw-Hill: Singapore, 1991
9. Jones SK. Solving methods and enumeration of Sudoku. Final Year Project. University of Glamorgan, 2006
10. Lynce, I and Ouaknine, J. Sudoku as a SAT problem. In: Golumbic M, Hoffman F and Zilberstein S (eds.), Proceedings of the Ninth International Symposium on Artificial Intelligence and Mathematics , AIMATH, 2006
11. Kwon G and Jain H. Optimized CNF Encoding for Sudoku Puzzles. In: Hermann M (ed.) Proceedings of the 13th International Conference on Logic Programming for Artificial Intelligence and Reasoning, available at http://www.lix.polytechnique.fr/~hermann/LPAR2006/short/submission_153.pdf , 2006
12. Moraglio A, Togelius J and Lucas S. Product Geometric Crossover for the Sudoku puzzle. In: Yen GG, Wang L, Bonissone P and Lucas SM (eds.), Proceedings of the IEEE Congress on Evolutionary Computation, IEEE Press, pages 470-476, 2006
13. Cazenave T and Labo IA. A Search Based Sudoku solver, available at http://www.ai.univ-paris8.fr/~cazenave/sudoku.pdf, 2006

14. Felgenhauer B and Jarvis F. Enumerating Possible Sudoku Grids. Internal Report. University of Sheffield, 2005
15. Inkala A. AI Escargot - The Most Difficult Sudoku Puzzle, Lulu Publishing, 2007
16. Michalewicz Z and Fogel DB. How to Solve It: Modern Heuristics, Springer: Berlin, 2000

Escaping Local Optima: Constraint Weights vs. Value Penalties

Muhammed Basharu[1], Inés Arana[2], and Hatem Ahriz[2]

[1] 4C, University College
Cork, Ireland
[2] School of Computing
The Robert Gordon University
Aberdeen, UK
mb@4c.ucc.ie, {ia,ha}@comp.rgu.ac.uk

Abstract. Constraint Satisfaction Problems can be solved using either iterative improvement or constructive search approaches. Iterative improvement techniques converge quicker than the constructive search techniques on large problems, but they have a propensity to converge to local optima. Therefore, a key research topic on iterative improvement search is the development of effective techniques for escaping local optima, most of which are based on increasing the weights attached to violated constraints. An alternative approach is to attach penalties to the individual variable values participating in a constraint violation. We compare both approaches and show that the penalty-based technique has a more dramatic effect on the cost landscape, leading to a higher ability to escape local optima.

We present an improved version of an existing penalty-based algorithm where penalty resets are driven by the amount of distortion to the cost landscape caused by penalties. We compare this algorithm with an algorithm based on constraint weights and justify the difference in their performance.

1 Introduction

There are two main categories of search algorithms in constraint satisfaction: constructive and iterative improvement/local search. While the former algorithms are complete, the latter offer the advantage of quicker convergence, albeit often to local optima. Techniques for escaping local optima can be categorised as: (i) Strategies based on the introduction of some non-improving decisions in order to attempt to move the search away to other regions of the search space where the algorithm can resume the search for a solution, e.g. a random move with a small probability; (ii) Strategies which try to determine the sources of the deadlocks (local optima) and seek moves that directly attempt to resolve them, e.g. the breakout algorithm (BA) [8]. In BA, the shape of the objective/cost landscape is modified by increasing the weight of the constraints which are not satisfied at a local optimum. The breakout approach has been shown to be very effective for solving several types of problems and a number of algorithms have been proposed which use this technique, e.g PAWS [9].

More recently, Basharu et al. [1] proposed a technique which associates penalties to domain values, rather than to constraints albeit for solving Distributed CSPs. They presented the DisPeL algorithm and included a comparison between DisPeL and the Distributed Breakout (DBA) [12] which showed that the former outperforms the latter in distributed graph colouring and random distributed constraint satisfaction problems.

In this paper, we analyse the weight-based and penalty-based techniques for escaping local optima (weights on constraints vs. penalties on domain values) and justify the difference in their performance. We also propose a modification to the penalty resetting strategy used in DisPeL which improves its overall performance.

The remainder of this paper is structured as follows. Section 2 gives some definitions and background knowledge. The two landscape modification techniques, i.e. constraint weights and value penalties are explained in Sections 3 and 4 respectively. We highlight a weakness of the weigthts-based approach and illustrate, through and example, why the penalty-based technique does not suffer from this disadvantage. We then propose a new penalty resetting strategy for the penalty-based algorithm DisPeL and show, empirically, its effectiveness (Section 5). Finally, Section 6 compares an algorithm based on constraint weights (DBA) with an algorithm based on value penalties (DisPeL) and justifies the latter's advantage over the former.

2 Background

A Constraint Satisfaction Problem (CSP) consists of a tuple $< X, D, C >$ where $X = \{x_1, ..., x_n\}$ is a set of variables; $D = \{d_1, ..., d_n\}$ is a set of domains, one for each variable in X and; C is a set of constraints which restrict the values that variables can take simultaneously. A solution to a CSP is an assignment for each variable in X which satisfies all the constraints in C.

A Distributed Constraint Satisfaction Problem (DisCSP) is a CSP where the problem is distributed over a number of agents $A = \{A_1, ..., A_k\}$. Each agent A_i represents a set X_i of variables it controls such that $\forall i \neq j, X_i \bigcap X_j = \phi$ and $\bigcup_{i=1..k} X_i = X$. It is often the case that an agent holds one variable only, i.e. $\forall i \in [1..k]|X_i| = 1$. Agents communicate with other agents they know of by sending messages. Without loss of generality, we assume that messages arrive to their destination in finite time and that messages are received in the order in which they were sent. We also assume that each agent is responsible for one variable only.

DisCSP are particularly challenging due to *privacy* and *partial knowledge* of a problem [11]. Thus, agents only know the domains and the constraints for the variables they represent. An agent may only reveal to other agents the current assignments to its variables. These features distinguish distributed constraint satisfaction from parallel or distributed approaches for solving traditional CSPs. DisCSPs are solved by a collaborative process, where each agent tries to find assignments for its variables that satisfy all associated constraints.

3 Modifying the cost landscape with constraint weights

Morris [8] introduced a strategy for dealing with local optima in boolean satisfiability (SAT) problem resolution by modifying the shape of the cost landscape. His technique enables the search to focus on resolving clauses (constraints) that are repeatedly unsatisfied and regularly associated with local optima by attaching weights to these constraints. The cost function of the problem to be solved is as follows:

$$h = \sum_{i=1}^{n} cw_i * viol(c_i) \tag{1}$$

where:
c_i is the ith constraint
cw_i is the weight of the ith constraint
$viol(c_i)$ is 0 if the constraint is satisfied, 1 otherwise.

Variables: [x,y]

Domains: Dx = Dy = [1..20]

Constraints: c1 : y < 10
c2 : not((y < 10) AND (x < 18) AND (x > 8))
c3 : x > 2

Constraint Weights: cw1 = 1
cw2 = 1
cw3 = 1

Current Assignment: x = 10, y = 16

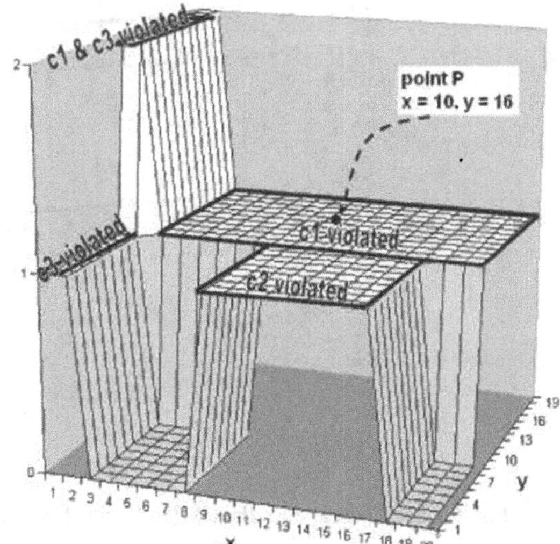

Fig. 1. A CSP and its cost landscape

We illustrate the use of weights on constraints using two examples. In these examples, when two or more variable values lead to the same maximal improvement, the first (lowest) value is chosen. First we look at the simple CSP and its cost landscape in Figure 1. There is a raised area at cost 1 where only c_1 is violated, another one where only c_2 is violated and a third one where only c_3 is violated. There is also a raised area at cost 2 where both c_1 and c_3 are violated. In addition, there are two regions with solutions, i.e. all constraints are satisfied.

Initially, the problem is in state $x = 10, y = 16$ (point P in Figure 1) and constraint c_1 is violated (cost 1). No change in an individual variable improves the situation: (i) changing the value of x does not affect the truth value for constraint c_1; (ii) changing the value of y could change the truth value of c_1, but only at the expense of violating constraint c_2. As both c_1 and c_2 have the same associated weight (1) changing the value of y does not improve the overall cost. Since c_1 is violated at point P, its weight cw_1 is increased to 2, changing the shape of the cost landscape (see Figure 2). The additional weight carried by constraint c_1 has raised point P making improvements possible as follows: (i) y can change its value to 1, hence satisfying the heavy constraint c_1, but violating the light constraint c_2 (point Q in Figure 2); (ii) finally, variable x can change its value to 3 so all constraints are satisfied (point R in Figure 2). Therefore, the problem has been solved and R $(x = 3, y = 1)$ is the solution found.

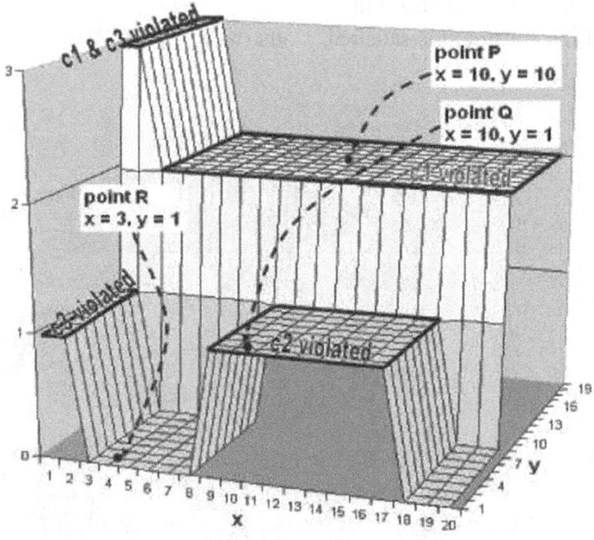

Fig. 2. Cost landscape for the CSP in Figure 1 with increased weights for c_1

It can be seen from the example that when the search is stuck at a local optimum - in this case within a plateau - the weights attached to violated constraints are increased, thus changing the shape of the cost landscape so that the search can resume downhill. However, there are problems for which this technique is ineffective because for some deadlocks it does not raise the current state compared to its surrounding areas so the search cannot find a path out of the local optimum. The example CSP in Figure 3 illustrates this problem and shows the cost landscape given the current assignment. Here, the search is in a deadlock state (point P) on a plateau where only c_1 is violated. There are two other plateaus in the landscape: the region where both constraints are violated and the region where just c_2 is violated. There is also a small region with solutions (e.g., $x = 11, y = 1$).

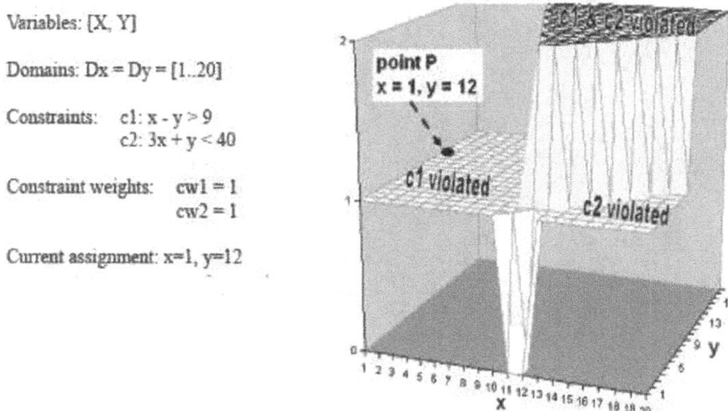

Fig. 3. A CSP and its cost landscape

An attempt to resolve the deadlock using constraint weights increases the weight cw_1 of the violated constraint c_1 to 2, producing the cost landscape in Figure 4. It can be seen from this figure that the problem solving is still in a deadlocked state, since not only the plateau containing the deadlock has been raised, but also every possible point the search could consider moving to within one step. The search is, therefore, unable to find a path out of the plateau and the deadlock remains unresolved. Increasing the weight on c_1 any further simply raises the plateau containing the deadlock and all points the search could consider moving to, but the conflict remains, albeit at a higher altitude. This problem with the given initialisation can, therefore, not be solved using the breakout technique (weights on constraints) alone.

4 Modifying cost landscapes with penalties on domain values

The DisPeL algorithm for solving Distributed CSPs [1], includes the technique of associating penalties with domain values, rather than weights on constraints, in order to escape local optima. Thus, the emphasis is on the assignments associated with constraint violations at local optima rather than on the constraints violated at that point. As a penalty is attached to each individual value in every variable's domain, the cost function to be minimised by the search for each variable is as follows:

$$h(d_i) = v(d_i) + p(d_i) \tag{2}$$

where:

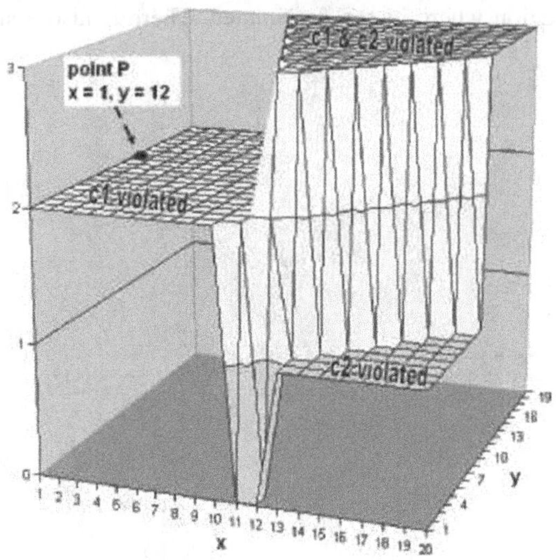

Fig. 4. Effect of constraint weight increase on the cost landscape for the CSP in Figure 3.

d_i is the ith value in the variable's domain
$v(d_i)$ is the number of constraints violated if d_i is selected
$p(d_i)$ is the penalty attached to d_i (initially 0)

When the underlying search is stuck at a local optimum, penalties attached to the values currently assigned to the variables involved in violated constraints are increased, therefore contorting the cost landscape around the deadlocked region. In order to illustrate landscape modification with this technique, the two examples from section 3 (Figures 1 and 3) are used. As with the breakout algorithm, when two or more variable values lead to the same maximal improvement, the first (lowest) value is chosen.

Let's first look at the example in Figure 1. Its initial cost landscape is shown in it. Since the search is stuck at a local optimum (point P in Figure 1) the penalty on the current value of y (i.e. the variable involved in the violated constraint c_1) is increased, resulting in the cost landscape shown in Figure 5. It can be seen from this figure that a new ridge has appeared which contains the point of the deadlock P. The search can now resume downhill with $y = 1$ (point Q), followed by $x = 3$ (point R). Note that if a value of y had been chosen which prevents x from changing its value too (e.g. $y = 14$) the penalties would have been applied to this value, causing a new ridge in the cost landscape from which the search could be resumed.

Let's now look at the example in Figure 3 which could not be solved using the breakout. The initial cost landscape is also shown in this figure. Since constraint c_1 is violated and there is no possible improvement, a penalty is attached to the values of variables involved in c_1. The values $x = 1$ and $y = 12$ are therefore penalised, contorting the cost landscape (see Figure 6) with new peaks and ridges from which the search can resume as follows: (i) variable x changes its value to 2 (point Q); (ii) y

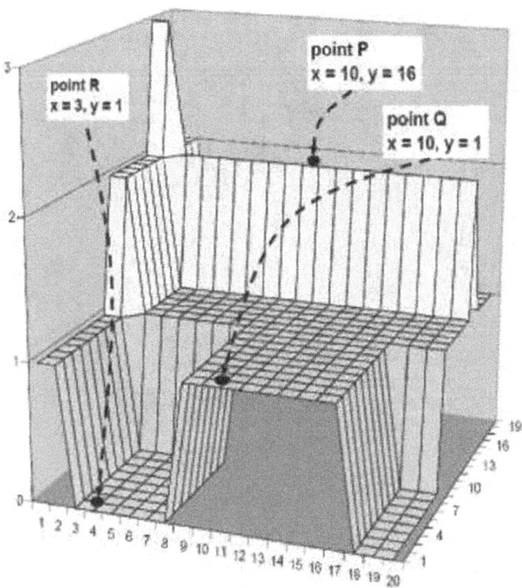

Fig. 5. Effect of penalty increases on the cost landscape for the CSP in Figure 1 i.e. increased penalty attached to $D_y(16)$ from 0 to 1.

changes its value to 1 (point R); (iii) finally, x changes its value to 11 (point S), and the problem is solved.

One contribution of this paper is the explanation of why a penalty-based approach can outperform a weight-based approach. The former technique is finer-grained and allows for more dramatic contortions in the cost landscape, causing peaks and ridges to appear, as illustrated with the example in Figure 3. Besides contorting plateaus, domain penalties may be thought of as a primitive form of learning. As penalties attached to particular values grow, the search is able to gradually *learn* of the association between the assignments and local optima. Hence, regions containing those assignments are excluded from further exploration as the search progresses.

5 Penalty resets guided by the cost landscape

Based on the technique of escaping local optima by associating penalties to domain values, DisPeL [1] uses two types of penalties (incremental and temporary) in a two phased strategy as follows:

1. In the first phase, the solution is perturbed by attaching a *temporary penalty* to the culprit variables values in an attempt to force agents to try other combinations of values, and allow exploration of other areas of the search space. This phase is used

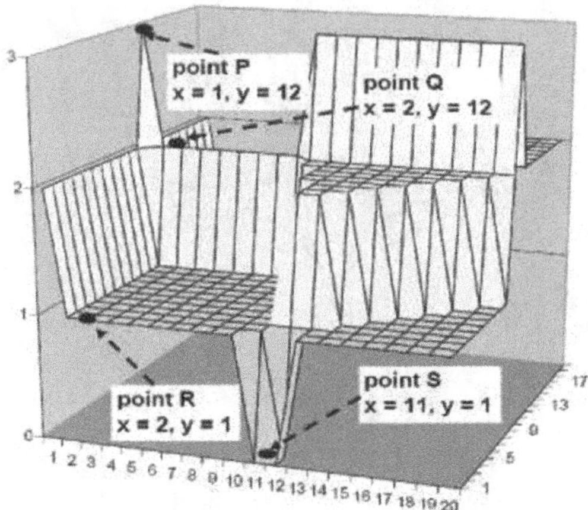

Fig. 6. Effect of penalty increases on the cost landscape for the CSP in Figure 3, i.e. increased penalties attached to $D_x(1)$ and $D_y(12)$ from 0 to 1.

when a local optimum is visited for the first time or when it hasn't been visited for a long time.

2. If the perturbation fails to resolve a deadlock, i.e. a recent deadlock is revisited, agents try to learn about and avoid the value combinations that caused the deadlock by increasing the *incremental penalties* attached to the culprit values.
3. Whenever an agent detects a deadlock and has to use a penalty, it imposes the penalty on its current assignment and asks its neighbours to impose the same penalty on their current assignments as well.
4. A no-good store is used to keep track of deadlocks encountered, and hence, used to help agents decide what phase of the resolution process to initiate when a deadlock is encountered.

The incremental penalty is small and accumulative and its effect lasts for a number of cycles. The temporary penalty, on the other hand, is larger and it is discarded as soon as it is used, i.e. it only lasts one cycle.

The use of weights on constraints has been shown to have undesirable effects on the cost landscape [8, 10] and, therefore, there are mechanisms to undo their impact. Similarly, the DisPeL algorithm uses a periodic penalty reset every 6 cycles, thus resetting all penalties to zero. The empirical justification for resetting every 6 cycles in [1] is not entirely convincing as other values appeared to give similar results. In addition, it is unclear how this reset policy affects different types of problems.

Here, we show that the penalties on values used by DisPeL can easily dominate cost functions, since they are given equal weighing with constraint violations (see Equation 2). This can drive the search away from promising regions because, as penalties grow, the search is moved towards regions where values have the least penalties rather than the least constraint violations. Moreover, the effect that penalties have in the cost landscape depends on the problem at hand, rather than on the number of cycles elapsed since the penalties were imposed.

A contribution of this paper is a resetting strategy based on the effect of penalties on the cost landscape, rather than on the number of cycles elapsed. Thus, the penalties of all values in a variable's domain are reset to zero, after variable assignment, in the following situations:

Consistency: When a variable has a consistent value as it is assumed that penalties become redundant when a variable has a consistent value.

Distortion: When a variable's cost function is distorted. This is detected when the following two conditions are satisfied simultaneously:

- **Condition 1:** The evaluation (h) of the current assignment is the least in a variables domain.
- **Condition 2:** There is another value in the domain which has fewer constraint violations than the current assignment.

The consistency rule simply states that if a variable's assignment is not causing problems currently, the cases when it was a problem in the past can now be ignored. This gives the algorithm room to manoeuver when the variable's assignment suddenly becomes inconsistent or has to partake in deadlock resolution with inconsistent neighbours.

The distortion rule is akin to an aspiration move (as in Tabu search [4]), where search memory is sometimes ignored. This is illustrated with the example in Figure 7.

$D_x = [w, r, b, g, k]$	$v(D_x) = [3, 5, 2, 3, 6]$	$p(D_x) = [2, 0, 4, 1, 0]$
therefore,		
$h(D_x) = [5, 5, 6, 4, 6]$ and the current assignment with the least $h(D_x)$ is $< x = g >$.		

Fig. 7. An example of a distorted cost function.

In this example, the cost function is distorted because the assignment $< x = g >$ has the least sum of constraint violations and penalties whereas the assignment $< x = b >$ violates fewer constraints and as such the cost function is being distorted by the penalties. Thus, penalties have become dominant in decision-making. Resetting penalties when this happens allows the algorithm to keep paths to solutions open.

Despite the clear advantage of penalty resets, using these too frequently could cause the search to oscillate as it continuously removes the (recently put up) barriers that prevent it from returning to previously visited (and infeasible) regions of the search space. An empirical analysis of the benefits of our new reset strategy when compared to the risks of frequent reset has been conducted. Table 1 shows the results of experiments for solving 100 randomly generated DisCSPs which clearly indicate that penalty resets are necessary. They also show the positive impact of the new penalty reset strategy on the percentage of problems solved (all problems used were solvable), and on the average search cost (100 run/problem instance were used).

Penalties differ from constraint weights fundamentally in the way they affect cost functions. While weights can be seen as fully integrated into an underlying function, penalties are more like modifiers of an underlying function. Hence, while solvers that rely on constraint weights can successfully solve problems without limiting the growth of weights, it appears that this is not the case with the penalty based strategy. It is clear that penalties do a very good job at blocking off paths to solutions if retained for too long a period. Performance improves when penalties are discarded frequently: more problems are solved and the search costs are at least 78% lower.

Table 1. Comparative evaluation of alternative reset policies for solving 100 randomly generated CSPs $< number\ of\ variables\ n = 60,\ domain\ size\ d = 10,\ density\ p_1 = 0.1,\ tightness\ p_2 = 0.5 >$.

Policy	% solved	average cost
No resets	1	n/a
Reset when consistent	87	1216
Reset when distorted	95	1063
Combined reset	99	275

We have incorporated our reset policy into the DisPeL algorithm and conducted experiments using both the old and the new penalty reset policies in DisPeL in order to solve graph colouring problems with 3 colours and 100 variables for which complexity peaks are well established [2]. We have considered graphs with varying degrees (constraint densities), and for each we have generated 100 solvable instances. Figure 8 shows the median search costs using both the old and the new reset policies. It is clear that the new reset policy leads to a substantial reduction in the cost of DisPeL. In the remainder of this paper, whenever we mention DisPeL we refer to the algorithm with the new penalty reset strategy unless otherwise stated.

Similar ideas of discarding search memory (in the form of weights or penalties) have been explored in the literature. For example, periodic penalty resets were proposed in [7], while regular [3] and probabilistic [6] weight decays have been shown to improve performance of weighted local search algorithms. There, the authors also argue that weights can block paths to solutions when retained. However, there is no equivalent in the literature for resetting penalties when variables find consistent assignments. Also, using both conditions in our distortion rule for resetting penalties is new, as far as we are aware.

6 DBA vs. DisPeL

In order to evaluate the two strategies for escaping local optima we have conducted a number of experiments comparing the constraint-weights and the value-penalty ap-

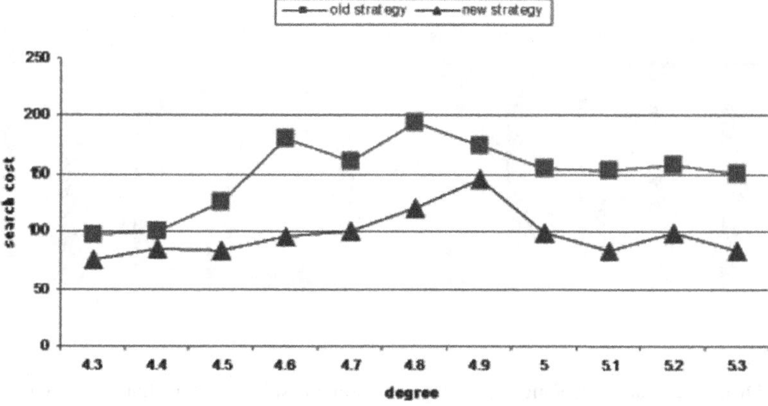

Fig. 8. Comparison of the median search cost of the old (every 6 cycles) and new (whenever the cost landscape is distorted) reset policies in solving graph colouring problems $< number\ of\ variables\ n = 100, number\ of\ colours\ k = 3, degree = 4.7 >$.

proaches. Since the original penalty-based algorithm (DisPeL) was distributed and there are successful distributed versions of the weighted constraint algorithms (e.g. DBA [12] and Multi-DB [5]) we have compared the two (weight- and penalty-based) strategies for escaping local optima by comparing DBA and DisPeL. The maximum number of iterations was set to $200n$ for DBA and $100n$ for DisPeL, thus taking into account DBA's 2-iteration cycles and making our experiments comparable to those reported in [1].We used graph colouring, random and car sequencing problems for our evaluation. Basharu et al. conducted experiments with the first two types of problems [1], albeit with their version of DisPeL (with the 6-cycle reset strategy). Their results showed that DisPeL outperformed DBA, solving substantially more problems at significantly smaller costs. The results that we have obtained show an even better performance for our version of DisPeL (with the new reset penalty) so, for reasons of space, these results are not included here.

Car sequencing is not one of the traditional test beds used for evaluating distributed algorithms, but it was used because DisPeL and DBA have not been previously compared on structured problems or problems with non-binary constraints and the car sequencing dataset [3] is one of the few publicly available problem sets where instances are entirely made up of non-binary constraints. Besides, it allows us to present results from problems which have not been randomly generated.

We used instances from the suite of feasible test problems. These are made up of 50 instances, grouped into 5 sets of 10 instances for each of the different workstation

[3] Prob001 from CSPLib at http://www.csplib.org [accessed 26 March 2007]

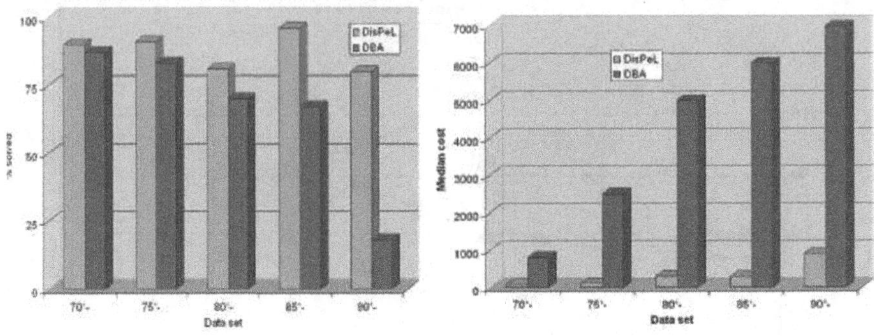

Fig. 9. Distributed car sequencing: percentage of problems solved and median costs by DisPeL and DBA.

capacity rates (or constraint tightnesses) which range from 70% to 90%. In each of these instances there are 200 cars to schedule, 5 workstations, and 17 to 30 configurations of options (or models) to be considered. To generate enough data for analysis, we made 5 attempts on each problem instance starting off with a different random initialisation in each run. The maximum number of iterations was set to 5,000 for DisPeL and 10,000 for DBA. Results of these experiments are presented in Figure 9 showing the percentage of problems solved and the median search costs for the problems solved.

The empirical results comparing DisPeL and DBA which we have obtained demonstrate the strengths of the penalty based strategy for dealing with local optima. We note that for reasons of space not all results are presented here, and remind the reader that the results that we have obtained on graph colouring and random problems show an improvement of DisPeL due to the new reset strategy which we have introduced when compared to results reported in [1]. DisPeL consistently solved more problems than DBA and it required fewer iterations. While the differences in performance of both algorithms vary from one problem class to the next, it appears that the gap widens as constraints get tighter. For example, in distributed graph colouring all constraints have a uniform tightness of 30% and DBA solves nearly as many problems as DisPeL. But as constraint tightness is increased to 50% in the experiments with random DisCSPs, DBA's performance degrades considerably. This is even more evident in the results of the experiments on the car sequencing problems which include constraints with even higher tightness. The experiments with the car sequencing problems illustrate how DBA is adversely affected by the structure of the constraint graph. Its coordination heuristic is designed to prevent connected agents from changing values concurrently to avoid oscillation. But in the case that each variable is connected to every other variable in the problem, only one variable's value is changed in every two iterations. Therefore, search costs are inevitably high.

We explain DisPeL's performance advantage over DBA as follows:

- Landscape modification with domain penalties is more effective at dealing with local optima and it allows quicker resumption of search by the underlying algorithm, compared to modifications with constraint weights.

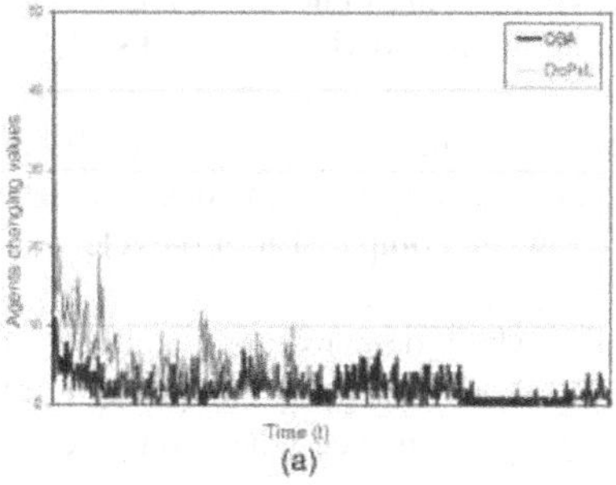

(a)

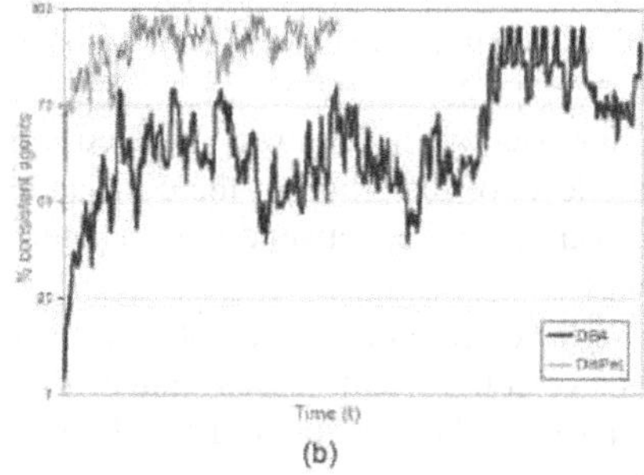

(b)

Fig. 10. Number of agents changing values and number of consistent agents in each iteration for sample runs of DBA and DisPeL.

- The new penalty reset strategy gives the algorithm opportunities to undo negative effects of penalties on the cost landscape. DBA, however, has no such opportunities and as such its performance can be severely hindered by bad decisions made early in the search or ill-advised weight increases.
- While parallel computation in DBA allows agents to reduce idle time, the coordination heuristic can slow the algorithm down considerably by inadvertently cutting down on the number of legal improvements that can take place in a single iteration (see Figure 10 (a)). We observed that there is a lot more activity in each iteration of DisPeL than DBA (in terms of agents changing values) especially in the first few iterations where high percentage of agents quickly become consistent, i.e. only 'critical' deadlocks remain unresolved. For DBA, however, few agents get to change values in each iteration therefore deadlocks tend to linger during the search. As a result, the number of consistent agents increases at a much slower pace than in DisPeL (see Figure 10 (b)).

In summary, the results of comparative evaluations of DisPeL and DBA show that on different problem types, DisPeL solved more problems than DBA and incurred lower search costs in the process. The results also suggest that DisPeL's advantage over DBA widens as constraint graphs become denser, especially since in highly connected graphs DBA's heuristics limit the number of concurrent changes per single iteration.

7 Conclusion

The contributions of this paper are threefold: a comparative analysis of the weight-based vs. the penalty based approach to escaping local optima in local search; a new reset strategy for the penalty-based approach to escaping local optima; an explanation for the difference in performance of the two landscape modification approaches to escaping local optima.

We have presented an analysis of weights on constraints (exemplified by the Breakout) and penalties on domain values (exemplified by DisPeL). We have discussed the way in which each technique modifies the cost landscape, uncovering a limitation of the first technique in cases where the problem gets stuck in a plateau. We have also justified the suitability of the penalty-based technique for solving deadlocks of this type.

Moreover, we have introduced a novel penalty resetting strategy in DisPeL based on the level of distortion to the cost landscape produced by the penalties. We have demonstrated the effectiveness of this new policy when compared to a 6-cycle reset strategy.

We have presented results of empirical studies which demonstrate a competitive advantage of the penalty-based strategy over the Breakout strategy by comparing DBA with DisPeL. We have then justified DisPeL's high performance when compared to DBA.

References

1. Muhammed Basharu, Inés Arana, and Hatem Ahriz. Solving DisCSPs with penalty-driven search. In *Proceedings of AAAI 2005 - the Twentieth National Conference of Artificial Intelligence*, pages 47–52. AAAI, 2005.
2. Peter Cheeseman, Bob Kanefsky, and William M. Taylor. Where the really hard problems are. In *Proceedings of the Twelfth International Joint Conference on ArtificialIntelligence, IJCAI-91, Sidney, Australia*, pages 331–337, 1991.
3. Jeremy Frank. Learning short-term weights for GSAT. In Martha Pollack, editor, *Proceedings of the 15th International Joint Conference on Artificial Intelligence (IJCAI97)*, pages 384–391, San Francisco, August 1997. Morgan Kaufmann.
4. Fred Glover. Tabu search - part I. *ORSA Journal on Computing*, 1(3):190–206, Summer 1989.
5. Katsutoshi Hirayama and Makoto Yokoo. Local search for distributed SAT with complex local problems. In *Proceedings of the first international joint conference on Autonomous agents and multiagent systems*, AAMAS 2002, pages 1199 – 1206, New York, NY, USA, 2002. ACM Press.
6. Frank Hutter, Dave A. D. Tompkins, and Holger H. Hoos. Scaling and probabilistic smoothing: Efficient dynamic local search for SAT. In P. Van Hentenryck, editor, *Proceedings of the 8th International Conference on Principles and Practice of Constraint Programming (CP02)*, volume 2470 of *LNCS*, pages 233–248, London, UK, September 2002. Springer-Verlag.
7. Patrick Mills. *Extensions to Guided Local Search.* PhD thesis, University of Essex, Essex, 2002.
8. Paul Morris. The breakout method for escaping from local minima. In *Proceedings of the 11th National Conference on Artificial Intelligence*, pages 40–45, 1995.
9. John Thornton, Duc Nghia Pham, Stuart Bain, and Valnir Ferreira Jr. Additive versus multiplicative clause weighting for SAT. In *Proceedings of AAAI'04*, pages 191–196, 2004.
10. Dave Tompkins and Holger Hoos. Warped landscapes and random acts of SAT solving. In *8th International Symposium on Artificial Intelligence and Mathematics (AMAI 2004)*, January 2004.
11. Makoto Yokoo, Edmund H. Durfee, Toru Ishida, and Kazuhiro Kuwabara. Distributed constraint satisfaction for formalizing distributed problem solving. In *12th International Conference on Distributed Computing Systems (ICDCS-92)*, pages 614–621, 1992.
12. Makoto Yokoo and Katsutoshi Hirayama. Distributed breakout algorithm for solving distributed constraint satisfaction problems. In *Proceedings of the Second International Conference on Multi-Agent Systems*, pages 401–408. MIT Press, 1996.

Dynamic Rule Mining for Argumentation Based Systems

Wardeh, M., Bench-Capon, T., Coenen, F.
The University of Liverpool
Liverpool L69 3BX, UK

Abstract

Argumentation has proved to be a very influential reasoning mechanism particularly in the context of multi agent systems. In this paper we introduce PADUA (Protocol for Argumentation Dialogue Using Association Rules), a novel argumentation formalism that dynamically mines Association Rules (ARs) from the case background as a means to: (i) generate the arguments exchanged among dialogue participants, and (ii) represent each participant's background domain knowledge, thus avoiding the traditional knowledge base representations. Dialogue participants mine ARs from their own case data and then use these rules as arguments and counter arguments. This paper fully describes the PADUA formalism and proposes a suite of dynamic ARM algorithms to provide support for the argumentation process.
Keywords: Dynamic rule mining, argumentation.

1 Introduction

Argumentation is an increasingly influential reasoning mechanism, particularly in the context of multi agent systems. One specific model of argumentation is a *Persuasion Dialogue* [11] during which each participant tries to persuade the other participant(s) of their own thesis, by offering arguments that support this thesis. Despite the increasing use of argumentation in a variety of applications, many of the studies in the literature give little importance to the background knowledge the dialogue participants rely on in their efforts to persuade each other. The focus has been on the protocols and the use of argumentation as a means of communication rather than on the content to be communicated. Typically some form of knowledge base is assumed to provide the participants with the necessary domain knowledge. This knowledge base is used to produce arguments according to some underlying argumentation model. (Note that each participant's knowledge base is similar, but not necessarily the same.)

The work described here does not assume that such a knowledge base has been constructed. Instead arguments are mined directly from some set of records providing examples relating to a particular domain. The repository of background knowledge used by each participant is considered to be a binary valued data set where each record represents a previous case and each column an attribute taken from the global set of attributes described by the background knowledge. Given this formalism we can apply *Association Rule*

Mining (ARM) [1] techniques to the data set to discover relations between attributes, expressed in the form of *Association Rules* (ARs), which in turn can be used to support the argumentation process. This approach offers a number of advantages over the knowledge based approach:
- It enjoys general applicability as it does not require the generation of specialised knowledge bases.
- It employs an automatic rule generation process using a "tried and tested" data mining technique and consequently avoids the need for reference to a domain expert.
- The proposed approach avoids the need for any knowledge re-engineering because it works directly with the case data.
- The advocated method generates knowledge "on the fly" according to the requirements of the participant in question (again because it operates with the raw case data).

In addition the approach provides for a natural representation of the participants experience as a set of records, and the arguments as ARs. The advocated approach also preserves the privacy of the information that each participant "knows", therefore it can be used in domains which involve sensitive data.

This paper introduces PADUA (Protocol for Argumentation Dialogue Using Association Rules); a novel argumentation formalism that implements the approach advocated above using a "just in time" approach to ARM; i.e. particular groups of ARs, that conform to some particular requirement as dictated by the PADUA protocol, are mined dynamically as required. The advantage is that the system avoids the overheads associated with the generation of the complete set of ARs represented in the case base. The PADUA system supports three different forms of dynamic ARM request:
1. Find a subset of rules that conform to a given set of constraints.
2. Distinguish a given rule by adding additional attributes.
3. Generalise a given rule by removing attributes.

The rest of this paper is organised as following: Section 2 gives some necessary background information. Section 3 introduces the PADUA protocol and its main components. Section 4 describes the dynamic ARM algorithms developed to support the PADUA protocol. In Section 5 an example of the PADUA systems operation is presented together with some analysis and discussion. Finally some conclusions are drawn in 6.

2 Previous Work

2.1 Argumentation, Dialogue and Dialogue games

Argumentation is a form of nonmonotonic defeasible reasoning, in which participants interact to decide whether to accept or reject a given statement. During the process of argumentation, each participant forms and asserts arguments that contradict or undermine arguments proposed by the other participant(s). The basic idea behind this *argumentational reasoning* is that a statement is acceptable if it can be argued successfully against attacking arguments.

Persuasion Dialogue is used to model this type of argumentation. The literature includes plenty of examples of dialogical argumentation that fall into several areas such as distributed planning [15], education [13], and modelling legal reasoning (a survey can be found in [6]). In their well known typology of dialogue types [14], Walton and Krabbe defined Persuasion Dialogue to be initiated by a conflict in the participants' points of view, the main goal of the dialogue is to resolve this conflict by verbal means, while each participant tries to persuade the other(s) of its own point of view. Their typology of dialogue types classifies five other primary dialogue types, besides persuasion, which are negotiation, information seeking, deliberation, enquiry and Eristic dialogue. This categorisation is based upon: the information each participant has at the commencement of the dialogue; the goals of each individual participant; and the goals of the dialogue itself.

Formal dialogue games have been used successfully to model most of the atomic dialogue types in the Walton and Krabbe typology including persuasion [10, 12, 14]. *Formal Dialogue Games* are defined as interactions between two or more players, where each player moves by making utterances, according to a defined set of rules known as a *Dialogue Game Protocol*. Each move has an identifying name associated with it and some statement which contributes to the dialogue. Players keep on exchanging such moves until the dialogue terminates, according to some termination rules. Dialogue games comprise the following components [11]:

1. *Commencement Rules*: Rules that define the circumstances under which the dialogue commences.
2. *Locutions*: Rules indicating what utterances are permitted at every stage of the dialogue.
3. *Combination Rules*: Rules that describe the dialogical contexts under which particular locutions are permitted or not, or obligatory or not.
4. *Commitments*: Rules that define the circumstances under which participants express commitment to a proposition.
5. *Termination Rules*: Rules that define the circumstances under which the dialogue ends.

2.2 Dynamic Association Rule Mining

The original objective of *Dynamic ARM* (D-ARM), also sometimes referred to as *On-line* ARM, was to address the increasing computational requirements for exploratory ARM (usually involving manual parameter tuning). Subsequently D-ARM has been used in the context of dynamic data mining applications where repeated ARM invocations are required to obtain different sets of rules either with different content (attributes or consequents) or different thresholds. The fundamental idea is to summarise the dataset so that all information required for future association rule mining is encoded in an appropriate data structure that will facilitate fast interaction.

D-ARM was, arguably, first proposed by Amir et al. [4] who used a trie data structure to store the data set and conducted experiments using the (sparse)

Reuters benchmark document set. Although Amir et al. allowed questions such as "find all the ARs with a given support and confidence threshold" to be answered, their system could not answer questions such as "find the association rules that contain a given item set". The approach by Amir et al. is essentially not dissimilar to later approaches to ARM, such as TFP [7] and FP-growth [8], that used an intermediate (summarising) data structure within the overall ARM process (P-trees and FP-trees respectively) although these later approaches did not explicitly considered the advantages with respect to D-ARM that their data structures offered.

The term On-line ARM was introduced by Aggarwal and Yu in 1997 in a technical report. In a subsequent publication, Aggarwal and Yu [2], the authors state that "The idea of on-line mining is that an end user ought to be able to query the database for association rules at differing values of support and confidence without excessive I/O or commutation". Aggarwal and Yu define an adjacency lattice, where two nodes are adjacent if one is a superset of the other, and use this structure for fast (on-line) rule generation. The lattice contains only itemsets whose support is greater than some minimum and consequently only ARs with support above this value can be generated. Hidber [9] also generate a lattice but the user can influence its growth by reducing the support threshold as the algorithm proceeds.

2.3 T-trees

As noted above, for D-ARM to operate successfully a summarising structure is required. In the work described here a T-tree (Total support tree) [7] is used. A T-tree is a "reverse" set enumeration tree data structure; Set enumeration trees impose an ordering on items and then enumerate the itemsets according to this ordering and T-trees are reverse in the sense that nodes are organized using reverse lexicographic ordering; the reason behind this reverse ordering is that T-tree differs from typical set enumeration trees in that the nodes at the same level at any sub-branch of the tree are organized as into 1D arrays so that array indexes represent column numbers, hence "reverse" version of the tree enables direct indexing based on the attribute (column) number.

An example of the T-tree structure is given in Figure 1. In the figure each record in the data set includes the items set x or y, these are the class attributes for the cases and are what the competing PADUA players will wish to establish. It should also be noted that each branch of the T-tree contains the itemsets rooted at a particular end itemset, thus all itemsets involving the class x (y) are contained in one branch of the T-tree (other branches are required for calculating individual AR confidence values). The implementation of this structure is illustrated in Figure 2, where each node in the T-tree is implemented as an object comprised of a support value and a reference to an array of child T-tree nodes.

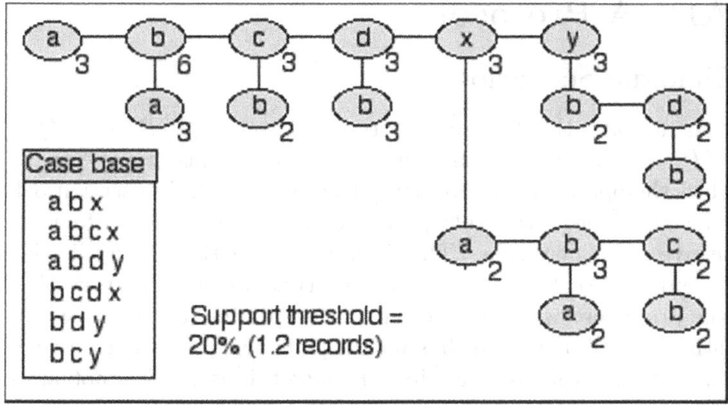

Fig. 1. Example T-tree

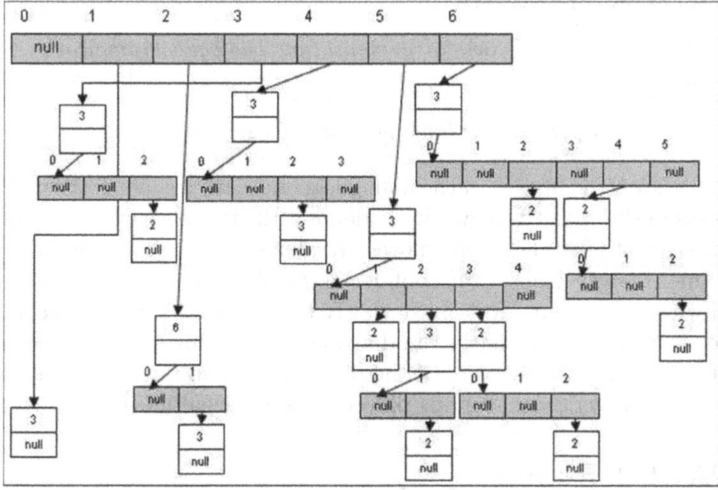

Fig.2. Example T-tree Implementation

The advantages offered by the T-tree structure are as follows:

1. Reduced storage requirements compared to those required by more traditional T-tree structures.
2. Fast look up facilities (by indexing from level to level)
3. Computational advantages because the frequent itemsets with particular consequence (classes) are stored in a single branch of the tree.

These advantages all serve to support D-ARM in general and the requirements for D-ARM supported argumentation in particular. Note that each PADUA player has its own T-tree (set of supported itemsets from which ARs can be obtained) generated from the player's individual case base.

3 PADUA Protocol

3.1 Dialogue Scenario

The proponent starts the dialogue by proposing some AR ($R : P \rightarrow Q$), which premises (P) match the case, and the conclusion (Q) justifies the agent's position. Then the opponent has to play a legal move (see Sub-section 3.4) that would undermine the initial rule proposed by the proponent: four of these moves involve some new rule. This is mined from the player's background database, and represents an attack on the original rule. The turn then goes back to the proponent which has to reply appropriately to the last move. The game continues until one player has no adequate reply. Then this player loses the game, and the other player wins. In fact this is the 'cannot argue any further' situation, and PADUA disallows playing rules that are weaker than previously played ones, which guarantees the dialogues's coherency.

3.2 PADUA Framework

The formal PADUA framework, *Argumentation Dialogue Framework* (ADF), is defined as follows:

$$ADF =< P, Attr, I, M, R, Conf, playedMoves, play > \quad (1)$$

Where P: denotes the players of the dialogue game. $Attr$: denotes the whole set of attributes in the entire framework. I: denotes the instance argued about. M: denotes the set of possible (legal) moves. R: denotes the set of rules that govern the game. $Conf$: denotes the confidence threshold, all the association rules proposed within this framework must satisfy this threshold. $playedMoves$: denotes the set of moves played in the dialogue so far, this set of played moves represents the commitment store of the dialogue system under discussion. Finally, $play$: is a function that maps players to some legal move.

3.3 PAUDA Players

Each player in a PADUA game ($\forall p \in P = Pro, Opp.$)is defined as a dialogical agent [3]:

$$\forall p \in P : p =< name_p, Attr_p, G_p, \Sigma_p, >>_p> \quad (2)$$

where: (i) $name_p$ is the *player* (*agent*) name, $\forall p \in P$ then $name(p) \in \{pro, opp\}$ (ii) $Attr_p$ is the set of attributes the player can understand (knows about), (iii) G_p: is the set of *goals* (class attributes) the player tries to achieve, G_p is defined as a subset of the attributes set $Attr_p$, i.e. G_p is the set of class attributes this player tries to demonstrate to be true, (iv) Σ_p: is the set of potential dynamic ARs the player can mine or has mined from its T-tree and (v) $>>_p$: represents the preferences order over Σ_p, a definition of this preference relationship is suggested as $>>_p$: $\Sigma_p \times \Sigma_p \rightarrow \{true, false\}$, but the exact implementation of this relation may differ from player to player. Σ_p is defined as follows:

$\forall p \in P : \Sigma_p =< T_p, R_p, Dr_p >$; where (i) T_p is the T-Tree representing the background data set, R_p is the set of association rules previously mined by this player and kept in store (thus $R_p = \{r : r =< Prem, Conc, Conf >\}$ where r is AR) and (iii) Dr_p is a function that maps between legal moves and suitable rules ($Dr_p : Tp \times M \rightarrow R$, where R is the set of all possible association rules).

3.4 PAUDA Legal Moves and Game Rules

The set (M) describes the six possible PADUA moves (M) that a player ($p \in P$) can play. The confidence measurement is used to compare the strength of the rules introduced by these moves, mainly because it's been implemented excessively in literature. PADUA moves are defined as follows.:
1. *Propose Rule*: Propose a new rule with a confidence higher than a given confidence threshold, the permises of this rule should be present in the instance under consideration.
2. *Distinguish*: Undermine the current rule proposed by the other player by adding a new attribute(s) satisfied by the instance, such that the confidence of the proposed rule is reduced below a confidence threshold.
3. *Unwanted Consequences*: Indicate that certain attributes in the consequent of the current rule are not present in the current instance.
4. *Counter Rule*: Propose a new rule, with a confidence value in excess of the previously proposed rule, that contradicts the consequent of the previous rule. The permises of the new rule should be present in the instance under consideration.
5. *Increase Confidence*: Add some new attribute, satisfied by the given instance, to the current rule so that the overall confidence rises.
6. *Withdraw Unwanted Consequences*: Remove unwanted attributes from the previously proposed rule while maintaining an appropriate level of confidence.

Not all of the above moves are "legal" moves at every stage of the game. The legal moves each player ($p \in P$) can play are determined by the following set of rules:
1. *Commencement Rules*: The dialogue always starts with a Propose Rule move played by the proponent.
2. *Locutions and Combination Rules*: Table 1 lists the possible moves that each player can play in respons to a move played by the other player. The next move column lists the legal moves according to desirability, according to one plausible strategy.
3. *Termination Rules*: The dialogue ends when a player can not find a suitable rule in its own data set to respond to a move played by the other player.

Move	*Label*	*Next Move*
1	Propose Rule	3, 2, 4
2	Distinguish	3, 5, 1
3	Unwanted Cons.	6, 1
4	Counter Rule	3, 2, 1
5	Increase Conf.	3, 2, 4
6	Withdraw Unwanted Cons.	3, 2, 4

Table 1. Possible Moves

4 Dynamic Association Rules Generation

The basic idea behind the PADUA approach is to mine ARs dynamically as needed according to: (i) desired minimum confidence, (ii) a specified consequent and (iii) a set of candidate attributes for the antecedent (a subset of the attributes represented by the current case). ARs are generated as required by traversing the T-Trees in such a way so that only the rules that match the content selection criteria of some move $m \in M$ are generated. Three dynamic AR retrieval algorithms were developed to support the PADUA protocol:
1. *Algorithm A*: Find a rule that conform to a given set of constraints.
2. *Algorithm B*: Distinguish a given rule by adding additional attributes.
3. *Algorithm C*: Revise a given rule by removing attributes.

Algorithm A (Fig 3) is used to find a new rule (moves 1, 2, 5 and 6) given (i) a current instance (I), (ii) a desired class attribute ($c \in G_p$) and (iii) a desired confidence threshold. The algorithm attempts to minimise the number of attributes in the rule. The algorithm operates by generating candidate itemsets, using the input values, in a level-wise manner; starting with the 2-itemset level in the T-tree(one attribute from the case and the class attribute). For every generated itemset ($S = (A \cup c)$), the T-tree is traversed for the node representing this itemset, if such a node exists, rules of the form ($P \rightarrow Q \cup c$)such that ($P \cup Q = A$), are generated, the algorithm returns the first rule that satisfies the given confidence threshold, otherwise the generation process continues until the entire T-tree has been processed.

Algorithm B (Fig 4) is used to distinguish an input rule $r = (P \rightarrow Q)$. The algorithm operates as follows: (i) generate the candidate itemsets ($P \cup Q \cup a_i$) where ($a_i \in I/(P \cup Q)$), (ii) search the T-tree subbranches for the node representing this itemset, (iii) if such a node exists generate a rule of the form $\acute{r} = ((P \cup a_i) \rightarrow Q)$ if the rule confidence is lower than the input rule confidence return the rule, otherwise traverse through the subtree which root is the candidate itemset for a rule of the form $\acute{\acute{r}} = (\acute{P} \rightarrow \acute{Q})$ that satisfies the conditions listed in the algorithm.

```
Algorithm A (inputs: instance I, class c,
           input T-Tree T,confidence threshold conf)
begin
 ∀s(a_i ∪ c : a_i ∈ I) ∈possible frequent 2-itemset
 if node(s) ∈ T
  generate rule r_dist(a_i ∪ P → Q)
  if r.confidence ≥ conf
   return r
  else
   level = 2
   while (no rules found) and (level ¡ T.max-level)
     ∀s(a_1, ..., a_level ∪ c : a_i ∈ I) ∈
    possible frequent(level+1)-itemset
     if node(s) ∈ T
      if ∃ association rule r(P → Q):
       c ∈ Q and (P ∪ Q = s) and r.confidence ≥ conf
       return r
      else
       Level++
end
```

Fig.3. Algorithm A - Propose New Rules.

```
Algorithm B (inputs: rule r(P → Q), instance I,
           class c,input T-Tree T,
           confidence threshold conf)
begin
 I_sub = I/(P ∪ Q)
 ∀ possible frequent itemset
 s(a_i ∪ P ∪ Q) : a_i ∈ I_sub
  if node(s) ∈ T
   generate rule r_dist(P ∪ a_i → c)
   if r_dist.confidence ≥ r.confidence
    return r_dist
   else
    traverse the sub T-Tree T(s)
    for every child node n ∈ T(s)
     if ∃ association rule r_dist(Ṕ → Q́):
     c ∈ Q́ and (Ṕ ∪ Q́ = n) and (Ṕ ⊆ I)
     and (r_dist.confidence ≤ conf)
      return r_dist
end
```

Fig.4. Algorithm B - Distinguish Rule.

In order to withdraw some unwanted consequences (X) from an input rule ($r = P \rightarrow Q \cup X$), *Algorithm C* (Fig 5) tries first to produce a rule ($\acute{r} = P \rightarrow Q$). If such a rule satisfies the confidence threshold, then the algorithm returns this rule, otherwise, the candidate itemsets are generated and rules are produced and tested in a very similar manner to *Algorithm B* to produce the rule ($\acute{r} = P \rightarrow Q \cup Y$) where ($X \cap Y = \phi$). A player ($p \in P$) may apply *Algorithm C*, both as a defender or attacker of some thesis under discussion. *Algorithm C* therefore takes the status of the player into consideration, so that if the player is defending its point of view the algorithm search for rules which confidence is equal or higher than the input rule. On the other hand, if the player is attacking its opponent's thesis, then the returned rules confidence must not be higher than the confidence of the input rule.

```
Algorithm C (inputs: rule r(P → Q ∪ X), instance I,
            class c,input T-Tree T,
            confidence threshold conf,player role role)
begin
 if (node(P ∪ Q) ∈ T)
  generate rule r_with(P → Q)
   if (role = defender) and
       (r_with.confidence ≥ r.confidence)
     return r_with
   else
    if (role = opponent) and
       (r_with.confidence ≤ r.confidence)
     return r_with
 else
   I_sub = I/(P ∪ Q)
   ∀s(a_i ∪ P ∪ Q : a_i ∈ I_sub) ∈
   possible frequent itemset
   if node(s) ∈ T
    ∀ association rule r_with(P → Q ∪ a_i)
     if (role = defender) and
        (r_with.confidence ≥ r.confidence)
      return r_with
     else
     if (role = opponent) and
        (r_with.confidence ≤ r.confidence)
      return r_with
    else
     traverse the sub T-Tree T(s)
     for every child node n ∈ T(s)
      if ∃ association rule r_with(Ṕ → Q́):
      c ∈ Q́ and (Ṕ ∪ Q́ = n) and (Ṕ ⊆ I)
       if (role = defender) and
          (r_with.confidence ≥ r.confidence)
        return r_with
       else
       if (role = attacker) and
          (r_with.confidence ≤ r.confidence)
        return r_with
end
```

Fig.5. Algorithm C - Withdraw Unwanted Consequences

```
Instance: [adoption-budget-resolution=y, physician-fee-freeze=y.
religious-groups-in-schools=n, el-salvador-aid=y,
superfund-right-to-sue=y, immigration=y, export-act-south-africa=y.]
(1)  proponent  Propose Rule
{physician-fee-freeze=y}->{className = democrat} 92.94%

(2)  opponent   Distinguish
{physician-fee-freeze=y, export-act-south-africa=y}->
{className = democrat, immigration=y} 53.33%

(3)  proponent  Propose Rule
{physician-fee-freeze=y, el-salvador-aid=y}->{className =
democrat} 92.68%

(4)  opponent   Counter Rule
{religious-groups-in-schools=n}->{className = republican} 93.33%

(5)  proponent  Distinguish
{adoption-budget-resolution=y, religious-groups-in-schools=n}->
{synfuels-corporation-cutback=y, className = republican} 37.17%

(6)  opponent   Unwanted Consequences
{synfuels-corporation-cutback=y} not in the case

(7)  proponent  Propose Rule
{physician-fee-freeze=y, immigration=y}->{className = democrat}
93.75%
...
(12) opponent   Propose Rule
{adoption-budget-resolution=y, religious-groups-in-schools=n}->
{className = republican} 96.0%

(13) proponent  Distinguish
{adoption-budget-resolution=y,religious-groups-in-schools=n,
export-act-south-africa=y}->{className = republican} 50.0%

(14) opponent   all moves fail
     proponent  wins --> class = democrat
```

Fig.6. Example Dialogue

5 Experimentation and Analysis

The dynamic AR algorithms (figures 3, 4, 5) were tested using the congressional voting records data set [5]. This dataset includes votes for each of the U.S. House of Representatives members of Congress (in the 1984 US congressional elections) on the 16 key votes identified by the CQA. The congressional voting records database contains 435 instances, among which 45.2% are Democrats and 54.8% are Republicans. The dataset, original comprising 17 binary attributes (including the class attribute) was normalised to 34 unique numerical attributes (numbered from 1 - 34) each corresponding to certain attribute value. The last two values (33 and 34) represents the two classes *Republican* and *Democrat* respectively). This dataset was horizontally divided into two equal size datasets, each of which was assigned to a player in PADUA framework. A T-tree was built for each player using a 10% support threshold, a minimum support threshold of 75% was adopted.

In the dialogue shown in (Figure 6) the two players (the proponent and the opponent) used the protocol rules discussed earlier (Sub-section 2.6), where the moves to be played are determined by the content of the moves played last. In the example the proponent (*pro*) starts the dialogue game by putting forward rule (1) ({`physician-fee-freeze =y`} `->` {`className = democrat`} `92.94%`), to establish that the given case falls under class *Democrat*, in the next move the opponent (*opp*) distinguishes the previous rule by adding the attribute (`export-act-south-africa=y`) to its premises, which causes the confidence to drop below the acceptable threshold. The dialogue continues with rules being proposed, distinguished and rejected for having unacceptable consequences, until step (12) where *opp* proposes a counter rule concluding that the class of the example case is *Republican*, with 96.0% confidence, but *pro* successfully distinguishes this rule in the following move (13). At this point the opponent has no valid moves to play, and thus the proponent wins this game, and persuades the opponent that the example case represents a *Democrat* candidate.

6 Conclusions

In this paper we have described a novel application of D-ARM to support argumentation, specifically dialogue games. The PADUA system (Dynamic Rule Mining for Argumentation Based Systems) is described. PADUA uses D-ARM to obtain ARs in a "just in time" manner that avoids generating all ARs with a confidence value above a given threshold. ARs are generated by interacting with the T-tree data structure that supports fast interaction times. Three specific D-ARM algorithms are described to either: (i) find a subset of rules that conforms to a given set of constraints, or (ii) distinguish a given rule by adding additional attributes or (iii) revise a given rule by removing attributes. The operation of the system is illustrated with an example taken from Congressional Voting benchmark data set. the approach introduced in this paper enjoy certain advantages when compared with other D-ARM techniques in the literature, specially regarding the generation of argumentation rules, mainly answering questions like "find the association rules that contain a given item set", "mine association rules with specific conclusions"... etc. another important advantage of the suggested techniques is that rules of various confidence thresholds can be mined from the auxiliary T-tree.

References

[1] R. Aggrawal, T. Imielinski, and A. N. Swami (1993). Association rules between sets of items in large databases. In Proc. ACM SIGMOD Int. Conf. on Management of Data, pp 207-216.

[2] C.C. Aggarwal and P.S. Yu (1998). Online Generation of Association Rules.Proc. i4th International Conference on Data Engineering (ICDE'98), IEEE, pp 402-411.

[3] L. Amgoud and S. Parsons (2001). Agent dialogues with conflicting preferences. Proc. 8th International Workshop on Agent Theories, Architectures and Languages, pp 1-15.

[4] A. Amir, R. Feldman and R. Kashi (1997). A New and Versatile Method for Association Generation. Proc. 1st Conf. Principles of Data Mining and Knowledge Discovery (PKDD), Springer LNCS, pp 221-231.

[5] C.L. Blake and C.J. Merz (1998). UCI Repository of machine learning databases http://www.ics.uci.edu/ mlearn/MLRepository.html, Irvine, CA: University of California, Department of Information and Computer Science.

[6] T.J.M. Bench-Capon and H. Prakken (2006).Argumentation. In Lodder, A.R. and Oskamp, A. (Eds),Information Technology and Lawyers: Advanced technology in the legal domain, from challenges to daily routine, Springer Verlag, pp 61-80.

[7] F. Coenen, P. Leng and G. Goulbourne (2004).Tree Structures for Mining Association Rules. Journal of Data Mining and Knowledge Discovery, Vol 8, No 1, pp25-51.

[8] J. Han, J. Pei and Y. Yiwen (2000).Mining Frequent Patterns Without Candidate Generation. Proceedings ACM-SIGMOD International Conference on Management of Data, ACM Press, pp1-12.

[9] C. Hidber (1999). Online association rule mining. Proc ACM SIGMOD international conference on Management of data, pp 145-156.

[10] P. Mcburney and S. Parsons (2001). Representing epistemic uncertainty by means of dialectical argumentation, In Annals of Mathematics and Artificial Intelligence 32, 125-169.

[11] P. Mcburney and S. Parsons (2002). Games That Agents Play: A Formal Framework for Dialogues between Autonomous Agents. In Jo. of logic, language and information, 11(3), pp 315-334.

[12] H. Prakken (2000).On dialogue systems with speech acts, arguments, and counterarguments. Proc, 7th European Workshop on Logic in Artificial Intelligence (JELIA 2000), Springer-Verlag, pp 224-238.

[13] E. Sklar and S. Parsons (2004).Towards the Application of Argumentation-Based Dialogues for Education. Proc. 3rd International Joint Conf. on Autonomous Agents and Multiagent Systems, Vol 3, pp 1420-1421.

[14] D. N. Walton and E. C. W. Krabbe. Commitment in Dialogue: Basic Concepts of Interpersonal Reasoning. SUNY Press, (1995), Albany, NY, USA.

[15] Y. Tang and S. Parsons (2005). Argumentation-based dialogues for deliberation. Proc. 4th Int. Joint Conf. on Autonomous Agents and Multiagent Systems, pp 552-559.

AI TECHNIQUES

Extending Jess to Handle Uncertainty

David Corsar, Derek Sleeman, and Anne McKenzie
Department of Computing Science
The University of Aberdeen
Aberdeen, UK
{dcorsar, d.sleeman}@abdn.ac.uk

Abstract

Computer scientists are often faced with the challenge of having to model the world and its associated uncertainties. One area in particular where modelling uncertainty is important are Expert Systems (also referred to as Knowledge Based Systems and Intelligent Systems), where procedural / classification knowledge is often captured as facts and rules. One of the earliest Expert Systems to incorporate uncertainty was MYCIN. The developers realized that uncertainty had to be associated with both the properties of the objects they were modelling and with the knowledge (the rules themselves). A popular engine for building Knowledge Based Systems currently is Jess, which has been extended to handle uncertain knowledge by using fuzzy logic. However, systems written using this extension are generally composed of two interrelated components – namely a Java program and a Jess knowledge base. Further, this technique has several other disadvantages which are also discussed. We have developed a system, Uncertainty Jess, which provides Jess with the same powerful, yet easy to use, uncertainty handling as MYCIN. Uncertainty Jess allows the user to assign certainty factors / scores to both the properties of their data and to the rules, which it then makes use of to determine the certainty of rule conclusions for single and multiple identical conclusions.

1. Introduction: Handling Uncertainty

Humans are good at handling uncertainty in both their everyday and professional lives, and so we perhaps underplay its pervasiveness and importance. There are many ways in which scientists and more recently computer scientists have attempted to model the world and its associated uncertainties. Many approaches to modelling devised by computer science, make the strong distinction between objects which have properties and values, and knowledge which says whether and how those objects should be classified / manipulated when certain conditions (on the objects themselves) are satisfied. One such approach is Expert Systems (also referred to as both Knowledge Based Systems (KBSs) and Intelligent Systems) which were introduced in the 1970s [4]. Here the procedural / classification knowledge is often captured as a rule. To effectively model domains, in this formalism, the developers realized that uncertainty had to be associated with both the properties of the object and with the knowledge (the rules themselves). In the next section (section 2) we discuss a concrete example from the domain of medical decision making, but in general such a formalism needs to address a variety of issues including:

- The need to represent uncertainty in both knowledge and data.
- The details of how such uncertainties are represented
- How the different pieces of evidence are combined.
- How the certainty level of an outcome affects decisions that the Knowledge Based System makes.

We recently developed a system to help medical technicians classify organisms present in blood samples, [5]. The decision was made to use the Jess system [3] as it was readily available here. However, it was soon clear that it was going to be essential in this domain to handle the inherent uncertainty in the *data* being provided by the technicians about various aspects of blood samples (for example the *shape* of the organism). Additionally, the pathologist was also clear that the classificatory rules used in this domain were always associated with uncertainties. That is, even if all the data values could be precisely determined, a range of diseases would virtually always be returned (each associated with a likelihood.) Thus if we were to use the Jess inference engine for this task it was essential that we were able to handle uncertainties at both these levels. This paper describes these investigations.

The structure of the rest of this paper is: section 2 gives an overview of how an early Expert System, MYCIN, handled uncertainty; section 3 give a brief overview of the Jess rule language; section 4 discusses extensions to Jess to enable it to handle uncertainty in a MYCIN-like way; section 5 presents alternative approaches for handling uncertainties in Jess; section 6 compares the several approaches for handling uncertainties; and section 7 provides conclusions and suggestions for future work.

2. Overview of how MYCIN Handled Uncertainty

As noted in the introduction, in many scientific domains there is uncertainty associated with the data which a user is able to provide and also in the domain knowledge. Below, we give a typical MYCIN rule [1] which classifies an organism (in this instance as enterobacteriaceae):

IF the stain of the organism is gram negative

AND the morphology of the organism is rod

AND the aerobicity of the organism is aerobic

THEN the class of the organism is enterobacteriaceae <u>with confidence 0.9</u>

This rule has 3 conditions, and if they are all satisfied then the rule is said to be satisfied when it reports a conclusion (the class of the organism is enterobacteriaceae) with a confidence level of .9, on a confidence scale of -1 (totally negative) to +1 (totally positive). MYCIN uses the term, Certainty Factor (CF), to represent confidence levels. These are discussed in more detail in Figure 1.

Definition of Certainty Factors (CF) in MYCIN

- Range: $-1 \leq CF \leq +1$
- CF level definitions:
  - CF = +1 the fact or rule is certainly true
  - CF = 0 we know nothing about whether the fact or rule is true or not
  - CF = -1 the fact or rule is certainly not true

Figure 1: A Summary of Certainty Factors in MYCIN

2.1 Uncertainty in MYCIN: Data and Rules

When the user inputs values which correspond to the three conditions in the rule shown above he is asked to specify his confidence in the data which he is reporting. Suppose the user has reached the following conclusions about the data (the organism he is analysing under a microscope):

- The stain of the organism is definitely gram negative (CF = 1.0)

- The morphology is rod, with confidence (CF = 0.8) **OR**
- The morphology is coccus, with confidence (CF = 0.2)

- The aerobicity is aerobic, with confidence (CF = 0.6) **OR**
- The aerobicity is anaerobic, with confidence (CF = 0.3) **OR**
- The aerobicity is both, with confidence (CF = 0.1)

Then when asked his confidence in the three conditions in the rule he would answer 1.0, 0.8 & 0.6 respectively. Further, MYCIN has a procedure for calculating the CF for a conclusion of a rule on the basis of the strength of belief in the rule itself and in the various data inputs:

$CF_{conclusion} = CF_{rule} * CF_{data}$, and

$CF_{data} = \min(CF_{d1}, CF_{d2} \ldots. CF_{dn})$ where the CF_{di} are the CFs for the several data inputs (Formula [I])

In this instance:

$CF_{rule} = 0.9$

$CF_{d1} = 1.0$, $CF_{d2} = 0.8$, and $CF_{d3} = 0.6$.

So

$CF_{conclusion} = .9 * \min(1.0, .8, .6)$

$CF_{conclusion} = .9 * .6 = .54$

2.2 Uncertainty in MYCIN: Multiple Conclusions

Not infrequently in rule bases like MYCIN's several rules reach the same conclusion. In fact one could argue that this is the normal situation in KBSs, where a variety of data sources and rules are required to be considered before one is able to reach a conclusion with any level of certainty, as generally KBSs are used in situations where deterministic algorithms do not exist. For these reasons MYCIN needed a mechanism to calculate the cumulative CF for a conclusion reached by several rules. So suppose one had a KB with the following rules:

Rule 1: IF A THEN B

Rule 2: IF C AND D AND E THEN B

The algorithm specifies that one should:

1. Calculate the CF for each rule (i.e. each conclusion, in this case B)
2. Combine the various CFs for that conclusion, using the procedure given below:

- Suppose a rule reports a conclusion with certainty CF_p and another rule reaches the same conclusion with certainty CF_n. How the combined CF (CF_{comb}) is calculated depends on the signs of CF_p and CFn
- IF $CF_p > 0$ & $CF_n > 0$ THEN $CF_{comb} = CF_p + CF_n - CF_p * CF_n$
- IF $CF_p < 0$ & $CF_n < 0$ THEN $CF_{comb} = CF_p + CF_n + CF_p * CF_n$
- ELSE $CF_{comb} = (CF_p + CF_n) / (1 - \min(abs(CF_p), abs(CF_n)))$

(Formula [II])

Figure 2 shows two rules which both have conclusions B. The two rules in this figure are in fact:

Rule1: IF A THEN CONCLUSION B <u>with confidence 1.0</u>

Rule2: IF C AND D AND E THEN CONCLUSION B <u>with confidence 0.9</u>

The above procedure indicates how to determine the conclusion and confidence of both of the rules (using Formula [I]) and then how to combine these confidences (using Formula [II]). So the result of this calculation is .862; the calculations are in fact summarized in Figure 2.

Further, if a third rule also concluded B with a CF of .6 then the overall CF would then become:

$$.862 + .6 - .862 * .6 \quad = .9448$$

and so on for each additional rule which concludes B. Note, too that if a particular CF (say CF_2) = 1 then the CF_{comb} will equal 1 as $(x + 1 - x * 1 = 1)$ (i.e. positive certainty). Analogously, if the CF =-1 then CF_{comb} can be shown to be -1 (i.e., negative certainty).

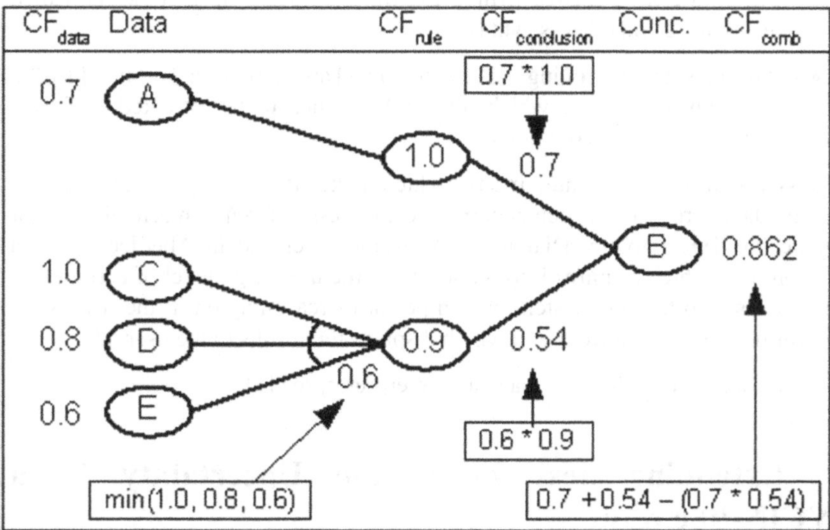

Figure 2: Illustration of how the CFs for data A (0.7), C (1.0), D (0.8), and E (0.6) are combined with the CF for rules Rule 1 (1.0) and Rule 2 (0.9), to give CFs for the conclusion B (0.7 for Rule 1, 0.54 for Rule 2) and how these are combined to give an overall CF for conclusion B (0.862).

So the overall algorithm for calculating the CF for a conclusion is:

- Follow up all conclusions regardless of their Certainty Factors
- Note that we cannot simply take the first chain that provides support, as the next could give more (or less) confidence in the result.
- The stopping condition is when the complete space has been searched OR we find a confidence level of 1.0 OR -1.0.

3. Brief Introduction to Jess

Jess:

- Is a forward chaining rule engine implemented in Java; it is a partial reimplementation / redevelopment of the CLIPS [2] Expert System shell.
- Stores facts in working memory (WM); decisions are made by running rules against the facts currently in WM.
- Allows one to define deftemplates, which specify the structure of facts, and deffacts which assert a series of facts (instances of the deftemplates) to WM.
- Allows users to define rules.
- Allows users to define functions directly in Jess; and user-functions, which are Java classes written externally to Jess, but that can be called using the standard Jess syntax.
- Provides the reasoning engine for JessTab, a plug-in for the Protégé ontology editor [7], which allows Jess rules to be executed against a populated Protégé ontology.

The Jess system is implemented in Java which makes it relatively straight forward to create Java programs which incorporate the Jess inference mechanism. For example, the Haematology Diagnostic Assistant developed in Aberdeen, has a Java front-end which acquires information from the user (e.g., level of certainty of data), passes it to the Jess system, which performs reasoning on it; the results are then returned to the Java front-end which displays the results to the user, [5].

For more details of the Jess language and interpreter, see [3].

4. Extending Jess to handle Uncertainty in a MYCIN-like way

The example discussed in section 2 is one of a number of rules that would be included in a system such as MYCIN. In this section we discuss how one would implement such a rule system in Jess; initially with a simple rule which excludes certainty factors, then one which includes them.

To implement the organism classification described previously, one is required to provide a deftemplate which describes the data that is being observed, and the organisms' classifications; a series of facts which provide the details of the actual observations; and some rules for generating classifications. Sample versions of these are provided in Figure 3.

This provides a simple (deterministic) implementation for classifying organisms of the enterobacteriaceae class, if they are of the gram negative strain, have a rod morphology and aerobic aerobicity. This is however, only part of the story: the example provided previously states that this classification only has a certainty of

0.9: however the implementation shown in Figure 3 does not take this into account.

To include uncertainty in the style of MYCIN into the system shown in Figure 3, we are required to make four changes:

1. The deftemplates for observations and classifications need to include a slot in which the certainty factor can be provided.
2. The rule then needs to be modified to generate a certainty factor for the classification.
3. Another rule is required which detects multiple identical conclusions and calls a function to calculate the certainty factor of multiple identical conclusions.
4. A function would be useful for calculating the combined certainty factor of multiple conclusions.

```
(deftemplate observable "The value of a property based on the
clinicians observations"
    (slot name) ; the name of the property being describes
    (slot value) ; the state, or value attached to the property
)
(deftemplate classification "The class to which the observed
organism has been classified"
    (slot class-name)
)
(deffacts some-observations
  (observable (name strain) (value GramNegative))
  (observable (name morphology) (value rod))
  (observable (name aerobicity) (aerobic))
)
(defrule enterobacteriaceae-classification
  (observable (name strain) (value GramNegative))
  (observable (name morphology) (value rod))
  (observable (name aerobicity) (aerobic))
  =>
  (assert (classification (class-name enterobacteriaceae) ) )
)
```

Figure 3: Example deftemplates and rule for enterobacteriaceae classification.

Changes 1 and 2 are relatively trivial steps, which the developer of the knowledge base would be expected to do. Change 3 is partially generic; so we provide a rule which the developer has to tailor to their own deftemplate used for classifications / conclusions; change 4 is generic enough for us to provide an implementation which developers can simply include in their system. The user / developer is then required to provide certainty factors for both the data (observations in Figure 3) and the rules. When defining the uncertainty factors for the data, a user interface can prompt the user to provide the necessary certainty factors, or these can be included directly in the deffacts. It is slightly different with the rules, however, in this application, the certainty factor must be included when each rule is created. Figure 4 shows the deftemplates, facts and rules initially introduced in Figure 3, extended with uncertainty data. Figure 5 shows a customisable rule for detecting multiple identical conclusions (classifications in this application); Figure 6 shows the Jess version of the generic function for calculating the certainty factor of multiple conclusions (deffunction calculate-combined-uncertainty). This system for MYCIN-like uncertainty reasoning in Jess is available as Uncertainty Jess.

```
(deftemplate observable "The value of a property based on the
clinicians observations"
   (slot name) ; the name of the property being described
   (slot value) ; the state, or value attached to the property
  (slot certainty-factor) ; the certainty of this observation
)

(deftemplate classification "The class to which the observed
organism has been classified"
   (slot class-name)
   (slot certainty-factor) ; the CF of this classification
)

(deftemplate combined-classification "Stores the result of
combining several classifications for the same class-name"
    (slot class-name)   (slot certainty-factor)
)
(deffacts some-observations
   (observable (name strain) (value GramNegative) (certainty-
factor 1.0))
   (observable (name morphology) (value rod) (certainty-factor
0.8))
   (observable (name aerobicity) (value aerobic) (certainty-
factor 0.6))
)

(defrule enterobacteriaceae-classification "a rule for
classification of enterobacteriaceae, including certainty
factors"
    ; variables in Jess start with ?var-name
    ; store the certainty-factors of the observations in variabes
?scf, ?mcf and ?acf
  (observable (name strain) (value GramNegative) (certainty-
factor ?scf))
   (observable (name morphology) (value rod) (certainty-factor
?mcf))
   (observable (name aerobicity) (value aerobic) (certainty-
factor ?acf))
    =>
   ; calculate CFConclusion as 0.9 (the CF for this rule) *
minimum CF of the data (stored in variables ?scf, ?mcf and
?acf), store it in the ?cfconc variable
    (bind ?cfconc (* 0.9 (min ?scf ?mcf ?acf) ) )
  (assert (classification (class-name enterobacteriaceae)
(certainty-factor ?cfconc)) )
)
```

Figure 4: The example deftemplates and rules from Figure 3 extended with CF information.

```
(defrule detect-and-calculate-multiple-conclusions "Combines all
the certainty factors for classifications with the same class-
name"
  ; declaring the salience to be -10 (the default for rules is
0) means this rule runs after all other rules have completed
  (declare (salience -10))
  ; find a classification with a certain name, stored in ?name
variable
  (classification (class-name ?name))
  ; create a new variable ?c, which will be a list of all the
certainty factors associated with classifications with the
class-name ?name
  ; the Jess accumulate function, first creates a new (empty
list), stored in ?cfs
  ?c <- (accumulate (bind ?cfs (create$))
  ; this line gets executed after the 'body' of the function and
adds ?cf to the list of certainty factors (?cfs)
      (bind ?cfs (create$ ?cfs ?cf))
      ?cfs ; this value gets returned
    ; the body of the function - find a classification with
class-name ?name and store its certainty-factor in ?cf
     (classification (class-name ?name) (certainty-factor ?cf)))
    =>
   ; ?c is now a list of certainty factors
  ; assert the combined classification for all the certainty
factors in ?c, by using the function calculate-combined-
certainty to calculate their combined certainty factor
 (assert (combined-classification (class-name ?name) (certainty-
factor (calculate-combined-uncertainty ?c) ) ))
)
```

Figure 5: A customisable rule which detects if multiple classifications to the same class have been concluded.

```
; This function calculates the combined uncertainty of the
values passed in the multislot CFConcs variable (a multislot
variable is a list variable in Jess)
(deffunction calculate-combined-uncertainty ($?CFConcs)
  // convert the first certainty factor in $?CFConcs to a float,
and store in ?cf
  (bind ?cf (float (nth$ 1 ?CFConcs)))
  // for every remaining certainty factor in $?CFConcs
  (foreach ?cfc (rest$ ?CFConcs)
    // convert the current certainty factor to a float
    (bind ?cfconc (float ?cfc))
    // combine the current ?cf with ?cfconc according to Formula
[II]
    (if (and (> ?cf 0.0) (> ?cfconc 0.0)) then
      (bind ?cf (- (+ ?cf ?cfconc) (* ?cf ?cfconc)))
    else (if (and (< ?cf 0.0) (< ?cfconc 0.0)) then
       (bind ?cf (+ (+ ?cf ?cfconc) (* ?cf ?cfconc)))
         else (bind ?cf (/ (+ ?cf ?cfconc) (- 1.0 (min (abs ?cf)
(abs ?cfconc)))))
        )
      )
   )
   ; return the final certainty factor value - ?cf
   ?cf
)
```

Figure 6: A generic function, calculate-combined-uncertainty, which calculates the combined uncertainty of several CFs.

5. Alternative Approaches to Handling Uncertainties in Jess

We have presented one approach to handling uncertainties in Jess, based on the use of certainty factors as implemented in the MYCIN system. An alternative method for dealing with uncertain knowledge in Jess is to use the FuzzyJess extension, [6]. Part of the FuzzyJ toolkit, FuzzyJess is built upon the concept of fuzzy logic and fuzzy set theory whereby knowledge is described in terms of its degree of membership of a fuzzy set. Membership is defined as a value between zero and one, where a value of zero indicates something is definitely not a member of that fuzzy set, and a value of one means it definitely is a member of that set[1]. FuzzyJess deals with three main concepts: fuzzy variables, fuzzy sets and fuzzy values. A fuzzy variable defines the basic components used to describe a fuzzy concept, providing the name of the variable, the units of the variable (if required), and the variables' universe of discourse. A fuzzy set defines a mapping of a real number onto a membership value in the range zero to one. A fuzzy value is an association of a fuzzy variable, a fuzzy set and a linguistic expression which describes the fuzzy variable. If a fuzzy value falls within the boundaries of the fuzzy set it is said to be a member of that set. Before a fuzzy value can be output from the system it has to be transformed to an actual value through the process of deffuzzification.

The problem with using FuzzyJess when dealing with uncertainty is that it does not naturally support certainty factors. This makes implementation more complex than the MYCIN style presented in section 4. The user is required to define various fuzzy variables that will be relevant to their application, along with relevant fuzzy values for describing the variables' universe of discourse. An example for defining certainty is provided in Figure 7.

Figure 7 also includes an example rule for the classification of enterobacteriaceae. As can been seen, one of the other problems is that FuzzyJess requires the rules to reference Java code to create the various fuzzy objects, which requires the author to be familiar with the FuzzyJess API, which is far larger and more complex than our Uncertainty Jess implementation, and so will require longer for the author to become familiar with. One of the other major problems is the number of rules that need to be written: in our approach, as long as there are the three observables for strain, morphology and aerobicity, the classification rule always fires, regardless of the certainty factors. The fuzzy-enterobacteriaceae-classification rule (Figure 7) on the other hand, only fires when the various certainty factors match (according to the fuzzy-match method) a certain fuzzy value. To ensure the classification is always generated, multiple versions of the rule will be required, dealing with the various different FuzzyValues each certainty-factor could have. For o observables, being matched against a single FuzzyVariable with v FuzzyValues, a minimum of v^o rules will be required. Another problem with FuzzyJess is that there does not seem to be any way of combining the strength of belief of multiple

---

1 Note this system uses a different scale from that used by the MYCIN CFs.

conclusions (which is possible in the MYCIN approach). That is, if several rules are fired and produce the same conclusions (with different or the same fuzzy output values), there is no built-in feature for combining them; one approach would be to provide a series of rules, one for each combinations of FuzzyValues, however, this approach obviously does not scale.

```
; create a new FuzzyVariable for Certainty, with a range from -1
to 1
(bind ?certainty (new FuzzyVariable "Certainty" -1 1));

; add a term to the Certainty FuzzyVariable for Highly Certain,
when the value is between 0.7 and 1
(?certainty addTerm "Highly Certain" (new SFuzzySet 0.7 1));
; add a term to the Certainty FuzzyVariable for Highly
Uncertain, when the value is between -1 and -0.7
(?certainty addTerm "Highly Uncertain" (new SFuzzySet -1 -0.7));
; add a term to the Certainty FuzzyVariable for Certain, when
the value is between 0.2 and 0.7, peaking at 0.45
(?certainty addTerm "Certain" (new TriangleFuzzySet 0.2 0.45
0.7));
; add a term to the Certainty FuzzyVariable for Uncertain, when
the value is between -0.7 and -0.2, peaking at -0.35
(?certainty addTerm "Uncertain" (new TriangleFuzzySet -0.7 -0.35
-0.2));
; add a term to the Certainty FuzzyVariable for Unsure, when the
value is between -0.2 and 0.2, peaking at 0
(?certainty addTerm "Unsure" (new TriangleFuzzySet -0.2 0 0.2));

(defrule fuzzy-enterobacteriaceae-classification "A FuzzyJess
version of the enterobacteriaceae classification rule"
   (observable (name strain) (value GramNegative) (certainty-
factor ?scf))
   ; fuzzy-match returns true if the value of ?scf maps to the
Highly Certain term for the Certainty FuzzyVariable
   (fuzzy-match ?scf "Highly Certain")
   (observable (name morphology) (value rod) (certainty-factor
?mcf))
   ; fuzzy-match returns true if the value of ?mcf maps to the
Highly Certain term for the Certainty FuzzyVariable
   (fuzzy-match ?mcf "Highly Certain")
   (observable (name aerobicity) (value aerobic) (certainty-
factor ?acf))
   ; fuzzy-match returns true if the value of ?acf maps to the
Certain term for the Certainty FuzzyVariable
   (fuzzy-match ?acf "Certain")
   =>
  ; assert the classification of enterobacteriaceae by
defuzzification using the Highly Certain term
  (assert (classification (class-name enterobacteriaceae)
(certainty-factor (new FuzzyValue ?certainty "Highly Certain") )
)
)
```

Figure 7: An example showing how the enterobacteriaceae classification rule could be written using FuzzyJess.

6. Comparing Approaches

FuzzyJess requires the user to define FuzzyVariables for every uncertain concept, along with a series of FuzzyValues which describe the various fuzzy concepts related to a FuzzyVariable, by defining a numeric range and natural language term for each FuzzyValue. It also requires that the rules specify which FuzzyValues the uncertainty associated with a piece of data (a fact) must match (as determined by the fuzzy-match function), in order to provide some conclusion. As we discuss in section 5, this has two disadvantages: firstly it means that the developer has to be familiar with Java and the FuzzyJess Java API, as they are required to use both within the Jess rules; and secondly rules only match very specific set of facts, and to cover a range of variable values, many rules have to be written. We believe these features reduce the maintainability of the FuzzyJess KBS; ideally a domain expert should be able to provide the system with the domain knowledge: a task we believe is made significantly more difficult if they have to specify fuzzy variables and values associated with the data. Further, the sizable number of rules required if the system should always produce a conclusion for a given set of facts (regardless of the uncertainty associated with them) also reduces maintainability. For these reasons, we believe our MYCIN-based approach to handling uncertainty in Jess is more practical.

Using the Uncertainty Jess system we have described, it is considerably less complex for the domain expert to specify uncertainties associated with both data and rules. Additionally the procedures needed to calculate combined uncertainties, as we have seen in section 4, are considerably simpler and more succinct than the various counterparts in FuzzyJess.

Essentially, the MYCIN-like approach involves the addition of one extra slot in the deftemplates used in a KBS, to represent the data CF, and the addition of a CF to each rule. In the most extensive application developed to date with Uncertainty Jess, a Haematology Diagnostic Assistant, [5], a Jess system (inference engine & rule set) was linked to a Java front-end program whose GUI presents the user with certainty scales to obtain the data's CF; the same GUI is effectively also used to acquire a CF for each rule from the expert. Once the combined certainty value for a particular conclusion has been calculated, the Java front-end system transforms this into a textual representation, e.g. "Highly Certain" or "Moderately Certain", etc., and the result and the CF are reported to the user.

From the perspective of a domain expert using the above system, the following steps occur:

1. The user inputs the degree of certainty associated with each of their data items.
2. The CF value of all the derived conclusions are calculated.
3. If there are multiple conclusions, the combined CF value is calculated.
4. The final CF value is transformed into a textual representation.
5. The conclusion and its CF are displayed to the user.

7. Conclusions / Future Work

The Uncertainty Jess system has so far only been used with one significant application. We are confident that it is a general approach, but we are now anxious that it is used extensively, so we can get much more feedback. For this reason we are making the following available for download:

1. the Uncertainty Jess rules for the main example used in this paper, i.e. the enterobacteriaceae rule; (deterministic and uncertain versions).
2. the Jess rules and functions needed to compute combined CFs, i.e. the deffunction: *calculate-combined-uncertainty.*
3. the Java classes to acquire uncertainty information from the domain expert and to report uncertainty information to the user (part of the Java front-end system).

This information can be downloaded from http://www.csd.abdn.ac.uk/~dcorsar/software/UncertaintyJess/

References

1. B.G. Buchanan and E.H. Shortliffe, editors. *Rule-Based Expert Systems: The MYCIN Experiments of the Stanford Heuristic Programming Project.* Addison-Wesley, Reading, MA., 1984.
2. CLIPS http://www.ghg.net/clips/CLIPS.html
3. E. Friedman-Hill. *Jess in Action: Rule-Based Systems in Java.* Manning Publications Co., Greenwich, CT, 2003.
4. F. Hayes-Roth, D.A. Waterman, and D. B. Lenat. *Building Expert Systems.* Publisher: Addison-Wesley, Reading, MA., 1983. pp. 444
5. A. McKenzie. *Identify: The Haematology Diagnostic Assistant.* BSc. Dissertation, Department of Computing Science, The University of Aberdeen, Aberdeen, 2006.
6. B. Orchard. *The FuzzyJ Toolkit.* http://www.iit.nrc.ca/IR_public/fuzzy/fuzzyJToolkit2.html
7. Protégé http://protege.stanford.edu

Modelling Affective-based Music Compositional Intelligence with the Aid of ANS Analyses

Toshihito Sugimoto[2], Roberto Legaspi[1], Akihiro Ota[2],
Koichi Moriyama[1], Satoshi Kurihara[1] and Masayuki Numao[1]
[1]Institute of Scientific and Industrial Research, Osaka University, Japan
[2]Dept. of Information Science and Technology, Osaka University, Japan
{sugimoto, roberto, a_ota, koichi, numao}@ai.sanken.osaka-u.ac.jp
www.ai.sanken.osaka-u.ac.jp

Abstract

This research investigates the use of emotion data derived from analyzing change in activity in the autonomic nervous system (ANS) as revealed by brainwave production to support the creative music compositional intelligence of an adaptive interface. A relational model of the influence of musical events on the listener's affect is first induced using inductive logic programming paradigms with the emotion data and musical score features as inputs of the induction task. The components of composition such as interval and scale, instrumentation, chord progression and melody are automatically combined using genetic algorithm and melodic transformation heuristics that depend on the predictive knowledge and character of the induced model. Out of the four targeted basic emotional states, namely, *stress*, *joy*, *sadness*, and *relaxation*, the empirical results reported here show that the system is able to successfully compose tunes that convey one of these affective states.

1. Introduction

It is no surprise that only a handful of research works have factored in human affect in creating an intelligent music system or interface (e.g., [1, 2, 3, 4 & 5]). One major reason is that the general issues alone when investigating music and emotion are enough to immediately confront and intimidate the researcher. More specifically, how can music composition, which is a highly structured cognitive process, be modelled and how can emotion, which consists of very complex elements and is dependent on individuals and stimuli, be measured? [6] The other is the fact that music is a reliable elicitor of affective response immediately raises the question as to what exactly in music can influence an individual's mood. For example, is it the case that musical structures contain related musical events (e.g., chord progression, melody change, etc.) that allow emotionally-stimulating mental images to surface? Although attempts have been made to pin-point which features of the musical structure elicit which affect (e.g., [7 & 8]), the problem remains compelling because the solutions are either partial or uncertain.

Our research addresses the problem of determining the extent by which emotion-inducing music can be modelled and generated using creative music compositional AI. Our approach involves inducing an affects-music relations *model* that describe musical events related to the listener's affective reactions and then using the *predictive* knowledge and character of the model to automatically control the music generation task. We have embodied our solution in a Constructive Adaptive User Interface (CAUI) that re-arranges or composes [3] a musical piece based on one's affect. We have reported the results of combining inductive logic programming (in [3 & 9]) or multiple-part learning (in [6]) to induce the model and a genetic algorithm whose fitness function is influenced by the model. In these previous versions of the CAUI, an evaluation instrument based on the semantic differential method (SDM) was used to measure affective responses. The listener rated musical pieces on a scale of 1-5 for a set of bipolar affective descriptor pairs (e.g., happy-sad). Each subjective rating indicates the degree of the positive or negative affect.

We argue that for the CAUI to accurately capture the listener's affective responses, it must satisfy necessary conditions that the SDM-based self-reporting instrument does not address. Emotion detection must capture the dynamic nature of both music and emotion. With the rating instrument, the listener can only evaluate after the music is played. This means that only one evaluation is mapped to the entire musical piece rather than having possibly varied evaluations as the musical events unfold. Secondly, the detection task should not impose a heavy cognitive load upon the listener. It must ensure that listening to music remains enjoyable and avoid, if not minimize, disturbing the listener. In our prior experiments, the listener was asked to evaluate 75 musical pieces, getting interrupted the same number of times. If indeed the listener experienced stress or anxiety in the process, it was difficult to factor this in the calculations. Lastly, the emotion detection task should be language independent, which can later on permit cross-cultural analyses. This flexibility evades the need to change the affective labels (e.g., Japanese to English).

We believe that the conditions stated above can be satisfied by using a device that can analyze emotional states by observing the change in activity in the autonomic nervous system (ANS). Any intense feeling has consequent physiological effects on the ANS [10]. These effects include faster and stronger heartbeat, increased blood pressure or breathing rate, muscle tension and sweating, accelerated mental activity, among others. This is the reason ANS effects can be observed using devices that can measure blood pressure, skin or heart responses, or brainwave production. Researchers in the field of affective computing are active in developing such devices (e.g., [11]). We have modified the learning architecture of the CAUI to incorporate an emotion spectrum analyzing system (ESA)[1] that detects emotional states by observing brainwave activities that accompany the emotion [12].

The learning architecture is shown in Figure 1. The relational model is induced by employing the inductive logic programming paradigms of FOIL and RX taking as inputs the musical score features and the ESA-provided emotion data. The musical score features are represented as definitions of first-order logic predicates and serve

[1]Developed by the Brain Functions Laboratory, Inc. (http://www.bfl.co.jp/main.html)

as background knowledge to the induction task. The next task employs a genetic algorithm (GA) that produces variants of the original score features. The fitness function of the GA fits each generated variant to the knowledge provided by the model and music theory. Finally, the CAUI creates using its melody-generating module an initial tune consisting of the GA-obtained chord tones and then alters certain chord tones to become non-chord tones in order to embellish the tune.

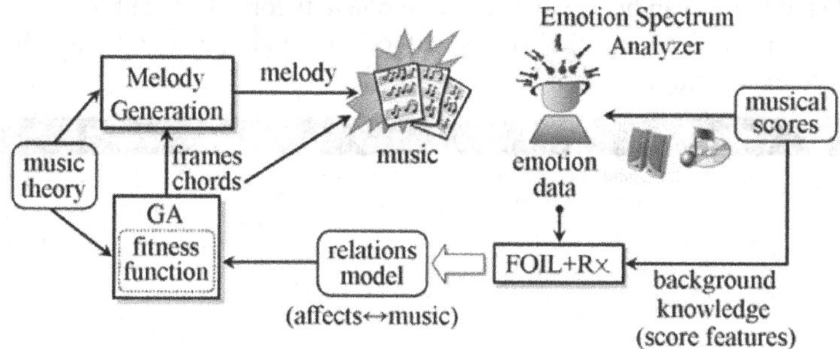

Figure 1. The learning architecture of the CAUI

Using the ESA has several advantages. The dynamic changes in both emotions and musical events can now be monitored and mapped continuously over time. Secondly, it allows mapping of emotion down to the musical *bar* level. This means that many training examples can be obtained from a single piece. Using the self-reporting instrument, the listener needed to hear and evaluate many musical pieces just to obtain fairly enough examples. Thirdly, more accurate measurements can now be acquired objectively. Lastly, it is unobtrusive thereby relieving the listener of any cognitive load and allowing him/her to just sit back and listen to the music.

In this paper, we first discuss the domain knowledge representations, learning parameters and learning tasks used for the CAUI in sections 2 to 3. Section 4 details our experimentation methodology and analysis of the empirical results we gathered. Section 5 briefly locates the contribution of the CAUI in the field. Discussions on what we intend to carry out as possible future works can be found part of our analysis and conclusion.

2. Knowledge Acquisition and Representation

In order to obtain a personalized model of the coupling of emotional expressions and the underlying music parameters, it is vital to: (1) identify which musical features (e.g., tempo, rhythm, harmony, etc.) should be represented as background knowledge, (2) provide an instrument to map the features to identified emotion descriptors, (3) logically represent the music parameters, and (4) automatically induce the model. Although the influence of various features have been well studied (e.g., refer to a comprehensive summary on the influence of compositional parameters [8] and an overview of recent investigations on the influence of performance parameters [13 & 14]), the task of the CAUI is to automatically find musical structure and sequence features that are influential to specific emotions.

2.1 Music Theory

The aspect of music theory relevant to our research is the interaction of music elements into patterns that can help the composition techniques. We have a narrow music theory that consists of a limited set of music elements (see Figure 2). The reason is that we need the predictive model to be tractable in order to perform controlled experimentations and obtain interpretable results. The definitions of the concepts listed below can be found in texts on music theory. The methods by which music theory is utilized by the genetic algorithm and melodic transformation heuristics are explained in section 3.

Frame features	
Tempo	adagio, lento, andante, moderato, allegretto, allegro, presto, larghetto
Rhythm	2/2, 2/4, 4/4, 6/8
Melodic instrument	piano, sax (soprano or tenor)
Accompaniment	piano, guitar
Key	As, B, Cis, D, Fis, G, A, H
Tonality	dur (major), moll (minor)
Cadence	complete (or authentic), half, other

Chord features	
Key	As, B, Cis, D, Fis, G, A, H
Tonality	dur (major), moll (minor)
Root	I, II, III, IV, V, VI, VII
Form	5th, 7th, 9th
Inversion	zero, 1, 2, 3
Semi-own	present, absent
Secondary dominant	II, IV, V, VI, absent
Special variations	Neopolitan 6th, sus4, absent
Function	tonic, dominant, subdominant

Figure 2. Basic aspects of music theory that are being used for this version of the CAUI

Fourteen (14) musical piece segments were prepared consisting of four pieces from classical music, three from Japanese Pop, and seven from harmony textbooks. The amount of time a segment may play is from 7.4 to 48 seconds (an average of 24.14 seconds). These pieces were selected, albeit not randomly, from the original 75 segments that were used in our previous experiments. Based on prior results, these selected pieces demonstrate a high degree of variance in emotional content when evaluated by previous users of the system. In other words, these pieces seem to elicit affective flavours that are more distinguishable.

2.2 Emotion Acquisition Features of the ESA

Through proper signal processing, scalp potentials that are measured by an electroencephalograph (EEG) can provide global information about mental activities and emotional states [12]. With the ESA, EEG features associated with emotional states are extracted into a set of 45 cross-correlation coefficients. These coefficients are calculated for each of the θ(5-8 Hz), α(8-13 Hz) and β(13-20 Hz) frequency components forming a 135-dim EEG state vector. Operating a transformation matrix on this state vector linearly transforms it to a 4-dim vector $E=<e_1,e_2,e_3,e_4>$, with the four components representing levels of *stress*, *joy*, *sadness* and *relaxation*, respectively. The maximum time resolution of the emotion analysis performed in real-time is 0.64 second. More detailed discussions on the ideas behind ESA can be found in [12]. The emotion charts in Figure 3 graphically show series of readings that were taken over time. The higher the value means the more evident is the emotion being displayed. The two wave charts at the bottom indicate levels of alertness and concentration, respectively. These readings help gauge the reliability of the emotion readings. For example, the level of alertness should be high when the music is being played indicating that the listener is being keen to the tune. Low alert points are valid so long as these correspond to the silent pauses inserted between tunes since there is no need for the user to listen to the pauses. However, acceptably high values for concentration should be expected at any point in time. The collected emotion data are used by the model induction task.

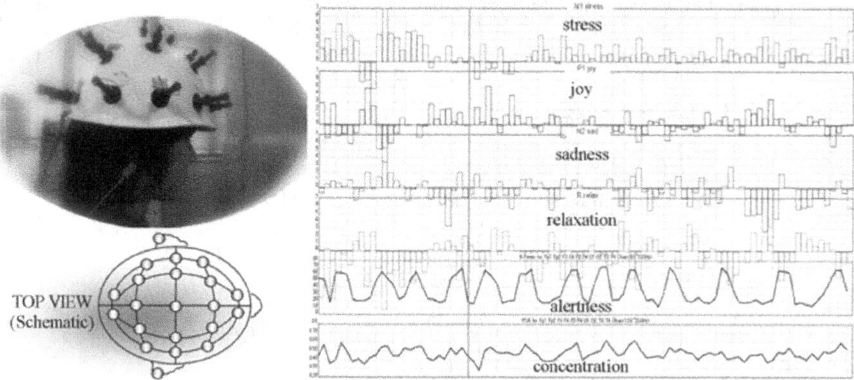

Figure 3. EEG signals used for emotion analyses are obtained using scalp electrodes

Brainwave analysis is a delicate task that can easily be distorted by external factors including an eye blink. Hence, careful attention need to be given when acquiring the readings. The listener needs to be in a closed room with minimal noise and other external distractions as possible. The listener is also required to close his/her eyes at all times. This set-up is necessary to obtain stable readings. Any series of measurements should be taken without disturbing the listener.

2.3 First-Order Logic Representation of the Score Features

The background knowledge of the CAUI are definitions in first-order logic that describe musical score features. The language of first-order logic, or predicate logic, is known to be well-suited both for data representation and describing the desired outputs. The representational power of predicate logic permits describing existing feature relations among data, even complex relations, and provides comprehensibility of the learned results [15]. Score features were encoded into a predicate variable, or *relation*, named *music*(·), which contains one *song_frame*(·) and a list of sequenced *chord*(·) relations describing the frame and chord features, respectively. Figure 4 shows the *music*(·) representation ('-' means NIL) of the musical score segment of the prelude of Jacques Offenbach's Orpheé aux Enfers.

The CAUI needs to learn three kinds of target relations or rules, namely, *frame*(·), *pair*(·) and *triplet*(·), wherein the last two represent patterns of two and three successive chords, respectively. These rules comprise the affects-music relational model. Figure 5-left, for example, shows structural information contained in the given sample relations and the actual musical notation they represent. Figure 5-right shows a segment of an actual model learned by the CAUI that can be used to construct a musical piece that is supposed to induce in one user a sad feeling.

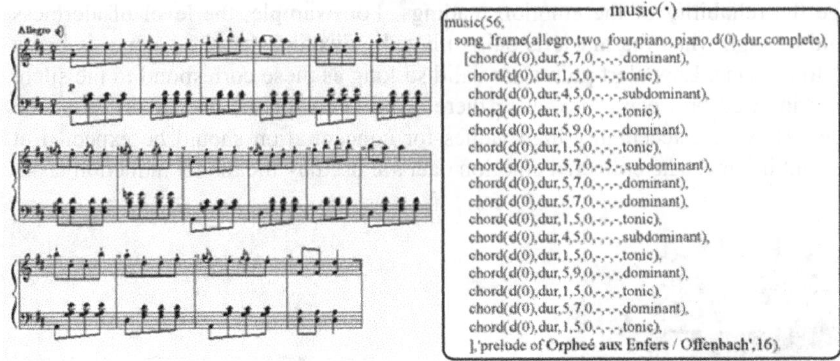

Figure 4. A musical score represented in *music*(·) predicate

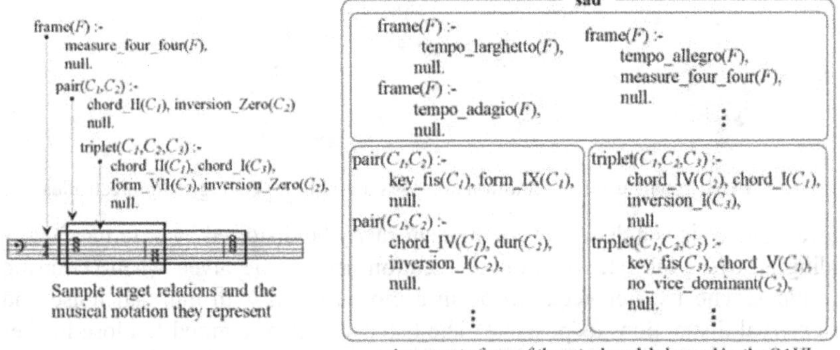

Figure 5. A segment of a set of rules that are supposed to stimulate a *sad* feeling

2.4 Model Induction Using FOIL and Rx

The CAUI employs the combination of FOIL and Rx (**Re**finement by **Ex**ample) to model the musical structures that correlate with the listener's emotions with the musical structures comprising the set of training examples.

FOIL [16] is a first-order inductive learning system that induces a theory represented as function-free Horn clauses. Each clause is a conjunction of literals, where each literal consists of a relation and an ordering of the variable arguments of the relation. The training examples are represented extensionally as sets of ground tuples, i.e., the constant values of the relations present in the examples. Tuples belonging or not belonging to the relation are labelled as ⊕ and ⊖ tuples, respectively. FOIL assumes that all ⊕ tuples exhibit a relationship R and the ⊖ tuples do not. FOIL iteratively learns a clause of the theory and removes from the training set the ⊕ tuples of the relation R covered by that clause until all ⊕ tuples are covered by one or more clauses.

Induction of a single clause starts with it having an empty body, and body literals are iteratively added at the end of the clause until no ⊖ tuple is covered by the clause. FOIL selects one literal to be added from a set of candidate literals based on an information gain heuristic that estimates the utility of a literal in discriminating ⊕ from ⊖ tuples. The information gained for adding a literal is computed as

$$Gain(L_i) = T_i^{++} \times \left(I(T_i) - I(T_{i+1})\right) \tag{1}$$

$$I(T_i) = -\log_2 \frac{T_i^+}{T_i^+ + T_i^-} \quad , \quad I(T_{i+1}) = -\log_2 \frac{T_{i+1}^+}{T_{i+1}^+ + T_{i+1}^-} \tag{2}$$

T_i^+ and T_i^- denote the number of ⊕ and ⊖ tuples in the training set T_i. Adding the literal L_m to the partially developing *clause*:=$R(v_1, v_2,\ldots, v_k)$:-$L_1, L_2,\ldots, L_{m-1}$ results to the new set T_{i+1}, which contains the tuples that remained from T_i. T_i^{++} denotes the number of tuples in T_i^+ that led to another ⊕ tuple after adding L_m. The candidate literal L_i that yields the largest gain becomes L_m.

RX [17] is a system that automatically refines the theory in the function-free first-order logic. It assumes that the induced theory can only be approximately correct, hence, needs to be refined to improve its accuracy using the training examples. RX implements a four-step theory revision process, i.e., (1) operationalization, (2) specialization, (3) rule creation, and (4) unoperationalization. Operationalization expands the theory into a set of operational clauses, detecting and removing useless literals. A literal is *useful* if its normalized gain, i.e., computing only for $I(T_i) - I(T_{i+1})$ of eq. (1), is > θ, where θ is a specified threshold, and if it produces new variables for the other literals in the clause, i.e., its generative [17]. RX considers the useless literals as faults in the theory. Specialization uses FOIL to add literals to the overly general clauses covering ⊖ tuples to make them more specific. Rule creation uses FOIL to introduce more operational clauses in case some ⊕ tuples cannot be covered by existing ones. Finally, unoperationalization re-organizes the clauses to reflect the hierarchical structure of the original theory.

The training examples suitable for inducing the model are generated as follows. Each musical piece is divided into musical bars or measures. A piece may contain eight to 16 bars (an average of 11.6 bars per piece). Every three successive bars in a piece together with the music frame are treated as one training example, i.e., $example_i$=(*frame*, bar_{i-2}, bar_{i-1}, bar_i). Each bar consists of a maximum of four chords. The idea here is that sound flowing from at least three bars are needed to elicit an affective response. The first two examples in every piece, however, will inherently contain only one and two bars, respectively. The components of each bar are extracted from *music*(•) and represented as ground tuples. A total of 162 examples were obtained from the 14 pieces with each bar having an average play-time of 2.1 seconds.

Recall that emotion readings are taken while the music is being played. Using the available synchronization tools of the ESA and music segmenting tools, the emotion measurements are assigned to the corresponding musical segments. Subsequently, each emotion measure is discretized to a value between 1-5 based on a pre-determined threshold. Using the same range of values as that of the SDM-based instrument permits us to retain the learning techniques in [9] while evaluating the new emotion detection scheme. It is also plausible for us to define a set of bipolar affective descriptor pairs ed_1-ed_2 (e.g., joyful-not joyful). It is important to note that antonymic semantics (e.g., stressed vs. relaxed and joyful vs. sad) do not hold for the ESA since the four emotions are defined along orthogonal dimensions. Hence, four separate readings are taken instead of just treating one as inversely proportional to the other. This is consistent with the circumplex model of affect [18] where each of the four emotions can be seen in different quadrants of this model. One relational model is learned for each affect in the four bipolar emotion pairs ed_1-ed_2 (a total of 4×2=8 models).

To generate the training instances specific to FOIL, for any emotion descriptor ed_1 in the pair ed_1-ed_2, the examples labelled as 5 are represented as ⊕ tuples, while those labelled as ≤ 4 as ⊖ tuples. Conversely for ed_2, ⊕ and ⊖ tuples are formed from bars which were evaluated as 1 and ≥ 2, respectively. In other words, there are corresponding sets of ⊕ and ⊖ tuples for each affect and a ⊖ tuple for ed_1 does not mean that it is a ⊕ tuple for ed_2. Examples are derived almost in the same way for FOIL+RX. For example, the ⊕ tuples of ed_1 and ed_2 are formed from bars labelled as ≥ 4 and ≤ 2, respectively.

3. Composing Using GA and Melody Heuristics

Evolutionary computational models have been dominating the realm of automatic music composition (as reviewed by [19]). One major problem in user-oriented GA-based music creation (e.g., [20 & 21]), however, is that the user is required to listen and then rate the composed musical sequences in each generation. This is obviously burdensome, tiring and time-consuming. Although the CAUI is user-oriented, it need not solicit user intervention since it uses the relational model as critic to control the quality of the composed tunes.

We adapted the conventional bit-string chromosome representation in GA as a columns-of-bits representation expressed in *music*(•) form (see Figure 6, where F is the *song_frame*(•) and C_i is a *chord*(•)). Each bit in a column represents a component of the frame (e.g., tempo) or chord (e.g., root). The performance of our GA depends on two basic operators, namely, single-point cross-over and mutation. With the first operator, the columns of bit strings from the beginning of the chromosome to a selected crossover point is copied from one parent and the rest is copied from the other. Mutation inverts selected bits thereby altering the individual frame and chord information. The more fundamental components (e.g., tempo, rhythm and root) are mutated less frequently to avoid a drastic change in musical events, while the other features are varied more frequently to acquire more variants.

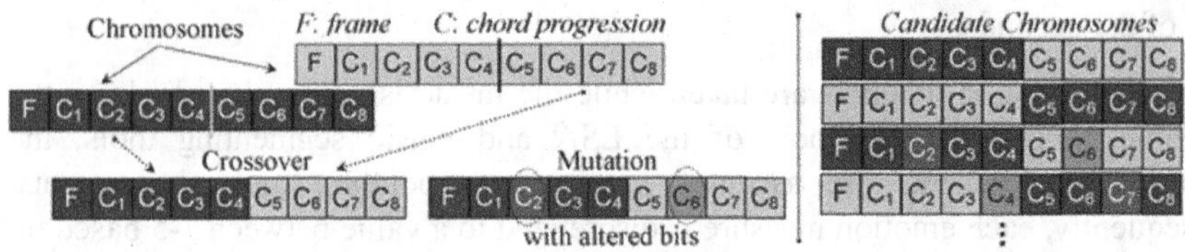

Figure 6. GA chromosome structure and operators

The fundamental idea of GA is to produce increasingly better solutions in each new generation of the evolutionary process. During the genetic evolution process, candidate chromosomes are being produced that may be better or worse than what has already been obtained. Hence, the fitness function is necessary to evaluate the utility of each candidate. The CAUI's fitness function takes into account the user-specific relational model and music theory:

$$fitnessChromosome(M) = fitnessUser(M) + fitnessTheory(M) \tag{3}$$

where M is a candidate chromosome. This function makes it possible to generate frames and chord progressions that fit the music theory and stimulate the target feeling. *fitnessUser(M)* is computed as follows:

$$fitnessUser(M) = fitnessFrame(M) + fitnessPair(M) + fitnessTriplet(M) \tag{4}$$

Each function at the right side of eq. (4) is generally computed as follows:

$$fitnessX(M) = \sum_{i=1}^{L} Average\left(\delta_F(P_i), \delta'_F(P_i), \delta_{FR}(P_i), \delta'_{FR}(P_i)\right) \tag{5}$$

The meanings of the objects in eq. (5) are shown in Table 1. The only variable parameter is P_i, which denotes the component/s extracted from M that will serve as input to the four subfunctions of *fitnessX*. If there are n *chord*(•) predicates in M, there will be L P_is formed depending on the *fitnessX*. For example, given chromosome M:=*music*(*song_frame*(•),*chord*$_1$(•),…,*chord*$_8$(•)), where the added subscripts denote chord positions, computing for *fitnessPair(M)* will have 7 P_is (L=8-1): P_1 = (*chord*$_1$(•), *chord*$_2$(•)) , …, P_7 = (*chord*$_7$(•), *chord*$_8$(•)). With *fitnessFrame(M)*, it will only be P_1=*song_frame*(•).

Table 1. Meanings of the objects in equation (5)

fitnessX	P_i (component/s of M)	L	*Target relation*
fitnessFrame	*song_frame*(•)	1	*frame*(•)
fitnessPair	(*chord*$_i$(•),*chord*$_{i+1}$(•))	n-1	*pair*(•)
fitnessTriplet	(*chord*$_i$(•),*chord*$_{i+1}$(•),*chord*$_{i+2}$(•))	n-2	*triplet*(•)

The values of the subfunctions in eq. (5) will differ depending on whether an ed_1 (e.g., sad) or ed_2 (e.g., not sad) music is being composed. Let us denote the target affect of the current composition as emo_P and the opposite of this affect as emo_N (e.g., if ed_1 is emo_P then emo_N refers to ed_2, and vice versa). δ_F and δ_{FR} (where F and FR refer to the models obtained using FOIL alone or FOIL+RX, respectively) return +2 and +1, respectively, if P_i appears in any of the corresponding target relations (see Table 1) in the model learned for emo_P. On the other hand, δ'_F and δ'_{FR} return -2 and -1, respectively, if P_i appears in any of the corresponding relations in the emo_N model. In effect, the structure P_i is rewarded if it is part of the desired relations and is penalized if it also appears in the model for the opposite affect since it does not possess a distinct affective flavour. The returned values ($\pm$2 and $\pm$1) were determined empirically.

fitnessTheory(M) seeks to reward chromosomes that are consistent with our music theory and penalize those that violate. This is computed in the same way as eq. (4)

except that each of the three functions at the right shall now be computed as

$$fitnessX(M) = \sum_{i=1}^{L} Average(\eta(P_i)) \quad (6)$$

The definitions of the objects in eq. (6) follow the ones in Table 1 except that P_i is no longer checked with the relational models but with the music theory. The subfunction η returns the score of fitting P_i with the music theory, which is either a reward or a penalty. Structures that earn a high reward include those whose frames have complete or half cadence, chord triplets that contain the transition T→S→D of the tonal functions tonic(T), subdominant(S) and dominant(D), and pairs that transition from dominant to secondary dominant (e.g., V/II→II). On the other hand, penalty is given to pairs or triplets that have the same root, form and inversion values, have the same tonal function and form, or have the transition D→S. All these heuristics are grounded in basic music theory. For example, the cadence types are scored based on the strength of their effects such that the complete cadence is given the highest score since it is the strongest. Another is that the transition T→S→D is rewarded since it is often used and many songs have been written using this. D→S is penalized since a dominant chord will not resolve with a subdominant.

Overall, the scheme we just described is defensible given that music theory can be represented using heuristics for evaluating the fitness of each GA-generated music variant. The character of each generated variant is immediately fit not just to the music theory, but more importantly, to the desired affective perception. It is also clear in the computations that the presence of the models permit the absence of human intervention during composition thereby relieving the user of unnecessary cognitive load and achieving full automation. Figure 7 shows one of the best-fit GA-generated chromosomes to stimulate a sad feeling.

```
music(0,
 song_frame(allegretto,two_two,soprano_sax,piano,h(-1),moll,other),
  [chord(h(-1),moll,2,5,1,true,-,-,-,-,-,subdominant), chord(h(-1),moll,4,5,1,-,-,-,-,-,-,subdominant),
   chord(h(-1),moll,3,5,2,-,-,-,-,-,-,-,-,subdominant), chord(h(-1),moll,6,7,1,-,-,-,-,-,-,tonic),
   chord(h(-1),moll,7,7,1,-,-,-,-,-,-,dominant), chord(h(-1),moll,2,5,1,-,-,-,-,-,-,subdominant),
   chord(h(-1),moll,6,7,0,-,-,-,-,-,-,tonic), chord(h(-1),moll,2,5,1,-,-,-,-,-,-,-,-,subdominant),
   ],GA generated Music,8).
```

Figure 7. An actual GA-generated musical piece

The outputs of the GA contain only chord progressions. Musical lines with only chord tones may sound monotonous or homophonic. A non-chord tone may serve to embellish the melodic motion surrounding the chord tones. The CAUI's melody-generating module first generates chord tones using the GA-obtained *music*(•) information and then utilizes a set of heuristics to generate the non-chord tones in order to create a non-monotonic piece of music.

To create the chord tones, certain aspects of music theory are adopted including the harmonic relations V7→I (or D→T, which is known to be very strong), T→D, T→S, S→T, and S→D, and keeping the intervals in octaves. Once the chord tones are created, the non-chord tones, which are supposed to be not members of the accompanying chords, are generated by selecting and "disturbing" the chord tones.

All chord tones have an equal chance of being selected. Once selected, a chord tone is modified into a non-chordal *broderie*, *appoggiatura* or *passing tone*. How these non-chord tones are adopted for the CAUI is detailed in [6].

4. Experimentation and Analysis of Results

We have performed a set of individualized experiments to determine whether the CAUI-composed pieces can actually stimulate the target emotion. Sixteen (16) subjects were asked to hear the 14 musical pieces, at the same time, wear the ESA's helmet. The subjects' were all Japanese male with ages ranging from 18 to 27 years. Although it is ideal to increase the heterogeneity of the subjects' profile, it seems more appropriate at this stage to limit their diversity in terms of their background and focus more on the possibly existing differences in their emotional reactions. For the subject to hear the music playing continuously, all the pieces were sequenced using a music editing tool and silent pauses of 15 seconds each were inserted before and after each piece with the exemption of the first which is preceded by a 30-second silence so as to condition the subject. Personalized models were learned for each subject based on their emotion readings and new pieces were composed independently for each. The same subjects were then asked to go through the same process using the set of newly composed pieces. Twenty-four (24) tunes were composed for each subject, i.e., three for each of the bipolar affective descriptors. Figure 8 shows that the CAUI was able to compose a *sad* piece, even without prior handcrafted knowledge of any affect-inducing piece.

Figure 8. A CAUI-composed *sad* musical piece

We computed for the difference of the averaged emotion readings for each ed_1-ed_2 pair. The motivation here is that the higher the difference is the more distinct/distinguishable is the affective flavour of the composed pieces. We also performed a *paired* t-test on the differences to determine if these are significant. Table 2 shows that the composed *sad* pieces are the only ones that correlate with the subjects' emotions. A positive difference was seen in many instances, albeit not necessarily significant statistically. This indicates that the system is not able to differentiate the structures that can arouse such impressions

The version of the CAUI reported in [9] is similar to the current except for two things: (1) it used self-reporting and (2) evaluated on a whole-music, instead of bar, level. Its compositions are significant in only two out of five emotion dimensions at level α=0.01 using student's t-test. The current version used only 14 pieces but was able to produce significant outputs for one emotion. This shows that we cannot easily dismiss the potential of the current version.

The results obtained can be viewed as acceptable if the current form of the research is taken as a proof of concept. The acceptably sufficient result for one of the emotion dimensions shows a promise in the direction we are heading and motivates to further enhance the system's capability in terms of its learning techniques. The unsatisfactory results obtained for the other emotion descriptors can also be attributed to shortcomings in creating adequately structured tunes due to our narrow music theory. For instance, the composed tunes at this stage consist only of eight bars and are rhythmically monotonic. Admittedly, we need to take more of music theory into consideration. Secondly, since the number of training examples has been downsized, the number of distinct frames, i.e., in terms of attribute values, became fewer. There is no doubt that integrating the more complex musical knowledge and scaling to a larger dataset are feasible provided that the CAUI sufficiently defines and represents the degrees of musical complexity (e.g., structure in the melody) and acquires the needed storage to store the training data (this has become our immediate obstacle). It is also an option to investigate the effect of just a single music element that is very influential in creating music and stimulating emotions (e.g., the role of beat in African music). This will permit a more focused study while lessening the complexity in scope.

Table 2. Results of empirical validation

Average difference of ed_1 (+) and ed_2 (-) emotion analyses				
Subject	Stressed	Joyful	Sad	Relaxed
A	1.67	2.33	– 0.67	– 3.00
B	0.67	0.33	– 1.33	1.33
C	1.00	– 1.00	0.67	– 1.33
D	– 1.00	0.67	0.67	2.33
E	– 2.67	1.00	1.33	1.00
F	0.67	0.33	0.00	– 0.67
G	0.67	0.33	1.67	1.33
H	1.00	0.00	1.33	– 0.67
I	0.67	– 0.33	1.67	– 0.67
J	0.67	0.33	– 0.33	– 2.00
K	0.33	– 0.33	0.67	0.00
L	0.67	0.33	2.33	0.00
M	– 0.67	0.33	0.33	– 1.33
N	– 0.33	– 2.33	1.00	2.00
O	0.33	0.33	0.67	1.00
P	– 1.67	– 1.67	0.00	1.00
average	0.13	0.04	0.63	0.02
sample variance	1.18	1.07	0.85	2.12
standard error	0.28	0.27	0.24	0.38
t value	0.45	0.16	2.63	0.06
significant (5%)	False	False	True	False
significant (1%)	False	False	True	False

5. Related Works

To comprehend the significant link that unites music and emotion has been a subject of considerable interest involving various fields (refer to [13]). For about five decades, artificial intelligence has played a crucial role in computerized music (reviewed in [22]), yet there seems to be a scarcity of research that tackles the compelling issues of a user affect-specific automated composition. As far as our limited knowledge of the literature is concerned, it has been difficult to find a study that aims to measure the emotional influence of music and then heads towards a fully automated composition task. This is in contrast to certain works that did not deal with music composition even if they have achieved detecting the emotional influence of music (e.g., [1 & 23]) or to systems that solicit user's ratings during composition (e.g., [5 & 21]). Other works attempt to compose music with EEG or other biological signals as direct generative source (e.g., refer to the concepts outlined in [24]) but may not necessarily distinguish the affective characteristics of the composed pieces. We single out the work of Kim and Andre [2] which deals with more affective dimensions whose measures are based on user's self-report and results of physiological sensing. It differs with the CAUI in the sense that it does not induce a relational model and it dealt primarily with generating rhythms.

6. Conclusion

This paper proposes the technique of composing music based on the user's emotions as analyzed from changes in brainwave activities. The results reported here shows that learning is feasible even with the currently small training set. The current architecture also permitted evading a tiring and burdensome self-reporting as emotion detection task while achieving partial success in composing an emotion-inducing tune. We cannot deny that the system falls a long way short of human composers, nevertheless, we believe that the potential of its compositional intelligence should not be easily dismissed.

The CAUI's learning architecture will remain viable even if other ANS measuring devices are used. The problem with the ESA is that it practically limits itself from being bought by ordinary people since it is expensive and it restricts user's mobility (e.g., eye blinks can easily introduce noises). We are currently developing a multi-modal emotion recognition scheme that will allow us to investigate other means to measure expressed emotions (e.g., through ANS response and human locomotive features) using devices that permit mobility and are cheaper than the ESA.

References

1. Bresin R, Friberg A. Emotional coloring of computer-controlled music performance. Computer Music Journal 2000; 24(4):44-62
2. Kim S, Andre E. Composing affective music with a generate and sense approach. In: Barr V, Markov Z (eds) Proceedings of the 17th International FLAIRS Conference, Special Track on AI and Music, AAAI Press, 2004
3. Numao M, Takagi S, Nakamura K. Constructive adaptive user interfaces – composing music based on human feelings. In: Proceedings of the 18th National Conference on AI, AAAI Press, 2002, pp 193-198

4. Riecken D. Wolfgang: 'emotions' plus goals enable learning. In: Proceedings of the IEEE International Conference on Systems, Man and Cybernetics, 1998, pp 1119-1120
5. Unehara M, Onisawa T. Music composition system based on subjective evaluation. In: Proceedings of the IEEE International Conference on Systems, Man and Cybernetics, 2003, pp 980-986
6. Legaspi R, Hashimoto Y, Moriyama K, Kurihara S, Numao M. Music compositional intelligence with an affective flavor. In: Proceedings of the 12th International Conference on Intelligent User Interfaces, ACM Press, 2007, pp 216-224
7. Sloboda JA. Music structure and emotional response: Some empirical findings. Psychology of Music 1991; 19(2):110-120
8. Gabrielsson A, Lindstrom E. The influence of musical structure on emotional expression. In: Juslin PN, Sloboda JA (eds) Music and emotion: Theory and research, Oxford University Press, New York, 2001, pp 223-248
9. Legaspi R, Hashimoto Y, Numao M. An emotion-driven musical piece generator for a constructive adaptive user interface. In: Proceedings of the 9th Pacific Rim International Conference on AI, 2006, pp 890-894 (LNAI 4009)
10. Roz C. The autonomic nervous system: Barometer of emotional intensity and internal conflict. A lecture given for Confer, 27th March 2001, [a copy can be found in] http://www.thinkbody.co.uk/papers/autonomic-nervous-system.htm
11. Picard RW, Healey J. Affective wearables. Personal and Ubiquitous Computing 1997; 1(4):231-240
12. Musha T, Terasaki Y, Haque HA, Ivanitsky GA. Feature extraction from EEGs associated with emotions, Artif Life Robotics 1997; 1:15-19
13. Juslin PN, Sloboda JA. Music and emotion: Theory and research. Oxford University Press, New York, 2001
14. Juslin PN. Studies of music performance: A theoretical analysis of empirical findings. In: Proceedings of the Stockholm Music Acoustics Conference, 2003, pp 513-516
15. Nattee C, Sinthupinyo S, Numao M, Okada T. Learning first-order rules from data with multiple parts: Applications on mining chemical compound data. In: Proceedings of the 21st International Conference on Machine Learning, 2004, pp 77-85
16. Quinlan JR. Learning logical definitions from relations. Machine Learning 1990; 5:239-266
17. Tangkitvanich S, Shimura M. Refining a relational theory with multiple faults in the concept and subconcept. In: Machine Learning: Proceedings of the Ninth International Workshop, 1992, pp 436-444
18. Posner J, Russell JA, Peterson BS. The circumplex model of affect: An integrative approach to affective neuroscience, cognitive development, and psychopathology. Development and Psychopathology 2005; 17:715-734.
19. Wiggins GA, Papadopoulos G, Phon-Amnuaisuk S, Tuson A. Evolutionary methods for musical composition. International Journal of Computing Anticipatory Systems 1999; 1(1)
20. Johanson BE, Poli R. GP-Music: An interactive genetic programming system for music generation with automated fitness raters. Technical Report CSRP-98-13, School of Computer Science, The University of Birmingham, 1998
21. Unehara M, Onisawa T. Interactive music composition system – composition of 16-bars musical work with a melody part and backing parts. In: Proceedings of the IEEE International Conference on Systems, Man and Cybernetics, 2004, pp 5736-5741
22. Lopez de Mantaras R, Arcos JL. AI and music: From composition to expressive performances. AI Magazine 2002; 23(3):43-57
23. Li T, Ogihara M. Detecting emotion in music. In: Proceedings of the 4th International Conference on Music Information Retrieval, 2003, pp 239-240
24. Rosenboom D. Extended musical interface with the human nervous system: Assessment and prospectus. Leonardo Monograph Series, Monograph No.1 1990/1997

Supporting Temporal Information in Medical Care Planning

Kirsty Bradbrook & Graham Winstanley
Computational Intelligence Group, University of Brighton
Brighton, UK

Abstract

The problems associated with planning and managing patient treatment through complex care settings are significant. It has long been realised that support tools are invaluable in ensuring quality and consistency of care in a domain characterised by complex information spread over widely differing contexts. This paper focuses on the temporal nature of medical support tools and describes structures designed to accommodate their representation and reasoning requirements. The paper discusses the temporal facilities of the CIG-Plan medical care planning system and critically compares our work with contemporary research in the medical guideline and AI Planning communities.

1. Introduction

In concert with global trends, the UK National Health Service (NHS) is currently undergoing an intensive review into the way patient care is designed, delivered and recorded. One important element of this is the development of computerised medical guidelines (CMG) that provide a reasoned plan of care for each patient journey, based on locally-agreed, evidence-based best practice. These care-pathways show the sequence of tasks (over time) which describe the treatment and progress of a patient [1, 2]. Our research has investigated the needs of such a system and has established a mapping between these requirements and a set of deliberative AI techniques [3]. In particular we have identified certain AI Planning techniques as offering strong potential for providing greatly enhanced representational and functional efficacy.

A major issue surrounding the problem of planning for patient care has been with providing methods for managing the temporal aspects of the patient journey. Preliminary research investigated the current and future capabilities of CMG systems and similar work from the AI Planning community. It has been concluded that the many complex temporal situations which arise through medical care planning are inadequately catered for by existing systems and methodologies. Neither are the current temporal representation and reasoning facilities of existing AI planning systems sufficient to support these requirements.

To further investigate the temporal requirements of CMG systems, a proof-of-concept research vehicle has been developed. This system, designated the

Computerised Integrated Guideline Planner (CIG-Plan), is a custom-designed hierarchical planner, used to demonstrate and evaluate the suitability of various techniques through design & implementation. This paper focuses on the expression and evaluation of the temporal information contained within CMGs.

2. Structuring the Temporal Information

2.1 Separating Relative and Actual Temporal Data

When investigating the temporal requirements of CMG systems it has been found that the problem could be most effectively handled by separating temporal data processing into two distinct issues: working with time-stamped data and working with relational temporal data. When initially developing or individualising a guideline, a CMG system would need to work primarily with relational temporal data (A before B, etc.). However, when instigating and monitoring a plan, the temporal data of the guideline would need to be transposed into calendar date-time information to allow for resource planning and success evaluation. This being the case, it is proposed that an effective guideline system should have the facilities to reason about relative and time-stamped temporal data separately, as well as being able to translate information between the two formats. This separation allows several actual-time scenarios to be examined by a user during guideline development without the involvement of extensive re-planning by the system. It also supports the handling of events whose actual timepoints are a priori unknown (such as birth date, death date etc.). These events can be defined as actions and then be expressed and evaluated relatively to the other guideline tasks during the development process without the need for instantiation.

When handling relative and actual temporal data separately, it is important to bear in mind that the translation of a guideline between the two states requires the retention of some information about the relative network to allow for plan modification at a later date. It would seem appropriate, therefore, to maintain the two temporal structures in parallel (one relative, one time-stamped), which can then be interchanged when plan modification or re-planning is necessary.

Within CIG-Plan, this separation occurs by the initial development of a plan in a purely relative format and then the application of that plan to an external temporal framework in order to generate actual time/dates for each action in the plan. This process entails allocating each plan action a time slot which is consistent with the constraints of the application domain (i.e. opening hours, resource allocations) as well as the constraints of the relative plan.

2.2 Core Temporal Structures

Our structuring of the temporal data has drawn heavy influence from the emerging AI community standard the Planning Domain Definition Language (PDDL) [4], as well as from existing guideline modelling languages such as PRO*forma* [5] and Asbru [6]. It is based on a point-based temporal framework with durational events, where the start and end limits of events are indicated by instantaneous points on a network. More complex temporal constructs are supported in CIG-Plan with the incorporation of PDDL's durative actions and the utilisation of intervals. All actions within CIG-Plan are considered to be durative in order to somewhat resolve the 'divided instant problem'. We can state that the duration of any action must be greater than 0 and that that duration is the length of time from the start point to the end point, excluding the duration of any conditions which extend beyond this period.

Unlike many existing AI planning systems, CIG-Plan actions contain a set of six types of conditions: *Achieve, Maintain, Avoid, Effect (including conditional effects), Suspend/Restart* and *Abort.* Each of these conditions needs to be supported by temporal structures which allow them to occur either at the end or the start of an action, through the duration of the action or outside the duration of the action. CIG-Plan does allow for instantaneous conditions within an action, but in the medical domain it is not sufficient to simply deal with conditions which occur within the duration of an action, nor is it sufficient to say that something happens 'sometime-before' or 'sometime-after' some other action or condition. This being the case, our work extends the basic temporal statements of PDDL (at start) (at end) and (over all) to include numeric values relative to the start and end points of the action.

This new numeric addition gives us the following structures for instantaneous conditions:

- *at start (num, granularity)*
- *at end (num, granularity)*
- *before start (num, granularity)*
- *before end (num, granularity)*
- *after start (num, granularity)*
- *after end (num, granularity)*

and for durative conditions:

- *over start (num1, granularity) start (num2, granularity)*
- *over start (num1, granularity) end (num2, granularity)*
- *over end (num1, granularity) end (num2, granularity)*

where *(num, num1 & num2)* are positive or negative numbers and where *(num1)* temporally precedes *(num2).*

For example, the condition '*at end (-2, day)*' means the condition would occur exactly 2 days before the end of the action, whereas the condition '*after end (3, hour)*' would make the condition occur sometime after 3 days after the end of the action. The condition '*over start(2, day) end(2, day)*' states that a condition holds true from 2 days after the start of the action until 2 days after the end of the action. This has been used to state that the effect of giving a patient Warfarin is 'anticoagulation' from 2 days after the drug is first given until 2 days after the drug as been stopped. Using 'start' and 'end' as relative points allows the condition to remain accurate regardless of how long the drug is given for.

It must be noted here that it would be unnecessary in a complete system to include the temporal granularity in these structures. However, due to the experimental nature of the CIG-Plan system, they were considered necessary to ensure optimum legibility during the development and analysis process.

These structures allow for conditions to extend outside the duration of the action, but ensures that conditions can only flow forwards in time. A condition may also precede the start of an action (i.e. the white blood count check must be performed up to 2 days before chemotherapy is given) or occur after the end of an action (i.e. alopecia will be present between 2 weeks and 6 months after having chemotherapy). These would be represented respectively as:

- *after start (-2, day) AND before start (0,day)*
- *over start(2, week) end(6,month)*

By having clear numeric statements of the time between two actions or conditions, the need for the slightly ambiguous statements 'sometime-before' and 'sometime-after' (found in PDDL3), is removed. CIG-Plan also makes the discretised durative actions from PDDL2.1 more transparent, by explicitly stating the moments during the action in which conditions and effects occur, whilst maintaining the essential complexity of continuous durative actions.

2.3 Delays Between Actions

The delay function is one which is found in many different temporal representations; the standard form being *(end(A), start(B), 5 days, 12 days),* which states that action B must start between 5 and 12 days after the end of action A. It is important to be able to define delays as they are an integral feature in medical care planning. Delays between actions can be defined using an extension to standard AIP ordering constraints. CIG-Plan's extension to standard ordering constraints also integrates a further feature of delays which is necessary in the medical domain; representing delays which are flexible but which have preferences as to the ideal delay time. To ensure the validity of an action, the ideal delay must be within the domain of the delay.

The CIG-Plan representation of an ordering constraint with delays is:

before/after/equal (n1,t1,n2,t2,(d1,d2),d3)

where

- n1/n2 are nodes on the network representing actions or events
- t1/t2 are timepoints relating to the start or end of the node
- d1/d2 are the minimum/maximum delays between t1 & t2
- d3 is the ideal delay between t1 & t2.

For example, figure 1 visualises the constraint:

before(n1,end(0,day),n2,start(-12,hour), (0,min,3,hour), (30,min))

where Timepoint 1 (representing the end of action n1) must end between 0-3 hours before Timepoint 2 (representing 12 hours before the start of action n2).

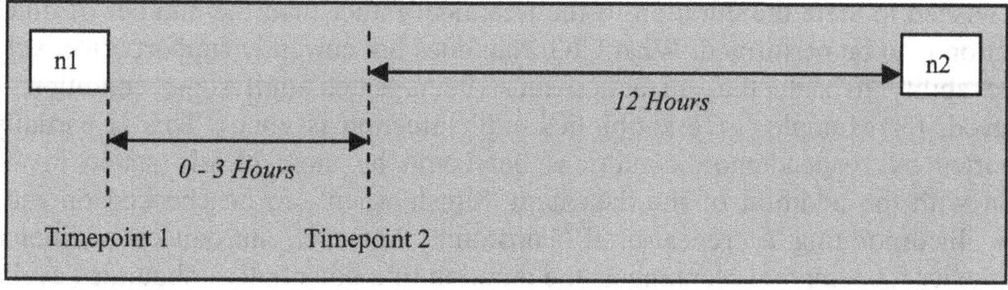

Figure 1 Representation of ordering constraint delays.

2.4 Temporal Cyclic Actions

One of the major complexities when dealing with the medical domain is to support complex cyclic actions. It is often the case that during a treatment plan a patient will be involved in a task or a set of tasks repeatedly, either for a specified number of repetitions or for a determinable period. For example, when giving chemotherapy to a patient the following cycle occurs until the patient has had chemotherapy 6 times:

- *check wbc (white blood count) (results remains valid for 2 days)*
- *if wbc >3000 give chemotherapy, wait at least 21 days and return to start*
- *if wcb 1500<>3000 wait 5 days and return to start*
- *if wbc 1500<>3000 after a 5 day wait then do CSF treatment and return to start*
- *if wbc <1500 then admit patient and treat, after treatment return to start*

There are also added complexities to this situation:

1) *there cannot be more than 42 days between chemotherapy treatments,*
2) *the preference is to be as close to 21 days between treatments as possible,*
3) *toxicity may occur and suspend the action or simply eradicate one cycle.*

In order to support complex cyclic actions, a standard CIG-Plan action has been extended to include details of the cycle. Each cyclic action identifies another (separate) action which is to be repeated a given number of times. The action to be repeated (called the 'use action') could be either a primitive action or a high-level action containing a sequence of tasks and possibly other cyclic actions. The details of the use action (its conditions, duration, score etc.) are not stored within the cyclic action, which creates a level of separation that is highly desirable for domain engineering and maintenance.

The cycle data states the number of repetitions to be performed, the delay range and ideal delay between each repetition, and the condition list which must be upheld for each individual repetition. The number of repetitions can be either an integer, stating explicitly how many times the use action must be performed, or a function from which this figure can be derived. The support of functions in the repetition counter adds flexibility to the domain and can be used, for example, if a user wished to state the duration of the treatment rather than the number of times an action is to be performed. What CIG-Plan does not currently support effectively is the ability to state that an action must be repeated until some condition is achieved, for example 'give antibiotics until infection is gone'. This is partially supported by suspend/abort conditions but could be more clearly stated in the action with the addition of the data item "finish when", to be checked on each cycle. Incorporating a 'repeat-until' constraint, however, introduces additional complexity for temporal planning as the duration of a potentially unbounded cyclic action cannot be stated and therefore any actions which follow it cannot be assigned actual temporal values. This can cause many problems for resource scheduling. It is also not good practice to have unbounded actions in medicine and there should always be a limit to the length of time / number of times an action can be performed. This is catered for in 'repeat-until' actions in PRO*forma* with the inclusion of a limiting statement which uses suspend and abort conditions to bound actions [7].

With regard to the delays and ideal delays between cycles, these can be stated in two ways. If the delay between each cycle is identical then the *betweenAll()* structure can be used. This states the temporal constraints between any two consecutive repetitions in the format:

betweenAll([start,end](int,gran), [start,end](int,gran), (minDelay,gran), (maxDelay,gran))

e.g.1 *betweenAll(end(1,day),end(0,day),(2,day),(3,day))*

e.g.1 There must be at least 2 days and no more than 3 days between one day after the end of the first action and the end of the second action

The delay can relate to either the start or the end of either repetition allowing for cycles to overlap if required. If there are a set number of repetitions and the delays between them are not all identical then the *between()* structure can be used. This states the temporal constraints between any two repetitions in the format:

between(RepNo,[start,end](int,gran),RepNo, [start,end](int,gran), (minDelay,gran), (maxDelay,gran))

e.g.2 *between(3,end(0,day),6,start(0,day),(7,day),(10,day))*

e.g.2 There must be at least 7 days and no more than 10 days between the end of the first action and the start of the second action

In this formalism RepNo relates to the number of times the cycle has been repeated, starting with the first cycle as RepNo = 1. So, the example above shows the delay constraint between the 3rd and 6th repetitions of the action.

This is useful, not only for stating repetitions with different temporal constraints, but also for stating extra temporal constraints over sets of repetitions as the two repetitions do not need to be consecutive. For example, if a person must attend physiotherapy 4 times a week for 3 weeks with no more than 2 days between each physiotherapy session, then the betweenAll() structure can be used to state that there must be not more than 2 days between each session (or repetition) and the between() structure can be used to state that there must be no more than 7 days between sessions 1 & 4, 5 & 8 and 9 & 12. This is shown in e.g.3 below.

e.g.3 *betweenAll(end(0,day),start(0,day),(1,day),(2,day))*
between(1,start(0,day),4,end(0,day),(0,day),(7,day))
between(5,start(0,day),8,end(0,day),(0,day),(7,day))
between(9,start(0,day),12,end(0,day),(0,day),(7,day))

The between() and betweenAll() structures can also be used to represent ideal delays between repetitions in the same manner as the structures for delays.

3. Maintaining Temporal Constraints

Alongside the development of structures in which medical temporal data can be contained, CIG-Plan has developed methods for maintaining and updating that temporal data throughout the planning process. The CIG-Plan algorithm is designed to specifically suit the needs of guideline systems and is based on (and reuses) many of the concepts that have proven effective in other areas of planning. It follows a recursive breadth-first search pattern, refining and resolving a plan completely at each level of decomposition before moving on to the next. Within each cycle, CIG-Plan first refines all complex plan actions and then attempts to solve any open goals.

When a new ordering constraint is added to the plan (either due to the addition of a new plan action or to solve a flaw/open goal) then its temporal requirements may affect existing plan constraints or even entire plan durations. CIG-Plan maintains temporal consistency by ensuring that the minimum and maximum delay durations of the new constraint do not conflict with the any existing constraints between related plan actions. If there are no conflicts then, where necessary, the original ordering constraints are modified to encompass the temporal restrictions of the new constraint.

During action decomposition, the overall duration of the plan may also be affected. The minimum and maximum durations of a complex action are the durations of its shortest and longest expansions. Therefore, when applying an expansion for a complex action the expansion's duration range may be smaller than that of the high level action. If this is the case then the plan's minimum and maximum durations must be edited accordingly. CIG-Plan maintains accurate overall plan durations throughout the planning process.

A concept that is not currently supported by CIG-Plan is the ability to use the temporal details of a condition as a reference point on which to base the temporal details of another condition or action. This would be useful for example if we wanted to model the effects of an effect, i.e. the effect of giving drug A is heart stops and the effect of heart stopping is death. The correlation of implied data such as this may, however, be derived from an external data source. As a step towards this capability, when actions are decomposed, the temporal placement of their conditions are used to update relational constraints between the actions in the decomposition and any actions associated with the high-level action. For example, the high level action A in fig 2 provides an effect which satisfies a precondition for action B, however in the decomposition this effect is provided by action D and therefore the temporal constraint can be updated accordingly.

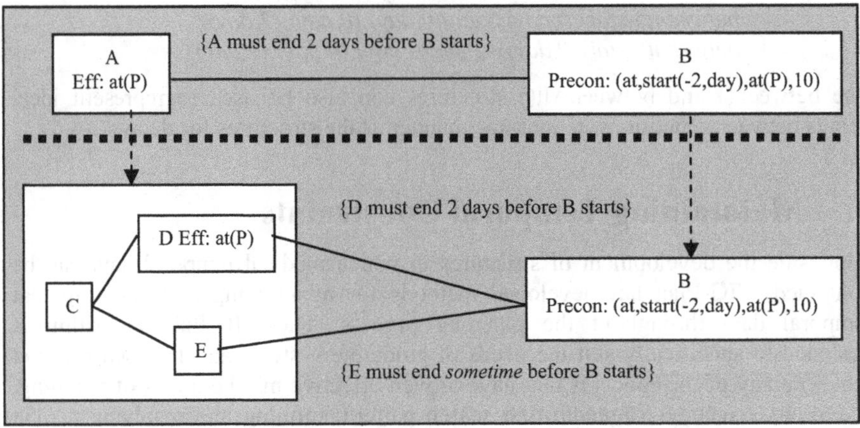

Figure 2 Movement of temporal constraints during decomposition

4. Comparative Evaluation against Existing Temporal Planning Structures

There are several existing AI planning & guideline modelling systems and methodologies which integrate some method of time handling into the planning process. It is important to note that time is used in many planning applications primarily for scheduling purposes, whereas in our case we have separated the scheduling of actions and resources onto real calendar time-dates from the abstract temporal allocation process.

4.1 PDDL Temporal Facilities

The current version of PDDL (PDDL3 [8]) caters for a number of temporal states and its temporal structure is based on points rather than intervals (which has shown to be more appropriate for the medical domain as discussed below).

Durative actions are supported with the ability to describe (pre- and post-) conditions and effects relative to the start and end points of an action using (at start) and (at end). Effects can also be durative over the length of an action with the use of the (over all) function. The (over all) statement is considered to cover the time period from the moment after the start of the action to the moment before the end of an action and therefore if a premise was required to hold true over the entire duration of the action, it would be necessary to state that the premise was true (at start) and (at end) as well as (over all). This set of functions is somewhat clumsy. However it does allow for more complex concurrent plans, whereby if a constraint holds true only at the start or end of an action (rather than over its duration) there is greater flexibility in what could potentially otherwise be mutex constraint situations.

The provision for temporal reasoning is further extended with the syntax:

(always <GD>), (sometime <GD>), (at-most-once <GD>),
(sometime-after <GD> <GD>), (sometime-before <GD> <GD>),
(within <num> <GD>), (always-within <num> <GD> <GD>),
(hold-during <num> <num> <GD>), (hold-after <num> <GD>)

where <GD> is a standard Goal Definition as described in Gerevini & Long [9].

Durative effects are further specialised with a distinction being made between discretised and continuous effects. Discretised effects are those which, although they occur over a period of time, can only be considered at the end of the action and cannot be accessed during the duration of the action. Continuous effects are those which are accessible and which "show the progress" of the effect throughout the duration of the action. For example, if we consider boiling a kettle, the discretised action effect would show that the kettle reached 100°C at the end of the action, whereas a continuous action effect could be queried to find the temperature of the water at some time point during the action.

CIG-Plan supports all of the temporal facilities currently available in PDDL and extends its complexity to a large degree, although it uses the standard CIG-Plan terminology and data structures rather than that offered by PDDL on occasion, for the sake of consistency.

4.2 O-Plan

O-Plan [10, 11] is a well known HTN planner which uses a time point network (TPN) containing time windows represented by upper and lower bounds to define limits for the start and finish of an action (max/min), its duration and separation between actions. This has the complexity to support the representation of "at, before, after and between" relationships with numerical values or symbolic expressions (symbolic expressions are currently represented but not supported). There are considered to be three types of time windows in O-Plan; the "at" function can be used to give a metric time value or a time relationship to a specific time point, a window can specify the duration of a plan element, and the time distance between two nodes can be specified.

O-plan2 uses an "Associated Data Structure" to provide a layer of separation between the temporal data tags and the reasoning about that data. All time points can be considered in relation to a nominal initial start point (or node) and time granularity is dealt with by measuring all time as integers in the format:

<days> ~ <hours> : <minutes> : <seconds>.

This temporal representation is similar to CIG-Plan in that it uses a structure based on the start and end points of each action and the interdependencies between those points. However, the CIG-Plan syntax is richer in that the individual effects and conditions of actions can be given unique temporal values in relation to the action as a whole. CIG-Plan does not have the separation of data from reasoning that O-plan has, but this is less important in CIG-plan as the scheduling process has already been removed from the abstract planning level.

4.3 TIMELINE

Timeline [12], a formalism for explicitly representing time in HTN planning, has the most similar temporal formalism to CIG-Plan in that it can represent durative actions and intermediate effects. It does not, however, appear to easily support durative conditions (like CIG-Plan's maintain conditions) or negative dependence between end points of actions.

4.4 ZENO

Zeno [13] is a sound and complete least commitment planner which can support concurrent actions, continuous change and deadline goals (although not as fully as SIADEX or CIG-Plan). Although the authors state that it is provably sound and complete, its focus is on the support of temporal metrics over continuous change situations and therefore it does not as fully support the broader functionality of the other planners noted here.

4.5 Duftschmid et al.

Duftschmid, et al. [14] define verification methods for checking the temporal and scheduling constraints of hierarchical guidelines during their creation phase and is based on the development of a minimal temporal network as shown in the work of Dechter et al. [15]. Their time annotation has the following structure:

[ESS,LSS], [EFS,LFS], [minDur,maxDur],Ref]

where ESS,LSS are the earliest & latest starting times for the action in relation to Ref (an arbitrary reference point on the timeline, possibly an actual calendar time) and EFS,LFS are the earliest and latest finishing times for the action in relation to Ref. The minimum and maximum durations are stated explicitly, although they do not support different temporal granularities.

Although the time ranges in CIG-Plan are not explicitly called {ESS,LSS}, they provide the same functionality as the metric properties on CIG-Plan's conditions and actions. Similarly to this work, CIG-Plan also has data structures to support minimum and maximum durations for actions. It does not, however, explicitly state the earliest and latest finishing times. The upper bounds for these can be implied from the ESS/LSS & durations, or if there are specific time restraints on the end of an action, they can again be encoded within the metric properties on CIG-Plan's conditions and actions.

Another similarity between the work of Duftschmid, et al. [14] and CIG-Plan is that both structures can support multiple timelines. In the case of Duftschmid, et al. [14] they have plan activations (PA's – essentially networks of constraints which each have their own timeline) with a priori unknown associations between reference points. In the work of CIG-Plan, a slightly different approach is taken, whereby relative networks (RN's) are used to hold the constraints of each complex action (with each action having its own timeline), and each RN is associated with the timeline on the next level of the hierarchy by its relation to the parent action, which appears on the RN of the higher level.

With regard to the decomposition of actions, Duftschmid, et al. [14] has a strong verification method for checking that decompositions do not extend the temporal constraints of a parent action. This keeps the durations of parent actions constant throughout the planning process, whereas CIG-Plan restricts the metric constraints of the minimal network by reducing the domain of a constraint when tighter restrictions are introduced through decomposition. For example, if action A had the duration 10 - 30 minutes and the expansion chosen for this action consisted of two sequential actions B & C with durations 10 - 15 minutes & 5 - 15 minutes respectively, then the domain for the duration of action A would become 15-30 minutes. The facility to alter the minimum network at each level when decomposition occurs is important to CIG-Plan as there is an intension to allow users to visualise plans at varying levels of decomposition, making it important to be able to show the minimum path network through the guideline accurately at all levels, not just the lowest level of decomposition.

4.6 Terenziani et al

The work of Terenziani, et al. [16] deals with the temporal structures of guidelines in a very similar fashion to CIG-Plan. Their formalisms and algorithms handle qualitative & quantative temporal constraints, cyclic actions, periodic events, imprecise/partially defined temporal constraints, structured (hierarchical) representation of actions and inherited constraint handling. The basic temporal constraint data structure is based on STP [17] with extensions to handle cyclic actions.

Terenziani, et al.[16] have separated their temporal constraint processing into two layers, low-level constraint representation and high-level temporal reasoning, executing the latter with a high-level language. Where CIG-Plan differs from this is that it separates the actual time handling (scheduling) from the relative time handling rather than the high level processing from the low. The CIG-Plan separation method would appear to be more appropriate in the guideline development and individualisation process as it separates the scheduling requirements from the care-planning requirements.

Terenziani, et al. [16] use the predicates *instanceOf*(I_1, *Action*$_1$, *p*) *and partOf*(A_1,A_2) to identify instances of actions and their hierarchical relations. In CIG-Plan, actions instances and decompositions automatically inherit the constraints of their parent action, which reduces both the need for consistency checking the problem of maintaining durations.

CIG-Plan's cyclic actions have extended the expressiveness of Terenziani, et al. [16] to allow a more clinically accurate view of the repeating cycle. Where

Terenziani, et al. [16] only states the minimum and maximum distance between the end of one cycle and start of next cycle, CIG-Plan allows for the delay between cycles to be related to either the start or the end of the repetitions. CIG-Plan does maintain Terenziani, et al.'s [16] premises that that only finite repetitions should be used (as infinite repetitions are not useful/possible in clinical practice) and that it is useful to separate the details. Both CIG-Plan and the work of Terenziani, et al. [16] can also support non-adjacency and nested repetitions by stating explicit metric constraints between different repetitions. Where the work of CIG-Plan goes beyond that of Terenziani, et al. [16] is that they have no constructs to define single repeating patterns with overlaps. CIG-Plan provides for this by enabling a delay to be associated with either the start or the end of a repetition, affording for overlaps in the pattern. It also supports nested repetition overlaps by separating the details of the repetition in a cyclic action from the contents of each repeated cycle.

CIG-Plan can handle standard repeating periodical events (such as shop open on Mondays) as well as providing for distinct periodic events which may or may not override existing events (such as the shop being closed on bank holidays).

Finally, while Terenziani, et al.'s [16] work extends that of Duftschmid, et al. [14] with the use of conditioned repetitions, CIG-Plan extends this further by adding to the complexity of the conditions, making them more closely match those used in real world medical situations, including the inclusion of PROforma's suspend and abort conditions [7].

5 Conclusion

The temporal knowledge representation format at the core of CIG-Plan has drawn influences from both PDDL and a number of existing medical guideline representations. It has provided an efficient and comprehensive framework for presenting the multifaceted information contained within guidelines, while retaining sufficient intricacy and flexibility to support detailed temporal structures and guideline flow information. The temporal structures of CIG-Plan extend those of existing guideline representations (and also many AI systems) with their support of highly accurate ordering specifications and cyclic actions. This is furthered by the inclusion (in the CIG-Plan system) of novel methods for manipulating the interaction between these complex temporal constraints. Full examples of how the formalisms shown here have been applied to guidelines for Breast Cancer Treatment and the treatment of Aortic Stenosis with Transient Ischemic Attacks can be found at [18].

References

1. Department of Health, *Summary of the overall procurement strategy*, in *Delivering 21st Century IT: Support for the NHS*. 2002.
2. NHS and NeLH. *Care Pathways*. Health Management Specialist Library 2006 11/08/06 [cited 2006 18/10/06]; Available from: http://www.library.nhs.uk/healthmanagement/ViewResource.aspx?resID=29626#1.

3. Bradbrook, K., et al. *AI Planning Technology as a Component of Computerised Clinical Practice Guidelines* in *10th Conference on Artificial Intelligence in Medicine (AIME-05)*. 2005. Aberdeen, UK: Springer.
4. McDermott, D. and The AIPS'98 Planning Committee, *PDDL: The Planning Domain Definition Language V1.2*. 1998, Department of Computer Science, Yale University: Technical Report.
5. Cancer Research UK. *PROforma*. 2005 [cited 2007 15/02/07]; Available from: http://www.acl.icnet.uk/lab/proforma.html.
6. Miksch, S. *Asbru*. 2005 24/05/05 [cited 2007 15/02/07]; Available from: http://www.openclinical.org/gmm_asbru.html.
7. Fox, J. and S. Das, *Safe and Sound: Artificial intelligence in Hazardous Applications*. 2000, London: MIT Press.
8. Gerevini, A. and D. Long, *Plan Constraints and Preferences in PDDL3*. 2006, Dept. of Electronics for Automation, University of Brescia: Italy. Technical Report, RT 2005-08-47.
9. Gerevini, A. and D. Long. *BNF Description of PDDL3.0*. 2006 7/10/05 [cited 2006 14/11/06]; Available from: http://zeus.ing.unibs.it/ipc-5/bnf.pdf.
10. Tate, A., B. Drabble, and R. Kirby, *O-PLAN2: An Architecture for Command, Planning and Control*, in *Intelligent Scheduling*, M. Aarup, M. Zweben, and M. Fox, Editors. 1994, Morgan Kaufmann: San Francisco.
11. Currie, K. and A. Tate, *O-PLAN: The Open Planning Architecture*. Artificial Intelligence, 1991. **52**(1): p. 49-86.
12. Yaman, F. and D.S. Nau, *TimeLine: An HTN Planner That can Reason About Time*, in *AIPS 2002 Workshop on Planning for Temporal Domains*. 2002: Toulouse.
13. Penberthy, J.S. and D. Weld, *Temporal Planning with Continuous Change*, in *National Conference on Artificial Intelligence (AAAI)*. 1994.
14. Duftschmid, G., S. Miksch, and W. Gall, *Verification of temporal scheduling constraints in clinical practice guidelines.* . Artificial Intelligence in Medicine 2002. **25**(2): p. 93-121.
15. Dechter, R., I. Meiri, and J. Pearl, *Temporal Constraint Networks*. Artificial Intelligence, 1991. **49**: p. 61-95.
16. Terenziani, P., et al., *Towards a Comprehensive Treatment of Repetitions, Periodicity and Temporal Constraints in Clinical Guidelines*. AI in Medicine, 2006. **38**(2): p. 171-195.
17. Terenziani, P. and L. Egidi, *A Lattice of Classes of User-Defined Symbolic Periodicities*, in *11th International Symposium on Temporal Representation & Reasoning (TIME 2004)*. 2004, IEEE Computer Society Tatihou Island, Normandie, France.
18. Bradbrook, K., G. Winstanley, and V. Patkar. *Benchmark Problem 1 Specification. CIG Technical Report TR0607-1*. July 2007 [cited 07/07]; Available from: http://www.cmis.brighton.ac.uk/research/cig/Publications.htm

Learning Sets of Sub-Models for Spatio-Temporal Prediction

Andrew Bennett and Derek Magee
School of Computing, University of Leeds
Leeds, UK, LS2 9JT
{andrewb,drm}@comp.leeds.ac.uk

Abstract

In this paper we describe a novel technique which implements a spatio-temporal model as a set of sub-models based on first order logic. These sub-models model different, typically independent, parts of the dataset; for example different spatio or temporal contexts. To decide which sub-models to use in different situations a context chooser is used. By separating the sub-models from where they are applied allows greater flexibility for the overall model. The sub-models are learnt using an evolutionary technique called Genetic Programming. The method has been applied to spatio-temporal data. This includes learning the rules of snap by observation, learning the rules of a traffic light sequence, and finally predicting a person's course through a network of CCTV cameras.

1 Introduction

Events over time may be described using a spatio-temporal data description. In all but the simplest events this may involve multiple (variable number of) objects; and multiple spatial, and temporal contexts. A description, and any model based on this description, must support this complexity. Our novel technique learns a set of sub-models that model different, typically independent, aspects of the data. To combine the sub-models into a single model a context chooser is used. This picks the most appropriate set of sub-models to predict in a certain context.

We have applied the technique to learning games by observation, and also for predicting how objects will move through a network of CCTV cameras. Both of these approaches benefit from breaking the solution down into its component parts, and modelling each part separately. In the game playing scenario this typically means finding a sub-model for each of the outcomes in the game. In the CCTV scenario this means learning the actions of single objects moving in the scene.

Global models typically will only be able to predict from data which has an exactly similar input structure to the training data. For example this means that if it was trained on a dataset containing single actions, it would fail to predict on a dataset containing multiple actions. This is because the system has not seen any data in this combined form, and may not be able to predict it. However, our technique can work in this scenario, because instead of having to find a model that matches all the combinations of actions, each of the actions occurring at the same time will be modelled by a separate sub-model, and the resulting output can simply be combined. The sub-model learning process has feature selection implicitly built in, so the learner can not only find and model the key actions in the dataset, but it also uses the most appropriate data items to detect and predict them. This can often simplify the models to be learnt.

There has been much previous work on learning from spatio-temporal domains. Traditional methods like decision trees, neural networks and support vector machines (SVMs) require a fixed length vector to represent the world. To construct this vector often requires knowledge of the domain, making these methods hard to use in a problem domain where the structure of the domain is variable, and not known a priori. In particular, only a subset of the data may be relevant, with the rest acting as a distractor. Feature selection is used to find this subset, which then allows for a more general model to be built. However, the relevant subset may change from one context to another. To perform feature selection, a set of variables is selected from the input set, and a goodness value is computed by using an objective function. By looking at the change in the function's value variables can be added or deleted. This will then repeat until convergence. An overview of feature selection can be found in [8]. One approach to modelling data of variable length is to take statistics of a variable size set [21] and [7]. This produces a fixed set description suitable for use with SVMs etc. However, spatial relationship information is lost in this process. If this information is important within a domain this leads to a poor model.

Temporal modelling approaches such as Markov chains, Hidden Markov Models (HMMs) [18] and Variable Length Markov Models (VLMMs) [6] use a description based on graphs to model state transitions. These methods still need a fixed size input vector, but can optimise their structure by using local optimisation approaches based on information theory [1]. In VLMMs this optimisation acts as kind of temporal feature selection, but as the input variables stay in the same fixed order spatial feature selection is not performed.

Bayesian networks are a generalisation of probabilistic graph based reasoning methods like HMMs and VLMMs. Again these networks require a fixed input vector, but again their relational structure can be optimised by local search [13], genetic algorithms [4], or MCMC [5] usually based on information theoretic criteria.

An alternative to using graph based methods is to use (1st order) logical expressions. Feature selection is implicit in the formalism of these expressions thus removing the need to use a fixed length vector. Logical expressions also make no assumptions about the ordering of variables, so there is no need to have a have them in a fixed ordering. Progol [15] and HR [2] are Inductive Logic Programming (ILP) methods. ILP in general takes data and generates a set of logical expressions describing the structure of the data. Progol does this by iterative subsumption using a deterministic search with the goal of data compression. HR does this by using a stochastic search using a number of specialist operators. These approaches suffer from a number of disadvantages.

Firstly, logical expressions are deterministic, so it is hard for then to model non-deterministic situations. However, there has been much work on combining (1st order) logic and probability to solve this problem [17] and [9]. Secondly Progol's search is depth bounded, which limits the size of problems it can work on, as explained in [16]. Thirdly Progol uses untyped data, this allows nonsensical models to be produced, and also increases the search time to find good models. Fourthly Progol only uses Horn clauses, which make it hard to represent some kind of logical expressions. Finally Progol's fitness function is only based on how well the model compresses the data, and not how well the model predicts the data. This can cause incorrect, or invalid models to be produced. [19] present a comparison of Progol and HR on a cognitive vision task, concluding that Progol performs better than HR. HR was produced to solve mathematical problems, so this probably shows that its representation, and operators are not well suited in a cognitive vision context. However, this work also shows that the performance of Progol is also limited.

Genetic Programming (GP) [10] is a evolutionary method, similar to genetic algorithms, for creating a program that model a dataset. In a similar way to HR, it takes a dataset data, a set of terminals, and a set of functions; and using a set of operators generates a binary tree that models the data.

There has been recent work on trying to build predictive models of basic games, using unsupervised approaches. [16] produced a system that could learn basic card games. It had three parts: an attention mechanism, unsupervised low-level learning, and high-level protocol learning. The attention mechanism uses a generic blob tracker, that locates the position of the moving objects. From this a set of features including: colour, position and texture are extracted. Clustering is used to cluster the data into groups. Using these clusters new input data is assigned its closest cluster prototype. A symbolic data stream is then created by combining together the clustered data, with time information. The symbolic stream is passed to Progol, which builds a model of the data. Once the model has been learnt it can be applied to new data. This allows the system to interact in the world.

Other related work in this area [3] looked at training a computer to play a peg-hole game. The game area was represented as an attributed relational graph. The vertices represent the objects in the scene, and the edges represent the 3D distance between a pair of objects. A percept distance metric is used to compare the similarity of two different game graphs. Using this metric a hierarchy can be founds that shows similar game playing scenarios across a dataset. Key scenes can then be extracted from the game data. These are typically when an object is moved or put down. To find the most appropriate action a particle filter is used. Initially the a set of hypothesis are set to the same (current) state, the actions are created by randomly sampling the set of actions that could cause the current state. Once the filter is initialised the actions are applied to the hypothesis, and the distance from the new state is taken off from the solved state. The worst hypothesises are then removed. Finally the next set of actions is calculated and the process repeats. After a number of iterations the optimal state is found.

[20] looked at learning event definitions from video. A raw video of a scene is converted into a polygon representation. This is then transformed into a force-dynamic model which shows how the objects in the scene are in contact with one another. Using this data and-meets-and (AMA) logic formulae describing the events are learnt using a specific-to-general ILP approach.

The reminder of this paper will take the following form. The second section talks about the architecture for the models. The subsequent section describes how these models are learnt by Genetic Programming. The subsequent section presents an evaluation of our system, and the final section shows the conclusions of the work and the further work.

2 Architecture for Models of Spatio-Temporal Data

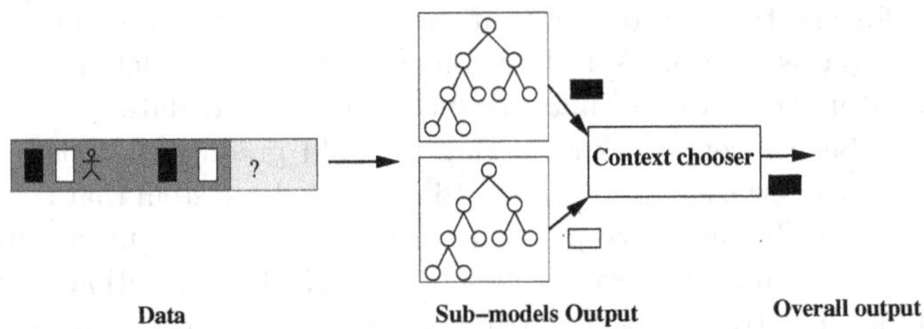

Figure 1: This figure shows the architecture of our model. It has two parts: a set of sub-models, and a context chooser to decide how to use the sub-models in different situations.

Figure 1 shows the architecture of our model. It is broken down into two parts: the sub-models, and the context chooser. The sub-models each model a separate part of the underlying process generating the data. Each sub-model contains two sections: a search section, and an output section. The search section looks for a particular pattern in the dataset. A query language, which has some similarity to SQL and Prolog, is used to describe the actual search, and a binary tree is used to represent it. The output section describes what is implied if the search returns true. This will be a set of entities and their properties the sub-model predicts will happen next. Figure 2 shows an example of a sub-model. The functions are standard logic functions: And, Or, and Not; as well as equally operators: Equals and Not Equals.

The context chooser is used to decide how to combine the sub-models in different situations. It takes as its input a boolean vector showing which sub-models have returned outputs, and makes a decision as to which ones will form the overall output. There are currently two kinds of chooser: a deterministic chooser, and a probabilistic chooser. The following sections will explain about them.

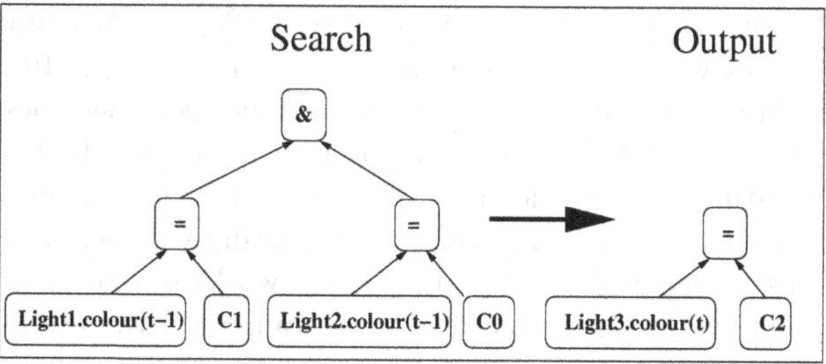

Figure 2: This shows a sub-model matching a traffic light with colour c1, and a different light having a colour c0 both at current time - 1. If the expression evaluates true it will output a new light which has a colour c2, at the current time.

2.1 Deterministic Chooser

The deterministic chooser is a transparent chooser. It simply returns the union of the outputs from all the sub-models that have evaluated true. It is only really useful for modelling deterministic datasets.

2.2 Probabilistic Chooser

The probabilistic chooser uses a probability distribution to decide what happens when a certain sub-set of sub-models produces an output. It can therefore be used to model stochastic datasets, where a particular input pattern can result in multiple possible outputs. It can also be applied to deterministic datasets giving potentially better results than using the deterministic chooser. With the deterministic chooser the sub-models must be modelling separate parts of the dataset, and interaction is limited. The probabilistic chooser works in a different way: a sub-model can be found that models a global concept in the dataset, and smaller sub-models can then be evolved to cover the cases where this global concept breaks down. This means the learner can find much simpler sub-models compared to the ones used with the deterministic chooser. This is analogous to the if/else constructs found in high level computer languages.

A context S_n is defined as a set of sub-models M producing an output in a given context, for example $S_n = M_1, M_2$ represents that M_1, and M_2 have produced an output at the same time. For each context a probability distribution over the overall output is defined for example $P_n(M_1), P_n(M_2), P_n(M_1, M_2)$. This distribution is formed from the frequency of occurrence of each situation in the training data in the given context. This then can be implemented as a sparse hash table.

2.3 Complexity of the problem

Every sub-model is stored as a binary tree. Assuming our query language has N_s functions and constants in it, and the number of nodes in the tree is N_n the complexity of generating every possible tree is: $O(N_s^{N_n})$. Assuming $N_n = 10$ the number of trees which can be generated at with depth 2 is 10^{2^2+1}, or 10^3. If we increase the depth to 3 the number of unique trees becomes 10^{2^3+1}, or 10^7, this is an increase of 10^4 for just one increase in the depth of the tree. We ran a test generating all possible trees of depth 2 for the Snap dataset, on a standard desktop machine which took 13s. Assuming the increase, generating all possible trees of depth 3 is $13 * 10^4$s, which works out to be more than 1 day of processing time. Once this has been completed there still leaves the problem of what subset of sub-models needs to be used to finding the optimal overall model. This clearly makes the problem of finding the optimal set of sub-models for anything other than a simple dataset an intractable problem to solve by exhaustive search. It should be noted that the complexity of searching for a global solution in a neural network by exhaustive search is similar to the problem just described. However the use of local search (an approximate method) makes the optimisation of the problem tractable.

3 Learning the Models from Data

As was shown in the previous section it is intractable to find the set of optimal sub-models by exhaustive search therefore an approximate search strategy needs to be used. We have decided to use Genetic Programming (GP) to learn our sub-models. It was chosen for two reasons, firstly it has already been successfully used to learning computer programs for pattern recognition tasks[11]. Secondly we have a discrete domain and it is not clear how local search would work here. Using a stochastic search seems like a better solution.

Genetic Programming (GP) [10] evolves a population of programs until a program with the desired behaviour is found. It is a type of genetic algorithm, but the programs are stored as binary trees, and not as fixed length strings. Functions are used for the nodes, and terminals (for example constants, and variables) are used for the leaf nodes. In order for the population to evolve a fitness function (in our case an accuracy score) must be defined. This score will be used by the GP system to decide which programs in the current generation to use to produce the next generation, and which ones to throw away. To initialise the system, a set of randomly generated programs must be created. Each then receive a score using the fitness function. Algorithms including crossover, mutation and reproduction use the programs from the current generation to create a new generation. Crossover takes two programs and randomly picks a sub-tree on each program, these two trees are swapped over, creating two new programs. Mutation takes one program, randomly picks a sub-tree on it, and replaces it with a randomly generated sub-tree. Reproduction copies a program exactly as it is into the new generation. The programs in the new generation are then scored, and the process is repeated. The GP system will stop when a certain fitness score is reached, or a certain number of generations has passed.

In GP it is assumed that every non-terminal will have closure. This means it will accept any type of data from any other terminal or non-terminal. For many problems this is an unrealistic assumption to make. [14] adds typing to the GP creation, and modification processes. This means that terminals have a data-type, and non-terminals have argument, and return data-types. The use of data-types puts restrictions on how trees can be created, and evolved. Montana works out for each non-terminal what terminals and non-terminals can be placed below it, so that the tree will still be valid. This prevents invalid trees being created. When crossover is performed checks are made to ensure that the types of each of the nodes are the same, to preserve the validity of the trees. We use GP with data typing for our system. In standard GP all the program code is placed in one main function. Normally when humans are writing code they make use of functions to break the code into re-usable sections. This approach was applied by Koza to create automatically defined functions (ADFs) [11]. Here functions were added to the GP trees. Crossover, and mutation can still be applied to evolve the trees, but structure preserving crossover is used to ensure that the new trees will still remain valid. Later work added the ability to add, duplicate, and delete functions, which allowed the GP system to specialise, and generalise, functions [12].

We also apply a structure to our trees to try and cut down the search space, and to make finding a solution more efficient. Our architecture can be seen as a ADF where the ADFs are replaced by the sub-models, and the main program by the context chooser. We, however, don't use all the methods from [11] to evolve our model because the ADF system is essentially still evolving single global models, and we need to evolve separate sub-models. Also, the basic structure of the chooser does not need to be evolved, we have a closed form solution that does not need refinement. Some of methods used to evolve ADFs evolve the structure of the solution, using these would make our search less efficient.

To initialise the population we generate a set of models just containing one randomly generated sub-model. The sub-model is produced using Koza's ramped half and half method [10]. We investigated creating an initial population with models containing multiple sub-models, however this approach did not perform well in ad-hoc tests. The models are then scored using the fitness function described below. To prevent overfitting a moving window which is 80% of the size of the dataset is placed over the dataset. At the start of each new generation the window is moved to a new random location. Next a new generation produced using the operators below. The learner will stop when a model of score 0 (this only will occur in non-noisy training sets) is produced, or it exceeds the maximum number of generations.

3.1 Operators

The system uses two kinds of operators. Firstly there are operators that try to optimise the sub-models used in the model, and secondly there are operators that optimise the sub-models themselves. A technique called tournament selection [10] is used to pick a model from the population. Tournament selection picks n models at random from the population, and returns the one with the lowest score, for our experiments we set n to be 10. The operators used to optimise the sub-models used in the model are shown below:

Reproduction A set number of models are picked via tournament selection and copied directly into the new population. (This occurs 10% of the time.)

Adding in a sub-model from another model Two models are picked by tournament selection. A sub-model from the first picked model is randomly selected, and added to the second chosen model. (This occurs 5% of the time.)

Replacing a sub-model Again two models are picked by tournament selection, and a sub-model from the first chosen model is then replaced by a sub-model randomly selected from the second chosen model. (This occurs 5% of the time.)

The only operator used to optimise the sub-models themselves is crossover. In crossover two models are picked using tournament selection. A sub-model from each model is then randomly selected, and standard crossover [10] is performed on these sub-models. (Crossover is performed 80% of the time.)

3.2 Fitness Function

To decide the fitness of a model (m), its prediction error (E), and coverage (C) over the dataset is computed. For each time point in the dataset the model is given a set of history data (h) and is queried to produce a prediction. This is then compared with the observed data (r). Coverage is the absolute difference between the number of data items (*Elements*) produced by the model, and the number of items in the observed data. The coverage score then acts as a penalty for overfitting or underfitting a part of the dataset. To compute the error the difference between the result returned by the model and the actual result is calculated. A penalisation penalty (p) is used as a penalty for models that incorrectly fire in the wrong part of the dataset. The overall score (S) is then the addition of the accuracy, and the coverage. This is then repeated over the rest of the dataset, and the results are summed together.

$$C(r, h) = Elements(m(h)) - Elements(r) \tag{1}$$

$$E(r, h) = (m(h) - r) * p \tag{2}$$

$$S = \sum_i E(r_i, h_i) + C(r_i, h_i) \tag{3}$$

4 Evaluation

The learner was evaluated on three different datasets, which were: handcrafted traffic light data, handcrafted snap data, and data from people walking through a network of mock CCTV cameras. More detail about these datasets is presented in the following section.

4.1 CCTV Data of a Path

A 10 minute video of people walking along a path containing a junction was filmed. This was then used to mock up a network of CCTV cameras. Figure 3 shows a frame from the video. Virtual motion detectors, representing CCTV cameras, were hand placed over the video has shown in Figure 3. Using frame differencing, and morphological operations the video was processed to determine the location of the motion. If the number of moved pixels in a region exceeded a fixed threshold then the virtual detector outputted that motion had occurred at that location. Hysteresis on the motion detection is implemented as a 2 state, state machine (where the states are motion/no motion). The state machine requires a numbers of frames (normally 10) of stability to change state. The data produced is then placed in a datafile with a motion event recorded per state change going from no motion to motion. This datafile was split into a test file containing 30 state changes and a training file containing 50 state changes.

Figure 3 shows the main actions that occurred in the video. People either walked from region 1 through state 0 to state 3, and then back to region 1 again via region 0, or they again walked from region 1 through region 0 to region 3, but this time they walked to region 2 via region 0, finally the other possible action is to walk directly to region 2 from region 1 via region 0.

4.2 Traffic Lights

The traffic light file was handcrafted and complies to the standard UK traffic light sequence. We chose this as it has a variable number of lights lit at any one time. Three datasets were prepared: a non-noisy training set, a noisy training set, and a test set. The non-noisy training set and the test set were identical, and contained 200 state changes, and 250 objects on total. The noisy training set was created by adding 10% noise to the non-noisy training set. The noise involved adding, and changing the order of the lights in traffic light sequence.

4.3 Snap

The snap dataset was handcrafted, but the format of it was the same as the snap dataset used in the work of [16]. The snap sequence is the following:

t_1	t_2	t_3	t_4	...
BLANK	PLAY	CARD 1	RESULT	...
		CARD 2		...

Initially the computer will see a blank scene, then it will hear the word play, next two coloured cards will be seen. If they are the same then the word equals will be heard, otherwise different will be heard. We ask the computer to only learn the sections where a human is speaking, as it would be impossible to accurately predict the next two cards because they are essentially random. Again three datasets were prepared: a non-noisy, and noisy training set, and a test set. The datasets were all contained 200 state changes, and typically had

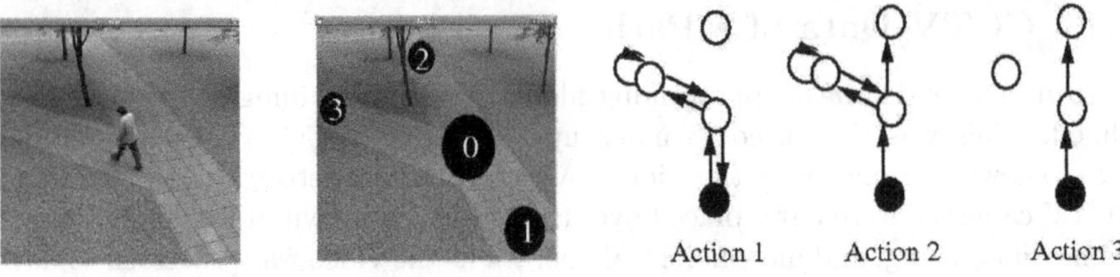

Figure 3: This figure firstly shows a frame of the video with a person taking a decision at the junction point, secondly it shows where the virtual detectors are on the video. Finally, it shows the three main actions in the video. Either people will walk from region 1 to region 3 and back again, or they will walk from region 1 to region 3 to region 2, or finally they can just walk directly from region 1 to region 2.

Dataset	Number of runs	Coverage(%)	Prediction Accuracy(%)
Snap No Noise with a Deterministic Chooser	2 3	100 92.8	100 100
Snap Noise with a Deterministic Chooser	2 1 1 1	100 94.4 95.6 88.4	100 100 100 100
Snap No Noise with a Probabilistic Chooser	5	100	100
Snap Noise with a Probabilistic Chooser	2 3	100 93	See Figure 6 See Figure 6

Figure 4: This figure shows the results for the snap datasets.

250 objects in total in them. The noisy data was generated by adding 10% noise to the non-noisy training set. The noise took the form of removing cards, removing the play state, and changing the output state, for example making the output not equal when it should be equal.

5 Results

To test the system five runs were allocated to each possible combination of dataset, and chooser. For each run a different random number seed was used to initialise the system.

To evaluate how well the models have been learnt they were tested on a test set. Two metrics were used to evaluate the results: coverage, and predic-

Dataset	Number of runs	Coverage score(%)	Prediction accuracy(%)
CCTV	3	94	See Figure 6
	1	83	See Figure 6
	1	77	See Figure 6

Figure 5: This figure shows the results for the CCTV dataset

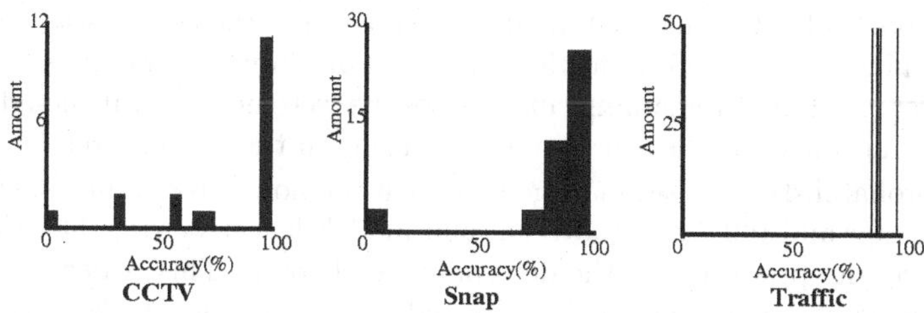

Figure 6: This shows the distribution of prediction accuracy for a typical model learnt for traffic, snap and path using noisy training data.

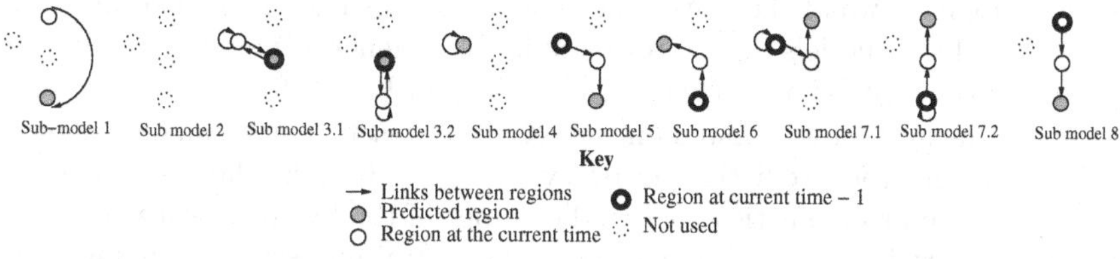

Figure 7: This figure shows the patterns matched for each sub-model from one of the results. Sub-models 3 and 7 have two possible outcomes. Note that the sub-models have different history lengths.

tion accuracy. Coverage scores if the system can correctly predict the dataset (ie. the probability of correct prediction is greater than 0%), and prediction accuracy scores with what probability the correct predicition is made. In non-deterministic scenarios this will not be 100%.

The system was initially tested on the traffic light dataset. Both the deterministic and the probabilistic choosers were used to learn from the noisy, and non-noisy training data. As this dataset is deterministic both of the choosers managed to learn all the non-noisy training data with 100% prediction accuracy , and 100% coverage. Almost all the results had three sub-models, with each sub-model modelling one of the lights. The deterministic chooser got 100% prediction accuracy and 100% coverage on all its runs from the noisy training set. Most of its results had multiple sub-models to model each different light. The probablistic chooser did get 100% coverage, but it did not get 100% prediction accuracy, this is because the probability distributions modelled some of the noise in the training set. The typical prediction accuracy for one of the runs is shown in Figure 6.

Next, the system was tested on the snap dataset. Again both the probabilistic, and deterministic choosers were used to learn from the training sets. The deterministic chooser managed to get 100% prediction accuracy in both learning from noisy and non-noisy training sets. In the non-noisy set only two runs got 100% coverage, these both found seperate sub-models for play, equal and not-equal. The runs for which the deterministic chooser did not get 100% coverage only had sub-models which only covered the not-equals and play states, and they had failed to find a sub-model which covered the equals state. In the noisy training set the deterministic chooser again only got two runs to have 100% coverage. In the remaining runs the results were not general enough, and the sub-models had only learnt patterns occuring in the training set.

The probabilistic chooser managed to learn the non-noisy training set with 100% coverage and 100% accuracy. The sub-models learnt were slightly simpler than the results produced by the deterministic chooser. This is because most of the models had a sub-model that covered a general concept like non-equal, and when this concept broke down a simplier sub-model like equals would cover it. This was all modelled in the chooser probability distribution. When the probablistic chooser learnt the noisy training data it only managed to get 100% coverage in two of the runs. The remaining runs like in the deterministic chooser found sub-models that were not sufficiently general enough. The typical prediction accuracy for one of the runs is shown in Figure 6

Finally the system was tested on the CCTV dataset. The results are shown in Figure 5, and the prediction accuracy in Figure 6. The dataset was only tested using the probabilistic chooser. Three out of the five results learnt every sub-model apart from one. From looking at the training set the missing sub-model appears to be not learnt due insufficient data. The actual sub-models learnt for one of the results are shown in a diagrammatic form in Figure 7. Looking at these you can see that the system has learnt small actions in the dataset, for example sub-model 6 shows the action of going to region 3 from region 1 (taking the left branch on the path). Figure 8 shows the probability distribution that decides how to use the sub-models. Two main parts of it are worth pointing out. Context 10 represents how the model deals with someone who has walked from region 1, to the junction point at region 0. The person can either go to region 3 (turn left) or region 2 (go straight on), and this entry models how likely they are to go to each region. Context 11 deals with a person who has already walked from region 1 to region 3, but now is coming back down the path and is at the junction point region 0 again. The two possible options are to go back to region 1 (turn right) or to go to region 2 (turn left), and again this entries models how likely each region is.

6 Conclusions

We have shown that that it is possible to learn a set of sub-models that can model different, typically disjoint, parts of a dataset. This technique is useful for a number of reasons. Firstly, it allows the system to learn from a dataset containing single actions, and then be able to predict from a dataset containing multiple overlapping actions. Secondly, model learning is easier and faster. If the dataset genuinely contains independent components then the complexity of the search is reduced to being linear in the number of contexts, rather than exponential (if every combination must be considered). Thirdly, being logical expressions, the sub-models are human readable, which makes them easy to check, and validate.

Context	Sub-Models giving Output	Output
1	sm3, sm4	sm4 (100%)
2	sm6	output nothing (50%), sm6(50%)
3	sm6, sm3	sm6 (100%)
4	sm6, sm1	sm3 (100%)
5	sm6, sm3, sm4	sm4 (100%)
6	sm3, sm4, sm5, sm6	sm4(100%)
7	sm7	output nothing (50%), sm7 (50%)
8	sm7, sm1	sm7 (100%)
9	sm4, sm7	sm4 (100%)
10	sm6, sm7	sm6 (25%), sm7 (75%)
11	sm5, sm7	sm5 (66%), sm7 (33%)
12	sm3, sm6, sm8	sm3 (100%)
13	sm6, sm7, sm8	sm8 (100%)

Figure 8: This shows the probability distribution for one of the results for the CCTV dataset.

The results show that using a probabilistic chooser performs better than a deterministic chooser, even in deterministic scenarios, because the probabilistic chooser can find a global sub-model that matches most of the dataset, and then learn simple sub-models to cover the cases where this global sub-model does not work. With the deterministic chooser the sub-models need to be more complex to represent the same scenario, and this makes the learning process harder, and slower.

In future work we will look into investigating more operators to improve the speed, and effectiveness of the GP learner. We are also looking into adding a compactness criterion to the learner, so that the models are of optimal size, and don't contain too many irrelevant terms. Finally we will be looking into using temporal, and spatio relations in both the datasets, and in the system.

References

[1] Matthew Brand. Pattern discovery via entropy minimization. In *Artificial Intelligence and Statistics*, 1998.

[2] Simon Colton, Alan Bundy, and Toby Walsh. Automatic identification of mathematical concepts. In *International Conference on Machine Learning*, 2000.

[3] Liam Ellis and Richard Bowden. A generalised exemplar approach to modeling perception action coupling. In *International Workshop on Semantic Knowledge in Computer Vision*, 2005.

[4] R. Etxeberria, P. Larranaga, and J.M. Picaza. Analysis of the behaviour of genetic algorithms when learning bayesian network structure from data. *Pattern Recognition Letters*, 13:1269–1273, 1997.

[5] Nir Friedman and Daphne Koller. Being bayesian about network structure. *Machine Learning*, 50:95–126, 2003.

[6] Aphrodite Galata, Neil Johnson, and David Hogg. Learning behaviour models of human activities. In *British Machine Vision Conference (BMVC)*, 1999.

[7] Kristen Grauman and Trevor Darrell. The pyramid match kernel:discriminative classication with sets of image features. In *International Conference on Computer Vision*, 2005.

[8] Isabelle Guyon and Andre Elissee. An introduction to variable and feature selection. *Journal of Machine Learning Research*, 2003.

[9] R Haenni. Towards a unifying theory of logical and probabilistic reasoning. In *International Symposium on Imprecise Probabilities and Their Applications*, pages 193–202, 2005.

[10] John Koza. *Genetic Programming.* MIT Press, 1992.

[11] John Koza. *Genetic Programming II.* MIT Press, 1994.

[12] John Koza, Forrest H Bennett III, David Andre, and Martin Keane. *Genetic Programming III.* Morgan Kaufmann, 1999.

[13] Philippe Leray and Olivier Francios. Bayesian network structural learning and incomplete data. In *Adaptive Knowledge Representation and Reasoning*, 2005.

[14] David Montana. Strongly typed genetic programming. In *Evolutionary Computation*, 1995.

[15] S.H. Muggleton and J. Firth. CProgol4.4: a tutorial introduction. In *Relational Data Mining*, pages 160–188. Springer-Verlag, 2001.

[16] Chris Needham, Paulo Santos, Derek Magee, Vincent Devin, David Hogg, and Anthony Cohn. Protocols from perceptual observations. *Artificial Intelligence*, 167:103–136, 2005.

[17] N. J. Nilsson. Probabilistic logic. *Artificial Intelligence*, 28:71–87, 1986.

[18] Lawrence R. Rabiner. A tutorial on hidden markov models and selected applications in speech recognition. *Proceedings of the IEEE*, 77(2):257–286, 1989.

[19] Paulo Santos, Simon Colton, and Derek Magee. Predictive and descriptive approaches to learning game rules from vision data. In *Ibero-American Artificial Intelligence Conference*, 2006.

[20] Jeffrey Mark Siskind. Grounding the lexical semantics of verbs in visual perception using force dynamics and event logic. *Articial Intelligence Research*, 15:31–90, 2000.

[21] C. Wallraven, B. Caputo, and A. Graf. Recognition with local features:the kernel recipe. In *International Conference on Computer Vision*, 2003.

DATA MINING AND MACHINE LEARNING

Frequent Set Meta Mining: Towards Multi-Agent Data Mining

Kamal Ali Albashiri, Frans Coenen, Rob Sanderson, and Paul Leng
Department of Computer Science, The University of Liverpool
Ashton Building, Ashton Street, Liverpool L69 3BX, United Kingdom
{ali,frans,azaroth,phl}@csc.liv.ac.uk

Abstract

In this paper we describe the concept of Meta ARM in the context of its objectives and challenges and go on to describe and analyse a number of potential solutions. Meta ARM is defined as the process of combining the results of a number of individually obtained Associate Rule Mining (ARM) operations to produce a composite result. The typical scenario where this is desirable is in multi-agent data mining where individual agents wish to preserve the security and privacy of their raw data but are prepared to share data mining results. Four Meta ARM algorithms are described: a Brute Force approach, an Apriori approach and two hybrid techniques. A "bench mark" system is also described to allow for appropriate comparison. A complete analysis of the algorithms is included that considers the effect of: the number of data sources, the number of records in the data sets and the number of attributes represented.

Keywords: Meta Mining, Multi Agent Data Mining, Association Rule Mining.

1 Introduction

The term *meta mining* describes the process of combining the individually obtained results of N applications of a data mining activity. This is typically undertaken in the context of Multi-Agent Data Mining (MADM) where the individual owners of agents wish to preserve the privacy and security of their raw data but are prepared to share the results of data mining activities. The mining activities in question could be, for example, clustering, classification or Association Rule Mining (ARM); the study described here concentrates on the latter — frequent set meta mining (which in this paper we will refer to as Meta ARM). The Meta ARM problem is defined as follows: a given ARM algorithm is applied to N raw data sets producing N collections of frequent item sets. Note that each raw data set conforms to some globally agreed attribute schema, although each local schema will typically comprise some subset of this global schema. The objective is then to *merge* the different sets of results into a single *meta* set of frequent itemsets with the aim of generating a set of ARs or alternative a set of Classification Association Rules (CARS).

The most significant issue when combining groups of previously identified frequent sets is that wherever an itemset is frequent in a data source A but not in a data source B a check for any contribution from data source B is required (so as to obtain a global support count). The challenge is thus to combine the results from N different data sources in the most computationally efficient manner. This in turn is influenced predominantly by the magnitude (in terms of data size) of returns to the source data that are required. There are a number of alternative mechanisms whereby ARM results can be combined to satisfy the requirements of Meta ARM. In this paper a study is presented comparing five different approaches (including a bench mark approach). The study is conducted using variations of the TFP set enumeration tree based ARM algorithm ([6, 4]), however the results are equally applicable to other algorithms (such as FP growth [7]) that use set enumeration tree style structures, the support-confidence framework and an Apriori methodology of processing/building the trees.

The paper is organised as follows. In Section 2 some related work is presented and discussed. A brief note on the data structures used by the Meta ARM algorithms is then presented in Section 3. The five different approaches that are to be compared are described in Section 4. This is followed, in Section 5, by an analysis of a sequence of experimental results used to evaluate the approaches introduced in Section 4. Finally some conclusions are presented in Section 6.

2 Previous Work

Multi-Agent Data Mining (MADM) is an emerging field concerned with the application and usage of Multi-Agent Systems (MAS) to perform data mining activities. MADM research encompasses many issues. In this paper the authors address the issue of collating data mining results produced by individual agents, we refer to this as *meta-mining.*

The Meta ARM problem (as outlined in the above introduction) has similarities, and in some cases overlap, with incremental ARM (I-ARM) and distributed ARM. The distinction between I-ARM, as first proposed by Agrawal and Psaila [1], and Meta ARM is that in the case of I-ARM we typically have only two sets of results: (i) a large set of frequent itemsets D and (ii) a much smaller set of itemsets d that we wish to process in order to update D. In the case of Meta ARM there can be any number of sets of results which can be of any (or the same) size. Furthermore, in this case each contributing set has already been processed to obtain results in the form of locally frequent sets. I-ARM algorithms typically operate using a relative support threshold [8, 11, 15] as opposed to an absolute threshold; the use of relative thresholds has been adopted in the work described here. I-ARM algorithms are therefore supported by the observation that for an itemset to be *globally frequent* it must be *locally frequent* in at least one set of results regardless of the relative number of records at individual sources (note that this only works with relative support thresholds). When undertaking I-ARM four scenarios can be identified according to whether a given itemset i is: (i) frequent in d, and/or (ii) frequent in D; these are itemised in Table 1.

	Frequent in d	Not frequent in d
Frequent in D (retained itemsets)	Increment total count for i and recalculate support	i may be globally supported, increment total count for i and recalculate support
NotFrequent in D	May be globally supported, need to obtain total support count and recalculate support (Emerging itemset)	Do nothing

Table 1. I-ARM itemset comparison options (relative support)

From the literature, three fundamental approaches to I-ARM are described. These may be categorised as follows:

1. Maintain itemsets on the border with maximal frequent item sets (the *negative border* idea) and hope that this includes all those itemsets that may become frequent. See for example ULI [14].
2. Make use of a second (lower) support threshold above which items are retained (similar idea to negative border). Examples include AFPIM [8]) and EFPIM [11].
3. Acknowledge that at some time or other we will have to recompute counts for some itemsets and consequently maintain a data structure that (a) stores all support counts, (b) requires less space than the original structure and (c) facilitates fast look-up, to enable updating. See for example [9].

Using a reduced support threshold results in a significant additional storage overhead. For example if we assume that given a data set with 100 ($n = 100$) attributes where all the 1 and 2 item sets are frequent but none of the other itemsets are frequent, the negative border will comprise 161700 item sets ($\frac{n(n-1)(n-2)}{3!}$) compared to 4970 supported item sets ($n + \frac{n(n-1)}{2!}$). The Meta ARM ideas presented here therefore subscribe to this last of the above categories. The data at each source is held using a P-tree (**P**artial Support Tree) data structure, the nature of which is described in further detail in Section 3 below.

The distinction between distributed mining and MADM is one of control. Distributed ARM assumes some central control that allows for the global partitioning of either the raw data (*data distribution*) or the ARM task (*task distribution*), amongst a fixed number of processors. MADM, and by extension the Meta ARM mining described here, does not require this centralised control, instead the different sets of results are produced in an autonomous manner without any centralised control. MADM also offers the significant advantage that the privacy and security of raw data belonging to individual agents is preserved, an advantage that is desirable for both commercial and legal reasons.

In both I-ARM and distributed ARM, as well as Meta ARM, the raw data typically conforms to some agreed global schema.

Other research on meta mining that includes work on meta classification. Meta classification, also sometimes referred to as meta learning, is a technique for generating a *global* classifier from N distributed data sources by first computing N *base* classifiers which are then collated to build a single *meta* classifier [13] in much the same way that we are collating ARM results.

The term *merge mining* is used in [3] to describe a generalised form of incremental association rule mining which has some conceptual similarities to the ideas behind Meta ARM described here. However Aref et al. define merge mining in the context of time series analysis where additional data is to be merged with existing data as it becomes available.

3 Note on P and T Trees

The Meta ARM algorithms described here make use of two data structures, namely P-trees and T-trees. The nature of these structures is described in detail in [4, 6]; however, for completeness a brief overview is presented here.

The P-tree (**P**artial support tree) is a set enumeration tree style structure with two important differences: (i) more than one item may be stored at any individual node, and (ii) the tree includes partial support counts. The structure is sued to store a compressed version of the raw data set with partial support counts obtained during the reading of the input data. The best way of describing the P-tree is through an example such as that given in Figure 1. In the figure the data set given on the left is stored in the P-tree on the right. The advantages offered by the P-tree are of particular benefit if the raw data set contains many common leading sub-strings (prefixes). The number of such sub-strings can be increased if the data is ordered according to the frequency of the 1-itemsets contained in the raw data. The likelihood of common leading sub-strings also increases with the number of records in the raw data.

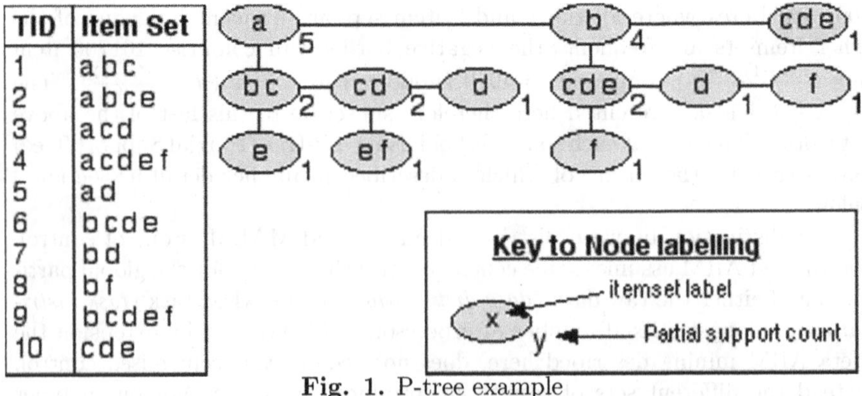

TID	Item Set
1	a b c
2	a b c e
3	a c d
4	a c d e f
5	a d
6	b c d e
7	b d
8	b f
9	b c d e f
10	c d e

Fig. 1. P-tree example

The T-tree (**T**otal support tree) is a "reverse" set enumeration tree structure that inter-leaves node records with arrays. It is used to store frequent item sets, in a compressed form, identified by processing the P-tree. An example, generated from the P-tree given Figure 1, is presented in Figure 2. ¿From the figure it can be seen that the top level comprises an array of references to node structures that hold the support count and reference to the next level (providing such a level exists). Indexes equate to itemset numbers although for ease of understanding in the figure letters have been used instead of numbers. The structure can be though of as a "reverse" set enumeration tree because child nodes only contain itemsets that are lexicographically before the parent itemsets. This offers the advantage that less array storage is required (especially if the data is ordered according to the frequency of individual items.

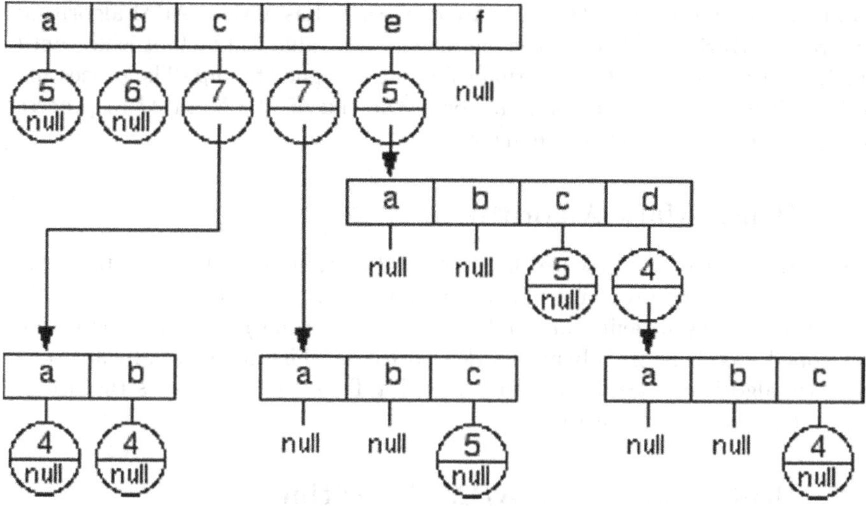

Fig. 2. T-tree example (support = 35%)

The T-tree is generated using an algorithm called Total From Partial (TFP) which is also described in [4, 6]. The TFP algorithm is essentially an Apriori style algorithm that proceeds in a level by level manner. At each level the P-tree is processed to generate appropriate support counts. Note that on completion of the TFP algorithm the T-tree contains details of all the supported itemsets, in a manner that provides for fast look up during AR generation, but no information about unsupported sets (other than that they are not supported). Referring to Figure 2 unsupported sets are indicated by a *null* reference.

4 Proposed Meta ARM Algorithms

In this section a number of Meta ARM algorithms are described, an analysis of which is presented in section 5. It is assumed that each data source will maintain the data set in either its raw form or a compressed form. For the experiments reported here the data has been stored in a compressed form using a P-tree (see above).

The first algorithm developed was a bench mark algorithm, against which the identified Meta ARM algorithms were to be compared. This is described in 4.1. Four Meta ARM algorithms were then constructed. For the Meta ARM algorithm it was assumed that each data source would produce a set of frequent sets using the TFP algorithm with the results stored in a T-tree. These T-trees would then be merged in some manner.

Each of the Meta ARM algorithms described below makes use of *return to data* (RTD) lists, one per data set, to contain lists of itemsets whose support was not included in the current T-tree and for which the count is to be obtained by a return to the raw data. RTD lists comprise zero, one or more tuples of the form $< I, sup >$, where I is an item set for which a count is required and sup is the desired count. RTD lists are constructed as a Meta ARM algorithm progresses. During RTD list construction the sup value will be 0, it is not until the RTD list is processed that actual values are assigned to sup. The processing of RTD lists may occur during, and/or at the end of, the Meta ARM process depending on the nature of the algorithm.

4.1 Bench Mark Algorithm

For Meta ARM to make sense the process of merging the distinct sets of discovered frequent itemsets must be faster than starting from the beginning (otherwise there is no benefit from undertaking the merging). The first algorithm developed was therefore a bench mark algorithm. This was essentially an Apriori style algorithm (see Table 2) that used a T-tree as a storage structure to support the generation process.

4.2 Brute Force Meta ARM Algorithm

The philosophy behind the Brute Force Meta ARM algorithm was that we simply fuze the collection of T-trees together adding items to the appropriate RTD lists as required. The algorithm comprises three phases: (i) merge, (ii) inclusion of additional counts and (iii) final prune. The merge phase commences by selecting one of the T-trees as the initial merged T-tree (from a computational perspective it is desirable that this is the largest T-tree). Each additional T-tree is then combined with the merged T-tree "sofar" in turn. The combining is undertaken by comparing each element in the top level of the merged T-tree sofar with the corresponding element in the "current" T-tree and then updating or extending the merged T-tree sofar and/or adding to the appropriate RTD lists as indicated in Table 3 (remember that we are working with relative support thresholds). Note that the algorithm only proceeds to the next branch in the merged T-tree sofar if an element represents a supported node in both the merged and current T-trees. At the end of the merge phase the RTD lists are processed and any additional counts included (the *inclusion of additional counts* phase). The final merged T-tree is then pruned in phase three to remove any unsupported frequent sets according to the user supplied support threshold (expressed as a percentage of the total number of records under consideration).

```
K = 1
Generate candidate K-itemsets
Start Loop
    if (K-itemsets == null break)
    forall N data sets get counts for K-itemsets
    Prune K-itemsets according to support threshold
    K ⇐ K+1
    Generate K-itemsets
End Loop
```

Table 2. Bench Mark Algorithm

	Frequent in T-tree N	Not frequent in T-tree N
Frequent in merged T-tree sofar	Update support count for i in merged T-tree sofar and proceed to child branch in merged T-tree sofar	Add labels for all supported nodes in merge T-tree branch, starting with current node, to RTD list N
Not Frequent in merged T-tree sofar	Process current branch in T-tree N, starting with current node, adding nodes with their support to the merged T-tree sofar and recording labels for each to RTD lists 1 to $N-1$	Do nothing

Table 3. Brute Force Meta ARM itemset comparison options

4.3 Apriori Meta ARM Algorithm

In the Brute Force approach the RTD lists are not processed until the end of the merge phase. This means that many itemsets may be included in the merged T-tree sofar and/or the RTD lists that are in fact not supported. The objective of the Aprori Meta ARM algorithm is to identify such unsupported itemsets much earlier on in the process. The algorithm proceeds in a similar manner to the standard Apriori algorithm (Table 2) as shown in Table 4. Note that items are added to the RTD list for data source n if a candidate itemset is not included in T-tree n.

```
K = 1
Generate candidate K-itemsets
Start Loop
   if (K-itemsets == null break)
   Add supports for level K from N T-trees or add to RTD list
   Prune K-itemsets according to support threshold
   K ⇐ K+1
   Generate K-itemsets
End Loop
```

Table 4. Apriori Meta ARM Algorithm

4.4 Hybrid Meta ARM Algorithm 1 and 2

The Apriori Meta ARM algorithm requires less itemsets to be included in the RTD list than is the case with the Brute Force Meta ARM algorithm (as demonstrated in Section 5). However, the Apriori approach requires the RTD lists to be processed at the end of each level generation, while in the case of the Brute Force approach this is only done once. A hybrid approach, that combines the advantages offered by both the Brute Force and Apriori meta ARM algorithms therefore suggests itself. Experiments were conducted using two different version of the hybrid approach.

The Hybrid 1 algorithm commences by generating the top level of the merged T-tree in the Apriori manner described above (including processing of the RTD list); and then adds the appropriate branches, according to which top level nodes are supported, using a Brute Force approach.

The Hybrid 2 algorithm commences by generating the top two levels of the merged T-tree, instead of only the first level, as in the Hybrid 1 approach. Additional support counts are obtained by processing the RTD lists. The remaining branches are added to the supported level 2-nodes in the merged T-tree sofar (again) using the Brute Force mechanism. The philosophy behind the hybrid 2 algorithm was that we might expect all the one itemsets to be supported and included in the component T-trees therefore we might as well commence by building the top two layers of the merged T-tree.

5 Experimentation and Analysis

To evaluate the five algorithms outlined above a number of experiments were conducted. These are described and analysed in this section. The experiments were designed to analyse the effect of the following:

1. The number of data sources.
2. The size of the datasets in terms of number of records .
3. The size of the datasets in terms of number of attributes.

All experiments were run using a Intel Core 2 Duo E6400 CPU (2.13GHz) with 3GB of main memory (DDR2 800MHz), Fedora Core 6, Kernel version 2.6.18 running under Linux. For each of the experiments we measured: (i) processing time (seconds / mseconds), (ii) the size of the RTD lists (Kbytes) and (iii) the number of RTD lists generated. The authors did not use the IBM QUEST generator [2] because many different data sets (with the same input parameters) were required and the quest generator always generated the same data given the same input parameters. Instead the authors used the LUCS KDD data generator [1].

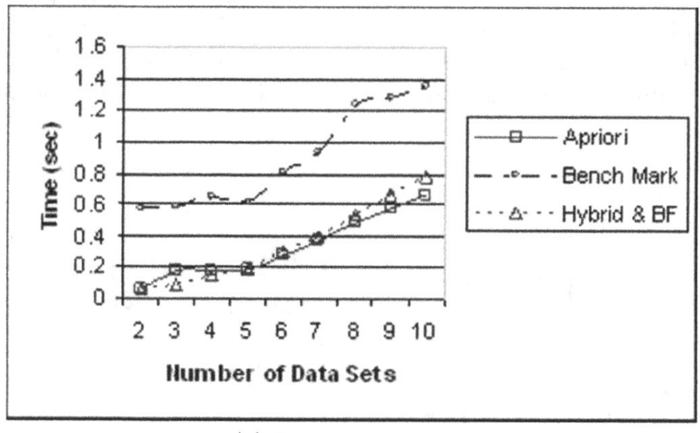

(a) Processing Time

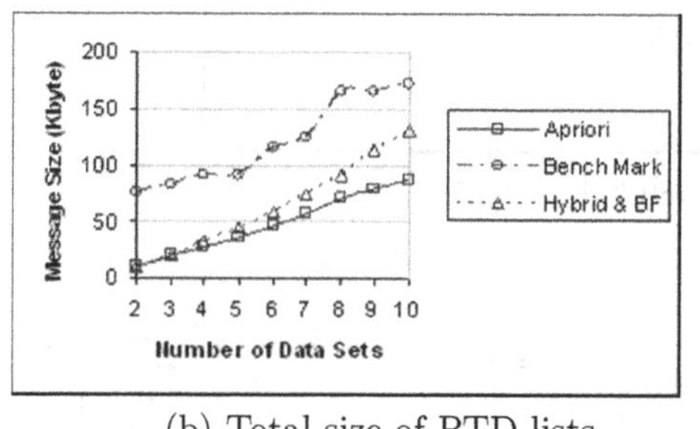

(b) Total size of RTD lists

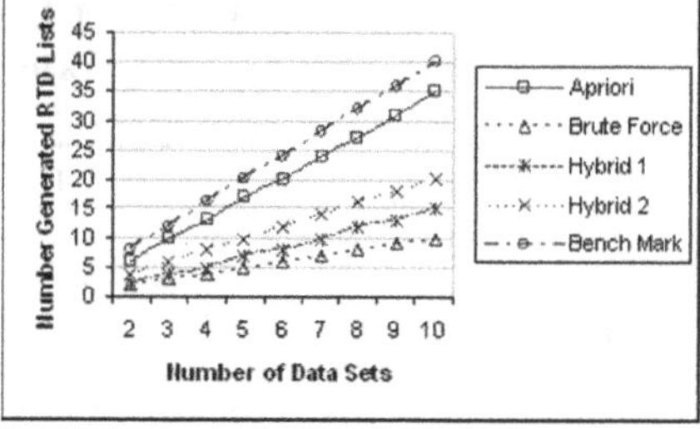

(c) Number of RTD lists

Fig. 3. Effect of number of data sources

Figure 3 shows the effect of adding additional data sources. For this experiment ten different artificial data sets were generated using $T = 4$ (average number of items per transactions), $N = 20$ (Number of attributes), $D = 100k$ (Number of transactions). Note that the selection of a relatively low value for N ensured that there were some common frequent itemsets shared across the T-trees. Experiments using $N = 100$ and above tended to produced very flat T-trees with many frequent 1-itemsets, only a few isolated frequent 2-itemsets and no frequent sets with cardinality greater than 2. For the experiments a support

[1] *http : //www.csc.liv.ac.uk/ frans/KDD/Software//LUCS − KDD − DataGen/*

threshold of 1% was selected. Graph 3(a) demonstrates that all of the proposed Meta ARM algorithms worked better then the bench mark (start all over again) approach. The graph also shows that the Apriori Meta ARM algorithm, which invokes the "return to data procedure" many more times than the other algorithms, at first takes longer; however as the number of data sources increases the approach starts to produce some advantages as T-tree branches that do not include frequent sets are identified and eliminated early in the process. The amount of data passed to and from sources, shown in graph 3(b), correlates directly with the execution times in graph 3(a). Graph 3(c) shows the number of RTD lists generated in each case. The Brute Force algorithm produces one (very large) RTD list per data source. The Bench Mark algorithm produces the most RTD lists as it is constantly returning to the data sets, while the Apriori approach produces the second most (although the content is significantly less).

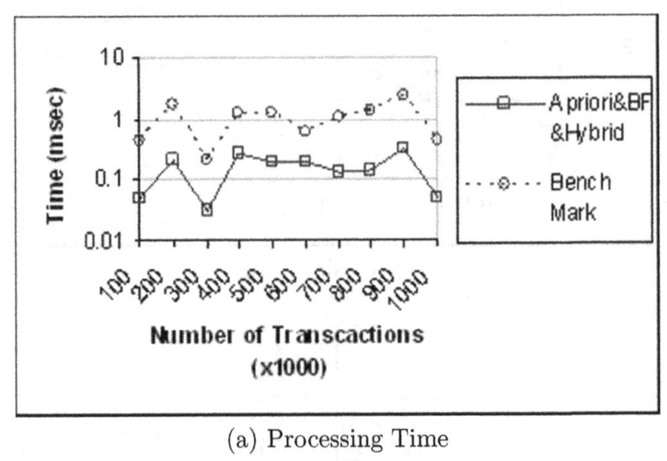

(a) Processing Time

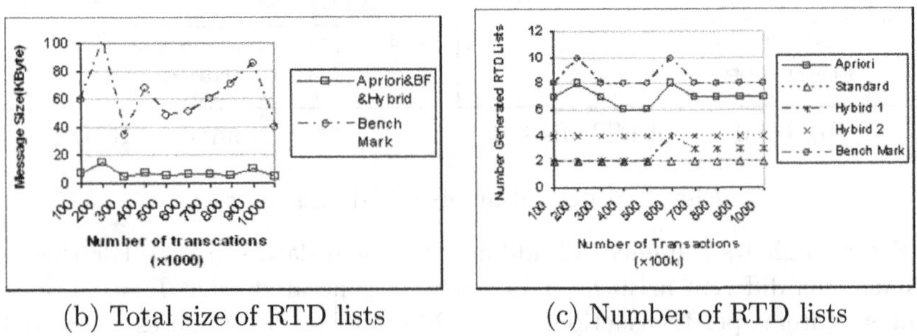

(b) Total size of RTD lists (c) Number of RTD lists

Fig. 4. Effect of increasing number of records

Figure 4 demonstrates the effect of increasing the number of records. The input data for this experiment was generated by producing a sequence of ten pairs of data sets (with $T = 4$, $N = 20$) representing two sources. From graph 4(a) it can be seen that the all algorithms work outperformed the bench mark algorithm because the size of the return to data lists are limited as no unnecessary candidate sets are generated. This is illustrated in graph 4(b). Graph 4(b) also shows that the increase in processing time in all case is due to the increase in the number of records only, the size of the RTD lists remains constant through as does the number of RTD lists generated (graph 4(c)). The few "bumps" at the results are simply from a vagary of the random nature of the test data generation.

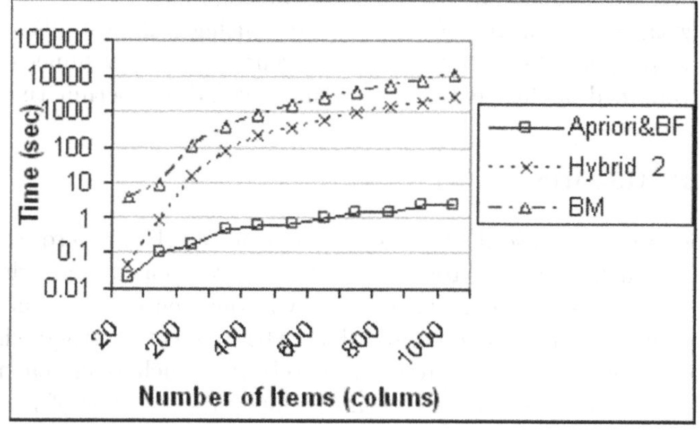

(a) Processing Time

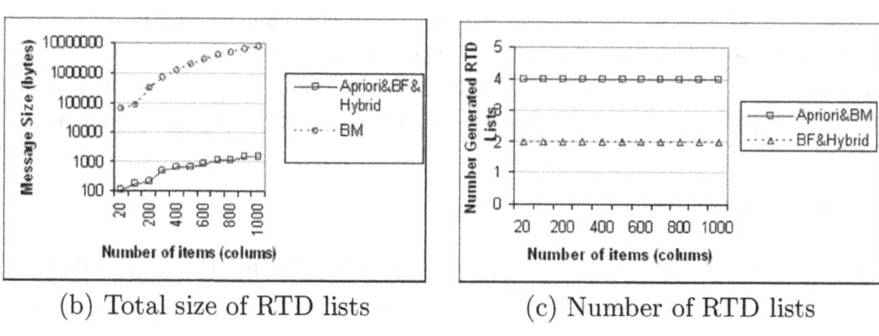

(b) Total size of RTD lists (c) Number of RTD lists

Fig. 5. Effect of increasing number of items (attributes)

Figure 5 shows the effect of increasing the global pool of potential attributes (remember that each data set will include some subset of this global set of attributes). For this experiment another sequence of pairs of data sets (representing two sources) was generated with $T = 4$, $D = 100K$ and N ranging from 100 to 1000. As in the case of experiment 2 the Apriori, Brute Force and Hybrid 1 algorithms work best (for similar reasons) as can be seen from graph 5(a,b). However in this case (compared to the previous experiment), the Hybrid 2 algorithm did not work as good. The reasoning behind the Hybrid 2 algorithm slower perfromance is that all the 1-itemsets tended not to be all supported and becuase there were not eliminated and included in 2-itemsets generation (graph 5(a)). For completeness graph 5(c) indicates the number of RTD lists sent with respect to the different algorithms.

All the Meta ARM algorithms outperformed the bench mark algorithm. The Hybrid 2 algorithm also performed in an unsatisfactory manner largely because of the size of the RTD lists sent. Of the remainder the Apriori approach coped best with a large number of data sources, while the Brute Force and Hybrid 1 approaches coped best with increases data sizes (in terms of column/rows) again largely because of the relatively smaller RTD list sizes.

It should also be noted that the algorithms are all complete and correct, i.e. the end result produced by all the algorithms is identical to that obtained from mining the union of all the raw data sets using some established ARM algorithm. In practice of course the MADM scenario, which assumes that data cannot be combined in this centralised manner, would not permit this.

6 Conclusions

In this paper we have described a novel extension of ARM where we build a meta set of frequent itemsets from a collection of component sets which have been generated in an autonomous manner without centralised control. We have termed this type of conglomerate Meta ARM so as to distinguish it from a number of other related data mining research areas such as incremental and distributed ARM. We have described and compared a number of meta ARM algorithms: (i) Bench Mark, (ii) Apriori, (iii) Brute Force, (iv) Hybrid 1 and (v) Hybrid 2. The results of this analysis indicates that Apriori Meta ARM approach coped best with a large number of data sources, while the Brute Force and Hybrid 1 approaches coped best with increases data sizes (in terms of column/rows). The work represents an important "milestone" towards a multi-agent approach to ARM that the authors are currently investigating.

References

[1] Agrawal, R. and Psaila, G. (1995). Active Data Mining. Proc. 1st Int. Conf. Knowledge Discovery in Data Mining, AAAI, pp 3-8.

[2] Agrawal, R., Mehta, M., Shafer, J., Srikant, R., Arning, A. and Bollinger, T. (1996). The Quest Data Mining System. Proc. 2nd Int. Conf. Knowledge Discovery and Data Mining, (KDD1996).

[3] Aref, W.G., Elfeky, M.G., Elmagarmid, A.K. (2004). Incremental, Online, and Merge Mining of Partial Periodic Patterns in Time-Series Databases. IEEE Transaction in Knowledge and Data Engineering, Vol 16, No 3, pp. 332-342

[4] Coenen, F.P. Leng, P., and Goulbourne, G. (2004). Tree Structures for Mining Association Rules. Journal of Data Mining and Knowledge Discovery, Vol 8, No 1, pp25-51.

[5] Dietterich, T.G. (2002). Ensemble Methods in Machine Learning. In Kittler J. and Roli, F. (Ed.), First International Workshop on Multiple Classifier Systems, LNCS pp1-15.

[6] Goulbourne, G., Coenen, F.P. and Leng, P. (1999). Algorithms for Computing Association Rules Using A Partial-Support Tree. Proc. ES99, Springer, London, pp132-147.

[7] Han,J., Pei, J. and Yiwen, Y. (2000). Mining Frequent Patterns Without Candidate Generation. Proc. ACM-SIGMOD International Conference on Management of Data, ACM Press, pp1-12.

[8] Koh, J.L. and Shieh, S.F. (2004). An efficient approach to maintaining association rules based on adjusting FP-tree structures. Proc. DASFAA 2004, pp417-424.

[9] Leung, C.K-S., Khan, Q.I, and Hoque, T, (2005). CanTree: A tree structure for efficient incremental mining of Frequent Patterns. Proc. ICDM 2005. pp274-281.

[10] Li W., Han, J. and Pei, J. (2001). CMAR: Accurate and Efficient Classification Based on Multiple Class-Association Rules. Proc. ICDM 2001, pp369-376.

[11] Li, X., Deng, Z-H. and Tang S-W. (2006). A Fast Algorithm for Maintenance of Association Rules in Incremental Databases. Proc. ADMA 2006, Springer-Verlag LNAI 4093, pp 56-63.

[12] Liu, B. Hsu, W. and Ma, Y (1998). Integrating Classification and Association Rule Mining. Proc. KDD-98, New York, 27-31 August. AAAI. pp80-86.

[13] Prodromides, A., Chan, P. and Stolfo, S. (2000). Meta-Learning in Distributed Data Mining Systems: Issues and Approaches. In Kargupta, H. and Chan, P. (Eds), Advances in Distributed and Parallel Knowledge Discovery. AAAI Press/The MIT Press, 2000, pp81-114.

[14] Thomas, S., Bodagala, S., Alsabti, K. and Ranka, S. (1997). An efficient algorithm for the incremental updation of association rules. In Proc. 3rd ACM SIGKDD Int. Conf. on Knowledge Discovery and Data Mining. pp263-266.

[15] Veloso, A.A., Meira, W., de Carvalho B. Possas, M.B., Parthasarathy, S. and Zaki, M.J. (2002). Mining Frequent Itemsets in Evolving Databases. Proc. Second SIAM International Conference on Data Mining (SDM'2002).

A Flexible Framework To Experiment With Ontology Learning Techniques

Ricardo Gacitua, Pete Sawyer, Paul Rayson
Computing Department, Lancaster University, UK
(r.gacitua, sawyer, p.rayson)@lancs.ac.uk

August 24, 2007

Abstract

Ontology learning refers to extracting conceptual knowledge from several sources and building an ontology from scratch, enriching, or adapting an existing ontology. It uses methods from a diverse spectrum of fields such as Natural Language Processing, Artificial Intelligence and Machine learning. However, a crucial challenging issue is to quantitatively evaluate the usefulness and accuracy of both techniques and combinations of techniques, when applied to ontology learning. It is an interesting problem because there are no published comparative studies. We are developing a flexible framework for ontology learning from text which provides a cyclical process that involves the successive application of various NLP techniques and learning algorithms for concept extraction and ontology modelling. The framework provides support to evaluate the usefulness and accuracy of different techniques and possible combinations of techniques into specific processes, to deal with the above challenge. We show our framework's efficacy as a workbench for testing and evaluating concept identification. Our initial experiment supports our assumption about the usefulness of our approach.

1 Introduction

The Semantic Web is an evolving extension of the World-Wide Web, in which content is encoded in a formal and explicit way, and can be read and used by software agents [1]. It depends heavily on the proliferation of ontologies. An ontology constitutes a formal conceptualization of a particular domain shared by a group of people. In complex domains to identify, define, and conceptualize a domain manually, can be a costly and error-prone task. This problem can be eased by semi-automatically generating an ontology.

Most domain knowledge about domain entities and their properties and relationships is embodied in text collections -with varying degrees of explicitness and precision. Ontology learning from text has therefore been among the most important strategies for building an ontology. Machine learning and automated language-processing techniques have been used to extract concepts and relationships from structured and unstructured data, such as text and databases. For instance, Cimiano et al.[2] use statistical analysis to extract terms and produce a taxonomy. Similarly, Reinberg et al. [3] use shallow linguistic parsing for concept formation and identify some types of relationships by using prepositions.

Most researchers have realized that the output for the ontology learning process is far from being perfect [4]. One problem is that in most cases it is not obvious to how to use, configure and combine techniques from different fields for a specific domain. Although there are a few published results about combinations of techniques, for instance [5], the problem is far from being solved. For example, some researchers use different text processing techniques such as stopwords filtering [6], lemmatization [7] or stemming [8] to generate a set of pre-processed data as input for the concept identification. However, there are no comparative studies that show the effectiveness of these linguistics pre-processing techniques. An additional problem for ontology learning is that most frameworks use a pre-defined combination of techniques. Thus, they do not include any mechanism for carrying out experiments with combinations or the ability to include new ones. Reinberg and Spyns [9, p. 604] point out that: *"To our knowledge no comparative study has been published yet on the efficiency and effectiveness of the various techniques applied to ontology learning".*

Our motivation is to help to make the ontology learning process controllable. Because of this, it is important to know the contribution of the available techniques and the efficiency of a technique combination. We think that the failure to evaluate the relative efficacy of different NLP techniques is likely to hinder the development of effective learning and knowledge acquisition support for ontology engineering. Due to the above problem, both a flexible framework and an integrated tool-suite to configure and combine techniques applied to ontology learning are proposed. The general architecture of our solution integrates an existing linguistic tool (WMatrix [10]), which provides part–of-speech (POS) and semantic tagging, an ontology workbench for information extraction, and an existing open source ontology editor called Protégé[11] [1]. This work is part of a larger project to build ontologies semi-automatically by processing a collection of domain texts. It involves dealing with four fundamental issues: extracting the relevant domain terminology, discovering concepts, deriving a concept hierarchy, and identifying and labeling ontological relations. Our work involves the innovative adaptation, integration and application of existing NLP and machine learning techniques in order to answer the following research question: *Can shallow analysis of the kind enabled by a range of linguistic and statistical NLP and corpus linguistic techniques identify key domain concepts? Can it do it with sufficient confidence in the correctness and completeness of the result?*

The main contributions of our project are:

- Providing ontology engineers with a coordinated and integrated tool for knowledge objects extraction and ontology modelling.

[1] http://protege.stanford.edu/

- Evaluating the contribution of different NLP and machine learning techniques and their combinations for ontology learning.
- Proposing a guideline to configure and combine techniques applied to ontology learning.

In this paper we present the results achieved so far:

- The definition of a framework which provides support for testing different NLP and machine learning techniques to support the semi-automatic ontology learning process.
- A prototype workbench for knowledge object extraction which provides support for the framework. This workbench integrates a set of NLP and corpus linguistics techniques for experimenting with them.
- Comparative analysis using a set of linguistic and statistical techniques.

The remainder of our paper is organized as follows. We begin by introducing related work. Then, we present the main parts of the framework by describing and characterizing each of the activities that form the process. Next, we present experiments using a set of linguistic and statistical techniques. Finally, we discuss the results of the experiments and present the conclusions.

2 Background

In recent years, a number of frameworks that support ontology learning processes have been reported. They implement several techniques from different fields such as knowledge acquisition, machine learning, information retrieval, natural language processing, artificial intelligence reasoning and database management, as shown by the following work:

- ASIUM [12] learns verb frames and taxonomic knowledge, based on statistical analysis of syntactic parsing of French texts.
- Text2Onto [13] is a complete re-design and re-engineering of KAON-TextToOnto.It combines machine learning approaches with basic linguistic processing such as tokenization or lemmatizing and shallow parsing. It is based on the GATE framework [14].
- Ontolearn [15] learns by interpretation of compounds by compositional interpretational.
- OntoLT [16] learns concepts by term extraction by statistical methods and definition of linguistic patterns as well as mapping to ontological structures.
- DODDLE II [17] learns taxonomic and non-taxonomic relations using coocurrence analysis, exploiting a machine readable dictionary (Wordnet) and domain-specific text.

- WEB->KB [18] combines Bayesian learning and First Order Logic rule learning methods to learn instances and instance extraction rules from World Wide Web documents.

All the above combine linguistic analyses methods with machine learning algorithms to find potentially interesting concepts and relationships between them. However, only Text2Onto has been designed with a central management component that allows various algorithms for ontology learning to be plugged in to. Since it is based on the GATE framework it is flexible with respect to the set of linguistic algorithms used, because GATE applications can be configured by replacing existing algorithms or adding new ones. Similarly, our framework uses a plug-in based structure so it can include new algorithms. However, in contrast, it can include techniques from existing linguistic and ontology tools by using java API's (Application Program Interface) directly where it is possible. In addition, Tex2Onto defines the user interaction as a core aspect whereas our framework provides support to process algorithms in an unsupervised mode as well.

In the next section we describe our Ontology Acquisition Framework before explaining in the subsequent section how our framework supports evaluation.

3 The Ontology Framework: OntoLancs

Our research project principally addresses the issue of quantitatively evaluating the usefulness or accuracy of techniques and combinations of techniques applied to ontology learning. We have integrated a first set of natural language processing, corpus linguistics and machine learning techniques for experimentation. They are: (a) POS grouping, (b) stopwords filtering, (c) frequency filtering, (d) POS filtering, (e) Lemmatization, (f) Stemming, (g) Frequency Profiling, (h) Concordance, (i) lexicon-syntactic pattern (j) coocurrence by distance, and (k) collocation analysis. Our framework facilitates experiments with different NLP and machine learning techniques in order to assess their efficiency and effectiveness, including the performances of various combinations of techniques. All such functions are being built into a prototype workbench to evaluate and refine existing techniques using a range of domain document corpora.

In this paper several existing knowledge acquisition techniques are selected for performing the concept acquisition process in order to evaluate the performance of the selected techniques.

3.1 Phases of the Ontology Framework

This section describes the ontology framework. The workflow of our ontology framework proceeds through the stages of (i) semi-automatic abstraction and classification of domain concepts, (ii) encoding them in the OWL ontology language [19], and (iii) editing them using an enhanced version of an existing editor - Protégé. This set of tools provides ontology engineers with a coordinated and integrated workbench for extracting terms and modelling ontology.

There are four main phases of process, as shown in Figure 1. Below we provide detailed descriptions of these phases.

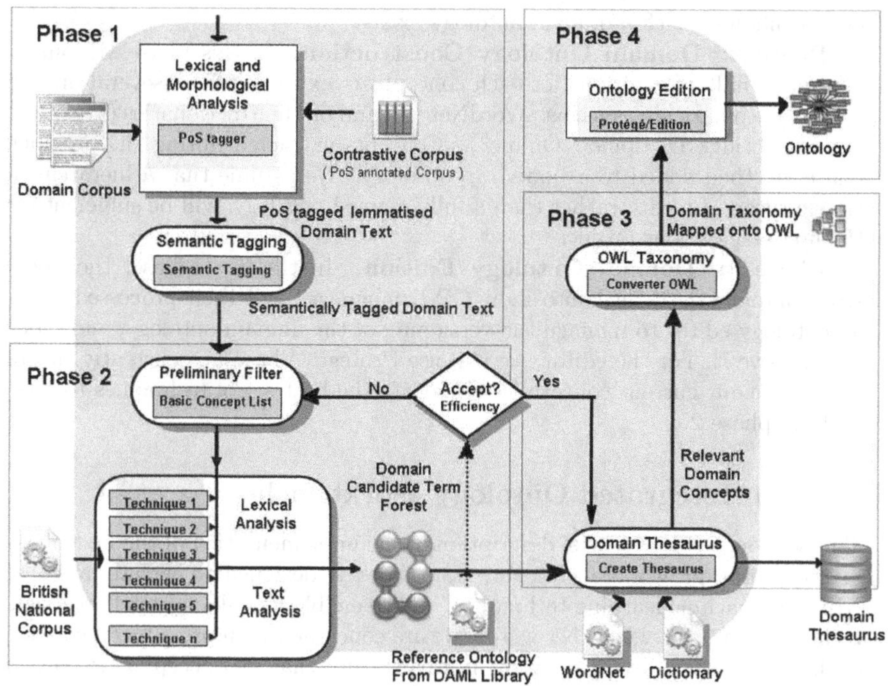

Figure 1: OntoLancs Framework

Phase 1: Part-of-Speech (POS) and Semantic annotation of corpus. Domain texts are tagged morpho-syntactically and semantically using Wmatrix. The system assigns a semantic category to each word employing a comprehensive semantic category scheme called The UCREL Semantic Analysis System (USAS)[20][2]. It is a framework for undertaking the automatic semantic analysis of text. The semantic tagset used by USAS has a hierarchical semantic taxonomy containing 21 major discourse fields and 232 fine-grained semantic fields. In addition, USAS combines several resources including the CLAWS POS tagger [21], which is used to assign POS tags to words.

Phase 2: Extraction of concepts. The domain terminology is extracted from the tagged domain corpus by identifying a list of candidate domain terms (Candidate Domain Term Forest). In this phase the system provides a set of NLP and machine learning techniques which an ontology engineer can combine for identifying candidate concepts. Where a domain ontology exists it can be used as a reference ontology and to calculate the precision and recall of the techniques used when applied to a set of domain documents. The DARPA

[2]http://www.comp.lancs.ac.uk/ucrel/usas/

Agent Markup Language (DAML) Library [3] provides a rich set of domain ontologies thus can be used as the basis for our experiment.

We initially plan to apply the framework and workbench to a set of domain documents for which a domain ontology exists.

Phase 3: Domain Ontology Construction. In this phase, a domain lexicon is built. Definitions for each concept are extracted from several on-line sources automatically, such as: WordNet [22] and on- line dictionaries (Webster[4] and Cambridge Dictionary Online[5]). Concepts extracted during the previous phase are then added to a bootstrap ontology. We assume that a hierarchical classification of terms, rather than a fully defined ontology, will be sufficient for the first stage of our project.

Phase 4: Domain Ontology Edition. In the final phase, the bootstrap ontology is turned into light OWL language, and then processed using an ontology editor to manage the versioning of the domain ontology, and modify/improve it. For the editor, we will use Protégé. Phase 4 is currently future work since our current concern is to identify the best set of techniques to integrate in phase 2.

3.2 An Integrated Ontology Workbench

This section provides a brief description of the implementation of the first phase in the prototype workbench. Our framework is designed to include a set of NLP and machine learning techniques, and to enable its enhancement with new techniques in future. In other words, we are concerned with providing a core set of linguistic utilities within an open architecture that can accept new plug-in techniques as they become available. Initially, the techniques are organized and executed as a pipeline (see figure 2), the output of one technique forms the input for another technique. When a technique is selected a new tab is created in the main panel. An optional linguistic technique (Grouping by POS) is included at the beginning. In future versions of our framework a graphical workflow engine will provide support for the composition of complex ensemble techniques.

The output from any technique is represented using XML format. In the first phase we use Wmatrix to get POS tags, lemmas and semantic tags for each word. The integration between both Wmatrix and the ontology workbench provides a platform for dealing with the scalability problem. Running in a powerful server, Wmatrix is capable of processing large volumes of corpora. Furthermore, the workbench has pre-loaded the BNC corpus - a balanced synchronic text corpus containing 100 million words with morphosyntactic annotation [6]. In order to identify a preliminary set of concepts the workbench provides functions to analyze the corpus and filter the candidates using POS tags and absolute frequency as preliminary filters. Figure 1 shows the GUI of the workbench. **Extraction of Concepts**: At present, a first set of linguistic techniques has

[3]http://www.daml.org/ontologies/
[4]http://www.m-w.com/
[5]http://dictionary.cambridge.org/
[6]http://www.natcorp.ox.ac.uk/

been implemented. It comprises:- *(i) POS grouping and filtering by POS Group.* This provides an option to select a set of POS tag categories and filter the list of terms, *(ii) Stopwords filtering.* This eliminates stop words when the texts are analyzed. However, stop words are not necessarily eliminated when extracting phrases (for example: "players of football"). As a result n-grams may contain stop words, *(iii) Frequency filtering.* This provides an option to filter the list of terms by frequency ranges, *(iv) Lemmatization.* This is a process wherein the inflectional and variant forms of a word are reduced to their lemma: their base form, *(v) Stemming.* This conflates terms in a common stem using Porter's algorithm [23], and *(vi) Frequency Profiling*[24]. This technique can be used to discover key words in a corpora which differentiate the domain corpus from a normative corpus, such as the British National Corpus as a normative corpus.

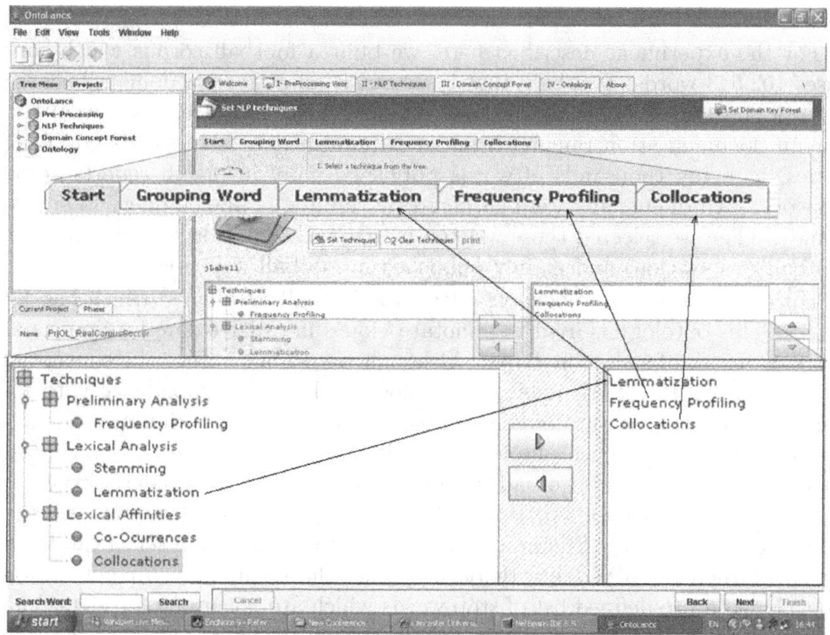

Figure 2: OntoLancs Workbench - Combining NLP techniques

4 Experiments

In this section we describe the mechanism our framework provides for evaluating the efficacy of different NLP techniques for the crucial second phase of the ontology learning process described in section 3.1.

The experiments were designed to extract a set of candidate concepts from a domain corpus using a combination of NLP and machine learning techniques and to check the correspondence between the candidate concepts and the classes of a DAML reference ontology. In order to assess the efficiency of the techniques we used the precision and recall values as a comparative measure. Note that although we do not believe that automatic ontology creation is possible or desirable, our experiments to select appropriate techniques are conducted in an unsupervised manner. In addition, it is important to remember here that we are not trying to validate the reference ontology itself. Our main aim is to validate NLP and machine learning techniques applied to concept identification. Clearly, the extent to which the chosen reference ontology reflects the consensus about the domain is a threat to validity. To try to minimise this, we selected reference ontologies from the DAML Library. Ontologies are not guaranteed to be validated, but their existence in the public domain provides an initial, weak, first level of confidence in their validity. A second threat to validity results from the corpus of domain documents. This can be mitigated by selecting domains for which much public-domain document is readily available.

For the experiment described here, we built a football corpus which comprises 102,543 words. Football, that is soccer, is an attractive domain because, at least one DAML football ontology already exists and there is a wealth of domain documentation ranging from rules published by the sport's governing bodies, to many thousands of words published daily in match reports across the world. All documents were gathered by running a Google query "Football Game". Then we selected those written by FIFA (Federation Internationale de Football Association) and mainly published in football web sites.

For our reference ontology, we selected a football ontology [7] which has 199 classes. This ontology is used to annotate videos in order to produce personalized summaries of soccer matches. Although we cannot ensure the conceptual correctness of the DAML reference ontology and its correspondence with the application context of our domain corpus, we assumed as a preliminary premise that the DAML reference ontology is valid in order to evaluate our concept extraction process. One we had assembled our football document corpus, we applied the following combination of linguistic techniques: Group & Filter by POS - Lemmatization / Stemming - Frequency Profiling - on a set of candidate terms returned by WMatrix. Before applying the techniques in combination, we excluded a pre-defined list of stop words which are not useful for identifying concepts. Note that these are presented here simply to illustrate how our evaluation mechanism works. We could have used any of the framework's in-built NLP techniques.

First, we grouped the initial list of candidate terms using different categories. These categories represent the results of applying different NLP techniques as described below:- (a) **Filter by Group by POS**, which provides an option for selecting a set of POS tag categories and filtering the list of terms. In this case, we used 3 sorts of word grouping: (i) *Using specific POS Tags.* For instance: **Kick _VV0** (base form or lexical verb) is considered different from **Kick_VVI** (infinitive), (ii) *Using a generic POS Tag.* In this case, we used a generic POS Tag. For instance **Kick_VV0** and **Kick_VVI** are turned into

[7] http://www.lgi2p.ema.fr/ ~ranwezs/ontologies/soccerV2.0.daml

Kick_"verb", (iii) *POS-independent*. In this case, we used only a word with a generic category: "any". For instance, **Kick_noun** and **Kick_verb** are turned into **Kick_any**. Second, we applied a morphological method - lemmatization or stemming - on the set of candidate terms in order to use a canonical form for each word. Third, we applied Frequency Profiling techniques and filtered the set of terms by using the log-likelihood measure (LL) which provides a measure of statistical significance. We used two filters: 95th percentile (5% level; $p<0.05$; critical value = 3.84. A LL greater 3.84 indicates that there is a 95% confidence in the result's reliability) and, 99.9th percentile(1% level; $p<0.01$; critical value = 6.63. A LL greater 6.63 indicates that there is a 99% confidence in the result's reliability). Finally, we checked the lexical correspondence between the candidate terms and the classes in the DAML reference ontology.

In order to evaluate quantitatively the results of this process we used the precision and recall values. Applied in this context, the metrics are defined as:

Precision: measures the number of classes of the reference ontology which were matched by a concept returned by applying the selected NLP techniques to the document corpus divided by the number of the candidate terms.

Recall: measures the number of classes of the reference ontology which were matched by a concept returned by applying the selected NLP techniques to the document corpus divided by the number of ontology classes.

We defined a set of NLP and machine learning techniques combinations, grouped by the use of a morphological technique, and then obtained precision and recall values for each combination (see figure 3).

	Filter Stop Words	Morphosyntactic		Grouping by POS			Frequency Profiling	
Code		Stemming	Lemmatization	Specific	Generic	Independent	95th	99th
A1	√			√			√	
A2	√			√				√
A3	√				√		√	
A4	√				√			√
A5	√					√	√	
A6	√					√		√
S1	√	√		√			√	
S2	√	√		√				√
S3	√	√			√		√	
S4	√	√			√			√
S5	√	√				√	√	
S6	√	√				√		√
L1	√		√	√			√	
L2	√		√	√				√
L3	√		√		√		√	
L4	√		√		√			√
L5	√		√			√	√	
L6	√		√			√		√

Figure 3: Technique combination

The results of the first evaluation, after applying grouping by POS, stemming or lemmatization and frequency profiling techniques, showed low values of recall and precision. This is a consequence of the fact that we used an unsupervised method and applied a limited number of techniques for identifying domain concepts.

In the above experiments, although we applied one NLP and one machine

Table 1: Performance using different techniques - Morphosyntactic technique independent

Combination	Recall	Precision
A1	45.45	2.36
A2	44.71	2.83
A3	44.98	2.39
A4	43.74	2.88
A5	44.02	2.42
A6	42.79	2.97

Table 2: Performance using different techniques - Stemming

Combination	Recall	Precision
S1	33.33	2.25
S2	32.52	2.65
S3	33.33	2.25
S4	32.52	2.65
S5	33.33	2.34
S6	32.25	2.77

learning technique only on the set of candidate terms, we collected a reasonable number of matched classes with the ontology - All experiments had a recall above 42 % (see Table 1). Applying the stemming technique before applying the frequency profiling technique on the set of candidates terms, produced the lowest values of recall. All were above 32% and below 34% (see Table 2). In the case of precision, the results were lower than the independent morphosyntactic technique. In contrast, applying lemmatization before applying the frequency profiling technique produced the best results. In particular, the set of candidate terms filtered by using a 95% confidence produced values of recall above 47% (see Table 3). In the case of precision, the results were higher than other cases (3.43% the highest value).

From the experiments, we can conclude that the lemmatization technique produces better results of precision and recall than the stemming technique for the domain concept acquisition process. Stemming just finds any base form, which does not even need to be a word in the language. Because of this, most of the stems generated by Porter's algorithm could not to be recognized as English words. For instance, in the soccer corpus the term: **referee** was reduced as **refere**. In contrast, lemmatization finds the actual *root* of a word, which comes from a morphological analysis. Our results are consistent with other studies. For instance, Alkula [25] suggested that lemmatization may be a better approach than stemming.

The precision and recall values obtained in the experiment are affected by the following factors:

Table 3: Performance using different techniques - Lemmatization

Combination	Recall	Precision
L1	47.62	2.98
L2	45.45	3.43
L3	47.62	2.98
L4	45.45	3.43
L5	47.14	3.16
L6	45.45	3.43

(1) **We used an unsupervised method**. The preliminary list of concepts tagged by POS has several words that carry general concepts, thus they should not be considered as domain concepts. For instance: *"following"*, *"greater"*, etc. These kinds of terms can be filtered by a human ontology engineer, and indeed, our overall aim is to develop our framework so that it provides effective support rather than full automation. Nevertheless, for the evaluation of the efficacy of individual or combinations of NLP techniques, objective results can only be acquired by applying them in an unsupervised way.

(2) **The reference domain ontology contains artificial classes which cannot be derived from a domain corpus automatically**. Most ontologies contain artificial classes defined for grouping classes generally. For instance, the soccer ontology which was used as a reference to appraise the knowledge extraction process contains classes such as: "Attribute", "Boolean-type", "False-value", etc. Such terms would not be expected to figure prominently in the domain corpus since they are an artifact of the ontology's taxonomic structuring mechanism rather than of the football domain.

In spite of this (2), the results provided a reasonable indication of the relative efficacy of the selected NLP and machine learning techniques, and offer a useful insights into, for example, the usefulness of filtering on different part of speech. In addition, we can confirm that applying lemmatization on a set of candidate terms produces better results than applying stemming, for ontology learning. Thus, values of recall and precision will become higher when new techniques to identify multiword are included, and also human supervision to filter general concepts is provided.

5 Conclusions and Further Work

In this paper we have described an ongoing project which proposes a flexible framework for the ontology learning process.This framework is designed as a cyclical process to experiment with different techniques and combinations of techniques. It provides support to determine what techniques or their combinations provide optimal performances for the ontology learning process. An ontology engineer can decide techniques or combinations which will be used to extract concepts and turn them into an ontology. In future versions of our framework a graphical workflow engine will provide support for the composition of complex ensemble techniques.

Our research project addresses an important challenge for ontology research, i.e., how to validate innovative natural language processing approaches for the purpose of capturing knowledge objects, which are contained in domain-specific texts. In a first stage, it involves dealing with three fundamental issues: extracting the relevant domain terminology, discovering concepts, and deriving a concept hierarchy. Additional future work includes using semantic filters. Our initial experiment supports our assumption about the usefulness of our approach: evaluating the effectiveness of the techniques for ontology learning acquisition. The experiments suggest that the lemmatization technique may be a better approach than stemming.

The preliminary results reinforce our belief that the availability of linguistic tools integrated into a practical ontology engineering process can potentially aid the rapid development of domain ontologies. Our ontology engineering environment, OntoLancs is unique in not only providing a framework for integrating linguistic techniques, but also the possibility of an experimental platform for identifying the most effective techniques or combinations.

6 Acknowledgments

Our thanks to Rosemary Peelo whose grammatical/proofreading corrections helped us to improve our paper.

References

[1] T. Berner-Lee, J. Hendler, O. Lassila, The Semantic Web - A new form of Web content that is meaningful to computers will unleash a revolution of new possibilities., Scientific American 284 (5) (2001) 34–+.

[2] P. Cimiano, L. Schmidt-Thieme, A. Pivk, S. Staab, Learning taxonomic relations from heterogeneous evidence, in: P. Buitelaar, P. Cimiano, B. Magnini (Eds.), Ontology Learning from Text: Methods, Applications and Evaluation, No. 123 in Frontiers in Artificial Intelligence and Appl, IOS Press, 2005, pp. 59–73.

[3] M.-L. Reinberger, P. Spyns, Discovering knowledge in texts for the learning of dogma-inspired ontologies., in: Proceedings of the workshop Ontology Learning and Population, ECAI04, Valencia, Spain, 2004, pp. 19–24.

[4] A. Maedche, S.Staab, Mining ontologies from text, in: EKAW-2000 - 12th International Conference on Knowledge Engineering and Knowledge Management, October 2-6, 2000, Juan-les-Pins, France. Springer, R.Dieng & O Corby, October 2000., 2000.

[5] M. Sabou, C. Wroe, C. A. Goble, H. Stuckenschmidt, Learning domain ontologies for semantic web service descriptions., J. Web Sem. 3 (4) (2005) 340–365.

[6] S. Bloehdorn, P. Cimiano, A. Hotho, Learning ontologies to improve text clustering and classification, in: M. Spiliopoulou, R. Kruse, A. Nürnberger, C. Borgelt, W. Gaul (Eds.), From Data and Information Analysis to Knowledge Engineering: Proceedings of the 29th Annual Conference of the German Classification Society (GfKl 2005), Magdeburg, Germany, March 9-11, 2005, Vol. 30 of Studies in Classification, Data Analysis, and, Springer, 2006.

[7] P. Buitelaar, S. Ramaka, Unsupervised ontology-based semantic tagging for knowledge markup, in: S. B. Wray Buntine, Andreas Hotho (Ed.), Proc. Of the Workshop on Learning in Web Search at the International Conference on Machine Learning, 2005.

[8] J.-U. Kietz, A. Maedche, R. Volz, A method for semi-automatic ontology acquisition from a corporate intranet, in: Proc. of Workshop Ontologies and Text, co-located with the 12th International Workshop on Knowledge Engineering and Knowledge Management (EKAW'2000), Juan-Les-Pins, France, 2000.

[9] M.-L. Reinberger, P. Spyns, J. Pretorius, W. Daelemans, Automatic initiation of an ontology, in: Proceedings of the Conference on Ontologies, Databases and Applications of Semantics (ODBASE), Lecture Notes in Computer Science, Springer Verlag, 2004, pp. 600–617.

[10] P. Rayson, Matrix: A statistical method and software tool for linguistic analysis through corpus comparison, Ph.D. thesis, Computing Department, Lancaster University, UK (2003).

[11] N. Noy, R. W. Fergerson, M. A. Musen, The knowledge model of protege-2000: Combining interoperability and flexibility, in: 12th International Conference on Knowledge Engineering and Knowledge Management (EKAW'2000), Juan-les-Pins, France, 2000., 2000.

[12] D. Faure, T. Poibeau, First experiences of using semantic knowledge learned by asium for information extraction task using intex., in: ECAI Workshop on Ontology Learning, 2000.

[13] P. Cimiano, J. Völker, Text2onto - a framework for ontology learning and data-driven change discovery, in: A. Montoyo, R. Munoz, E. Metais (Eds.), Proceedings of the 10th International Conference on Applications of Natural Language to Information Systems (NLDB), Vol. 3513 of Lecture Notes in Computer Science, Springer, Alicante, Spain, 2005, pp. 227–238.

[14] H. Cunningham, D. Maynard, K. Bontcheva, V. Tablan, GATE: A framework and graphical development environment for robust NLP tools and

applications, in: Proceedings of the 40th Anniversary Meeting of the Association for Computational Linguistics, 2002.

[15] P. Velardi, R. Navigl, A. Cucchiarelli, F. Neri, Ontology Learning from Text: Methods, Evaluation and Applications, ios press Edition, Vol. 123, Frontiers in Artificial Intelligence and Applications, 2005, Ch. Evaluation of OntoLearn, a Methodology for Automatic Learning of Domain Ontologies.

[16] P. Buitelaar, M. Sintek, Ontolt version 1.0: Middleware for ontology extraction from text, in: Proc. of the Demo Session at the International Semantic Web Conference, 2004.

[17] T. Yamaguchi, Acquiring conceptual relationships from domain-specific texts., in: A. Maedche, S. Staab, C. Nedellec, E. H. Hovy (Eds.), Workshop on Ontology Learning, Vol. 38 of CEUR Workshop Proceedings, CEUR-WS.org, 2001.

[18] M. Craven, D. DiPasquo, D. Freitag, A. K. McCallum, T. M. Mitchell, K. Nigam, S. Slattery, Learning to construct knowledge bases from the World Wide Web, Artificial Intelligence 118 (1/2) (2000) 69–113.
URL `citeseer.ist.psu.edu/craven00learning.html`

[19] M. Dean, G. S. and, OWL Web Ontology Language Reference, W3C Recommendation 10.

[20] P. Rayson, D. Archer, S. L. Piao, T. McEnery, The ucrel semantic analysis system., in: In proceedings of the workshop on Beyond Named Entity Recognition Semantic labelling for NLP tasks in association with 4th International Conference on Language Resources and Evaluation (LREC 2004), 25th May 2004, Lisbon, Portugal, pp. 7-12., 2004.

[21] R. Garside, The CLAWS Word-tagging System. The Computational Analysis of English: A Corpus-based Approach, Longman.London, 1987.

[22] G. A. Miller, Wordnet: A lexical database for english., in: HLT, Morgan Kaufmann, 1994.

[23] M. F. Porter, An algorithm for suffix stripping, Program 14 (3) (1980) 130–137.

[24] P. Rayson, R. Garside, Comparing corpora using frequency profiling, in: Proceedings of the workshop on Comparing corpora, Association for Computational Linguistics, Morristown, NJ, USA, 2000, pp. 1–6.

[25] R. Alkula, From plain character strings to meaningful words: Producing better full text databases for inflectional and compounding languages with morphological analysis software, Inf. Retr. 4 (3-4) (2001) 195–208.

Evolving a Dynamic Predictive Coding Mechanism for Novelty Detection

Simon J. Haggett
Computing Laboratory, University of Kent
Canterbury, UK
simon.haggett@acm.org

Dominique F. Chu
Computing Laboratory, University of Kent
Canterbury, UK
D.F.Chu@kent.ac.uk

Ian W. Marshall
Lancaster Environment Centre, Lancaster University
Lancaster, UK
I.W.Marshall@lancaster.ac.uk

Abstract

Novelty detection is a machine learning technique which identifies new or unknown information in data sets. We present our current work on the construction of a new novelty detector based on a dynamical version of predictive coding. We compare three evolutionary algorithms, a simple genetic algorithm, NEAT and FS-NEAT, for the task of optimising the structure of an illustrative dynamic predictive coding neural network to improve its performance over stimuli from a number of artificially generated visual environments. We find that NEAT performs more reliably than the other two algorithms in this task and evolves the network with the highest fitness. However, both NEAT and FS-NEAT fail to evolve a network with a significantly higher fitness than the best network evolved by the simple genetic algorithm. The best network evolved demonstrates a more consistent performance over a broader range of inputs than the original network. We also examine the robustness of this network to noise and find that it handles low levels reasonably well, but is outperformed by the illustrative network when the level of noise is increased.

1 Introduction

A novelty detector is a machine learning system that identifies new or unknown data that it was not aware of during its training phase [1]. Novelty detection is important in practical applications where large data sets are being processed. In a sensor array which continuously monitors an unpredictable environment, a constant stream of data is produced by each sensor. A large proportion of this data will be redundant since it describes information already known. The crucial information is that which indicates that change has occurred, since this may require some action to take place. Novelty detection can be used in this case to highlight such data.

Because novelty detection is an extremely challenging task, there are currently a number of different approaches [2]. A comprehensive survey of approaches using neural networks is given by [1]. Marsland *et al.* [3] propose a novelty detector which employs a Habituating Self Organising Map (HSOM). An input layer is connected to a clustering layer which represents the feature space. Each input vector is classified by associating it with a neuron in the clustering layer as follows. The neuron in the clustering layer with the smallest distance to the input vector (where distance is defined by the sum of the squared difference between each element of the input vector and the value held in the given node in the clustering layer) fires for that input vector. Each node in the clustering layer is connected to the output neuron via a habituable synapse, which not only weakens (habituates) when the corresponding node in the clustering layer fires frequently, but also strengthens (dishabituates) when the node fires infrequently. The value of the output neuron for a given input vector indicates the novelty of that vector. Habituation enables the network to learn on-line and cope with changing environments. However, since the size of the network remains fixed one limitation is that on-line learning can cause saturation in the network. This is when all synapses habituate, resulting in novel input vectors being misclassified as normal [4]. Marsland *et al.* [4, 5] extend this work by proposing the 'Grow When Required' (GWR) network as an improvement to the HSOM. The GWR network is a new type of clustering map that allows new nodes to be created as required, thus overcoming the problem of saturation seen in the HSOM.

Predictive coding is a technique used in areas such as image and speech compression [6]. In image compression, this technique attempts to predict the value of a given pixel based on the values of neighbouring pixels. A difference signal, holding the difference between the predicted and observed values of the given pixel, is then used to represent that pixel. When the predicted value is close to the observed value, this difference signal will have a smaller magnitude, which means that it can be represented more compactly. In turn, this allows the image as a whole to be represented in a compressed form. If we assume that novel values are likely to be unpredictable, then the difference signal can be used to determine the novelty of the observed value.

Hosoya *et al.* [7] propose a possible neural network model of circuits in the retina. This model performs a dynamical version of predictive coding in that it adapts on-line to the changing visual scene. As animals move through their environment, they tend to encounter visual scenes which differ strongly in their statistical properties. For example, the scene in a woodland environment is likely to have strong correlation between vertically separated points and weak correlation between horizontally separated points, whilst the scene in a sandy environment, such as a desert or beach, is likely to have correlation between points only in small localities. By adapting to the changing image statistics, a predictive coder is able to maintain its efficiency as the visual scene changes.

We wish to develop a new novelty detector which is based on dynamic predictive coding. This form of predictive coding is a promising model to base a novelty detector on because of its capability to learn on-line the current norm conditions and adapt to changes in these conditions over time. Unlike Marslands GWR [4, 5], which is also capable of on-line learning, this method of novelty detection will learn the statistical relationships between values and report novelty when those relationships change. Inputs are classified depending on the statistical relationships between their elements, as opposed to Euclidean distance to a feature prototype. Therefore, inputs which are represented by multiple classes in GWR may be represented by a single class in our proposed approach.

In this paper, we present our current work on the construction of a new novelty detector based on dynamic predictive coding. We compare three evolutionary algorithms for the task of evolving a neural network structure to give an optimal performance over stimuli from a number of artificially generated visual environments. We also examine the robustness of the evolved structure when noise is introduced to its inputs. The remainder of this paper is organised as follows. In section 2, we describe a neural network capable of dynamic predictive coding and identify a limitation of this network. Section 3 describes three evolutionary algorithms used to search for a neural network structure which gives an optimal performance according to two basic criteria. In section 4, we present experimental results from using these algorithms and examine the robustness of the best evolved network to random noise. Section 5 discusses these results and the comparative performance of the evolutionary algorithms. Finally, section 6 concludes this paper and briefly outlines how we plan to continue this work.

2 Novelty Detection using Dynamic Predictive Coding

The neural network model proposed by Hosoya *et al.* [7] is a feedforward network which represents a neural circuit found in the retina [8]. In this model, input neurons connect to output neurons via fixed-weight synapses and/or modifiable synapses. The fixed-weight synapse from input x_j to output y_i is represented as b_{ij}, and the modifiable synapse between these neurons is represented as a_{ij}. The output y_i of the i-th output neuron is given by equation 1.

$$y_i = \sum_j (b_{ij} + a_{ij}) x_j \quad (1)$$

At each output neuron, the network attempts to predict the sum of the inputs received through fixed synapses and subtract this prediction from the neurons input. The modifiable synapse weights are modulated according to the anti-hebbian learning rule shown in equation 2 to form this prediction.

$$\frac{da_{ij}}{dt} = \frac{-a_{ij} - \beta \langle y_i x_j \rangle}{\tau} \quad \tau, \beta > 0 \quad (2)$$

$\langle y_i x_j \rangle$ is the time-averaged correlation between input x_j and output y_i and is sampled over m previous time steps up to the current time step t:

$$\langle y_i x_j \rangle = \frac{1}{m} \sum_{k=t-m+1}^{t} y_i(k)\, x_j(k) \tag{3}$$

where $y_i(k)$ and $x_j(k)$ are the values of y_i and x_j respectively at time k. This anti-hebbian learning rule causes the modifiable synapses to weaken when the activity at the presynaptic and postsynaptic neurons is correlated and strengthen when the activity is anti-correlated. The parameters β and τ control the networks sensitivity to the correlation signal and the rates of learning and decay respectively.

To illustrate this model, the following single layer example neural network was given by [7]. Consider a 4x4 pixel greyscale image where each pixel provides a single input to the network. The network has a single output neuron y which aims to predict the sum of the centre 2x2 pixels given the correlational relationships between those pixels and the neighbouring 'surround' pixels. All pixels are connected to the output neuron by modifiable synapses. In addition, the 2x2 centre pixels are also connected to the output neuron via fixed-weight synapses with weight 1. In the networks initial state, each modifiable synapse has a weight of 0, meaning that the output of the network is initially the sum of the centre 2x2 pixels. Over time, the modifiable synapses have their weights updated by the anti-hebbian learning rule (equation 2) such that a prediction of the sum of the 2x2 pixels is formed and subtracted from the observed sum.

Hosoya *et al.* [7] demonstrate the operation of this illustrative neural network over a number of artificially generated visual 'environments'. Four of these environments were flickering greyscale images with perfect correlational relationships and one of these environments, titled "random", was a flickering environment with no correlation between pixels. The four environments with perfect correlational relationships were a flickering uniform field, a flickering checkerboard pattern and flickering vertical and horizontal bars. Each pixel was updated every u timesteps with an independently drawn value from a standard normal distribution. Finally, a "none" environment was used which was defined as a steady grey screen. Figure 1 illustrates the environments. To analyse the performance of the network, Hosoya *et al.* [7] observed how the sensitivity of the output neuron to the uniform, checkerboard, vertical bar and horizontal bar environments varied during the simulation. Sensitivity of the output neuron y to a given environment E is defined by [7] as the square root of the averaged variance of y, taken over stimuli from environment E (equation 5 in section 3).

We use this network as the basis for a novelty detector utilising dynamic predictive coding. To improve our understanding and identify any limitations, we constructed a simulation in which we observed how this network responded when shown a series of visual environments. In this simulation, each environment was shown for 2500 time steps. After every time step, the weights of the network were frozen and the variance of the output neuron $var(y)$ sampled for stimuli from each environment (except "none" and "random"). After every 100

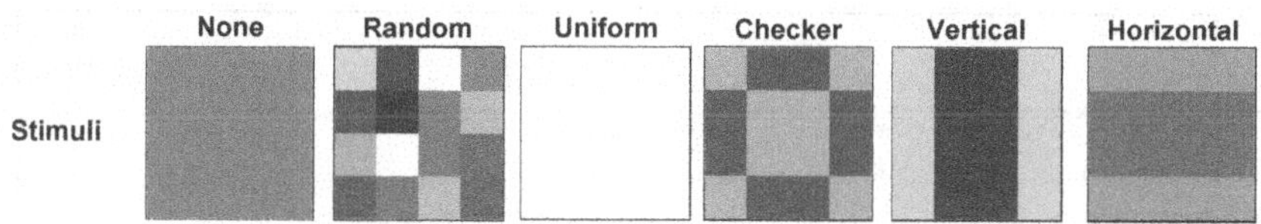

Figure 1: The artificial environments specified in [7].

time steps, these variances were averaged and the sensitivity to each environment calculated. We used a value of 0.4 for β and a value of 500 for τ, both determined experimentally. The parameter u was set to 1 to give maximum flicker.

We also introduced two new diagonal environments (shown in figure 2) and observed how the network responded to these. As with the existing environments, each diagonal environment was shown to the network for 2500 time steps.

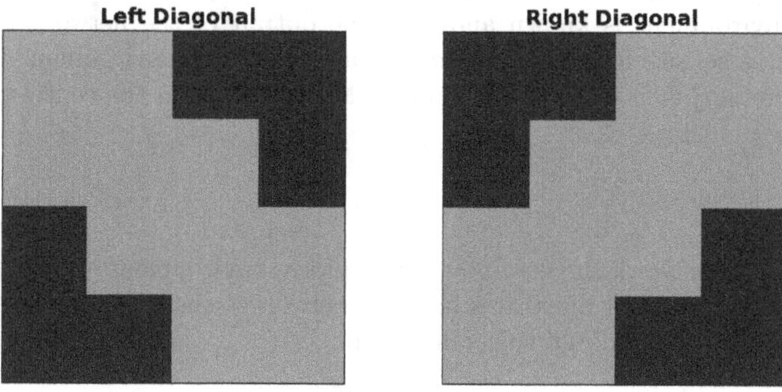

Figure 2: The new diagonal environments.

To verify our implementation of this example network, we first tested it with the original environments used in [7]. Figure 3 illustrates how the networks sensitivity to the uniform environment varies during the time course of the simulation. For this network, sensitivity is scaled such that a sensitivity of 1 is defined by the sensitivity of the network to environments in its unadapted state. The network was shown each environment in the order implied by the horizontal axis.

When the network was shown the "random" environment, its sensitivity to the uniform environment fell slightly. This behaviour was observed for all environments monitored and is also demonstrated in [7]. When the network adapted to the uniform environment, its sensitivity to that environment fell considerably. In this state, the network considers the uniform environment to be known and therefore not novel. When the network was subsequently shown the checkerboard environment, its sensitivity to the uniform environment

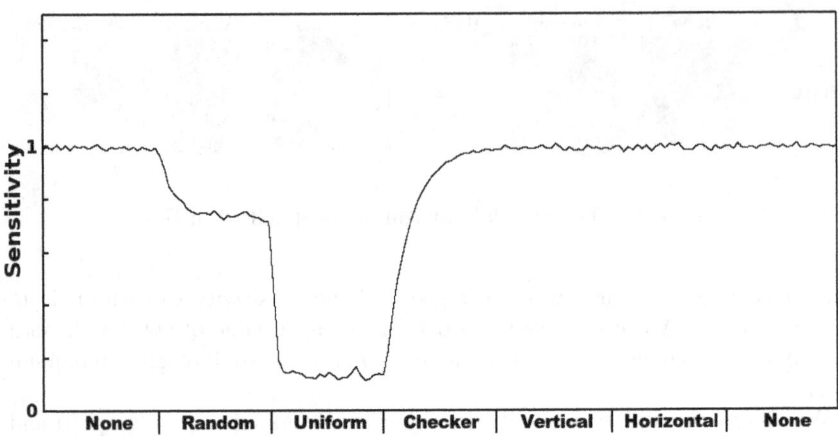

Figure 3: The sensitivity graph produced by the illustrative neural network given in [7]. This shows how sensitivity to the uniform environment varies during the time course of the simulation. A sensitivity close to zero indicates that the environment is known and that the output of the network is small. Conversely, a sensitivity close to one indicates that the environment is novel and that the output is close to the sum of the intensities in the centre patch.

recovered. The network forgets about the uniform environment and classifies it as novel again. Figure 4 illustrates how the networks sensitivity to the original environments varied through this simulation.

We also performed a simulation using the diagonal environments. Figure 5 shows how the networks sensitivity varied through the simulation. As the network adapts to the uniform, checkerboard, vertical bar and horizontal bar environments, its sensitivity to the diagonal environments falls to approximately 0.75. As the network adapts to one diagonal environment, the sensitivity to the other diagonal environment rises above 1. Here, the output of the network is greater than the sum of the centre 2x2 patch. Since the goal of predictive coding is to compress the observed value, this behaviour is undesired.

To explain this result, we considered the original network when adapted to a non-diagonal environment. In this case, sensitivity to diagonal environments is reduced because similarities between the diagonal and non-diagonal environments are used to form a partial prediction (this can also be seen vice-versa as the network adapts to the diagonal environments). If the original network is adapted to a diagonal environment, sensitivity to the alternative diagonal environment rises above 1. This was caused by a limitation of the network in handling symmetry between environments.

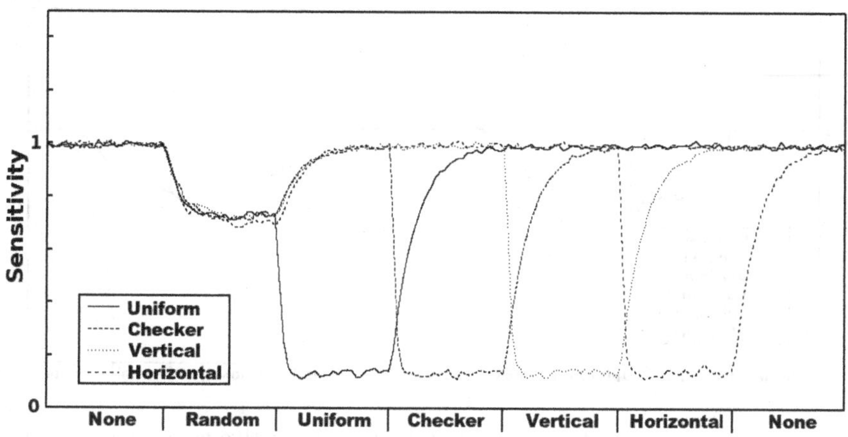

Figure 4: The sensitivity graph produced by the illustrative neural network given in [7]. This shows how sensitivity to the uniform, checkerboard, vertical bar and horizontal bar environments vary as the network adapts to each environment during the time course of the simulation.

3 Optimising Structure using Evolution

To optimise the neural network, we searched for a structure which gave the best performance according to two basic criteria of novelty detection. We wished to find a solution which (a) maximises the difference in sensitivity between known and novel environments and (b) remains at a similar level of sensitivity for all novel environments. We first attempted to construct a new structure by hand but this proved to be time consuming and none of the networks developed gave any significant improvement in performance. We then considered a genetic algorithm (GA) based approach, since such an approach is good in cases when the search space is not well understood [9]. We compared three GA's for this task; a simple textbook-based genetic algorithm, and two neuroevolution methods which are specifically designed to evolve neural network structure.

The simple genetic algorithm is based on that described by [10]. Each gene is represented by the quadruple *(inID, outID, weight, type)*, which is in turn encoded as a 25 character bitstring. A genome holds a collection of these genes and thus has a connection-centric view of the neural network. Point mutation and single-point crossover are both used, as well as a 'gene-replicate' and 'gene-remove' mutation (to allow the addition or removal of new structural elements).

The first neuroevolution method used was NeuroEvolution of Augmenting Topologies (NEAT), proposed by Stanley [11]. NEAT is specifically designed to evolve neural networks. New structure is introduced gradually so as minimise the dimensionality of the search space. Speciation is used to encourage diversity and help prevent bloat from occurring (solutions containing unnecessary elements). In crossover, NEAT uses historical markings to discover which

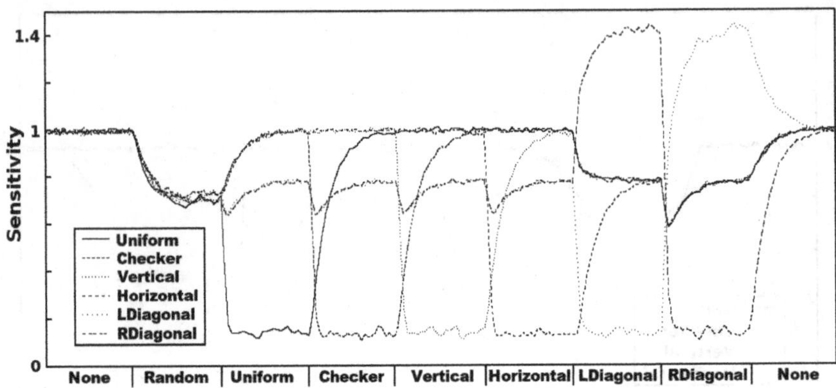

Figure 5: The sensitivity graph produced by the illustrative neural network. In addition to the environments seen in figure 4, this graph shows the networks response to the left diagonal and right diagonal environments.

genes in two genomes match and which do not, solving the competing conventions problem (whereby two identical solutions have different genetic representations). The competing conventions problem is important to solve because crossover of similar solutions with different representations is likely to produce damaged offspring [11].

We also used a variation of NEAT proposed by Whiteson *et al.* [12], Feature Selective NEAT (FS-NEAT). Unlike NEAT, which usually starts with a population of fully connected networks, FS-NEAT starts with a population where each network has only a single connection between a randomly chosen input and output. This allows FS-NEAT to begin its search in a space of an even lower dimensionality. FS-NEAT then proceeds in the same manner as NEAT. Experiments conducted in an autonomous car racing simulation showed that FS-NEAT was capable of outperforming NEAT in evolving solutions that both scored higher and were also less complex in terms of their structure [12].

All three approaches use the same measure of fitness, based on our performance criteria stated earlier. We define the following fitness function over N environments (not including "none" or "random"):

$$F(c) = \sum_{i=1}^{N} \frac{1}{N-1} \left(\sum_{j=1, \quad j \neq i}^{N} S_c(i,j) \right) - S_c(i,i) \tag{4}$$

The sensitivity of a network to a given environment E is defined as the square root of the variance of the output neuron y averaged over stimuli from environment E [7]:

$$S_E = \sqrt{\langle var(y) \rangle_E} \tag{5}$$

We then define $S_c(i,j)$ as the sensitivity of candidate network c to environment j when adapted to environment i. Sensitivity is scaled such that a sensitivity of 1 is defined as the sensitivity of the original neural network (described in section 2) to each environment when in an unadapted state. To encourage sensitivity to novel environments to remain at a similar level, candidates which allow sensitivity to any environment to rise above 1 should be punished. However, such candidates should not simply be awarded a fitness of zero since they may yet evolve into good solutions. Also, sensitivity values greater than 1 that have a small distance from 1 should be awarded a higher fitness than those with a large distance. From experimentation, we found that the following non-linear adjustment gave the best results:

$$S_c(i,j) = \begin{cases} 2.0 - S_c(i,j)^4 & S_c(i,j) > 1.0 \\ S_c(i,j) & \text{otherwise} \end{cases} \tag{6}$$

After this adjustment, $S_c(i,j)$ may be negative. However, the lowest fitness the network can achieve when adapted to a single environment i is constrained to 0. Thus, a network performing badly when adapted to one environment but not when adapted to another is punished for its poor performance only.

4 Results

Table 1 shows how the sensitivity of the best network evolved by the simple GA varies when it is unadapted (shown the "none" environment) and when it is adapted to the environments with perfect correlational relationships. Tables 2 and 3 show these results for the best networks evolved by NEAT and FS-NEAT respectively. The highest scoring network overall was that found by NEAT. Figure 6 shows the sensitivity graph produced by this best overall network.

In each experiment, 10 runs of the GA were executed, with each run performing 500 generations of evolution and returning the best network evolved during that time. The best network from the 10 runs was taken to be the best network for that method. Table 4 shows the average, best and worst performances of each GA method and table 5 shows the average hidden node and synapse count of solutions produced by each method.

Comparing the GA approaches, we can see that the fitness of their best networks are all at a similar level. The average fitness after 500 generations was highest for NEAT (4.169) with a standard deviation of 0.032, demonstrating a more consistent performance. Looking at the complexity of networks evolved, NEAT tended to evolve networks with fewer hidden nodes, but with a similar average synapse count to that seen for the simple GA. FS-NEAT tended to evolve networks with more fixed-weight synapses. The networks evolved by the simple GA also showed evidence of bloat in that they had both nodes with no inputs (unstimulated nodes) and hidden nodes which did not connect to, or influence in any way, the output neuron. However, such obsolete structure can easily be pruned from these networks.

Environment Adapted	Sensitivity To Uniform	Checker	Vertical	Horizontal	LDiag	RDiag
None	0.831	0.829	0.845	0.830	0.835	0.850
Uniform	**0.134**	0.785	0.884	0.783	0.697	0.976
Checker	0.792	**0.129**	0.796	0.895	0.996	0.704
Vertical	0.881	0.777	**0.134**	0.790	0.700	0.974
Horizontal	0.793	0.899	0.796	**0.118**	0.983	0.700
LDiag	0.697	0.987	0.698	0.970	**0.138**	0.415
RDiag	0.987	0.692	0.996	0.691	0.390	**0.102**

Table 1: Sensitivity of the best network evolved by the simple GA to the uniform, checkerboard, vertical bar, horizontal bar and diagonal environments as the network adapts to each environment. The sensitivity to the adapted environment is highlighted in bold.

Environment Adapted	Sensitivity To Uniform	Checker	Vertical	Horizontal	LDiag	RDiag
None	0.871	0.854	0.873	0.853	0.857	0.854
Uniform	**0.127**	0.902	0.894	0.896	0.988	0.605
Checker	0.893	**0.113**	0.897	0.905	0.997	0.592
Vertical	0.895	0.875	**0.112**	0.891	0.612	0.987
Horizontal	0.900	0.892	0.895	**0.117**	0.598	1.004
LDiag	0.987	0.999	0.609	0.599	**0.125**	0.506
RDiag	0.610	0.617	0.996	1.006	0.510	**0.120**

Table 2: Sensitivity of the best network evolved by NEAT to the uniform, checkerboard, vertical bar, horizontal bar and diagonal environments as the network adapts to each environment. The sensitivity to the adapted environment is highlighted in bold.

Environment Adapted	Sensitivity To Uniform	Checker	Vertical	Horizontal	LDiag	RDiag
None	0.684	0.687	0.682	0.686	0.683	0.675
Uniform	**0.041**	1.026	0.661	1.023	0.673	1.005
Checker	1.031	**0.063**	1.046	0.675	0.319	0.690
Vertical	0.669	1.002	**0.045**	0.993	0.683	0.351
Horizontal	1.009	0.678	1.013	**0.042**	0.993	0.658
LDiag	0.672	0.340	0.682	0.990	**0.031**	0.350
RDiag	1.013	0.669	0.341	0.663	0.342	**0.044**

Table 3: Sensitivity of the best network evolved by FS-NEAT to the uniform, checkerboard, vertical bar, horizontal bar and diagonal environments as the network adapts to each environment. The sensitivity to the adapted environment is highlighted in bold.

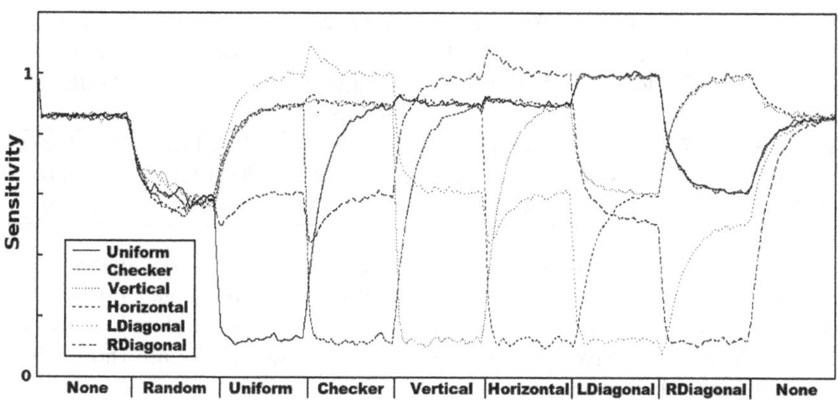

Figure 6: The sensitivity graph produced by the best network found by NEAT.

Method	Average Fitness	Standard Deviation	Best Fitness	Worst Fitness
Simple GA	3.537	0.220	4.122	3.405
NEAT	4.169	0.032	4.208	4.096
FS-NEAT	3.708	0.201	4.167	3.532

Table 4: Average, best and worst fitness observed for each GA method over 10 500-generation runs.

In most practical applications, data is likely to contain a noise component. Therefore, a novelty detector used in such applications should be resilient to noise. To investigate this, we tested the performance of the best evolved network when independent noise was introduced to each input. The noise component was a value drawn independently from a standard normal distribution and scaled by a constant factor k. We varied k from 0.0 to 5.0, with a step size of 0.2. Figure 7 shows how the fitness of both the original illustrative neural network and the best evolved network varies as noise is introduced. This reduces in a non-linear fashion for both networks as the noise factor k is increased. The best evolved network is able to distinguish between novel and known environments until $k = 0.8$, after which it struggles to reliably differentiate between the diagonal environments. At $k = 1.6$, the best evolved network is unable to distinguish between any of the environments. The original network is unable to distinguish between environments at $k = 2.2$.

5 Discussion

The networks evolved by the GA methods show a more consistent handling of a broader range of environments than either the example neural network given

Method	Average Hidden Nodes	Average Modifiable Synapses	Average Fixed-Weight Synapses	Unstim. Nodes	Ineffective Hidden Nodes
Simple GA	7.7 (9.76)	16.5 (1.9)	4.6 (1.07)	3.1 (4.51)	6.8 (9.17)
NEAT	3.6 (2.84)	18 (2.87)	8.2 (4.02)	0.0 (0.0)	0.0 (0.0)
FS-NEAT	8.1 (4.01)	9.7 (4.69)	14.1 (5.34)	0.0 (0.0)	0.0 (0.0)

Table 5: Average hidden node, synapse and ineffective/unstimulated node counts for solutions produced by each GA method over 10 500-generation runs. Numbers in brackets represent standard deviation. Unstimulated nodes are those which do not receive any input. Ineffective hidden nodes are those which do not influence the output neuron.

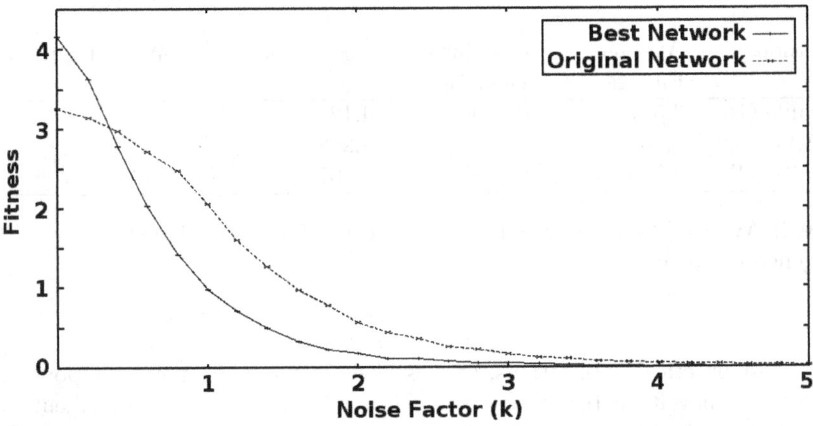

Figure 7: Fitness of the best evolved network as noise is applied to its inputs, with noise factor k varied from 0.0 to 5.0

by [7] or any of the networks we designed by hand. The network with the highest fitness, found using NEAT, has a complexity similar to that of the example network. For most novel environments, this networks sensitivity remains at a similar level throughout the simulation. Unlike the example network, this network does not see a dramatic increase in sensitivity to one diagonal environment when adapted to the alternative diagonal environment. This is important as it ensures a more consistent separation between novel and known environments. However, a drop in sensitivity to the diagonal environments is still observed when the network is adapted to non-diagonal environments, and vice versa. This is again caused by the network being able to form partial predictions of stimuli due to similarities between environments.

Interestingly, the structure of the best network has demonstrated, from a predictive coding standpoint, a change in function. The fixed-weight synapses between the centre patch inputs and the output neuron have been removed and a new fixed-weight synapse introduced connecting a single peripheral input to the output neuron. Thus, the network has changed from predicting the sum of the centre patch to predicting the selected periphery input. However, from a novelty detection perspective this network retains the intended function of indicating the novelty of a given input vector. The high-scoring candidates from all three GA approaches demonstrate similar changes in network structure. This may indicate that a network which preserves the function of predicting the sum of the centre patch does not exist.

A surprising result is the comparatively high best fitness score achieved by the simple GA. For this problem, the best network evolved by the simple GA was of a similar fitness to the best networks evolved by both NEAT and FS-NEAT. This is despite the relative complexity of these two neuroevolution techniques, compared to the simple GA. Improvements can easily be made to the simple GA, such as adding new nodes using a similar method to that used by NEAT to reduce the observed bloating of networks. Whilst NEAT has been demonstrated to give a more reliable performance, investigating the effect of such improvements to the performance of the simple GA would be instructive.

The best network presented in section 4 has been shown to cope reasonably well with noise. At $k = 0.8$, the variance of the noise component was 0.64 times the variance of the signal component. Despite this, the network was still capable of distinguishing between known (adapted) and novel (unadapted) environments. However, with increasing noise, the network is shown to perform worse than the original network in terms of the fitness criteria defined in section 3. This demonstrates that performance over noisy data should be considered by the GA approaches when searching for new neural network structures.

6 Conclusions and Future Work

We have described a neural network used by [7] to illustrate dynamic predictive coding and identified a limitation of this network. For the task of optimising the structure of the network, we have demonstrated that whilst NEAT outperforms two other evolutionary algorithms, it does not produce a solution which is significantly better than that produced by a simple genetic algorithm. The optimised network evolved by NEAT distinguishes more consistently between a broader range of environments than either the original neural network or any of the networks we designed by hand. It also performs well when a low level of noise is introduced but its performance degrades quickly as this noise increases. This is because noise sensitivity was not part of the fitness criteria used by the GA approaches. Since we plan to test this approach to novelty detection on data that is inherently noisy, this will need to be addressed in future work.

In order to extend this work, we plan to investigate using a neural network, capable of dynamic predictive coding, for novelty detection over recorded weather data. A vector of metrics would be passed to the network, which would then learn the correlational relationships between those metrics and detect novelty when these relationships change. We consider it likely that the structure of the neural network used will need to be evolved to give optimal performance in this task, and this process of evolution will need to take into consideration noise applied to the data.

References

[1] Markou, M., Singh, S. Novelty detection: a review part 2: neural network based approaches. Signal Process. 2003; 83:2499–2521

[2] Markou, M., Singh, S. Novelty detection: a review part 1: statistical approaches. Signal Process. 2003; 83:2481–2497

[3] Marsland, S., Nehmzow, U., Shapiro, J. Detecting novel features of an environment using habiutation. In: Proc. Simulation of Adaptive Behaviour, MIT Press, 2000, 189–198

[4] Marsland, S., Nehmzow, U., Shapiro, J. On-line novelty detection for autonomous mobile robots. Robo. Auto. Syst. 2005; 51:191–206

[5] Marsland, S., Shapiro, J., Nehmzow, U. A self-organising network that grows when required. Neural Netw. 2002; 15:1041–1058

[6] Jiang, J. Image compression with neural networks - a survey. Signal Process., Image Commun. 1999; 14:737–760

[7] Hosoya, T., Baccus, S.A., Meister, M. Dynamic predictive coding by the retina. Nature 2005; 436:71–77

[8] Stirling, P. Retina. In: Shepherd, G.M. (ed.) The Synaptic Organization of the Brain. 3rd edn. Oxford University Press, 1990, 170–213

[9] Mitchell, M. An Introduction to Genetic Algorithms. 6th edn. MIT Press, 1999

[10] Mitchell, T. Machine Learning. Int. edn. McGraw-Hill Higher Education, 1997

[11] Stanley, K.O. Efficient Evolution of Neural Networks Through Complexification. PhD thesis, University of Texas at Austin, 2004

[12] Whiteson, S., Stone, P., Stanley, K.O., Miikkulainen, R., Kohl, N. Automatic feature selection in neuroevolution. In: Proc. Genetic and Evolutionary Computation, ACM Press, 2005, 1225–1232

Selecting Bi-Tags for Sentiment Analysis of Text

Rahman Mukras, Nirmalie Wiratunga, and Robert Lothian

School of Computing
The Robert Gordon University
St Andrew Street
Aberdeen UK, AB25 1HG
{ram,nw,rml}@comp.rgu.ac.uk

Abstract. Sentiment Analysis aims to determine the overall sentiment orientation of a given input text. One motivation for research in this area is the need for consumer related industries to extract public opinion from online portals such as blogs, discussion boards, and reviews. Estimating sentiment orientation in text involves extraction of sentiment rich phrases and the aggregation of their sentiment orientation. Identifying sentiment rich phrases is typically achieved by using manually selected part-of-speech (PoS) patterns. In this paper we present an algorithm for automated discovery of PoS patterns from sentiment rich background data. Here PoS patterns are selected by applying standard feature selection heuristics: Information Gain (IG), Chi-Squared (CHI) score, and Document Frequency (DF). Experimental results from two real-world datasets suggests that classification accuracy is significantly better with DF selected patterns than with IG or the CHI score. Importantly, we also found DF selected patterns to result in comparative classifier accuracy to that of manually selected patterns.

1 Introduction

Sentiment Analysis involves the discovery and extraction of opinions contained in text. Recently this area has received much attention due to its potential applicability to lucrative industries such as marketing and the media. A typical application would be the classification of sentiments expressed within the widely uncharted domain of consumer generated media (e.g. online reviews and blogs). These domains play an increasingly important role in consumer related industries by providing direct and spontaneous feedback on public opinion [1, 11].

Much of the work in sentiment analysis has been devoted to the task of sentiment extraction by identifying subjective text [20]. Closely related to this is the need to establish intensity of extracted sentiment by measuring the deviation from non-subjective text [21]. A more constrained form of analysis involves the classification of text into two distinctive classes of positive and negative sentiment orientation [18, 12] In this paper we propose a part-of-speech (PoS) pattern selection algorithm to address the first problem area. A PoS pattern is composed of a sequence of consecutive PoS tags and is used to extract a set of phrases from an input text [8]. For example, the PoS pattern "JJ NN1" (an adjective followed by a singular noun) can be used to extract bi-grams such as "fast car," "great person," or "evil motive." A bi-tag refers to a PoS pattern containing two consecutive PoS tags.

The algorithm we propose makes use of a background dataset to learn a set of bi-tags for extracting sentiment rich bi-grams. Each word in the background dataset is replaced with its respective PoS tag after which bi-tags are formed. Standard feature selection heuristics such as Information Gain (IG) [15, 22], Document Frequency (DF) [15, 22], and the Chi-Squared (CHI) score [22] are then applied to select the top discriminative bi-tags. Our hypothesis behind this is that bi-tags that are predictive of a particular sentiment orientation, should also extract bi-grams that are predictive of the same.

We evaluated the three feature selection heuristics on two test datasets by assessing their utility in sentiment classification, and found DF to yield best performances over IG and CHI. These results were contrary to what we expected, and were also in direct opposition to what is normally observed in text classification, where IG and CHI have traditionally been superior to DF [22, 15]. Given that both IG and CHI are designed to return relatively more discriminative bi-tags than DF [6], we speculate that these results indicate the absence of a one-to-one correspondence between the discriminative ability of a bi-tag, and the sentiment orientation of the bi-grams it extracts. Rather a useful bi-tag is one that occurs frequently across documents. We found also that the performance of DF is dependant on the availability of a sentiment-rich background dataset, whilst IG and CHI are unaffected by the choice of background data.

The remainder of this paper is organised as follows. Section 2 describes the process of selecting bi-tags for sentiment classification. Experimental results on two datasets are presented in Section 3. Related work appear in Section 4, followed by conclusions in Section 5.

2 Selecting Bi-Tags for Sentiment Classification

Fig. 1 illustrates a semisupervised approach to sentiment classification. Input text is tagged with corresponding PoS tags (we used the RASP PoS tagger[1] [2]). Bi-tags, obtained from a sentiment rich background dataset, are then used to extract sentiment rich bi-grams from the tagged text. The sentiment orientation of each bi-gram is then computed by comparing its association to two predefined sets of positive and negative words. These individual orientations are then aggregated to obtain the overall sentiment orientation of the input text.

Crucial to this semisupervised sentiment classification approach is the availability of bi-tags for bi-gram extraction. Existing approaches typically use manually selected bi-tags. Turney [18], for example, employs a set of manually crafted bi-tags similar to those listed in Table 1. In this Table, J refers to adjective forms (JJ, JJT, or JJR), NN1 and NN2 to a singular and plural nouns respectively, R to adverb forms (RR, RG, RGA, or RGR), and VV0 to a verb.

[1] Uses the CLAWS2 Tagset: http://www.comp.lancs.ac.uk/ucrel/claws2tags.html

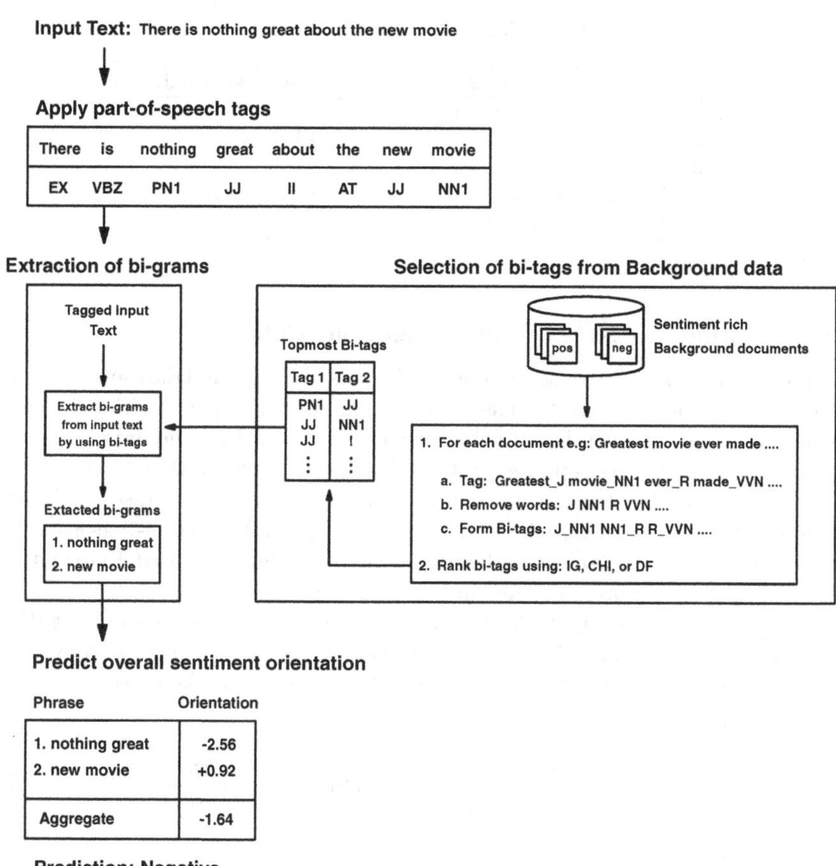

Fig. 1. Semisupervised Sentiment Classification.

To describe the patterns in Table 1, consider the fourth one which means that two consecutive words are extracted if the first is a noun and the second is an adjective, but the third (not extracted) cannot be a noun. The third word is checked so as to avoid extracting two consecutive bi-grams such as "very fast" and "fast car" from the initial phrase "very fast car." Note also that bi-grams are used instead of uni-grams so as to preserve context. For instance, "very good" and "not good" clearly posses opposing polarities. This information would be lost if we only use unigrams such as "good."

An obvious drawback of using manually selected bi-tags is that they need to be created by a domain expert in the first place. This can be a setback in practical applications such as blog-opinion filtering where maintenance of bi-tags is difficult. Consequently, in this paper we present an alternative procedure that automates the creation of bi-tags by use of a set of background documents.

Table 1. Manually Selected Bi-Tags.

	Tag 1	Tag 2	Tag 3 (Not Extracted)
1.	J	NN1 or NN2	anything
2.	R	J	not NN1 or NN2
3.	J	J	not NN1 or NN2
4.	NN1 or NN2	J	not NN1 or NN2
5.	R	VV0	anything

2.1 Selection of Bi-Tags from Background Data

As shown in Fig. 1, we use a sentiment rich bi-polar background dataset for bi-tag selection. A bi-polar dataset consists of documents belonging to either a sentiment positive or negative class. Each document in the background dataset is processed so that words are replaced by their PoS tag. Assuming that $t_1, t_2, \ldots, t_M$ is a sequence of PoS tags in an arbitrary document of this dataset, a bi-tag would be defined as $t_m t_{m+1}$ where $m = 1, 2, \ldots, M-1$. All such bi-tags are then ranked using a feature selection heuristic. In this study, we used Information Gain, Chi-Squared score, and document frequency.

Let q_k be the kth bi-tag in the corpus, c^+ and c^- be the positive and negative classes respectively, and N be the total number of documents in the corpus. The following is how we implemented the above feature selection heuristics:

1. Information Gain:

$$IG(q_k) = \sum_{c \in \{c^+, c^-\}} \sum_{q \in \{q_k, \bar{q_k}\}} P(q, c) \log \frac{P(q, c)}{P(q)P(c)} \tag{1}$$

2. Chi-Squared score:

$$CHI(q_k) = \max_{c \in \{c^+, c^-\}} \left\{ \frac{N \cdot [P(q_k, c)P(\bar{q_k}, \bar{c}) - P(q_k, \bar{c})P(\bar{q_k}, c)]^2}{P(q_k)P(\bar{q_k})P(c)P(\bar{c})} \right\} \tag{2}$$

3. Document frequency:

$$DF(q_k) = N \cdot P(q_k) \tag{3}$$

We only recognise the presence of a bi-tag in a document when estimating the probabilities in Equations 1, 2, and 3. Once ranked, the topmost bi-tags are used to extract bi-grams from the input text. Table 2 illustrates, for each feature selection heuristic, a sample of the topmost bi-tags that were returned, along with a few of the bi-grams that they extracted.

Note that bi-grams extracted using DF such as "worst actor," and "terrible breakfast" are relatively more intuitive (in terms of sentiment richness) than the those extracted by IG and CHI such as "shrug ?" and "moron ?." We shall later show that classification performances also tend to follow the same trend.

Singular and plural proper nouns are avoided because they can adversely influence sentiment classification by being contextually associated with both positive and negative sentiments [18].

Table 2. Sample of top ranked bi-tags selected using IG CHI and DF.

Heuristic	Tag 1	Tag 2	Examples of extracted phrases
IG	NN1	?	shrug ?, glory ?, loser ?
	NN1	!	joke !, understatement !, menace !, perfection !
	VVZ	NN2	grate nerve, play scene, think woman
	NN2	NN2	work life, year job, concert movie
	J	VVG	good look, serious think, good fall
CHI	NN1	J	guy worst, personality decent, spelling unattractive
	NN1	?	shrug ?, moron ?, fear ?, glory ?, loser ?
	NN1	!	joke !, understatement !, menace !, perfection !
	NN1	VVZ	planet act, man pray, character play
	VV0	NN1	walk sunset, get sitcom, show emotion
DF	J	NN1	worst actor, terrible actress, worst breakfast
	NN1	NN1	example non-talent, quality style, courage range
	NN1	J	guy worst, personality decent, spelling unattractive
	NN1	NN2	going look, education work, world affair
	J	NN2	cute star, decent performance, outspoken topic

2.2 Predicting the Sentiment Orientation of the Input Text

Once the sentiment rich bi-grams have been extracted, then the next step is to compute their respective sentiment orientations. These orientations are later aggregated to compute the overall orientation of the input text.

Let b_i be the ith extracted bi-gram from the input text. The sentiment orientation of b_i is computed by comparing its association to a set of positive words $\mathcal{P}$, against its association to a set of negative words $\mathcal{N}$ [18]. The words in these two sets are normally based on antonym pairs. For example, given an entry "good" in set $\mathcal{P}$, there would be a corresponding antonym such as "bad" in set $\mathcal{N}$.

Adjectives are known to be good carriers of sentiment [7], and therefore we compiled the two sets $\mathcal{P}$ and $\mathcal{N}$ from a list of manually selected adjectives as follows. For each word, we recorded an antonym set using a thesaurus, and a *familiarity score* using WordNet [5]. The familiarity score is a measure of a words usage in normal language. A high score would imply a commonly used word, whereas a low score would imply an uncommon word. This score is crucial in selecting the right words as computing association is difficult with either uncommon or excessively common words. We further augmented the familiarity score with word usage statistics obtained from a search engine.

Table 3 illustrates a sample of the list that we made. The two fields within the brackets of each word correspond to its familiarity score, and the number of hits it returned when queried in a search engine. Note that "good" would be unsuitable as it occurs too frequently. Similarly, "used" is also unsuitable due to its infrequent occurrence. The following are the words we finally chose:

$\mathcal{P}$ = {glad, rich, smart, great, wise, huge}
$\mathcal{N}$ = {sad, poor, stupid, terrible, foolish, little}

Table 3. A sample of the adjectives and their respective usage statistics.

Adjective Word	Corresponding Antonyms
new (11,1268194)	old (8,354828), used (3,3)
good (21,719768)	awful (6,29714), terrible (4,38042), bad (14,409)
general (6,574866)	special (7,195450)
right (14,549695)	wrong (9,180121), erroneous (1,2660)
great (6,514301)	terrible (4,38042), ordinary (2,28635)
big (13,410606)	small (10,248872), little (8,505147)
simple (7,245606)	complex (1,44198), difficult (2,77048)
poor (6,113213)	rich (12,74127)
huge (1,109800)	small (10,248872), little (8,505147)
glad (4,103213)	sad (3,82949), bittersweet (2,4273)
smart (7,86815)	stupid (3,104053), weak (12,28502)
foolish (2,10510)	wise (4,32497), all-knowing (1,0)

Association between two entities is computed using Pointwise Mutual Information [4] defined as follows:

$$I(x, y) = \log\left[\frac{P(x, y)}{P(x)P(y)}\right] \tag{4}$$

Here $I(x, y)$ has a minimum value of zero when x and y are independent of each other, and its value increases with the dependency between the two. This idea can be used to compute the sentiment orientation (SO) of b_i as follows,

$$SO(b_i) = I(b_i, \mathcal{P}) - I(b_i, \mathcal{N}) = \log\left[\frac{P(b_i, \mathcal{P})P(\mathcal{N})}{P(b_i, \mathcal{N})P(\mathcal{P})}\right] \tag{5}$$

Note that if b_i is equally associated to both $\mathcal{P}$ and $\mathcal{N}$, then $SO(b_i)$ would yield a value of zero. However, if b_i is more associated to either $\mathcal{P}$ or $\mathcal{N}$, then the value of $SO(b_i)$ would either be positive or negative respectively. To estimate the probabilities in Equation 5, we use the number of hits returned by a search engine given a query [18]. This was done as follows:

$$\begin{aligned} P(\mathcal{P}) &\simeq \mathit{hits}\,(\text{glad} \vee \ldots \vee \text{huge}) \\ P(\mathcal{N}) &\simeq \mathit{hits}\,(\text{sad} \vee \ldots \vee \text{little}) \\ P(b_i, \mathcal{P}) &\simeq \mathit{hits}\,(b_i\ \textbf{near}\ (\text{glad} \vee \ldots \vee \text{huge})) \\ P(b_i, \mathcal{N}) &\simeq \mathit{hits}\,(b_i\ \textbf{near}\ (\text{sad} \vee \ldots \vee \text{little})) \end{aligned}$$

Here $hits(\cdot)$ is a function that returns the number of documents that satisfy its query parameter, and **near** is a binary operator that constrains the search to documents containing its two query parameters, within 10 words of each other in any order (a similar approach was used in [18]). Finally the sentiment orientation of the input text is computed as the sign of the aggregate orientation

```
SEMANTIC-ORIENTATION(d, Q, P, N)
SO^d = 0
B ← EXTRACT-BIGRAMS(d, Q)
for each b ∈ B do
    SO^d += SO(b) // Accumulates the orientation of bi-grams.
return sign [SO^d]

EXTRACT-BIGRAMS(d, Q)
B ← {}
for i = 1 to length(d) − 1 do // length(d) returns the number of words in d.
    t = PoS(w_i^d w_{i+1}^d) // PoS returns the part-of-speech tags of the phrase.
    if t ∈ Q and w_i^d w_{i+1}^d ∉ B then
        B ← B ∪ {w_i^d w_{i+1}^d}
return B
```

Fig. 2. The Semantic Orientation Algorithm.

of its extracted bi-grams,

$$SO^d = sign\left[\sum_i SO(b_i)\right] \tag{6}$$

A positive aggregate would imply a positive orientation whereas a negative aggregate would imply a negative orientation. The algorithm is summarised in Fig. 2 whereby d is an input document consisting of all its words $w_1^d \dots w_{length(d)}^d$, and Q is a set of bi-tags extracted using the approach discussed in Section 2.1.

3 Evaluation

The evaluation was performed on two Test datasets and two separate Background datasets. We also used the Trec Blog06 collection[2] [9] as a Query dataset to return the hits required to estimate the probabilities in Equation 5.

3.1 Datasets and Performance Metrics

The Test Datasets: Two bi-polar datasets were employed:

1. The Edmunds Dataset [10]: This dataset was composed of consumer reviews on used motor vehicles from the *Edmunds.com* website. Each review contained an ordinal label ranging from 1.0 to 9.8 step 0.2 (1.0 containing the most negative sentiment and 9.8 the most positive). Due to sparsity, we only used reviews within the range of 4.4 to 9.8. All reviews with less than 10 words were discarded and an equal class distribution was formed by randomly retaining 100 reviews per class. We then reduced the resultant into

[2] See http://ir.dcs.gla.ac.uk/test_collections/blog06info.html

Table 4. Comparison of bi-tag selection with IG, CHI and DF.

No of	Actors			Edmunds		
Patterns	IG	CHI	DF	IG	CHI	DF
1	0.49	0.50	**0.62**	0.50	0.50	**0.61**
2	0.49	0.55	**0.60**	0.50	0.51	0.62
3	0.49	0.55	**0.62**	0.50	0.51	0.59
4	0.52	0.55	**0.61**	0.51	0.51	0.59
5	0.53	0.57	**0.63**	0.52	0.52	0.60
6	0.54	0.57	**0.64**	0.52	0.54	0.59
7	0.53	0.57	**0.63**	0.51	0.53	0.60
8	0.53	0.57	**0.63**	0.50	0.53	0.59
9	0.52	0.57	0.62	0.50	0.50	**0.60**
10	0.53	0.57	**0.62**	0.50	0.50	**0.60**
11	0.53	0.57	**0.63**	0.50	0.50	**0.60**
12	0.53	0.58	0.62	0.50	0.54	**0.60**
13	0.52	0.59	0.62	0.51	0.55	**0.61**
14	0.53	0.59	**0.62**	0.52	0.55	0.58
15	0.53	0.60	0.62	0.52	0.55	0.58

bi-polar classes by assigning reviews labelled 4.4 and 4.6 to c^- and reviews labelled 9.6 and 9.8 to c^+.

2. The Actors Dataset [3]: This dataset was composed of reviews from the actors and actresses sub-topic of the *Rateitall.com* opinion website. Each review contained an ordinal integer label ranging from 1 to 5 (1 containing the most negative sentiment and 5 the most positive). All reviews that had less than 10 words were discarded. We restricted the number of reviews per author per rating to a maximum of 15, so as to avoid the bias of any prolific author from dominating the corpus [12]. We then reduced the resultant into bi-polar classes by assigning reviews labelled 1 to c^- and reviews labelled 5 to c^+. Finally, we formed an equal class distribution by randomly retaining 500 reviews per class.

Note that the formation of the bi-polar classes is sensible as classes at extremes of an ordinal scale possess opposite sentiment orientations and hence are essentially bi-polar. Both datasets were preprocessed using the sequence of tokenization, conversion to lowercase, PoS tagging, stemming, and finally stopword removal. We used a customised stopword list as we found that words such as "not," which is present in most stopword lists, to be quite useful in bi-grams such as "not good."

The Background Datasets: We employed a sentiment rich, and a non-sentiment-rich background dataset. For the former one, we used the Polarity dataset [12] which is composed of 2000 movie reviews (1000 positive reviews and 1000 negative ones). For the latter dataset, we used the ACQ, and EARN categories of the Reuters-21578 corpus [13]. These two categories are business

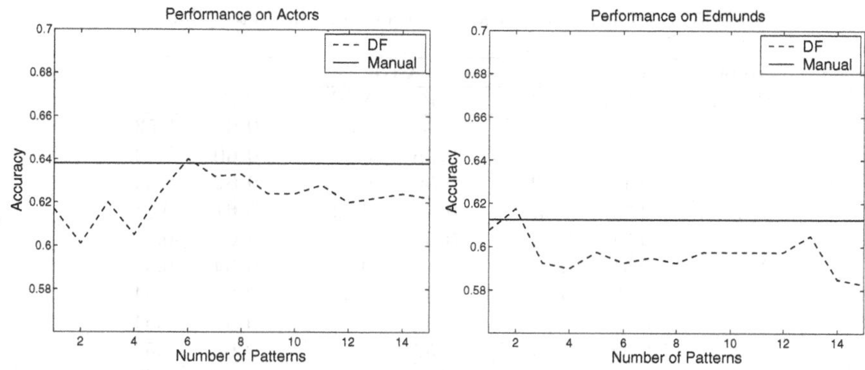

Fig. 3. Performance of manual and auto-generated bi-tags.

related and hence contain little, if any, sentiment rich information. We prepared this dataset by randomly selecting 1000 documents from each class such that each document belongs to at most one class. Both datasets were preprocessed in a fashion similar to the Test datasets.

The Query Dataset: We used the Trec Blog06 collection [9] to perform the queries that allowed us to realise the *hits*(.) function. This collection was compiled by the University of Glasgow and is composed of over 3.2 million blog posts. A blog post refers to an entry into a personal site that archives the posts in a reverse chronological order. Blogs are typically rich in opinion as they are authored by individuals who aim at expressing their opinions to the world. The Trec Blog06 collection was meant to be a realistic snapshot of the blogsphere (the collective term for all blogs), making it an excellent query dataset.

To prepare this collection, we extracted the text from the initial HTML format discarding all tokens that contained non-printable characters. We then preprocessed it using the sequence of tokenization, conversion to lowercase, stemming and stopword removal (with the specialised stopword list). We finally indexed the resultant collection, containing 2,466,650 documents, using the lucene[3] search engine.

Performance Metrics: Once bi-tags are learnt from the background dataset we used these to predict the sentiment orientation of unseen test data. The accuracy on test data is calculated for performance comparison. All reported results are the averages of 10 fold cross validation and significance is reported using the two-tailed paired t-test.

We also note that the semantic orientation of an input text can evaluate to zero. This often happens when extracted bi-grams are sparse in that they may

[3] http://lucene.apache.org

Table 5. Comparison of background data on the Actors dataset.

No of	IG		CHI		DF	
Patterns	SR	NSR	SR	NSR	SR	NSR
1	0.49	0.50	0.50	0.50	**0.62**	0.53
2	0.49	0.50	**0.55**	0.50	**0.60**	0.53
3	0.49	**0.52**	**0.55**	0.50	**0.62**	0.53
4	0.53	0.53	**0.55**	0.50	**0.61**	0.53
5	0.53	0.53	**0.57**	0.50	**0.63**	0.53
6	0.54	0.53	0.57	0.53	**0.64**	0.53
7	0.53	0.53	0.57	0.53	**0.63**	0.54
8	0.53	0.53	0.57	0.53	**0.63**	0.54
9	0.52	0.53	0.57	0.54	**0.62**	0.54
10	0.53	0.53	0.57	0.55	**0.62**	0.55
11	0.53	0.53	0.57	0.55	**0.63**	0.55
12	0.53	0.53	0.58	0.57	**0.62**	0.55
13	0.53	0.53	0.59	0.57	**0.62**	0.55
14	0.53	0.53	0.59	0.57	**0.62**	0.55
15	0.53	0.54	0.60	0.57	**0.62**	0.55

not co-occur with words in $\mathcal{P}$ or $\mathcal{N}$. It can also occur when no bi-grams are extracted from the input text. In such situations we chose the most commonly predicted class, and if this was a tie then we chose the positive class.

3.2 Experimental Results

We performed three main experiments: Firstly, we compared the three bi-tag selection heuristics (IG, CHI, and DF). Secondly, we compared the performance of automatically selected bi-tags against that of manually selected ones. Lastly, we assessed the effect of a non-sentiment-rich background dataset on performance.

Comparison of the Bi-Tag Selection Heuristics: Table 4 contains the classification accuracy achieved by the three bi-tag selection heuristics on the Actors and Edmunds datasets. Here we use the sentiment rich Polarity dataset as Background. Each row corresponds to results obtained with a particular PoS pattern size. For each row of each dataset, performances significantly better than the rest ($p < 0.05$) are shown in bold.

Note, in both datasets, that DF is on average better than both CHI and IG. Indeed this result was unexpected given the number of numerous studies that have reported the opposite trend in performance [22, 15]. Given that both IG and CHI are known to return relatively more discriminative bi-tags than DF [6], these results strongly suggest that the discriminative ability of a bi-tag does not directly influence that of the bi-grams it extracts.

Comparison with Manually Acquired Bi-Tags: Fig. 3 illustrates the results of comparing bi-tags selected from background data against manual bi-tags

Table 6. Comparison of background data on the Edmunds dataset.

No of	IG		CHI		DF	
Patterns	SR	NSR	SR	NSR	SR	NSR
1	**0.50**	0.47	0.50	0.51	**0.61**	0.55
2	**0.50**	0.47	0.51	0.47	**0.62**	0.55
3	0.50	0.51	0.51	0.47	**0.59**	0.55
4	0.51	0.50	0.51	0.48	0.59	0.55
5	0.52	0.50	0.52	0.47	0.60	0.55
6	0.52	0.50	0.54	0.53	0.59	0.55
7	0.51	0.50	0.53	0.52	**0.60**	0.53
8	0.50	0.49	0.53	0.52	**0.59**	0.53
9	0.50	0.50	0.50	0.53	**0.60**	0.52
10	0.50	0.50	0.50	0.52	**0.60**	0.54
11	0.50	0.50	0.50	0.50	**0.60**	0.54
12	0.50	0.49	0.54	0.53	**0.60**	0.54
13	0.51	0.49	0.55	0.53	**0.61**	0.54
14	0.52	0.48	0.55	0.53	**0.59**	0.53
15	0.52	0.52	0.55	0.54	**0.58**	0.53

shown in Table 1. Note, in this Figure, that the performance of manually selected bi-tags is independent of the x-axis and hence is a straight line.

Note that manual bi-tags perform, on average, better than bi-tags selected by DF. We, however, found this difference not to be statistically significant. These results were not unexpected as experience tells us that manual PoS pattern construction is rigorous and time-consuming. Each pattern, once derived, must be tested against a representative collection and fine tuned in light of the results. This is an iterative process that must be done by a domain expert. It is therefore not surprising to expect better performance when using such carefully designed patterns. However the advantage of the automatically generated bi-tags is that it reduces the demand on the knowledge engineer. This makes it suitable in applications whereby the data structure morphs rapidly making it infeasible to employ hand-crafted techniques.

Comparison with Non-Sentiment-Rich Background Data: We sought to investigate the role of a sentiment rich (SR) background dataset on the quality of generated bi-tags. To do this, we reran our experiments using the Reuters corpus as a non-sentiment-rich (NSR) background dataset and compared the results against the previous ones. Table 5 and 6 illustrate the results obtained on the Actors and Edmunds datasets. For each row of each feature selection heuristic, a significantly better ($p < 0.05$) performance is shown in bold.

Note, in both datasets, that DF performs significantly better on almost all pattern sizes when using a sentiment rich background dataset. This result strongly indicates the necessity of employing a sentiment rich background dataset to generate bi-tags. In contrast, there is almost no difference in the performances of both CHI and IG on the two background datasets. This further supports our conclusion that the discriminative ability of a bi-tag does not necessarily translate to that of the bi-grams it extracts.

4 Related Work

We are aware of at least three other closely related efforts that focus on extracting sentiment rich information from text. Pang *et al* [12] noted that negation plays an important contextual role in identifying the sentiment orientation of text. For example, the word "not" in "not good" clearly flips the orientation of the word "good." To model this effect, Pang *et al* adapted a technique called negation tagging whereby a `NOT_` tag is added to every word between a negation word ("not," "isn't," "shouldn't," etc.), and the next punctuation mark. They found this procedure to be, on average, beneficial to sentiment classification performance. In contrast to our work, by extracting bi-grams rather than uni-grams, our system is by default capable of handling the problem of negation.

In another study, Rillof *et al* [14] employs PoS patterns to learn a dictionary of subjective nouns. Their algorithm starts with a set of patterns and ranks them based on their ability to extract a set of manually selected seed words. The approach is iterative in that, at each iteration patterns are ranked and the best once are carried over to the next iteration. The set of seed words is also updated with words extracted by the selected patterns at each iteration. A clear advantage of this method over ours is its iterative nature which provides it with the opportunity to incrementally refine the pattern set. However the bootstrapping method relies on the availability of a manually selected set of seed words at the start.

Finally, Turney [18] presents an unsupervised algorithm that classifies a review as *recommended* or *not recommended.* The algorithm performs the classification by computing the aggregate semantic orientation of a set of selected phrases extracted from the review [17, 16, 19]. The approach is similar to the one presented here except for the fact that it employs manually crafted bi-tags rather than mining them as we do. In Section 3.2 we found that comparative performance can be achieved with our approach. Importantly, the demand on the knowledge engineer is greatly reduced making it far more suited to dynamic environments, such as opinion filtering from blogs.

5 Conclusion

This paper presents a novel approach to PoS pattern selection for sentiment analysis of text. To the best of our knowledge, this is the first study in sentiment analysis that explores the possibility of applying feature selection heuristics to PoS pattern selection. Our approach achieves comparative performance against existing approaches that rely on manually selected PoS patterns.

An empirical evaluation of three bi-tag selection heuristics, showed DF to be the most effective over both IG and CHI. These results contradict previous work on feature selection for text classification where IG and CHI have consistently outperformed DF [22]. Therefore we conclude that there exists a disparity between the sentiment orientation of a bi-tag and that of its extracted bi-grams. Instead, we find that bi-tags occurring frequently in a sentiment rich dataset, are good carriers of sentiment.

In future work we plan to extend the approach to accommodate a mixture of PoS pattern sizes. This would enable us to extract longer phrases such as "extremely superb vehicle," which occur frequently in sentiment rich text. We would also intend to improve the aggregation of extracted patterns when calculating sentiment orientation.

References

1. Lada Adamic and Natalie Glance. The Political Blogosphere and the 2004 U.S. Election: Divided They Blog. In *Proc. of 2nd Annual Workshop on the Weblogging Ecosystem: Aggregation, Analysis and Dynamics*, 2005.
2. Ted Briscoe and John Carroll. Robust Accurate Statistical Annotation of General Text. In *Proc. of LREC*, pages 1499–1504, Las Palmas, Canary Islands, May 2002.
3. Sutanu Chakraborti, Rahman Mukras, Robert Lothian, Nirmalie Wiratunga, Stuart Watt, and David Harper. Supervised Latent Semantic Indexing using Adaptive Sprinkling. In *Proc. of IJCAI*, pages 1582–1587. AAAI Press, 2007.
4. Kenneth Ward Church and Patrick Hanks. Word association norms, mutual information, and lexicography. *Comput. Linguist.*, 16(1):22–29, 1990.
5. Christiane Fellbaum, editor. *WordNet: An Electronic Lexical Database.* MIT Press, 1998.
6. George Forman. An Extensive Empirical Study of Feature Selection Metrics for Text Classification. *JMLR*, 3:1289–1305, 2003.
7. Vasileios Hatzivassiloglou and Janyce M. Wiebe. Effects of Adjective Orientation and Gradability on Sentence Subjectivity. In *Proc. of Computational Linguistics*, pages 299–305, Morristown, NJ, USA, 2000. ACL.
8. John S. Justeson and Slava M. Katz. Technical Terminology: Some Linguistic Properties and an Algorithm for Identification in Text. *Natural Language Engineering*, 1:9–27, 1995.
9. Craig Macdonald and Iadh Ounis. The TREC Blogs06 Collection : Creating and Analysing a Blog Test Collection. Technical report, Department of Computing Science, University of Glasgow, Glasgow, UK, 2006.
10. Rahman Mukras, Nirmalie Wiratunga, Robert Lothian, Sutanu Chakraborti, and David Harper. Information Gain Feature Selection for Ordinal Text Classification using Probability Re-distribution. In *Proc. of IJCAI Textlink Workshop*, 2007.
11. Shinsuke Nakajima, Junichi Tatemura, Yoichiro Hino, Yoshinori Hara, and Katsumi Tanaka. Discovering Important Bloggers based on Analyzing Blog Threads. In *Proc. of 2nd Annual Workshop on the Weblogging Ecosystem: Aggregation, Analysis and Dynamics*, 2005.
12. Bo Pang, Lillian Lee, and Shivakumar Vaithyanathan. Thumbs up? Sentiment Classification using Machine Learning Techniques. In *Proc. of EMNLP*, pages 79–86, 2002.
13. Reuters. Reuters-21578 text classification corpus. daviddlewis.com/resources/testcollections/reuters21578/, 1997.

14. Ellen Riloff, Janyce Wiebe, and Theresa Wilson. Learning Subjective Nouns using Extraction Pattern Bootstrapping. In *Proc. of CoNLL , ACL SIGNLL*, 2003.
15. Fabrizio Sebastiani. Machine Learning in Automated Text Categorization. *ACM Computing Surveys*, 34(1):1–47, 2002.
16. P.D. Turney and M.L. Littman. Unsupervised Learning of Semantic Orientation from a Hundred-Billion-Word Corpus. Technical report, National Research Council, Institute for Information Technology, 2002.
17. Peter D. Turney. Mining the Web for Synonyms: PMI-IR versus LSA on TOEFL. In *Proc. of EMCL*, pages 491–502, London, UK, 2001. Springer-Verlag.
18. Peter D. Turney. Thumbs Up or Thumbs Down? Semantic Orientation Applied to Unsupervised Classification of Reviews. In *Proc. of ACL*, pages 417–424, Morristown, NJ, USA, 2002. ACL.
19. Peter D. Turney and Michael L. Littman. Measuring praise and criticism: Inference of semantic orientation from association. *ACM Trans. Inf. Syst.*, 21(4):315–346, 2003.
20. Janyce Wiebe and Ellen Riloff. Creating Subjective and Objective Sentence Classifiers from Unannotated Texts. In *Proc. of CICLing*, pages 486–497, 2005.
21. Theresa Wilson, Janyce Wiebe, and Rebecca Hwa. Just How Mad Are You? Finding Strong and Weak Opinion Clauses. In *Proc. of AAAI*, pages 761–769. AAAI Press, 2004.
22. Yiming Yang and Jan O. Pedersen. A Comparative Study on Feature Selection in Text Categorization. In *Proc. of ICML*, pages 412–420. Morgan Kaufmann, 1997.

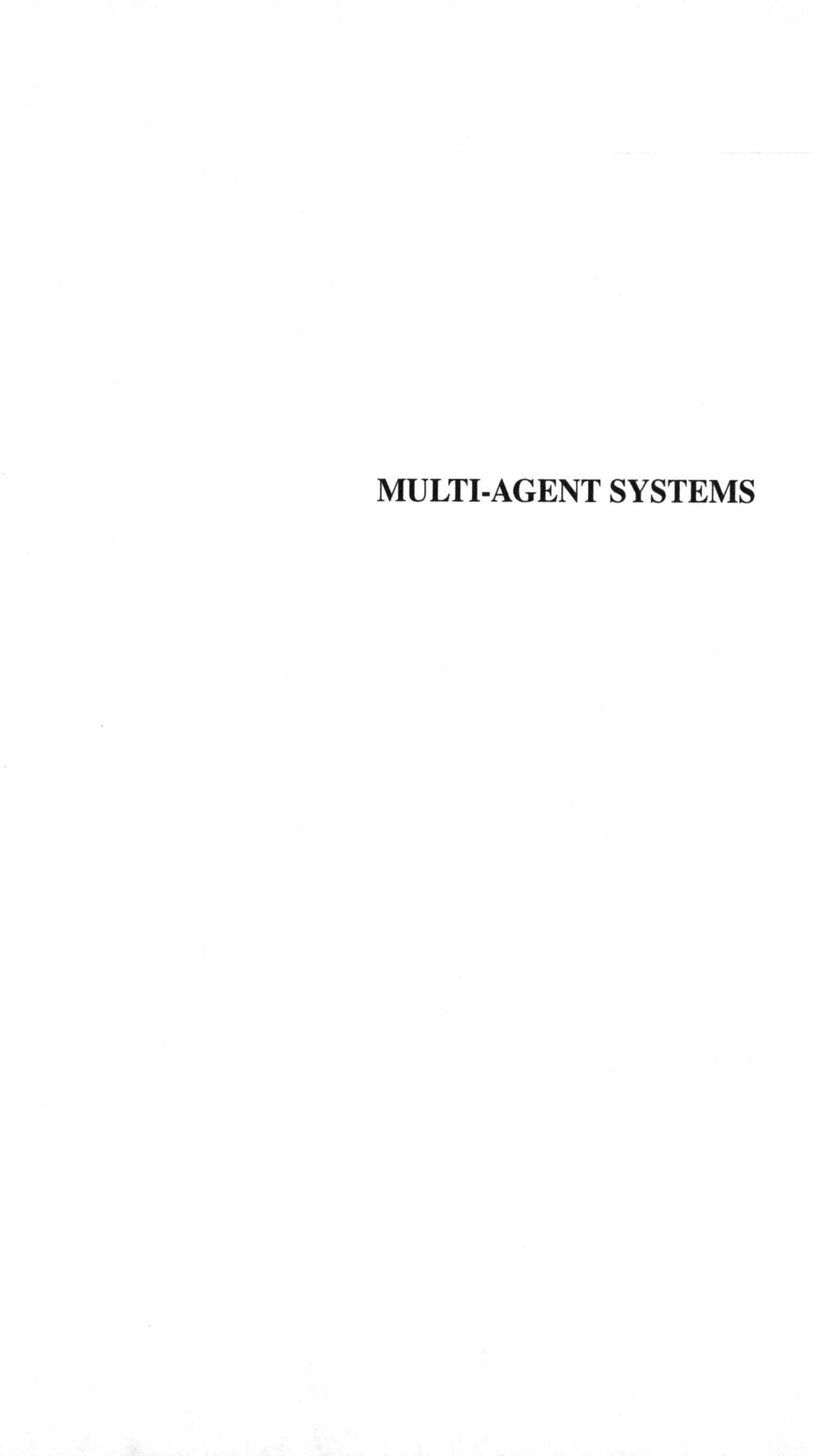

MULTI-AGENT SYSTEMS

Merging Intelligent Agency and the Semantic Web

John Debenham[1] and Carles Sierra[2]

[1] University of Technology, Sydney, Australia debenham@it.uts.edu.au
[2] Institut d'Investigació en Intel·ligència Artificial - IIIA,
Spanish Scientific Research Council, CSIC
08193 Bellaterra, Catalonia, Spain sierra@iiia.csic.es

Abstract. The semantic web makes unique demands on agency. Such agents should: be built around an ontology and should take advantage of the relations in it, be based on a grounded approach to uncertainty, be able to deal naturally with the issue of semantic alignment, and deal with interaction in a way that is suited to the co-ordination of services. A new breed of 'information-based' intelligent agents [1] meets these demands. This form of agency is founded on ideas from information theory, and was inspired by the insight that interaction is an information revelation and discovery process. Ontologies are fundamental to these agent's reasoning that relies on semantic distance measures. They employ entropy-based inference, a form of Bayesian inference, to manage uncertainty that they represent using probability distributions. Semantic alignment is managed through a negotiation process during which the agent's uncertain beliefs are continually revised. The co-ordination of services is achieved by modelling interaction as time-constrained, resource-constrained processes — a proven application of agent technology. In addition, measures of trust, reputation, and reliability are unified in a single model.

1 Introduction

The Semantic Web is a *data* sharing effort, a colossal human effort to liberate data currently confined to each one's private space. The main social objective of the Semantic Web is to permit the best possible data retrieval from this potentially huge distributed collection of data repositories. This extension of the classical *document* sharing approach of the web offers a great potential for human users but puts a series of technical challenges to the data retrieval tools: (1) heterogeneity in the representation of data, (2) inconsistency of the data appearing in different sites, and (3) uncertainty on the values associated to properties.

We argue in this paper that agent technology based on information theory is a sound way of addressing these challenges and at the same time is a feasible engineering approach to build actual web applications: agents permit to incorporate proactive behaviour into web services, or to co-ordinate in flexible ways P2P or Grid nodes, while facilitating a personalised interaction with users. Moreover, agent technology permits to keep track of interactions and provenance, as well as to build world models that facilitate the interpretation of the information gathered to assess the behaviour of other agents in the network. In this way agent technology can be used, as we show here, to give a clear operational meaning to the elusive top layer of the Semantic Web tower, that is, to the concept of *trust* [2].

Information-based agency is grounded on information-based concepts [3]. The agent architecture admits a game-theoretical reading and an information-theoretical reading. This approach contrasts with previous work on interaction that did not take information exchange into account, but focused on the similarity of offers [4, 5], game theory [6], or first-order logic [7]. This preoccupation with information and its integrity, together with the fundamental role played by ontologies, is the basis for their affinity with the semantic web. We use the following notation: a multiagent system $\{\alpha, \beta_1, \ldots, \beta_o, \xi, \theta_1, \ldots, \theta_t\}$, contains an agent α that interacts with other agents, β_i, information sources wrapped as agents, θ_j, and an *institutional agent*, ξ, that represents the prevailing norms of behaviour that may include laws and rules [8].

We will describe a *communication language* $\mathcal{C}$ that incorporates the specification of an *ontology* and permits us both to structure the dialogues and to structure the processing of the information gathered by agents. Agents have an *internal language* $\mathcal{L}$ used to build a probabilistic *world model*. We understand agents as being built on top of two basic functionalities. First, a *proactive machinery*, that transforms *needs* into *goals* and these into *plans* composed of *actions*. Second, a reactive machinery, that uses the received messages to revise the world model by updating the probability distributions in it. Agents summarise their world models using a number of measures (e.g. trust, reputation, and reliability [9]) that can then be used to define strategies for "exchanging information" — in the sense developed here, this is the only thing that an agent can do. Each agent has its own ontology that, together with the ontology identified as the context for each incoming illocution, plays a fundamental role in the agent's operation.

We introduce the communication language and its attendant ontological machinery in Section 2, the agent architecture in Section 3, measures of trust, reliability and reputation based on the architecture in Section 4, the way in which these agents deal with semantic alignment is described in Section 5, in Section 6 the agents co-ordinate services by employing goal-driven process management technology and treating the co-ordination problem as a time-constraiined, resource-constrained processes, and finally Section 7 concludes.

2 Communication Language $\mathcal{C}$

The shape of the language that α uses to represent the information received and the content of its dialogues depends on two fundamental notions. First, when agents interact within an overarching institution they explicitly or implicitly accept the *norms* that will constrain their behaviour, and accept the established sanctions and penalties whenever norms are violated. Second, the dialogues in which α engages are built around two fundamental actions: (i) passing information, and (ii) exchanging proposals and contracts. A *contract* is any agreement between two agents such as to provide some service over the Web or access to data — formally, a contract $\delta = (a, b)$ between agents α and β is a pair where a and b represent the activities that agents α and β are respectively responsible for. *Contracts* signed by agents and *information* passed by agents, are similar to norms in the sense that they oblige agents to behave in a particular way, so as to satisfy the conditions of the contract, or to make the world consistent with the information passed. Contracts and Information can then be thought of as normative statements that restrict an agent's behaviour.

Norms, contracts, and information have an obvious temporal dimension. Thus, an agent has to abide by a norm while it is operating within the Semantic web, a contract has a validity period, and a piece of information is true only during an interval in time. The set of norms affecting the behaviour of an agent define the *context* that the agent has to take into account.

The communication language that α needs requires two fundamental primitives: $\mathrm{Commit}(\alpha,\beta,\varphi)$ to represent, in φ, the state of affairs that α aims to bring about and that β has the right to verify, complain about or claim compensation for any deviations from, and $\mathrm{Done}(a)$ to represent the event that a certain action a[3] has taken place. In this way, norms, contracts, and information chunks will be represented as instances of $\mathrm{Commit}(\cdot)$ where α and β can be individual agents or the Semantic Web, $\mathcal{C}$ is:

$$
\begin{aligned}
a &::= illoc(\alpha,\beta,\varphi,t) \mid a; a \mid \textbf{Let}\ context\ \textbf{In}\ a\ \textbf{End}\\
\varphi &::= term \mid \mathrm{Done}(a) \mid \mathrm{Commit}(\alpha,\beta,\varphi) \mid \varphi \wedge \varphi \mid \\
&\quad\ \varphi \vee \varphi \mid \neg\varphi \mid \forall v.\varphi_v \mid \exists v.\varphi_v\\
context &::= \varphi \mid id = \varphi \mid prolog\_clause \mid context; context
\end{aligned}
$$

where φ_v is a formula with free variable v, *illoc* is any appropriate set of illocutionary particles, ';' means sequencing, and *context* represents either previous agreements, previous illocutions, or code that aligns the ontological differences between the speakers needed to interpret an action a.

For example, we can represent the following offer: "If you spend a total of more than €100 on my information service during October then I will give you a 10% discount on all of my services in November", as:

$$
\begin{aligned}
&\mathrm{Offer}(\alpha,\beta,\mathtt{spent}(\beta,\alpha,\mathtt{October},X) \wedge X \geq €100 \rightarrow\\
&\quad \forall y.\ \mathrm{Done}(\mathrm{Inform}(\xi,\alpha,\mathrm{pay}(\beta,\alpha,y),\mathrm{November})) \rightarrow\\
&\qquad \mathrm{Commit}(\alpha,\beta,\mathrm{discount}(y,10\%)))
\end{aligned}
$$

Note the use of the institution agent ξ to report the payment.

2.1 The Ontological Context

In order to define the language introduced above that structures agent dialogues we need an ontology that includes a (minimum) repertoire of elements: a set of *concepts* (e.g. quantity, quality, material) organised in a is-a hierarchy (e.g. platypus is a mammal, australian-dollar is a currency), and a set of relations over these concepts (e.g. price(beer,AUD)).[4] We model ontologies following an algebraic approach [10] as:

An ontology is a tuple $\mathcal{O} = (C, R, \leq, \sigma)$ where:

[3] Without loss of generality we will assume that all actions are dialogical.

[4] Usually, a set of axioms defined over the concepts and relations is also required. We will omit this here.

1. C is a finite set of concept symbols (including basic data types);
2. R is a finite set of relation symbols;
3. $\leq$ is a reflexive, transitive and anti-symmetric relation on C (a partial order)
4. $\sigma : R \to C^+$ is the function assigning to each relation symbol its arity

where $\leq$ is a traditional *is-a* hierarchy, and R contains relations between the concepts in the hierarchy.

The concepts within an agent's ontology are closer, semantically speaking, depending on how far away are they in the structure defined by the $\leq$ relation. Semantic distance plays a fundamental role in strategies for information-based agency. How signed contracts, *Commit*$(\cdot)$ about objects in a particular semantic region, and their execution *Done*$(\cdot)$, *affect* our decision making process about signing future contracts on nearby semantic regions is crucial to model the common sense that human beings apply in managing business relationships. A measure [11] bases the *semantic similarity* between two concepts on the path length induced by $\leq$ (more distance in the $\leq$ graph means less semantic similarity), and the *depth* of the subsumer concept (common ancestor) in the shortest path between the two concepts (the deeper in the hierarchy, the closer the meaning of the concepts). For agent α semantic similarity could then be defined as:

$$\mathrm{Sim}(c, c', \mathcal{O}_\alpha) = e^{-\kappa_1 l} \cdot \frac{e^{\kappa_2 h} - e^{-\kappa_2 h}}{e^{\kappa_2 h} + e^{-\kappa_2 h}}$$

where l is the length (i.e. number of hops) of the shortest path between the concepts in $\mathcal{O}_\alpha$, h is the depth of the deepest concept subsuming both concepts, and κ_1 and κ_2 are parameters scaling the contribution of shortest path length and depth respectively.

Given a formula $\varphi \in \mathcal{C}$ in the communication language and an ontology $\mathcal{O}_\alpha$ we define the vocabulary or *ontological context* of the formula, $C(\varphi, \mathcal{O}_\alpha)$, as the set of concepts in $\mathcal{O}_\alpha$ used in φ. Thus, we extend the previous definition of similarity to sets of concepts in the following way:

$$\mathrm{Sim}(\varphi, \psi, \mathcal{O}_\alpha) = \max_{c_i \in C(\varphi, \mathcal{O}_\alpha)} \min_{c_j \in C(\psi, \mathcal{O}_\alpha)} \{\mathrm{Sim}(c_i, c_j, \mathcal{O}_\alpha)\}$$

The following relies on *a* measure of semantic distance but not necessarily this one.

3 Agent Architecture

The vision here is intelligent agents managing each service across the Semantic Web. An agent α receives all messages expressed in $\mathcal{C}$ in an in-box $\mathcal{X}$ where they are time-stamped and sourced-stamped. A message μ from agent β (or θ or ξ), expressed in the sender's ontology, is then moved from $\mathcal{X}$ to a *percept repository* $\mathcal{Y}^t$ where it is appended with a subjective belief function $\mathbb{R}^t(\alpha, \beta, \mu)$ that normally decays with time. α acts in response to a message that expresses a *need*. A need may be exogenous such as a need for information and may be triggered by another agent offering to supply it, or endogenous such as α deciding that it wishes to offer its information or services across the Web. Needs trigger α's goal/plan proactive reasoning described in Section 3.1, other messages are dealt with by α's reactive reasoning described in Section 3.2.

Fig. 1. The *information-based* agent architecture in summary — the notation has been simplified from the complete version in the text.

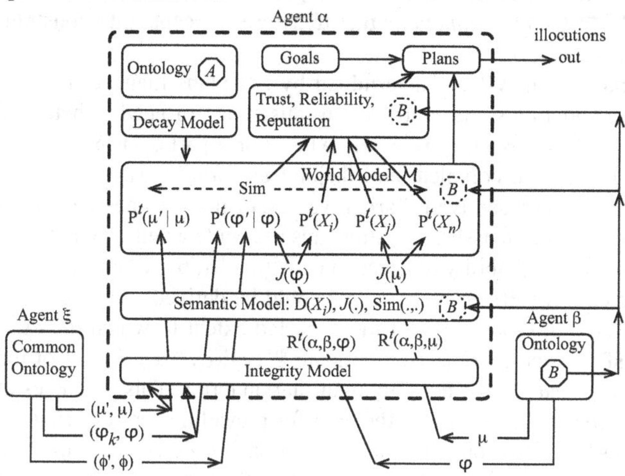

Figure 1 shows the agent architecture of agent α using ontology A in summary using notation that has been simplified from the version in the text. All communication is in the illocutionary communication language $\mathcal{C}$ — Section 2 — in the context of an ontology that is the foundation for the Semantic Model and the Sim similarity measure — Section 2.1. Agent β sends information μ to agent α in the context of ontology B, the integrity model adds a belief to it and the semantic model converts it to a set of constraints $\{J_s^{X_i}(\cdot)\}_{i\in T(s)}$ on the set of distributions $\{X_i\}_{i\in T(s)}$ in the world model — Section 3.2 — determined by each active plan s. Agent β makes commitment φ to agent α — agent α's expectation of what will occur is the distribution $\mathbb{P}^t(\varphi'|\varphi)$ — Section 3.4. The institution agent ξ reports on what occurs — (μ', μ) and (φ_k, φ) — that feeds into the Integrity Model — Section 3.3. Given β's commitment φ, the outcome, (φ_k, φ) updates α's expectation $\mathbb{P}^{t+1}(\varphi'|\varphi)$ using the method in Section 3.4 — likewise all of ξ's reports update other distributions in a way that is moderated by semantic distance as denoted by the double arrow labelled "Sim" that is derived from the ontology B. The decay model is described in Section 3.1. General measures of trust, reliability and reputation, that are so important on the Semantic Web, are given in Section 4 and summarise the World Model $\mathcal{M}^t$. α uses these summary measures and the world model to feed into its plans as described below.

3.1 Information Integrity

The Semantic Web provides a context of changing uncertainty and so α's goal/plan machinery typically will pursue multiple sub-goals concurrently. This applies both to securing agreements with service providers, and to interaction with public information sources that either may be unreliable or may take an unpredictable time to respond.

Each plan contains constructors for a *world model* $\mathcal{M}^t$ that consists of probability distributions, (X_i), in first-order probabilistic logic $\mathcal{L}$. $\mathcal{M}^t$ is then maintained from percepts received using *update functions* that transform percepts into constraints on $\mathcal{M}^t$ — described in Section 3.2.

The distributions in $\mathcal{M}^t$ are determined by α's plans that are determined by its needs. If α is negotiating some contract δ in satisfaction of need χ then it may require the distribution $\mathbb{P}^t(\text{eval}(\alpha, \beta, \chi, \delta) = e_i)$ where for a particular δ, $\text{eval}(\alpha, \beta, \chi, \delta)$ is an evaluation over some complete and disjoint *evaluation space* $E = (e_1, \ldots, e_n)$ that may contain hard (possibly utilitarian) values, or fuzzy values such as "reject" and "accept". This distribution assists α's strategies to decide whether to accept a proposed contract leading to a probability of acceptance $\mathbb{P}^t(\text{acc}(\alpha, \beta, \chi, \delta))$.

For example, $\mathbb{P}^t(\text{eval}(\alpha, \beta, \chi, \delta) = e_i)$ could be derived from the subjective estimate $\mathbb{P}^t(\text{satisfy}(\alpha, \beta, \chi, \delta) = f_j)$ of the expected extent to which the *execution* of δ by β will satisfy χ, and an objective estimate $\mathbb{P}^t(\text{val}(\alpha, \beta, \delta) = g_k)$ of the expected valuation of the *execution* of δ possibly in utilitarian terms. This second estimate could be derived by proactive reference to the $\{\theta_i\}$ for prevailing service pricing. In a negotiation α's plans may also construct the distribution $\mathbb{P}^t(\text{acc}(\beta, \alpha, \delta))$ that estimates the probability that β would accept δ — we show in Section 3.2 how α may derive this estimate from the information in β's proposals.

α's plans may construct various other distributions such as: $\mathbb{P}^t(\text{trade}(\alpha, \beta, o) = e_i)$ that β is a good agent to sign contracts with in context o, and $\mathbb{P}^t(\text{confide}(\alpha, \beta, o) = f_j)$ that α can trust β with confidential information the context o that consists of the interaction history and β's ontology $\mathcal{O}_\beta$.

The integrity of percepts decreases in time. α may have background knowledge concerning the expected integrity of a percept as $t \to \infty$. Such background knowledge will be expressed in terms of α's ontology $\mathcal{O}_\alpha$, and is represented as a *decay limit distribution*. If the background knowledge is incomplete then one possibility is for α to assume that the decay limit distribution has maximum entropy whilst being consistent with the data. Given a distribution, $\mathbb{P}(X_i)$, and a decay limit distribution $\mathbb{D}(X_i)$, $\mathbb{P}(X_i)$ decays by:

$$\mathbb{P}^{t+1}(X_i) = \Delta_i(\mathbb{D}(X_i), \mathbb{P}^t(X_i)) \tag{1}$$

where Δ_i is the *decay function* for the X_i satisfying the property that $\lim_{t\to\infty} \mathbb{P}^t(X_i) = \mathbb{D}(X_i)$. For example, Δ_i could be linear: $\mathbb{P}^{t+1}(X_i) = (1-\nu_i) \times \mathbb{D}(X_i) + \nu_i \times \mathbb{P}^t(X_i)$, where $\nu_i < 1$ is the decay rate for the i'th distribution. Either the decay function or the decay limit distribution could also be a function of time: Δ_i^t and $\mathbb{D}^t(X_i)$.

3.2 New Information

In the absence of in-coming messages the integrity of $\mathcal{M}^t$ decays by Eqn. 1. The following procedure updates $\mathcal{M}^t$ for all percepts expressed in $\mathcal{C}$. Suppose that α receives a message μ from agent β in terms of ontology $\mathcal{O}_\beta$ at time t. Suppose that this message states that something is so with probability z, and suppose that α attaches an epistemic belief $\mathbb{R}^t(\alpha, \beta, \mu)$ to μ — this probability reflects α's level of personal *caution*. Each of α's active plans, s, contains constructors for a set of distributions $\{X_i\} \in \mathcal{M}^t$ together with associated *update functions*, $J_s(\cdot)$, such that $J_s^{X_i}(\mu)$ is a set of linear constraints on the posterior distribution for X_i. Examples of these update functions are given in Section 3.4. Denote the prior distribution $\mathbb{P}^t(X_i)$ by $\boldsymbol{p}$, and let $\boldsymbol{p}_{(\mu)}$ be the distribution with minimum relative entropy[5] with respect to $\boldsymbol{p}$: $\boldsymbol{p}_{(\mu)} = \arg\min_{\boldsymbol{r}} \sum_j r_j \log \frac{r_j}{p_j}$ that satisfies the constraints $J_s^{X_i}(\mu)$. Then let $\boldsymbol{q}_{(\mu)}$ be the distribution:

$$\boldsymbol{q}_{(\mu)} = \mathbb{R}^t(\alpha, \beta, \mu) \times \boldsymbol{p}_{(\mu)} + (1 - \mathbb{R}^t(\alpha, \beta, \mu)) \times \boldsymbol{p} \tag{2}$$

and then let:

$$\mathbb{P}^t(X_{i(\mu)}) = \begin{cases} \boldsymbol{q}_{(\mu)} & \text{if } \boldsymbol{q}_{(\mu)} \text{ is more interesting than } \boldsymbol{p} \\ \boldsymbol{p} & \text{otherwise} \end{cases} \tag{3}$$

A general measure of whether $\boldsymbol{q}_{(\mu)}$ is more interesting than $\boldsymbol{p}$ is: $\mathbb{K}(\boldsymbol{q}_{(\mu)} \| \mathbb{D}(X_i)) > \mathbb{K}(\boldsymbol{p} \| \mathbb{D}(X_i))$, where $\mathbb{K}(\boldsymbol{x} \| \boldsymbol{y}) = \sum_j x_j \ln \frac{x_j}{y_j}$ is the Kullback-Leibler distance between two probability distributions $\boldsymbol{x}$ and $\boldsymbol{y}$.

Finally merging Eqn. 3 and Eqn. 1 we obtain the method for updating a distribution X_i on receipt of a message μ:

$$\mathbb{P}^{t+1}(X_i) = \Delta_i(\mathbb{D}(X_i), \mathbb{P}^t(X_{i(\mu)})) \tag{4}$$

This procedure deals with integrity decay, and with two probabilities: first, the probability z in the percept μ, and second the belief $\mathbb{R}^t(\alpha, \beta, \mu)$ that α attached to μ.

In a simple multi-issue contract negotiation α may estimate $\mathbb{P}^t(\text{acc}(\beta, \alpha, \delta))$, the probability that β would accept δ, by observing β's responses. Using shorthand notation, if β sends the message $\text{Offer}(\delta_1)$ then α may derive the constraint:

$$J^{\text{acc}(\beta,\alpha,\delta)}(\text{Offer}(\delta_1)) = \{\mathbb{P}^t(\text{acc}(\beta, \alpha, \delta_1)) = 1\},$$

and if this is a counter offer to a former offer of α's, δ_0, then: $J^{\text{acc}(\beta,\alpha,\delta)}(\text{Offer}(\delta_1)) = \{\mathbb{P}^t(\text{acc}(\beta, \alpha, \delta_0)) = 0\}$. In the not-atypical special case of multi-issue contracting where the agents' preferences over the individual issues *only* are known and are complementary to each other's, maximum entropy reasoning can be applied to estimate the probability that any multi-issue δ will be acceptable to β by enumerating the possible worlds that represent β's "limit of acceptability" [14].

3.3 Reliability of an Information Source

$\mathbb{R}^t(\alpha, \beta, \mu)$ is an epistemic probability that represents α's belief in the validity of μ taking account of α's personal caution concerning β. An empirical estimate of $\mathbb{R}^t(\alpha, \beta, \mu)$

[5] Given a probability distribution $\boldsymbol{q}$, the *minimum relative entropy distribution* $\boldsymbol{p} = (p_1, \ldots, p_I)$ subject to a set of J linear constraints $\boldsymbol{g} = \{g_j(\boldsymbol{p}) = \boldsymbol{a}_j \cdot \boldsymbol{p} - c_j = 0\}, j = 1, \ldots, J$ (that must include the constraint $\sum_i p_i - 1 = 0$) is: $\boldsymbol{p} = \arg\min_{\boldsymbol{r}} \sum_j r_j \log \frac{r_j}{q_j}$. This may be calculated by introducing Lagrange multipliers $\boldsymbol{\lambda}$: $L(\boldsymbol{p}, \boldsymbol{\lambda}) = \sum_j p_j \log \frac{p_j}{q_j} + \boldsymbol{\lambda} \cdot \boldsymbol{g}$. Minimising L, $\{\frac{\partial L}{\partial \lambda_j} = g_j(\boldsymbol{p}) = 0\}, j = 1, \ldots, J$ is the set of given constraints $\boldsymbol{g}$, and a solution to $\frac{\partial L}{\partial p_i} = 0, i = 1, \ldots, I$ leads eventually to $\boldsymbol{p}$. Entropy-based inference is a form of Bayesian inference that is convenient when the data is sparse [12] and encapsulates common-sense reasoning [13].

may be obtained by measuring the 'difference' between commitment and enactment. Suppose that μ is received from agent β at time u and is verified by ξ as μ' at some later time t. Denote the prior $\mathbb{P}^u(X_i)$ by $\boldsymbol{p}$. Let $\boldsymbol{p}_{(\mu)}$ be the posterior minimum relative entropy distribution subject to the constraints $J_s^{X_i}(\mu)$, and let $\boldsymbol{p}_{(\mu')}$ be that distribution subject to $J_s^{X_i}(\mu')$. We now estimate what $\mathbb{R}^u(\alpha, \beta, \mu)$ should have been in the light of knowing *now*, at time t, that μ should have been μ'.

The idea of Eqn. 2, is that $\mathbb{R}^t(\alpha, \beta, \mu)$ should be such that, *on average* across $\mathcal{M}^t$, $\boldsymbol{q}_{(\mu)}$ will predict $\boldsymbol{p}_{(\mu')}$ — no matter whether or not μ was used to update the distribution for X_i, as determined by the condition in Eqn. 3 at time u. The *observed reliability* for μ and distribution X_i, $\mathbb{R}^t_{X_i}(\alpha, \beta, \mu)|\mu'$, on the basis of the verification of μ with μ', is the value of k that minimises the Kullback-Leibler distance:

$$\mathbb{R}^t_{X_i}(\alpha, \beta, \mu)|\mu' = \arg\min_k \mathbb{K}(k \cdot \boldsymbol{p}_{(\mu)} + (1-k) \cdot \boldsymbol{p} \parallel \boldsymbol{p}_{(\mu')})$$

The predicted *information* in the enactment of μ with respect to X_i is:

$$\mathbb{I}^t_{X_i}(\alpha, \beta, \mu) = \mathbb{H}^t(X_i) - \mathbb{H}^t(X_{i(\mu)}) \tag{5}$$

that is the reduction in uncertainty in X_i where $\mathbb{H}(\cdot)$ is Shannon entropy. Eqn. 5 takes account of the value of $\mathbb{R}^t(\alpha, \beta, \mu)$.

If $\mathbf{X}(\mu)$ is the set of distributions that μ affects, then the *observed reliability* of β on the basis of the verification of μ with μ' is:

$$\mathbb{R}^t(\alpha, \beta, \mu)|\mu' = \frac{1}{|\mathbf{X}(\mu)|} \sum_i \mathbb{R}^t_{X_i}(\alpha, \beta, \mu)|\mu' \tag{6}$$

If $\mathbf{X}(\mu)$ are independent the predicted *information* in μ is:

$$\mathbb{I}^t(\alpha, \beta, \mu) = \sum_{X_i \in \mathbf{X}(\mu)} \mathbb{I}^t_{X_i}(\alpha, \beta, \mu) \tag{7}$$

Suppose α sends message μ to β where μ is α's private information, then assuming that β's reasoning apparatus, but *not* β's ontology, mirrors α's, α can estimate $\mathbb{I}^t(\beta, \alpha, \mu)$.

For each formula φ at time t when μ has been verified with μ', the *observed reliability* that α has for agent β in φ is:

$$\mathbb{R}^{t+1}(\alpha, \beta, \varphi) = (1-\nu) \times \mathbb{R}^t(\alpha, \beta, \varphi) + \nu \times \mathbb{R}^t(\alpha, \beta, \mu)|\mu' \times \text{Sim}(\varphi, \mu, \mathcal{O}_\beta)$$

where Sim measures the semantic distance between two sections of the ontology $\mathcal{O}_\beta$ as introduced in Section 2, and ν is the learning rate. Over time, α notes the context of the various μ received from β, and over the various contexts calculates the relative frequency, $\mathbb{P}^t(\mu)$. This leads to an overall expectation of the *reliability* that agent α has for agent β: $\mathbb{R}^t(\alpha, \beta) = \sum_\mu \mathbb{P}^t(\mu) \times \mathbb{R}^t(\alpha, \beta, \mu)$.

3.4 Expectation and Execution

The interaction between agents α and β will involve β making contractual commitments and (perhaps implicitly) committing to the truth of information exchanged. No matter what these commitments are, α will be interested in any variation between β's commitment, φ, and what is actually observed (as advised by the institution agent ξ), as the enactment, φ'. We denote the relationship between commitment and enactment, $\mathbb{P}^t(\text{Observe}(\varphi')|\text{Commit}(\varphi))$ simply as $\mathbb{P}^t(\varphi'|\varphi) \in \mathcal{M}^t$.

In the absence of in-coming messages the conditional probabilities, $\mathbb{P}^t(\varphi'|\varphi)$, should tend to ignorance as represented by the *decay limit distribution* and Eqn. 1. Eqn. 4 is used to revise $\mathbb{P}^t(\varphi'|\varphi)$ as observations are made. Let the set of possible enactments be $\Phi = \{\varphi_1, \varphi_2, \ldots, \varphi_m\}$ with prior distribution $\boldsymbol{p} = \mathbb{P}^t(\varphi'|\varphi)$. Suppose that message μ is received, we estimate the posterior $\boldsymbol{p}_{(\mu)} = (p_{(\mu)i})_{i=1}^m = \mathbb{P}^{t+1}(\varphi'|\varphi)$.

First, if $\mu = (\varphi_k, \varphi)$ is observed then α may use this observation to estimate $p_{(\varphi_k)k}$ as some value d at time $t+1$. We estimate the distribution $\boldsymbol{p}_{(\varphi_k)}$ by applying the principle of minimum relative entropy as in Eqn. 4 with prior $\boldsymbol{p}$, and the posterior $\boldsymbol{p}_{(\varphi_k)} = (p_{(\varphi_k)j})_{j=1}^m$ satisfying the single constraint: $J^{(\varphi'|\varphi)}(\varphi_k) = \{p_{(\varphi_k)k} = d\}$.

Second, we consider the effect that the enactment ϕ' of another commitment ϕ, also by agent β, has on $\boldsymbol{p}$. This is achieved in two ways, first by appealing to the structure of the ontology using the $\text{Sim}(\cdot)$ function, and second by introducing a valuation function.

The $\text{Sim}(\cdot)$ *method.* Given the observation $\mu = (\phi', \phi)$, define the vector $\boldsymbol{t}$ by

$$t_i = \mathbb{P}^t(\varphi_i|\varphi) + (1 - \mid \text{Sim}(\phi', \phi, \mathcal{O}_\beta) - \text{Sim}(\varphi_i, \varphi, \mathcal{O}_\beta) \mid) \cdot \text{Sim}(\varphi', \phi, \mathcal{O}_\beta)$$

for $i = 1, \ldots, m$. $\boldsymbol{t}$ is not a probability distribution. The factor $\text{Sim}(\varphi', \phi, \mathcal{O}_\beta)$ limits the variation of probability to those formulae whose ontological context is not too far away from the observation. The posterior $\boldsymbol{p}_{(\phi',\phi)}$ is defined to be the normalisation of $\boldsymbol{t}$.

The valuation method. α may wish to value φ in some sense. This value will depend on the future use that α makes of it. So α estimates the value of φ using a probability distribution $(p_1, \ldots, p_n)$ over some *evaluation space* $E = (e_1, \ldots, e_n)$. $p_i = w_i(\varphi)$ is the probability that e_i is the correct evaluation of the enactment φ, and $\boldsymbol{w} : \mathcal{L} \times \mathcal{L} \rightarrow [0, 1]^n$ is the *evaluation function*.

For a given φ_k, $(\mathbb{P}^t(\varphi_1|\varphi_k), \ldots, \mathbb{P}^t(\varphi_m|\varphi_k))$ is the prior distribution of α's estimate of what will be observed if β committed to φ_k. $\boldsymbol{w}(\varphi_k) = (w_1(\varphi_k), \ldots, w_n(\varphi_k))$ is α's evaluation over E of β's commitment φ_k. α's expected evaluation of what will be observed that β has committed to φ_k is $\boldsymbol{w}^{\text{exp}}(\varphi_k)$: $w^{\text{exp}}(\varphi_k)_i = \sum_{j=1}^m \mathbb{P}^t(\varphi_j|\varphi_k) \cdot w_i(\varphi_j)$ for $i = 1, \ldots, n$. Now suppose that α observes the enactment ϕ' of another commitment ϕ also by agent β. Eg: α may acquire information about both the weather and the stock market from the same supplier. α may wish to revise the prior estimate of the expected valuation $\boldsymbol{w}^{\text{exp}}(\varphi_k)$ in the light of the observation (ϕ', ϕ) to:

$$\begin{aligned}&(\boldsymbol{w}^{\text{rev}}(\varphi_k) \mid (\phi'|\phi)) = \\ &\quad \boldsymbol{g}(\boldsymbol{w}^{\text{exp}}(\varphi_k), \text{Sim}(\phi', \phi, \mathcal{O}_\beta), \text{Sim}(\varphi, \phi, \mathcal{O}_\beta), \boldsymbol{w}(\varphi), \boldsymbol{w}(\phi), \boldsymbol{w}(\phi'))\end{aligned}$$

for some function $\boldsymbol{g}$ — the idea being, for example, that if the commitment, ϕ, to supply accurate weather information was not kept by β then α's expectation that the commitment, φ, to supply accurate stock market information should decrease. We estimate the posterior $p_{(\phi',\phi)}$ by applying the principle of minimum relative entropy as in Eqn. 4 with prior p and $p_{(\phi',\phi)} = (p_{(\phi',\phi)j})_{j=1}^{m}$ satisfying the n constraints:

$$J^{(\varphi'|\varphi)}((\phi',\phi)) = \Big\{\sum_{j=1}^{m} p_{(\phi',\phi)j} \cdot w_i(\varphi_j) = \\ g_i(w^{\exp}(\varphi_k), \text{Sim}(\phi',\phi,\mathcal{O}_\beta), \text{Sim}(\varphi,\phi,\mathcal{O}_\beta), w(\varphi), w(\phi), w(\phi'))\Big\}_{i=1}^{n}$$

This is a set of n linear equations in m unknowns, and so the calculation of the minimum relative entropy distribution may be impossible if $n > m$. In this case, we take only the m equations for which the change from the prior to the posterior value is greatest.

4 Trust, Reliability and Reputation

The measures here generalise what are commonly called *trust*, *reliability* and *reputation* measures into a single computational framework that may be applied to information, information sources and information suppliers across the Semantic Web. It they are applied to the execution of contracts they become trust measures, to the validation of information they become reliability measures, and to socially transmitted overall behaviour they become reputation measures.

Ideal enactments. Consider a distribution of enactments that represent α's "ideal" in the sense that it is the best that α could reasonably expect to happen. This distribution will be a function of α's *context* with β denoted by e, and is $\mathbb{P}^t_I(\varphi'|\varphi, e)$. Here we measure the relative entropy between this ideal distribution, $\mathbb{P}^t_I(\varphi'|\varphi, e)$, and the distribution of expected enactments, $\mathbb{P}^t(\varphi'|\varphi)$. That is:

$$M(\alpha,\beta,\varphi) = 1 - \sum_{\varphi'} \mathbb{P}^t_I(\varphi'|\varphi,e) \log \frac{\mathbb{P}^t_I(\varphi'|\varphi,e)}{\mathbb{P}^t(\varphi'|\varphi)} \tag{8}$$

where the "1" is an arbitrarily chosen constant being the maximum value that this measure may have. This equation measures one, single commitment φ. It makes sense to aggregate these values over a class of commitments, say over those φ that are in the context o, that is $\varphi \leq o$:

$$M(\alpha,\beta,o) = 1 - \frac{\sum_{\varphi:\varphi\leq o} \mathbb{P}^t_\beta(\varphi)\,[1 - M(\alpha,\beta,\varphi)]}{\sum_{\varphi:\varphi\leq o} \mathbb{P}^t_\beta(\varphi)}$$

where $\mathbb{P}^t_\beta(\varphi)$ is a probability distribution over the space of commitments that the next commitment β will make to α is φ. Similarly, for an overall estimate of β's *reputation* to α: $M(\alpha,\beta) = 1 - \sum_\varphi \mathbb{P}^t_\beta(\varphi)\,[1 - M(\alpha,\beta,\varphi)]$.

Preferred enactments. The previous measure, 'Ideal enactments', requires that an ideal distribution, $\mathbb{P}^t_I(\varphi'|\varphi, e)$, has to be specified for each φ. Here we measure the extent to which the enactment φ' is preferable to the commitment φ. Given a predicate

$\text{Prefer}(c_1, c_2, e)$ meaning that α prefers c_1 to c_2 in environment e. An evaluation of $\mathbb{P}^t(\text{Prefer}(c_1, c_2, e))$ may be defined using $\text{Sim}(\cdot)$ and the evaluation function $w(\cdot)$ — but we do not detail it here. Then if $\varphi \leq o$:

$$M(\alpha, \beta, \varphi) = \sum_{\varphi'} \mathbb{P}^t(\text{Prefer}(\varphi', \varphi, o))\mathbb{P}^t(\varphi' \mid \varphi)$$

$$M(\alpha, \beta, o) = \frac{\sum_{\varphi:\varphi \leq o} \mathbb{P}^t_\beta(\varphi) M(\alpha, \beta, \varphi)}{\sum_{\varphi:\varphi \leq o} \mathbb{P}^t_\beta(\varphi)}$$

Certainty in enactment. Here we measure the consistency in expected acceptable enactment of commitments, or "the lack of expected uncertainty in those possible enactments that are preferred to the commitment as specified". If $\varphi \leq o$ let: $\Phi_+(\varphi, o, \kappa) = \{\varphi' \mid \mathbb{P}^t(\text{Prefer}(\varphi', \varphi, o)) > \kappa\}$ for some constant κ, and:

$$M(\alpha, \beta, \varphi) = 1 + \frac{1}{B^*} \cdot \sum_{\varphi' \in \Phi_+(\varphi, o, \kappa)} \mathbb{P}^t_+(\varphi' | \varphi) \log \mathbb{P}^t_+(\varphi' | \varphi)$$

where $\mathbb{P}^t_+(\varphi' | \varphi)$ is the normalisation of $\mathbb{P}^t(\varphi' | \varphi)$ for $\varphi' \in \Phi_+(\varphi, o, \kappa)$,

$$B^* = \begin{cases} 1 & \text{if } |\Phi_+(\varphi, o, \kappa)| = 1 \\ \log |\Phi_+(\varphi, o, \kappa)| & \text{otherwise} \end{cases}$$

5 Semantic Alignment

Information-based agents treat *everything* in the Semantic Web as uncertain — including the meaning of terms expressed in other agents' ontologies. They model their uncertain beliefs using random variables and probability distributions that are in a constant state of decay (as described in Section 3.1) and incorporate incoming information using entropy-based inference (as described in Section 3.3).

This discussion is from the point of view of agent α with ontology A who receives an illocution from agent β containing a term c expressed in β's ontology B. We assume that there is a term in A that corresponds precisely to $c \in B$.[6] Let $\Psi_{AB}(c)$ denote the term in ontology A that corresponds to $c \in B$, and let $F_{AB}(c)$ be a random variable over a subset of A representing α's beliefs about the meaning of c. $F_{AB}(c)$ may be defined at some level of abstraction determined by the $\leq$ relation — ie: not necessarily at the lowest level on the *is-a* hierarchy. In the absence of any information, the probability distribution for $F_{AB}(c)$ will be a maximum entropy distribution. We now consider how α can increase the certainty in $F_{AB}(c)$.

Suppose that α has signed a contract with β and that β's commitment b is described as having property $d \in B$. When β enacts that commitment, as b', it may not necessarily be as promised, and, as described in Section 2, ξ will advise α accurately of b'

[6] This assumption can be avoided by simply adding another layer to the analysis and constructing a probability distribution for c across the space $\{$may be represented in A, may not be represented in $A\}$ — we ignore this complication.

in terms of A, d'. So α will have the evidence that α promised $d \in B$ and delivered $d' \in A$. This evidence can be used to reduce the uncertainty of $F_{AB}(c)$ using one of the methods described in Section 3.4. Another means of reducing the entropy $\mathbb{H}(F_{AB}(c))$ is through dialogue with β, or any other agent, who may communicate information about the meaning of d. α will temper any such advice in line with the estimated trustworthiness of the agent as described in Section 4, and with an estimate of the agent's reliability in this context as described in Section 3.3, and will then permit the qualified advice to update $F_{AB}(c)$ as long as the condition in Equation 3 is satisfied. We have described how α reduces $\mathbb{H}(F_{AB}(c))$ following the receipt of messages — we now discuss proactive action that α may take to achieve this goal.

A simple example of proactive behaviour is to ask questions that require a "yes/no" response. This leads to the issues of which question to ask, and to whom should the question be directed? A simple, but powerful, strategy is to construct the question whose answer will yield maximum reduction in entropy — ie: maximum information gain. These estimates are made in reference to the $J_s^{X_i}$("yes/no") update functions that determine the affect that each illocution has on the set of distributions that make up the world model. The update functions $J_s^{F_{AB}(c)}(\cdot)$ have to do two separate jobs: (i) they translate a message expressed in B into an expectation in terms of α's ontology A, then (ii) using this expectation they induce constraints on α's world model derived from that expectation. The update functions are the only means of updating the world model, and so they enable us to identify information that has the capacity to reduce the entropy to an acceptable level.

6 Interaction Models

From an agent perspective, the co-ordination of services is naturally seen as a complex process management problem — an area where agent technology has proved itself. We do not consider mobile agents due to security concerns — in any case, the value of mobility in process management is questionable as the agents are typically large. A conventional multiagent system that tracks both the process constraints (generally time and cost) and the process ownership[7] is eminently suitable. Constraints are essential to managing processes that are co-ordinating the quality of service delivery — where sub-processes have, and maintain, a budget that is passed from agent to agent with the process. The processes involved in the co-ordination of services will be unpredictable and prone to failure. This indicates that they should be formalised as *goal-driven* processes [15], that is they should be conceptualised as agent plans expressed in terms of the goals that are to be achieved. This abstraction enables *what* is to be achieved and *when* that has to happen to be considered separately from *how* it will be achieved and *who* will do the work. Here each high-level goal has at least one plan whose *body* is a state-chart of goals, and atomic goals are associated with some procedural program. To cope with plan failure at each level in this framework, each plan has three exits: success (✓), fail (✗) and abort(**A**), with appropriate associated conditions and actions. This

[7] If an agent sends a process off into a distribute multiagent system then it relinquishes immediate control over it. To maintain this control the whole system abides by an ownership convention so that the agent who initiates a process will not "loose" control of it.

means that the plans are near-failure-proof but are expensive to construct. This expense is justified by the prospect of reusing plans to manage similar processes.

Dialogical interaction takes place not simply for the purpose of clarification but to reach some sort of service level agreement or contract — that could be a contract deliver a service with particular characteristics. Given two contracts δ and δ' expressed in terms of concepts $\{o_1, \ldots, o_i\}$ and $\{o'_1, \ldots, o'_j\}$ respectively, the (non-symmetric) distance of δ' from δ is given by the vector $\boldsymbol{\Gamma}(\delta, \delta') = (d_k : o''_k)_{k=1}^{i}$ where $d_k = \min_x\{\text{Sim}(o_k, o'_x) \mid x = 1, \ldots, j\}$, $o''_k = \sup(\arg\min_x\{\text{Sim}(o_k, x) \mid x = o'_1, \ldots, o'_j\}$ $, o_k)$ and the function $\sup(\cdot, \cdot)$ is the supremum of two concepts in the ontology. $\boldsymbol{\Gamma}(\delta, \delta')$ is a simple measure of how dissimilar δ' is to δ and enables α to metricate contract space and to "work around" or "move away from" a contract under consideration. Every time an agent communicates it gives away information. So even for purely self-interested agents, interaction is a semi-cooperative process. If agent β sends α a proposed contract δ then the information gain observed by α, $\mathbb{I}(\alpha, \beta, \delta)$, is the resulting reduction in the entropy of α's world model $\mathcal{M}$. An approach to issue-tradeoffs is described in [5]. That strategy attempts to make an acceptable offer by "walking round" the iso-curve of α's previous proposal towards β's current proposal δ. We extend that idea here, and respond to δ with a proposed contract δ' that should be optimally acceptable to β whilst giving β equitable information gain: $\arg\max_{\delta'}\{\ \mathbb{P}^t(\text{acc}(\beta, \alpha, \delta')) \mid \mathbb{I}^{t-1}(\alpha, \beta, \delta) \approx \mathbb{I}^t(\beta, \alpha, \delta')\ \}$, where the predicate $\text{acc}(\cdot)$ is as described in Section 3.2. This strategy aims to be *fair* in revealing α's private information. Unlike quasi-utilitarian measures, both the measure of information gain and the $\boldsymbol{\Gamma}(\cdot, \cdot)$ measure apply to *all* illocutions.

7 Conclusion

Information-based agency meets the demands identified for agents and the Semantic Web. The agents' communication language is quite general and accommodates on each agent's ontology (Section 2.1). These agents treat everything in their world as uncertain and model this uncertainty using probability distributions. They employ minimum relative entropy inference to update their probability distributions as new information becomes available (Section 3.2) — information-based agency manages uncertainty using probability theory and Bayesian inference. These agents deal with semantic alignment, and with *all* interaction, as an uncertainty reducing exercise until the cost of further reduction of uncertainty out-weighs expected benefits (Section 5). The interaction model for the co-ordination of services capitalises on the track-record of multiagent systems in process management applications, and models service co-ordination as a time-constrained, resource-constained process management problem — the co-ordination of services is then achieved by managing these processes as goal-driven processes (Section 6). The estimation of trust, that is so important to the Semantic Web, is achieved here with a computationally grounded method that is unified with the estimation of reliability of information and the reputation of information providers. The information-based agency project is on-going — recent work [16] describes how agents can build working relationships in the information world.

Acknowledgements. Carles Sierra's research is supported by the OpenKnowledge STREP project, sponsored by the European Commission under contract number FP6-027253.

References

1. Sierra, C., Debenham, J.: Information-based agency. In: Proceedings of Twentieth International Joint Conference on Artificial Intelligence IJCAI-07, Hyderabad, India (2007) 1513–1518
2. Berners-Lee, T., Hall, W., Hendler, J.A., OHara, K., Shadbolt, N., Weitzner, D.J.: A framework for web science. Foundations and trend in Web Science **1** (2006) 1–130
3. MacKay, D.: Information Theory, Inference and Learning Algorithms. Cambridge University Press (2003)
4. Jennings, N., Faratin, P., Lomuscio, A., Parsons, S., Sierra, C., Wooldridge, M.: Automated negotiation: Prospects, methods and challenges. International Journal of Group Decision and Negotiation **10** (2001) 199–215
5. Faratin, P., Sierra, C., Jennings, N.: Using similarity criteria to make issue trade-offs in automated negotiation. Journal of Artificial Intelligence **142** (2003) 205–237
6. Rosenschein, J.S., Zlotkin, G.: Rules of Encounter. The MIT Press, Cambridge, USA (1994)
7. Kraus, S.: Negotiation and cooperation in multi-agent environments. Artificial Intelligence **94** (1997) 79–97
8. Arcos, J.L., Esteva, M., Noriega, P., Rodríguez, J.A., Sierra, C.: Environment engineering for multiagent systems. Journal on Engineering Applications of Artificial Intelligence **18** (2005)
9. Sierra, C., Debenham, J.: Trust and honour in information-based agency. In Stone, P., Weiss, G., eds.: Proceedings Fifth International Conference on Autonomous Agents and Multi Agent Systems AAMAS-2006, Hakodate, Japan, ACM Press, New York (2006) 1225 - 1232
10. Kalfoglou, Y., Schorlemmer, M.: IF-Map: An ontology-mapping method based on information-flow theory. In Spaccapietra, S., March, S., Aberer, K., eds.: Journal on Data Semantics I. Volume 2800 of Lecture Notes in Computer Science. Springer-Verlag: Heidelberg, Germany (2003) 98–127
11. Li, Y., Bandar, Z.A., McLean, D.: An approach for measuring semantic similarity between words using multiple information sources. IEEE Transactions on Knowledge and Data Engineering **15** (2003) 871 – 882
12. Cheeseman, P., Stutz, J.: On The Relationship between Bayesian and Maximum Entropy Inference. In: Bayesian Inference and Maximum Entropy Methods in Science and Engineering. American Institute of Physics, Melville, NY, USA (2004) 445 – 461
13. Paris, J.: Common sense and maximum entropy. Synthese **117** (1999) 75 – 93
14. Debenham, J.: Bargaining with information. In Jennings, N., Sierra, C., Sonenberg, L., Tambe, M., eds.: Proceedings Third International Conference on Autonomous Agents and Multi Agent Systems AAMAS-2004, ACM Press, New York (2004) 664 – 671
15. Debenham, J.: A multiagent system manages collaboration in emergent processes. In Dignum, F., Dignum, V., Koenig, S., Kraus, S., Singh, M., Wooldridge, M., eds.: Proceedings Fourth International Conference on Autonomous Agents and Multi Agent Systems AAMAS-2005, Utrecht, The Netherlands, ACM Press, New York (2005) 175 – 182
16. Sierra, C., Debenham, J.: The LOGIC Negotiation Model. In: Proceedings Sixth International Conference on Autonomous Agents and Multi Agent Systems AAMAS-2007, Honolulu, Hawai'i (2007)

Can Agents Without Concepts Think? An Investigation Using a Knowledge Based System

Nicky Moss*, Adrian Hopgood** and Martin Weller*
*The Open University, Milton Keynes, MK7 6AA, UK
**Faculty of Computing Sciences & Engineering, De Montfort University, The Gateway, Leicester, LE1 9BH, UK

n.g.moss@open.ac.uk
aah@dmu.ac.uk

Abstract

Grid-World is a working computer model which has been used to investigate the search capabilities of artificial agents that understand the world in terms of non-conceptual content. The results from this model show that the non-conceptual agent outperformed the stimulus response agent, and both were outperformed by the conceptual agent. This result provides quantitative evidence to support the theoretical argument that animals and pre-linguistic children may use non-conceptual content to understand the world. Modelling these ideas in an artificial environment provides an opportunity for a new approach to artificial intelligence.

1 Introduction

There does not seem to be a universally agreed definition of intelligence [1]. There are, however, some general characteristics that can be attributed to intelligent behaviour, and when witnessed in a particular situation a judgement can be made about whether a given agent is intelligent or not. One way of explaining thinking is to refer to concepts. Many philosophers [2] believe that only language users can have concepts, and along with this a view of the world that is objective. Others [3] argue that conceptual content has developed out of non-conceptual content, and that there must be some sort of objective understanding as a pre-cursor to developing into an agent with full conceptual capabilities.

It is the reflective nature of intentions which provides the mechanism to enable agents to think about their actions in ways that can lead to goal directed or purposeful behaviour. Intentions also form a key element in the belief, desire and intention (BDI) architecture and follow on from Bratman's [4] systematic framework for characterising mind and actions in terms of intentions. The relationship between beliefs, desires and intentions is easy for us to comprehend as it reflects the way we reason about the world in our own conscious minds. It is a perfectly reasonable, and largely practical, way to construct an artificial agent. However, human reasoning is a conscious process that is intrinsically tied into our conceptual understanding of the world. For this reason most of our practical reasoning will use conceptual content, hence the success of the BDI architecture as an AI technique.

The approach adopted here is one that is based upon the multi-disciplinary principles of Cognitive Science. The idea that there is an intentional capacity that can be explained in terms of non-conceptual content is important because it frees us from linking an intelligent understanding of the world to agents that possess language. One difficulty with the general progression of non-conceptual content is that it has been largely based on discussion in the philosophical literature. Although there is plenty of supportive evidence from experiments using infants and animals, there have been few attempts to use computers to model non-conceptual content. Grid-World provides an environment that enables the characteristics that embody non-conceptual content to be modelled and investigated using artificial agents.

2 Non-conceptual Content

Our understanding of concepts is so dominant in our view of how things are in the world, that it is very hard for adult humans to think of anything in the world that is not defined conceptually. Holding concepts is clearly a conscious thinking activity, so it is the one that we are very aware of. Conceptual content is therefore about perceptual beliefs; it is how we believe the world to be. Non-conceptual content, on the other hand, is about perceptual experience, it is how the world is presented to us. An analogy can be drawn with the difference between analogue and digital. Information in the world is basically analogue in nature. For our minds to be able to grasp and manipulate concepts it needs to abstract away from the detail, and one way to do this is to encode it digitally with a certain level of quantisation.

Non-conceptual content can be defined [5] as a mental state that represents the world but which does not require the bearer of that mental state to possess the concepts required to specify the way in which they represent the world. According to this definition, it is possible for an agent to act as if it holds a concept, when in fact it does not. For example, an agent may search a problem space as if it has the concept of planning, but upon further investigation it may be revealed that the agent did not hold this concept at all.

Agents that are intentional will use intentions to work towards their goal (mean-end reasoning), maintain their intentions unless there is good evidence not to, constrain the range of options they may consider (constrain future deliberation) and allow them to change their beliefs (reason practically) as they discover new features of their environment. The ability to hold an intentional attitude has long been attributed to concept holders. Non-conceptual content provides an explanative mechanism that allows intentions to be attributed to non-language using agents.

Affordance has been established as the term used most frequently to reflect Gibson's ecological view of sensation, first put forward by him in 1950. Affordances offer a good mechanism for capturing information about the environment, and one that is sufficiently rich to provide the basis for action according to a non-conceptual view. If affordance can provide the opportunity, then non-conceptual content provides the mechanism to turn perception into action. The most immediate source of affordance comes from the agent itself, especially the role that the agent's own body plays in perception. This role of affordance in perception may be crucial for implementing artificial agents.

Bermudez draws upon some experimental work from psychology concerning object permanence. An agent is said to hold the idea of object permanence if it believes an object exists, even when that object is not being directly perceived. The basic experimental methodology is to place objects in full view of a very young child and then remove the object from view (usually by obscuring it behind a screen). The child is then tested to see if it appreciates the fact that the object could still be there. In other words to test the child's conceptual understanding of objects, and in particular its understanding of object permanence. The general conclusion has been that object permanence only comes with mastery of the concept of objects. Bermudez argues, by the following alternative explanation, that this need not be the case. It is possible for the child to be 'aware' of the object, for example, by showing surprise when it apparently moves through a solid screen, yet the same child will not search for the object behind the screen. This seems to provide some evidence that the child has representational capability, with respect to the object, even when that object is out of view, however, the same child obviously does not have the concept of an object.

3 Grid-World

Grid-World has been built using an expert system toolkit called Flex[1] (and associated prolog compiler) which uses its own English-like knowledge specification language (KSL). Flex supports frame-based reasoning with inheritance, rule-based programming and data-driven procedures. Grid-World makes extensive use of rule-based logic and uses frames to organise data. The features of Flex make it an attractive option for investigating agents that have basic sensory and memory capabilities.

Grid-World has drawn upon some of the ideas behind Brooks' subsumption architecture [6]. Brooks' general approach is to build robots with relatively simple rules and see what sort of behaviours emerge as a result. Grid-World also uses relatively simple rules, and behaviours do emerge. This bottom up approach is also important in the principal relationship between non-conceptual and conceptual content, as it can be argued that creatures that hold concepts may have evolved from

[1] Developed and maintained by Logic Programming Associates (LPA) Ltd.

others that had simpler capabilities. However, Grid-World falls well short of Brooks' approach where real robots are used in the real world.

Three different agents are implemented in Grid-World. The first agent – called stimulus response (SR) – searches using a combination of wall following and random searching and is modelled on the principles of stimulus response conditioning. The second agent – called non-conceptual content (CC) – is given the capability to recognise and remember features of the environment it has previously learned. It is then able to use these to aid any subsequent search. These capabilities model a form of non-conceptual content that uses affordances to recognise places. The third agent – called conceptual content (CC) – also has memory and place recognition capabilities, but it can also form a plan to join the affordances together. The ability to plan is a conceptual skill. The three agents can be viewed as steps from the simplest to the most sophisticated, and in each case the capabilities of each agent build upon those of its predecessor, to ensure that this reflects development rather than diversification.

The simple aim for each of the agents in Grid-World is to find its way from home to the goal. This choice of task, within an artificial world, has been chosen because it mirrors the actions of simple animals. This idea follows the work of Campbell [7] who suggests that basic navigation skills are ones that could be explained using non-conceptual content. Picking up on Gibson's [8] ecological approach to vision, Grid-World has affordances built into the environment, and these can be used by the two more sophisticated agents in helping them to reach their goal when searching. So the overall design principle of Grid-World is one that draws upon comparison with real world agents, and this principle is reflected in both the architecture and the rules that govern the behaviour of the three types of agent.

3.1 Grid-World Environment

The name 'Grid-World' was chosen because the space occupied by the world is defined in terms of x and y co-ordinates, where each co-ordinate defines a single square within the world. For example, the co-ordinate (4,5) is a single square 4 spaces to the right (x) and 5 spaces up (y), taking the co-ordinates (1,1) as a point of reference that represents the bottom left hand corner of Grid-World. So the whole world can be seen as a grid of intersecting lines, with the spaces between the lines defining a large number of squares. Each co-ordinate contains either a blank square, or a tile representing some feature of the world as will be described below. A visual representation of Grid-World, as appears on the computer screen when the program is running, is shown in figure 1.

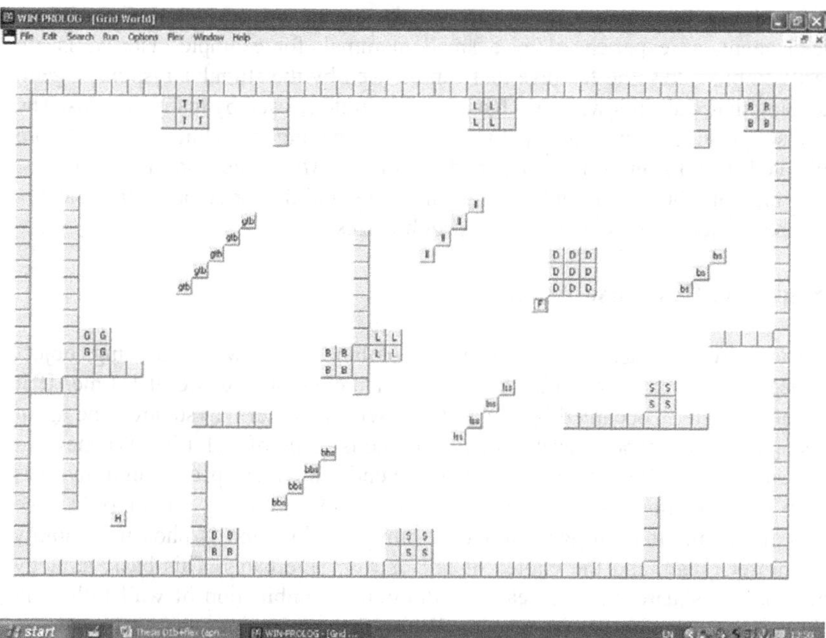

Figure 1. Screen view of Grid-World

The entire space is bounded by a continuous wall that occupies all the outer grid squares. Each square that makes up a wall contains a blank tile with no labels. In the example shown this is a boundary measuring 48 by 30, giving a large internal space of 1440 squares. Horizontal and vertical walls are added to introduce features into what would otherwise be an open space. These are also shown as blank tiles. A goal is defined as a block of one or more squares, and each one is marked with the letter D.

Other features of the landscape are also shown as blocks of tiles, each labelled with a letter. These represent various landmarks. For example, the block labelled ‘L’ is a lake, and the block labelled ‘T’ is a group of trees. The main purpose of the landmarks is to provide some visual cues, things in the environment that the agent may recognise, and for this reason the agent is able to pass through the landmarks. The blocks that have two or three lower case letters represent areas of Grid-World that lay between two or more landmarks. These are called affordances as they provide the agent with information directly about the environment. One way to think of them is as points in the landscape where one or more distant cues intersect. The tile marked with an ‘H’ is the home location and is where the agent starts its search. The position of the agent at any given point during a search is shown by a tile with the letter ‘F’. This was chosen to represent forager, and this tile moves as the agent searches the landscape.

Grid-World has been designed to provide the same sort of complexity, for an artificial agent, as experienced by a small mammal, for example. The walls are primarily to provide some features that can be used by the stimulus response agent, recognising that wall following is a basic search strategy used by many animals. The walls also provide some variety to the space, making searching a little more complicated for all agents. The cues, and associated affordances, are intended to be used by the non-conceptual and conceptual agents and mirror some of the features used in experiments where mice or rats search mazes.

3.2 Stimulus Response Agent

The basic search characteristics used are a combination of wall following, object avoidance and searching open space. An agent moves one square at a time. If it finds that a square is occupied by a wall tile it will not enter that square. The agent will recognise a wall whenever it finds a continuous string of wall tiles. Whenever it finds a wall it will follow it until it reaches the end. The open space search involves going in one direction for a number of squares, before turning left or right. The number of squares that an agent moves in any one direction is chosen randomly from a preset range, and the choice of left or right alternates. This basic strategy ensures that all squares can be searched through a combination of wall following and the random searching of open space. With this basic strategy the goal is always found. The more sophisticated skills needed for the agent to search intelligently are built upon these basic characteristics. All agent types will fall back to a random search when there is no better choice.

The agents location, and the location of all the Grid-World features, are stored in a range of databases. Information is read to and from these databases using actions of the format:

```
read_changes (position(X,Y,T))
```

In this example position is the name of the database, x and y are the location co-ordinates and T is the data being read.

A combination of rules and actions are then used to move the agent according to the information retrieved. For example, an action that would start an agent searching open space has the format:

```
Action random_search_left;
  do n := 0
  and random_number(12)
  and while in_open_space
  and n<random_range
    do move_left
    and n :=(n+1)
  end while .
```

The agent continues searching until it finds the goal. The program then records a range of quantitative data including the number of steps taken to move from home to the goal and a list of the affordances visited.

3.2 Non-conceptual Agent

The non-conceptual agent learns during the initial search phase which can follow the same path as the stimulus response agent. During this phase, whenever the agent finds a point of affordance, it makes an entry into a memory frame. The principle behind the memory is for the agent to record the direction of the next point of significance, either another affordance or the goal. For this purpose it makes a note of its current location and then records the net direction when it reaches the next point of significance. This memory also includes the name of the affordance at which it was initiated.

An instance of a completed frame is created whenever an affordance is found during an initial search. Each instance is given a number and records a start point (starting), an end point (ending) and the direction from start to end. The direction is simply recorded as a compass bearing that divides the area around any square into four quadrants.

In the non-conceptual search mode the agent has access to the additional information held in the frames created during the initial search. It uses this data whenever it finds an affordance. The principle behind the agent that searches using non-conceptual content is that it gains a benefit from understanding the significance of the affordances found in the initial search. This significance comes from recognising the place and knowing something about the last time it visited this place. What it knows is that setting off in a particular direction moves it towards another place it would recognise. It does not know that this may eventually lead to the goal it just recognises that it did set off in a particular direction last time, so it chooses to go this way again. The non-conceptual agent gains this benefit from reading the frames made during the initial search.

All other aspects of the search remain the same and the agent still follows walls, for example. To ensure that the agent is given no other advantage, apart from setting off in a particular direction, when it sets off in the remembered direction it still uses the same range of random numbers to move as it does when it is in open space. One way to think of the advantage that this agent has is just being ‘nudged’ in a potentially successful direction.

The consequence of the data in the memory frame is to point the agent in the general direction of the next affordance and set it off in that direction. For affordances that are near the goal, it is possible that the agent will be pushed towards the goal. There is no guarantee that any instance will point the agent towards another affordance closer to the goal. If, during the initial search, the agent happened to find an affordance that was further away from the goal, then this is the direction it records, and this is the one the non-conceptual agent will use.

3.3 Conceptual Agent

The last search phase, as used by the conceptual agent, is modelled on an agent that holds navigational concepts. Most significantly it is able to take a detached view of what it has done and plan accordingly. The difference between this search strategy and the one used by the non-conceptual agent is best understood by looking at two aspects of that search that may not be optimised. During the initial search phase the creation of memories is dependent upon the agent finding an affordance and moving from that affordance to one that takes it closer to the goal. It is possible (although unlikely) for the agent to find the goal during an initial search without finding any affordances. Any subsequent non-conceptual search would be identical to an initial search as there is no additional information to help the agent. It is more likely that the agent will not create a memory for each affordance type as it will not visit them all. It is also possible that an agent will move from one affordance to another that is further away from the goal. Neither of these will optimise the agent's chances of finding the goal.

Because the conceptual agent can take a detached view of the search space, and it is capable of planning, it can be given the optimum memory for each of the affordance types before it searches. This plan is created by having a frame for each affordance that always points the agent in the direction of the goal. The agent then uses the same search strategy as the non-conceptual agent, but one that draws on this optimal memory and not what is learned by any other search.

4 Experimental Results

There are three agents. Each one has the same basic sensory and search capabilities. The three differ in the way they represent sensations that they detect in the environment. The first agent (SR) responds in a strictly law like way to any stimulus when choosing the next step. The second agent (NCC) uses sensory information that is immediately available to it, combined with memory to assist it in making a choice about where to go next. The third agent (CC) uses sensation together with a plan to choose the next move.

4.1 Experimental Design

The difference between each agent is the way in which they represent sensory data in their environment. Therefore, there is one independent variable; the type of representation. In this design there are three levels for the independent variable that correspond directly to the implementation of the three agents. The dependent variable is the data that records the number of steps it takes the agent to move from home to goal.

The experimental hypothesis predicts the relationship between the independent and dependent variable. In this case this is the prediction that the search performance (dependent variable) will improve as the agent's search capabilities become more sophisticated (independent variable).

Statistical tests were applied to the results to determine whether observed differences in the mean were due to the experimental conditions or chance. A result was deemed significant if there was a probability of less than 5% that the result occurred by chance.

4.2 Results

The statistical data for 40 searches carried out by the stimulus response (SR), non-conceptual (NCC) and conceptual (CC) agents are shown in figure 2. In this experiment the SR agent followed 40 different paths, and each one of these paths were used as the initial search (training) for the NCC agent. The CC agent used the same pre-set memories for each search.

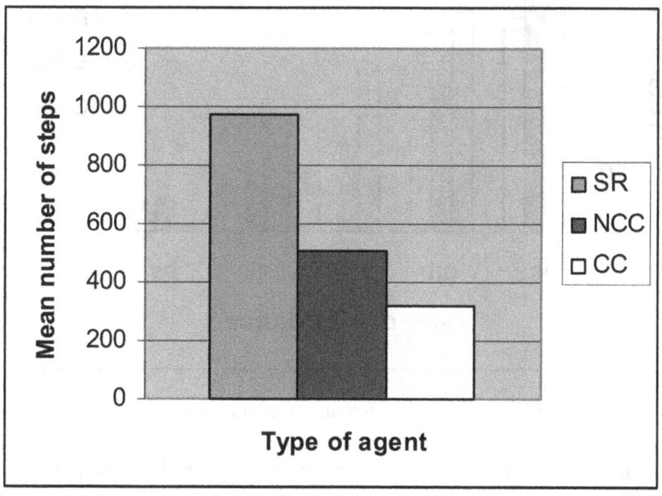

Figure 2 – 40 searches, with 3 types of agent

The mean values for the stimulus response, non-conceptual and conceptual agents are 1174, 419 and 290 respectively. These results show a significant difference in the search performance of the three agents.

By looking at the data for individual searches, aided by information on the distribution of step counts, it can be seen that all three agents manage to find the goal in fewer than 100 steps in at least one search. This represents a very good search performance, as the minimum path length is 40 steps. At the other end of the spectrum it can be seen that the stimulus response agent takes the longest single search time of more than 5000 steps. The fact that the stimulus response agent reaches both extremes is not surprising as any basically random search method is likely, over enough runs, to find the extremes. The overall distribution of searches shows more clearly that the non-conceptual and conceptual agent are able to find the goal in fewer steps on many more occasions. This is particularly true for the conceptual agent which only once took more than a 1000 steps out of 80 searches.

While the results show that there is a clear difference between the search times for each of the three agents, the range of search times varies considerably for the stimulus response and non-conceptual agents. Other data also shows that the number of frames generated by the stimulus response agent also varies across a wide range. Figure 3 shows the total number of times that each affordance was used, for each of the three agents, during another set of 20 searches.

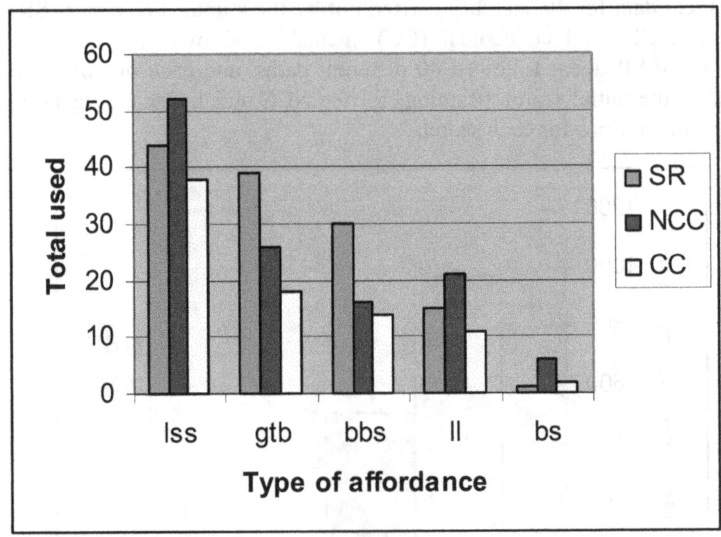

Figure 3 – How often an affordance is used

As can be seen in figure 1, the affordances are located in the 'open space' areas of Grid-World. These locations were chosen to make sure that the agent would have to find the affordances, and not be led directly to them by following the wall, or stepping directly into one when it left the end of a wall. The largest affordance (gtb) occupies five tiles, and the smallest (bs) three. These sizes were chosen because these were respectively placed in larger and smaller areas of open space.

The lss affordance is visited most often by all three types of agent, and bs is visited least often. The other three affordances are visited often, and normally occur in each search. Looking at which of the affordances is visited just before the goal is reached (the last affordance) shows that lss is very dominant in this role, occupying this position in just over 73% of the searches carried out in experiment 4. By comparison, bs only occupied the last position in just one search.

From these results, it would appear that lss is playing a dominant role in the search strategy used by all three agents. This is partly explained by the proximity of lss to the goal, although it is not immediately obvious, from the results, or looking at figure 1, why lss should be more dominant than ll, for example. After all, both are close to the goal and on the same side as the agent's home. The fact that bs is situated on the far side of the goal, which means that the agent has to pass the goal to visit it, could be part of the reason that it is often not included in a search very often.

Other arrangements of Grid-World were used to explore the impact of different environments on the search performance of the agents. As a general rule, the non-conceptual agent outperformed the stimulus response agent, and both were outperformed by the conceptual agent. However, the location of affordances, both in absolute numbers and in their relationship to each other and wall, was significant in the effect upon both the non-conceptual and conceptual agents. Another set of experiments was also able to show that if the non-conceptual agent could string together affordances in the correct order, then it could match the performance of the conceptual agent. This result re-enforces the idea that the difference between the two is rooted in the latter's ability to plan.

5 Conclusion

The overall aim of developing Grid-World has been to provide a flexible experimental environment that can be used to explore non-conceptual content using qualitative data. Using Artificial Intelligence techniques in this way is consistent with a cognitive science approach where computer models are used to investigate theoretical ideas. Grid-World has provided a robust artificial environment in which it has been possible to implement different agents and to test their search capabilities. The implementation has also enabled the test environment to be altered to explore agent behaviours as they emerged from earlier experiments.

The results from all of the experiments using the stimulus response agent have shown that a combination of wall following and searching in open space was sufficient to always lead the agent to the goal. However, with search values ranging between 40 and 5,000 steps, there was considerable variation and this cannot really be called a successful search strategy.

The non-conceptual and conceptual agents both use a memory of affordances to give significance to proximal features of their environment that they sense. The location and size of affordances within the search space was shown to have a measured impact upon the search performance of both agents. These characteristics of affordances provide further evidence to support the idea that there is a real proximity limit to an agent's capacity to grasp the significance of an object. If it is too far, it is just beyond the agent's reach. So the distance between any two points of affordance must fit with the agent's capabilities, and when searching there must be a sufficient number of well spaced affordances to provide a path. This conclusion is supported by the actions of the conceptual agent, which even with a path linking affordances, still did less well when affordance were moved near the goal.

Only a very basic memory capability has been given to the non-conceptual agent. In particular the memory instance for each affordance is only significant to the agent at that unique location and it cannot access memories from one location at any other. Further, although the agent can visit an affordance more than once during an initial search, it always recalls the result of the last visit. So it cannot learn the best direction from many visits. All of these parameters were carefully chosen so as not to give the agent any concepts, yet the non-conceptual agent has still consistently found the goal in fewer steps than the stimulus response agent. In some way it has operated as if it had a concept of searching, not one as sophisticated as the plan held by the conceptual agent, but nevertheless one that might convince an observer that it held a concept of planning.

This is an exciting conclusion as there is little other experimental evidence to support the case for non-conceptual content. However, a more critical reflection tells us that much of the performance improvement is closely related to the positions of the affordances within a particular environment. This is not to deny that there is an agent in Grid-World that can be said to have non-conceptual content, just that it is necessary to appreciate the close relationship between such an agent and the affordances in its environment.

If the behaviour of animals can be explained in terms of non-conceptual content, then there are reasons to believe that conceptual content has evolved from this simpler representational capability. If this is the case, then the evolution of conceptual content from non-conceptual content provides evidence to support a bottom up approach to artificial intelligence.

References

1. Weiss, G. (1999). Multiagent Systems: A Modern Approach to Distributed AI. Cambridge MA: MIT Press.
2. Gunter, Y.H. (2003). Essays on Nonconceptual Content. Cambridge, MA: MIT.
3. Byrne, A. (2003). Consciousness and Non-conceptual Content. Philosophical Studies 113: 261–274.
4. Bratman, M.E. (1987). Intention, Plans and Practical Reason. Cambridge, MA: Harvard University Press.
5. Bermudez, J.L. (2003). Thinking Without Words. Oxford: Oxford University Press.
6. Brooks, R.A (1999). Cambrian Intelligence – The Early History of the New AI. Cambridge, MA: MIT Press.
7. Campbell, J (1994). Past, Space & Self. Cambridge, MA: MIT Press.
8, Gibson, J.J. (1986). The Ecological Approach to Visual Perception. Boston: Houghton Mifflin.

Effective Selection of Abstract Plans for Multi-Agent Systems*

Toshiharu Sugawara
Dept. of Computer Science and Engineering
Waseda University
Tokyo 169-8555, Japan
sugawara@waseda.jp

Satoshi Kurihara
Institute of Industrial Science
Osaka University
Osaka 567-0047, Japan
kurihara@ist.osaka-u.ac.jp

Toshio Hirotsu
Department of Computer Science
Toyohashi Univ. of Technology
Aichi 441-8580, Japan
hirotsu@ics.tut.ac.jp

Kensuke Fukuda
National Institute of Informatics
Tokyo 101-8430, Japan
kensuke@nii.ac.jp

Toshihiro Takada
NTT Communication Science Laboratories
Kanagawa 243-0198, Japan
takada@brl.ntt.co.jp

Abstract

This paper proposes a situation-based conflict estimation method that efficiently generates quality plans for multi-agent systems (MAS) by appropriately selecting abstract plans in hierarchical planning (HP). In HP, selecting a plan at an abstract level affects planning performance because an abstract plan restricts the scope of concrete-level (or primitive) plans and thus can reduce the planning cost. However, if all primitive plans under the selected abstract plan have serious and difficult-to-resolve conflicts with the plans of other agents, the final plan after conflict resolution will be inefficient or of low quality. This issue originates in the uncertainty of MAS, where other agents also have individual plans for their own goals and it is difficult to clearly anticipate which abstract plan will cause fewer conflicts with other agents' plans. In the proposed method, by introducing conflict patterns that express the situations of conflicts among agents' plans, agents learn and estimate which abstract plans are less likely to cause conflicts or which conflicts will be easy to resolve; thus, after conflict resolution, they can induce probabilistically higher-utility primitive plans. This paper also describes an experiment to evaluate our method. The results indicate that our method can improve the efficiency of plan execution.

*All authors were supported largely by SCOPE program of the Ministry of Internal Affairs and Communications under contract 071607001 in this work. This work was also supported in part by Global COE Program of the Ministry of Education, Culture, Sports, Science and Technology, Japan.

1 Introduction

An agent in a multi-agent system (MAS) has to generate plans for its individual goal, but these plans may conflict with those that are already being scheduled or executed by other agents. It must also be able to complete its planning and resolution of these conflicts within a reasonable time to have an acceptable quality plan.

Although we adopt hierarchical planning (HP, for example, see [7, 12]) using the decision-theoretic planning (DTP) approach [6] for efficient planning, it is not trivial to apply HPO to MAS. In HP, appropriate (abstract) plans are selected level by level to maximize the utility $U(p)$, where where p is the expected final plan comprising a sequence of primitive actions. However, in the MAS context, conflicts between agents affect the efficiency and quality of resulting plans. When a conflict is found at lower levels, an additional sophisticated process for avoiding it (*conflict resolution*) must be invoked and some extra actions (such as waiting for synchronization and detouring) may have to be added to the plan. The conflict resolution process may become costly or fail. Even a single conflict, if it is difficult to resolve, will result in a plan with considerably lower quality than it otherwise would have. As a result, in multi-agent systems, the second- or third-best plans may result in better overall performance.

The objective of our research is to predict which tasks in an abstract plan will conflict with other agents' plans at a lower level with higher probability and either involve a costly conflict resolution process and/or result in a low-quality plan after it has been resolved. For this issue, Sugawara *et al.* [14] introduced *conflict patterns (CP)* at a certain abstract level called the *screening level (SL)*. They then introduced a negative utility, called *conflict discount*, which cumulatively predicts the probability of conflicts in the subsequent refinement process, the cost of resolutions, and the quality/performance of the resulting plans on the basis of CPs in the SL plans and past experience. The conflict discount is calculated and updated by using statistically learned expected values or by reinforcement learning, so that the agents select the appropriate refinement at the SL. We assume that the initial utility is good for selecting plans for single-agent cases. This utility may lead to acceptable but minimum quality plans after conflict resolution in the MAS context. Thus, agents learn the conflict discount appropriate for the environment in order to select better SL plans. While reference [14] illustrated the way in which the conflict discount is adjusted, it did not experimentally tackle the question of whether or not the final plans were actually efficient.

In this paper, we formally define conflict patterns and discuss the estimation of their conflict discounts. We then introduce the notion of sub-conflict patterns for avoiding redundant calculations of conflict discounts and reducing memory space. We also clarify the distributed version of the planning framework with our conflict estimation, which is an extension of that in [14]. Then we present an experimental evaluation of the efficiency of plans generated by our method for a simulated laboratory room, which was not described in [14], either. This paper is organized as follows: First, we discuss the issue addressed here and the planning framework used in our application systems. We then explain the process of conflict detection and resolution. Following that, we introduce the use of conflict patterns to classify situations involving conflicts with other agents' plans. Then, the experimental results to evaluate our approach are presented. Finally, we cover related work and offer some concluding remarks.

2 Conflict estimation in hierarchical planning

In HP, plans are generated using an abstract hierarchy of the domain model, which includes tasks and resources in an abstract form. Initial states and goals are first described in the most abstract model, and a number of task sequences are generated to achieve these goals. One of the sequences is then selected according to a particular planning strategy (A utility is used in the case of DTP.[1]), and each task in the sequence is further refined into task sequences in the less-abstract model. This refine-and-select process is iterated until all tasks have been refined to primitive tasks in the lowest model. In general, while abstract (higher-level) models are simple and thus do not contain complete information, they are appropriate for understanding the global and long-term picture of activities. Naturally, the lower-layer models are more informative and complicated, so they are used for detailed descriptions of local and sectional plans.

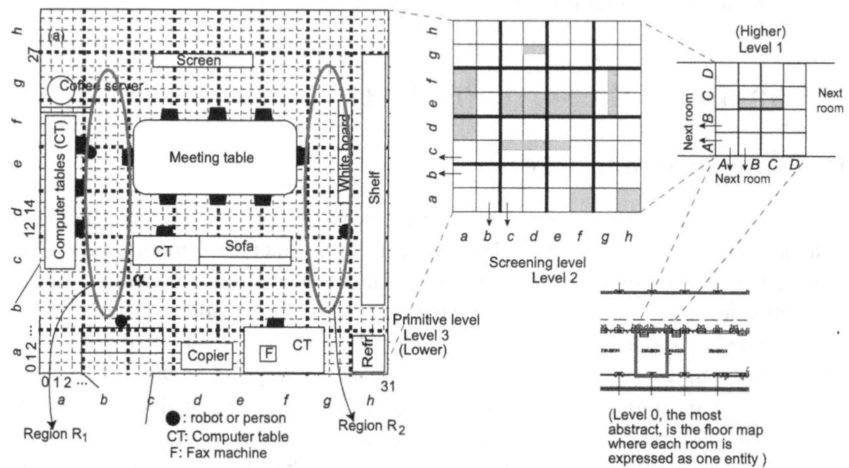

Figure 1: Example of a hierarchical description.

Actual conflicts are identified when all tasks have been expanded into primitive tasks, since the required amount of resources and time needed for executing the plan are precisely determined at this level. This may not prevent an agent from investigating the possibility of conflicts at an abstract level, however. For example, if a certain room is roughly modeled as a single object at an abstract level such as the level-0 model in Fig. 1 and two agents have plans to work in this room at the same time, they can

[1] An agent selects the plan that may lead to the highest utility. However, the utility value is determined from the primitive task/plan, so the utility of a non-primitive task/plan is expressed as a range calculated according to the possible lower-level refined plans. It has been reported that agents should choose the plan that contains the highest utility and expand it to the next layer for effective planning [6].

resolve this possible conflict by one agent deciding to work at another time. However, this conflict may not occur after the plans have been expanded into primitive ones, because it might turn out that the agents are able to work at different places in the room. In general, the process of conflict detection and resolution in abstract layers is simple because its domain model and related operators are simple. However, it usually results in redundant and inefficient plans.

Normal utilities for making efficiet or high-quality plans do not usually take into account possible conflicts with other agents. As a result, although they can create acceptable plans when there is no interference between plans, they might not be able to do so when there is interference. Furthermore, in applications where real-time performance is stipulated, it is preferable that agents predict which conflicts will vanish or be easy or difficult to resolve during the remainder of the planning period. It is important, therefore, to provide another utility for plan selection when there is the possibility of conflict. However, determining what the conflicts are and which tasks easily cause them is a function of the location of scarce or heavily used resources and the type of agent; thus, the outcome strongly depends on the situation and environment. This type of information cannot be provided *a priori* during the design time. Therefore, agents have to learn an additional utility for MAS contexts.

3 Planning at the screening level

3.1 Planning architecture

In our planning architecture, agents first exchange only the presently being generated, scheduled and executed plans described in a certain abstract-level model, called the *screening level (SL)*. We assume that the plans at this level are simpler than ones at the primitive level but are enough to classify the conflicting situations. The SL plans presently scheduled or being executed are called *SL-valid* plans, and the SL plans that are currently being generated (so are pending) are called *SL-pending plans*.

When agent a_i starts to create its plan for this environment, it first generates a number of SL plans and tentatively selects one of them (using conventional utility). It then requests SL-valid and SL-pending plans from other agents to investigate the possible conflicts between a_i's new plan and other plans, by using an estimation based on the utility with the learned conflict discount as described in Section 4. According to this result, a_i selects one of the SL plans to refine further. This plan is marked as 'SL-pending'. If a_i is requested to send its plans during this process, it immediately notifies the request for that it is 'SL planning' and sends the SL-pending plan right after it is determined. Agent a_i then waits for a short while for other unreceived plans; if it receives no other SL plans that have high conflict discounts, it proceeds to the next stage described below. Otherwise, one of the agents selects another SL plan instead of the current SL-pending plan; this may slow down the system in an extremely busy environment, so a tailored method for this issue will need to be developed in the future.

For further conflicts analysis, a_i requests primitive plans only from the agents whose plans are predicted to conflict with a_i's SL plan. When a_i completes a primitive plan without conflicts, the plan is scheduled or executed immediately; and its SL-plan is marked 'SL-valid'. Section 4 discusses how a_i learns to predict conflicts at the SL and how the utilities with a conflict discount are estimated.

We focus on applications where the same or similar plans are frequently reproduced. Examples of target applications are planning the behavior of multiple robots (Fig. 1) and ubiquitous computing with many devices, such as sensors and effectors, where agents reside in these devices to control them [16]. Examples of application scenarios are described in [9]. In this sort of application, e.g., robots moving in a room and assisting in people's daily activities, certain actions are repeated. We assume that other plans that are already scheduled or being executed are not modified (at least, the plans that have already been approved should be preferred) in the current implementation. Often this restricts the quality of the resulting plan. Our aim, however, is to select the most appropriate SL plan in a timely manner. If all of the plans generated at the SL appear to have high-discount conflicts, the agent can backtrack and select another plan at the SL or at a higher level; the agent still creates an abstract plan, which is simpler than creating a primitive plan, so the cost is not so high.

3.2 Conflict detection at screening level

The agent detects possible conflicts, according to resource and task information at the SL, by identifying the possibility of whether multiple plans will use the same resources, such as locations (e.g., squares in Fig. 1). An example is illustrated in Fig. 2, for which the SL is level 2 in Fig. 1; a square at this SL (specified by a pair of lowercase letters) corresponds to 4x4 squares in the primitive model (A square in the primitive level is specified by a pair of positive integers.). In Fig. 2, the agent can suggest that task t_l = *move(**cd**→ **dd**)* in the new plan may conflict with task t'_n =*move(**cd**→ **bd**)* in the SL-valid plan, where *move(**cd**→ **dd**)* is the SL plan expressing the agent's movement from somewhere in area *(**c**,**d**)* to area *(**d**,**d**)*. This conflict can be expected if some squares in area *(**c**,**d**)* can be simultaneously occupied by two agents during a certain time interval.

An agent has to take into account time relationships between tasks in the plans. The duration of each task in the SL-valid plans has already been determined, but not that of the new plan. Thus, it uses the expected average duration of each SL task. This value is initially given as part of the SL model; for example, *move(**cd**→ **bd**)* takes four ticks if agents (that is, robots) can move to the next small square in a tick. The expected duration is then statistically adjusted according to the generated primitive plans induced from this SL task.

The questions of when and where conflicts likely occur and whether their resolutions are difficult depend upon the system's environment. Suppose that three agents want to pass through area *(**b**,**d**)*. In the SL model, this area (place is a resource) is expressed as a single entity, so conflicts can be expected. However, this area has enough room for three agents if each agent occupies a small square at the primitive level; hence, the conflicts might not actually occur or might be easily resolved. However, in *(**c**,**d**)* where agents move only left or right, there is not enough room for three agents. Thus, it seems probable that the agents' plans will have conflicts there. Of course, this probability is influenced by the temporal relationships of the agents entering area *(**c**,**d**)*. If a conflict is detected, one of the agents must step out of the other agent's way

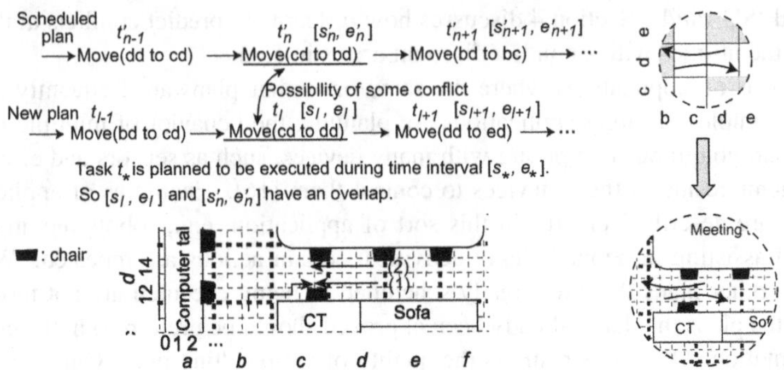

Figure 2: Example of a detected conflict.

and wait for it to pass by before resuming its movement.

4 Conflict estimation from conflict patterns

4.1 Conflict pattern — an expression of conflicting situations

A *conflict pattern (CP)* expresses a conflict between SL plans. First, we focus on an SL task identified as having a conflict. Let t be an SL task in a new SL plan p, denoted by $t \in p$. Suppose that SL plans $p_1, \ldots, p_k$ of other agents are SL-valid. Then CP, denoted here by $\mathcal{P}(t)$, is expressed as

$$\mathcal{P}(t) = (t, (t'_1, o_1), \ldots, (t'_h, o_h))$$

where $t'_i \in p_j$ $(1 \leq \exists j \leq h)$ and o_i is optional data. CP describes the situation where t is expected to conflict with $t'_1, \ldots, t'_h$ in SL-valid plans.

The optional data o_i can be any information that can be used to distinguish conflicting situations more accurately. For instance, it may be information about (relative) the time of execution and agents' names or types that suggest their ability/performance or physical size (when agents, such as robots and vehicles, have physical bodies). In the example of Fig. 2, CP is expressed as

$$\mathcal{P}_1(t_l) = (t_l, (t'_n, (\max(s'_n - s_l, 0), \min(e_l - s_l, e'_n - s_l)))),$$

where the optional data is the relative time interval during which the expected conflict may occur. To simplify the expression of this example, we describe the optional data in a more abstract form. For this purpose, we can use the expressions of time relativity; the duration of t'_n overlaps the anterior half (*ah*) or posterior half (*ph*) of the duration of t_l. Other cases of time relativity are expressed as 'overlap (*ol*).' Thus, $\mathcal{P}_1(t_l) = (t_l, (t'_n, r'_l))$, where r'_l = *ah*, *ph* or *ol*.

The situation in Fig. 3 shows that t_l may conflict with t'_{n+1} and t''_{m-1}. The following CP corresponds to this situation:

$$\mathcal{P}_2(t_l) = (t_l, (t'_{n+1}, r'_l), (t''_{m-1}, r''_l))$$

where r'_l, r''_l = *ah*, *ph* or *ol*.

4.2 Concept of conflict discount

Let $U(p)$ (or $U(t)$) be the initial utility for a primitive plan p (or a primitive task t). $U(p)$ for a non-primitive plan (or task) is the range that cumulatively indicates possible lower-primitive plans/tasks. We introduce the *conflict discount* for a CP, $cd(\mathcal{P})$. The conflict discount is conceptually defined as

$$cd(\mathcal{P}) = U(pp) - U(pp_m) + CCR(\mathcal{P}) \qquad (1)$$

where pp is the primitive plan of SL plan p before conflict resolution, and pp_m is the modified primitive plan for resolving conflict $\mathcal{P}$. The term *CCR* indicates the cost of conflict detection and resolution at the primitive level, which is calculated by combining the costs of requesting, receiving, and analyzing primitive plans from other agents and applying conflict resolution rules to modify the new plan. So even if no conflict actually occurs at the primitive level ($U(pp) = U(pp_m)$), $cd(\mathcal{P}) \neq 0$. This is because, if a conflict is expected at SL, the cost of conflict detection will be incurred. Define $cd'(\mathcal{P}) = U(pp) - U(pp_m)$ as the difference in utilities. The estimation of $cd(\mathcal{P})$ is described in the next section.

When an agent has a new SL plan p that is expected to have CPs $\mathcal{P}_1 \ldots \mathcal{P}_N$,

$$cd(p) = \sum_{i=1}^{N} cd(\mathcal{P}_i).$$

The agent uses the modified utility $U(p) - cd(p)$ instead of $U(p)$. When no conflicts are predicted, the agent uses $U(p)$ since $cd(p) = 0$. Our method statistically adjusts the conflict discounts for frequently appearing CPs. Because we focus on the efficiency of plans, we assume that $U(p)$ is the estimated execution time of the primitive plan in the example below.

4.3 Estimation of conflict discount

The conflict discount for a CP, $cd(\mathcal{P})$, is iteratively adjusted by the average or update function as follows when CP is observed s times.

$$cd_s(\mathcal{P}) = \sum_{i=1}^{s} d_i/s \qquad (2)$$

$$cd_s(\mathcal{P}) = \lambda * cd_{s-1}(\mathcal{P}) + (1-\lambda) * d_s \qquad (3)$$

where $0 < \lambda < 1$ and d_s indicates the s-th CCR_s plus the s-th observed utility difference between the original primitive plan and the plan after the resolution of the conflict corresponding to $\mathcal{P}$. Eq. (3) is more sensitive to environmental changes than Eq. (2). Note that the conflict of $\mathcal{P}$ might not occur at the primitive level after all; if so, $d_s = 0 + CCR_s$. For example, if the partner agent takes route (1) in Fig. 2, and this conflict can be resolved by taking a detour or by using “wait for two ticks” to wait until the partner agent passes by. In this case, $d_s = 2 + CCR_s$. However, if the partner agent takes route (2) in Fig. 2, no conflict actually occurs and $d_s = 0 + CCR_s$.

To acquire the CCR value for each plan, we assume that agents can monitor their planning activities by themselves. More precisely, CCR consists of the time for (1) requesting and receiving primitive plans from other agents that are suggested to have conflicts, (2) detecting actual conflicts between these plans and the local plan, and (3) modifying the local plan to resolve these conflicts. Agents keep the times for these activities. The conflict discount is re-calculated using the value of *CCR* plus the differential utility for each CP acquired by each agent from Eq. (2) or (3).

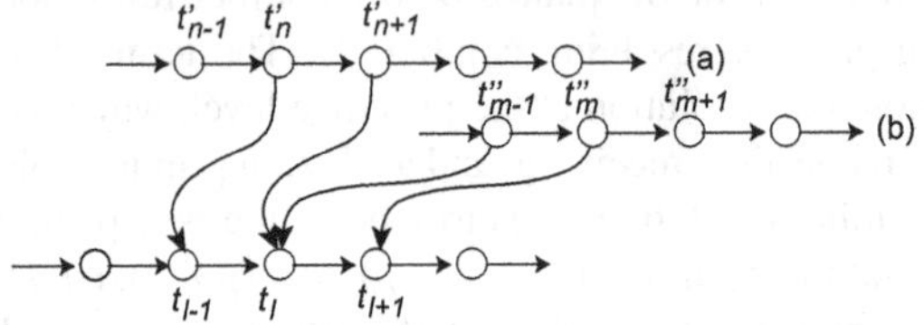
Plans (a) and (b) are scheduled or executing plans;
some conflicts with the new plan have been detected by the manager agent.
t'n-1 t'n t'n+1
(a)
t''m-1 t''m t''m+1
(b)
tl-1 tl tl+1
tl-1 has a conflict with t'n during [s e] (the relative time interval where this
conflict is expected to occur. If s=0, this conflict will occur when tl-1 starts.).

Figure 3: Example of conflicts between plans.

The calculation of $cd(p)$ of SL plan p, like the conflict resolution process, is an iteration of the procedures for (1) searching for, from the first task, the task t that has a conflict pattern $\mathcal{P}$ with other plans, and (2) predicting the conflict discount $cd(\mathcal{P})$. In procedure (2), the additional cost of avoiding conflicts is predicted, and thus the start times of subsequent tasks may be delayed for this amount of time. Since a number of conflicts may appear and disappear in the remaining part of the plan because of this delay, the agent detects the next conflicting task by using the adjusted duration.

4.4 Sub-conflict patterns

It is probable that many CPs will be created, and storing many CPs in the casebase would require a large amount of memory. This also incurs a large search cost, which degrades scalability. It also lowers the performance of conflict estimations of the CPs. Here, we can try to reduce the memory taken up by the CPs.

Suppose that $\mathcal{P}_1$ and $\mathcal{P}_2$ are CPs:

$$\mathcal{P}_1 = (t, (t_1, r_1), \ldots, (t_n, r_n)) \mathcal{P}_2 = (t', (t'_1, r'_1), \ldots, (t'_m, r'_m))$$

If $t = t'$ and $\{(t_1, r_1), \ldots, (t_n, r_n)\} \subseteq \{(t'_1, r'_1), \ldots, (t'_m, r'_m)\}$, then $\mathcal{P}_1$ is the sub-conflict pattern (sub-CP) of $\mathcal{P}_2$, denoted by $\mathcal{P}_1 \subseteq \mathcal{P}_2$. Now, we assume that $cd(\mathcal{P}_1) \leq cd(\mathcal{P}_2)$ if $\mathcal{P}_1 \subseteq \mathcal{P}_2$. This is a natural assumption because $\mathcal{P}_1$ is resolved if the conflict with $\mathcal{P}_2$ is resolved.

To save memory, the agent only stores CPs whose conflict discount values are near the turning point of the decision. For example, if $cd(\mathcal{P}_2)$ is sufficiently small, the *cd* value for $\mathcal{P}_1$ ($\subseteq \mathcal{P}_2$) will not necessarily be stored, so its *cd* estimation can be eliminated. Similarly, if $cd(\mathcal{P}_1)$ is large, which means that the agent will give up the current SL plan, the *cd* value for $\mathcal{P}_2$ ($\supseteq \mathcal{P}_1$) does not have to be stored.

5 Experiments

5.1 Conflict discount estimation

We experimentally investigated how cd' (instead of *cd*) changes depending on the ways that agents interfere in a simulated laboratory room (Fig. 1). Agent A randomly selects a starting point in region R_1 and a goal in region R_2 and then tries to generate a new plan for this movement. Another agent, B, already has an approved plan whose start and goal are also randomly selected in R_1 and R_2. In this setting, these agents do not cause any conflict when they may take different routes, such as to the north or south of the meeting table. However, they are likely to have conflicts when they both have to pass through area ***(c,d)*** because chairs and computer tables slightly narrow the route through it. Hence, we focused on the cases in which a conflict would be expected there at the SL and iterated the experiment until A's task *move(**cd**→ **dd**)* conflicted with B's task, which were both expressed as *move(**cd**→ **dd**)* (same direction) at the SL. Note that the duration of A's SL plan was an estimated value that may differ from the actual duration of execution. This estimated duration was not used in the experiments in [14]; thus, some of the experimental values shown below are slightly different from the ones reported in that paper.

The SL plan was expanded into a primitive plan, and we investigated the conflict discount after conflict resolution. Because B requests A's primitive plan, extra costs may be incurred even if no conflicts end up occurring. Therefore, in the following experiments, the number of plans of other agents that were predicted to have conflicts with the new plan was used as the approximate value of *CCR* (hence, a constant for each $\mathcal{P}$) of Eq. (1), because it is proportional to the number of these plans. This assumption means that it takes a tick to request and receive a primitive plan from another agent, check for conflicts between the received and local plans, and resolve these conflicts. We iterated this experiment a few hundred times to calculate cd'.

The task *move(**cd**→ **dd**)* usually takes four to six ticks in this environment. Note that we assumed the SL-task $move(X, Y)$ during interval $[s, e]$ occupies resource X during s to e and resource Y at e and that the primitive-level task $move(x, y)$ during $[s, s+1]$ (a primitive task takes 1 tick) occupies x and y during s to $s+1$. If the agent finds a possible conflict within the first two ticks, the relative time relationship is denoted by *ah*; Additionally note that if it finds such a possibility within the last two ticks, the relative time relationship is denoted by *ph*. Otherwise, the relative time relationship is denoted by *ol*. Hence, we estimated the values of cd' for the following conflict patterns:

$$\mathcal{P}_3 = (\mathit{move}(\mathbf{cd}\rightarrow \mathbf{dd}), ((\mathit{move}(\mathbf{cd}\rightarrow \mathbf{dd}), r)))$$

where r is *ah, ph* or *ol*, meaning that these two agents move in the same direction.

Tables 1 and 2 show the average values from ten experiments based on ten different random seeds, and the graphs in Fig. 4 are from one of these experiments.

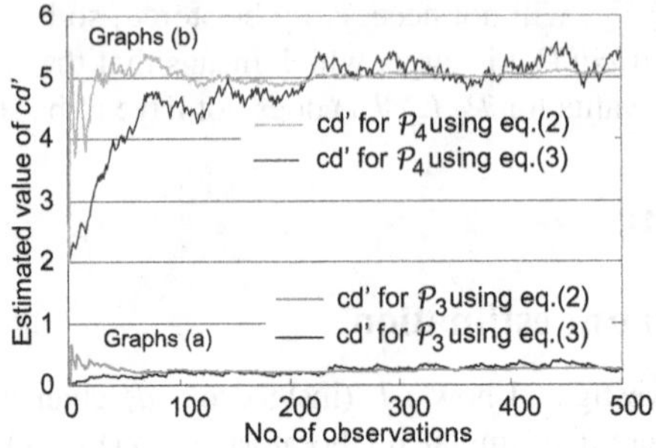

Figure 4: Estimated *cd′* and average values.

Graphs (a) in Fig. 4 show the estimated values of cd'_m ($\lambda = 0.98, 1 \leq m \leq 500$) derived from Eqs. (2) and (3) when r = *ol*. In these cases, $cd'(\mathcal{P}_3) = 0.71$ (so $cd(\mathcal{P}_3) = cd'(\mathcal{P}_3) + CCR(\mathcal{P}_3) = 1.71$), which is reasonably small. This is because the two-square-wide path is wide enough for two agents to pass through the area, but agent A sometimes has to take a detour to avoid conflicts. Other cases, such as moving in the opposite direction, are shown in [14].

However, the *cd′* values largely differ when two agents, B and C, which have approved plans (i.e., plans that do not conflict with each other), move in the same direction *move(**cd**→ **dd**)* and agent A begins to create a plan to move in the opposite direction though the same area. The conflict pattern of this situation is expressed as

$$\mathcal{P}_4 = (move(\mathbf{cd}\rightarrow \mathbf{bd}), ((move(\mathbf{cd}\rightarrow \mathbf{dd}), ol), (move(\mathbf{cd}\rightarrow \mathbf{dd}), ol))).$$

The estimated $cd'(\mathcal{P}_4) = 5.12$ ($cd(\mathcal{P}_4) = 7.12$) is quite different from the previous cases, as shown by graphs (b) in Fig. 4. Because B and C move almost simultaneously without conflicts, they usually occupy the narrow route in area *(**c,d**)* together. Thus, agent A always has to move aside, wait for several ticks until B and C pass, and then move back to the original route. If the agent's new plan is predicted to have this conflict pattern at the SL, it can select, after learning, another route, such as one taking it north of the meeting table or another taking it south of the sofa in Fig. 1, provided the route is shorter than the one in the original plan plus 7.12.

Table 1 shows the estimated *cd′* values in time-relativity cases other than $\mathcal{P}_4$. For example, if one of the relative time relationships in $\mathcal{P}_4$ is *ah* (This CP is denoted by $\mathcal{P}'_4$), the estimated $cd'(\mathcal{P}'_4) = 1.80$. This is small because if B and C move a slight distance away from each other, A can weave its way around them. In the case of *ph-ph*, A's planned task *move(**cd**→ **bd**)* may conflict in the latter half of its execution, so the agents will usually not meet in the narrow area (A moves right to left). However, because of uncertainty, they infrequently meet at different times in the narrow area. Table 1 suggests that the values of *cd′* depend on the resource structure of the routes, especially area *(**c,d**)* in Fig. 1.

Suppose that in another situation the agent finds a CP $\mathcal{P}_5$ such that $\mathcal{P}_4 \subseteq \mathcal{P}_5$. This CP may appear when conflict among more than four agents at *(**c,d**)* is expected. In

Table 1: Experimentally estimated conflict discount *cd'*

	ol-ol ($\mathcal{P}_4$)	*ah-ah*	*ph-ph*	*ah-ol* ($\mathcal{P}'_4$)	*ah-ph*	*ph-ol*
Value of *cd'*	5.12	3.67	3.30	1.80	0.75	1.87

this case, $cd'(\mathcal{P}_5)$ must be larger than 5.12. If this value is larger than the predefined threshold, the agent can calculate that $cd(\mathcal{P}_5) \geq 7.12$ (or $cd(\mathcal{P}_5) \geq 8.12$ if this conflict occurs among more than four agents), suggesting that it should try to find another route or shift (delay) its start time to avoid this conflict, even if it has no data about $\mathcal{P}_5$. Conversely, $cd'(\mathcal{P}'_4) = 1.80$ can induce $cd'(\mathcal{P}_3) \leq 1.80$. If this value is small enough, the agent does not need to calculate $cd(\mathcal{P}_3)$. Table 1 also indicates that $cd'(\mathcal{P}_3) \leq 0.70$ if $r = ah$ or ph in $\mathcal{P}_3$.

5.2 Cost (length) of generated plans

We investigated how efficient plans are generated with lower cost after a conflict pattern is found. In our planning strategy, agent A tries to select or generate another SL plan that is expected to have no conflict with other plans and whose estimated utility (in our case, the length of the plan) is less than the estimated utility of the original SL plan plus *cd* (if the CP is $\mathcal{P}_4$, then $cd(\mathcal{P}_4)$ is 7.12). The cost of selecting or generating another SL-plan is relatively low because we can set the upper limit of plan length. If A can find the new SL plan, it is selected and further refined. If A cannot find one, the original plan is selected (so conflict detection and resolution may be required). In the conventional planning strategy, the first SL plan to be generated would always be refined even if some conflicts were expected. (Of course, there might be no conflicts after all).

We examined, in our simulated room, the improvement of our planning strategy that resulted from using the estimated conflict discount value in Table 1. The results of this experiment (Table 2) show that our planning strategy provides an improvement of 2.65 ticks on average when a conflicting situation corresponding $\mathcal{P}_4$ is detected. In other cases, our planning method can generate efficient plans except when the conflict time relativity is *ph-ol*. This improvement is not very large. However, the ability to provide some information for deciding whether the agent should continue to refine the current plan even if the conflict resolution process will very likely be invoked or try to find another plan that does not have conflict with other agents is significant in applications like ours. In the *ph-ol* case, *cd'* is low so A cannot find any other better route.

The improvement shown in Table 2 seems fairly small, but our simulated laboratory room is based on an actual room; we believe that our method would be more significant in other situations/environments. For example, (1) if more robots were to move right to left in the narrow area in Fig. 2, (2) if the chair there were a bench (a longer chair), or (3) if there were a shorter detour, the improvement would be larger, thus the resulting plans would be of relatively higher quality than the ones obtained

Table 2: Cost (length) of resulting primitive plans

CPs	Conventional strategy	Our planning strategy	Improvement
$\mathcal{P}_4$ (*ol-ol*)	33.34	30.69	2.65
ah-ah	32.39	30.44	1.95
ph-ph	30.93	29.40	1.53
ph-ol	23.80	23.80	0

Column 1 and 2 respectively show the average cost of primitive plans derived from the original SL plans and that of primitive plans derived under our planning strategy. In both cases, the cost of conflict detection and resolution is included.

by a conventional planning strategy. We finally note that, although the start and goal positions were selected randomly in our experiments, agents (including persons) in actual applications usually have fixed start and goal points. Therefore, we believe that the improvements derived from the experimental results would appear more when this is actually applied to this kind of systems.

6 Discussion and related work

There have been a number of studies on efficient planning in the MAS context. For example, GPGP [3] is a general framework for generating effective plans using task and resource relationships among agents. Our method can be used in this framework to identify which abstract plan (task) should be refined first so that the map of the task relationships related to the plan can be created.

Hierarchical planning and coordination issues for improving MAS planning have also been discussed. For example, Ref. [2] proposed choosing the most appropriate abstract task/plan on the basis of summary information derived from the primitive tasks and plans in a bottom-up fashion. This method can avoid hopeless planning if some resources are recognized to be insufficient at an abstract level. It also introduced *fewest-threats-first* (FTF) heuristics to choose a lower (deeper) plan. Our approach focuses on the cases where conflicts can be accurately identified at only deeper levels, because the tasks, resources, and their environment in an abstract model are described in an abstract way. Furthermore, a plan with fewer conflicts does not always lead to a better plan; it is possible that only one conflict may fail to be resolved but that conflict is nonetheless a critical one. The idea behind our research is that, although conflicts may be invisible at abstract levels (including the SL), there is a tendency that conflicts often occur depending on the environmental factors related to the availability and use of resources, such as the location of agents, the kind of resources, and type of agents, as well as on the kind of task. Hence, we aim at expressing and distinguishing these situations by using CPs in order to enable agents to statistically learn the difficulty of conflict resolution and the quality of a resulting plan.

A number of issues related to MAS planning have been investigated in case-based reasoning (CBR) or its related domains. For example, Ref. [5] proposed a conversational case-based reasoner, called NaCoDAE, which is a type of agent in their MAS applications and helps users decide a course of action by engaging them in a dialogue in which they must describe the problem or situation of assigning missions to platoons. Plan reuse for the same/similar situations in a MAS context has also been proposed for MAS coordination [13] and collaboration [11]. A remarkable work similar to our approach is [10], where a case is used to expand an abstract plan to a less abstract one in HTN, although we focus on avoiding conflicts and/or selecting costless conflicts. In this sense, our motivation is more similar to that in [1] which applied CBR to a real-time strategy game.

Our work is also related to hierarchical reinforcement learning, such as [4, 8, 15], because an abstract task is considered to be a subroutine or a subfunction to be learned. For example, in the MAXQ approach [4], a task is divided into subroutines that are individually learned by RL methods. Our approach is to select an appropriate subroutine for each situation. In MAXQ, the conflict discount is assumed to have been learned at lower levels. However, in a multi-agent setting, it is naturally difficult to define the task hierarchy for all agents simultaneously.

One clear limitation of our method is that the reliability of *cd* values heavily depends on the accuracy of the SL conflict detection and time-estimation processes. Thus, it is very important to select the appropriate SL and carefully describe the SL model. For example, if level 1 in Fig. 1 is the SL, our method does not work well since that level is too abstract. As mentioned above, another issue is that the use of optional data in CPs is important for distinguishing one situation from another. To distinguish situations, our method needs the location of task execution (which may determine available resources), type of agent (which may determine required resources), and (relative) time information. Additionally, if many CPs are expected in a plan, conflict detection at the SL may be ambiguous regarding the scheduled time and resources of the SL tasks, which would affect the quality and cost of the plans. Finally, our method will have to be extended before it can deal with situations where multiple plans are created simultaneously; this extension is important for effective planning, and it will be addressed in a future work.

7 Conclusion

This paper proposed a method to predict, at an abstract level called the screening level, the cost of possible conflict resolution, and the quality of the resulting plan, to generate better primitive (concrete) plans. In our framework, an agent called the manager agent maintains the plans that are scheduled or being executed at the screening level and predicts possible conflicts between these plans and the newly proposed plan. Then, if necessary, a detailed analysis of primitive plans is performed by individual agents. We conducted experiments to reveal the estimated additional cost (estimated cd and cd' values) of the plans after conflict resolution and the efficiency of plans derived from our method. Our method enables agents to decide whether the current plan should be refined or another plan should be created at an earlier stage, that is, before an agent creates its primitive plan; this decision makes agents' planning efficient.

References

[1] D. W. Aha, M. Molineaux, and M. Ponsen. Learning to win: Case-based plan selection in a real-time strategy game. *Proc. of ICCBR 2005*, pages 5–20, 2005.

[2] B. J. Clement, A. C. Barrett, G. R. Rabideau, and E. H. Durfee. Using abstraction in planning and scheduling. *Proc. of 6th European Conf. on Planning*, 2001.

[3] K. Decker and V. Lesser. Generalizing the Partial Global Planning Algorithm. *Int. Jour. on Intelligent Cooperative Information Systems*, 1(2):319 – 346, 1992.

[4] T. G. Dietterich. The MAXQ Method for Hierarchical Reinforcement Learning. *Proc. of ICML-98*, pages 118–126, 1998.

[5] J. A. Giampapa and K. Sycara. Conversational case-based planning for agent team coordination. *Proc. of ICCBR 2001*, LNAI 2080, pages 189–203, 2001.

[6] R. Goldwin and R. Simmons. Search Control of Plan Generation in Decision-Theoretic Planners. *AIPS 1998*, pages 94–101, 1998.

[7] J. H. K. Erol and D. S. Nau. HTN planning: Complexity and expressivity. *Proc. of AAAI-94*, pages 1123–1128, 1994.

[8] L. P. Kaelbling. Hierarchical Learning in Stochastic Domains: Preliminary Results. *Proc. of Int. Conf. on Machine Learning*, pages 167–173, 1993.

[9] S. Kurihara, S. Aoyagi, T. Takada, T. Hirotsu, and T. Sugawara. Agent-Based Human-Environment Interaction Framework for Ubiquitous Environment. *Proc. of Int. Workshop on Networked Sensing Systems*, pages 103 – 108, 2005.

[10] L. Macedo and A. Cardoso. Case-Based, Decision-Theoretic, HTN Planning. *Proc. of ECCBR 2004*, LNAI 3155, pages 257 – 271. Springer-Verlag, 2004.

[11] E. Plaza. Cooperative reuse for compositional cases in multi-agent systems. *Proc. of ICCBR 2005*, LNAI 3620, pages 382–396, 2005.

[12] E. Sacerdoti. Planning in a hierarchy of abstraction spaces. *Artificial Intelligence*, 5(2):115 – 135, 1974.

[13] T. Sugawara. Reusing Past Plans in Distributed Planning. *Proc. of the 1st Int. Conf. on Multi-Agent Systems (ICMAS95)*, pages 360 – 367, 1995.

[14] T. Sugawara, S. Kurihara, T. Hirotsu, K. Fukuda, and T. Takada. Predicting Possible Conflicts in Hierarchical planning for Multi-Agent Systems. *Proc. of 4th Int. Conf. on Auton. Agents and Multiagent Systems*, pages 813 – 820, 2005.

[15] R. S. Sutton, D. Precup, and S. Singh. Intra-Option Learning about Temporary Abstract Actions. *Proc. of Int. Conf. on Machine Learning (ICML)*, pages 556–564, 1998.

[16] T. Takada, S. Kurihara, T. Hirotsu, and T. Sugawara. Proximity Mining: Finding Proximity using Sensor Data History. *Proc. of IEEE Workshop on Mobile Computing Systems and Applications*, pages 129 – 138, 2003.

Expressive security policy rules using Layered Conceptual Graphs

Madalina Croitoru, Liang Xiao, David Dupplaw, Paul Lewis
University of Southampton
Southampton, UK

Abstract

A method must be provided to support the analysis of security policy rules interdependencies in a (possibly distributed) environment. We propose a Conceptual Graphs based language that will allow us to represent the structure of information and to employ reasoning for consistency checking. We motivate our choice of language by the gained expressivity, the potential for depicting policy associations rigourously and by associated reasoning capabilities. We explain our approach in the context of security requirements for medical systems. We evaluate our work theoretically, by means of an example of a real world policy rule.

1 Introduction

In every organization there are business rules, that is compact statements that lay down what must or must not be the case in some aspect of a business [8]. According to the Object Management Group [9], rules are "declarations of policy or conditions that must be satisfied". Rules capture requirements including the decisions, guidelines and controls which make up the functionality. As long as inconsistency and ambiguity are identified, either in rules or by rules, they are supposed to be useful for capturing and resolving conflicts, both at the requirements level and at the design level [7]. However, even for explicitly captured rules, (human readable and/or machine process-able form) their interdependencies are usually far from obvious. Usually the rules are set-up separately by stakeholders with different views on the system. This results in the existence of contradictory rules that may affect the behavior of the running system. Therefore, a method must be provided to support the detection of conflicting rules specified in its (possibly distributed) environment as well as the connection of the relevant ones for aggregation applications.

To this end we propose a Conceptual Graphs [13] based language, Layered Conceptual Graphs [6] for representing the interdependencies amongst policy rules. The visual, logic based language will advance the state of the art by allowing the hierarchical depiction of information and consistency checking of policy rules interdependencies. Our choice of Layered Conceptual Graphs is thus motivated by the gained expressivity, the potential for depicting policy associations rigourously and by associated reasoning capabilities.

We explain our approach in the context of security requirements for medical systems. As an application scenario we use HealthAgents [1], an agent-based, distributed decision support system that employs clinical information, Magnetic Resonance Imaging (MRI) data, Magnetic Resonance Spectroscopy (MRS) data and genomic DNA profile information. The aim of this project is to help and improve brain tumour classification by providing alternative, non invasive techniques. To increase the number of cases HealthAgents is decentralizing its predecessor project, Interpret [14], by building a distributed decision support system (d-DSS). Decentralizing such a system poses interesting challenges from a security point of view. These challenges are further explained in Section 2 along with the motivation for this work. Section 3 explains the security mechanisms for the HealthAgents prototype and how policy rules complement these security mechanisms. Finally, Section 4 presents our proposed language for expressing the policy rules. A real-life example is given and the advantages of this approach are evaluated theoretically by analyzing their expressive power. Section 5 concludes the paper and lays down future work directions.

2 Motivation and background

Security is a growing concern in designing such systems that organizations can trust and use. Well-studied data encryption algorithms and publicly available libraries can alleviate some of the problems, yet more complex considerations are related with the management of the different levels of access rights to multiple types of resources by users distributed among and managed by multiple organizations. Some systems embed security policy modules within the application code. The tight coupling of software architecture with policies that spread all over the application, but which intend to change, makes such systems hard to maintain [15]. A recent access control model that supports efficient management is the widely accepted US National Institute of Standards and Technology model of role based access control (RBAC) [12]. In RBAC roles represent job functions in an organization. They bring together users and permissions. Permissions that describe operations upon resources are associated with roles. Users are assigned to roles to gain permissions that allow them to perform particular job functions.

A major benefit of using this type of model is that the reconfiguration of user-role, role-permission, and role-role relationships, directed by administrators, can reflect changing organizational policies. The maintenance of such a sub-system that is independent from the core application minimizes the impact on the overall system of requirements changes with regard to security. RBAC is widely accepted as a best practice and implemented in one form or another in systems including Microsoft Active Directory, SELinux, FreeBSD, Solaris, and Oracle DBMS. However, several weaknesses have been identified. In a hospital, different users with the same clinician role may have different permissions to particular resources. For example, one clinician that created a patient case in a hospital might have more rights than other clinicians in the same hospital. Clinicians in one hospital could have more rights to data in that hospital than clinicians from another hospital. Since permissions are not directly assignable to individual users, it is impossible to use RBAC to differentiate users with practically different capabilities in the system. Another insufficiency in the RBAC model is the lack of context access modelling.

The DAFMAT approach [4] is based on the RBAC model and applied to healthcare applications. Concepts of user, role, subject and domain are used and their mappings in pairs are defined to declare access modes. Authorization requests are validated using the access modes. However, their subjects represent executable domain functions and other resource types, such as data resources, are not protected. Moreover, the presentation of this model is only for human comprehension. A mechanism of forming security policies in an executable manner has not been considered. The importance of security in the healthcare domain has also been recognized in [16], particularly for managing patient data and its communication in a distributed environment. Security tags are used to mark information with regard to privacy within the patient record structure so that access is restricted to trusted agents only. This approach is limited to secure patient data access and has paid no attention to the many security issues involved in the healthcare service provision process.

As a direct consequence we believe that an adaptive security model that is configurable and reusable across applications would represent a significant advance. Therefore we extend the "role" concept, incorporating both role-based agent behavior and role-based access control in a single role interaction model. The easily re-configurable model maintains not only functional requirements but also security constraints in Multi-Agent Systems. Our novel adaptive security model is expressed using a knowledge rich language. This model is applied to HealthAgents, a multi agent distributed decision support system for brain tumor diagnosis. Our approach avoids weaknesses of traditional RBAC approaches and provides a practically usable security model for Multi-Agent Systems (MAS). The proposed unified role interaction model framework incorporates not only functional requirements but also security constraints in MAS. The security policy rule scheme has been used to express security requirements in relation to effective roles. The language proposed for expressing these requirements is an extension to Conceptual Graphs, Layered Conceptual Graphs. Layered Conceptual Graphs are a visual, logic based, knowledge representation formalism allowing for depiction of hierarchical knowledge.

To conclude, the major contribution of this work is two fold. First, little redevelopment effort will be required when security is to be engineered into the overall architecture, minimizing the impact of security requirements changes to the MAS. Second, by employing a knowledge rich formalism for expressing policy rules we can then (i) use deduction to minimize the number of written rules for the system (inheritance), (ii) be able to check for consistency and (iii) rigourously depict the policy rules interdependencies.

3 Security mechanisms for HealthAgents

The use of a distributed system for data collection and management is a necessity for medical decision support systems, especially when the number cases to be analyzed is limited per single node. However, the medical context poses extra interesting security requirements including ethical approval and informed consent of the participants. For multinational projects, ethical approval is devolved to regional bodies without any coordinated or uniform decision making. As a consequence, data gathered from different centers may be subject to different restrictions. Allowing for flexibility within the data security model is therefore essential. This section presents the basic security architecture implemented in the prototype for HealthAgents and how policy rules complement the existing security mechanisms. We then explain the expressivity requirements for policy rules and hence motivate the proposed Conceptual Graphs based language detailed in Section 4. In order to put our work in context a brief introduction to HealthAgents and its security requirements is also presented.

3.1 HealthAgents

The HealthAgents project, a Specific Targeted Research or Innovation Project (STREP) plans to create a multi-agent distributed Decision Support System (d-DSS) based on novel medical imaging and laboratory tests to help determine the diagnosis and prognosis of brain tumours. The HealthAgents decision support system implements a series of automated classifiers based on pattern recognition methodologies for the diagnosis and prognosis of brain tumours. These classifiers (implemented as agents) will need to access the data stored in the hospitals both for training and for decision making purposes.

Prior to incorporation into clinical practice such methods must be fully tested within a clinical trials setting. Clinical trials commonly use data from which personal information (e.g. name, address, date of birth) is removed but to which a unique patient identifier is added, often termed link-anonymised data. Such a scheme has the advantage of having a high chance of preserving patient anonymity whilst allowing data from the same patient to be added at a later date. This scheme also allows a specific patients data to be located and removed from the project at any time they request, a condition usually imposed by ethics committees.

Clinical trials are usually supported by a centralized database where the link-anonymised data are stored. For a distributed system, similarly robust arrangements must be designed to reassure ethics committees and patients that the data are secure. Security systems will need to be in place which can allow each center to potentially limit the type of data transmitted and the locations it is transmitted to.

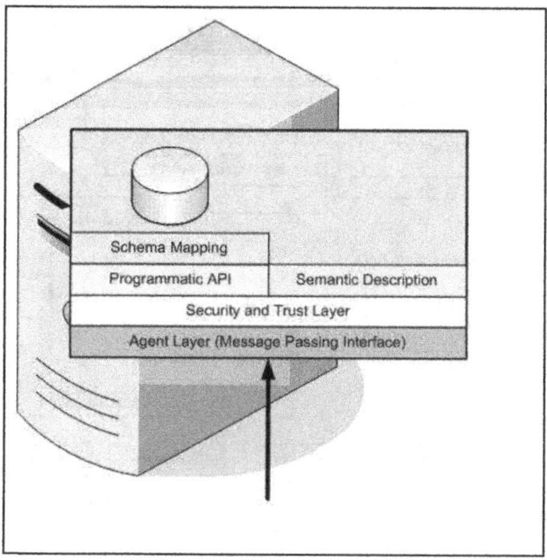

Figure 1: HealthAgents security levels

3.2 Basic Architecture

The HealthAgents framework provides an abstraction of the underlying agent platform, such that developers may implement new agents in a platform–independent way. The framework abstraction is built upon a layered architecture that provides fundamental services to the final agent. Messages that enter the agent are effectively filtered through the layers and only if all layers understand and accept the message's credentials will the message be acted upon. Therefore, perhaps the most important of these layers is the security layer that will determine whether the credentials in the message are valid for interpretation on this particular agent.

The framework has been built such that security modules, that are designed to check the credentials of a message, have to adhere to a specific pattern; that is, an application programmer's interface has been defined for this module. The agent's kernel will call upon the appropriate security module (defined by the agent's configuration) to authenticate the message. Only when a message has been authenticated will the message be provided to the functionality provider of the agent, signified by the Programmatic API in Figure 1.

3.3 Enhanced security: policy rules

In HealthAgents most of the policy rules regulate the access to data of different centers. According to their type, different users/agents will have different access rights to data. In this paper we are going to focus on the following rules (agreed upon clinician feedback):

- Only clinicians in the same hospital as the data can fully access them.

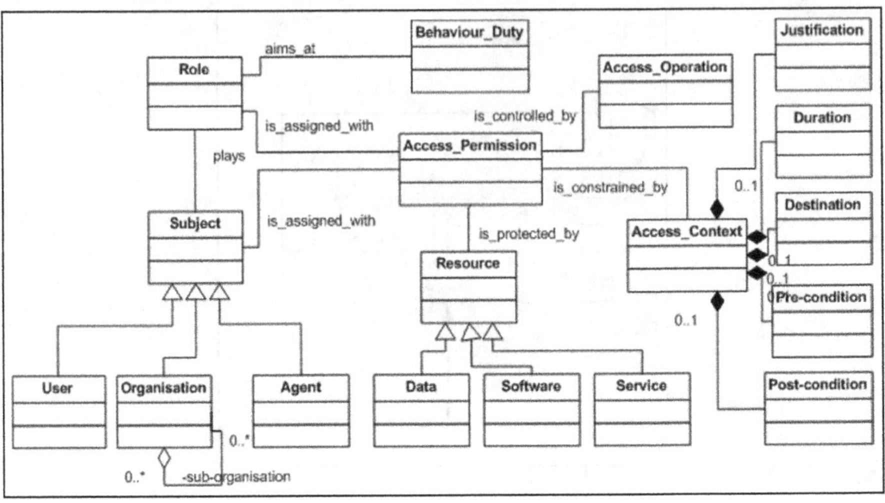

Figure 2: HealthAgents Security Model

- Clinicians have access to a non empty subset of data from other hospitals.
- Classifier sites have access to data only upon accreditation.
- Classifiers are not to further redistribute the data.

Note that other intrinsic policy rules (such as the fact that one should only access the relevant data for diagnostic purposes) are also considered within HealthAgents but, due to certain knowledge representation challenges, are beyond the scope the current paper.

In [17] we extended the RBAC model to avoid its weakness and to meet the unique characteristics of MAS. A security model has been proposed (see Figure 2), motivated by the particular requirements of the HealthAgents project but generic enough so that other domains and applications may use it.

In the security model depicted in Figure 2, agent behavior is specified in roles which not only meet functional requirements but also enforce security policy requirements. Figure 3 shows a prototype interaction model for invoking a classification in the HealthAgents system. In [17] we provided an analysis of the security requirements for this prototype model based on the security model shown in Figure 2. The application of the security model was discussed and sample security policies were given in a XML format.

However, when expressed in a syntactic language with no attached logical semantics (such as UML, XML etc), policy rule frameworks suffer from a number of drawbacks:

- Policy rules are usually presented in natural language. They are often embedded directly into the final software product as part of the implementation. The misinterpretation of policy rules from their original natural

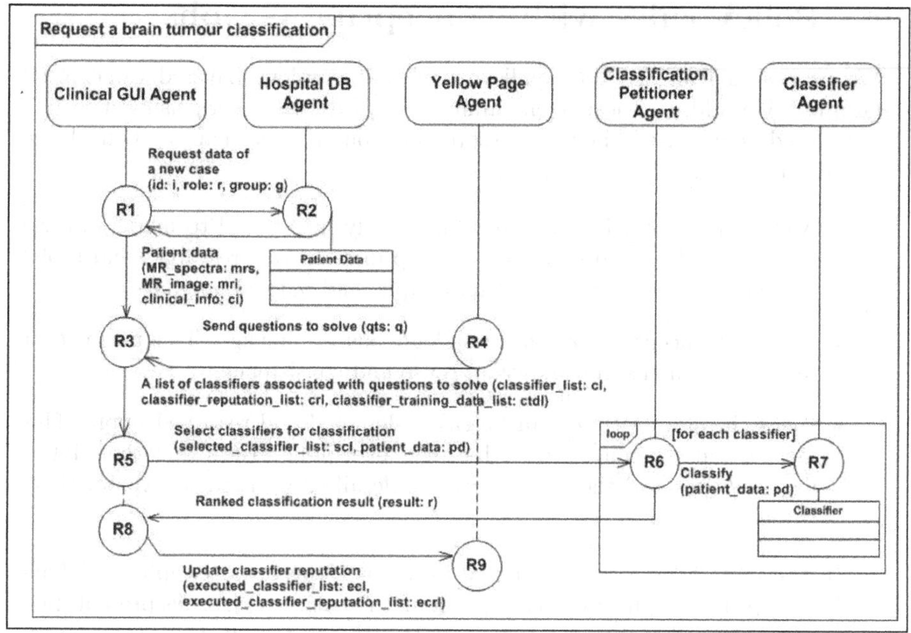

Figure 3: HealthAgents Interaction Model

language representation into code by developers with their own assumptions will lead to later re-development. A means must be provided for explicit representation of rules in the running system that supports direct execution (and reasoning).

- Inconsistency and ambiguity in policy rules are hard to identify since they may be set-up by various responsible people with different views. This will confuse the running system when contradictory rules come into play at the same time.

- Inter-relationships among policy rules must be established but little work so far is in this direction. When a set of rules are found to be applicable and others irrelevant, the system may actually need to be sufficiently intelligent in not ruling out the seemingly irrelevant ones. This is due to the fact that when some rules are applied, extra knowledge is obtained by the system, and then the pre-conditions of other policy rules become satisfied. A graph that interconnects the policy rules to check for their relationships while ensuring validation would support the overall system decision making and human analysis.

4 Policy rules with Conceptual Graphs

We propose a framework for policy rules that employs Layered Conceptual Graphs. We address the current limitations of existing work using a visual, structured, logic based knowledge representation (KR) formalism. Our choice of KR means that we benefit from:

- An extension of a KR formalism originally introduced to model natural language. This means that we can tap into existing research (and tools) looking at modelling Conceptual Graphs and natural language.
- Layered Conceptual Graphs are a logic based language. This means that reasoning can ensure validation, reuse and consistency.
- Hierarchical knowledge can be easily depicted and reasoned upon. This means that we can express the high level policy rules and their interdependencies and then get into more detail as we need to expand those rules.

In the remainder of the section we present Conceptual Graphs and Layered Conceptual Graphs informally (for a mathematically rigorous presentation please refer to [5, 6]). We then show how HealthAgents policy rules can be expressed using Layered Conceptual Graphs and what expressivity and reasoning power we gain.

4.1 Conceptual Graphs

During the past 30 years, a wide variety of knowledge representation schemes have been developed, each of which have their own benefits and drawbacks. Expressiveness and efficiency are the key factors that greatly affect the competence of a representational scheme. The system KL-ONE [3] and its descendants are the main representative descendants of semantic networks [11]. The lack of a clear formal semantics of the first members of KL-ONE family has been successfully repaired by the most prominent KR languages, Description Logics (DLs) [2]. John Sowa developed Conceptual Graphs (CGs) on the basis of semantic networks and Peirce's Existential Graphs [10]. These graphs can be viewed as a diagrammatic system of logic, with the purpose "to express meaning in a form that is logically precise, humanly readable, and computationally tractable" [13].

Conceptual Graphs(CGs) represent background knowledge, i.e. basic ontological knowledge, in a structure called support, which is implicitly used in the representation of factual knowledge as labelled graphs. A support consists of a concept type hierarchy, a relation type hierarchy, a set of individual markers that refer to specific concepts and a generic marker, denoted by *, which refers to an unspecified concept. The support defines the main concepts and relations that exist in the world we are trying to describe. These concepts and relations are going to be linked together by the means of an ordered bipartite graph that will describe the facts we are interested in. The ordered bipartite graph is going to represent the "stencil" which is going to be "filled in" with the concepts/relations taken from the support. A CG can be viewed as a bipartite graph that provides a semantic set of pointers to two ontologies. This means that we can reuse sources' ontologies, database schemas etc. for the purpose of describing those sources by means of a CG. Moreover, the attached semantics of Conceptual Graphs make them a powerful reasoning knowledge representation and reasoning formalism [5].

Layered Conceptual Graphs (LCGs for short) is a rigorously defined representation formalism evolved from Conceptual Graphs. It allows highlighting a new type of rendering based on the additional expansion of concept / relation nodes. This way hierarchical knowledge can be represented in a mathematically sound manner. The semantics associated with layered conceptual graphs are based on the semantics of conceptual graphs and are described in more detail in [6].

LCGs preserve the bipartite graph structure of the original model by defining transitional descriptions which allow a successive construction of bipartite graphs. Unlike existing approaches the knowledge detailed on a level of a hierarchy is put in context by using descriptions for relation nodes as well.

A transitional description of a bipartite graph G provides a set D of complex nodes in one of the classes of the bipartition, each complex node having associated a description. Complex nodes are visually depicted in bold. Their descriptions are disjoint bipartite graphs.

The neighbors of complex nodes either have empty descriptions or are described as bipartite graphs. These bipartite graphs contain in one of the classes of the bipartition, (V_C), all the atomic neighbors of the initial graph. The remaining nodes in each of these classes are new nodes or are taken from the descriptions of the corresponding complex neighbors of the initial graph.

In other words, if we have a interconnected world described by a CG and if we can provide details about both some complex concepts and their relationships, then we can construct a second level of knowledge about this world, describing these new details as Conceptual Graphs and applying the corresponding substitutions. This process can be similarly performed with the last constructed level, thus obtaining a coherent set of layered representations of the initial world.

We will use Layered Conceptual Graphs for representing the policy rules and then their associated "expansion" properties for highlighting the interdependencies between such rules.

4.2 Intelligent policy rules

This section will present a simple real-world example of policy rules for HealthAgents. Figure 4 depicts the support for our framework. Please note that the support is not exhaustive, being intended for illustration purposes only.

The concept hierarchy is comprised of the top, universal type, further refined as a subject, resource, policy rule or attribute. Policy rule is a stand alone

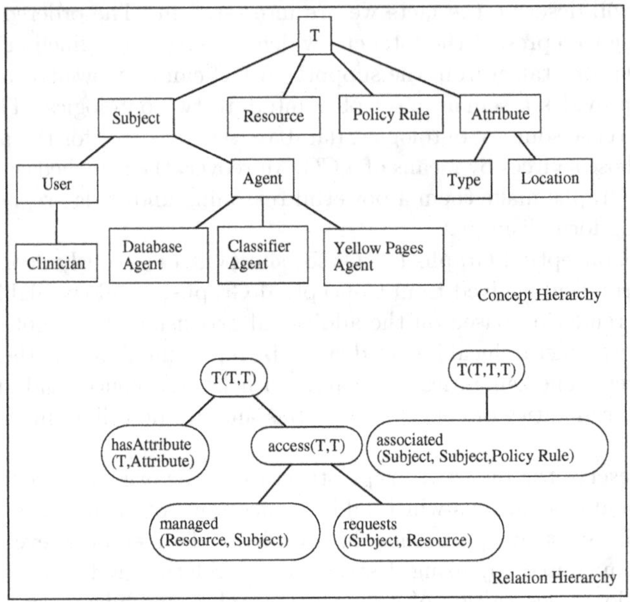

Figure 4: Intelligent Policy Rules Support

concept as one of our aims is to represent their interdependencies. The agents are further specialised in database agent, classifier agent and yellow pages agent. The relation hierarchy is made out of binary relations: access and attribute; and ternary relations: associate. For simplicity reasons we only consider two very generic access relations: managed and requests.

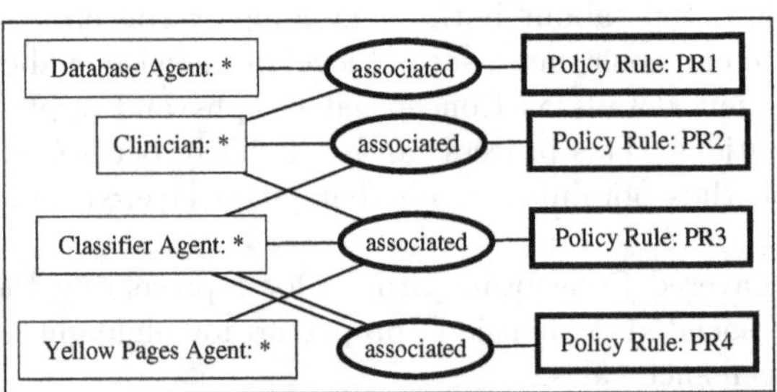

Figure 5: Some Policy Rules between Different Agents

In Figure 5 a bipartite graph is depicted for four policy rules. The policy rules are depicted on the right hand side of the picture while the subjects are represented on the left. To increase readability the edges are not explicitly ordered in the Figure. The bolded out nodes stand for complex nodes, that is, nodes can be further expanded. The four agents from the interaction are:

- **Clinical GUI Agent**: the clinician, working in a given hospital, requesting the d-DSS for a case to be classified. In Figure 5 we used the term "clinician" for clarity purposes.
- **Database Agent**: gives access to the data from a given hospital.
- **Classifier Agent**: a software that classifies brain tumor cases based on their characteristics (MRS spectra, case meta-data, etc.)
- **Yellow Pages Agent**.

The policy rules depicted in Figure 5 address the following scenarios:

- PR_1: A clinician wants to view data from a hospital.
- PR_2: A clinician directly asks a specific classifier for a case to be categorized.
- PR_3: A user asks the yellow pages for a classifier and the classifier is found by the yellow pages.
- PR_4: Classifiers want to exchange information for combination.

Due to space limitations we only focus on a subset of the first scenario, namely the clinicians accessing data from a hospital. We want to reinforce the fact that only clinicians within the same hospital as the data have access to them. This information is captured in Figure 6. Indeed, the bolded out nodes (the relation node associates and the concept node policy rule) will be expanded to capture this information. Please note that the concepts database agent and clinician remain unchanged, but are now linked to several relations to express the required information. Figure 6 represents the fact that a clinician, which has a certain location, is allowed to access a resource which is at the same location as him and is managed by a database agent.

Based on the example above we have demonstrated that we can represent hierarchical information in a consistent, mathematically correct manner. However, beside their representational capabilities, Layered Conceptual Graphs also have attached rigorous reasoning mechanisms. In the remainder of the section we will present a simple example that illustrate some of the reasoning capabilities we can benefit from.

Consider the example presented in Figure 7. On the left hand side the expanded PR_1 policy rule graph is depicted. On the right hand side we consider the query graph that wants to check if Maurice, a user from Birmingham is allowed to request data from Valencia. Checking whether the rules allow for that query is done by the means of projection, a labelled graph homomorphism between the query graph and the rules graph. More precisely, the relation nodes are projected into relation nodes and concept nodes into concept nodes. The structure of the graph also has to be preserved. We can see that, in this example, the answer to the query is "no". This is due to the fact that the structure of the query graph does not match the rule (more precisely, there is

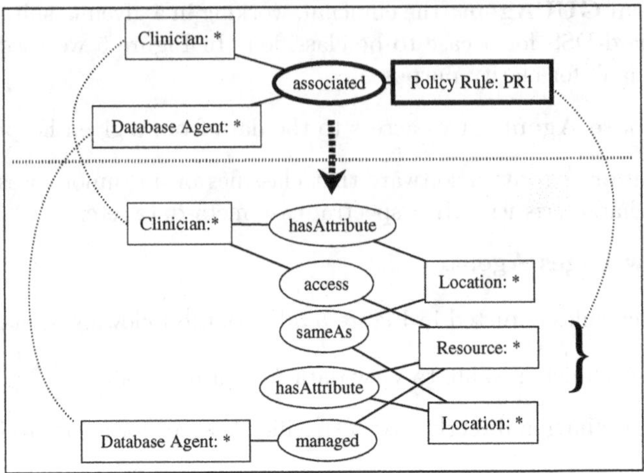

Figure 6: Policy Rule 1 expanded

no "sameAs" relation in the query graph). Please note that information from the support is also considered while performing the projection. For example the concept type user from the query graph has been projected onto the concept type clinician (according to the concept type hierarchy). In the same way, according to the relation hierarchy, the relation node request was projected onto the relation node access.

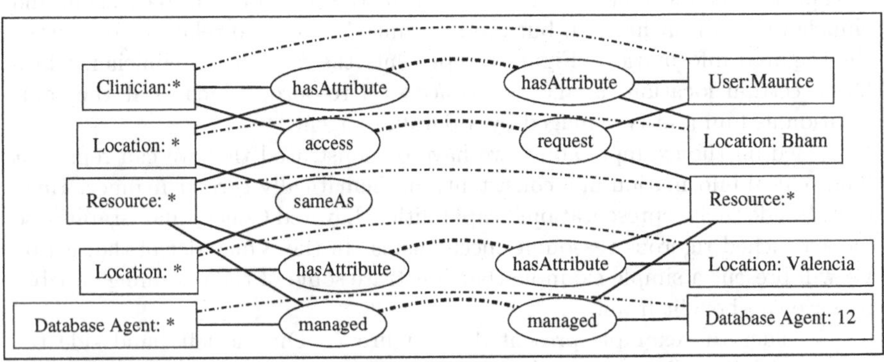

Figure 7: Policy Rule 1 Query Projection

5 Conclusions and future work

In this paper we proposed a knowledge intensive approach to expressing policy rules. We have motivated our approach based on current limitations of existing work: no reasoning capabilities to manage rule interdependencies. Our work was explained in the context of HealthAgents, a distributed decision support system for brain tumor diagnosis. We evaluated our work theoretically, by showing gained representational and reasoning power. The examples were based on real-life policy rules considered for the HealthAgents prototype.

Future work will consider looking at further exploring policy rules interdependencies from a knowledge representation point of view. It will be interesting (both from a policy rule and a conceptual Graph research point of view) to clearly state what redundancy or incoherence means. For instance it would be interesting to investigate the reasons why a policy rule cannot be projected onto another policy rule (structural mismatch, type mismatch etc).

6 Acknowledgements

This work is supported under the HealthAgents STREP project funded by EU Framework 6 under Grant number IST-FP6- 027213. We would also like to thank Javier Vincente Robledo, Srinandan Dasmahapatra, Andrew Peet, Horacio Gonzalez-Velez and Alex Gibb for useful feedback on earlier versions of this paper.

References

[1] C. Arús, B. Celda, S. Dasmahapatra, D. Dupplaw, H. González-Vélez, S. van Huffel, P. Lewis, M. Lluch i Ariet, M. Mier, A. Peet, and M. Robles. On the design of a web-based decision support system for brain tumour diagnosis using distributed agents. In *WI-IATW'06: 2006 IEEE/WIC/ACM Int Conf on Web Intelligence & Intelligent Agent Technology*, pages 208–211, Hong Kong, December 2006. IEEE.

[2] F. Baader et al., editors. *The Description Logic Handbook.* Cambridge Univ. Press, 2003.

[3] R. J. Brachman and J. G. Schmolze. An Overview of the KL-ONE Representation System. *Cognitive Science*, 9(2):171–216, 1985.

[4] R. Chandramouli. A framework for multiple authorization types in a healthcare application system. *Proceedings of the 17th Annual Computer Security Applications Conference*, 1:137–148, 2001.

[5] M. Chein and M.-L. Mugnier. Conceptual graphs: Fundamental notions. *Revue d'Intelligence Artificielle*, 6(4):365–406, 1992.

[6] M. Croitoru, E. Compatangelo, and C. Mellish. Hierarchical knowledge integration using layered conceptual graphs. In *Proc. of the 13th Int'l Conf. on Conceptual Structures (ICCS'2005)*, number 3596 in Lect. Notes in Artif. Intell., pages 267–280. Springer, 2005.

[7] A. Kleppe, J. Warmer, and W. Bast. *MDA Explained: The Model Driven Architecture: Practice and Promise.* Addison, 2003.

[8] T. Morgan. *Business Rules and Information Systems.* Addison, 2002.

[9] Object Management Group (OMG). The OMG Unified Modeling Language (UML) Specification Ver. 1.5, March 2003.

[10] C. S. Peirce. Manuscript 514, 1909. Available at http://www.jfsowa.com/peirce/ms514.htm.

[11] M. Quillian. Semantic memory. In M. Minsky, editor, *Semantic Information Processing*, pages 227–270. MIT Press, 1968.

[12] R. Sandhu, E. Coyne, H. Feinstein, and C. Youman. Role-based access control models. *Computer*, 29:38–47, 1996.

[13] J. F. Sowa. *Conceptual Structures: Information Processing in Mind and Machine.* Addison-Wesley, 1984.

[14] A. R. Tate, J. Underwood, D. M. Acosta, M. . Julia-Sape, C. Majos, A. Moreno-Torres, F. A. Howe, M. van der Graaf, M. M. Lefournier, F. Murphy, A. Loosemore, C. Ladroue, P. Wesseling, J. L. Bosson, A. W. Simonetti, W. Gajewicz, J. Calvar, A. Capdevila, P. Wilkins, A. C. Bell, C. Remy, A. Heerschap, D. Watson, J. R. Griffiths, and C. Arus. Development of a decision support system for diagnosis and grading of brain tumours using in vivo magnetic resonance single voxel spectra. *NMR Biomed*, 19:411–434, 2006.

[15] T. Verhanneman, F. Piessens, E. Win, B.D. andTruyen, and W. Joosen. A modular access control service for supporting application-specific policies. *IEEE Distributed Systems Online*, 7:367–398, 2006.

[16] J. Wimalasiri, P. Ray, and C. Wilson. Maintaining security in an ontology driven multi-agent system for electronic health records. *Proceedings of the 6th International Workshop on Enterprise Networking and Computing in Healthcare Industry*, 1:19–34, 2004.

[17] L. Xiao, L. Peet, P. Lewis, S. Dasmahapatra, C. Saez, M. Croitoru, J. Vicente, H. Gonzalez-Valez, and M. Lluch. An adaptive security model for multi-agent systems and application to a clinical trials environment. In *The First IEEE International Workshop on Security in Software Engineering*, 2007.

DATA MINING

Relevance Feedback for Association Rules by Leveraging Concepts from Information Retrieval

Georg Ruß
Institute for Knowledge and Language Engineering
University of Magdeburg
Germany

Mirko Böttcher
Intelligent Systems
Research Centre, BT Group
Ipswich, United Kingdom

Detlef Nauck
Intelligent Systems
Research Centre, BT Group
Ipswich, United Kingdom

Rudolf Kruse
Institute for Knowledge and Language Engineering
University of Magdeburg
Germany

Abstract

The task of detecting those association rules which are interesting within the vast set of discovered ones still is a major research challenge in data mining. Although several possible solutions have been proposed, they usually require a user to be aware what he knows, to have a rough idea what he is looking for, and to be able to specify this knowledge in advance. In this paper we compare the task of finding the most relevant rules with the task of finding the most relevant documents known from Information Retrieval. We propose a novel and flexible method of relevance feedback for association rules which leverages technologies from Information Retrieval, like document vectors, term frequencies and similarity calculations. By acquiring a user's preferences our approach builds a repository of what he considers to be (non-)relevant. By calculating and aggregating the similarities of each unexamined rule with the rules in the repository we obtain a relevance score which better reflects the user's notion of relevance with each feedback provided.

1 Introduction

Association rule mining [1, 2] originally has been developed for market basket data analysis, where each basket, also referred to as a transaction, consists of a set of purchased items. The goal of association rule mining is to detect all those items which frequently occur together and to form rules which predict the co-occurrence of items. However, association rule mining is not just bound to this specific purpose. It can be applied, for example, to every relational database.

Nowadays, the discovery of association rules is a relatively mature and well-researched topic. Many algorithms have been proposed to ever faster discover and maintain association rules. However, one of the biggest problems of association rules still remains unresolved. Usually, the number of discovered associations will be immense, easily in the thousands or even tens of thousands. Clearly, the large numbers make rules difficult to examine by a human user. Moreover, many of the discovered rules will be obvious, already known, or not relevant to a user. For this reason several methods have been proposed to assist a user in detecting the most interesting or relevant ones. The vast majority of these approaches either calculate a relevance score or determine rules that contradict a user's prior knowledge based on Boolean logic.

In this paper we argue that such approaches only insufficiently reflect the way a user searches for relevant rules because a user's perception of relevance is not a static but rather a dynamic process due to several reasons: firstly, when a user starts to explore a set of discovered association rules he only has a very vague notion about which rules might be relevant to him. Secondly, while seeing more rules his knowledge about the domain of interest changes, some aspects might gain while others might lose importance. His notion of relevance depends on these changes and thus changes too, almost always becoming clearer. The more rules a user examines, the more knowledge he gathers about the domain of interest. This knowledge then helps him to decide for newly encountered rules whether they are (non-)relevant for him, for example, because they are kind-of similar to previously seen (non-)relevant ones.

The importance of user dynamics and incremental knowledge gathering in assessing the relevance of data mining results only recently gained attention in the research community [3, 4]. However, it is a rather well-researched topic in the field of information retrieval where it is known for a long time that a user cannot express his information need from scratch. For example, when using a internet search engine to search documents about a non-trivial topic most users start with a rather simple query. By analysing the search results they gain more knowledge about what they actually look for and thus are able to further refine their initial query, i.e. to express their notion of relevance more clearly. To support a user in this process techniques like relevance feedback based on document similarities have been developed.

In fact, the way a user builds up his internal notion of relevancy when searching for the most relevant association rules described above is very similar to the models of user behaviour used in information retrieval (cp. [5]). Based on these similarities we present a new approach to the problem of finding the most relevant rules out of a large set of association rules which is inspired by ideas from information retrieval. Our approach uses relevance feedback to acquire users' preferences and to build a knowledge base of what he considers to be relevant and non-relevant, respectively. By calculating the (dis-)similarity of each unexamined rule with the rules in the knowledge base and aggregating the scores we obtain a relevance score which—with each feedback provided—better reflects the user's notion of relevance.

The remainder of this paper is organised as follows: Section 2 gives the background on association rules, Section 3 shows the related work that is most relevant to our topic. Section 4 will further elaborate the link between information retrieval and interestingness assessment of association rules. Section 5 introduces a novel notion of association rules based on features vectors which are inspired by document vectors from information retrieval. This representation is closely related to our notion of rule similarity explained in Section 6 and Section 7. The relevance scoring metric will be derived in Section 8 before Section 9 concludes the paper.

2 Association Rules

Formally, association rule mining is applied to a set $\mathcal{D}$ of *transactions* $\mathcal{T} \in \mathcal{D}$. Every transaction $\mathcal{T}$ is a subset of a set of items $\mathcal{L}$. A subset $\mathcal{X} \subseteq \mathcal{L}$ is called *itemset*. It is said that a transaction $\mathcal{T}$ *supports* an itemset $\mathcal{X}$ if $\mathcal{X} \subseteq \mathcal{T}$.

An association rule r is an expression $\mathcal{X} \rightarrow \mathcal{Y}$ where $\mathcal{X}$ and $\mathcal{Y}$ are itemsets, $|\mathcal{Y}| > 0$ and $X \cap Y = \varnothing$. Its meaning is quite intuitive: Given a database $\mathcal{D}$ of transactions the rule above expresses that whenever $\mathcal{X} \subseteq \mathcal{T}$ holds, $\mathcal{Y} \subseteq \mathcal{T}$ is likely to hold too. If for two rules $r : \mathcal{X} \rightarrow \mathcal{Y}$ and $r' : \mathcal{X}' \rightarrow \mathcal{Y}$, $\mathcal{X} \subset \mathcal{X}'$ holds, then it is said that r is a *generalization* of r'. This is denoted by $r' \prec r$.

As usual, the reliability of a rule $r : \mathcal{X} \rightarrow \mathcal{Y}$ is measured by its *confidence* $\operatorname{conf}(r)$, which estimates $P(\mathcal{Y} \subseteq \mathcal{T} \mid \mathcal{X} \subset \mathcal{T})$, or short $P(\mathcal{Y} \mid \mathcal{X})$. The statistical significance of r is measured by its *support* $\operatorname{supp}(r)$ which estimates $P(\mathcal{X} \cup \mathcal{Y} \subseteq \mathcal{T})$, or short $P(\mathcal{X}\mathcal{Y})$. We also use the support of an itemset $\mathcal{X}$ denoted by $\operatorname{supp}(\mathcal{X})$.

3 Related Work

The strength of an association rule learner to discover all patterns is likewise its weakness. Usually the number of discovered associations can be immense, easily in the thousands or even tens of thousands. Clearly, the large numbers make rules difficult to examine by a human user. Therefore significant research has been conducted into methods which assess the relevance, or interestingness, of a rule. Studies concerning interestingness assessment can roughly be divided into two classes. The first class are objective measures. These are usually derived from statistics, information theory or machine learning and assess numerical or structural properties of a rule and the data to produce a ranking [6]. Objective measures do not take any background information into account and are therefore suitable if an unbiased ranking is required, e.g. in off-the-shelf data mining tools. The second class are subjective measures which incorporate a user's background knowledge. In this class a rule is considered interesting if it is either *actionable* or *unexpected*.

Actionability of a rule means that the user "can act upon it to his advantage" [7]. Their focal point is on rules that are advantageous for the user's goals. The actionability approach needs detailed knowledge about the current goals and also about the cost and risks of possible actions. Systems that utilise it are hence very domain specific, like the *KEFIR* system described in [8].

A rule is unexpected if it contradicts the user's knowledge about the domain. Systems that build upon this approach require the user to express his domain knowledge – a sometimes difficult, long and tedious task. The methods are usually based on pairwise comparison of a discovered rule with rules representing the user knowledge. This comparison can be logic-based [9, 10, 11] or syntax-based [12]. In logic-based systems a contradiction is determined by means of a logical calculus, whereas in syntax-based systems a rule contradicts if it has a similar body but a dissimilar head.

In [9, 10, 11] the authors connect belief models with association rules. In particular, they assume that a belief system has been provided by the user whereby beliefs are defined as association rules. Based on this definition they provide a set of conditions to verify whether a rule $\mathcal{X} \rightarrow y$ is *unexpected* with respect to the belief $\mathcal{X} \rightarrow z$ on the rule database D. They propose an algorithm *ZoomUR* which discovers the set of unexpected rules regarding a specified set of beliefs. The algorithm itself consists of two different discovery strategies: *ZoominUR* discovers all unexpected rules that are refinements (or specialisations). On the other hand, *ZoomoutUR* discovers all unexpected rules that are more general.

In [12] the authors address the insufficiency of objective interestingness measures by focusing on the unexpectedness of generalised association rules. They assume that taxonomies exist among association rules' attributes. In subsequent work [13], human knowledge is recognised to have different degrees of certainty or preciseness. Their system allows for three degrees, notably *general impressions, reasonably precise concepts* and *precise knowledge.* The approach they propose accounts for these degrees and uses the gathered knowledge to find rules which are unexpected in regard to the expressed knowledge. The approach works iteratively: first, the user specifies his knowledge or modifies previously specified knowledge, supported by the specification language; second, the system analyses the association rules according to conformity and unexpectedness; and third, the user inspects the analysis results (aided by visualisation), saves interesting rules and discards uninteresting rules.

How to incorporate user dynamics into the relevance assessment has been studied in [3]. They propose an approach based on two models which a user has to specify prior to any analysis: a model of his existing knowledge and a model of how he likes to apply this knowledge. The degree of unexpectedness of each discovered rule is calculated with respect to these two models. Their approach is based on what they call the See-and-Know assumption. Once a user has seen a rule, the rule itself and similar rules are not of interest anymore. Our approach, in contrast, uses two classes of seen rules, relevant and non-relevant ones. The ranking is calculated by aggregating the (dis-)similarity of a rule with respect to rules in both classes. Our approach also does not require a user to specify any kind of prior model of a his knowledge.

4 Using Concepts from Information Retrieval

Existing approaches to assess the relevance of association rules strongly require a user to explicitly specify his existing knowledge in advance. This leads to two major drawbacks. In the first place, when specifying their existing knowledge, domain experts often forget certain key aspects or may not remember others which come into play under rarer circumstances. This problem can be termed 'expert dilemma' and has already been observed by designers of expert systems in the 1980s [14]. Secondly, at the beginning of an analysis session a user can only very vaguely specify what he considers to be relevant. His notion of relevance only becomes clearer the more rules he examines. This problem, that a user is incapable of specifying his information need from scratch, is very well-known in the field of information retrieval [5] where it lead to the development of relevance feedback methods.

Relevance feedback is an intuitive technique that has been introduced to information retrieval in the mid-1960s [15]. In information retrieval it is a controlled, semi-automatic, iterative process for query reformulation, that can greatly improve the usability of an information retrieval system [16]. Relevance feedback allows a user to express what he considers to be relevant by marking rules as relevant and non-relevant, respectively. Whenever a rule has been marked as relevant, it is added to the set of relevant rules R_{r}. Whenever a rule is marked as non-relevant, it is added to the set of non-relevant rules R_{n}. For simplicity, we will assume that in each feedback cycle exactly one rule is marked.

After each feedback cycle the remaining rules are compared with the set of annotated rules and a new relevance score is calculated. The set of annotated rules, in turn, can be seen as a representation of the user's notion of relevance. Hence it also provides a solution to the first of the above-mentioned drawbacks by supporting an iterative, easy way for a user to specify his knowledge about a domain. For example, he may annotate rules that are already known as non-relevant and some novel rules as relevant.

In order to develop a feedback system for association rules the following questions need to be answered:

- How do we represent association rules for the purpose of relevance feedback?
- How do we score the likely relevance of a rule in relation to a rule already marked as (non-)relevant?
- How do we aggregate those scores to an overall relevance score?

We will provide answers to these questions in the subsequent sections. In particular we are aiming at adapting established methods from information retrieval.

5 Rule Representation

To be the core building block of a relevance feedback approach it is necessary to transform the rules into an equivalent representation. In particular, such a representation should have a couple of properties. Firstly, rather than relying on generalisation and specialisation relationships among rules as a key to rule similarity it should support a less crisp and thus more flexible definition. For example, rules that have the same head and share items in their body should be regarded as similar to a certain degree. Secondly, items have a different importance to a user. For example, an item that is contained in almost every rule does not contribute much towards a user's understanding of the domain, whereas an item that is only contained in a few rules can contribute considerably. This importance should be reflected in the rule representation. Thirdly, it should be easy to extend the rule representation by further numeric properties of a rule. For example, recently there has been an increasing interest into the change of a rule's support and confidence values (e.g. [17]) as a key to rule interestingness. In this scenario the rule representation should incorporate the timeseries of support or confidence in order to enable similarity calculations based on rule change. To illustrate the usage of further information about rules for relevance feedback we will use the example of rule change throughout this paper.

As a representation that fulfills all of the above requirements we define a *feature vector $\vec{r}$ of an association rule r* whose elements are numerical values and which consists of three components: a representation of the rule's body, a representation of the rule's head and a rule's time series. The latter component can easily be replaced by other numeric features of a rule or completely omitted. Formally, a feature vector thus is defined as

$$\vec{r} = (\underbrace{\overbrace{r_1, \ldots, r_b}^{\texttt{body}}, \overbrace{r_{b+1}, \ldots, r_{b+h}}^{\texttt{head}}}_{\texttt{symbolic}}, \underbrace{r_{b+h+1}, \ldots, r_{b+h+t}}_{\texttt{timeseries}}) \tag{1}$$

The different components can be seen as a projection of $\vec{r}$ and will be referred to as follows:

$$\vec{r}_{\texttt{body}} = (r_1, \ldots, r_b) \tag{2}$$

$$\vec{r}_{\texttt{head}} = (r_{b+1}, \ldots, r_{b+h}) \tag{3}$$

$$\vec{r}_{\texttt{sym}} = (r_1, \ldots, r_{b+h}) \tag{4}$$

$$\vec{r}_{\texttt{time}} = (r_{b+h+1}, \ldots, r_{b+h+t}) \tag{5}$$

To calculate the *item weights* r_i we adapted the well-known TF-IDF approach [18] from information retrieval. The TF-IDF approach weights terms according to their appearance in a document and in the overall document collection. A high term weight, which is correlated with a high importance of that particular term, is achieved if the term appears frequently in the document (term frequency, TF) but much less frequently in the document collection (inverse document frequency, IDF). This approach filters out commonly used terms and tries to capture the perceived relevance of certain terms.

This method, carried over to association rules, means that items that appear in the vast majority of rules will get a very low weight whereas items that are rather infrequent will get a rather high weight. Since item appearance in rules is linked to item appearance in a data set this also means that infrequent attribute values in the data set will receive a high weight.

The term frequency tf of an item x in an association rule r is calculated as follows:

$$tf(x,r) = \begin{cases} 1 & \text{if } x \in r, \\ 0 & \text{otherwise.} \end{cases} \tag{6}$$

The inverse document frequency idf of an item x in an association rule r and in regard to a rule set R is calculated as follows:

$$idf(x,R) = 1 - \frac{\ln |r : r \in R \wedge x \in r|}{\ln |R|} \tag{7}$$

To generate $\vec{r}_{\mathtt{body}}$ and $\vec{r}_{\mathtt{head}}$, a series of steps has to be performed. For body and head separately, a set of items is generated: $I_{body} = \{x_1, \ldots, x_b\}$ and $I_{head} = \{x_1, \ldots, x_h\}$ where the x_i are the items that occur in body or head of the association rules in R, respectively. Each item of these sets is assigned exactly one vector dimension in $\vec{r}_{\mathtt{body}}$ or $\vec{r}_{\mathtt{head}}$, respectively. Hence, the values for b and h in (1) are the cardinalities of the respective itemsets: $b = |I_{body}|$ and $h = |I_{head}|$

The part of the feature vector of an association rule r which covers body and head consists of TF-IDF values. Let x_i the i-th item of the alphabetically ordered set I_{body} and let r_i be the i-th component of $\vec{r}_{\mathtt{body}}$. Then, $\vec{r}_{\mathtt{body}}$ is defined as follows:

$$r_i = tf(x_i, r) \cdot idf(x_i, R), \quad i = 1, \ldots, b \tag{8}$$

$\vec{r}_{\mathtt{head}}$ is treated in the same way, except that x_j is the j-th item of the alphabetically ordered set I_{head}

$$r_{b+j} = tf(x_j, r) \cdot idf(x_j, R), \quad j = 1, \ldots, h \tag{9}$$

6 Pairwise Similarity

A relevance feedback system must have the ability to compare unrated rules, or features of those, with rules previously rated as (non-)relevant. Instead of utilizing the generalisation and specialisation relationships among rules we choose a more flexible approach based on a notion of similarity among rules. As a similarity measure we have chosen the cosine similarity. It calculates the cosine of the angle between two n-dimensional vectors r and s as follows:

$$sim(\vec{r}, \vec{s}) = \frac{\sum_{i=1}^{n} r_i s_i}{\sqrt{r_i^2}\sqrt{s_i^2}} \tag{10}$$

Since the cosine measure yields values in $[0, 1]$, the corresponding dissimilarity measure therefore is:

$$dissim(\vec{r}, \vec{s}) = 1 - sim(\vec{r}, \vec{s}) \tag{11}$$

The cosine similarity compared to other similarity measures, like ones based on the Euclidean distance, has the advantage that it does not take missing items in a rule into account. For example, when measuring the similarity between a rule $\mathcal{X}y \rightarrow z$ and its more general rule $\mathcal{X} \rightarrow z$ only the item weights contained in both rules (i.e. $\mathcal{X}$ and z) contribute towards the similarity measure. This property of the cosine measure is also the reason why it is frequently used in information retrieval systems. When comparing, for example, a query with a document it is desirable only to take the actual words contained in the query into account and not each of the many words the user did not specify.

The similarity between rules' bodies or rules' heads can be calculated straightforwardly using the cosine measure, yielding $sim(\vec{r}_{\texttt{body}}, \vec{s}_{\texttt{body}})$ and $sim(\vec{r}_{\texttt{head}}, \vec{s}_{\texttt{head}})$, respectively. By averaging both we obtain the similarity of a rule $\vec{r}_{\texttt{sym}}$ with regard to a rule $\vec{s}_{\texttt{sym}}$:

$$sim(\vec{r}_{\texttt{sym}}, \vec{s}_{\texttt{sym}}) = 0.5sim(\vec{r}_{\texttt{body}}, \vec{s}_{\texttt{body}}) + 0.5sim(\vec{r}_{\texttt{head}}, \vec{s}_{\texttt{head}}) \tag{12}$$

The cosine measure is also suitable as a measure of time series similarity $sim(\vec{r}_{\texttt{time}}, \vec{s}_{\texttt{time}})$ which we use in this paper as an example of further information about rules embedded into the rule vector. For time series the cosine measure has the advantage only to reflect the magnitude of the angle between two vectors but—compared with other distance measures (e.g. Euclidean distance)—to ignore the magnitude difference between the two vectors. This means, it is robust w.r.t. different variation ranges of the time series. It is, however, not robust w.r.t. shifts of the time series mean value. Nevertheless, robustness can be achieved by subtracting from both time series their respective mean value prior to similarity calculation.

7 Similarity Aggregation

So far, we have discussed how to calculate pairwise similarities between vectors which represent certain features of a rule like its head, body or a time series of rule measures. For the purpose of relevance feedback it is necessary to measure the similarity of a feature of an unrated rule r relative to the features contained in the elements of a rule set R which may represent relevant and non-relevant rules. Generally, we define the similarity of a vector $\vec{r}$ relative to a set $R = \{\vec{s}_1, \ldots, \vec{s}_m\}$ as

$$sim_{rs}(\vec{r}, R) = \Omega(\{sim(\vec{r}, \vec{s}_1), \ldots, sim(\vec{r}, \vec{s}_m)\}) \tag{13}$$

whereby Ω denotes a suitable aggregation operator which we will describe in the next section. As in Section 6, the dissimilarity of a vector relative to a set is defined as

$$dissim_{rs}(\vec{r}, R) = 1 - sim_{rs}(\vec{r}, R) \tag{14}$$

7.1 The OWA Operator

Our choice of the aggregation operator Ω is guided by two requirements: firstly, the user should be able to influence the aggregation operator, either implicitly or explicitly. Secondly, to obtain comparable results, the aggregation operator should be able to represent also simple aggregation operators like min, max or median. These two requirements are met by the family of OWA operators, which originate in the Fuzzy Domain and have been introduced by [19]. An OWA operator Ω is a mapping $\Omega : S \to \mathbf{R}$, where S is a set of numerical values s_i with $S \neq \varnothing$ and $|S| = n$. The OWA operator Ω has an associated weighting vector $W = (w_1, w_2, \ldots, w_n)^T$ with $w_j \in [0, 1]$ and $\sum_{j=1}^{n} w_j = 1$. It is defined as

$$\Omega(\{s_1, s_2, \ldots, s_n\}) = \sum_{j=1}^{n} w_j b_j \quad , \tag{15}$$

with b_j being the j-th largest of the s_i.

The most important feature of this operator is the ordering of the arguments by value. The OWA operator is in a way very general in that it allows different conventional aggregation operators. This is achieved by appropriately setting the weights in W – different arguments can be emphasised based upon their position in the ordering.

Min, *max*, *mean*, and *median* are special cases for the OWA operator and were described by [20]. They illustrate the generality and flexibility of the OWA operator. By setting the weights accordingly, the user can influence the relevance score to suit the needs of his particular application scenario. For example, $(1/n, 1/n, \ldots, 1/n)^T$ yields the mean, whereas $(1, 0, \ldots, 0)^T$ yields the maximum operator.

Furthermore, the OWA operator is strongly related to the concept of linguistic quantifiers, such as *many, a few, most.* In [19] the connection to linguistic quantifiers is presented by explaining how the weights of the OWA expression can be obtained by using the membership function of any linguistic quantifier.

7.2 Relative Importance of Recent Relevance Choices

The retrieval of relevant association rules is a consecutive, iterative process. The user's knowledge, his beliefs and assumptions change during the relevance feedback cycle as he sees more rules. Therefore, the user's latest choices should be considered as having a higher priority over the first, relatively uninformed ones. This concept can be captured as the *decay of a relevant or non-relevant* rule's importance over time. The similarity aggregation should account for this and thus should weight recently selected rules higher than older ones.

Let $t(r)$ be the *age* of a relevant or non-relevant association rule r. This means, $t(r)$ is the number of feedback cycles that have been performed since the rule r was marked as being (non-)relevant, thereby a newly selected rule receives $t = 0$. Two possibilities to model such a relevance decay are:

$$\tau_{exp}(r) = (1-\delta)^{t(r)} \quad (16)$$
$$\tau_{lin}(r) = max(1 - t(r) \cdot \delta, 0) \quad (17)$$

with (16) for an exponential type of decay and (17) for a linear decay down to a minimum of zero, whereby $\delta \in [0, 1]$ is a decay constant that controls the speed of decay.

This concept can also be described as a kind of *memory* of the relevance feedback engine. The higher the decay factor δ, the faster the system forgets what has been chosen in an earlier step. If we set $\delta = 1$ then our approach would only consider the user's latest relevance decision in its relevance score calculation. The value of $\delta = 0$ would deactivate the decay completely. Values of δ in between those bounds activate a gradual decay. Using the time weighted importance we refine our definition of a vector $\vec{r}$ its similarity relative to a set R and yield

$$sim_{rs}(\vec{r}, R) = \Omega(\{\tau(\vec{s}_1)sim(\vec{r}, \vec{s}_1), \ldots, \tau(\vec{s}_m)sim(\vec{r}, \vec{s}_m)\}) \quad (18)$$

8 Relevance Scoring

Based on the similarity measure we defined in the last section we can develop a notion of a rule's pairwise score, i.e. its relevance score with respect to a certain rule that was marked as relevant. While in information retrieval it is mostly assumed that those documents which are similar to (non-)relevant ones are (non-)relevant too, we use a slightly different approach.

For rules marked as relevant we assume that once a user has seen such a rule rather than being interested in similar ones his attention is attracted by those which are similar in certain features but dissimilar in others. This means, a user aims for rules which have an element of surprise. For example, a rule could have a very similar antecedent, but a rather dissimilar head when compared to a relevant one. It would therefore be surprising to a user because it is an exception to his previous knowledge. This approach also captures the case of rule contradiction employed by other authors [12, 11], albeit in a fuzzy, less crisp way.

Table 1 shows three of such interesting combinations of rule features. The case discussed above is named C_1 in this table. Another example is C_2. It assigns a high score to those rules that are very different in their symbolic representation, but exhibit a similar time series. Such a combination can hint at an unknown hidden cause for the observed changes, which in turn are of interest to a user who typically will assume that only similar rules change similarly. The remaining entry C_3 is basically the inversion of the last one. A rule is considered interesting if it is similar to a relevant one, but has a very dissimilar time series

For rules marked as non-relevant we use an approach similar to the one used in information retrieval, i.e. rules that are similar to non-relevant ones are also considered non-relevant.

similar \ *dissimilar*	head	time series	symbolic
body	C_1	-	-
time series	-	-	C_2
symbolic	-	C_3	-

Table 1: Interestingness Matrix

Based on these considerations our calculation of the overall relevance score is split into two parts: one each for the relevant and non-relevant rules, respectively.

Our definition of the relevance of a rule with regard to the set of relevant rules is rather straightforward and shown in (19),(20) and (21) for the three cases mentioned above. To pick up on our examples from the previous section, using C_1 a rule receives a high relevance score if its body is similar to the rule bodies in $R_\mathtt{r}$ and its head dissimilar to the rule heads in $R_\mathtt{r}$. Likewise, the score for C_2 is calculated by multiplying the similarity of the rule/rule set combination for the time series with the dissimilarity of the rule/rule set combination for the symbolic representation.

$$C_1 \;:\; \Phi(\vec{r}, R_\mathtt{r}) = sim_{rs}(\vec{r}_\mathtt{body}, R_\mathtt{r}) dissim_{rs}(\vec{r}_\mathtt{head}, R_\mathtt{r}) \quad (19)$$

$$C_2 \;:\; \Phi(\vec{r}, R_\mathtt{r}) = sim_{rs}(\vec{r}_\mathtt{time}, R_\mathtt{r}) dissim_{rs}(\vec{r}_\mathtt{sym}, R_\mathtt{r}) \quad (20)$$

$$C_3 \;:\; \Phi(\vec{r}, R_\mathtt{r}) = sim_{rs}(\vec{r}_\mathtt{sym}, R_\mathtt{r}) dissim_{rs}(\vec{r}_\mathtt{time}, R_\mathtt{r}) \quad (21)$$

For the non-relevant rules we assume that rules in $R_\mathtt{n}$ specify a subspace of the rule space where more non-relevant rules are located. To direct the user away from this subspace, rules that are far away from it will receive a higher score, whereas those in the vicinity will receive a low score. An unrated rule r should therefore receive a high interestingness score the more dissimilar it is from the set of non-relevant rules, i.e.

$$\Psi(\vec{r}, R_\mathtt{n}) = dissim(\vec{r}, R_\mathtt{n}) \quad (22)$$

Our final relevance score of an unrated rule r under consideration of the set of relevant and (non-)relevant rules consists of two parts, $\Phi(\vec{r}, R_\mathtt{r})$ and $\Psi(\vec{r}, R_\mathtt{n})$, which are both weighted to give the user more influence on the scoring.

$$F(\vec{r}, R_\mathtt{r}, R_\mathtt{n}) = w_\mathtt{rel} \Phi(\vec{r}, R_\mathtt{r}) + w_\mathtt{nrel} \Psi(\vec{r}, R_\mathtt{n}) \quad (23)$$

After every feedback cycle, i.e. after every update of $R_\mathtt{r}$ or $R_\mathtt{n}$, each unrated rule r is being reevaluated whereby a new score $F(\vec{r}, R_\mathtt{r}, R_\mathtt{n})$ is assigned. Rules which previously have been ranked as rather non-relevant can now receive a higher score whereas others may lose their relevance.

9 Conclusion

In this paper we have dealt with the well-known issue of finding the most relevant rules within a large set of association rules. By leveraging techniques and concepts from Information Retrieval we have proposed a novel method for association rule relevance feedback which has several advantages compared to existing methods. Firstly, it allows a user to refine his notion of relevancy over time by providing feedback. Secondly, it utilizes a more flexible notion of related rules based on vector similarity. Thirdly, it allows to incorporate further information about rules into the exploration process by turning the symbolic notion of a rule into a numeric feature vector.

Our approach is currently being trialed within BT Group to assist users in exploring association rule changes with the CRM (Customer Relationship Management) domain. So far, the results we obtained are quite promising and underlining the usefulness of our relevance feedback method.

References

[1] Rakesh Agrawal, Tomasz Imielinski, and Arun N. Swami. Mining association rules between sets of items in large databases. In *Proc. ACM SIGMOD 1993*, pages 207–216, Washington, DC, 1993.

[2] Rakesh Agrawal and Ramakrishnan Srikant. Fast algorithms for mining association rules. In Jorge B. Bocca, Matthias Jarke, and Carlo Zaniolo, editors, *Proc. 20th Int. Conf. Very Large Data Bases, VLDB*, pages 487–499. Morgan Kaufmann, 12–15 1994.

[3] Ke Wang, Yuelong Jiang, and Laks V. S. Lakshmanan. Mining unexpected rules by pushing user dynamics. In *Proceedings of the 9th ACM SIGKDD International Conference on Knowledge Discovery and Data Mining*, pages 246–255, 2003.

[4] Dong Xin, Xuehua Shen, Qiaozhu Mei, and Jiawei Han. Discovering interesting patterns through user's interactive feedback. In *Proceedings of the 12th ACM SIGKDD International Conference on Knowledge Discovery and Data Mining*, pages 773–778, New York, NY, USA, 2006. ACM Press.

[5] Ricardo A. Baeza-Yates and Berthier A. Ribeiro-Neto. *Modern Information Retrieval.* ACM Press / Addison-Wesley, 1999.

[6] Pang-Ning Tan, Vipin Kumar, and Jaideep Srivastava. Selecting the right objective measure for association analysis. *Information Systems*, 29(4):293–313, 2004.

[7] Abraham Silberschatz and Alexander Tuzhilin. What makes patterns interesting in knowledge discovery systems. *IEEE Transactions on Knowledge and Data Engineering*, 8(6):970–974, 1996.

[8] G. Piatesky-Shapiro and C. J. Matheus. The interestingness of deviations. In *Proceedings AAAI workshop on Knowledge Discovery in Databases*, pages 25–36, 1994.

[9] Balaji Padmanabhan and Alexander Tuzhilin. Unexpectedness as a measure of interestingness in knowledge discovery. *Decision Support Systems*, 27, 1999.

[10] Balaji Padmanabhan and Alexander Tuzhilin. Small is beautiful: discovering the minimal set of unexpected patterns. In *Proceedings of the 6th ACM SIGKDD International Conference on Knowledge Discovery and Data Mining*, pages 54–63, 2000.

[11] Balaji Padmanabhan and Alexander Tuzhilin. Knowledge refinement based on the discovery of unexpected patterns in data mining. *Decision Support Systems*, 33(3):309–321, 2002.

[12] Bing Liu, Wynne Hsu, and Shu Chen. Using general impressions to analyze discovered classification rules. In *Proceedings of the 3rd ACM SIGKDD International Conference on Knowledge Discovery and Data Mining*, pages 31–36, 1997.

[13] Bing Liu, Wynne Hsu, Shu Chen, and Yiming Ma. Analyzing the subjective interestingness of association rules. *IEEE Intelligent Systems*, 15(5):47–55, 2000.

[14] David B. Fogel. The advantages of evolutionary computation. In D. Lundh, B. Olsson, and A. Narayanan, editors, *Bio-Computing and Emergent Computation*. World Scientific Press, Singapore, 1997.

[15] Gerard Salton. *The SMART Information Retrieval System*. Prentice Hall, Englewood Cliffs, NJ, 1971.

[16] Tommi Jaakkola and Hava Siegelmann. Active information retrieval. In *Advances in Neural Information Processing Systems 14*, pages 777–784. MIT Press, 2001.

[17] Mirko Boettcher, Detlef Nauck, Dymitr Ruta, and Martin Spott. Towards a framework for change detection in datasets. In *Proceedings of the 26th SGAI International Conference on Innovative Techniques and Applications of Artificial Intelligence*, pages 115–128. Springer, 2006.

[18] Gerard Salton and Chris Buckley. Term weighting approaches in automatic text retrieval. *Information Processing and Management*, 5(24):513– 523, 1987.

[19] Ronald R. Yager. On ordered weighted averaging aggregation operators in multicriteria decisionmaking. *IEEE Trans. Syst. Man Cybern.*, 18(1):183–190, 1988.

[20] Ronald R. Yager. On the inclusion of importances in owa aggregations. In *The ordered weighted averaging operators: theory and applications*, pages 41–59, Norwell, MA, USA, 1997. Kluwer Academic Publishers.

Visualization and Grouping of Graph Patterns in Molecular Databases

Edgar H. de Graaf Walter A. Kosters
Joost N. Kok
Leiden Institute of Advanced Computer Science
Leiden University, The Netherlands

Jeroen Kazius
Leiden/Amsterdam Center for Drug Research
Leiden University, The Netherlands

Abstract

Mining subgraphs is an area of research where we have a given set of graphs, and we search for (connected) subgraphs contained in these graphs. In this paper we focus on the analysis of graph patterns where the graphs are molecules and the subgraphs are patterns. In the analysis of fragments one is interested in the molecules in which the patterns occur. This data can be very extensive and in this paper we introduce a technique of making it better available using visualization. The user does not have to browse all the occurrences in search of patterns occurring in the same molecules; instead the user can directly see which subgraphs are of interest.

1 Introduction

Mining frequent patterns is an important area of data mining where we discover substructures that occur often in (semi-)structured data. The research in this work will be in the area of frequent subgraph mining. These *subgraphs* are connected vertex- and edge-labeled graphs that are subgraphs of a given set of graphs. A subgraph is considered to be frequent if it occurs in at least *minsupp* transactions, where *minsupp* is a user-defined threshold above which patterns are considered to be frequent. The *frequent subgraph mining* algorithm will discover all these frequent subgraphs. Figure 1 shows an example graph and two of its subgraphs.

This work is motivated by bio-chemists wishing to view co-occurrences of subgraphs in a dataset of molecules (graphs):

- For a bio-chemist it is very interesting to know which fragments occur often together, for example in so-called active molecules. This is because frequent co-occurrence implies that the fragments are needed simultaneously for biological activity.

- Pharmaceutical companies provide generated libraries of molecules. A visualization of co-occurrences in molecule libraries gives a bio-chemist insight how the libraries are constructed by the company.

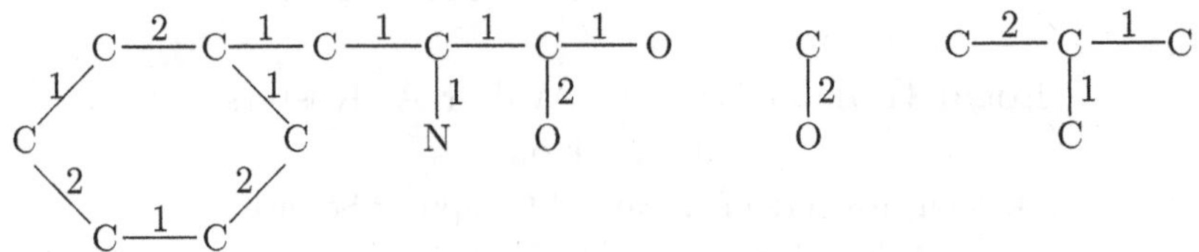

Figure 1: An example of a graph (the amino acid Phenylalanine) in the molecule data set and two of its many (connected) subgraphs, also called patterns or fragments.

The distance between patterns, the amount of co-occurrence, can be measured by calculating in how many graphs (or transactions) only one of the two patterns occurs: if this never happens then these patterns are very close to each other and if this always happens then their distance is very large.

We will define our method of building a co-occurrence model and show its usefulness. To this end, this paper makes the following contributions:
— The visualization of co-occurring graph patterns.
— We improve the clarity of the visualization by grouping.
— We will define a measure of calculating distances between patterns and show how it can be calculated (Section 2 and Section 3).
— An empirical discussion of model construction for visualizing co-occurrence (Section 5).

The mining techniques for molecules in this paper make use of a graph miner called GSPAN, introduced in [17] by Yan and Han.

For the visualization a method of pushing and pulling points in accordance with a distance measure is used. The main reason to choose this particular method was because it enables us to put a limit on the number iterations and still have a result. Similar techniques were used in [1] to cluster criminal careers and in [8] for clustering association rules.

This research is related to research on clustering, in particular of molecules. Also our work is related to frequent subgraph mining and frequent pattern mining when lattices are discussed. In [18] Zaki et al. discuss different ways for searching through the lattice and they propose the ECLAT algorithm.

Clustering in the area of biology is important because of the visualization that it can provide. In general our work is related to SOMs as developed by Kohonen (see [7]), in the sense that SOMs are also used to visualize data through a distance measure. A Self-Organizing Map (SOM) is a type of artificial neural network that is trained to produce a low dimensional representation of the training samples. A SOM is constructed by moving the best matching point and its neighbours (within a lattice of neurons) towards the input node. SOMs have been used in a biological context many times, for example in [5, 11]. In some cases molecules are clustered via numeric data describing each molecule, in [16] clustering such data is investigated. Also our work is related to work done on the identification *structure activity relationships* (SARs) where one relates biological activity of molecules by analyzing their chemical structure [3, 6] in the sense that in our work the structure of a graph is used to build a model. In [2, 13, 14] a statistical analysis was done on the presence of fragment substructures in active and inactive molecules. However our work is not concerned with the discovery of SARs, but with co-occurrence of subgraphs occurring in a collection of graphs. More related is the work done by Lameijer et al. in [9]. This work is concerned with co-occurring fragments discovered with a graph splitting. Graph splitting breaks molecules at topologically interesting points. Also they use a frequency threshold to filter out some fragments after they were generated, however they do not use frequent pattern mining techniques. Furthermore they do not build a co-occurrence model or a similar visualization of co-occurrence. Figure 2 shows two co-occurring subgraphs (fragments) discovered by Lameijer et al. in their dataset of molecules.

In [4] the current setup is used to cluster data; that paper discusses an application that enables the user to further explore the results from a frequent subgraph mining algorithm, by browsing the lattice of frequent graphs.

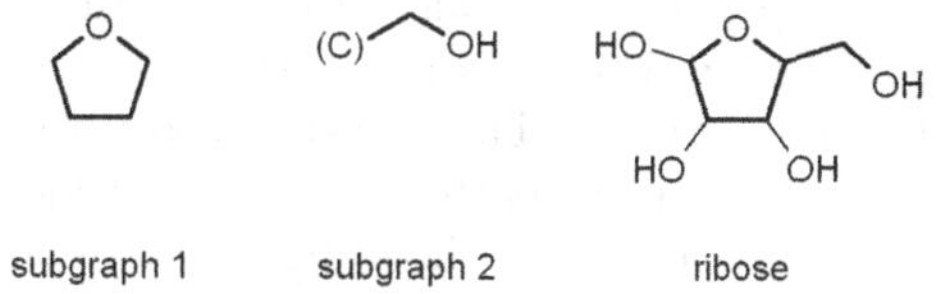

Figure 2: An example of co-occurring subgraphs from [9] with an example molecule.

The overview of the rest of the paper is as follows. In Section 2 our distance measure is introduced, in Section 3 we discuss our method of grouping, in Section 4 we introduce the visualization and finally in Section 5 we discuss our experimental results.

2 Distance Measure

As was mentioned in the introduction, we are interested to know if patterns occur in the same graphs in the dataset of graphs. Patterns in this work are *connected subgraphs.*

The distance measure will compute how often subgraphs occur in the same graphs of the dataset. In the case of our working example it will show if different patterns (subgraphs) exist in the same molecules in the database. This distance measure is known as the Jaccard metric and was primarily chosen for its common use in Bio-informatics (see [15]). It is also easy to compute, given the appropriate supports; it doesn't make use of complicated graph comparisons, that would slow down the process. Formally we will define the distance measure in the following way (for graphs g_1 and g_2):

$$dist(g_1, g_2) = \frac{support(g_1) + support(g_2) - 2 \cdot support(g_1 \wedge g_2)}{support(g_1 \vee g_2)} \tag{1}$$

Here $support(g)$ is the number of times a (sub)graph g occurs in the set of graphs; $support(g_1 \wedge g_2)$ gives the number of graphs (or transactions) with both subgraphs g_1 and g_2 and $support(g_1 \vee g_2)$ gives the number of graphs with at least one of these subgraphs. The numerator of the *dist* measure computes the number of times the two graphs do not occur together in one graph of the dataset. We divide by $support(g_1 \vee g_2)$ to make the distance independent from the total occurrence, thereby normalizing it. We can reformulate *dist* in the following manner:

$$dist(g_1, g_2) = \frac{support(g_1) + support(g_2) - 2 \cdot support(g_1 \wedge g_2)}{support(g_1) + support(g_2) - support(g_1 \wedge g_2)} \tag{2}$$

In this way we do not need to separately compute $support(g_1 \vee g_2)$ by counting the number of times subgraphs occur in the graphs in the dataset.

The measure is appropriate for our algorithm because it exactly calculates the number of transactions in which both patterns *do not* exist, hence a small distance means much co-occurrence. This measure also normalizes the exact co-occurrence, otherwise very frequent patterns can be considered mutually more distant compared to other points with the same proportional co-occurrence.

The distance measure satisfies the usual requirements, such as the triangular inequality. Note that $0 \leq dist(g_1, g_2) \leq 1$ and $dist(g_1, g_2) = 1 \Leftrightarrow support(g_1 \wedge g_2) = 0$, so g_1 and g_2 have no common transactions in this case. If $dist(g_1, g_2) = 0$, both subgraphs occur in exactly the same transactions, but they are not necessarily equal.

3 Optimization: Restriction to Frequent Subgraphs and Grouping

In practice it is possible for the user to select a set of patterns for visualization. In this context we consider an optimization to be an automated selection of patterns such that the algorithm faster provides a model within reasonable time. The **first** optimization is to restrict the patterns to frequent patterns. Patterns (subgraphs) are considered to be frequent if they occur in at least *minsupp* graphs in the dataset. If we do not use frequent patterns we simply have too many patterns and, the frequent patterns give a comprehensive overview of the patterns. Efficient algorithms exist for finding frequent subgraphs, e.g., [17].

The **second** optimization is grouping: we group subgraphs and we will treat them as one point in our co-occurrence model. This will reduce the number of points. Moreover, the visualization will now show more directly the structural unrelated patterns, since related patterns are grouped. This will show to a biochemist the structural unrelated patterns that suggest to be together needed for biological activity.

The formula for the distance between supergraph g_2 and subgraph g_1 originates from Equation 2, where $support(g_1 \wedge g_2) = support(g_2)$:

$$
\begin{aligned}
dist(g_1, g_2) &= \frac{support(g_1) + support(g_2) - 2 \cdot support(g_2)}{support(g_1) + support(g_2) - support(g_2)} \\
&= \frac{support(g_1) - support(g_2)}{support(g_1)}
\end{aligned}
$$

The frequent pattern mining algorithm gives rise to a so-called lattice, in which the frequent subgraphs are ordered with respect to supergraphs. All information used to compute these distances can be retrieved from the lattice information provided by the graph mining algorithm, when we focus on the subgraph-supergraph pairs. This information is needed by the graph mining algorithm to discover the frequent subgraphs and so the only extra calculating is done when *dist* does a search in this information.

Of course, many graphs have no parent-child relation and for this reason we define *lattice_dist* in the following way:

$$
lattice\_dist(g_1, g_2) = \begin{cases} dist(g_1, g_2) & \text{if } g_2 \text{ is a supergraph of } g_1 \\ & \text{or } g_1 \text{ is a supergraph of } g_2 \\ 1 & \text{otherwise} \end{cases} \tag{3}
$$

Note that $lattice\_dist(g_1, g_2) < 1$ if g_1 is a subgraph of g_2 and has non-zero support, or the other way around.

We will now organize "close" patterns into groups. The algorithm forms groups hierarchically, but this can be done fast because only related subgraphs are compared and also as a consequence all distances can be computed with the lattice. Now we need a distance between groups of patterns $C_1 = \{g_1, g_2, \ldots, g_n\}$ and $C_2 = \{h_1, h_2, \ldots, h_m\}$:

$$
grdist(C_1, C_2) = \begin{cases} max(PG) & \text{if } PG \neq \emptyset \\ -1 & \text{otherwise} \end{cases} \tag{4}
$$
$$
PG = \{lattice\_dist(g, h) \mid g \in C_1, h \in C_2, lattice\_dist(g, h) \neq 1\}
$$

Two clusters should not be merged if their graphs do not have a supergraph-subgraph relation, so we do not consider graphs where $lattice\_dist(g, h) = 1$. The value of *grdist* is -1 if no maximal distance exists, and clusters will not be merged in the algorithm.

The parameter *maxdist* is a user-defined threshold giving the largest distance allowed for two clusters to be joined. Note that grouping is efficient due to the fact that we can use the lattice information stemming from the frequent graph mining algorithm.

The outline of the algorithm is the following:

initialize $\mathcal{P}$ with sets of subgraphs of size 1 from the lattice
while $\mathcal{P}$ was changed or was initialized
 Select C_1 and C_2 from $\mathcal{P}$ with minimal *grdist* $(C_1, C_2) \geq 0$
 if $grdist(C_1, C_2) \leq maxdist$ **then**
  $\mathcal{P} = \mathcal{P} \cup \{C_1 \cup C_2\}$
  Remove C_1 and C_2 from $\mathcal{P}$

GROUPING

4 Visualization

We will visualize co-occurrence by positioning all groups in a 2-dimensional area. We take the Euclidean distance $eucl\_dist(C_1, C_2)$ between the 2D coordinates of the points corresponding with the two groups (of frequent subgraphs) C_1 and C_2.

The graphs in a group occur in almost all the same transactions, hence the distance between groups is assumed to be the distance between any of the points of the two groups. We choose to define the distance between groups as the distance between a smallest graph of each of the two groups (*size* gives the number of vertices): for $g_1 \in C_1$ and $g_2 \in C_2$ with $size(g_1) = min(\{size(g) \mid g \in C_1\})$ and $size(g_2) = min(\{size(g) \mid g \in C_2\})$, we let $group\_dist(C_1, C_2) = dist(g_1, g_2)$.

The coordinates (x_{C_1}, y_{C_1}) and (x_{C_2}, y_{C_2}) of the points corresponding with C_1 and C_2 are adapted by applying the following formulas:

1. $x_{C_1} \leftarrow x_{C_1} - \alpha \cdot (eucl\_dist(C_1, C_2) - group\_dist(C_1, C_2)) \cdot (x_{C_1} - x_{C_2})$
2. $y_{C_1} \leftarrow y_{C_1} - \alpha \cdot (eucl\_dist(C_1, C_2) - group\_dist(C_1, C_2)) \cdot (y_{C_1} - y_{C_2})$
3. $x_{C_2} \leftarrow x_{C_2} + \alpha \cdot (eucl\_dist(C_1, C_2) - group\_dist(C_1, C_2)) \cdot (x_{C_1} - x_{C_2})$
4. $y_{C_2} \leftarrow y_{C_2} + \alpha \cdot (eucl\_dist(C_1, C_2) - group\_dist(C_1, C_2)) \cdot (y_{C_1} - y_{C_2})$

Here α $(0 \leq \alpha \leq 1)$ is the user-defined learning rate.

Starting with random coordinates for the groups, we will build a 2D model of relative positions between groups by randomly *choosing two groups r times and applying the formulas.* This is a kind of push and pull algorithm which yields a visualization in which the distances in 2D correspond to the distances in the pattern space. Note that we always have a visualization: the longer we run the algorithm, the better the Euclidean distances correspond to the distances between groups in the pattern space.

5 Performance

The experiments are organized such that we first show that the distances are approximated correctly. Secondly we will discuss runtime in the case of different *minsupp* settings for different datasets. Finally through experiments we analyze the speed-up due to making groups first.

One dataset we use, the `4069.no_aro` *dataset*, containing 4,069 molecules; from this we extracted a lattice containing the 1,229 most frequent subgraphs. This dataset was provided by Leiden/Amsterdam Center for Drug Research (LACDR). Other datasets we use are datasets of the National Cancer Institute (NCI), and can be found in [12]. One of these datasets contains 32,557 2D structures (molecules, average size is 26.3 nodes) with cancer test data as of August 1999; we will call this dataset the `NCI.normal.99` *dataset*. The other NCI dataset contains 250,251 molecules and we will call this dataset the `NCI.large.99` *dataset*.

All experiments were performed on an Intel Pentium 4 64-bits 3.2 GHz machine with 3 GB memory. As operating system Debian Linux 64-bits was used with kernel 2.6.8-12-em64t-p4.

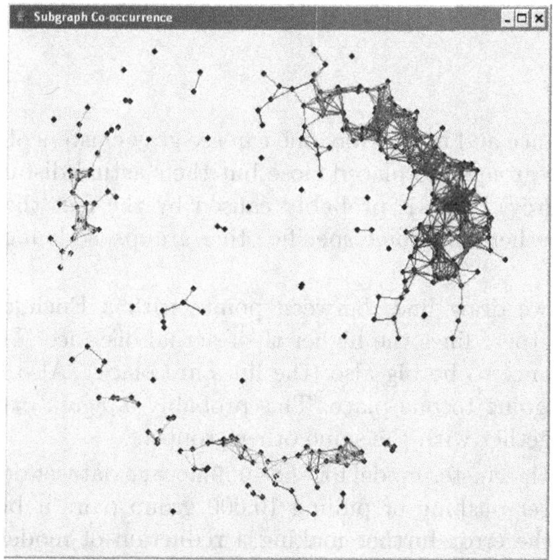

Figure 3: Clusters for graphs in the `4069.no_aro` dataset built in 24.5 seconds, connecting points at distance 0.05 or lower (α = 0.1, *maxdist* = 0.1, r = 1,000,000).

Figure 3 shows how points, that represent subgraphs occurring in the same graphs (transactions) of the dataset, are close together. We draw lines between points if their Euclidean distance is ≤ 0.05. The darker these lines the lower

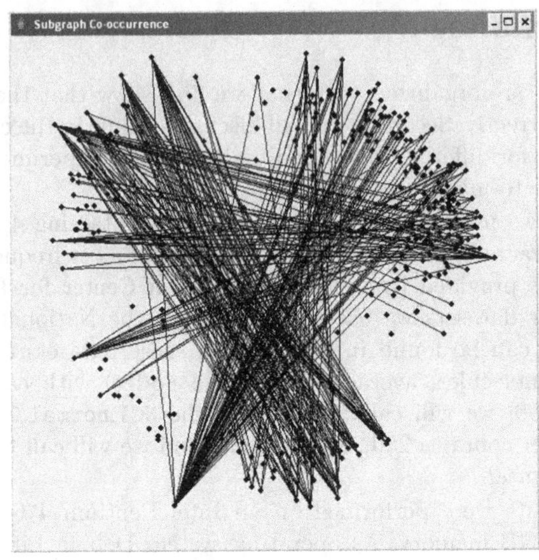

Figure 4: Clusters of graphs in the 4069.no_aro dataset built in 24.5 seconds, connecting points at distance 0.95 or higher ($\alpha = 0.1$, $maxdist = 0.1$, $r = 1,000,000$).

their actual distance and in this way one can see gray clusters of close groups of subgraphs. Some groups are placed close but their actual distance is not close (they are light grey). This is probably caused by the fact that these groups do not occur together with some specific other groups, so being far away from these other ones.

In Figure 4 we draw lines between points with a Euclidean distance ≥ 0.95. The darker these lines the higher their actual distance. The figure shows their actual distance to be big also (the lines are black). Also Figure 4 shows bundles of lines going to one place. This probably is again caused by groups not occurring together with the same other groups.

The error for the cluster model for the 4069.no_aro dataset decreases quickly, see Figure 5. After pushing or pulling 10,000 group pairs it becomes already hard to reduce the error further making a reduction of model building time possible.

In one experiment we assumed that the distances could not be stored in memory. In this experiment we first clustered 1,229 patterns without grouping, taking 81 seconds. However, grouping reduced the number of requests to the compressed occurrence data and because of this with grouping model construction was done in 48 seconds ($\alpha = 0.1$, $r = 1,000,000$, $maxdist = 0.1$, dataset is 4069.no_aro).

Table 1 shows the runtime where *minsupp* varies. Obviously for a lower

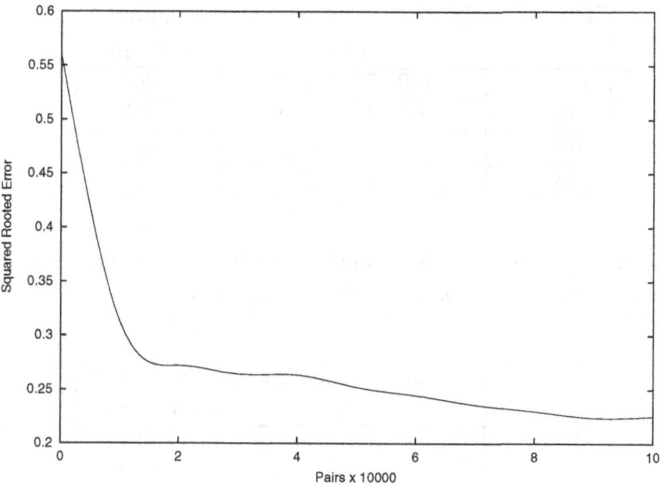

Figure 5: Root squared error for distance given by the cluster model for the `4069.no_aro` dataset ($\alpha = 0.1$).

minsupp it takes longer to build the model, but for 12,734 subgraphs a model is still built within an acceptable time frame.

Table 2 and 3 show the runtime where *minsupp* varies, it is set to a percentage of the total dataset size. Results show that the algorithm is able to handle the `NCI.normal.99` dataset of 32,557 molecules and `NCI.large.99` dataset of 250,251 molecules, even with a low *minsupp*, within a reasonable time frame.

Our final experiments were done to show how the runtime is influenced by the *maxdist* threshold and how much the preprocessing step influences runtime. Here we assume that the distances can be stored in memory. In Figure 6 the influence on runtime is shown and to each line a Bézier curve is fitted (the degree is the number of datapoints). The figure displays preprocessing to proceed more or less stable.

minsupp	average runtime (sec) $\pm$ *stdev*	number of subgraphs
200	2204.60 $\pm$ 6.36	12,734
300	335.10 $\pm$ 2.00	4,571
400	45.75 $\pm$ 0.17	2,149
500	17.95 $\pm$ 0.23	1,229

Table 1: Runtime performance in seconds for different *minsupp* settings for the `4069.no_aro` dataset ($\alpha = 0.1$, $r = 10,000$, $maxdist = 0.2$).

minsupp	average runtime (sec) $\pm$ *stdev*	number of subgraphs
5%	1495.57 $\pm$ 5.41	5,663
10%	160.82 $\pm$ 0.42	1,447
20%	17.09 $\pm$ 0.13	361
30%	4.64 $\pm$ 0.01	158

Table 2: Runtime performance in seconds for different *minsupp* settings for the `NCI.normal.99` dataset ($\alpha = 0.1$, $r = 10,000$, $maxdist = 0.2$).

minsupp	average runtime (sec) $\pm$ *stdev*	number of subgraphs
5%	2080.12 $\pm$ 9.40	2,391
7%	840.49 $\pm$ 11.67	1,313
10%	301.58 $\pm$ 3.57	648
15%	91.35 $\pm$ 0.59	332

Table 3: Runtime performance in seconds for different *minsupp* settings for the `NCI.large.99` dataset ($\alpha = 0.1$, $r = 10,000$, $maxdist = 0.2$).

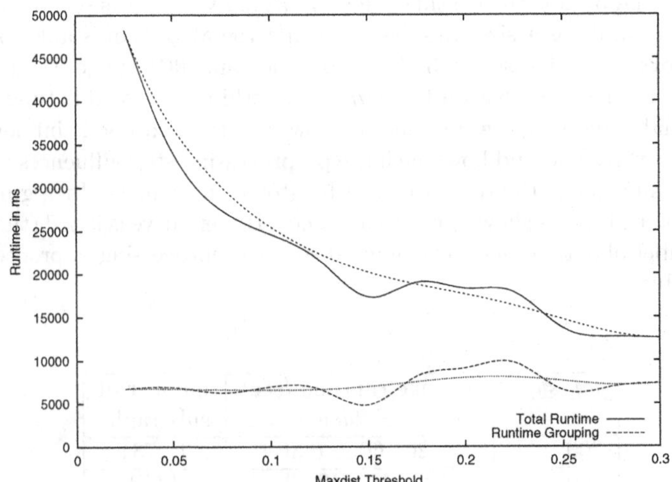

Figure 6: Average runtime for the `4069.no_aro` dataset with varying *maxdist* ($\alpha = 0.1$, nr. of patterns = 1,229, $r = 1,000,000$).

In Figure 7 results show the runtime for the `NCI.normal.99` dataset with approximately an equal number of patterns. The performance for grouping is nearly the same as for the `4069.no_aro` dataset. This performance depends more on the number of patterns that are grouped. The results indicate that the total runtime depends on the size of the dataset, but that runtime can be improved strongly by better selecting the *maxdist* threshold.

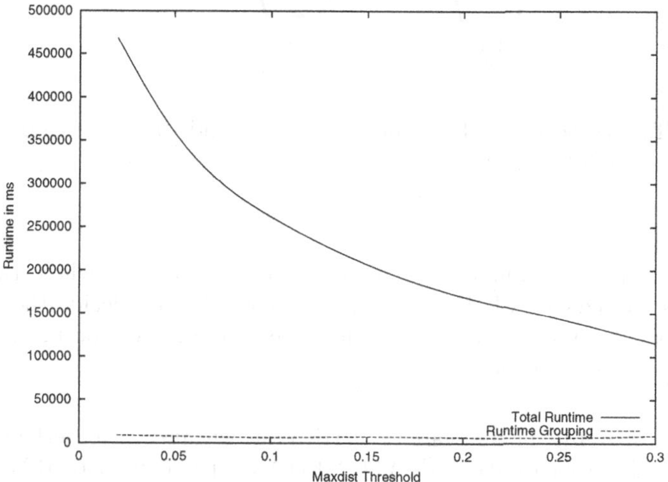

Figure 7: Average runtime for the `NCI.normal.99` dataset with varying *maxdist* ($\alpha = 0.1$, nr. of patterns = 1,447, $r = 1,000,000$).

The first analysis of results shows promising patterns, see Figure 8. The results show two frequent subgraphs (a) and (b) occurring together. This suggests that patterns (c) and (d) might also occur together, requiring further research.

Also biochemists in Leiden are actively researching the development of simple biologically active molecules consisting of fragments (subgraphs) not co-occurring frequently [10]. Modeling co-occurrence will hopefully help improve their analysis.

6 Conclusions and Future Work

Presenting data mining results to the user in an efficient way is important. In this paper we propose a visualization of a co-occurrence model for subgraphs that enables quicker exploration of occurrence data.

The forming of groups improves the visualization. The visualization enables the user to quickly select the interesting subgraphs for which the user wants to investigate the graphs in which the subgraphs occur. Additionally the model can be built faster because of the grouping of the subgraphs.

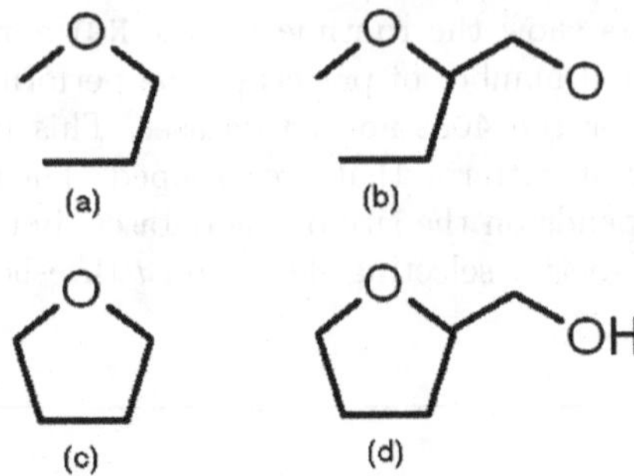

Figure 8: Two co-occurring frequent patterns (a) and (b), and two potentially interesting ones (c) and (d).

In the future we want to take a closer look at grouping where the types of vertices and edges and their corresponding weight also decide their group. Furthermore, we want to investigate how we can compress occurrence more efficiently and access it faster.

Acknowledgments This research is carried out within the Netherlands Organization for Scientific Research (NWO) MISTA Project (grant no. 612.066.304). We thank Siegfried Nijssen for his implementation of GSPAN.

References

[1] Bruin, J.S. de, Cocx, T.K., Kosters, W.A., Laros, J.F.J. and Kok, J.N.: *Data Mining Approaches to Criminal Career Analysis*, in Proc. 6th IEEE International Conference on Data Mining (ICDM 2006), pp. 171–177.

[2] Gao, H., Williams, C., Labute, P. and Bajorath, J.W.: *Binary Quantitative Structure-Activity Relationship (QSAR) Analysis of Estrogen*, Journal of Chemical Information and Computer Sciences, 39 (1999), pp. 164–168.

[3] Gedeck, P. and Willett, P.: *Visual and Computational Analysis of Structure-Activity Relationships in High-Throughput Screening Data*, Current Opinion in Chemical Biology 5 (2001), pp. 389–395.

[4] Graaf, E.H. de, Kok, J.N. and Kosters, W.A.: *Improving the Exploration of Graph Mining Results with Clustering*, in Proc. 4th IFIP Conference on Artificial Intelligence Applications and Innovations (AIAI2007), to appear.

[5] Hanke, J., Beckmann, G., Bork, P. and Reich, J.G.: *Self-Organizing Hierarchic Networks for Pattern Recognition in Protein Sequence*, Protein Science Journal 5 (1996), pp. 72–82.

[6] Izrailev, S. and Agrafiotis, D.K.: *A Method for Quantifying and Visualizing the Diversity of QSAR Models*, Journal of Molecular Graphics and Modelling 22 (2004), pp. 275–284

[7] Kohonen, T.: *Self-Organizing Maps*, Volume 30 of Springer Series in Information Science, Springer, second edition, 1997.

[8] Kosters, W.A. and Wezel, M.C. van: *Competitive Neural Networks for Customer Choice Models*, in E-Commerce and Intelligent Methods, Volume 105 of Studies in Fuzziness and Soft Computing, Physica-Verlag, Springer, 2002, pp. 41–60.

[9] Lameijer, E.W., Kok, J.N., Bäck, T. and IJzerman, A.P.: *Mining a Chemical Database for Fragment Co-Occurrence: Discovery of "Chemical Clichés"* Journal of Chemical Information and Modelling 46 (2006), pp. 553–562.

[10] Lameijer, E.W., Tromp, R.A., Spanjersberg, R.F., Brussee, J. and IJzerman, A.P.: *Designing Active Template Molecules by Combining Computational De Novo Design and Human Chemist's Expertise* Journal of Medicinal Chemistry 50 (2007), pp. 1925–1932.

[11] Mahony, S., Hendrix, D., Smith, T.J. and Golden, A.: *Self-Organizing Maps of Position Weight Matrices for Motif Discovery in Biological Sequences*, Artificial Intelligence Review Journal 24 (2005), pp. 397–413.

[12] National Cancer Institute (NCI), DTP/2D and 3D structural information, `http : //cactus.nci.nih.gov/ncidb2/download.html`.

[13] Rhodes, N., Willet, P., Dunbar, J. and Humblet, C.: *Bit-String Methods for Selective Compound Acquisition*, Journal of Chemical Information and Computer Sciences 40 (2000), pp. 210–214.

[14] Roberts, G., Myatt, G.J., Johnson, W.P., Cross, K.P. and Blower Jr, P.E.: *LeadScope: Software for Exploring Large Sets of Screening Data*, Journal of Chemical Information and Computer Sciences 40 (2000), pp. 1302–1314.

[15] Willet, P., Barnad, J.M. and Downs, G.M.J.: *Chemical Similarity Searching*, Journal of Chemical Information and Computer Sciences 38 (1999), pp. 983–996.

[16] Xu, J., Zhang, Q. and Shih, C.-K.: *V-Cluster Algorithm: A New Algorithm for Clustering Molecules Based Upon Numeric Data*, Molecular Diversity 10 (2006), pp. 463–478.

[17] Yan, X. and Han, J.: *gSpan: Graph-Based Substructure Pattern Mining*, in Proc. 2002 IEEE International Conference on Data Mining (ICDM 2002), pp. 721–724.

[18] Zaki, M., Parthasarathy, S., Ogihara, M. and Li, W.: *New Algorithms for Fast Discovery of Association Rules*, in Proc. 3rd International Conference on Knowledge Discovery and Data Mining (KDD 1997), pp. 283–296.

A Classification Algorithm based on Concept Similarity

João Paulo Domingos-Silva
Universidade Federal de Minas Gerais (UFMG)
Belo Horizonte, Minas Gerais, Brazil
jpaulo@dcc.ufmg.br

Newton José Vieira
Universidade Federal de Minas Gerais (UFMG)
Belo Horizonte, Minas Gerais, Brazil
nvieira@dcc.ufmg.br

Abstract

Due to its mathematical foundation and intuitive diagrams (concept lattices), formal concept analysis (FCA) is an attractive alternative for data mining. This work proposes a FCA-based classification algorithm called "Similar Concepts". Unlike previous proposals, the algorithm searches the concept lattice for similar formal concepts, which classify unseen objects. Despite its complexity limitations (inherent to FCA algorithms), "Similar Concepts" usually presents better accuracy than previous FCA-based classification algorithms.

1 Introduction

Due to the huge volume of data stored in repositories, data mining performs nowadays an essential role in the process of information and knowledge discovery. Classification is a common data mining task, for instance in diagnosis applications. This work proposes a classification algorithm that uses concept lattices (from formal concept analysis), represented by diagrams that explicitly show the search space to be explored. Besides a theoretical presentation, this work also discusses practical issues, comparing different proposals for classification.

This paper is organized in the following way: Section 2 introduces classification and formal concept analysis; Section 3 examines previous approaches to classification that use lattices; the new algorithm – called "Similar Concepts" – is presented in Section 4; experimentation and comparison are the subject of Section 5; the last section contains some final remarks.

2 Foundations

This section briefly introduces classification and formal concept analysis, mainly for reasons of terminology agreement. The reader is invited to search for further details in the literature (some suggested readings are [1, 2, 3, 4]).

2.1 Classification

Data mining is an essential step in knowledge discovery in databases (KDD), which is the process of converting data into information and ultimately into knowledge. Data mining tasks are expected to discover useful patterns in large repositories. Such repositories are usually represented by simple tables, with rows and columns. Classification is the task covered here, but before presenting it, it is appropriate to introduce its input.

The input for the classification task is a collection of objects and attributes[1]. Each object consists of attribute values, which are in the attribute domains. For classification, a "special" attribute is called class. Table 1 is an example of classification input; the last column is the class.

Table 1: Contact lenses database (adapted from [5])

	Age	Spectacle prescription	Astigmatism	Tear production rate	Recommended lenses
1	Young	Myope	No	Reduced	None
2	Young	Hypermetrope	Yes	Normal	Hard
3	Pre-presbyopic	Myope	Yes	Reduced	None
4	Pre-presbyopic	Hypermetrope	No	Normal	Soft
5	Presbyopic	Myope	Yes	Normal	Hard
6	Presbyopic	Hypermetrope	No	Normal	Soft

Classification is the task of learning a target function (also called classification model) that maps attribute values to one of the class values. Such function can be used both for descriptive or predictive modeling. In the latter case, the learning algorithm consists of two steps. First, a database with known class values is used for producing the classification model; then, the model can predict missing class values in unseen databases.

This work organizes a classification input in the following way:

- $O = O' \cup O''$ is the set of objects used in the learning process;
- O' are the objects for the 1st classification step (learning);
- O'' are the objects for the 2nd classification step (operation);
- $A = B \cup \{c\}$ are the attributes, including the class c;

[1] Although data mining literature uses a different terminology, "objects" and "attributes" are preferred here due to FCA terminology.

- B are the "normal" attributes (there are four in the example);
- c is the "special" attribute called class (*lenses*, in the example);
- $A' = B' \cup C'$ are the attribute values, including the class ones;
- B' are the attribute values, excluding the class ones;
- C' are the class values ($\{none, soft, hard\}$, in the example).

So, in the first step, O' is used for producing the classification function, then, in the second step, this function classifies objects in O''. For instance, the object $(Young, Myope, No, Normal)$ can be used in the operation step, so that its class must be predicted. Classification has different applications, such as medical diagnosis, evaluation of customers profiles, detection of spam messages etc.

2.2 Formal Concept Analysis

Formal concept analysis (FCA) is a mathematical framework, based on the theory of complete lattices. This section briefly introduces its basic notions: formal context, formal concept and concept lattice.

A formal context (O, A, R) consists of objects O, attributes A and the relation $R \subseteq O \times A$. Table 2 is an example of a formal context; it is the one valued version of Table 1, produced by nominal scaling. Each $(o, a) \in R$ (also written as oRa) is read as "the object o has the attribute a". For sets $E \subseteq O$ and $I \subseteq A$, derivation operators are defined:

$$\begin{aligned} E^{\uparrow} &:= \{a \in A \mid \forall o \in E \; oRa\} \\ I^{\downarrow} &:= \{o \in O \mid \forall a \in I \; oRa\} \end{aligned}$$

Table 2: Contact lenses formal context

	Young	Pre-presbyopic	Presbyopic	Myope	Hypermetrope	No	Yes	Reduced	Normal	None	Soft	Hard
1	×			×		×		×		×		
2	×				×		×		×			×
3		×		×			×	×		×		
4		×			×	×			×		×	
5			×	×			×		×			×
6			×		×	×			×		×	

A formal concept of a context (O, A, R) is a pair (E, I) with $E \subseteq O$, $I \subseteq A$, $E^{\uparrow} = I$ and $I^{\downarrow} = E$. E is called extent and I is called intent. The reader can notice that each object of the extent has all the attributes of the intent (and vice versa). $\mathfrak{B}(O, A, R)$ is the set of all concepts of a context (O, A, R).

For formal concepts (E_1, I_1) and (E_2, I_2), if $E_1 \subseteq E_2$ then such concepts have the relation $(E_1, I_1) \leq (E_2, I_2)$. In this relation, (E_1, I_1) is called subconcept and (E_2, I_2) is called superconcept. If all concepts $\mathfrak{B}(O, A, R)$ of a context are ordered according to that relation, they produce a concept lattice, denoted by $\underline{\mathfrak{B}}(O, A, R)$. Figure 1 is the line diagram of the concept lattice of Table 2. Each node represents a formal concept and each edge connects direct subconcept and superconcept. Many algorithms [6] have been proposed for producing concept lattices, but they are not discussed here.

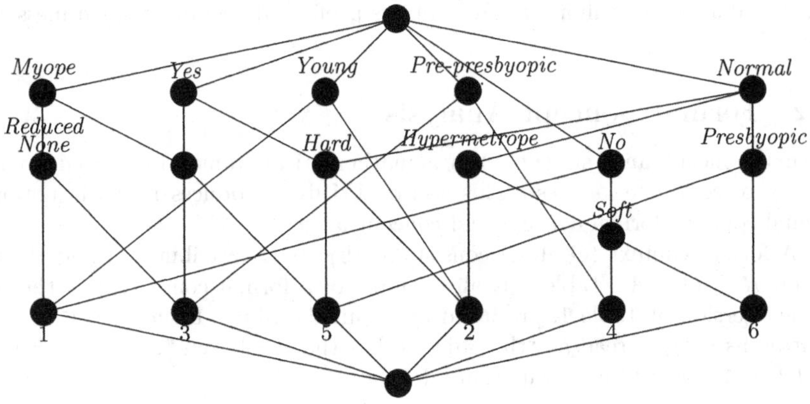

Figure 1: Contact lenses concept lattice

Figure 1 show the concept labels in reduced mode. A simple example helps in better understanding the diagram: the node labeled $\{reduced, none\}$ has the extent $\{1, 3\}$ and the intent $\{myope, reduced, none\}$. For each node, the intents of superconcepts make up its intent, while the extents of subconcepts make up its extent. So, the organization in levels of a concept lattice must not be ignored.

3 Previous Algorithms

Several algorithms using lattices for classification have already been proposed [7]; some of them are briefly presented here. Some produce concept lattices, but others produce pseudo lattices. This last structure is not a complete lattice; it has attribute nodes (the upper ones), object nodes (the lower ones), and intermediary nodes (between attribute and object nodes). Some algorithms produce rules, but others use only the concept lattice.

"Grand" [8] and "Rulearner" [9] are classification algorithms that use pseudo lattices and rules. In the learning step, they produce a pseudo lattice for the formal context (O', A', R_1) ("Rulearner" ignores class values). Then, they produce classification rules (with attribute values in the antecedent and class value in the consequent) based on that structure. "Grand" explores class nodes ant their children to produce the rules; "Rulearner" uses several labels for selecting the best nodes. Both algorithms search for rules with few attributes in their antecedents, but covering many objects. In the operation step, such rules classify (O'', A', R_2).

"Legal" [10] produces a concept lattice and rules in the learning step. It has the advantage of producing a partial lattice, with only some upper formal concepts. However, the algorithm has disadvantages, like its limitation to binary classification and the quantity of required parameters (two for the learning step, two for the operation step). In the last step, rules classify unseen objects as positive or negative (binary classification).

"Galois" [11] (the name is actually adopted in a previous work [12]) uses the lattice produced in the learning step for classifying unseen objects in the operation step. The result of the learning step is only the lattice, which ignores class values. In the operation step, for each unseen object, the algorithm searches for formal concepts in which intents are subsets of the object attributes and selects the class value most voted among such concepts.

4 Algorithm "Similar Concepts"

"Similar Concepts" [13] is an algorithm that uses the notion of similar formal concepts (rather than formal concepts with many objects and few attributes, as in the proposals discussed in section 3) in its classification process. In the step of learning the classification function, the algorithm requires a formal context (O', A', R_1) and produces the ordinary concept lattice $\mathfrak{B}(O', B', R_2)$. Although the objects have class values in the formal context, such values are ignored in the concept lattice. For instance, if Fig. 1 was the output of the classification step, it would not have the labels $\{none, soft, hard\}$.

In its second step, "Similar Concepts" classifies each object of a formal context (O'', A', R_3), using the previously generated concept lattice $\mathfrak{B}(O', B', R_2)$. An important point is that no object in the formal context has class values. In this step, for each object, the algorithm searches for its similar formal concepts and then classifies it. Algorithm 1 presents the pseudocode of the process.

For each object in the formal context, Algorithm 1 searches the concept lattice, using two sets of formal concepts: `current` and `next`. In each search, the most similar concepts to the considered object are stored in `similar`. During the search, if any concept is considered more similar, the maximum similarity `maxsim` and the set `similar` are then altered; otherwise, if any concept has an identical similarity to the maximum one, the set `similar` is then only increased. The process of updating the maximum similarity and the similar concepts have been described here, but it is also necessary to define a similarity measure.

Algorithm 1 Pseudocode for the second classification step.

```
Require: concept lattice 𝔅(O', B', R_2);
  formal context (O'', A', R_3).
Ensure: classes for objects in O''.
  for all object ∈ O'' do
    maxsim ← 0
    similar ← {}
    current ← {(O', O'↑)}
    next ← {}
    for all (E, I) ∈ current do
      sim ← similarity (object, (E, I))
      if sim > maxsim then
        similar ← {(E, I)}
        maxsim ← sim
      else if sim = maxsim then
        similar ∪ {(E, I)}
      end if
      if (E, I) is a promising concept then
        next ← unseen subconcepts of (E, I)
      end if
      current ← next
      next ← {}
    end for
    classify object according to similar
  end for
```

Such measure must say how similar an object and a formal concept are. Since objects have attributes and concepts have extent (subset of objects) and intent (subset of attributes), the measure should consider the quantities of identical and different attributes between the compared entities. Attributes shared by object and concept are called positive here, and attributes that only the object has (they are not in the concept) are called negative. For any object $o \in O''$ and any formal concept (E, I), the similarity measure proposed in this work is increased by positive attributes and decreased by negative ones:

$$\begin{aligned} similarity\ (o, (E, I)) \ &= \ \text{number of positive attributes} - \\ & \quad\ \text{number of negative attributes} \end{aligned}$$

Once the most similar formal concepts have been stored, how does the algorithm classify an object? The question is pertinent, because the set `similar` can have more than one element and they can suggest different classes. An important point is that although the class values are ignored in the concept lattice, they must remain accesible for recovering the classes suggested by the concepts (the most frequent class value among the extent elements is the suggested one). This work proposes two simple approaches for solving this problem; they are called "Similar Concepts 1" and "Similar Concepts 2" in section 5.

The first approach consists in finding, among the most similar formal concepts, the most convincing one. This concept has the greatest percentage of its extent elements with the same class value (if the entire extent has the same class value, the concept is 100% convincing). Then, the class value suggested by that concept is assigned to the object. The second approach consists in classifying the object with the class value most voted by the similar concepts. In this case, the algorithm can require a parameter for ignoring concepts that, despite of the similarity, are not very convincing. For instance, only similar concepts 80% convincing or more could have their suggestions considered.

It is important to present here some details of the search process. For instance, it is necessary to mark concepts as visited or unvisited to prevent the repeated processing of them. It is also desirable to search only regions of the concept lattice which can really increase the maximum similarity. So, after calculating the similarity between an object $o \in O''$ and a formal concept (E, I), the algorithm checks if that concept is promising. In other words, it is checked if any subconcept of that node can increase the maximum similarity to a greatest value. The following analysis says if a formal concept is promising or not:

$$similarity(o, (E, I)) + (|A'| - |I|) \geq maxsim \quad \rightarrow \text{Concept is promising.}$$
$$similarity(o, (E, I)) + (|A'| - |I|) < maxsim \quad \rightarrow \text{Concept is not promising.}$$

The algorithm tolerates, as shown by the similarity measure, the presence of negative attributes in the concepts considered similar, but a restriction is necessary. It is not desirable that any negative attribute determine the class value; it must be implied by positive attributes only. So, for any formal concept (E_1, I_1) and a subconcept (E_2, I_2) that adds only negative attributes, the subconcept is visited only if both nodes suggest the same class.

5 Experimental results

"Similar Concepts" and the previous algorithms presented here have been implemented and their results compared. The programs have been coded in Java (classification accuracy is evaluated rather than execution performance) according to pseudocodes presented in literature. For each program, datasets have been turned into formal contexts and partitioned into O' and O''. The following accuracy measure has been applied to the algorithms after the operation step:

$$\text{accuracy (\%)} = \frac{\text{number of correct predictions}}{\text{number of predictions}} \times 100$$

Several datasets [14] (widely used in the classification literature) have been turned into formal contexts and used as inputs:

BA: "balance scale weight and distance database";

HR: "Hayes-Roth and Hayes-Roth (1977) database";

LE: "database for fitting contact lenses";

M: "the monk's problems";

PO: "postoperative patient data";

SH: "space shuttle autolanding domain";

VO: "1984 United States congressional voting records database";

ZO: "zoo database".

This work organizes the datasets in O' and O'' according to the experiments (it is important to remark that M has 3 versions, but its intersection form here one dataset). Objects with missing values as well as attributes for indexing have been discarded. Table 3 summarizes some datasets information. For producing formal contexts, PO had a numeric attribute converted into categorical, and VO had its attribute domains decreased from 3 to 2 elements (the original attribute values $\{yes, no, ?\}$ have been mapped into $\{yes, no\}$).

Table 3: Original datasets.

	BA	HR	LE	M	PO	SH	VO	ZO
$\|O\|$	625	132	24	432	87	15	435	101
$\|A\|$	5	5	5	7	9	7	17	17
$\|B'\|$	20	15	9	17	26	22	16	36
$\|C'\|$	3	3	3	2	3	2	2	7

The algorithms accuracies have been computed and compared according to different methods – holdout and cross-validation. This last method has its results presented here. In k-fold cross-validation, the dataset is segmented into k partitions, then the program is run k times; during each run, one partition is chosen for testing (the operation step) and the others are used for training (the learning step). The algorithm accuracy is the average of all k runs.

The following tables present the results of the cross-validation method. "Galois" and "Rulearner" have been tested with different parameters values (40%-10% is the tolerated percentage of different classes in each node). "Legal" has been run only for binary classification. In the following tables, "SC" denotes "Similar Concepts"; "SC1" selects the most convincing formal concept for classifying, and "SC2" classifies (with or without parameter) according to the most voted class value (as mentioned in section 4).

Table 4 presents the results of four-fold cross-validation. "Grand" has the lowest accuracies for 3 sets (BA, M, VO) and also the lowest average accuracy. "Rulearner" (in its several tests) has the lowest results for 4 sets (LE, M, SH, ZO). The average accuracy of "Legal" is low, if compared to the other algorithms. "Galois" (in its several tests) has the highest result for PO, but the lowest one for M. "SC1" has the highest results for several sets (BA, LE, M, ZO) and "SC2" (with parameter 40%) has the best average accuracy.

Table 4: Classification accuracy (%) in four-fold cross-validation.

	BA	HR	LE	M1	PO	SH	VO	ZO	Avg
Grand	46.89	69.70	75.00	30.56	57.68	41.67	53.11	84.04	57.33
RL 40%	50.72	71.22	62.50	75.00	67.86	31.25	81.34	65.19	63.14
RL 30%	59.08	79.55	75.00	52.78	64.34	20.83	89.18	76.08	64.60
RL 20%	53.30	74.25	79.17	31.48	62.18	33.33	91.25	76.12	62.63
RL 10%	50.42	75.76	75.00	30.56	51.95	45.83	90.34	84.04	62.99
Legal				55.56		37.50	85.51		59.52
Galois 40%	66.43	69.70	79.17	51.39	71.27	37.50	92.40	77.08	68.12
Galois 30%	65.15	76.52	75.00	53.71	71.27	29.17	91.71	78.08	67.57
Galois 20%	57.14	74.25	79.17	31.48	69.00	35.42	92.17	76.08	64.34
Galois 10%	50.09	71.97	75.00	30.56	57.68	41.67	91.72	83.04	62.72
SC1	69.95	69.70	83.33	75.00	49.62	33.33	91.96	95.00	70.99
SC2	63.86	63.64	83.33	75.00	52.92	41.67	92.64	93.00	70.76
SC2 40%	65.31	69.70	75.00	75.00	57.63	50.00	93.55	93.00	72.40
SC2 30%	66.27	72.73	75.00	75.00	53.09	45.83	93.55	93.00	71.81
SC2 20%	65.16	71.97	75.00	75.00	50.81	45.83	93.32	93.00	71.26
SC2 10%	65.16	71.97	75.00	75.00	49.68	45.83	91.49	93.00	70.89
Best	69.95	79.55	83.33	75.00	71.27	50.00	93.55	95.00	72.40
Worst	46.89	63.64	62.50	30.56	49.62	20.83	53.11	65.19	57.33

Table 5 presents the results of the ten-fold cross-validation. The oldest proposals ("Grand", "Legal", "Rulearner") have the weakest results – "Legal" has the lowest average accuracy. "Galois" (in its several tests) has the highest results for several sets (BA, PO, SH). "SC2" (with parameter 30%) has the best average accuracy once more; despite of the weak performance for PO, such algorithm has the highest results for many sets (LE, M, VO, ZO).

6 Conclusion

Several classification algorithms (including a new proposal) are presented and compared in this work. Some of them use concept lattices, others use pseudo lattices; some use the diagram for classifying, others use classification rules; some require parameters, others do not etc. Unlike previous algorithms, which usually search for formal concepts with "few" attributes and "many" objects, "Similar Concepts" uses the notion of concept similarity. The similarity measure presented here is quite simple and can be improved in future researches.

As previously mentioned, due to its mathematical foundation and intuitive diagrams, FCA is an attractive alternative for data mining. However, FCA proposals are usually limited by complexity issues, because concept lattices grow in an exponential manner, depending on the formal context dimensions (in particular, the incidence relation R). Since the dimensions of data repositories are a motivation for data mining, solving or minimizing the complexity problems in FCA algorithms is essential to enable their wider application.

Table 5: Classification accuracy (%) in ten-fold cross-validation.

	BA	HR	LE	M1	PO	SH	VO	ZO	Avg
Grand	62.03	68.19	75.00	46.33	54.31	70.00	51.26	86.09	64.15
RL 40%	70.88	76.65	58.33	75.08	67.92	60.00	77.44	67.27	69.20
RL 30%	75.82	78.19	68.33	41.69	64.45	65.00	89.63	82.09	70.65
RL 20%	67.84	74.34	86.67	45.38	62.36	65.00	91.48	81.09	71.77
RL 10%	63.65	63.65	78.33	44.23	48.47	55.00	88.75	85.09	65.90
Legal				50.09		35.00	85.52		56.87
Galois 40%	76.00	69.89	70.00	64.19	71.39	45.00	92.86	78.09	70.93
Galois 30%	72.95	73.63	75.00	48.64	71.39	75.00	92.17	78.09	73.36
Galois 20%	70.54	72.80	83.33	46.08	72.17	70.00	92.40	76.09	72.93
Galois 10%	65.58	72.80	75.00	45.86	55.42	70.00	92.41	82.09	69.89
SC1	73.49	67.36	86.67	75.31	49.31	70.00	91.49	95.00	76.08
SC2	63.89	65.16	90.00	75.08	51.81	70.00	92.17	96.00	75.51
SC2 40%	67.37	69.78	78.33	75.08	52.92	70.00	93.55	96.00	75.38
SC2 30%	70.26	73.52	81.67	75.08	51.81	70.00	93.78	96.00	76.51
SC2 20%	70.41	72.75	78.33	75.08	44.86	70.00	92.86	96.00	75.04
SC2 10%	70.41	72.75	78.33	75.78	46.11	70.00	90.80	96.00	75.02
Best	76.00	78.19	90.00	75.78	72.17	75.00	93.78	96.00	76.51
Worst	62.03	63.65	58.33	41.69	44.86	35.00	51.26	67.27	56.87

References

[1] I. Witten and E. Frank. *Data mining - Practical machine learning tools and techniques.* Morgan Kaufmann, 2 edition, 2005.

[2] P. Tan, M. Steinbach, and V. Kumar. *Introduction to data mining.* Addison Wesley, 2006.

[3] B. Davey and H. Priestley. *Introduction to lattices and order.* Cambridge University Press, 1990.

[4] B. Ganter and R. Wille. *Formal concept analysis - Mathematical foundations.* Springer Verlag, 1996.

[5] J. Cendrowska. PRISM: An algorithm for inducing modular rules. *International Journal of Man-Machine Studies 27*, 1987.

[6] S. Kuznetsov and S. Obiedkov. Comparing performance of algorithms for generating concept lattices. In *ICCS workshop on Concept Lattices for Knowledge Discovery in Databases*, 2001.

[7] H. Fu, H. Fu, P. Njiwoua, and E. Nguifo. A comparative study of FCA-based supervised classification algorithms. In *2nd International Conference on Formal Concept Analysis*, 2004.

[8] G. Oosthuizen. *The use of a lattice in knowledge processing.* PhD thesis, University of Strathclyde, Scotland, 1988.

[9] M. Sahami. Learning classification rules using lattices. In *8th European Conference on Machine Learning*, 1995.

[10] M. Liquière and E. Nguifo. LEGAL: un système d'apprentissage de concepts à partir d'exemples. *Journées Françaises sur l'Apprentissage*, 1990.

[11] C. Carpineto and G. Romano. *Concept data analysis: Theory and applications*. John Wiley and Sons, 2004.

[12] C. Carpineto and G. Romano. GALOIS: An order-theoretic approach to conceptual clustering. In *10th International Conference on Machine Learning*, 1993.

[13] J. P. Domingos-Silva. Algoritmos de classificação baseados em análise formal de conceitos. Master's thesis, Universidade Federal de Minas Gerais, Brazil, 2007. (in portuguese).

[14] D. Newman, S. Hettich, C. Blake, and C. Merz. UCI repository of machine learning databases, 1998.
http://www.ics.uci.edu/~mlearn/MLRepository.html.

Metrics for Mining Multisets

Walter A. Kosters and Jeroen F. J. Laros

Leiden Institute of Advanced Computer Science
Leiden University, The Netherlands
jlaros@liacs.nl

Abstract. We propose a new class of distance measures (metrics) designed for multisets, both of which are a recurrent theme in many data mining applications. One particular instance of this class originated from the necessity for a clustering of criminal behaviours.
These distance measures are parameterized by a function f which, given a few simple restrictions, will always produce a valid metric. This flexibility allows these measures to be tailored for many domain-specific applications.
In this paper, the metrics are applied in bio-informatics (genomics), criminal behaviour clustering and text mining. The metric we propose also is a generalization of some known measures, e.g., the Jaccard distance and the Canberra distance. We discuss several options, and compare the behaviour of different instances.

1 Introduction

In many fields data mining is applied to find information in the overwhelming amounts of data. A few example areas are bio-informatics, crime analysis and of course computer science itself. In data mining, *multisets* (also referred to as bags) are a recurring theme. Finding *distance measures* or *metrics* (for multisets) is one aspect of data mining [7]. When a suitable measure is found, many types of analysis, such as clustering, can be performed on specific documents, DNA and other instances of multisets.

The reasons for finding distance measures are very diverse. In crime analysis [2] for example, it is possible to determine the distance between two criminals based on their behaviour (their crime record). In bio-informatics comparing two species with only the information of their DNA (or short fragments of it) can be done. This is especially useful in forensic applications where DNA strands are frequently damaged, so the fragments that are extracted from samples cannot be given a place on the genome. Even without the information of the placement of the DNA fragments found, it is possible to differentiate between species and even individuals by using techniques described in this paper. We finally mention market basket analysis, where distances between multisets are basic for further analysis. As a motivating example, the distance between two customers can or cannot take into account the numbers of purchases of individual products (thus providing either multisets or sets), and it is also possible to stress the difference between 1 and 2 sales on the one hand and, e.g., 41 and 42 sales on the other hand.

In Section 3 we give a new class of distance measures that are suitable for comparing multisets. The class has a parameter f (a function) that has a couple of simple properties which, if met, will always produce a valid metric. To the best of our knowledge, the class is new, and generalizes several of the more well-known distance measures mentioned in Section 2 and Section 3.4.

For different domains, different problems arise and different distance measures will be needed. For many of them, a tailor made function f can be provided and if the given restrictions apply to f, no further effort has to be made with respect to the validity of the metric. We mention several examples in the applications in Section 4. Different choices of f may lead to different visualizations. Furthermore, choosing such a function f is rather straightforward and intuitively easier to do than constructing a metric directly.

2 Background

Finite multisets from a universe with n elements can be viewed as points in n-dimensional space. For example, the multiset $\{a, b, a, a, b, a\}$ can be abbreviated to $\{a^4, b^2\}$ (since the order of elements is irrelevant) and by leaving out the element names, we get the vector $(4, 2)$ in 2-dimensional space. Several known distance measures can be applied. We mention the most important ones. In Section 3.4 we will show the relation with our metric. In all cases, we consider multisets X, Y over $\{1, 2, \ldots, n\}$, and let $x_i \in \mathbb{R}_{\geq 0}$ (resp. y_i) be the number of times that i ($i = 1, 2, \ldots, n$) occurs in X (resp. Y).

- Minkowski distance of order p [7]

$$d(X,Y) = \left(\sum_{i=1}^{n} |x_i - y_i|^p \right)^{1/p}$$

  For $p = 1$, we get the Manhattan distance; for $p = 2$, we get the well-known Euclidean distance; if we let $p = \infty$, we get the Chebyshev distance or L_∞ metric.
- Canberra distance

$$d(X,Y) = \sum_{i=1}^{n} \frac{|x_i - y_i|}{x_i + y_i}$$

  When both x_i and y_i are zero, the fraction is defined as zero. Often the distance is divided by the number of indices i for which at least one of x_i or y_i is nonzero.
- Jaccard distance for sets [4]

$$d(X,Y) = \sum_{i=1}^{n} |x_i - y_i| \;/\; \left(n - \sum_{i=1}^{n} (1 - x_i)(1 - y_i) \right)$$

– Bray-Curtis (Sorensen) distance (often used in botany, ecology and environmental science) [1]

$$d(X,Y) = \sum_{i=1}^{n} |x_i - y_i| \;/\; \sum_{i=1}^{n} (x_i + y_i)$$

– Mahalanobis distance (generalized form of the Euclidean distance) [6]
This is an example of a metric that requires a more complicated scheme: the covariance matrix of the data must be computed, which is quite time-consuming. We will not further discuss this type of metric here.

3 The metric

In this section we will define our new *class of metrics*. As a parameter we have a function f that must meet several properties.

3.1 Definition

Let f be a function $f : \mathbb{R}_{\geq 0} \times \mathbb{R}_{\geq 0} \to \mathbb{R}_{\geq 0}$ with finite supremum M and the following properties:

$$f(x,y) = f(y,x) \qquad \text{for all } x,y \in \mathbb{R}_{\geq 0} \tag{1}$$
$$f(x,x) = 0 \qquad \text{for all } x \in \mathbb{R}_{\geq 0} \tag{2}$$
$$f(x,0) \geq M/2 \qquad \text{for all } x \in \mathbb{R}_{>0} \tag{3}$$
$$f(x,y) \leq f(x,z) + f(z,y) \qquad \text{for all } x,y,z \in \mathbb{R}_{\geq 0} \tag{4}$$

For a multiset X, let $S(X)$ denote its underlying set. For multisets X, Y with $S(X), S(Y) \subseteq \{1,2,\ldots,n\}$ we define $d_f(\emptyset,\emptyset) = 0$ and

$$d_f(X,Y) = \frac{\sum_{i=1}^{n} f(x_i, y_i)}{|S(X) \cup S(Y)|}$$

if both X and Y are non-empty. Again, $x_i \in \mathbb{R}_{\geq 0}$ (resp. y_i) is the number of times that i ($i = 1,2,\ldots,n$) occurs in X (resp. Y; usually x_i and y_i are integers); $|S(X) \cup S(Y)|$ is the number of elements in $X \cup Y$, seen as set. Note that $0 \leq d_f(X,Y) \leq M$, $d_f(X,Y) = d_f(Y,X)$ and $d_f(X,Y) = 0 \Rightarrow S(X) = S(Y)$. If f also satisfies

$$f(x,y) = 0 \Rightarrow x = y \qquad \text{for all } x,y \in \mathbb{R}_{\geq 0} \tag{5}$$

we have $d_f(X,Y) = 0 \Rightarrow X = Y$. It is clear that properties (1), (2) and (4) must hold in order to ensure that we have a metric; indeed, just consider the case where $n = 1$.

The function f specifies the difference between the number of occurrences of a particular element in two multisets. Constructing such a function is natural and can easily be done by domain experts. Also note that the function f is defined for all positive real numbers; this property is only used when weights are involved (see Section 3.3), and it also makes the proof below more general.

3.2 Triangle inequality

We now show that d_f satisfies the *triangle inequality*, and therefore is a metric.

Theorem 1. *For all X, Y, Z with $S(X), S(Y), S(Z) \subseteq \{1, 2, \ldots, n\}$ we have:*

$$d_f(X,Y) \leq d_f(X,Z) + d_f(Z,Y)$$

Proof. We may assume that not both X and Y are $\emptyset$. If $d_f(X,Z)+d_f(Z,Y) \geq M$ we are done, since $d_f(X,Y) \leq M$. So we may assume that $d_f(X,Z)+d_f(Z,Y) < M$. Now

$$\begin{aligned} d_f(X,Y) &= \frac{\sum_{i=1}^{n} f(x_i,y_i)}{|S(X) \cup S(Y)|} = \frac{\sum_{i \in S(X) \cup S(Y)} f(x_i,y_i)}{|S(X) \cup S(Y)|} \\ &\leq \frac{\sum_{i \in S(X) \cup S(Y)} f(x_i,z_i) + \sum_{i \in S(X) \cup S(Y)} f(z_i,y_i)}{|S(X) \cup S(Y)|} \\ &= \frac{\sum_{i \in S(X) \cup T} f(x_i,z_i) + \sum_{i \in S(Y) \cup T} f(z_i,y_i)}{|S(X) \cup S(Y)|} \end{aligned}$$

where the set T is defined by $T = S(Z) \cap (S(X) \cup S(Y))$. We have

$$\begin{aligned} \sum_{i \in S(X) \cup T} f(x_i,z_i) &= \sum_{i \in S(X) \cup S(Z)} f(x_i,z_i) - \sum_{i \in S(Z) \setminus T} f(0,z_i) \\ &\leq \sum_{i \in S(X) \cup S(Z)} f(x_i,z_i) - \frac{tM}{2} \end{aligned}$$

with $t = |S(Z) \setminus T|$. We conclude

$$\begin{aligned} d_f(X,Y) &\leq \frac{\sum_{i \in S(X) \cup S(Z)} f(x_i,z_i) + \sum_{i \in S(Y) \cup S(Z)} f(z_i,y_i) - tM}{|S(X) \cup S(Y)|} \\ &= \frac{d_f(X,Z)|S(X) \cup S(Z)| + d_f(Z,Y)|S(Y) \cup S(Z)| - tM}{|S(X) \cup S(Y)|} \end{aligned}$$

Now $-tM \leq -t(d_f(X,Z)+d_f(Z,Y))$ (because of the assumption that $d_f(X,Z)+d_f(Z,Y) < M$). So, noting that $|S(X) \cup S(Z)| = t + |S(X) \cup T|$ (and similarly for $|S(Y) \cup S(Z)|$) we get

$$\begin{aligned} d_f(X,Y) &\leq \frac{d_f(X,Z)|S(X) \cup T| + d_f(Z,Y)|S(Y) \cup T|}{|S(X) \cup S(Y)|} \\ &\leq d_f(X,Z) + d_f(Z,Y) \end{aligned}$$

since $|S(X) \cup T| \leq |S(X) \cup S(Y)|$ (and similarly for $|S(Y) \cup T|$). □

3.3 Remarks

Before studying several properties of the metric, we first notice that its behaviour deviates from that of standard distance measures. As an example, if we have two given points, and we move one of these in a "new" dimension, the distance changes considerably whereas in the Euclidean case it does not.

Interesting properties of this measure are:

- If X and Y are "normal" sets, i.e., $x_i, y_i \in \{0,1\}$ $(i = 1, 2, \ldots, n)$, we note that

$$d_f(X,Y) = f(1,0)\frac{|X \setminus Y| + |Y \setminus X|}{|X \cup Y|} = f(1,0)\left(1 - \frac{|X \cap Y|}{|X \cup Y|}\right)$$

- $d_f(\emptyset, (\underbrace{1, \ldots, 1}_{n})) = nf(1,0)/n = f(1,0)$.

Here we use the notation $(x_1, x_2, \ldots, x_n)$ for the multiset X, where again x_i denotes the number of times the element i occurs in X (cf. the example in Section 2).

A variant of this measure can be defined as follows:

$$\widetilde{d}_f(X,Y) = \frac{\sum_{i=1}^{n} f(x_i, y_i)}{|S(X) \cup S(Y)| + 1}$$

By using this measure, we can drop the separate definition of $\widetilde{d}_f(\emptyset, \emptyset)$. Another advantage of this measure is that $d(\emptyset, \{x\}) = d(\emptyset, \{x, y\}) = \ldots = \frac{1}{2}f(1,0)$, while $\widetilde{d}(\emptyset, \{x\}) = \frac{1}{2}f(1,0)$, $\widetilde{d}(\emptyset, \{x, y\}) = \frac{2}{3}f(1,0)$ and so on. All conditions for a distance measure hold, since this function is still symmetric, the distance between identical multisets is zero, and the triangle inequality holds. To show the latter property, we can use a proof that is analogous to the one above, except for the last step, in which we replace $|S(X) \cup T|/|S(X) \cup S(Y)| \leq 1$ by $|S(X) \cup T|/(|S(X) \cup S(Y)| + 1) \leq 1$. Another way of proving it is by adding a new element $*$ that is present once in each multiset. This reduces the problem to the property shown above: $\widetilde{d}_f(X,Y) = d_f(X \cup \{*\}, Y \cup \{*\})$.

The application of weights for certain elements can be done by multiplying the number of elements to which the weight must by applied by the weight. These weights need not be integers, which is the reason why f is defined on real numbers in Section 3.1. As an example, suppose we have the multiset $X = (1, 2, 1)$ and we want to apply the weight 10 to the first element. The resulting multiset X' is defined by $X' = (10, 2, 1)$. We shall return to this issue in Section 4.

In order to obtain more reasonable and intuitive measures, the following restriction can be posed upon f:

$$f(x,y) \leq f(x', y') \quad \text{if } x' \leq x \leq y \leq y' \tag{6}$$

It then follows that $\lim_{k \to \infty} f(k, 0) = M$. In this case it is easy to show that the condition that $f(x, 0) \geq M/2$ is mandatory for the triangle inequality to hold. Indeed, let $X = (k, 0, \ldots, 0)$, $Y = (0, \ldots, 0)$ and $Z = (0, \ell, \ldots, \ell)$. With $|S(X)| = 1$, $|S(Y)| = 0$ and $|S(Z)| = n - 1$, we have

$$d_f(X,Y) = f(k,0) \to M \text{ when } k \to \infty$$

$$d_f(X,Z) = \frac{f(k,0) + (n-1)f(\ell,0)}{n} \to \frac{M + (n-1)f(\ell,0)}{n} \text{ when } k \to \infty$$

$$d_f(Z,Y) = \frac{(n-1)f(\ell,0)}{n-1} = f(\ell,0)$$

Now $d_f(X,Y) \leq d_f(X,Z) + d_f(Z,Y)$ implies $f(k,0) \leq 2f(\ell,0)$ (let $n \to \infty$). With $f(\ell,0) < M/2$ for some $\ell > 0$ this is not true, so the triangle inequality does not hold.

A natural way to generate a suitable f is the following. Start with a function $g : \mathbb{R}_{\geq 0} \to \mathbb{R}_{\geq 0}$, and put $f(x,y) = |g(x) - g(y)|$. Clearly, properties (1), (2) and (4) hold for f. We may take $g(0) = 0$. If in addition g is an increasing function with $\lim_{x\to\infty} g(x) = M$ and $g(x) \geq M/2$ for $x \in \mathbb{R}_{>0}$, f also satisfies properties (3) and (6). If g is injective, e.g., if g is strictly increasing, (5) holds too.

Typical examples include:

- $g(x) = 1$ for x with $0 < x \leq 1$ and $g(x) = M = 2$ for x with $x \geq 1$
- $g(x) = 1/2$ for x with $0 < x < L$ and $g(x) = M = 1$ for x with $x \geq L$; here L is a (large) constant
- $g(x) = 1/2$ for x with $0 < x \leq 1$ and $g(x) = x/(x+1)$ for x with $x > 1$ ($M = 1$), see Section 4; note that if we only use integer arguments, we just need the "$x/(x+1)$ part"
- $g(x) = 1/2$ for x with $0 < x \leq 1$ and $g(x) = (2^x - 1)/2^x$ for x with $x > 1$ ($M = 1$)

We conclude with a more intuitive explanation of the metric. Consider two vases filled with marbles of different colours. We first take a look at the marbles of the first colour. If both vases contain many marbles of this colour, the difference should be small, but the difference between one marble and no marbles should be large. The exact difference can be tuned by altering the function f, which specifies the distance between groups with a different number of marbles of the same colour.

When looking at all colours, we repeat the procedure above and divide by the amount of colours we have encountered. This differs from division by the total number of marbles, or by (some variation of) the total number of possible colours. This latter option, for instance chosen in case of the Euclidean distance, does not keep track of the "sizes" of the multisets under consideration. Choosing the total number of marbles as denominator — as the Bray-Curtis distance does — has the disadvantage that adding one marble of a fresh colour is hardly noticed, while our metric is much more sensible to this. Our metric emphasizes the number of different colours.

3.4 Relation with other distance measures

Many well-known distance measures are special cases of the one we describe here. For example the Jaccard distance can be constructed by any f with $f(1,0) = 1$, where the multisets must be "normal" sets, so $A = S(A)$ and $B = S(B)$. As noted before, this results in the following formula for sets:

$$d(X,Y) = \frac{|X \backslash Y| + |X \backslash Y|}{|X \cup Y|}$$

To produce the Canberra distance (with the extended denominator) we use the following f:

$$f(x,y) = \frac{|x-y|}{x+y} \text{ for } (x,y) \neq (0,0)$$

and $f(0,0) = 0$. Note that this f cannot be constructed by a function g in the way explained above.

4 Applications

In this section we use the following function for f:

$$f_O(x,y) = \frac{|x-y|}{(x+1)(y+1)}$$

This function satisfies properties (1)–(6) mentioned in the previous section; it is a result of using $g(x) = x/(x+1)$. This function has the interesting property that if both x and y are large, the resulting value is small. For example, the (pairwise) distance between 0 and 1 is larger than the distance between 8 and 9, which is intuitive in many applications concerning multisets.

The visualization algorithm we use in this section is a randomized push-and-pull oriented algorithm [5], comparable to a competitive neural network. It gives a projection of the original points in a 2-dimensional space. The reason we use this algorithm is because it is fast and able to give a clustering for many data points, where normal dimension reduction algorithms perhaps would fail. For the purpose of this paper, there is no need to go into detail concerning this algorithm. We only state here that the Euclidean distances between points in the 2-dimensional space approximate the original distances as good as possible.

4.1 Plagiarism

When comparing two documents while ignoring the context and the semantics, we can make a multiset of words in the documents. To accommodate for the difference in lengths of two documents, we can increase the weight for each word in the smallest document by the relative size of the documents. In this way, identical copies of the same text will be detected.

In this paper we will not further elaborate on this; we only mention the flexibility of the measures, which allows for many user-defined alterations.

4.2 Genomics

In this section we will give an example of an instance of our distance measure in the genomics domain. We do not claim this particular instance is the best for clustering species, but from the illustrative example it can be seen that this instance does work.

A *genome* of some biological species can be considered as a long string over a small finite alphabet, usually {A, C, G, T}; it can be converted into a multiset by using a sliding window of length n to count the occurrence of each substring (or factor) of length n (see [3]). Of course the number of occurrences will depend on n: the larger n is, the lower the number of occurrences will be on average.

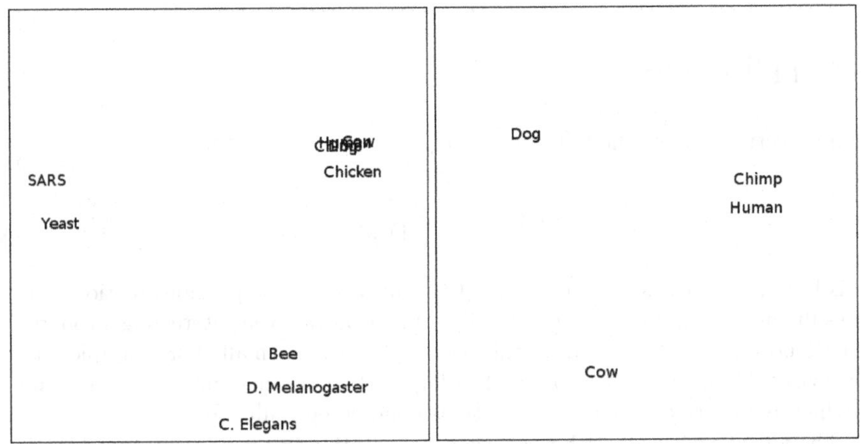

Fig. 1. Visualization for ten species; left: all ten; right: the four mammals

By determining the number of occurrences of each factor in two genomes, we obtain two multisets that can be compared to each other. If we use our distance measure with the function mentioned above, the occurrences of unique or almost unique substrings will account for most of the difference between the genomes. Factors that occur many times in both genomes are accounted for accordingly.

In this way we compare two species mostly on the number of differences between rare substrings in their DNA. In Figure 1 a clustering based on this distance is shown; DNA [8] of ten species (SARS, Yeast, Bee, C. Elegans, Drosophila Melanogaster, Chicken, Cow, Dog, Chimp and Human) is used; the right part of the figure zooms in on the four mammals, which are very close together in the left part of the figure (the labels are practically on top of each other). The sizes of the genomes vary from $3.69 \cdot 10^4$ for SARS to $3.60 \cdot 10^9$ for Cow. As in the case of Plagiarism, we here also compensate for the difference in sizes.

Apart from this type of clustering, other visualizations are possible too: the metric can also be used to generate a phylogenetic tree, for example.

4.3 Criminal records

For comparing criminal records [2], the above function is very well suited. When we make a multiset from criminal records, we get for example a multiset where the first element represents bicycle theft, the second one represents violent crimes, and so on. The difference between no crime and one or more crimes in each category accounts for a large difference, while having two large numbers in each category accounts for almost no difference at all. This is rather useful, since two people who steal bikes on a regular basis, can be seen as much alike.

Of course there are some differences between the categories which one might want to accentuate. For example, a murder is considered a much more severe offense than a bicycle theft. One way to accommodate for this difference is to use a vector of weights $W = (w_1, w_2, \ldots, w_n)$ with $w_i \in \mathbb{R}_{\geq 0}$ and to make the following adjustments to the distance measure:

$$d_f^W(X,Y) = \frac{\sum_{i=1}^{n} f(w_i x_i, w_i y_i)}{|S(X) \cup S(Y)|}$$

It is easy to prove that this adjustment does not change the fact that the distance formula is still a good metric.

Now, by choosing the vector of weights carefully (this must be done by an expert in criminology) we can assign relative weights for crimes. In our example, we can set the weight for bicycle theft to 1 and the weight for murder to a large integer to accentuate the severity of the crime.

As a test case, we made the following synthetic dataset with fictional crimes $\mathcal{A}$, $\mathcal{B}$, $\mathcal{C}$ and $\mathcal{D}$ of increasing severity, and criminals ranging from 1 to 10. For each criminal the number of crimes in each category is given. For instance, 1 is innocent, 2 is an incidental small criminal, 6 is a one-time offender of a serious crime, and 10 is a severe all-round criminal.

	1	2	3	4	5	6	7	8	9	10
$\mathcal{A}$	0	2	10	0	0	0	0	2	0	2
$\mathcal{B}$	0	0	0	2	0	0	2	4	0	2
$\mathcal{C}$	0	0	0	0	1	0	2	0	3	2
$\mathcal{D}$	0	0	0	0	0	1	1	0	5	2

Table 1. Ten criminals, four crimes

In the top-left picture of Figure 2 we see a clustering of these ten criminals with the standard f_0. In the picture right next to it, we applied weights $1, 10, 100, 1000$, respectively, to the crimes, to specify the weight of the crime. We now see that criminals 7 and 10 are very close together, but at the same time, criminals 2 and 3 also stay close. "Criminal" 1 is surprisingly rather close to the two criminals who have committed relatively light crimes. The reason that

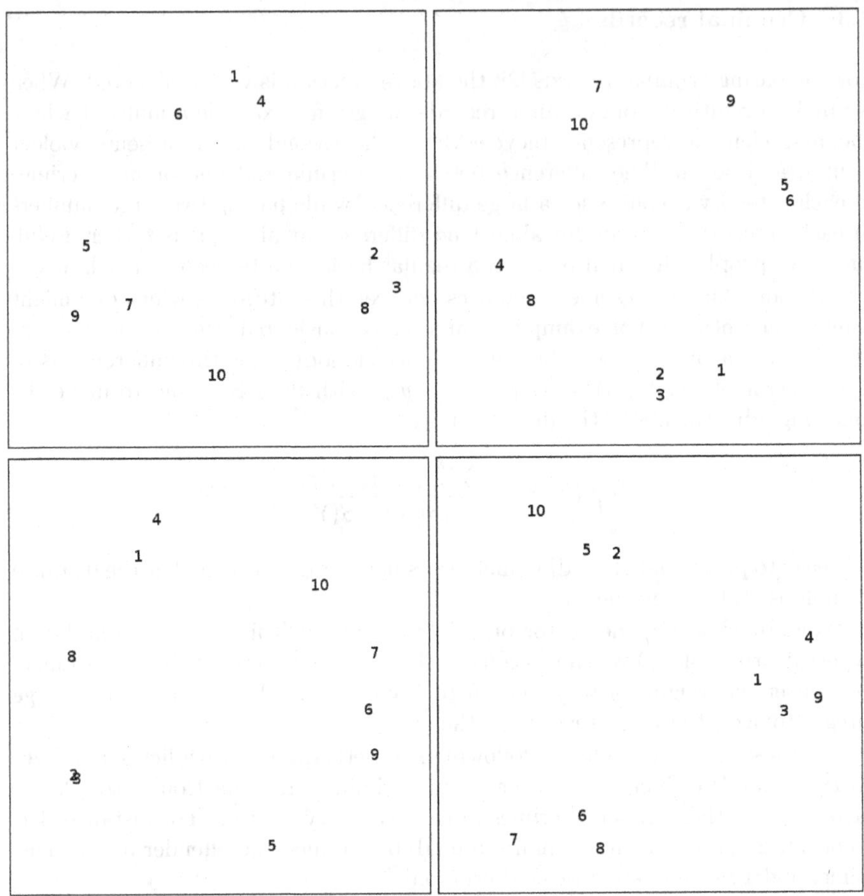

Fig. 2. Four different clusterings for ten criminals

criminals 5 and 6 are close together is because they are one-time offenders, and have a large distance to the rest of the group.

In the bottom-left picture, we see a clustering with f chosen in such a way that we get the Jaccard distance, so we treat the criminals as sets. Notice that criminals 2 and 3 now have distance zero to each other (the labels are on top of each other in this picture). The bottom-right clustering uses a totally different f: $f_1(x,y) = \frac{3}{2} - f_0(x,y)$ for $(x,y) \neq (0,0)$ and $f_1(0,0) = 0$. Note that, e.g., $f_1(0,1) = 1 > \frac{3}{4} = f_1(0,3)$, so property (6) does not hold for f_1. Now criminals with disjoint behaviour are grouped, leading to a "dissimilarity" clustering.

5 Conclusions and further research

In this paper we have proposed a new flexible distance measure, that is suitable in many fields of interest. It can be fine tuned to a large extent.

We can use this measure as a basis for further analysis, like the analysis of criminal careers. In that case, we suggest that the distance measure is used as a basis for alignment to make the best match between two careers. By doing this, and by comparing sub-careers, we might be able to extrapolate criminal behaviour based upon the criminal record through time. We also want to apply the measure to a real, large database. Finally, we would like to examine the relation with more statistically oriented measures.

Acknowledgements

This research is part of the DALE (Data Assistance for Law Enforcement) project as financed in the ToKeN program from the Netherlands Organization for Scientific Research (NWO) under grant number 634.000.430. We would like to thank Jeroen de Bruin and Tim Cocx.

References

1. Bray J.R., Curtis J.T., An ordination of the upland forest communities of southern Wisconsin, Ecol. Monogr. 27 (1957): 325–349.
2. Bruin, J.S. de, Cocx, T.K., Kosters, W.A., Laros, J.F.J., Kok, J.N., Data mining approaches to criminal career analysis, Sixth IEEE International Conference on Data Mining (ICDM 2006), Proceedings pp. 171-177.
3. Hoogeboom, H.J., Kosters, W.A., Laros, J.F.J., Selection of DNA markers, to appear in IEEE Transactions on Systems, Man, and Cybernetics Part C, 2007.
4. Jaccard, P., Lois de distribution florale dans la zone alpine, Bull. Soc. Vaud. Sci. Nat. 38 (1902): 69–130.
5. Kosters, W.A., Wezel, M.C. van, Competitive neural networks for customer choice models, in E-Commerce and Intelligent Methods, volume 105 of Studies in Fuzziness and Soft Computing, Physica-Verlag, Springer, 2002, pp. 41–60.
6. Mahalanobis, P. C., On the generalised distance in statistics, Proceedings of the National Institute of Science of India 12 (1936): 49–55.
7. Tan, P.-N., Steinbach, M., Kumar, V., Introduction to data mining, Addison-Wesley, 2005.
8. UCSC Genome Bioinformatics, `http://genome.ucsc.edu/`.

KNOWLEDGE ACQUISITION AND MANAGEMENT

Knowledge Management for Evolving Products

Thorsten Krebs
HITeC e.V. c/o University of Hamburg
Hamburg, Germany

Abstract

Modern product manufacturers face the problem of managing a variety of products that change over time. A product catalog is constantly subject to change due to increasing technical capabilities and customer demands. This paper introduces a novel approach to handle a product catalog using representation facilities of structure-based configuration. Configurable components from which a product can be assembled are represented in a configuration model and product types are represented in product models. A sophisticated evolution mechanism preserves consistency of the configuration model despite changes and suggests suitable repair operations in case the intended change entails inconsistency. Mismatches between product models and the corresponding configuration model that result from changes are identified and give input for managing the product catalog.

1 Introduction

Modern product manufacturers face the problem of managing a variety of products that change over time. A *product catalog* defines different product types, each of them offering alternative and optional choices to the customer. Such a variety of products is typically needed to satisfy customers with different demands. In order to stay competitive, product manufacturers need to diversify the product variety and improve existing product types over time.

Example. A car manufacturer offers a variety of models from each of which a customer can choose between certain alternatives and options. Alternative selections are, the color of the Car and its Seats, the type of Motor (Gasoline or DieselEngine), and so on. Optional selections are, for example, the possibility to have a Sunroof, a Turbocharger, a Hitch, etc. The development of new Motors that consume less fuel or electronic applications like a ParkingAssistanceSystem, drive the interest of customers in buying a new Car, just to name a few examples. Such developments are not specific to a type of car. Instead, new developments that is integratable into all car types improves return on investment.

On the surface, product manufacturers have to cope with launching new product types or phasing out product types that are no longer sold. Looking a bit deeper into what happens in production, typical changes are the development of new types of components, new versions or variants of existing components and that certain components are no longer produced and thus become obsolete.

Obsolete components need to be replaced in products that will be sold further on. All this has direct influence on the product catalog. It is apparent that sophisticated tool support is needed for managing knowledge about products, the configurable components from which products are assembled and dependencies between them and impacts that changes to components have on products.

Configuration is a well-known approach to support the composition of products from a given set of components. *Configuration tools* have been used successfully for about three decades in different domains. Traditional application areas of configuration are technical or electronic domains, but the approach is not limited to these domains [8]. One of the major benefits the configuration approach offers is that a solution to the given configuration problem is guaranteed to be consistent and complete.

Structure-based configuration, in particular, employs hierarchical specialization structures and composition structures in a *configuration model*. Within a configuration model, all potentially configurable products of a domain (e.g. the car domain) are implicitly represented by defining the components from which a product can be composed, component attributes and relations between the components. Similar products are configured from a common set of components while diversity is realized with different compositions. The hierarchical representation of structure-based configuration is especially appropriate to model products that are assembled from smaller components.

The remainder of this paper is organized as follows. Section 2 describes modeling facilities used for specifying configuration models and product models as well as the notion of consistency and how consistency can be preserved using pre-defined invariants. Section 3 addresses evolution and describes a flexible way of defining change operations. Section 4 introduces the evolution process, which is a four-step process consisting of change identification, compilation of change operations, execution of change operations and evaluation of product coverage. Section 5 describes a prototypical model editor implementing this evolution process. After Section 6 presents related work, Section 7 concludes this paper with a summary and an outlook on future topics.

2 Knowledge Representation

In the following we define a knowledge representation that is based on description logics [2] with Tarski-style model theoretic semantics to formally represent domain knowledge (Sections 2.1 & 2.2). The notions of consistency and product coverage are defined later in Section 2.3.

2.1 Modeling Facilities

A *concept* is a description which gathers common features of a set of components. Concepts are modelled containing two different hierarchical relationships: *is-a* and *has-parts*. The taxonomic *is-a* relation concerns commonalities and differences of the concept definitions while the partonomic *has-parts* relation involves spatial and functional correlation. Concepts are denoted with upper case names, e.g. C, D or Car, and specify exactly one parent concept, and an arbitrary number of *attributes* and *composition relations* collectively called *properties*.

Concepts describe classes of objects from which multiple *instances* may be generated during the configuration process. Instances are instance of exactly one concept (e.g. $i \in C$) and inherit all properties from this concept. Property values may be partly specified and are only allowed to specify subsets of the original values defined in the concepts of which they are an instance.

The taxonomic hierarchy is defined by $D \sqsubseteq C$. Concept C is called *parent* and concept D is called *child*. A concept D is a subconcept of concept C if and only if every potential instance of D is also an instance of C ($i \in D \Rightarrow i \in C$). Within the taxonomy properties of concepts are monotonically inherited. Additional properties may be defined for more specific concepts and inherited properties may be *overwritten* with more specific values.

Attributes define characteristics of concepts and are denoted as roles with lower case names and a concrete domain as role filler, e.g. $a.\mathsf{Integer}$, $b.\mathsf{String}$ or $\mathsf{color.String}$. The name is uniquely identifiable within the taxonomy. Three value domains are pre-defined for specifying attribute values: integer numbers, real numbers and strings. In implementations, however, the potential values of concrete domains are dictated by the programming language.

Composition relations define the partition of complex concepts into simpler concepts and are denoted as roles with lower case names and concepts as role fillers, e.g. $r.C$, $p.D$ or $\mathsf{hasParts.Motor}$. A composition relation between a *composite* Car and a *part* Motor is denoted by $\mathsf{Car} \sqsubseteq \exists \mathsf{hasParts.Motor}$. A number restriction denotes how many instances of the part concept may be related to an instance of the composite concept, i.e. minimum $\exists^{\geq m}\mathsf{hasParts.Motor}$ and maximum $\exists^{\leq n}\mathsf{hasParts.Motor}$ with $m, n \in \mathbb{N}$ and $m \leq n$.

Restrictions between concepts and their properties are expressed with *constraints*. Constraints represent non-hierarchical dependencies between concepts and concept properties, as well as between the existence of instances of certain concepts. A constraint definition consists of an antecedent and a consequent. The antecedent specifies a *pattern* consisting of a conceptual structure, an expression that evaluates to true whenever the pattern matches a corresponding instance structure. The consequent, i.e. a set of relations restricting attribute values or composition relations, is executed when the pattern evaluates to true.

Example. A constraint that enforces equal values for the size attributes of Tire and Rim is denoted with:

$$\mathsf{Tire} \sqsubseteq \forall \mathsf{size.Integer} \wedge \mathsf{Rim} \sqsubseteq \forall \mathsf{size.Integer} \Rightarrow \mathsf{Tire.size} = \mathsf{Rim.size}$$

2.2 Building a Configuration Model

We assume a set of concept names N_C and a set of property names N_P. The latter consists of two disjoint subsets N_A and N_R denoting attribute names and composition relation names, respectively ($N_P = N_A \cup N_R$). Complex concept expressions can be formed from concept names, property names, number restrictions ($\geq n$ and $\leq n$), set intersection ($\sqcap$), and set complement ($\neg$).

Example. A Car concept that consists of a Motor, four Tires and has a color represented with a String is specified as follows:

$$\mathsf{Car} \sqsubseteq \exists^{=1}\mathsf{hasParts.Motor} \sqcap \exists^{=4}\mathsf{hasParts.Tire} \sqcap \forall \mathsf{color.String}$$

Note that the specified characteristics are necessary conditions for a Car (that is why $\sqsubseteq$ is used), not necessary and sufficient conditions (in which case $\equiv$ was used). This means that every instance of concept Car has these characteristics but not every instance with such characteristics is necessarily instance of Car.

2.3 Consistency and Product Coverage

The effectiveness of a configuration application heavily depends on the quality of the underlying knowledge, that is the configuration model. It is thus a fundamental tenet that the model unambiguously represents the knowledge about components from which products can be assembled.

Well-formedness of the configuration model is based on the language specification. A configuration model is well-formed if it adheres to the underlying language specification. *Consistency*, in addition, goes beyond the specification by semantically interpreting the specified knowledge: a well-formed specification may still be inconsistent, for example, when a constraint restricts two attributes in a way that cannot be fulfilled with the specified attributes values.

Example. The size of Rims is constrained to equal the size of Tires, but the Rim and Tire concepts do not specify overlapping values for their size attributes. The constraint can not be satisfied for any combination of instances.

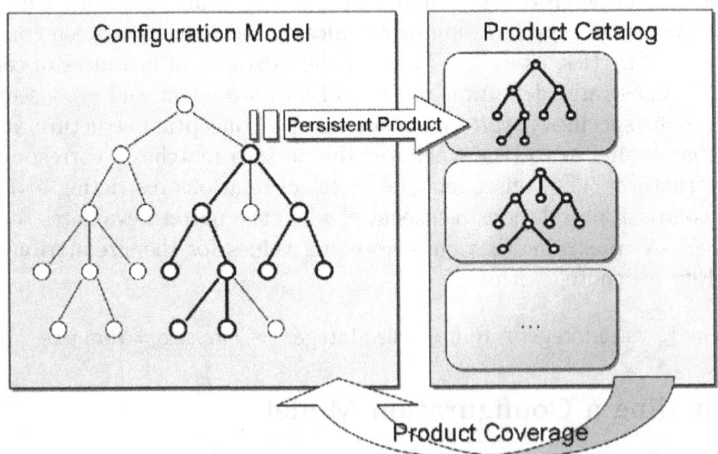

Figure 1: Configuration model and product catalog containing persistent product models.

On top of a consistent configuration model, *product coverage* describes a situation in which a given set of products (the product catalog) is covered by the corresponding configuration model (see Figure 1). A configuration model *covers* a product model when the latter represents a consistent and complete product that is configurable with this configuration model. Both the configuration model and product models are defined using modeling facilities from structure-based configuration. A *product model* in this sense is a subset of the configuration model and a *product catalog* is a set of product models that refer to the same configuration model. Product models are persistent copies of the corresponding subset of the configuration model. Persistent copies are needed because implicit knowledge about products were lost when evolving the configuration model. This way mismatches between product models and the configuration model can be identified and give valuable input for managing the product catalog.

While well-formedness and consistency are enforced, product coverage is not. When a product model is not covered by the corresponding configuration model the product is not configurable using this model. But this may be wanted! When components evolve, they are modified, added to or removed from the configuration model. When some component is no longer produced it can not be used to assemble a product. Therefore, mismatches between product models and configuration models are natural impacts of evolution. These mismatches help deciding how to react to changes and how to adapt the product catalog.

Well-formedness and consistency of configuration model can be ensured by using invariants. *Invariants* are formulae that have a particular status: they must be guaranteed to hold at every quiescent state of the model, that is before and after a change is executed [3]. If changes follow these invariants, it can be guaranteed that the configuration model stays well-formed and consistent.

Well-formedness invariants ensure that a configuration model is well-formed. Every well-formedness invariant has to be satisfied. Consistency invariants ensure that the configuration model is consistent. But the notion of consistency may vary based on the represented domain or the configuration tool. An example for differently understood notions of consistency is the semantics of composition relations, which varies according to three main criteria: whether the relation from the part to the whole is functional or not, whether the parts are homeomerous or not, and whether the part and whole are separable or not. [14] distinguish six major types: (1) component - integral object, (2) member - collection, (3) portion - mass, (4) stuff - object, (5) feature - activity, and (6) place - area. Although product configuration is mainly concerned with type 1, different domains or configuration tools treat composition relations sometimes reflexive or irreflexive, symmetric or antisymmetric and sometimes allow that parts are shared by different composites or not.

A complete list of well-formedness invariants covers that all specified expressions are unambiguous and that references to all neighbored expressions point to indeed specified expressions, the taxonomy specifies a tree structure, overwritten properties may only define more specific values and cardinality definitions of composition relations specify a correct integer interval: the minimum cardinality may not be greater than the maximum cardinality.

Consistency invariants cover, for example, that composition relations may not be reflexive, symmetric or share parts, or that constraint relations need to be satisfiable. Other domain-specific invariants are conceivable.

Due to space limitations we define two well-formedness invariants at this point that are needed by examples in the following:

Taxonomy Tree Invariant A concept has exactly one superconcept.

$$D \in N_C \Rightarrow C \in N_C \mid D \sqsubseteq C \wedge \#\{\text{parent}(D)\} = 1$$

Attribute Inheritance Invariant An attribute overwriting an inherited attribute may only specify a subset (or equal) value of the original value.

$$C, D \in N_C \wedge a, b \in N_A \mid D \sqsubseteq \exists b \wedge C \sqsubseteq \exists a \wedge a = b :$$
$$D \sqsubseteq C \Rightarrow \text{value}(b) \sqsubseteq \text{value}(a)$$

3 Evolution

Configuration models are used to configure products over long time periods. New functionality is implemented, new products are launched, components and products are dropped. Components and products are represented by concepts in a configuration model. An impact of evolution is that the configuration model has to evolve in parallel with the domain it represents.

The evolution support described in this paper offers a set of pre-defined *change operations* from which a knowledge engineer can select. The system preserves consistency of the configuration model by evaluating the necessary invariants. In case an invariant is violated, i.e. inconsistency is identified, potential repair operations are suggested.

3.1 Changes

Change operations, like any kind of actions, are specified through preconditions and postconditions. The *preconditions* for a change operation encode what the model must be like in order for the change to be executable. The *postconditions* describe immediate consequences resulting from the change. In addition, it is known which invariants need to be evaluated after change execution.

Base operations represent elementary changes that cannot be further decomposed into smaller units. This means that a base operation describes an explicit action: the way this action reaches its intended goal does not vary depending on the knowledge specified in the configuration model. There are three types of meta changes: addition, removal and modification. The set of all base operations is the cross-product of modeling facility types and the meta changes. Base operations concerning concepts, for example, are $\text{addConcept}(C)$, $\text{removeConcept}(C)$ and $\text{renameConcept}(C, \mathsf{NewName})$. Addition and removal are defined analogously for all types of modeling facilities. Modifications include, next to renaming, also changing attribute values, composition parts and cardinalities, etc.

Compound operations are compiled from a set of base operations. The way their intended goal is reached may vary based on the current state of the configuration model.

Example. A car manufacturer no longer produces DieselEngine engines. The corresponding concept is removed from the configuration model, which is a simple operation when that concept is a leaf node in the taxonomic hierarchy. However, when there is a descendant TurboDiesel $\sqsubseteq$ DieselEngine, for example, the DieselEngine concept cannot be simply removed (due to the Taxonomy Tree Invariant). There are two viable alternatives: TurboDiesel (including potential further children) is also removed (removeSubtree(DieselEngine)), or TurboDiesel is moved upwards, as a child of the generic Motor concept.

3.2 Composing Change Operations

The compilation of a compound operation is based on *essential operations*, *dependent operations* and *repair operations*:

Essential operations explicitly realize the semantics of the intended change, they are always executed. Removing the DieselEngine or its subtree, for example, removeConcept(DieselEngine) is an essential operation.

Dependent operations are identified and compiled according to the current state of the model. Removing a subtree of DieselEngine, all its children are computed via the transitive closure over the taxonomy. For every (indirect) child, the dependent change (e.g. removeConcept(TurboDiesel)) is added to the compound operation.

Repair operations repair inconsistencies that may occur as side effects of the intended change. Removing the subtree of DieselEngine some specific Car concept may specify the TurboDiesel as a part in a composition relation. Further action is required: either the composition relation is also removed or the part is exchanged with an existing concept expression. It is obvious that a Car without Motor does not make sense – but how to identify a suitable substitute? The taxonomic hierarchy of the structure-based approach helps in identifying siblings or parents, i.e. similar concepts, of the missing part concept.

The ability to construct compound operations from a pre-defined set of base operations offers a flexible and extendable way to define new change operations with minimal effort. This helps defining new types of (maybe domain-dependant or tool-specific) changes. Compound operations are treated as *transactions* [4]: either all or none of the operations are executed.

4 Evolution Process

For every change that is executed, four steps are run through (see Figure 2):

Change Identification: The knowledge engineer initiates the evolution process by choosing one of the change operations the system offers.

Compilation of change operations: The system compiles compound change operations based on the current state of the configuration model: dependent changes are identified and added. In case the intended change introduces inconsistency, repair operations are computed and selected.

Execution of change operations: The compiled change operations are sequentially executed.

Evaluation of product coverage: When a change has been successfully executed, product coverage is evaluated. Impacts a change has on the product models are computed and mismatches are identified.

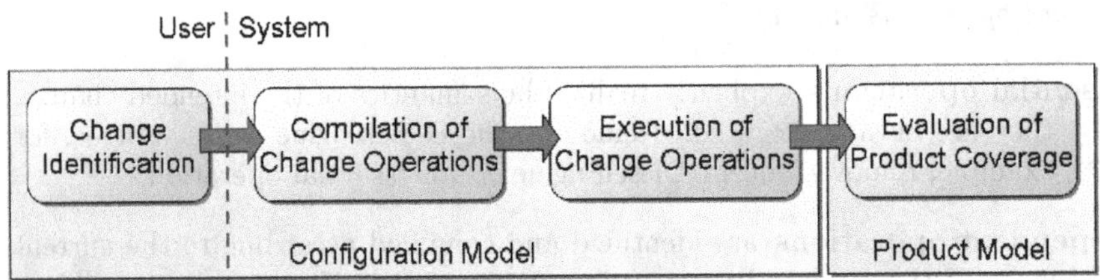

Figure 2: The four steps of the evolution process.

4.1 Change Identification

Not all change operations are executable at any time. Removing a single concept definition, for example, is only possible when it does not have children (see Section 3.1). The knowledge engineer can select a change operation from the set of change operations that are executable at the moment. Multiple operations may be needed to fulfill the intended change, for example removing more than one concept. They can be sequentially selected and executed.

Change identification includes the possibility to undo previous changes. It is obvious that for every base operation there is exactly one inverse operation that, when executed, reverses the original change. For example, the inverse operation of addConcept(C) is removeConcept(C). To revert the effect of a sequence of base operations, as within compound operations, simply a new sequence of inverse changes in reverse order needs to be created and executed.

4.2 Compilation of Change Operations

Essential operations are pre-defined for every compound operation. Dependant changes are identified based on the neighborhood of affected modeling facilities.

Changes define a list of invariants that may be affected by their execution. When executing a compound operation, all inherent base operations are known and their invariants are accumulated. Computation time is kept minimal by only evaluating those invariants that may be affected.

For every invariant a set of potential inconsistencies is known. Evaluating an invariant has one of two possible outcomes: it is satisfied or it is violated. The former means that the configuration model is consistent. The latter means that inconsistency has been identified.

The system automatically generates a list of suitable repair operations which leads to a click-and-repair process. These repair operations are disjoint: every operation is able to repair the inconsistency and one has to be chosen. The selection of the most appropriate repair operation cannot be automated. This is an expert's task since the configuration model has to represent the configurable components of the product domain.

Example. A car vendor no longer offers red Cars. The Car concept represents all models in general. Specific Cars are modeled as children of this concept. This parent concept specifies an color attribute containing a String set representing all varieties of offered colors. The value red is removed from this set. Concepts representing specific car types overwrite the attribute value since not every Car type is offered in every color. Those color attributes of specific Car types containing the value red also need to be changed (due to the Attribute Inheritance Invariant). The appropriate operations are computed (e.g. changeAttributeValue({black, white, red}, {black, white})).

4.3 Execution of Change Operations

The change operations compiled in the previous step are sequentially executed. The sequence in which change operations are executed is determined based on their preconditions and postconditions. A change operation is executable when all preconditions are satisfied, else other operations have to be executed first [11]. For testing validity of an implementation, the postconditions of change operations may be checked after their execution.

4.4 Evaluation of Product Coverage

Changes to components have different impacts on configurable products. Different scenarios are conceivable, including richer or poorer variety from which a customer can choose. When a certain component is no longer available, some car types may be affected while others are not. Furthermore, some car types can still be sold with a restricted choice of variability while others cannot persist and should be removed from the product catalog.

Deciding how to react to a change is an expert's task. Knowledge about product types and their components is needed as well as an estimation of customer reaction. In the end all boils down to return-on-investment. Hence, we leave this decision to the knowledge engineer, but a list of mismatches between a product model and the corresponding configuration model gives valuable input.

Product coverage depends on a consistent configuration model. Therefore, this step is done subsequent to execution of change operations. Impacts of a change are evaluated for all product models by addressing the following aspects:

1. Every component referred to in the product model is defined as a concept in the configuration model.
2. The part definitions and cardinalities of all composition relations defined in the product model are equal to or specializations of the corresponding values defined in the configuration model.
3. Every attribute value of every component in the product model is a subset of the original value of the concept in the configuration model.
4. The relevant constraints (i.e. those constraints where patterns are satisfied through instances in the product model) are free of conflicts.

Note that results of constraint propagation are only reliable when the product model does not contain variability. When a product model contains variability, conflicts may be identified that can never occur within a single product. This problem can be tackled by creating all potential instances for every concept and propagating the constraints for every combination of instances.

Example. Two different types of NavigationSystems exist, each of which relying on one CommunicationModule. One of the NavigationSystems requires a GPSModule, the other one requires a GalileoModule. Two constraint relations enforce the specialization of the CommunicationModule to GPSModule and GalileoModule, accordingly. However, this is not possible for both of them: a car can contain only one navigation system.

5 Proof of Concept

For proving viability of the conceptual ideas presented in this paper, a prototype has been implemented. This prototypical model editor is implemented in *Java 1.6* (http://java.sun.com), using the *Standard Windows Toolkit* (*SWT* – http://www.eclipse.org/swt) for a graphical user interface. Constraint propagation is based on the *Java Constraint Library* (*JCL* – http://liawww.epfl.ch/JCL) which offers integer, float and string domains for variables and different strategies for solving unary and binary constraints; including support for continuous domains. The representation used for storing configuration models is based on the *Extensible Markup Language* (*XML* – http://www.w3.org/XML).

5.1 Architecture

Different configurators use different representations for storing configuration models. The natural response to this aspect is providing an internal representation that can be mapped to external languages, and vice versa (see Figure 3).

This means that different languages[1] can be imported and exported. For being able to import an external language, the internal language needs to accommodate all facilities used for modelling within the external language specification. For supporting a new external language, additional modelling facilities, base operations and invariants may need to be implemented.

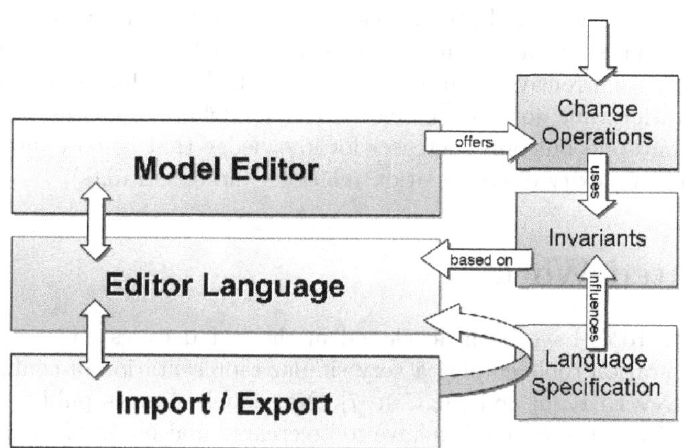

Figure 3: Model Editor Architecture.

The model editor offers a pre-defined set of change operations from which a knowledge engineer can choose in a drop-down menu. Only executable operations are offered. Invariants defined for executed changes are evaluated. Those invariants that are not part of the current language specification need not be computed and are simply ignored.

5.2 Scalability

While the set of base operations is fixed, there are many compound operations one can think of. The possibility to compose compound operations from base operations facilitates their definition because preconditions, postconditions and invariants are pre-defined for all base operations and are automatically accumulated for compound operations.

First tests show that the implemented prototype is able to handle configuration models of reasonable size and from different sources. A test model containing knowledge about a fictious car domain and an EngCon [7] model containing knowledge about a car periphery supervision system [9], created in the ConIPF project (Configuration in Industrial Product Families)[2], were used for extensive testing. The car domain contains 52 concepts, 24 attributes, 33

[1] Actually, during development of the model editor, configuration models in the format of the EngCon configurator [7] have been used extensively. The representation of EngCon models is also based on XML syntax.

[2] http://www.conipf.org

composition relations and 9 constraint relations. The car periphery supervision domain contains 72 concepts, 107 attributes, 34 composition relations and 62 constraint relations. The model editor identifies inconsistencies and suggests suitable repair operations. All consistency tests were computed in less than a second for both models.

Scalability tests with hundreds or thousands of modeling facilities still have to be done, but the first results look very promising and so long as the configuration model is consistent before change execution, only those invariants that may be affected by a currently executed change need to be evaluated. This means that computation time does not increase as the model grows in size (in terms of number of concepts) but only increases for knowledge that is more interweaved (in terms of complexity of composition relations and constraints).

6 Related Work

Configuration tools have been developed in the last decades. Two structure-based configuration tools employ a very similar representation of configuration models: KONWERK [6] and EngCon [7]. No model editor is publically available so that configuration models have to be created and maintained using text editors, which is error-prone, of course. Kumbang Modeler [10] is an editor for Kumbang models [1], which focus on variability in software product families. However, it only offers a validity check for models, not giving detailed information about errors nor helping in resolving them. The evolution approach presented in this paper is novel in the sense that it identifies all potential inconsistencies (incl. constraint satisfaction) and automatically computes repair options. The four-step evolution process is based on earlier work [11].

To the knowledge of the author, no prior approach for maintaining knowledge about evolving products is based on structure-based configuration. The product coverage approach is novel in the sense that mismatches between product models and the corresponding configuration model are identified, explained to the knowledge engineer and serve as input for managing the product catalog.

Invariants are known from knowledge base and database communities, typically called *integrity constraints* [5]. To distinguish this domain-independent language restricting notion from the domain-dependent problem solving notion of constraints introduced in Section 2.1, we stick to the terms *invariant* and *constraint*, respectively in this paper. Invariants were first introduced in [3] for evolution of database schemata. [12] and [13] also define invariants to preserve consistency in the course of ontology evolution. Ontology editors are readily available but only handle a portion of the knowledge needed for configuration.

7 Summary and Outlook

In this paper we have introduced a novel approach for handling evolution of a product catalog. The set of configurable components is represented in a configuration model and the product types are represented in product models referring to concept definitions in the corresponding configuration model. Well-formedness and consistency of the configuration model are preserved by dynamically compiling change operations, evaluating change-dependent invariants and identifying repair operations in case of inconsistency. Major contributions of this paper are a formal definition of modeling facilities and change operations, an adaptive definition of consistency (depending on the represented domain or configuration tool), a consistency-preserving evolution process that minimizes computation effort by dynamically evaluating only those parts of the configuration model that depend on the executed change, exploiting the representation structure for automatically generating repair operations in case an inconsistency is identified (leading to a click-and-repair process) and computing impacts that evolution of the configuration model has on the product catalog.

Mismatches between product models and the configuration model are identified and give valuable input for managing the product catalog. The model editor introduced in this paper helps identifying such situations. With only small extra effort, this approach can be extended to embody reconfiguration of product models: the change operations needed to "repair" a product model can be computed analogously to those repairing configuration models. A list of changes is the output and describes changes that, when applied to a product individual, bring this product up-to-date.

Current research focuses on identifying suitable repair operations for identified inconsistency. An inconsistency is identified when two expressions contradict one another, e.g. $\mathsf{Car} \sqsubseteq \exists \mathsf{hasParts.DieselEngine}$ and $\mathsf{DieselEngine} \notin N_C$, and can be repaired by replacing one of the two expressions with its opposite: removing the composition relation or adding a concept named DieselEngine. But other repair operations may be more suitable, e.g. replacing DieselEngine with a general Motor. An obvious problem is that a representation has no access to the represented domain and thus the repair process cannot be automated.

Another topic of current research is the import / export of different modeling languages. This includes both translating the represented knowledge into the internal language and handling potentially different semantics. Importing OWL (Web Ontology Language) and SWRL (Semantic Web Rule Language) files, for example, are interesting additions. But for being able to import OWL the internal taxonomy needs to be extended for allowing non-tree structures.

References

[1] T. Asikainen, T. Männistö, and T. Soininen. Kumbang: A domain ontology for modelling variability in software product families. *Advanced Engineering Informatics*, 21(1):23–40, 2007.

[2] F. Baader, D. Calvanese, D. L. McGuinness, D. Nardi, and P. F. Patel-Schneider. *The Description Logic Handbook: Theory, Implementation, and Applications.* Cambridge University Press, 2003.

[3] J. Banerjee, W. Kim, H.-J. Kim, and H. F. Korth. Semantics and implementation of schema evolution in object-oriented databases. In *Proceedings of the 1987 ACM SIGMOD International Conference on Management of Data (SIGMOD 1987)*, pages 311–322, New York, NY, USA, 1987. ACM Press.

[4] J. Gray. The transaction concept: Virtues and limitations (invited paper). In *Very Large Data Bases, 7th International Conference*, pages 144–154, Cannes, France, 1981.

[5] P. M. Gray, S. M. Embury, K. Y. Hui, and G. J. Kemp. The evolving role of constraints in the functional data model. *Journal of Intelligent Information Systems*, 12(2-3):113–137, 1999.

[6] A. Günter and L. Hotz. KONWERK - a domain independent configuration tool. In *Proceedings of Configuration (AAAI Workshop)*, pages 10–19, Orlando, FL, USA, 1999. AAAI Press.

[7] O. Hollmann, T. Wagner, and A. Günter. EngCon: A flexible domain-independent configuration engine. In *Proceedings Configuration (ECAI 2000-Workshop)*, pages 94–96, 2000.

[8] L. Hotz and T. Krebs. Configuration – state of the art and new challenges. In *Proceedings of 17. Workshop Planen, Scheduling und Konfigurieren, Entwerfen (PuK2003) – KI 2003 Workshop*, pages 145–157, 2003.

[9] L. Hotz, T. Krebs, K. Wolter, J. Nijhuis, S. Deelstra, M. Sinnema, and J. MacGregor. *Configuration in Industrial Product Families - The ConIPF Methodology.* AKA Verlag, 2006.

[10] H. Koivu, M. Raatikainen, M. Nieminen, and T. Männistö. Kumbang modeler: A prototype tool for modeling variability. In M. R. Tomi Männistö, Eila Niemelä, editor, *Software and Service Variability Management Workshop - Concepts, Models, and Tools.* Helsinki University of Technology, Software Business and Engineering Institute, 2007.

[11] T. Krebs. Evolution of configuration models – a focus on correctness. In *Proceedings of Configuration - ECAI 2006 Workshop*, pages 31–37, Riva del Garda, Italy, 2006.

[12] A. Maedche, B. Motik, L. Stojanovic, R. Studer, and R. Volz. An infrastructure for searching, reusing and evolving distributed ontologies. In *Proceedings of the 12th international conference on World Wide Web (WWW '03)*, pages 439–448, New York, NY, USA, 2003. ACM Press.

[13] L. Stojanovic. *Methods and Tools for Ontology Evolution.* PhD thesis, Universität Karlsruhe, 2004.

[14] M. E. Winston, R. Chaffin, and D. Herrmann. A taxonomy of part-whole relations. *Cognitive Science*, 11(4):417–444, 1987.

Recovery from Plan Failures in Partially Observable Environments

Roberto Micalizio Pietro Torasso
Dipartimento di Informatica, Università di Torino
Corso Svizzera 185, 10149 Torino (Italy)

Abstract

The paper discusses a distributed approach to multi-agent plan execution and control, where a team of agents may perform actions concurrently in a partially observable environment. Each agent is able to supervise the execution of the actions it is responsible for by means of an on-line monitoring step and to perform agent diagnosis when a failure in the execution of an action has been detected.
The emphasis of the paper is on the mechanism for synthesizing a recovery plan in presence of an action failure. One contribution of the paper concerns an in depth analysis of the characteristics the recovery plan has to satisfy. The most stringent requirement regards that the recovery plan has to be conformant, as the partial observability of the system allows just to estimate the status of the agent and the action effects may be non deterministic.
The paper proposes an approach for synthesizing such a conformant recovery plan based on the adoption of symbolic methods. In particular, the recovery planning is implemented in terms of operations on Ordered Binary Decision Diagrams used for encoding both the belief states and the action models.

1 Introduction

The need of diagnosing planning failures has been singled out a long time ago [1] since the execution of a plan can be *threatened* by the occurrence of unexpected events, such as faults in the agents functionalities.
The impact of plan failures is even more dramatic when we consider multi-agent plans, where a complex task is distributed among a team of cooperating agents and agents can perform concurrent actions. In fact, in such a scenario, a failure in the action of an agent can cause a global failure of the plan because of the existence of causal dependencies among the actions performed by different agents.
While the multi-agent systems are widely recognized as a powerful methodology for efficiently solving complex tasks in a distributed way, distributed problem solving presents also a number of challenges to deal with (see e.g., [12]). First of all innovative planning techniques (such as the ones introduced in [2]) must be devised to define plans where actions that can be executed concurrently are distributed among agents. Moreover the execution of a multi-agent plan needs to be monitored and diagnosed.
In the recent years, the problems of monitoring and diagnosing the execution of a multi-agent plan have been deeply discussed and different approaches have been proposed (e.g., see [12, 13, 5, 9]). However, while these approaches provide solutions for detecting and explaining action failures, they do not discuss how these pieces of information can be exploited for overcoming such failures.

In principle, the process of recovering from an action failure could be seen as a reactive step; i.e., whenever a specific anomalous situation is detected the recovery consists in resuming a precompiled (recovery) plan, which overcomes such a situation (see [10]). However, in many real cases, the system is just partially observable and its status can not be precisely determined; as a consequence precompiled solutions which recover from specific failures can not be applied since the failures can not be always univocally determined. In these cases the recovery process require a re-planning process which takes into account the ambiguous status of the system. More precisely, the recovery plan (if exists) must be executable regardless the actual health status of the system; i.e., the recovery plan must be *conformant*.

To deal with uncertainty, many approaches to planning propose the adoption of symbolic formalisms: for example, in [4] an Universal Planner is proposed which exploits the formalism of Ordered Binary Decision Diagrams (OBDDs) for dealing with the system ambiguity, while the possibility of synthesizing a conformant plan via symbolic model checking has been investigated in [3].

In this paper we address the problem of recovering the execution of a multi-agent plan from an action failure. In particular, we consider the case of systems which are just partially observable and we propose a distributed architecture where each agent has to monitor and diagnose the actions it executes ([9]). Whenever an agent detects the failure of an action, it has to recover (if possible) from such a failure by means of a local re-planning step, which has to take into account that the agent has suffered from some fault and therefore its health status is impaired. Since the system is just partially observable, the re-planning process must guarantee that the recovery plan is conformant.

The paper is organized as follows. In the next section we introduce the distributed architecture and formalize the notion of multi-agent plan. In section 3 we sketch the task of plan execution supervision, involving the activities of on-line monitoring and diagnosis. In section 4 we characterize the recovery mechanism; in particular we specify which requirements must be satisfied by a local plan in order to recover from an action failure. In section 5 we discuss how the high level requirements introduced in the previous section can be accomplished by means of a relational-based solution to the problem of conformant planning and provide some preliminary results on the effectiveness of the proposed approach. The paper closes with some concluding remarks in section 6.

2 Setting the framework

The paper addresses the problem of recovering the execution of a multi-agent plan P after the detection of an action failure. Before discussing the recovery mechanism, we focus our attention on the main characteristics of the multi-agent system and of the environment. We assume that a team T of agents has to solve a complex goal G, which requires some form of co-operation among the agents in the team (at least they have to avoid interferences in accessing to critical resources). The multi-agent plan P (whose main features are described below) is executed by the agents of the team; in particular, the actions are executed synchronously and each action in P takes a time unit to be executed (this is a common assumption, see e.g. [13]). For controlling the plan execution, at each instant some observations are available to the agents, but in general the system is just partially observable; thus the agents have just a limited view of the changes occurred in the environment.

By exploiting the experience gained in previous works (see e.g., [9]), not only the actual execution of the plan is distributed among the agents of the team, but also the problem of controlling the execution of the global plan P is decomposed in as many sub-plans as the agents in the team $\mathcal{T}$. Each sub-plan P_i is assigned to agent i, which is responsible for executing and controlling the actions in P_i; it follows that each agent i reaches, by means of P_i, just a portion of the global plan goal G, i.e., a sub-goal G_i.

Observe that the partitioning of the control task among agents does not guarantee that the sub-problems are completely independent of one another. In fact, in many domains the agents in $\mathcal{T}$ have to cooperate in order to achieve a common global goal G by exchanging services (the notion of *service* will be formalized in the following of this section).

The agents need to communicate during the plan execution phase in order to notify whether a service has been achieved. More precisely, an action a assigned to agent i is executable if and only if all its preconditions $pre(a)$ are satisfied; however, some of these preconditions may be services which another agent j in $\mathcal{T}$ has to provide i with. Agent i waits for the satisfaction of these services by performing a *Wait* action as long as agent j notifies agent i the achievement or the failure of the expected services. The communication among the agents avoids that an agent waits indefinitely for the services it requires and, as we will see in the following of this section, it is ruled by the causal links included in the multi-agent plan P.

The control task performed by each agent involves two main activities:

1) the agent i *on-line supervises* the actions it executes and infers action's outcome (success or failure)

2) whenever an action failure is detected, the agent i tries to *recover* from the action failure in order to achieve (in a different way) the sub-goal G_i.

For controlling the execution of the sub-plan P_i, the agent i exploits the set of observations obs_t^i that i receives at each time t; the observations in obs_t^i convey important pieces of information about the status of agent i itself, but given the partial observability, in general there is not sufficient information for uniquely inferring the i's status. Relying on the observations obs_t^i, the agent i can determine, at least for some actions, the outcome of the action a_t^i i has executed at time t: the outcome of an action is *succeeded*, when the action is executed in the nominal way and all the intended direct effects have been achieved, or *failed* otherwise.

It is worth noting that the cooperative behavior of the agents introduces causal dependencies among the actions the agents have to execute; therefore, when an action failure occurs in the sub-plan P_i (i.e., a *primary failure* occurs), the failure may affect the sub-plans of other agents; i.e., the harmful effects of the primary failure may cause *secondary failures* (see e.g., [11]) not only in P_i, but even in the global plan P.

The Structure of the Multi-Agent Plan. A partial order plan (POP) is classically defined as a directed acyclic graph POP=$\langle A, E, C\rangle$, where A is the set of nodes representing the action instances the agents have to execute; E is a set of precedence links between actions (a precedence link $a \prec a'$ in E indicates that the execution of action a must precede the execution of the action a'); C is a set of causal links of the form

$l : a \xrightarrow{q} a'$; the link l indicates that the action a provides the action a' with the service q, where q is an atom occurring in the preconditions of a'.
The class of multi-agent plans we deal with in the present paper is a subclass of the POP defined above. In fact, as in the POP case, we define P as the DAG $\langle A, E, C \rangle$, where A, E and C have the same meanings, but we introduce the following requirements:

- Every action instance $a \in A$ is assigned to a specific agent $i \in \mathcal{T}$.
- All the actions assigned to the same agent i are totally ordered, i.e., for any pair of actions a and a' assigned to i, either a precedes a' or a' precedes a.
- The access to critical resources is ruled by means of causal links. For example, let's assume that both actions a, assigned to agent i, and a', assigned to agent j, require the same critical resource res: in the plan P the causal link $l : a \xrightarrow{free(res)} a'$ imposes that the action a' must be executed after action a, in particular the link l states that action a provides a' with the service of releasing the resource res.

Observe that a multi-agent plan instance P satisfying the previous requirements can be synthesized by exploiting planning algorithms similar to the POMP planner proposed by Boutilier et al. in [2].
Given the global plan P, the sub-plan for agent i is the tuple P_i=$\langle A_i, E_i, C_i, X_i^{in}, X_i^{out} \rangle$ where: A_i is the subset of actions in A that agent i has to execute; E_i is a total order relation defined over the actions in A_i; C_i is a set of causal links $a \xrightarrow{q} a'$ where both a and a' belong to A_i; X_i^{in} is a set of incoming causal links where a' belongs to A_i and a is assigned to another agent j in $\mathcal{T}$; X_i^{out} is a set of outgoing causal links where a belongs to A_i and a' is assigned to another agent $j \in \mathcal{T}$.
In the following we will denote as a_t^i the action that agent i executes at time t.
Running Example. In the paper we will use a simple example from the blocks world. We distinguish between two type of blocks: *small* and *large*; we assume that, under the nominal behavior an agent can carry either two small blocks or a large one. Let us consider two agents `A1` and `A2`, which have to cooperate to build two "walls" in target positions `T1` (where the large block `B3` must be put on the small ones `B1` and `B2`) and `T2` (consisting of the large block `B4` only). At the initial time instant agent `A1` is located in `S1` and agent `A2` is located in `S2`, also the blocks to be moved are initially located in the two source positions: `B1`, `B2` and `B3` are in `S1`, while `B4` is in `S2`. The access to the source and target locations is constrained since just one agent at a time can load (unload) a block within them. However, there exists a further location, called `PRK` (i.e. parking area), which is not constrained and where the agents are positioned when they complete their sub-plans. Table 1 reports the STRIPS-like definition of a subset of actions the agents can execute (for lack of space the definitions of the other actions are omitted).

Figure 1 shows the global plan produced by a POMP-like planner for achieving the goal of building the walls. The dashed rectangles highlight the sub-plans assigned to the agents. The plan is a DAG where nodes correspond to actions and edges correspond to precedence (dashed) or causal (solid) links. The causal links are labeled with the services an action provides to another one, for example the causal link between actions `1` and `4` is labeled with the service `LOADED(A1,B1)`, which is both one of the effects of the action `1` and one of the preconditions for the execution of action `4`.

Move(A,P1,P2)	LoadS(A,OBJ,P)	PDownS(A,OBJ,P)	LoadL(A,OBJ,P)
PRE: AT(A,P1)	**PRE**: SMALL(OBJ)	**PRE**: AT(A,P)	**PRE**: LARGE(OBJ)
FREE(P2)	AT(A,P) AT(OBJ,P)	LOADED(A,OBJ)	AT(A,P) AT(OBJ,P)
	EMPTY(A)	HALF-LOADED(A)	EMPTY(A)
EFF: ~AT(A,P1)	**EFF**: ~EMPTY(A)	**EFF**: ~LOADED(A,OBJ)	**EFF**: ~EMPTY(A)
~FREE(P2)	~AT(OBJ,P)	AT(OBJ,P)	~AT(OBJ,P)
AT(A,P2)	LOADED(A,OBJ)	EMPTY(A)	LOADED(A,OBJ)
FREE(P1)	HALF-LOADED(A)	~HALF-LOADED(A)	FULL-LOADED(A)

Table 1: The preconditions and the effects of the actions in the plan of Figure 1.

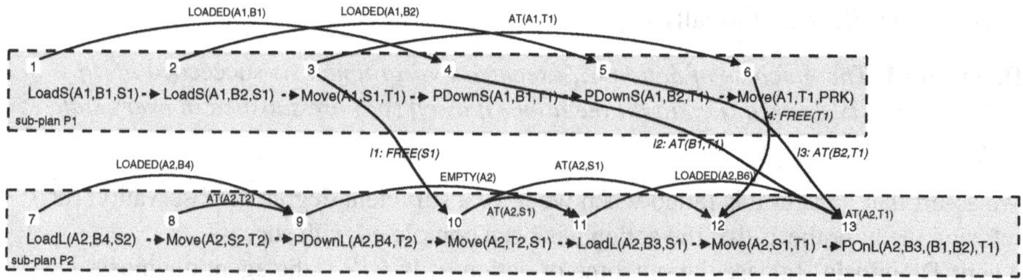

Figure 1: The plan built by a POMP-like planner.

The information associated with the causal link play a critical role in evaluating the effect of a failure: in fact, when the action 1 fails the action 4 fails too since one of its preconditions is not satisfied.

3 On-line Plan Supervision: Basic concepts

In this section we sketch the basic concepts of the on-line supervision task (monitoring + diagnosis) that each agent i has to perform over the execution of the actions it is responsible for. A formal and detailed description of the problem of supervising the plan execution has been addressed in [9, 7].

At each time instant t, the supervision process performed by agent i over the execution of action a_t^i has to provide three main results: 1) an estimation of the status of agent i after the execution of a_t^i; 2) the outcome of the action a_t^i (in case there is sufficient observability) and 3) in case a_t^i is failed, an agent diagnosis D_t^i which explains the failure of a_t^i in terms of faults occurred in some functionalities of agent i.

Agent Status. The status of agent i is represented in a qualitative way by means of a set of status variables VAR^i, where each variable $v \in VAR^i$ takes values in a finite domain $Dom(v)$. The set VAR^i is partitioned into two sets:

- $HEALTH^i$ denotes the set of variables concerning the health status of an agent functionalities (e.g., mobility and power). Since these variables are not directly observable, their actual value can be just estimated.
- $ENDO^i$; denotes the set of all endogenous status variables (e.g., the agent's *position*). Their value may be directly observed by agent i; however, since agent i receives just partial observations about the changes occurring in the system, at

each time instant t the agent i observes the value of just a subset of variables in $ENDO^i$.

Therefore, agent i is in general unable to precisely determine its own status; rather i can determine just a set of states after the execution of a^i_t, this set is known in literature as *belief state* and will be denoted as $\mathcal{B}^i_t$.

Action Outcome. As said above, the actual execution of an action is threatened by the occurrence of unexpected events, such as faults, hence the outcome of an action may be not nominal. The outcome of action a^i_t is considered as *succeeded* when all the nominal effects of the action have been achieved, the outcome is *failed* otherwise. Since at each time instant t we have to deal with an ambiguous belief states $\mathcal{B}^i_t$, the action a^i_t is succeeded only when all the expected effects of action a hold in every state s included in $\mathcal{B}^i_t$; more formally.

Definition 1 *The outcome of action a^i_t, executed by i at time t, is* succeeded *iff* $\forall q \in$ *eff*(a^i_t), $\forall s \in \mathcal{B}^i_t$, $s \models q$; *i.e., iff all the atoms q in eff(a^i_t) are satisfied in every state s in $\mathcal{B}^i_t$.*

We assert that an action is failed when we have a sufficient degree of observation for refusing the hypothesis that the action has been completed with success.

Agent Diagnosis. In case the outcome of action a^i_t is *failed*, the agent diagnosis D^i_t has to explain this failure by singling out which functionalities of agent i may behave in a faulty mode (i.e., in which functionalities a fault may have occurred). The diagnosis for agent i can be inferred just projecting the current belief state $\mathcal{B}^i_t$ over the status variables regarding the health status of the agent functionalities; more formally, D^i_t=PROJECT$_{HEALTH^i}\mathcal{B}^i_t$. It is easy to see that the precision of the diagnosis strongly depends on how much the belief state is accurate. In general, since the belief state $\mathcal{B}^i_t$ is ambiguous, the agent diagnosis will be ambiguous too containing a number of alternative explanations.

Extended Action Model. In order to supervise the execution of P_i, the agent i must have at disposal extended action templates, which model not only the nominal behavior of the actions, but also the actions behavior when faults occur. For such a modeling task we adopt a relational representation, which has been proved to be useful for the on-line monitoring and diagnosis of multi-agent systems (see [9]). In particular, this formalism is able to capture non deterministic effects of the action execution.

The extended model of an action a^i_t is a transition relation $\Delta(a^i_t)$, where every tuple $d \in \Delta(a^i_t)$ models a possible change in the status of agent i, which may occur while i is executing a^i_t. More precisely, each tuple d has the form $d = \langle s_{t-1}, fault, s_t \rangle$; where s_{t-1} and s_t represent two agent states at time $t-1$ and t respectively, each state is a complete assignment of values to the status variables VAR^i of agent i; *fault* denotes the fault which occurs to cause a change of status from s_{t-1} to s_t (of course, in the transitions which model the nominal behavior *fault* is empty).

Table 2 shows the extended model of a `Move` action from a location `P1` to a location `P2`; due to space reasons we show just a subset of tuples of the transition relation $\Delta($`Move`$)$. Moreover, for sake of readability, the agent states are expressed just in the subset of status variables directly affected by the `Move` action, in particular they are: *position*, the position of the agent; *carried* the amount of load carried by the agent, this variable assumes values in the set *empty*, *half-loaded* and *full-loaded*; *pwr*, the power

	s_{t-1}				*fault*	s_t			
	endogenous		**health variables**			**endogenous**		**health variables**	
	position	*carried*	*power*	*mobility*		*position*	*carried*	*power*	*mobility*
1	P1	*	High	OK	*null*	P2	*	High	OK
2	P1	HALF	High	OK	f-BRY	P2	HALF	Low	OK
3	P1	FULL	High	OK	f-BRY	P1	FULL	Low	OK
4	P1	HALF	High	OK	f-MOB	P2	HALF	High	SD
5	P1	FULL	High	OK	f-MOB	P1	FULL	High	SD
6	P1	HALF	Low	OK	*null*	P2	HALF	Low	OK
7	P1	FULL	Low	OK	*null*	P1	FULL	Low	OK
8	P1	HALF	High	SD	*null*	P2	HALF	High	SD
9	P1	FULL	High	SD	*null*	P1	FULL	High	SD

Table 2: The extended model of action Move(A,P1,P2).

of the agent's battery, which can be *high* (the nominal mode) or *low* (a degraded mode) and *mobility*, the health status of the agent's mobility functionality which can be *ok* (nominal) or *sd* (i.e., slowdown). Observe that, while the STRIPS model of the Move action just represents the nominal behavior of the action (assuming that both power and mobility are in their nominal mode), the corresponding extended model represents also how the Move action behaves in any combination of power and mobility modes, included the faulty ones. In fact the nominal behavior of the Move action is modeled by transition 1, the $*$ symbol (don't care) indicates that, when the agent's functionalities behave nominally, the actual carried load does not impact the outcome of the action. In our example the Move action can fail as a consequence of two types of faults: f-BRY and f-MOB. f-BRY affects the battery by reducing the level of power from the nominal *high* to the degraded *low*. An agent can complete a move action with battery power *low* iff the agent is not carrying any block or the agent is carrying a small block, the action fails otherwise (see transitions 2, 3). Moreover, the degraded mode of the power affects also the handling functionality of the agent and, as a consequence, the agent can not execute some types of actions; in fact, when the power is in the *low* mode an agent can not load a large block (i.e. the LoadL action can not be executed) and can not put either a small or a large block on another one (i.e., the actions POnS and POnL are not executable). The fault f-MOB affects the health status of the mobility functionality, which changes from the nominal *ok* to the anomalous *sd* (slowdown); even under this health status the agent can move only when it is either empty or half loaded, but in this case the f-MOB affects the mobility functionality only (see transitions 4 and 5). Finally, transitions 6 to 9 show that the consequences of a fault are persistent and may cause the failure of the Move action (see in particular transitions 7 and 9).

4 Recovery Mechanism

Running example. Given the multi-agent plan in Figure 1, it is easy to see that the sub-plans P_1 and P_2 have causal dependent actions; thereby a failure in P_1 (P_2) may have harmful effects in P_2 (P_1). To point out this fact let's assume that, at time t,

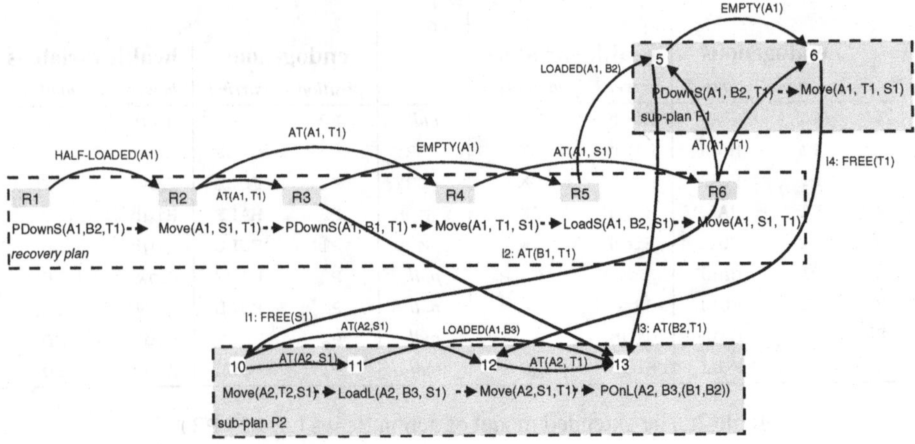

Figure 2: The plan synthesized for recovering from the failure of action 3.

action 3 fails (primary failure) as a consequence of a fault in the functionalities of agent A1. It is easy to see that this failure affects the whole plan since many actions, even assigned to agent A2, can no longer be executed (secondary failures). Instead of immediately notifying the occurrence of an action failure, agent A1 tries to overcome the failure by means of local recovery plan. To this end, the first step consists in inferring the agent diagnosis D^i_t, which provides the causes of the failure of action 3: in this case the agent diagnosis is ambiguous since the amount of available observations does not allow to discriminate between a fault in the power and a fault in the mobility functionality; i.e., D^i_t={*power* = *reduced* $\vee$ *mobility* = *slowdown*}. As we will discuss in the following of the section, the agent diagnosis D^i_t plays an important role for determining which actions can be included in the plan for recovering from the failure of action 3.

Characteristics of the Recovery Plan. When the failure of an action a^i_t is detected, the agent i tries to synthesize a new sub-plan P^*_i, which overcomes the failure of action a^i_t by taking into account that the non nominal health status (in fact, at least a fault is occurred in one of its functionalities). To this end, the agent i individuates a *safe status* $\mathcal{S}$ such that: 1) the sub-goal G_i assigned to i holds in $\mathcal{S}$ and 2) all the services that agent i provides to other agents in the original plan P_i, are achieved in $\mathcal{S}$. The safe status represents a new sub-goal that agent i intends to reach for overcoming the action failure: the recovery plan P^*_i, if exists, leads agent i in a state where all the harmful effects of the action failure have been canceled.

The safe status can be determined by exploiting the structure of the plan P_i (in particular the set of causal links outgoing from the failed action a^i_t) and by considering the services (if any) that agent i provides to other agents; for instance, in the previous example from the blocks world, given the failure of action 3, it is easy to see that the safe status consists of the atoms $\mathcal{S} = \{\texttt{AT(B1,T1)}, \texttt{AT(B2,T1)}\}$. The status $\mathcal{S}$ is safe as the original sub-goal assigned to agent A1 is reached and all the services the agent A1 must provide to A2 are accomplished.

Once the safe status $\mathcal{S}$ has been determined, the agent i has to synthesize a recovery plan P_i^* which, given the current status $\mathcal{B}_t^i$, achieves $\mathcal{S}$. However, since the system is only partially observable, the belief state $\mathcal{B}_t^i$ may not be a precise representation of the agent status, in particular as concerns the health status of agent i itself. Dealing with ambiguous belief state reduces the precision of the diagnostic inferences, as we have seen in the blocks world example.

The ambiguity in the belief state requires that the recovery plan has to guarantee the achievement of the safe status $\mathcal{S}$ starting from any state in the belief state while its current health status is *not nominal*. The planning process aimed at synthesizing P_i^* has to exploit *recovery action models* which consider the possibly not nominal health status of agent i; these action models can be easily derived from the extended action models by selecting the tuples which are consistent with the agent diagnosis D_t^i and which do not assume the occurrence of new faults. More formally, given the failure of action a_t^i and the corresponding agent diagnosis D_t^i, the *recovery action model* of an action a (to be used during the synthesis of P_i^*) is determined as $\Delta^*(a)$=SELECT$_{fault=null}(\Delta(a)) \cap D_t^i$; where: SELECT$_{fault=null}(\Delta(a))$ selects from $\Delta(a)$ all the transitions where no new fault occurs (e.g., in $\Delta(Move)$ model of Figure 2, SELECT$_{fault=null}(\Delta(Move))$=$\{$1,6,7,8,9$\}$); the intersection with the current diagnosis of agent i filters out all those transitions which are not consistent with the health status of agent i currently assumed (e.g., in this simple case the only transition filtered out is transition 1, the nominal one).

A further issue the recovery process has to face concerns the inability of the agent i to determine the outcome of some actions it executes (see [7] for details). In other words, during the plan execution the agent i has not the guarantee that the value of each status variables in $ENDO^i$ is actually observed at each time instant; this fact puts a strong requirement on the recovery plan P_i^*. In fact P_i^* can not be a conditional plan, as a conditional approach to planning assumes to get enough observations during the execution phase, so that the agent executing the plan is able to select the next action to be executed. Instead, the recovery plan P_i^* has the characteristics of a *conformant* plan. More precisely, the recovery plan P_i^* must be a sequential plan, which must ensure to achieve the safe status in all possible circumstances included in $\mathcal{B}_t^i$.

Of course, imposing P_i^* to be a conformant plan is a very strong requirement and in some cases the recovery process may fail; in these cases we assume that the failure of action a_t^i is reported to a human user, which has to handle it (see e.g., [8]).

Finally, we impose that the recovery plan P_i^* must not include a sequence of actions larger than a domain-dependent threshold $planLength$; this threshold is imposed in order to avoid that that the local recovery plan is too complex and, therefore, has a potential negative impact on the execution of the whole plan.

The specification of a conformant planning algorithm. By taking into account the requirements discussed above, the process for building the recovery plan can be sketched according to the high-level specifications of figure 3: in particular, we discuss the $k+1$-th step of the planning process.

The PLAN function takes in input the belief state $\mathcal{B}_k^i$ which represents the set of possible states reachable by the agent i when a specific sequence of recovery actions $\{ra_1, \ldots, ra_k\}$ would be applied starting from the belief state $\mathcal{B}_t^i$; the sequence of recovery actions to get $\mathcal{B}_k^i$ will be denoted as $actSeq(\mathcal{B}_k^i)$ and represents the tentative

partial solution built so far. Observe that $actSeq(\mathcal{B}^i_k)$ identifies univocally the belief state $\mathcal{B}^i_k$.
The first step of the algorithm checks whether a solution has been found, i.e. the safe status $\mathcal{S}$ has been achieved, in particular the GOAL_ACHIEVED function (step `01`) assesses whether, for each state $s \in \mathcal{B}^i_k$, the atoms included in the safe status $\mathcal{S}$ hold in s; i.e., $s \vdash \mathcal{S}$. If this condition holds, the recovery plan P^*_i can be synthesized from the sequence of recovery actions $actSeq(\mathcal{B}^i_k)$.
In case a solution is not found, the second step checks whether the threshold on the plan length is reached (line `02`), in such a case the planning process terminates returning the empty set (i.e., a recovery plan with less than *planLength* actions does not exist).

In the general case, given the belief state $\mathcal{B}^i_k$ and the set $ACTS_{k+1}$ of all the actions agent i can execute, the FIND_APPLICABLE_ACTIONS function (step `03`) determines the subset of actions $\overline{ACTS_{k+1}} \subseteq ACTS_{k+1}$ which can be applied to $\mathcal{B}^i_k$. In particular, since the recovery plan must be conformant, a recovery action ra is included in $\overline{ACTS_{k+1}}$ iff ra is applicable in every state $s \in \mathcal{B}^i_k$. If the set $\overline{ACTS_{k+1}}$ is empty, the recursive call terminates immediately returning the empty set as a solution (step `04`); i.e., there are no conformant actions to be applied to $\mathcal{B}^i_k$.
On the contrary (step `05`), when $\overline{ACTS_{k+1}}$ is not empty, the planning process has to predict all the possible states reachable via the actions in $\overline{ACTS_{k+1}}$. As discussed above, the recovery process is performed in not nominal conditions, therefore the planning algorithm has to exploit the extended models of the actions in $\overline{ACTS_{k+1}}$ and in particular their recovery model (which is consistent with the agent diagnosis D^i_t). In the following the set of recovery models used at the $k+1$-th step is denotes as Φ_{k+1}; more precisely, Φ_{k+1}=\{recovery action models $\Delta^*(ra) | ra \in \overline{ACTS_{k+1}}$ \}.
The PREDICT_STATES function (step `06`) generates all the possible states reachable via actions in $\overline{ACTS_{k+1}}$; in particular, the result $BSET^i_{k+1}$ is a set of belief states, where each belief state $\mathcal{B}^i_{k+1} \in BSET^i_{k+1}$ is obtained by applying an action $ra \in \overline{ACTS_{k+1}}$ to each state $s \in \mathcal{B}^i_k$.
For each belief state $\mathcal{B}^i_{k+1} \in BSET^i_{k+1}$, $\mathcal{B}^i_{k+1}$ is marked univocally with the sequence of actions that have been applied so far; i.e., let ra be the recovery action used to get $\mathcal{B}^i_{k+1}$, then $actSeq(\mathcal{B}^i_{k+1})$ equals the sequence of recovery actions $actSeq(\mathcal{B}^i_k)$ concatenated with ra (see lines `07` and `08`).
Finally, at line `10`, the PLAN function is recursively invoked on each $\mathcal{B}^i_{k+1}$ previously determined.

5 Implementing the recovery mechanism

In principle, the PLAN function in Figure 3 could be used for synthesizing a plan P^*_i for recovering from the failure of an action a^i_t: in fact, it is sufficient to invoke the function as PLAN$(\mathcal{B}^i_t, \emptyset, 0)$, where the belief state $\mathcal{B}^i_t$ represents the set of consistent states of the agent i when the failure of action a^i_t has been detected. However, a direct implementation of the specification of figure 3 would be extremely expensive as it requires backtracking mechanisms and involves a number of iterations. In order to face these issues, we have devised an algorithm which neither requires backtracking

PLAN($\mathcal{B}_k^i$, $actSeq(\mathcal{B}_k^i)$, k)
if GOAL_ACHIEVED($\mathcal{B}_k$, $\mathcal{S}$) **return** $actSeq(\mathcal{B}_k^i)$;
if $k \geq planLength$ **return** $\emptyset$;
$\overline{ACTS}_{k+1}$=FIND_APPLICABLE_ACTIONS($\mathcal{B}_k^i$);
if $\overline{ACTS}_{k+1}=\emptyset$ **return** $\emptyset$;
$\Phi_{k+1}=\{\ \Delta^*(ra)|ra \in \overline{ACTS}_{k+1}\ \}$.
$\mathcal{B}SET_{k+1}^i$=PREDICT_STATES($\mathcal{B}_k^i$, Φ_{k+1});
for each $\mathcal{B}_{k+1}^i \in \mathcal{B}SET_{k+1}$
  let $ra \in \overline{ACTS}_{k+1}$ the action used for predicting $\mathcal{B}_{k+1}^i$;
  $actSeq(\mathcal{B}_{k+1}^i)$=$append(actSeq(\mathcal{B}_k^i), ra)$;
  P_i^*=PLAN($\mathcal{B}_{k+1}^i$, $actSeq(\mathcal{B}_{k+1}^i)$, $k+1$);
  if $P_i^* \neq \emptyset$ **return** P_i^*;
return $\emptyset$;

Figure 3: The high level specification of $k+1$-th step of the recovery planning process.

mechanisms nor iterative functions. This algorithm progresses forward from step k-th to step $k+1$-th until the safe status $\mathcal{S}$ is achieved (as done in the PLAN function) but, at each k-th step, the algorithm keeps track of all the partial solutions inferred so far and considers them as a whole; thus, at the $k+1$-th step, all the possible predictions are made in just one shot.

This is made possible by adopting a relational approach for modeling both the $\mathcal{B}SET_k$ and the transition function Φ_{k+1} and by exploiting the symbolic formalism of the Ordered Binary Decision Diagrams (OBDDs), which encode in a compact and efficient way the possibly huge relations handled by the algorithm. Due to space reasons, we refer to [6] for a thorough discussion on the algorithm, while in the following we describe some of the steps of the algorithm by means of an example. Figure 4 outlines the first steps of the conformant planning process, which leads to the recovery plan in Figure 2. The initial uncertainty is a consequence of the fact that the causes of the failure of action 3 have not been univocally determined. At the first step the algorithm applies all the actions which are conformant w.r.t. the initial belief state; i.e., all the actions which are applicable in states 1 and 2: there are just two actions which satisfy this requirement: `PDownS(A1,B1)` and `PDownS(A1,B2)`. The result consists of the $\mathcal{B}SET_1$, which maintains two belief states: the first, `B`, includes states 4 and 5; the second, `C`, includes states 6 and 7. At the second step the algorithm applies all the actions which are conformant, respectively, for the belief states `B` and `C`. It is easy to see that action `LoadS(A1,B1)` is conformant w.r.t. belief `B`, however the application of the action would lead back to the initial belief state; as discussed in [3], it is possible to avoid the presence of loops by pruning off all the belief states which have been already determined. For the same reason, the application of action `LoadS(A1,B2)` to belief `C` leads to an empty belief. Action `Move(A1,S1,T1)` is conformant both in `B` and in `C`, and it leads to the belief states `D` and `E` at the second step. It is worth noting that the relational-based approach keeps track of all the possible conformant solutions built so far, therefore the algorithm finds all the optimal solutions (i.e., all the conformant plans including the least number of actions). In this specific example, it is easy to see that there are two optimal solutions with length 8: one delivers first block `B2`, whereas the other delivers first block `B1`, this second solution is the one

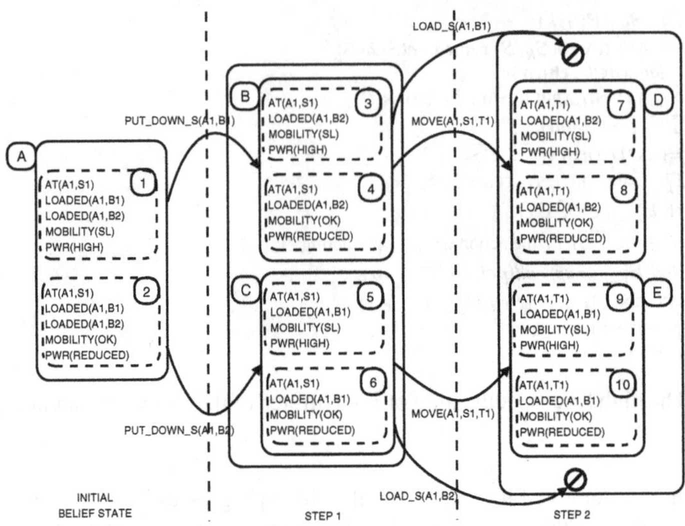

Figure 4: First steps of the conformant planning process.

shown in Figure 2.

Formal results and preliminary experiments. As discussed in the previous example, a first important property of the approach is its ability in determining, all the conformant plans with the least number of actions (if a conformant plan exists). Concerning the computational complexity, it is possible to demonstrate that the algorithm based on OBDDs is polynomial in the number of relational operations. However, the cost of each operation strongly depends on the size of the involved relations which could (in the worse case) grows exponentially in the number of steps. The adoption of the OBDDs plays a critical role for mitigating the computational cost due to the dimension of the relations.

The effectiveness of the approach is proved by the preliminary experimental results we have collected in a world blocks domain involving 10 positions, 8 small blocks and 4 large blocks. In this scenario we have assumed that the recovery plans can not be longer than 15 actions. The test-set includes 30 cases partitioned into two sets: *no-solution* and *with-solution*; the former contains 15 cases where no conformant recovery plan exists to reach the safe status starting from the (ambiguous) belief state determined after an action failure, and the latter contains 15 cases where such a recovery plan exists. The OBDD encoding in quite effective, since the average size (in number of nodes) of the OBDD encoding Φ_{k+1} is just 1696, while on average Φ_{k+1} includes the recovery models of 18 actions. Considering the cases with solutions, the average CPU time[1] for inferring the recovery plan is 1428±548 msec.; and the recovery plan includes on average 6.5±0.5 actions. The longest plan consists of 8 actions, the corresponding $\mathcal{BSET}_8$, including the solution, has been encoded by an OBDD

[1]The cases have been simulated on a laptop Intel Core2 2.16 GHz, 1 GB RAM, equipped with Windows XP OS; the OBDDs are made available via the JavaBDD library.

with 92033 nodes.
As concerns the cases in *no-solution* set, the planning process behaves very well since it terminates as soon as the set $\overline{ACT}_{k+1}$ results to be empty, in particular the average time for determining the failure of the planning process is 47$\pm$16 msec. and on average, the planning process terminates after 2$\pm$0.5 steps.

6 Conclusions

In the present paper we have sketched the global architecture for a distributed control of a team of agents each one carrying on a set of actions possibly executed in concurrency with other agents. In particular, the paper addresses the problem of automatically synthesizing a recovery plan for the agent that has detected a failure in its local plan. While the problem of plan diagnosis has received an increasing amount of interest in recent years, ([5, 13, 9, 12]), not so much attention has been devoted to the problem of recovery plan in such a multi-agent environment.

We have addressed the problem by taking into account a set of tough environmental conditions in order to develop solutions that are applicable in real world contexts. In particular we have considered the case where:

- The actions have non deterministic effects
- The system observability is just partial, so in general it is not possible to know univocally the status of the agents at any time instant.
- The agent diagnosis, performed when an action failure is detected, is ambiguous

The combination of these characteristics requires that the recovery plan has to be a conformant plan and such a conformant plan (if exists) has to allow the agent to go from the state resulting from an action failure to a safe status where there is the guarantee of providing the required services to the other agents related by causal dependencies.

In order to synthesize the recovery plan, we have adopted symbolic methods for representing both the set of belief states as well as the model of the actions. In particular we have adopted Ordered Binary Decision Diagrams (OBDDs) and the planning process has been implemented in terms of OBDD operations. The use of OBDDs in planning has been already proved useful, in particular Jensen and Veloso [4] have shown how to exploit OBDDs for universal planning, a kind of generalized conditional planning. However the approach by Veloso is not directly applicable to the problem of recovery plan since we need to synthesize a conformant plan. The use of model checking techniques for conformant planning have been investigated by Cimatti and Roveri [3]; the methodology they propose assumes that both the initial and the final states are completely instantiated and requires the construction of a system model, represented as a finite state machine, where each node represents a possible global system state and transitions between nodes represent the execution of the actions, which possibly have non deterministic effects. The construction of the system model, however, may represent a critical step as it strongly depends on the dimension of the domain under consideration (see for example [11]). On the contrary, the methodology we have proposed does not require a global model of the system as the action models are directly used (in the disjunctive transition relation Φ_{k+1}) to determine, at each iteration of the algorithm, the set of conformant actions. Moreover, we have shown that the conformant planning is just a step of a closed loop of control finalized to the development of agents which exhibit some form of autonomy. To this end we have enriched the model of the actions with the notion of faults and we have related the planning process with the notion of agent diagnosis.

The preliminary experimental results reported in the present paper are encouraging since they show that the planning process is efficient both when a solution exists and when a conformant plan does not exist. In the first case an agent is able to recover from an action failure avoiding too expensive solutions by imposing a limit on the length of the recovery plan.

References

[1] L. Birnbaum, G. Collins, M. Freed, and B. Krulwich, 'Model-based diagnosis of planning failures', in Proc. AAAI90, pp. 318-323, (1990).

[2] C. Boutilier and R. I. Brafman, 'Partial-order planning with concurrent interacting actions', Journal of Artificial Intelligence Research, 14, pp. 105-136 (2001).

[3] A. Cimatti and M. Roveri, 'Conformant Planning via Symbolic Model Checking', Journal of Artificial Intelligence Research **13**, pp. 305-338 (2000).

[4] R. M. Jensen and M. M. Veloso, 'OBDD-based Universal Planning for Synchronized Agents in Non-Deterministic Domains', Journal of Artificial Intelligence Research **13**, pp. 189-226 (2000).

[5] M. Kalech and G.A.Kaminka, 'Towards Model-Based Diagnosis of Coordination Failures', in Proc. AAAI05, pp. 102-107 (2005).

[6] R. Micalizio and P. Torasso, 'Recovery from Plan Failure in Partially Observable Environments: the long report', Technical Report www.di.unito.it\ ~micalizi.

[7] R. Micalizio and P. Torasso, 'Diagnosis of Multi-Agent Plans under Partial Observability', in Proc. 18th International Workshop on Principles of Diagnosis (DX07), pp. 346-353 (2007).

[8] R. Micalizio, P. Torasso and G. Torta, 'Intelligent Supervision of Plan Execution in Multi-Agent Systems' in International Transactions on Systems Science and Applications, **1**(3), pp. 259-267 (2006).

[9] R. Micalizio, and P. Torasso, 'On-Line Monitoring and Diagnosis of Multi-Agent Systems: a Model Based Approach', Knowledge-Based Systems (special issue on AI 2006), **20**(2), pp. 134-142 (2007).

[10] M. D. R-Moreno, G. Brat, N. Muscettola and D. Rijsman, 'Validation of a Multi-Agent Architecture for Planning and Execution' in Proc. 18th International Workshop on Principles of Diagnosis (DX07), pp. 368-374 (2007).

[11] Y. Pencole and M.O. Cordier, 'A formal framework for the decentralised diagnosis of large scale discrete event systems and its application to telecommunication networks', Artificial Intelligence, 164, 121-170, (2005).

[12] N. Carver and V. Lesser, 'Domain monotonicity and the performance of local solutions strategies for cdps-based distributed sensor interpretation and distributed diagnosis', AAMAS Journal, 6, 35-76, (2003).

[13] C. Wittenven, N. Roos, R. van der Krogt, and M. deWeerdt, 'Diagnosis of single and multi-agent plans', in Proc. AAMAS05, pp. 805-812 (2005).

Automatic Character Assignation

Gerard Lynch & Carl Vogel
Computational Linguistics Group
Department of Computer Science and Statistics
Trinity College
Dublin 2,Ireland
{gplynch,vogel}@tcd.ie

Abstract

This article outlines a simple method for parsing an ASCII-format dramatic work from the Project Gutenberg Corpus into separate characters. The motivation for the program is a upcoming study in computational stylistics and characterization in drama. Various previous approaches involving interactive media are examined and the parser is evaluated by comparing the output to data annotated by hand and parsed automatically by the Opensourceshakespeare.org project parser. An acceptable level of accuracy is achieved, and it is identified how to improve accuracy to extremely high levels.

1 Introduction

The need for a program to parse drama files into constituent characters was born out of ongoing research on stylistics and character strengths in written drama. A script that parsed a play and separated characters was needed, as carrying this out by hand would be an arduous task, at great risk of introducing human error. Although there are XML annotated drama files available for some playwrights, the largest repository of drama files, Project Gutenberg, are for the most part in the ASCII text format, and do not all confirm to a common formatting style. A Java program was developed, named *PlayParser* which takes ASCII play files from Project Gutenberg as input and extracts a group of individual character files. It is important to note that wherever parsing is mentioned in the text, it refers to extracting the utterances from different characters and not any form of sentence-level grammatical parsing. This paper proceeds by situating the work with respect to its background motivations for parsing plays, and related work in information extraction from semi-structured texts. The operation of the parser is detailed, and the result is evaluated with respect to gold-standard annotations of ten Shakespeare plays, from the Opensourceshakespeare.org project.

2 Contextualization

2.1 Computational Stylistics

A number of points relevant to this paper can be usefully illustrated by recourse to the following excerpt from the screen play of *Dead Poet's Society*, [20]

```
                    KEATING
      Gentlemen, open your text to page
      twenty-one of the introduction. Mr.
      Perry, will you read the opening
      paragraph of the preface, entitled
      "Understanding Poetry"?

                    NEIL
      Understanding Poetry, by Dr. J. Evans
      Pritchard, Ph.D. To fully understand
      poetry, we must first be fluent with
      its meter, rhyme, and figures of speech.
      Then ask two questions: One, how artfully
      has the objective of the poem been
      rendered, and two, how important is that
      objective. Question one rates the poem's
      perfection, question two rates its
      importance. And once these questions have
      been answered, determining a poem's
      greatness becomes a relatively simple
      matter.

Keating gets up from his desk and prepares to draw on the chalk board.

                    NEIL
      If the poem's score for perfection is
      plotted along the horizontal of a graph,
      and its importance is plotted on the
      vertical, then calculating the total
      area of the poem yields the measure of
      its greatness.

Keating draws a corresponding graph on the board and the students
dutifully copy it down.

                    NEIL
      A sonnet by Byron may score high on the
      vertical, but only average on the
      horizontal. A Shakespearean sonnet, on
      the other hand, would score high both
      horizontally and vertically, yielding a
      massive total area, thereby revealing the
      poem to be truly great. As you proceed
      through the poetry in this book, practice
      this rating method. As your ability to
      evaluate poems in this matter grows, so
      will - so will your enjoyment and
      understanding of poetry.

Neil sets the book down and takes off his glasses. The student sitting
across from him is discretely trying to eat. Keating turns away from
the chalkboard with a smile.

                    KEATING
      Excrement. That's what I think of Mr. J.
      Evans Pritchard. We're not laying pipe,
      we're talking about poetry.

Cameron looks down at the graph he copied into his notes and quickly
scribbles it out.
```

The first point is that quantitative approaches to text stylistics may well not be "excrement". Suppose one wants to examine the spoken contributions of each character within a play to the overall play. One might want to apply authorship attribution techniques, or methods for corpus classification to assess whether on the basis of the text alone one can track the development of a character in a play. This could be viewed as a sort of sentiment analysis, applied to literary purposes. The second point that this excerpt illustrates from a typographical perspective is the sort of information that would want to extract from a script is nontrivial to receive: one must decide if stage instructions interrupting a speech are in fact a continuation of the same character's speech, or constitutes a new speech (presumably by the same character), or even a long name for the next character to speak (with inconsistent capitalization conventions indicating speaking turn owners); one must accept that not all of the text intended to be spoken by a character is directly the speech of the character (in the example here, the first contribution by Keating uses the speech of the character to provide a stage instruction that lets the audience know that Neil's speech is indirect); one must account for variability in the conventions that offset indication of the character speaking from the speech and from accompanying stage instructions and background narrative. These issues specific to plays are detailed further in §2.2.2.

While applying computational stylistics to character analysis is novel, computational stylistics is not at all new. [19] provides an overview of such work beginning with the middle of the 19th Century. Much of the work is in authorship attribution in a context in which some work is available with unquestioned provenance for an author, but also where attributions are doubtful. This sort of work is in contrast to that of [5] in which subjective analysis of textual features and information external to the texts are applied to a range of attribution problems. An open problem even within the attribution task is noted by [25], typically attribution research makes the idealizing assumption that (for example) the complete works of Shakespeare were written all at the same instant. An exception is in the work of [27] which attempts to leverage information about distributions of syllable stress and pauses indicated by line breaks in the Shakespeare plays over time of composition to date works whose temporal origin is less certain. Statistical methods have been applied to comparisons of political speeches [9] and political party manifestos [24]. However, this form of sentiment analysis, which has currency in the political science literature ([13, 14]), attempts to discern *content*. Certainly, [8] demonstrates that an algorithmic approach to textual analysis can also support fine-grained *stylistic* characterization of, for example, cohesion.

The approach we have in mind to support with the research described in this paper is rather more like that of [26], which performs a sort of cluster analysis on the poetry of Brendan Kennelly in order to identify poems with one or more of the narrative voices that Kennelly appeals to in the composition of his works: "the woman", "the child", "Ozzie", "the chorus", etc. Here we want to consider the textual contributions of characters in plays and identify, among other things, how homogeneous the contributions of each character are. Using authorship attribution tools, if all of the contributions of a character cluster together (without attracting the contributions of other characters), then that character is textually very strong. It is intriguing to know whether, across a playwright's canon, their characters are strong. Further, it is interesting to know whether the character is stronger than the author—this is the situation if the textual contributions of the character are easier to predict as contributions of the character than they are to be spotted as the product of the author, using only textual internal features. This would bolster any claim about the author's ability to construct strong characters, as opposed to constructing characters that are all alter egos of the author. The point is perhaps nuanced, but the claim is that it is in general more difficult to write characters that are strong in the above sense than to write characters whose authorship can be guessed.

In order to perform this sort of analysis, it is necessary to extract from the plays the relevant information associated with each character, and assigning it appropriately. This gives rise to the problem of parsing a play.

2.2 Information Extraction from Semi-Structured Text

The task of parsing a play is a problem in the area of parsing of semi-structured documents. Much of the literature on document parsing presupposes that the the text begins with XML mark-up (e.g. [12]), and set the task of identifying larger discourse structure in the text. In our case, the relevant information is within unannotated text; nonetheless, the text has implicit information packaging in the formatting. The problem exists in other tasks in extracting information from text.

2.2.1 The problem in general

More challenging problems in this field include dictionary parsing and the parsing of business cards. [17] describes methods for parsing machine readable copies of dictionaries using a grammar-based parser written in Prolog. This is a complicated procedure due to the fact that a dictionary entry may contain different fields including parts of speech markers, explanation, examples of usage, related words and phrases and various other categories including dialectical and cultural information.

[4] describes work done on using a similar Definite Clause Grammar based system for parsing business cards.This article describes how although the information on a business card is usually fairly uniform, fields such as name, address, professional degrees, organization, email address and website occur in nearly all instances, there is no fixed order as to how they should appear, which means any parser must be very flexible in order to capture all of the information contained on the card. [11] describes using OCR data to parse track names from CD covers for an imagined scenario in which the custodian of a large CD library equipped with a mobile phone with a camera can communicate with a library-based server to identify whether a CD found at a car-boot sale contains tracks not already in the library. This task also requires a good deal of flexibility in order to tackle the various different fonts and styles of layout that are encountered.

These are all instances of the general problem of information extraction from raw data into templates [6]. [18] discusses how to generalize across domains to enable re-use of information extraction methods. However, this sort of information has the harder problem of linguistic processing as the relevant information is embedded in the sentences of the document. They appeal to shallow linguistic processing to make progress. In the context of filling templates from business cards, or dictionaries, or CD covers or plays, one has to engage in meta-linguistic processing to understand document structure, rather than content. Yet, essentially finite state methods still apply [1]. Thus, the risks pointed out by [7] do not apply directly: named entity recognition is an issue, though, as discussed in the second step of our method (see §3). Ours is a specialization of the information extraction task orthogonal to scanning documents for particular sorts of information [23].

2.2.2 The problem of parsing plays

In contrast, parsing a play is a relatively straightforward process. The majority of plays written since the Renaissance have contained the same structure, a piece of writing, divided into a number of acts, each act divided into a number of scenes, each scene containing a dialogue(or monologue) between at least one character, with the utterance of each character clearly marked at the beginning by a string identifying the character and normally some stage instructions which inform the reader when and where the scene takes place, what characters are present and when characters enter and leave.

The constancy of conventions in structuring a play as a document is slightly surprising if one reflects on other changes of form that occur in the period that stretches even just from iambic pentameter to free verse to flat prose. However, the conventions of recording interactive dialogue in writing has shown little innovation since antiquity.

Assume D is the *dramatis personae* or the set of characters in the play, S is the set of all stage directions in the play, L is the sequence of all utterances.[1] It is possible to model a play as a structure as in (1), the semantic structure that corresponds to a template for a play.

(1) $P = \langle D, S, L, \lhd, \leq \rangle$

A binary relation ($\lhd$) maps characters to their lines (2).

(2) $\lhd \subseteq D \times L$

Finally, $\leq$ is a partial order on $\lhd$, which thus models the order of spoken lines, and allows for overlapping turns. Any information extraction device tailored to plays must aspire to approximating the structure P that corresponds to the play. In general it suffices to approximate $\leq$ by simply keeping track of all of the lines uttered by each character in the order the lines are uttered, without separating them as individual turns.

[1]It is a sequence rather than a set because the same sentence may be uttered more than once, and each instance is a line, by union rules.

The difficulty lies in the different formats that are present in the Gutenberg corpus. Some random examples from the Gutenberg corpus illustrate this. from Henrik Ibsen's *The Feast at Solhoug*

```
ERIK.

  [Rising at the table.]  In one word, now, what answer have you to
make to my wooing on Knut Gesling's behalf?

BENGT.

  [Glancing uneasily towards his wife.]  Well, I--to me it seems-- [As
she remains silent.]  H'm, Margit, let us first hear your thought in
the matter.
```

from *The Blue Bird : A Fairy Play in Six Acts* by Maurice Maeterlinck

```
TYLTYL Of course; there's no one to stop us.... Do you hear the
music?... Let us get up....

(_The two_ CHILDREN _get up, run to one of the windows, climb on to
the stool and throw back the shutters. A bright light fills the room.
The_ CHILDREN _look out greedily_.)

TYLTYL We can see everything!...
```

from *The Jew of Malta* by Christopher Marlowe

```
MERCHANT. I go.

BARABAS. So, then, there's somewhat come.-- Sirrah, which of my ships
art thou master of?

MERCHANT. Of the Speranza, sir.
```

from *Volpone, the Fox* by Ben Jonson

```
VOLP: I thank you, signior Voltore; Where is the plate? mine eyes are
bad.

VOLT [PUTTING IT INTO HIS HANDS.]: I'm sorry, To see you still thus
weak.

MOS [ASIDE.]: That he's not weaker.
```

There are other elements that are present in some plays, for example *dramatis personae* provided in a block at the outset. A lot of transcriptions also contain historical information about the play, when and where the play was first staged, and the actors that played the various roles. However, this information is not always provided and it would be unwise to rely on a *dramatis personae* as the ultimate authority on which characters are in a drama.

2.3 Available tools for interactive drama

There are several resources already available for interactively dealing with drama files on the Internet. [10] is a website implementing fully searchable versions of all the major works of Shakespeare. The website is built around a database coupled with an interactive interface written in PHP. One of the options available is to search for a particular character in any Shakespeare play and display all of the utterances of the character, including line numbers and corresponding act and scene markers. A concordancer and statistics based on word counts and frequencies are also available. In addition to being available for use via the internet, the source code for this system is freely available, which allows for modification. The drawbacks of this system for the task at hand is the fact that the plays must be annotated in a specific format to be read by the parser, and as the forthcoming study mentioned in §2.1 deals with a number of different playwrights, this would be necessary for each piece of work. If successful *PlayParser* will abet reliable automatic annotation of all plays that adhere to the conventions mentioned in §2.2.2, even with variability within those conventions.

[22] describes an prototype interactive Flash-based system called *Watching the Script* for displaying interactive scripts. It displays a number of views including the basic play text, and creates small character avatars on a stylized stage for students of directing to control. This system doesn't perform any pre-parsing of characters, simply displaying them as encountered and also takes plays in a special input format, though the possibility of incorporating non-formatted drama files is mentioned. Success in our endeavor would provide theirs with usefully structured input.

Scenario [16] is a commercially available interactive stage directors tool for all of Shakespeare's major works. It features drag and drop graphically represented characters and props, sound effects and allows creation of different frames. It does not appear to feature any concordancing elements or searching tools and is restricted to the plays of William Shakespeare.

3 Specification & Realization

The *PlayParser* is a two pass parser. The algorithm and input/output assumptions are as follows.

Input

Raw files of plays, except for manual preprocessed removal of headers and footers like glossaries, from the Project Gutenberg archive are supplied as input.

Output

The output is a set of files, one file for each character in each input play, and an index. Each file consists of all of the lines in the play spoken by the character. The index is a list of files and unique character identifiers.

Algorithm

1. The first pass reads through the play and compiles a list of character specifiers
2. The list is then presented to the user and the user is expected to remove any invalid entries. The number of occurrences of the character is displayed beside the name, to aid disambiguation, certain names may look like characters but in fact not be.
3. The parser then reads through the play again using the list of character specifiers as definitive points for termination and divides the file into the utterances of the different characters

Thus, *PlayParser* can be described as function mapping a text T to a structure P' that approximates (1) as (4).

(3) $PP(T) \mapsto P'$

(4) $P' = \langle D, \emptyset, L \cup S, \triangleleft, \leq \rangle$

In particular, in its current form, stage instructions are not eliminated, but are identified with the character whose speech they apply to.

There are two main advantages over the system described in [10] The first is the fact that the *PlayParser* does not rely on uniquely formatted input and is relatively flexible. The other is in the way the list of characters is created. [10] requires that the user enter the list of characters manually for the play that will be extracted. Although most of the Shakespeare plays contain a *dramatis personae* this is not always the case for other playwrights, and even when it is provided, it is not always possible to deduce some of the lesser characters' names from it. A solution to this would be of course to skim through the play manually looking for all unique character names, but this could take some time. It was decided to use algorithms trained on a base set of plays to determine whether a line contained a character specifier, check whether this character specifier is contained in the list of characters, if this is not the case, add it to the list and then move on. The list is then presented to the user who can look over the list of character specifiers and remove anything that is not a character specifier.

If one were to push the system away from manual intervention altogether, it would be in this second step that one would do so. One could imagine heuristics for guessing whether two strings refer to the same character. This is a rich open problem, as big as the puzzles of naming and definite reference in the philosophy of language and the problems of named entity recognition and anaphor resolution in computational linguistics.

The time complexity of the method is tractable (essentially finite-state, with a look-up operation), measured in terms of n, the number of tokens of text in a play's file. The worst case is defined by the situation in which the play consists of n characters who have one turn each of silence.

1. $n*log(n)$: This is the amount of time to read each line and decide whether the speaker's character has been encountered before.

2. n: Each character name is shown to the user once.

3. $n * log(n)$: This is the amount of time to process each line and decide whether it is a turn.

Thus, the complexity is dominated by $n * log(n)$.

Although the current prototype of the parser is flexible in the sense that it does not require a specific file format to parse, it does have some limitations. The dataset that it was developed on consists of the Project Gutenberg ASCII versions of plays by the following playwrights: William Shakespeare, Ben Jonson, W.B Yeats, George Bernard Shaw and Oscar Wilde. The formatting of all plays by each playwright was not necessarily consistent and was often undertaken by a number of different transcribers. The character specifier formatting fell into two main categories. The first example is taken from the Gutenberg file of *A Woman of No Importance* by Oscar Wilde

```
LADY CAROLINE.  I believe this is the first English country house you
have stayed at, Miss Worsley?

HESTER.  Yes, Lady Caroline.

LADY CAROLINE.  You have no country houses, I am told, in America?

HESTER.  We have not many.
```

In this case, the formatting for character name is given by the full character name in capitals. This particular formatting style is relatively easy to parse, as the character name is distinguishable from any proper noun occurring in the text. The second most popular formatting style is the following.

```
Ham. Whither wilt thou lead me? Speak! I'll go no further.
Ghost. Mark me.
 Ham. I will.
```

This short extract from the Project Gutenberg file of Shakespeare's *Hamlet* illustrates constructions that must be overcome by the parser. Here, the characters utterances are marked by an abbreviated form of their name written in conventional English writing style with a capital letter at the beginning. The names are not always abbreviated, as in the case of the Ghost character in this extract. In the current prototype of the parser, it looks for strings terminated by a full stop at the beginning of a sentence to indicate a character marker. The parser could read the two second sentences as unique characters in their own right, and add them to the list of characters. These would then have to be removed by the user.

There are issues that are beyond the reach of the program, such as keeping a character consistent when the character's name is changed. Many plays have characters who for one reason or another, begin with one name and then later take on a different name, sometimes when we learn the name of the character or when his or her status changes, for example, being crowned king or queen in some Shakespearean drama. For example, in Shaw's *Pygmalion*, the character of "Flower Girl" subsequently becomes named "Eliza". Moreover, annotations of characters speaking lines in plays within plays are also complex. Inconsistency on the part of the human transcriber is also not handled by the program, for example, if the transcriber suddenly decides to abbreviate a character name halfway through a play, the program will create two separate files for each version of the name it occurs if in the second pass, human intervention has not normalized the spelling to that of an established orthography for the character. Improvements that take some of these issues into account are a source for future work.

4 Evaluation

The parser was evaluated by comparing its output to the gold standard data from Opensourceshakespeare.org. Ten plays were chosen for the comparison. [2] claim that 90% precision is the threshold of accuracy necessary for information to be acceptable in "live" applications. It has been noted [6] that by the end of the 1990s, precision in the Message Understanding Conferences was around 70%. However, our task involves not text understanding, but document structure recognition. A wide range of evaluation statistics beyond precision and recall are available [3]. The problem of parsing a play is different from information retrieval, certainly. There precision and recall correspond to having correctly retrieved relevant documents and all relevant documents, respectively. It is in fact normal to distinguish information retrieval and information extraction. In the context of document understanding, as opposed to template filling from interpretation of sentences the documents contain, recall is nearly equivalent to precision because all segments of the document get classified in terms of the relevant document definition. Thus, like [15], we compute evaluation statistics more directly. A simple value for parsing accuracy was used, which is calculated as in (5).

(5) $Accuracy = \frac{CorrectlyAssignedLines}{TotalNumberofLines}$

Correctly parsed lines were lines that were assigned correctly to a character as marked in the source text. Ambiguities in the original text markup were not considered as errors, for example if the original text gave a number of character X's lines to character Y, this was ignored. Examples of errors include, skipping a number of lines because of the lack of correct formatting for the character specifier, the creation of a new character that does not exist in the text, or the inclusion of stage directions in the text of a character. Table 1 gives a simple but immediate view of the accuracy of the parser.

Results		
Playname	Average accuracy	Average accuracy less stage directions
A Comedy Of Errors	89	100
Loves Labour Lost	91.8	99.4
A Midsummer Night's Dream	81	100
Macbeth	80.1	99.7
Much Ado About Nothing	88.9	98.3
Romeo And Juliet	82	100
The Taming Of The Shrew	91	100
The Tempest	90	99.9
Twelfth Night	85.1	97.3
Coriolanus	88.7	99.5
Average accuracy	86.76	99.94

Table 1: Benchmarking Results

The two columns indicate accuracy under two different standards of success. The first column gives the method a penalty for each line of stage instructions that is mistakenly attributed as a part of a character's speech. This is clearly in the neighborhood of acceptability suggested by [2]. More interestingly, the second column displays the accuracy under the idealization of stage instructions having been hand tagged. The average resulting accuracy of 99.94 compellingly suggests that the next important open question to address in this area is connected to the binary decision about whether a line of text is a stage instruction or not.

5 Speculation

From the evaluation done on the parser, it is clear that a more flexible algorithm is needed that can deal with issues like missing full stops after character specifiers and indented character specifiers. The program should be able to deal with misspelt character specifiers and at the very least report to the user where possible parse errors may have occurred. Another extension, as discussed above, would be to implement a system to automatically detect stage directions. There are many transcribed works where stage directions and scene descriptions are given no particular marking and are not bracketed in any clear way. One such indicator could be to look for certain verb inflection and large concentrations of character names. For example, while much of the content of a play is written in second person as characters speak to each other, or third person past, stage instructions tend to be in third person present. However, they range from very terse, simple Shakespearean instructions (e.g. "exeunt") to rather involved descriptions (e.g. those of Shaw's plays). A large enumeration of character names would tend to signal a description of the action that is set to happen rather than, forming a constituent of a character's speaking part. The algorithm that detects character specifiers could be revised to incorporate regular expressions which might improve the accuracy by detecting slight differences in character specifiers that would otherwise be passed over.

6 Rumination

This paper has detailed a prototype parser for separating a play into characters, and assigning the text intended to be spoken by each character correctly to the character. It performed relatively well as compared to hand annotated input but although flexible, is still in need of streamlining in order to be fully autonomous. The character data will be used in a study on character strengths in different styles of drama. Although this was the initial task of the parser, it could also be a useful tool for parsing speech transcripts, minutes of meetings, screenplays or chatroom and instant messenger dialogues with some minor adjustments. It works without XML annotation of documents but could put to use in generating textual markup appropriate to the structure of plays. And, [21], "The play's the thing."

References

[1] D. Appelt, J. Hobbs, J. Bear, and D. I. M. Tyson. Fastus: a finite-state processor for information extraction from real-world text. In *Proceedings of the 13 International Joint Conference on Artificial Intelligence*, pages 1172–1178, 1993.

[2] J. Cowie and W. Lehnert. Information extraction. *Communications of the ACM*, 39(1):80–90, 1996.

[3] T. Fawcett. Roc graphs: Notes and practical considerations for researchers. Technical report, HP Laboratories, Page Mill Road, Palo Alto CA, 1994.

[4] R. Ferguson. Parsing business cards with an extended logic grammar. Technical report, CCRIT, 1988.

[5] D. Foster. *Author Unknown. On the trail of Anonymous.* Macmillan: London, Basingstoke and Oxford, 2001.

[6] R. Gaizauskas and Y. Wilks. Information extraction: Beyond document retrieval. *Journal of Documentation*, 54(1):70–105, 1998.

[7] R. Grishman. Information extraction: Techniques and challenges. In M. Pazienza, editor, *Information Extraction - a Multidisciplinary Approach to an Emerging Information Technology*, Lecture Notes in Artificial Intelligence, pages 10–27. Springer-Verlag: Berlin, 1997.

[8] M. Hoey. *Patterns of Lexis in Text.* Oxford University Press, 1991.

[9] L. Hogan. A corpus linguistic analysis of american, british and irish political speeches. Master's thesis, Centre for Language and Communication Studies, Trinity College, University of Dublin, 2005.

[10] E. M. Johnson. http://www.opensourceshakespeare.org, 2004. last verified 1st May 2007.

[11] P. Kilkenny. Information retrieval from cd covers using ocr text. Department of Computer Science, Trinity College, University of Dublin. Bachelor in Computer Science. Final Project Dissertation., 2006.

[12] H. Langer, H. Lüngen, and P. S. Bayerl. Text type structure and logical document structure. 2004. Proceedings of the ACL-Workshop on Discourse Annotation, Barcelona.

[13] M. Laver, editor. *Estimating the Policy Position of Political Actors.* Routledge, 2001.

[14] M. Laver, K. Benoit, and J. Garry. Extracting policy positions from political texts using words as data. *American Political Science Review*, 97, 2003.

[15] J. Makhoul, F. Kubala, R. Schwartz, and R. Weischedel. Performance measures for information extraction. In *Proc. of the DARPA Broadcast News Workshop*, pages 249–252, 1999. Virginia, USA.

[16] I. Media. http://ise.uvic.ca/Annex/ShakespeareSuite/scenario.html, 2004. last verified 1st May 2007.

[17] M. S. Neff and B. K. Boguraev. Dictionaries, dictionary grammars and dictionary entry parsing. In *Proceedings of the 27th annual meeting on Association for Computational Linguistics*, pages 91–101, Morristown, NJ, USA, 1989. Association for Computational Linguistics.

[18] G. Neumann and T. Declerck. Domain adaptive information extraction. In *Proceedings of the International Workshop on Innovative Language Technology and Chinese Information Processing (ILT & CIP '01), April*, Shanghai, 2001.

[19] M. P. Oakes. *Statistics for Corpus Linguistics.* Edinburgh Textbooks in Empirical Linguistics. Edinburgh: Edinburgh University Press, 1998.

[20] T. Schulman. http://www10.pair.com/crazydv/weir/dps/script.html. last verified August 23, 2007.

[21] W. Shakespeare. Hamlet, prince of denmark. In M. Mack, B. Knox, J. McGalliard, P. M. Pasinetti, H. Hugo, R. Wellek, and K. Douglas, editors, *World Masterpieces: Through the Renaissance*, volume 1. New York: Norton, 1973.

[22] S. Sinclair, S. Gabriele, S. Ruecker, and A. Sapp. Digital scripts on a virtual stage: the design of new online tools for drama students. In *WBE'06: Proceedings of the 5th IASTED international conference on Web-based education*, pages 155–159, Anaheim, CA, USA, 2006. ACTA Press.

[23] J. Thomas, D. Milward, C. Ouzounis, S. Pulman, and M. Carroll. Automatic extraction of protein interactions from scientific abstracts. In *Pacific Symposium on Biocomputing*, volume 5, pages 538–549, 2000.

[24] S. Van Gijsel and C. Vogel. Inducing a cline from corpora of political manifestos. In M. A. et al., editor, *Proceedings of the International Symposium on Information and Communication Technologies*, pages 304–310, 2003.

[25] C. Vogel. N-gram distributions in texts as proxy for textual fingerprints. In A. Esposito, E. Keller, M. Marinaro, and M. Bratanic, editors, *The Fundamentals of Verbal and Non-Verbal Communication and the Biometrical Issue*. IOS Press, 2007.

[26] C. Vogel and S. Brisset. Hearing voices in the poetry of brendan kennelly. In *Varieties of Voice*, 2006. 3rd international BAAHE conference. Leuven, 7-9 December 2006.Revised version to appear in *Belgian Journal of English Language & Literature*.

[27] M. R. Yardi. A statistical approach to the problem of the chronology of shakespear's plays. *Sankhya: The Indian Journal of Statistics*, 7(3):263–8, 1946.

SHORT PAPERS

An Agent-Based Algorithm for Data Reduction

Ireneusz Czarnowski and Piotr Jędrzejowicz
Department of Information Systems, Gdynia Maritime University
Morska 83, 81-225 Gdynia, Poland
E-mail: irek@am.gdynia,pl, pj@am.gdynia.pl

Abstract

The paper proposes an agent-based algorithm for data reduction, implemented using JABAT (**JA**DE **B**ased **A**-**T**eam) environment designed for solving a variety of computationally hard optimization problems. The approach aims at reducing the original dataset in two dimensions including selection of reference instances and removal of irrelevant attributes. Several agents representing different local-search based strategies are employed in parallel to achieve a synergetic effect. The paper includes also computational experiment results.

1. Introduction

In the supervised learning, a machine-learning algorithm is shown a training set, which is a collection of training examples called instances. After learning from the training set, the learning algorithm is presented with additional input vectors, and the algorithm should generalize, that is to decide what the output value should be.

It is well known that in order to avoid excessive storage and time complexity and to improve generalization accuracy by avoiding noise and overfitting, it is often advisable to reduce original training set by selecting the most representative information [8]. Reducing the size of the dataset can also result in diminishing the size of formulas obtained by an induction algorithm on the reduced data sets [1].

Data reduction can be achieved by selecting instances and by selecting features. Instance reduction, often referred to as the selection of reference vectors, becomes especially important in case of large data sets, since overcoming storage and complexity constraints might become computationally very expensive. Although a variety of instance reduction methods has been so far proposed in the literature (see, for example the review [8]), no single approach can be considered as superior nor guaranteeing satisfactory results in terms of the learning error reduction or increased efficiency of the supervised learning.

Equally important is the reduction of the number of features by removing features that are irrelevant for classification results. In the real-world situations, relevant features are often unknown a priori and, therefore, many features are introduced with a view to better represent the domain [3]. Many of these features are not only irrelevant for classification results but also can have a negative influence on the accuracy and on the required learning time of the classifier. The presence of redundant features introduces unnecessary noise to the data mining analysis and results in the increased computational complexity of the learning process. As it has been observed in [5], the number of instances needed to assure the required classification accuracy grows exponentially with the number or irrelevant features present. The feature selection problem belongs to the group of NP-hard problem [9], [5]. The discussion of the feature selection approaches can be found in [3].

The idea of simultaneously reducing both discussed dimensions of the training dataset has been recently investigated in [1], [7]. In both papers the suggested approach was based on using genetic algorithm to train the respective classifiers. In [9] the data reduction problem was combined with the belief revision in the adaptive classification systems. The belief revision is understood as modification and updating of the dataset in two dimensions. The modification and the updating of the dataset occur in the adaptive classification systems when the size of the dataset increases or when the dataset is huge and a decision system operates on subset of data.

The proposed approach is an agent-based algorithm for data reduction in two dimensions, implemented using JABAT environment. The paper contains a short overview of the functionality and structure of the JABAT as well as provides details of the proposed data reduction approach. To validate the approach computational experiment results are shown. Conclusions focus on evaluation of the proposed approach.

2. Overview of the JABAT

The instance reduction and feature selection are computationally difficult combinatorial problems [2], [3], [5]. To overcome some of the difficulties posed by computational complexity of the data reduction problem it is proposed to apply the population-based approach with optimization procedures implemented as an asynchronous team of agents (A-Team).

An A-Team is a cyclic network of autonomous agents and shared, common memories. Each agent contains some problems solving skills and each memory contains a population of temporary solutions to the problem to be solved. All the agents can work in parallel. During their work agents cooperate by selecting and modifying solutions. In the reported approach the A-Team was designed and implemented using JADE-based A-Team (JABAT) environment [4].

The JABAT produces solutions to combinatorial optimization problems using a set of optimising agents, each representing an improvement algorithm. To escape getting trapped into a local optimum an initial population of solutions called individuals is generated or constructed. Individuals forming an initial population are, at the following computation stages, improved by independently acting agents, thus increasing chances for reaching a global optimum.

To perform the above two classes of agents are used. The first one includes *OptiAgents*, which are implementations of the improvement algorithms. The second are *SolutionManagers*, which are agents responsible for maintenance and updating of individuals in the common memory. All agents act in parallel. Each *OptiAgent* is representing a single improvement algorithm. An *OptiAgent* has two basic behaviours defined. The first is sending around messages on readiness for action including the required number of individuals (solutions). The second is activated upon receiving a message from some *SolutionManager* containing the problem instance description and the required number of individuals. This behaviour involves improving fitness of individuals and resending the improved ones to a sender. A *SolutionManager* is brought to life for each problem instance. Its behaviour involves sending individuals to *OptiAgents* and updating the common memory.

Main feature of the proposed approach is its independence from the problem definition and solution algorithms. Hence, main classes *Task* and *Solution* upon which agents act, have been defined at a rather general level. Interfaces of both classes include function *ontology*(), which returns JADE's ontology designed for classes *Task* and *Solution*, respectively.

3. Agent-Based Data Reduction Algorithm

The JABAT environment has served as the tool for solving instances of the data reduction problem. All the required classes have been defined in the package called *IFS (Instance and Feature Selection)*. The *IFS* includes the following two classes: *IFS_Task* inheriting form the *Task* class and *IFS_Solution* inheriting from the *Solution* class.

The *IFS_Task* identifies the task and data set. *IFS_Task* creates clusters of the potential reference instances. In this case *IFS_Task* using the following algorithm that was original proposed in earlier paper of the authors [2]:

Step 1. Transform X normalizing value of each x_{ij} into interval [0, 1] and then round it to the nearest integer, that is 0 or 1, where $X = \{x_{ij}\}$ denotes the matrix containing values of all instances from the original training set denoted as T, N denote the number of instances in T and n – the number of attributes (total length of each instance - training example, is equal to n+1, where element numbered n+1 contains the output value).

Step 2. Calculate for each instance from the original set the value of its similarity coefficient I_i:

$$I_i = \sum_{j=1}^{n+1} x_{ij} s_j, \; i = 1,...,N,$$

where:

$$s_j = \sum_{i=1}^{N} x_{ij}, \; j = 1,...,n+1.$$

Step 3. Map instances (i.e. rows from X) into clusters denoted as Y_v, v=1...t. Each cluster contains input vectors with identical value of the similarity coefficient I and t is a number of different values of I.

In next step the JABAT uses the following rules for selecting instances:

- If $|Y_v| = 1$ then $S = S \cup Y_v$, where S denotes reduced training set and $|Y_v|$ denotes a number of instances in the cluster v.
- If $|Y_v| > 1$ then $S = S \cup \{ x_j^v \}$, where x_j^v are reference instances from the cluster Y_v selected by *OptiAgents*.

IFS_Solution contains representation of the solution. It consists of: the list of the selected reference instances from original data set - the list, on the first t positions, defines how many elements from Y_v are contained in the cluster v, the next positions represent input vector number from Y_v; the list of the selected features i.e. the number of selected features; the list of values of the quality factors including the classification accuracy, the percentage of compression of the training set and the number of rules - to obtain value of the last parameter the C 4.5 classification tool is used and or each decision tree produced by the C 4.5 the size of the respective tree is calculated and recorded.

To enable communication between optimization agents and the solution manager the *IFS_TaskOntology* and *IFS_SolutionOntology* classes have been also defined. The *TaskOntology* is needed to enable the transmission of task parameters and instance numbers belonging to respective clusters and representing potential reference instances. This communication involves agents and the common memory. The *SolutionOntology* is required to enable sending around potential solutions.

Each optimization agent operates on a single individual (solution) randomly selected form the population by the *SolutionManager*. An optimization agent tries to improve quality of the solution provided by the *SolutionManager*. This is done iteratively using some local search procedure. After the stopping criterion has been met the resulting individual is resend to the *SolutionManager*, which, in turn, updates common memory by replacing a randomly selected individual with the improved one. Generally, the *SolutionManager* manages the population of solutions, which on initial phase is generated randomly.

To solve the data reduction problem four types of agents representing different improvement procedures have been implemented. In each case the agent's classes are inherited from the *OptiAgent* class. The first and the second procedure aim at improving current solution through modification and exchange of the reference vectors in clusters. The third procedure improves a solution by changing, randomly, numbers on the feature list. The fourth improvement procedure modifies a solution by changing values on both lists - of reference vectors and features. The modification of both lists is a random move performed under the uniform distribution. The first and the third improvement procedure use the tabu search algorithm, where the tabu list (short term memory) contains moves that, for some number of iterations, are disallowed. If, during the search, an agent successfully improves the received solution then it stops and the improved solution will be transmitted to the respective *SolutionManager*. Otherwise, agents stop searching for an improvement after having completed the prescribed number of iterations.

4. Computational Experiment Results

To validate the proposed approach several benchmark classification problems have been solved. They include: Cleveland heart disease (303 instances, 13 attributes, 2 classes), credit approval (690, 15, 2), Wisconsin breast cancer (699, 9, 2), sonar problem (208, 60, 2) and adult (30162, 14, 2) [6]. Experiment plan has been based on the 10-cross-validation approach. For each run the respective training set T has been then reduced to a subset S containing reference vectors with relevant features only. Each reference vectors set has been, in turn, used to produce a decision tree. This has been evaluated from the point of view of the classification accuracy. Each decision tree has been created using only the instances in S and each C 4.5 classifier has been trained without pruned leaves and with pruned leaves. In case of the sonar problem the experiment has been carried out using the available training and test sets. Training set has been reduced as in all remaining cases.

The reported values of the quality measures have been averaged over all 30 runs. All optimization agents have been allowed to continue iterating until 100 iterations have been performed. The common memory size in JABAT was set to 100 individuals. The number of iterations and the size of common memory have been set out experimentally at the fine-tuning phase.

Table 1. Average classification accuracy (%), average number of rules and average size of the decision tree

Problem	Pruned leaves					Unpruned leaves				
	Average accuracy (%)									
	A	B	C	D	E	A	B	C	D	E
credit	84.9	77.2	90.7	81.3	92.6	83.2	74.8	90.4	76.7	90.9
cancer	94.6	94.4	97.4	95.0	98.1	95.0	94.4	98.4	86.5	97.9
heart	77.9	79.9	91.2	81.7	93.0	76.9	79.5	92.4	81.3	92.2
sonar	74.0	72.1	83.7	78.4	87.5	74.0	71.2	83.7	76.4	88.8
adult	83.2	80.1	83.9	83.3	86.1	81.4	82.4	83.5	82.4	85.3
average	82.43	80.74	89.05	83.94	91.46	82.1	81.70	89.50	81.40	91.05
	Average number of rules									
credit	12.0	36.0	16.4	15.5	10.5	54.0	75.0	24.5	15.4	13.9
cancer	15.0	8.0	8.2	2.3	6.5	20.0	19.0	12.8	2.7	7.7
heart	17.0	11.0	17.6	8.7	11.5	44.0	26.0	23.8	8.4	14.3
sonar	8.0	10.0	9.0	16.0	11.0	8.0	12.0	10.0	14.0	11.4
adult	215.3	225	37.2	45.5	23.4	274	197.2	34.6	52.4	27.4
	Average size of the tree									
credit	23.0	71.0	31.8	30.0	20.0	107.0	149.0	48.0	29.8	26.8
cancer	29.0	15.0	15.4	3.6	12.0	39.0	37.0	24.6	4.4	14.3
heart	33.0	21.0	34.3	16.4	22.0	87.0	35.0	46.6	15.8	27.6
sonar	15.0	20.0	17.0	19.0	21.0	15.0	25.0	19.0	17.0	21.8
adult	1432	654	87.6	40.5	28.4	1765	721	94.2	68.2	32.1

Experiment results are shown in Table 1. The results have been averaged over all experiment runs carried. Table 1 show accuracy of classification performed on the test set by the trained C 4.5 classifier without pruned leaves and with pruned leaves. Additionally, Table 1 includes the average number of rules and the average size of the resulting tree. The results in Table 1 are presented for following cases: **A** – classification accuracy (percentage of rightly classified instances) – all instances from the original dataset with all features; **B** – classification accuracy – all instances from the original dataset with the reduced number of features produced by the *wrapper* technique [3], where subsets of features are evaluated using the C 4.5 algorithm; **C** - classification accuracy - reference vectors with all features; **D** - classification accuracy - as in C with the *wrapper*-based selection of features; **E** – classification accuracy - reference vectors and feature selection as proposed in Section 2.

It can be observed that the proposed approach guarantees good classification results together with quite a satisfactory reduction of the original dataset. In case of all of the considered problems data reduction have increased the classification accuracy as compared with accuracy obtained by training the C 4.5 classifier using the original dataset. Gains in classification accuracy seem to be quite substantial.

The experiment results show also that the data reduction can result in a decreased complexity and size of the decision tree as compared with the decision tree created using the full dataset. It can be concluded that the proposed approach to data reduction results in a decreasing complexity of knowledge representation as well as in a reduction of computation time required. This remains true not only for decision trees but also for other machine learning techniques.

5. Conclusion

Main contribution of the paper is proposing and validating the agent-based approach to data reduction. Effective and dependable data reduction procedures are of vital importance to machine learning and data mining. Computational experiment results support author's claim that reducing training set size still preserves basic features of the analyzed data. It has been also shown that a set of simple, local-search based agents can produce very good solutions achieving a synergetic effect. Properties of the proposed algorithm will be further studied.

Acknowledgements: The research has been supported by the KBN grant no. 3T11C05928

References

1. Cano J.R., Herrera F., Lozano M. On the combination of evolutionary algorithms and stratified strategies for training set selection in data mining. Pattern Recognition Letters, Elsevier, 2004 (in press)
2. Czarnowski I., Jędrzejowicz, P. An approach to instance reduction in supervised learning. In: Coenen F., Preece A. and Macintosh A. (eds.) Research and Development in Intelligent Systems XX. Springer, London, 2004, pp 267-282
3. Dash, M. Liu H. Feature selection for classification. Intelligence Data Analysis 1(3), 1997, 131-156
4. Jędrzejowicz P., Wierzbowska I. JADE-based A-Team environment. Lecture Notes in Computer Science, 3993, Springer Berlin/Heidelberg, 2006, pp 719-726
5. Meiri R., Zahavi J. Using simulated annealing to optimize the feature selection problem in marketing applications. EURO Summer Institute (ESI) N°21, Nida-Neringa, Lituanie 2006, 171(3), 842-858
6. Merz, C.J. Murphy, M. UCI Repository of machine learning databases. [http://www.ics.uci.edu/~mlearn/MLRepository.html]. Irvine, CA: University of California, Department of Information and Computer Science, 1998
7. Rozsypal A., Kubat M. Selecting representative examples and attributes by a genetic algorithm. Intelligent Data Analysis 7(4), 2003, 291-304
8. Wilson, D. R., Martinez, T. R. Reduction techniques for instance-based learning algorithm. Machine Learning, Kluwer Academic Publishers, Boston 2000, 33-3: 257-286
9. Wróblewski J. Adaptacyjne metody klasyfikacji obiektów. PhD thesis, University of Warsaw, Warsaw, 2001 (in Polish)

Towards a Computationally Efficient Approach to Modular Classification Rule Induction

Frederic Stahl, Max Bramer
School of Computing, University of Portsmouth, PO1 3HE, UK
{Frederic.Stahl; Max.Bramer}@port.ac.uk

Abstract

Induction of classification rules is one of the most important technologies in data mining. Most of the work in this field has concentrated on the Top Down Induction of Decision Trees (TDIDT) approach. However, alternative approaches have been developed such as the Prism algorithm for inducing modular rules. Prism often produces qualitatively better rules than TDIDT but suffers from higher computational requirements. We investigate approaches that have been developed to minimize the computational requirements of TDIDT, in order to find analogous approaches that could reduce the computational requirements of Prism.

1. Introduction

In research areas such as bioinformatics and cosmology researchers are confronted with huge amounts of data to which they wish to apply data mining algorithms such as association rule mining or artificial intelligence techniques such as pattern matching. Constructing a model from a dataset in the form of classification rules is often the method of choice to enable the classification of previously unseen data. However most of these algorithms are faced with the problem of scaling up to large datasets. The most common method of inducing classification rules is the Top Down Induction of Decision Trees (TDIDT) algorithm [1], which is the basis for well-known classification algorithms such as C5.0.

There have been several attempts to improve the scalability of TDIDT, notably the Scalable Parallelisable Induction of Decision Trees (SPRINT[1]) algorithm, which promises to scale up well without loss of any accuracy. The basic techniques used by SPRINT are pre-sorting of the data and parallelisation [2]. However, using the intermediate representation of a decision tree is not necessarily the best way to induce decision rules, especially if the data contains a lot of noise and clashes. The Prism algorithm presented by Cendrowska [3] is an alternative approach to developing classification rules which can often produce rules of a higher quality when there are clashes, noise or missing values in the dataset [4]. Unfortunately Prism has much higher computational requirements than TDIDT and thus in practice is seldom used, especially for large datasets. This work transfers the

---

[1] SPRINT stands for **S**calable **PaR**allelisable **IN**duction of decision **T**rees

approach used by SPRINT [2] in a modified form to the Prism algorithm. We will consider only the case where all attributes are continuous.

2. Inducing Decision Rules: The Prism Algorithm

Cendrowska [3] identified as a serious disadvantage of TDIDT that it generally constructs rules with substantial redundancies. Rulesets such as:

IF a = 1 AND b = 1 THEN CLASS = 1
IF c = 1 AND d = 1 THEN CLASS = 1

which have no common variable cannot be induced directly by TDIDT. Using TDIDT will frequently result in unnecessarily large and confusing decision trees, and that in turn causes unnecessary problems, for example if the values of redundant attributes are not known or are expensive to find out for an unseen instance, resulting in the decision rules needing to be pruned to remove redundant rule terms. Cendrowska presents Prism as an alternative to decision tree algorithms with the aim of generating rules with significantly fewer redundant terms compared with those derived from decision trees, from the beginning.

The basic Prism algorithm for a dataset D can be summarised as follows, assuming that there are n (>1) possible classes and that all attributes are continuous.

```
For each class i from 1 to n inclusive:

   (a) working dataset W = D
       delete all records that match the rules that have
       been derived so far for class i.
   (b) For each attribute A in W
       - sort data according to A
       - for each possible split value v of attribute A
         calculate the probability that the class is i
         for both subsets A < v and A ≥ v
   (c) Select the attribute that has the subset S with
       the overall highest probability
   (d) build a rule term describing S
   (e) W = S
   (f) Repeat b to d until the dataset contains only
       records of class i. The induced rule is then
       the conjunction of all the rule terms built at
       step d.
   (g) Repeat a to f until all records of class i have
       been removed.
```

The computational requirements of Prism are considerable. The basic algorithm comprises five nested loops and thus is not suitable for massive training sets. Nevertheless it can offer a higher quality of rules than TDIDT, for example it is less vulnerable to clashes. A clash occurs when a rule induction algorithm encounters a subset of the training set which has more than one classification but which cannot be processed further [4]. Prism has a bias towards leaving a test record unclassified rather then giving it a wrong classification. Furthermore Prism can produce rules with many fewer terms than the TDIDT algorithm, if there are missing values in the training set [4]. Loosely speaking Prism produces qualitatively strong rules, but suffers from its high computational complexity.

3. Data Decoupling and Pre-Sorting to Improve Prism

In the SPRINT [2] version of TDIDT the data is initially decoupled into attribute lists. This enables each attribute to be processed independently of the others and thus overcomes memory constraints. The decoupling is performed by building data structures of the form *<record id, attribute value, class value>* for each attribute. A detailed description of the SPRINT algorithm is given in [2], on which the figures given in this section are based.

Figure 1 illustrates the creation of attribute lists from a sample data table, which is the part of SPRINT which we are using in an analogous way in our new version of Prism. Note that each list is sorted and each comprises a column with identifiers (ids) added so that data records split over several lists can be reconstructed.

Split & Sort

savings	salary	classes
30.1	65.5	G
23.5	15.9	B
40.2	75	B
55.9	40.8	B
55.9	100.7	G
45.4	60.4	G

id	salary	classes
1	15.9	B
3	40.8	B
5	60.4	G
0	65.5	G
2	75	B
4	100.7	G

id	savings	classes
1	23.5	B
0	30.1	G
2	40.2	B
5	45.4	G
3	55.9	B
4	55.9	G

Figure 1 The building of sorted attribute lists

In contrast to SPRINT, Prism removes records that are not covered by a found rule term. When our Prism, which works with attribute lists, finds a rule term, it removes all records in the corresponding attribute list that are not covered by that term. By using the ids of the deleted list records, Prism further deletes all records in its other attribute lists that match these ids.

Figure 2 shows how data records are removed from the attribute lists. Assume we are generating rules for the class value G, Prism would find the highest probability of the class being G for the term *salary* $\geq$ *60.4*. In the salary list the records with ids 1 and 3 are the only ones not covered by this term, thus the records with ids 1 and 3 are removed from all the attribute lists. The shaded records in both lists are those that are covered by this term.

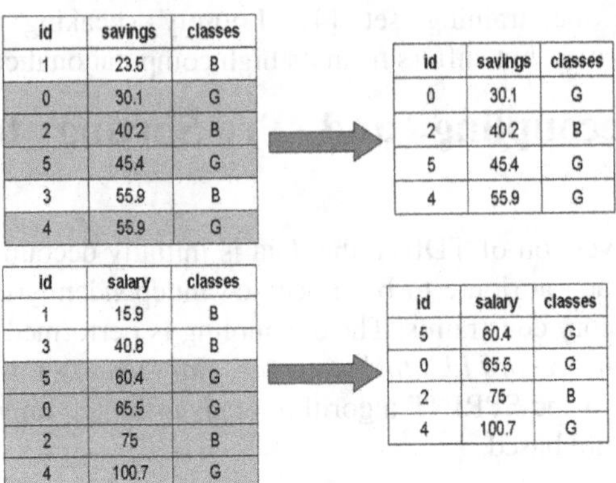

Figure 2 Removing records from the attribute lists

What is important here is that the resulting attribute lists shown on the right-hand side of Figure 2 are still sorted. Thus we have eliminated the multiple sorting which formed part of step (b) in the original algorithm description in Section 2. This removal of one of the five nested loops in Prism makes its runtimes considerably faster. A further effect of the usage of attribute lists is that memory constraints are removed. Our version of Prism now only needs to hold one attribute list in memory at any stage of the algorithm instead of the complete dataset. This allows us to process datasets that are too large to fit wholly into memory, which is clearly desirable but imposes the requirement for many I/O operations in order to buffer unneeded attribute lists onto the hard disc.

4. Evaluation of Improved Prism

We used a test dataset containing 100 attributes and 1000 records. The data consists of continuous double precision values with three classes. We implemented three algorithms:

(1) Prism without pre-sorting.
(2) Prism using attribute lists and pre-sorting of attributes.
(3) Prism using attribute lists, pre-sorting of attributes and buffering of unneeded attribute lists to the hard disc.

We want to show by comparing algorithms (1) and (2) that pre-sorting in Prism has a positive impact on efficiency and thus makes it scale better on bigger datasets. Although all the attribute lists were held in memory simultaneously for experiments (1) and (2), we conducted a further experiment (3) to investigate the overhead imposed by I/O operations in cases where we need to deal with memory constraints that make it necessary to hold only one attribute in memory at any time. We ran each algorithm on the training set 100 times and recorded the runtimes. We also checked that all the results were reproducible.

Table 1 shows the average runtimes of each implemented algorithm on the dataset described above. The average runtime values are based on 100 runs. In each case the first run was not taken into account as it is influenced by the operating system which caches the algorithm. Comparing Prism with and without pre-sorting we can see that the pre-sorting approach speeds up Prism by about a factor of 1.8. We can also see the substantial overhead imposed by the buffering of unneeded attribute lists onto the hard disc.

Table 1 Average runtimes of the test algorithms on the test dataset

Algorithm	Average Runtime in ms
Prism without pre-sorting	230995
Prism with pre-sorting	128189
Prism with I/O and pre-sorting	1757897

5. Ongoing Work

5.1 Ongoing Work on Serial Prism

Pre-sorting has a high potential to improve the complexity of Prism, but (as for SPRINT) it involves many time consuming I/O operations if the attribute lists do not fit into the memory. Thus one part of our present work lies in the reduction of the size of the attribute lists. Here we describe how we can reduce the size of attribute lists in the case of continuous attributes. The size of the data that needs to be held in memory by the conventional Prism is (8*n+1)*m bytes, where n is the number of attributes and m is the number of records. Eight bytes is the amount of storage needed for an attribute value (assuming double precision values) and one byte corresponds to the size of a class value assuming a character. The storage needed to hold all the attribute lists in memory is (8+4+1)*n*m bytes. The eight bytes are the size of an attribute value; the four bytes correspond to a record id and the one byte to a class value. However we could reduce these memory requirements simply by working without the attribute value in the attribute lists. We only need the complete attribute list structure *<record id, attribute value, class value>* to sort the attribute list according to its values. After sorting, the Prism algorithm could work with only the distribution of the class values in the attribute list. *<record id, class value>* for each attribute would need to be held in memory. Thus the memory requirement after sorting could be reduced to (4+1)*n*m bytes, which would be considerably less than the memory required by the conventional Prism. (The memory requirement of categorical attributes can be reduced in a similar way.) A version of Prism that works with this reduced list approach is currently in development.

5.2 Ongoing Work on Parallel Prism

We are currently focussing on data parallelisation on a *shared nothing* machine. In a shared nothing system, in contrast to a shared memory system, each processor has its own memory assigned to it. From the hardware point of view the shared nothing system could be realised by a cluster of PCs, thus it would be the cheapest and most flexible hardware configuration. It is especially flexible as it is easy to upgrade by simply adding more PCs into the cluster. Data parallelism in Prism could be achieved by having n processors that work on portions of the training set and consequently generate a global set of classification rules. The data parallelism that SPRINT uses is called *attribute data parallelism.* The basic approach is to divide the attribute lists equally among different processors. Thus each processor is responsible for 1/n attributes [5]. This approach could be used analogously by Prism but we expect it to cause work balancing problems after the first iteration as Prism removes parts of the attribute lists during its iterations. Thus it could easily happen that part attribute lists are completely removed on some processors and not on others. We are currently developing a further distributed workload balancing mechanism by assigning not only one but two or more chunks of each attribute list which are not in ascending order to a processor. Thus we would ensure that the records removed by Prism are less concentrated on a certain processor.

6. Conclusions

This paper presents ongoing work and first results in the attempt to speed up a classification rule induction algorithm that is an alternative to decision trees. It points out some weaknesses of the traditional TDIDT algorithm and the computational inefficiency of the alternative Prism algorithm. We propose (a) pre-sorting of the data and (b) parallelisation as methods to improve Prism's computational efficiency. With regard to (a) we mapped the attribute list structure used in the SPRINT algorithm onto Prism. In comparison with the runtimes of the conventional Prism algorithm the runtimes of Prism with pre-sorting are about a factor of 1.8 faster. However, the data in the form of attribute lists is much bigger in size then the raw data and for large datasets this can result in massive I/O operations between the hard disc and the memory. Our ongoing work is on a new attribute list structure that is smaller in size and thus promises to reduce the data volume of the I/O operations. With regard to (b) we introduced a more advanced attribute list parallelisation strategy than those of SPRINT in order to overcome work balancing problems caused by the nature of Prism. Future work will comprise with regard to (a) the implementation of Prism with a smaller attribute list structure and with regard to (b) the implementation of data parallel Prism with a novel work balancing structure.

References

1. Quinlan, J.R., Induction of decision trees. Machine learning, 1986. 1(1): p. 81-106.
2. Shafer, J.C., R. Agrawal, and M. Mehta. SPRINT: A Scalable Parallel Classifier for Data Mining. in 22th International Conference on Very Large Data Bases. 1996.
3. Cendrowska, J., PRISM: an Algorithm for Inducing Modular Rules. International Journal of Man-Machine Studies, 1987. 27: p. 349-370.
4. Bramer, M. Automatic Induction of Classification Rules from Examples Using N-Prism. in Research and Development in Intelligent Systems XVI. 2000: Springer Verlag.
5. Zaki, M.J., C.-T. Ho, and R. Agrawl. Parallel Classification for Data Mining on Shared Memory Multiprocessors. in 15th International Conference on Data Engineering. 1999.

Mobile Robots and EEG - A Review

K. A. Plant, P.V.S Ponnapalli and D.M. Southall.
Department of Engineering and Technology, Manchester Metropolitan University, Manchester M1 5GD.

Abstract — In this paper we present an overview of recent methods of controlling mobile robots with emphasis on evolutionary approaches of robot control. Development of recent electroencephalogram (EEG) based Brain-computer interfaces (BCI) are discussed with the main reference to EEG analysis where brain electrical activity is classified with the intent of generating output commands. Recent attempts to control a mobile robot with a BCI are discussed with future plans for further research in this field.

1. Introduction

Research in Artificial Intelligence (AI) is concerned with producing machines to automate tasks requiring intelligent behaviour. AI applications are generally divided into two types: classifiers and controllers; controllers do however also classify conditions before inferring actions and therefore classification forms a central part of most AI systems. Classifiers make use of pattern recognition for condition matching. Techniques to achieve this fall roughly into two categories: Conventional AI and Computational intelligence. Conventional AI mostly involves methods now classified as machine learning, characterized by formalism and statistical analysis. Methods in this category include: Expert systems, Case based reasoning, Bayesian networks and Behaviour based AI. Computational intelligence involves iterative development or learning e.g. parameter tuning in connectionist systems. Learning is based on empirical data methods, mainly including: Neural networks, Fuzzy systems and Evolutionary computation.

2. Autonomous Robots

Typically robots are used for tasks which are unfriendly to human operatives in hostile and hazardous environments. While many robots can be fixed in an industrial setting in manufacturing plants where the environment is highly controlled it is necessary for others to be more flexible and mobile. These criteria often result in the robot requiring some intelligence. Information transmission and reactions to real time events make it inevitable that such robots need their own controllers leading to autonomous behaviours. A high degree of autonomy is particularly desirable in fields such as space exploration, other more mundane applications benefit from having some level of autonomy. An important area of robotics research is to enable the robot to cope with its environment whether on land, underwater or in space. For the past twenty years several researchers have looked at novel methods of setting up autonomous mobile robots including Behaviour Based Robotics, Artificial life, Robot Learning, and Evolutionary

Robotics [2-4, 6-8, 14, 17-20]. The use of robot platforms has, in recent years, been made significantly easier with the range and complexity of sensors now available which are able to monitor most if not all, environmental conditions. This allows an increasing number of stimuli on which an autonomous robotic platform can base its decisions. Various applications for autonomous robots have been previously researched, e.g. predator avoidance [20], reactive navigation [17], maze exploration [18]. Such research is fundamental in refining our understanding of the process of artificial learning and decision making, providing industrial and general applications of autonomous robotics in addition to planetary exploration, hostile and hazardous environment applications.

3. Recent Approaches in Mobile Robot Control

Much research has taken place with regard to controlling the robot paradigm; the influence from biology is evident already in the structure of the artificial brains used in autonomous robots. In Behaviour-Based Robotics (BBR) robots are equipped with a collection of simple behaviours which are generally running concurrently and are organized to form a complete robotic brain. This branch of robotics incorporating modular or behaviour based AI (BBAI) techniques were applied to building real robots incrementally in the subsumption architecture [4, 14]. The control system is built up layer by layer and each layer is responsible for a single basic behaviour. The coordination mechanism of basic behaviours is usually designed through a trial and error process and the behaviours are coordinated by a central mechanism. By contrast, classical (AI), with its sense-plan-act structure, has much less in common with biological systems. The traditional approach of AI is a top down methodology where the overall goal is partitioned into smaller subsystems which were then developed individually. The main disadvantage of this method is the potential incompatibility of the subsystems and the control mechanisms such as symbolic reasoning systems. In contrast to AI, Artificial Life (AL) generally works from the bottom up. AL studies the evolution of agents or populations of computer simulated life forms in artificial environments. The goal is to study phenomena found in real life evolution in a controlled manner and specifically how different levels of organizational elements within the agent or population interact with each other [3]. Robot learning is a subset of machine learning and robotics which is closely related to adaptive control. While machine learning is frequently used by computer vision algorithms, robot learning relates to the specified task, based on a system's ability to learn sensory-motor mapping or develop subsystems of the controller which is typically an Artificial Neural Network (ANN). Robot learning can use different algorithms for learning e.g. reinforcement learning [22], self organising maps and classifier systems.

4. Evolutionary Robotics

Evolutionary robotics (ER) aims to develop a suitable control system of the robot through artificial evolution. Evolution and learning are two forms of biological adaptation that operate on different time scales. Evolution is capable of capturing slow environmental changes that might occur through several generations, whereas learning may produce adaptive changes in an individual during its lifetime. Recently, researchers have started using artificial evolution techniques, such as genetic algorithms (GAs) [9, 10] and learning techniques, namely ANNs [11], to study the interaction between evolution and learning. ANNs have proven to be a powerful computational tool widely applied to science and engineering. They are often used to implement robot controllers because of their ability to capture nonlinear dynamics, inherent fault-tolerance and parallel implementation, properties that facilitate real time control and potentially modular implementation of complex perception-to-action functions. ANNs can be designed and trained using various techniques including those based on evolutionary computation. Evolutionary Algorithms (EAs) are methods for search and optimization based on Darwinian evolution; an EA allows structural as well as parametric optimization of the system under study. This is particularly important in ER, where it is rarely possible to specify the structure of e.g. the artificial brain of a robot in advance and, therefore, parametric optimization would not be sufficiently versatile for the problem at hand. Evolution, whether artificial or natural, under the right conditions has the ability to avoid getting stuck at local optima in a search space, and given enough time, an evolutionary algorithm usually finds a solution close to the global optimum. Due partly to its stochastic nature, evolution can find several different and equally viable solutions to a given problem. ER is a methodology that uses evolutionary computation to develop controllers for autonomous robots. EAs in ER frequently operate on populations of controllers, initially selected from some distribution. This population is then repeatedly modified according to a fitness function. In the case of GAs, the population of controllers is repeatedly grown according to crossover and mutation, and then culled according to the fitness function. In ER the designer plays a passive role and the basic behaviours emerge automatically through evolution due to the interactions between the robot and its environment. The designer defines the fitness function, which measures the ability of a robot to perform a desired task. The robot and the environment form a highly dynamical system, in which the robot's decision at a particular time depends on the sensory information and its previous actions. Developing a suitable adaptive ANN-controller for a robot is the prime aim of evolutionary robotics. A binary-coded GA is used to provide training to the ANN. The GA starts with a population of binary strings, created at random and each string indicates the weights of the ANN. The fitness of each string is determined by creating a number of training scenarios at random and each scenario differs from the other in terms of the initial position, size and velocity of the moving obstacles. For each training scenario, a robot collects information about its dynamic environment using its sensors. The sensory information is then fed as input to the robot controller and it determines the output, which is realised through motor action. The fitness values of all the GA-strings contained in the population are determined similarly. The initial population of solutions is then modified using the GA-operators, namely reproduction, crossover and mutation. Optimal/near-optimal weights of the ANN are determined by the evolution technique. The robot controller may not behave in an optimal sense initially, but the controller improves its performance and produces better results gradually, a suitable robot controller evolves through a self-organizing process. In ER the environment plays a central role by determining which basic behaviour is active at any given time. Evolutionary robotics may solve this problem in a more effective way as compared to alternative methods discussed previously, as the evolution of behaviours and their coordination mechanism can be obtained through a self-organizing process rather than by an explicit design. ER is done with many different objectives, often at the same time, these include creating useful controllers for real-world robot tasks, exploring the intricacies of evolutionary theory, reproducing psychological phenomena, and finding out about biological neural networks by studying ANNs.

5. Electroencephalogram (EEG)

The brain function test electroencephalogram (EEG) is the neurophysiologic measurement of the electrical activity of the brain by recording from electrodes placed on the scalp. The resulting traces are known as EEG and represent the global activity of millions of neurons as an electrical signal. Electrical voltage differences are measured between different parts of the brain. EEGs are frequently used in experimentation because the process is non-invasive to the research subject. The EEG is capable of detecting changes in electrical activity in the brain on a millisecond-level. It is one of the few techniques available that has such high temporal resolution.

6. Brain-Computer Interfaces

The research interest of direct brain-computer communication first became apparent just over 30 years ago. Now more than 20 research groups worldwide are working on various aspects of this problem [16, 25]. Many different approaches from a variety of disciplines (medicine, biology, physics, mathematics, computer science, mechanical and electrical engineering, etc) have produced valuable research for a variety of applications. A brain-computer interface is intended to enable communication with a computer by thought patterns alone; this is achieved by training a subject to become familiar with meditation techniques and controlling mental tasks. The resulting EEG signals can then be classified into patterns which can be processed as a means of communication. The popularity of this method of communication has increased because it requires no physical effort compared with other input methods such as keyboard and mouse. This method allows thought to direct an action such as controlling a computer curser [3] or operating a wheelchair [13], mobile robot or mechanisms such as a prosthetic or robotic arm. This makes people with severe disabilities a target for a vast amount of this research. Electroencephalogram (EEG) is the foundation of current BCI research, although other methods include Electromyography (EMG) which is a medical technique for evaluating and recording physiologic properties of muscles at rest, and while contracting. EMG is performed using an instrument called an electromyograph, to record signals of electrical potential generated by muscle cells when contracting and at rest. Electrooculography (EOG) is a technique for measuring the resting potential of the retina. The resulting signal is called the electrooculogram which records eye movements. Although EMG and EOG can be used as a means of BCI communication they also can cause problems in the form of interference artifacts when EEG signals are recorded and classified, these artifacts are usually filtered to avoid distorted data.

7. Related Work

Several studies on mobile robots controlled by brainwaves have been reported; the control of a small four-wheeled mobile robot using combinations of EEG, EOG and EMG [1] was observed. EEG was used only as speed control, EMG as a jaw clench action was used for forward/reverse motion and EOG eye movements controlled direction. Although the work was a preliminary exercise, the paper did not report any success or failure of the robot reaching any desired destinations. Two further studies were carried out, the first on a small two wheeled mobile robot controlled only by EEG [12], and this study was then extended to the control of an electric wheelchair [13]. In the experiments the mobile robot/wheelchair were controlled by EEG but the motion was either left-forward or right-forward by a pre-programmed 45 degree angles. A Gaussian classifier [15] was developed to recognise three mental states plus an unknown state, applied to a small khepera robot in which the design mimics an electric wheelchair. This approach uses an asynchronous protocol that analyses on-going EEG signals to determine which mental state is active at any moment, this allows effective control of a mobile robot as the robot does not have to stop while the EEG measurements are recorded and classified. The controller uses a finite state machine to maximise robot instructions by assigning two instructions per mental state, if a left turn mental state is detected the robot will turn left or follow any obstacle to the left while keeping a specific distance from it. Forward motion and stop can also be toggled.

8. Conclusion

Our intention is to build on previous ER and EEG research activities; our proposed research is to develop an evolutionary EEG based teleoperated mobile robot control system, with specific emphasis on evolutionary techniques. Our proposed research is to develop an intelligent mobile robot which interacts with a changing environments with the view to executing complex tasks. ER facilitates our requirements as it looks at robots as autonomous artificial organisms that develop their own skills in close interaction with the environment without human interaction. Further research on BCIs with regard to mobile machines, suggests the possibility for humans to mentally operate wheelchairs, prosthetic limbs and other devices, helping people with motor diseases and those severely disabled.

References

[1] Amai, W., Fahrenholtz, J., Leger, C. Hands-Free Operation of a Small Mobile Robot, Autonomous Robots July 2001, 11 (1) pp. 69 - 76.

[2] Beer, R.D., Gallagher, J.C. (1992). Evolving dynamical neural networks for adaptive behaviour. Adaptive Behavior 1 (1) pp. 91-122.

[3] Beer, R.D, Toward the Evolution of Dynamical Neural Networks for Minimally Cognitive Behavior, in P. Maes, M. Mataric, J. Meyer, J. Pollack and S. Wilson (Eds.), From animals to animats 4: Proceedings Bajaj of the Fourth International Conference on Simulation of Adaptive Behavior, 1992 pp. 421-429. MIT Press.

[4] Brooks, R.A. The Role of Learning in Autonomous Robots. Proceedings of the Fourth Annual Workshop on Computational Learning Theory (COLT '91), Santa Cruz, CA, Morgan Kaufmann Publishers, August 1991, pp. 5-10.

[5] Fabiani, G.E.; McFarland, D.J.; Wolpaw, J.R.; Pfurtscheller, G. Conversion of EEG activity into cursor movement by a brain-computer interface (BCI). IEEE Transactions on Neural Systems and Rehabilitation Engineering. Sept. 2004. 12 (3) pp 331 - 338.

[6] Floreano, D. and Mondada, F. Evolution of Homing Navigation in a Real Mobile Robot. IEEE Transactions on Systems, Man, and Cybernetics - Part B: Cybernetics. 1996. 26 (3) pp. 396-407.

[7] Floreano, D., Godjevac, J., Martinoli, A., Mondada, F. and Nicoud, J.D. Design, Control, and Applications of Autonomous Mobile Robots. In Advances in Intelligent Autonomous Agents, Boston: Kluwer Academic Publishers, 1998.

[8] Floreano, D. and Mondada, F. Evolutionary Neurocontrollers for Autonomous Mobile Robots. Neural Networks. 1998. 11 (7-8) pp 1461-1478.

[9] Goldberg, D.E. Genetic Algorithms in search, optimization and machine learning. Reading MA: Addison-Wesley. 1989.

[10] Holland, J.H. Adaptation in Natural and Artificial Systems. Ann Arbor, MI: University of Michigan Press. 1975.

[11] Kosko, B. Neural Networks and Fuzzy Systems. Prentice-Hall 1994.

[12] Tanaka,K.,Matsunaga,K.,Kanamori,N.,Hori,S.,Wang,H.O. Electroencephalogram-based control of a mobile robot. In Computational Intelligence, Robotics and Automation, July 2003, 2 (16-20) pp 688 - 693.

[13] Tanaka, K., Matsunaga, K., Wang, H.O. Electroencephalogram-Based Control of an Electric Wheelchair. Robotics, IEEE Transactions on Robotics and Automation. Aug. 2005. 21 (4) pp 762 - 766.

[14] Maes, P. and R. A. Brooks, Learning to Coordinate Behaviors. AAAI, Boston, MA, August 1990 pp. 796-802.

[15] Millan, J., Renkens, F., Mourino, J., Gerstner, Wulfram. Non-Invasive Brain-Actuated Control of a Mobile Robot. Proceedings of the 18th International Joint Conference on Artificial Intelligence, Acapulco, Mexico. August 2003.

[16] Millan, J., Renkens, F., Mourino, J., Gerstner, Wulfram. Brain-actuated interaction. Artificial Intelligence. November 2004. 159 (1-2) pp. 241 - 259.

[17] Nelson, A.L. Grant, E. Barlow, G. White, M. Evolution of Complex Autonomous Robot Behaviors using Competitive Fitness. Integration of Knowledge Intensive Multi-Agent Systems. Oct 2003. pp. 145 - 150.

[18] Nelson, A.L., Grant, E., Galeotti, J.M., Rhody, S. Maze Exploration Behaviors using an Integrated Evolutionary Robotics Environment. Robotics and Autonomous Systems, 2004. 46 (3) pp. 159-173.

[19] Nolfi, S., Floreano, D., Miglino, O. and Mondada, F. How to Evolve Autonomous Robots: Different Approaches in Evolutionary Robotics. 4th International Workshop on Artificial Life. 1994.

[20] Ricardo A. Tellez, C.A., Evolving Cooperation of Simple Agents for the Control of an Autonomous Robot. Proceedings of the 5th IFAC Symposium on Intelligent Autonomous Vehicles (IAV04) Lisbon, Portugal, 2004.

[21] Tanev, Ivan., Brzozowski, Michael., Shimohara, Katsunori. Evolution, Generality and Robustness of Emerged Surrounding Behavior in Continuous Predators-Prey Pursuit Problem in Genetic Programming and Evolvable Machines. September 2005. 6(3) pp. 301-318.

[22] Wiering, M., Salustowicz, R. Schmidhuber, J. Model-based reinforcement learning for evolving soccer strategies. In Computational Intelligence in Games, chapter 5. Editors N. Baba and L. Jain. 2001 pp. 99-131.

[23] Wolpaw, J.R, Birbaumer, N., McFarland, D.J., Pfurtscheller, G., Vaughan, T.M. Brain- computer interfaces for communication and control. Clinical Neurophysiology. 2002. 113 pp. 767-791.

Studying Anticipation Behavior in ALife Simulator

Ahmed M. Elmahalawy and Pavel Nahodil
Department ofCybernetics, Czech Technical University,
Karlovo námestí 13, 121 35 Prague 2, Czech Republic.
a_elmhalaway@hotmail.com, nahodil@fel.cvut.cz
http://cyber.felk.cvut.cz/

Abstract

We present two original systems in *Artificial Life* (ALife) domain, a new designed simulator *World of Artificial Life* (WAL) and an *Anticipatory Agent System* (AAS). Both of them are based on the concept of M*ulti Agent Systems* (MAS). We made some modification in WAL basing on the anticipation behavior. Further, we use *Genetic Algorithms* (GA) within anticipatory module in ASS and evaluate the system. We have verified that anticipation behavior could be one of the most frequent behaviors in ALife, too. Our results confirmed that the system's performance is much better in this case.

1. Introduction

In this paper, we introduce *World of Artificial Life* (WAL) simulator [1] and *Anticipatory Agent System* (AAS) [2] as two examples of *Artificial Life* (ALife) systems. These two systems are based on the concept of *Multi Agent Systems* (MAS). The development of such agent-based systems has been largely increased in the last years. One of the applications of the agent technology is in simulation systems. Artificial Life simulations become the most useful application. It helps us to understand the concepts of life and find a solution for the unexpected problems in our life [3].

Initially, *ALife* was defined as a broad field of work in which attempts are made to simulate or recreate one or more natural processes using artificial methods. Nevertheless, applications in this field have quickly exceeded purely biological applications [4]. However, only recently has the concept of anticipations acquired more recognition in artificial learning systems.

The study of anticipation behavior is referring to behavior that is dependent on predictions, expectations, or beliefs about future states. Hereby, behavior includes actual decision making, internal decision making, internal preparatory mechanisms, as well as learning. The term "anticipation" is often understood as a synonym for prediction or expectation—the simple act of predicting the future or expecting a future event or imagining a future state or event. [5]

The paper is organized as follows: Section 2 gives a briefly description of the anticipation behavior. Section 3 presents the architecture of two different systems that we used. In Section 4, a proposed prototype modification of the WAL has been represented, and section 5 shows the evaluation of using genetic algorithms within AAS. Finally, a conclusion is briefly described in the last section 6

2. Anticipation Behavior

Anticipation is a mental activity that humans, but also some other living organisms, are capable of and one which is frequently practiced. A tennis player, for instance, has to anticipate the trajectory of the ball in order to make a good hit. A stockbroker makes forecasts of stock prices in order to make a good deal. In short, they use knowledge of future states to guide their current behavior. To do this they make use of an internal model of particular phenomenon. [6]

Basic definition of anticipatory systems was published in 1985 by cyberneticist R. Rosen in his book Anticipatory systems (Rosen, 1985). He defined an anticipatory system as follows: *"A system containing a predictive model of itself and/or its environment, which allows it to change state at an instant in accord with the model's predictions pertaining to a latter instant"*. [7]

More sophisticated anticipatory systems are those which also contain its own model, are able to change model and to maintain several models, which imply that such systems are able to make hypotheses and also that they can comprehend what is good and bad. One can infer from this statement that true agent systems are only those that have a clear anticipatory ability, both at the level of the individual agents themselves, and also at the whole MAS. [8]

3. The used Environment

3.1. World of Artificial Life

One of the last MAS architectures for ALife domain is *World of Artificial Life* (WAL). WAL architecture is based on hybrid architecture for ALife agent that would be emergent, proactive, sociable, autonomous and adaptive. Agent's learning is based on AI algorithms where a movement planning agent uses the concept of artificial potential field known from mobile robotics. These algorithms were chosen as an alternative to evolutionary algorithms and Artificial Neural Networks, which are also commonly used in ALife domain. This simulator has been developed by the *Mobile Robotics Group* "MRG" (leaded by P. Nahodil) in previous years [1].

The whole WAL is based on the idea that the only information agent gets data from sensors and awareness of action he should react to.

In the following, we will concentrate our attention to the architecture of the agent itself. It will be called *Architecture Lemming*. There is much hybrid architecture that used in mobile robotics but we can be simply adjusted for ALife purposes. *Architecture Lemming* could be classified as hybrid architecture with strong adaptive and generalizing abilities. [1]

The *architecture Lemming* is based on processing data from sensors and inner states. If we follow data flow, we start in the block Environment. Environment supplies agent through *Sensors* with sensory data and through *Inner States block* with information about inner variables. Data are filtered by *Mood Filter* and passed to *Action Selection Mechanism* and Memory. *Action Selection Mechanism* compiles available data and using *Knowledge Base* and *Long-Term Goals* agent makes decision about future actions which are performed by *Actuators*. History, Rules Generator and New Rules Repository are used for generalization [1].

3.2. Anticipatory Agent System (AAS)

The framework for anticipatory agents is based on the concept of anticipatory systems as described by Rosen. It is a hybrid approach that synthesizes low-level reactive behavior and high-level symbolic reasoning. An anticipatory agent consists of three main entities: an object system (*S*), a world model (*M*), and a meta-level component (*Anticipator*). The object system is an ordinary (i.e., non-anticipatory) dynamic system. *M* is a description of the environment including *S*, but excluding the *Anticipator*. The *Anticipator* should be able to make predictions using *M* and to use these predictions to change the dynamic properties of *S*. Although the different parts of an anticipatory agent certainly are causal systems, the agent taken as a whole will nevertheless behave in an anticipatory fashion. [2].

To summarize: The sensors receive input from the environment. This data is then used in two different ways: (1) to update the World Model and (2) to serve as stimuli for the *Reactor*. The *Reactor* reacts to these stimuli and provides a response that is forwarded to the *effectors*, which then carry out the desired action(s) in the environment. Moreover, the *Anticipator* uses the World Model to make predictions and on the basis of these predictions the *Anticipator* decides if, and what, changes of the dynamical properties of the *Reactor* are necessary. Every time the *Reactor* is modified, the *Anticipator* should, of course, also update the part of the World Model de-scribing the agent accordingly. Thus, the working of an anticipatory agent can be viewed as two concurrent processes, one reactive at the object level and one more deliberative at the meta-level. [2]

4. Results

4.1. Suggested Modification of WAL Simulator

The drawback that was found in the previous architecture of agent in WAL is missing the real values of inner state values. It was assumed that all inner state values have ideal in the beginning of the experiment. So, our modification is adding a new block to this architecture to test the inner state values at the beginning of the experiment. If they have not its ideal values so do action to adjust them to its ideal values. This modification is based on the principles of anticipation. That is shown in Figure 1.

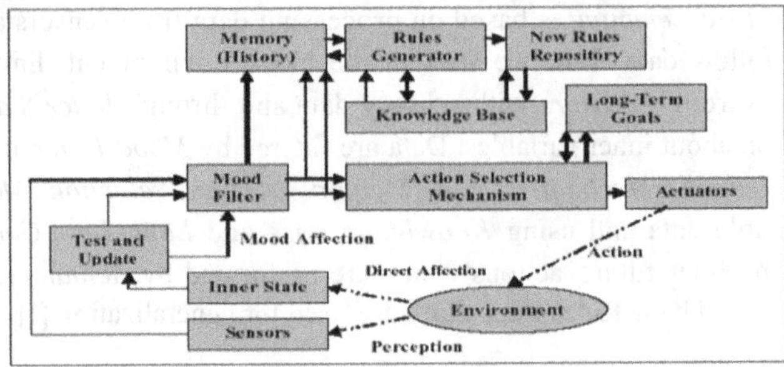

Figure 1 A modification of agent's architecture in WAL

4.2. Adding a New Behavior in WAL

Here, we add a new behavior in the WAL that is called fire behavior. When the creature is near to the source of the fire, he feels its affect to him. He then goes fare it. Figure 2 shows a screenshot for this new behavior.

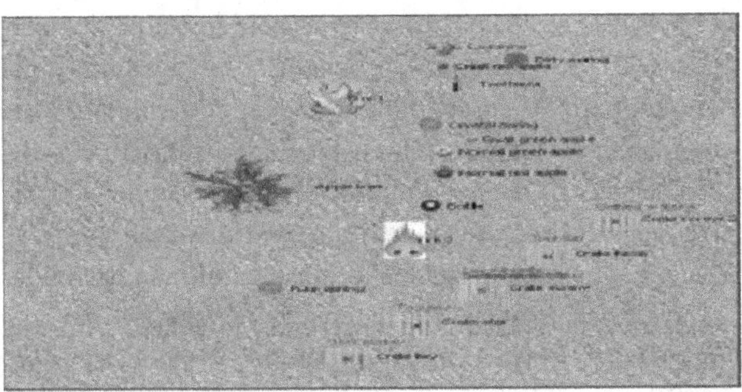

Figure 2 A screenshot of Fire Behavior.

5. Evaluation

We will present many experiments using the simple maze problem. The AAS will be used in the experiments. The anticipatory module depends on the GA to anticipate the next step in the maze problem until the agent reaches to his goal. In each experiment, we use different maze configuration that is, we change the obstacles position. Also, we change the number of agents and goals in the maze. From the following cases, we can calculate the range of the change in the agent's steps as follows:

Range = (max number of steps – min number of steps)/2

We present our result in the following cases, where the numbers of obstacles are changed from 0 to 35. The number of steps that agent will take to reach its goal is calculated. Table1 presents the summery of our experiments for evaluation of system's performance.

Table.1. Summery of System performance

Case	Range value	Comments
Single Agent, Single Goal	T1=51, T2=48, T3= 52	The system is stable as the change in the *Range* is small among the three tries. Its value is 4
Single Agent, Multi Goals	T1-G1=66,T2-G1= 50, T3-G1=40,T1-G2= 51, T2-G2= 60,T3-G2= 52	We can see that for *Goal1*, the system is not more stable as the change in the value of range from different tries is now 26. But with *Goal2*, the system is more stable where the change in the value of the *Range* among three tries is 9.
Multi Agents, Single Goal	T1-A1= 0, T2-A1 =0, T3-A1= 0, T1-A2= 72, T2-A2=76,T3-A2= 86.	The system predicts that *Agent2* has a good chance to go to goal rather than *Agent1*. So, *Agent1* doesn't move from its initial position and *Agent2* goes to goal. The change in the value of *Range* among different tries is 14.
Multi Agents, Multi Goals	T1-A1 =0, T2-A1 =0, T3-A1 =8, T1-A2= 75, T2-A2 =71,T3-A2 =72	The system tries to predict which A*gent* is suitable for which *Goal* to go to it. As shown, the system is stable for both *Agent1* and *Agent2* where the value of range of them is 8 and 3 respectively.

6. Conclusions

This paper presents our research in two insights. The first one is the modification in WAL simulator where the new block has added. It causes that the system begins in its ideal state. Adding the fire behavior in our experiments evokes that the agent is prevented from the fire affect. So, both modifications improve the system performance. Secondly we used Genetic Algorithms (GA) in ASS.

We conclude from the previous figures the following: in almost all cases was shown that the anticipatory system is much more stable, while the value of the *Range* is small. It is benefit of our reach because it is good and expected results. Although there is a great amplitude vibration in the number of steps to reach the goal and sometimes the number of steps is quite large. The reason for that the GA population has random value in each beginning of the used algorithm. Also, GA has more parameters that must be adjust very well to have good results. These parameters are for example number of iteration, population size, crossover probability and mutation probability. We argue that such parameters are new challenges to get the best system's performance. But, further investigations should be carried out to adjust these parameters towards improving the performance of the system.

References

1. Foltýn L. Realization of Intelligent Agents Architecture for Artificial Life Domain. Diploma Thesis on Dept. of Cybernetics, supervised by Nahodil, P., Faculty of Electrical Engineering, CTU in Prague, Prague 2005

2. Davidsson P. A Framework for Preventive State Anticipation. In M. Butz et al. (Eds.): Anticipatory Behavior in Adaptive Learning Systems (2004), LNCS, Vol. 2684. Springer-Verlag Berlin Heidelberg (2004), 151–166

3. Canuto A. Campos A. Santos A. Moura E. Santos E. Soares R. and Dantas K. Simulating Working Environments Through the Use of Personality-Based Agents. In J.S. Sichman et al. (Eds.): IBERAMIA-SBIA 2006, LNAI, Vol. 4140. Springer-Verlag Berlin Heidelberg (2006), 108 – 117

4. Aznar F. Pujol M. and Rizo R. Specifying Complex Systems with Bayesian Programming. An Alife Application. In:V.S. Sunderam et al. (Eds.): ICCS 2005, LNCS, Vol. 3514. Springer Berlin, Heidelberg (2005), 828–836

5. Butz M. Sigaud O. and G´erard P. Anticipatory Behavior: Exploiting Knowledge About the Future to Improve Current Behavior. In M. Butz et al. (Eds.): Anticipatory Behavior in Adaptive Learning Systems (2004), LNCS, Vol. 2684. Springer-Verlag Berlin Heidelberg (2004), 1–10

6. Davidsson P. Astor E. and Ekdahl B. A Framework for Autonomous Agents Based on the Concept of Anticipatory Systems. In Proc. of Cybernetics and Systems 1994, 1427-1431, World Scientific (1994)

7. Kohout K.and Nahodil P. Simulation of Anticipatory Behavior in the Artificial Life Domain. In WSEAS Transactions on Information Science and Applications. March 2007, Vol. 4, Issue 3, 568-575.

8. Meyer G. and Szirbik N. Behaviour Alignment as a Mechanism for Anticipatory Agent Interaction. In M. Butz et al. (Eds.): Proc. of the Third Workshop on Anticipatory Behavior in adaptive Learning Systems (ABiALS 2006). Rome: Istituto di Scienze e Tecnologie della Cognizione, Consiglio Nazionale delle Ricerche (ISTC-CNR).

Acknowledgement

The project was supported by the Ministry of Education, Youth and Sport of the Czech Republic with the grant No. MSM6840770012 entitled "Trandisciplinary Research in Biomedical Engineering II".

A Mereological Semantics of Contexts*

Ander Altuna

School of Computing
University of Leeds, Leeds, LS2 9JT, UK
ander@comp.leeds.ac.uk

Abstract. The aim of this paper is to present a formal semantics inspired by the notion of Mental Imagery that grasps the full significance of the concept of context. The outcomes presented here are considered important for both the Knowledge Representation and Philosophy of Language communities for two reasons. Firstly, the semantics that will be introduced allows to overcome some unjustified constraints imposed by previous quantificational languages of context, like flatness or the use of constant domains among others, and increases notably their expressive power. Secondly, it attempts to throw some light on the debate about the relation between meaning and truth by formally separating the conditions for a sentence to be meaningful from those that turn it true within a context.

1 Introduction

Although the interest in a formal theory of context within the AI community had already been present years before, there was no official research programme in this direction until in 1993 McCarthy [8] presented it as a candidate solution for the problem of generality [9]. Since then, many logics [4, 1–3] have emerged with the aim of capturing all of the common-sense intuitions about contextual reasoning that were introduced in [8]. However, only the quantificational logic of context presented in [2] deals with contexts as first-class citizens and is capable of quantifying over them. Nevertheless, its semantics is too restrictive and imposes counter-intuitive restrictions like flatness [1] or the use of constant domains [10].

In parallel with the research in contextual reasoning developed in AI, the theory of a mental representation of ideas in the form of mental images has been largely researched by cognitive scientists, experimental psychologists and philosophers [13]. According to the *analog* or *quasi-pictorial* theory of imagery [6], the human ability for the interpretation of symbols is equivalent to the recreation of quasi-perceptual experiences by mind. We endorse the quasi-pictorial theory of imagery and argue that by taking it as an inspiration we can develop a logic of context that meets the challenges introduced by [8]. This inspiration is mainly realized in two features of our semantics. Firstly, in contrast with

* This work has been funded by Tecnalia-Labein (Building 700, Bizkaia Technology Park, 48160 Derio, Spain) under the FCT-Iñaki Goenaga doctoral scholarship programme.

the truth-conditional theory of meaning, in our logic the meaning of a sentence will be regarded as a set of quasi-perceptual experiences instead of as a set of worlds. Secondly, a sentence will be considered to be supported by a context if its meaning is part of the image produced by the interpretation of that context. We claim that this separation between meaning and truth is necessary to grasp the concept of context in its full extent.

In this paper we present a semantics that formalizes a conceptualization of a quasi-pictorial theory of Mental Imagery by which the expressiveness of predicate calculus with identity is increased with the following capabilities: First, like in previous logics of context [4, 1–3], formulas can be stated in a context. Therefore, there is no contradiction in asserting a formula and its negation while they occur in different contexts. Second, the formulas of our language can refer to contexts and quantify over them like in [4, 2]. In our logic it is not allowed, however, to predicate on any context, but only on those that are accessible from the context under which the formula in question is being asserted. Third, a given contextualized formula can be quoted or not depending on the context in terms of which that formula is being expressed. Fourth, like suggested in [12], we differentiate between internal and external negations. And last, the formulas can express a parthood relation between two individuals, which will be particularly useful when formalizing normalcy assumptions between contexts [5].

2 Formal System

2.1 Syntax

A language $\mathcal{L}$ of our logic is any language of classical two-sorted predicate calculus with identity, together with an extra number of logical symbols, namely, two kinds of parthood relations ($\leq_g, \leq_f$), quotation marks (",") and a symbol for the internal negation of formulas ($^-$). Like [2] we call the sorts the *discourse* sort and the *context* sort. For simplicity we will make no use of functions.

We will use the following notational conventions: $a, a_1, \ldots$ range over constants of the discourse sort; $k, k_1, \ldots$ range over constants of the context sort;x, x_1, ... range over variables any sort;$P^n, P^n_1, \ldots$ range over n-ary predicates. Given a language $\mathcal{L}$, we will use $\mathbb{C}$ to refer to the set of constants of the discourse sort, and $\mathbb{K}$ to refer to the set of constants of the context sort. The set of variables of both sorts will be given by $\mathbb{V}$, while $\mathbb{P}$ will denote the set of predicates.

Definition 1. *The set of terms $\mathbb{T}$ and well-formed formulas (wffs) $\mathbb{W}$ are inductively defined on their construction by using the following formation rules:*

1. *Each variable or constant of any sort is a term.*
2. *If $t_1, \ldots, t_n$ are terms and P^n is an n-ary predicate, then $P^n(t_1, \ldots, t_n)$ and $\overline{P^n}(t_1, \ldots, t_n)$ are wffs.*
3. *If t_1 and t_2 are terms, then $t_1 = t_2$, $t_1 \leq_g t_2$ and $t_1 \leq_f t_2$ are wffs.*
4. *If A is a wff, then $[\neg A]$ is a wff.*
5. *If A and B are wffs, then $[A \vee B]$, $[A \wedge B]$ and $[A \supset B]$ are wffs.*

6. *If A is a wff and x is a variable of any sort, then* $(\forall x)[A]$ *and* $(\exists x)[A]$ *are wffs.*
7. *If A is a wff and k is a constant of the context sort, then* $[k : A]$ *and* $[k : \text{"}A\text{"}]$ *are wffs.*

It must be noted that the treatment of the parthood relations as logical symbols of our logic entails that their axiomatization as transitive, reflexive and antisymmetric relations will be included in the set of axioms of the logic itself. We will refer to the axioms of Extensional Mereology [11] for this. In addition, for the elaboration of the semantics, we will make use of the part-expansion operator represented by the symbol $\downarrow$. Given an object Γ, its part-expansion $\downarrow \Gamma$ will be the set containing every part of Γ: $\downarrow \Gamma = \{x : x \preccurlyeq \Gamma\}$.

2.2 A Model of Interpretation

In our attempt to elaborate a formal semantics inspired by a quasi-pictorial theory of mental imagery, we consider that an image is a mereologically structured object and therefore it is a whole composed of parts. An image will be said to model the set of facts that its parts support and consequently the truth value assigned to a sentence will be relativized to the context under which is being considered. However, we will differentiate between two kinds of parts of which images may consist, namely *grounded* and *figured* parts. While the former will determine the domain of those objects of the discourse sort, the latter will determine the domain of those objects of the context sort and their accessibility.

Definition 2. *In this system a model,* $\mathfrak{M}$, *is a structure* $\mathfrak{M} = \langle \mathcal{I}, \preccurlyeq_g, \preccurlyeq_f, \Omega, \mathcal{M} \rangle$ *whose components are defined as follows:*

1. $\mathcal{I}$ *is a non-empty set. It consists of all the imagery an agent can recreate at the moment she is performing the interpretation.*
2. $\preccurlyeq_g$ *is a partial ordering on* $\mathcal{I}$. *It is therefore a transitive, reflexive, and antisymmetric relation on* $\mathcal{I}$. *It denotes the mereological parthood relation on the members of* $\mathcal{I}$ *in a grounded sense.*
3. $\preccurlyeq_f$ *is a partial ordering on* $\mathcal{I}$. *It is therefore a transitive, reflexive, and antisymmetric relation on* $\mathcal{I}$. *It denotes the mereological parthood relation on the members of* $\mathcal{I}$ *in a figured sense.*
4. Ω *is a distinguished member of* $\mathcal{I}$. *It represents the image of actuality constructed by the agent performing the interpretation.*
5. $\mathcal{M}$ *is a function from the non-logical symbols of* $\mathcal{L}$ *to a mapping from members of* $\mathcal{I}$ *to subsets of* $\mathcal{I}$. $\mathcal{M}$ *denotes the meaning function that assigns each constant of* $\mathcal{L}$ *a mapping from contexts to its set of possible denotations and each predicate of* $\mathcal{L}$ *a mapping from contexts to its extension over* $\mathcal{I}$. *In the definition of* $\mathcal{M}$ *given below we use the standard mathematical notation* $\mathcal{P}(X)$ *to refer to the powerset of* X.

$$\mathcal{M} : \begin{cases} \mathbb{C} \rightarrow [\mathcal{I} \rightarrow \mathcal{P}(\mathcal{I})] \\ \mathbb{K} \rightarrow [\mathcal{I} \rightarrow \mathcal{P}(\mathcal{I})] \\ \mathbb{P} \rightarrow [\mathcal{I} \rightarrow \mathcal{P}(\mathcal{I}^n)] \end{cases} \tag{1}$$

Below we proceed with the definition of assignment, x-variant assignment and valuation function.

Definition 3. *If x is a variable of any sort, an assignment into $\mathfrak{M}$ is a function φ such that $\varphi(x)$ is a mapping from contexts to the set of possible denotations of x. Formally, $\varphi : \mathbb{V} \rightarrow [\mathcal{I} \rightarrow \mathcal{P}(\mathcal{I})]$. On the other hand, an assignment ψ is an x-variant of an assignment φ if φ and ψ agree on all variables except possibly x.*

Definition 4. *Given a model $\mathfrak{M} = \langle \mathcal{I}, \preccurlyeq_g, \preccurlyeq_f, \Omega, \mathcal{M} \rangle$, an assignment φ and a context Δ member of $\mathcal{I}$, a valuation $\mathcal{V}^{\mathfrak{M}}_{\varphi,\Delta}$ of the non-logical symbols of $\mathcal{L}$ into $\mathfrak{M}$ under φ and in terms of Δ is defined as follows:*

1. $\mathcal{V}^{\mathfrak{M}}_{\varphi,\Delta}(t) = \varphi(t)(\Delta)$ *if t is a variable.*
2. $\mathcal{V}^{\mathfrak{M}}_{\varphi,\Delta}(t) = \mathcal{M}(t)(\Delta)$ *if t is a constant of any sort.*
3. $\mathcal{V}^{\mathfrak{M}}_{\varphi,\Delta}(P^n) = \mathcal{M}(P^n)(\Delta)$ *if P^n is an n-ary predicate.*

Whether a formula is meaningful or not will only depend on the valuation of the terms and predicates it contains. We will say that a sentence is meaningful with regard to a model constructed by an agent if this agent can recreate some image for each of the terms in the sentence and at least one of these images is included in the extension that she would attribute to the predicate in question.

Definition 5. *$P^n(t_1, \ldots, t_n)$ is a meaningful formula iff*
$\left|\left[\mathcal{V}^{\mathfrak{M}}_{\varphi,\Delta}(t_1) \times \cdots \times \mathcal{V}^{\mathfrak{M}}_{\varphi,\Delta}(t_n)\right] \cap \mathcal{V}^{\mathfrak{M}}_{\varphi,\Delta}(P^n)\right| \geq 1$

2.3 Truth

In our logic the truth value of a formula is relativized to the context in which it is asserted. If a formula is to be supported by a context, exactly one counterpart of each of the terms of that sentence must be part of the image of that context.

Definition 6. *The denotation of an unambiguous term t that succeeds to denote, what will be expressed by $\mathbf{D}^{\mathfrak{M},\Gamma}_{\varphi,\Delta}(t)$, is defined as*

$$\mathcal{V}^{\mathfrak{M},\Gamma}_{\varphi,\Delta}(t) =_{def} (\iota x) \begin{cases} x \in \left[\mathcal{V}^{\mathfrak{M}}_{\varphi,\Delta}(t) \cap \downarrow_g \Gamma\right] & \text{if } t \text{ is of the discourse sort,} \\ x \in \left[\mathcal{V}^{\mathfrak{M}}_{\varphi,\Delta}(t) \cap \downarrow_f \Gamma\right] & \text{if } t \text{ is of the context sort.} \end{cases} \quad (2)$$

Below we proceed with the characterization of the truth function into the model we have presented in the previous section.

Definition 7. *Truth ($\Vdash$), with respect to an assignment φ into a model $\mathfrak{M} = \langle \mathcal{I}, \preccurlyeq_g, \preccurlyeq_f, \Omega, \mathcal{M} \rangle$, is characterized as follows:*

$$\begin{aligned} &\mathfrak{M}, \Gamma \Vdash_{\varphi,\Delta} P^n(t_1, \ldots, t_n) \text{ iff } \mathbf{D}^{\mathfrak{M},\Gamma}_{\varphi,\Delta}(t_1), \ldots, \mathbf{D}^{\mathfrak{M},\Gamma}_{\varphi,\Delta}(t_n) \\ &\quad \text{and } \langle \mathcal{V}^{\mathfrak{M},\Gamma}_{\varphi,\Delta}(t_1), \ldots, \mathcal{V}^{\mathfrak{M},\Gamma}_{\varphi,\Delta}(t_n) \rangle \in \mathcal{V}^{\mathfrak{M}}_{\varphi,\Delta}(P^n) \end{aligned} \quad (3)$$

$$\begin{aligned} &\mathfrak{M}, \Gamma \Vdash_{\varphi,\Delta} \overline{P^n}(t_1, \ldots, t_n) \text{ iff } \mathbf{D}^{\mathfrak{M},\Gamma}_{\varphi,\Delta}(t_1), \ldots, \mathbf{D}^{\mathfrak{M},\Gamma}_{\varphi,\Delta}(t_n) \\ &\quad \text{and } \langle \mathcal{V}^{\mathfrak{M},\Gamma}_{\varphi,\Delta}(t_1), \ldots, \mathcal{V}^{\mathfrak{M},\Gamma}_{\varphi,\Delta}(t_n) \rangle \in \left[\mathcal{V}^{\mathfrak{M}}_{\varphi,\Delta}(P^n)\right]^C \end{aligned} \quad (4)$$

$$\begin{aligned}\mathfrak{M}, \Gamma \Vdash_{\varphi,\Delta} t_1 = t_2 \textit{ iff } \mathbf{D}^{\mathfrak{M},\Gamma}_{\varphi,\Delta}(t_1) \textit{ and } \mathbf{D}^{\mathfrak{M},\Gamma}_{\varphi,\Delta}(t_2) \\ \textit{and } \mathcal{V}^{\mathfrak{M},\Gamma}_{\varphi,\Delta}(t_1) = \mathcal{V}^{\mathfrak{M},\Gamma}_{\varphi,\Delta}(t_2)\end{aligned} \tag{5}$$

$$\begin{aligned}\mathfrak{M}, \Gamma \Vdash_{\varphi,\Delta} t_1 \leq_g t_2 \textit{ iff } \mathbf{D}^{\mathfrak{M},\Gamma}_{\varphi,\Delta}(t_1) \textit{ and } \mathbf{D}^{\mathfrak{M},\Gamma}_{\varphi,\Delta}(t_2) \\ \textit{and } \mathcal{V}^{\mathfrak{M},\Gamma}_{\varphi,\Delta}(t_1) \preccurlyeq_g \mathcal{V}^{\mathfrak{M},\Gamma}_{\varphi,\Delta}(t_2)\end{aligned} \tag{6}$$

$$\begin{aligned}\mathfrak{M}, \Gamma \Vdash_{\varphi,\Delta} t_1 \leq_f t_2 \textit{ iff } \mathbf{D}^{\mathfrak{M},\Gamma}_{\varphi,\Delta}(t_1) \textit{ and } \mathbf{D}^{\mathfrak{M},\Gamma}_{\varphi,\Delta}(t_2) \\ \textit{and } \mathcal{V}^{\mathfrak{M},\Gamma}_{\varphi,\Delta}(t_1) \preccurlyeq_f \mathcal{V}^{\mathfrak{M},\Gamma}_{\varphi,\Delta}(t_2)\end{aligned} \tag{7}$$

$$\mathfrak{M}, \Gamma \Vdash_{\varphi,\Delta} \neg A \textit{ iff not } \mathfrak{M}, \Gamma \Vdash_{\varphi,\Delta} A \tag{8}$$

$$\mathfrak{M}, \Gamma \Vdash_{\varphi,\Delta} A \wedge B \textit{ iff } \mathfrak{M}, \Gamma \Vdash_{\varphi,\Delta} A \textit{ and } \mathfrak{M}, \Gamma \Vdash_{\varphi,\Delta} B \tag{9}$$

$$\mathfrak{M}, \Gamma \Vdash_{\varphi,\Delta} A \vee B \textit{ iff } \mathfrak{M}, \Gamma \Vdash_{\varphi,\Delta} A \textit{ or } \mathfrak{M}, \Gamma \Vdash_{\varphi,\Delta} B \tag{10}$$

$$\mathfrak{M}, \Gamma \Vdash_{\varphi,\Delta} A \supset B \textit{ iff not } \mathfrak{M}, \Gamma \Vdash_{\varphi,\Delta} A \textit{ or } \mathfrak{M}, \Gamma \Vdash_{\varphi,\Delta} B \tag{11}$$

$$\begin{aligned}\mathfrak{M}, \Gamma \Vdash_{\varphi,\Delta} (\forall x)\,[A] \textit{ iff for every } x\textit{-variant assignment } \psi, \\ \textit{if } \mathbf{D}^{\mathfrak{M},\Gamma}_{\psi,\Delta}(x) \textit{ then } \mathfrak{M}, \Gamma \Vdash_{\psi,\Delta} A\end{aligned} \tag{12}$$

$$\begin{aligned}\mathfrak{M}, \Gamma \Vdash_{\varphi,\Delta} (\exists x)\,[A] \textit{ iff for some } x\textit{-variant assignment } \psi, \\ \mathbf{D}^{\mathfrak{M},\Gamma}_{\psi,\Delta}(x) \textit{ and } \mathfrak{M}, \Gamma \Vdash_{\psi,\Delta} A\end{aligned} \tag{13}$$

$$\mathfrak{M} \Vdash_{\varphi} A \textit{ iff } \mathfrak{M}, \Omega \Vdash_{\varphi,\Omega} A \tag{14}$$

$$\mathfrak{M}, \Gamma \Vdash_{\varphi,\Delta} k : A \textit{ iff } \mathbf{D}^{\mathfrak{M},\Gamma}_{\varphi,\Delta}(k) \textit{ and } \mathfrak{M}, \mathcal{V}^{\mathfrak{M},\Gamma}_{\varphi,\Delta}(k) \Vdash_{\varphi,\Delta} A \tag{15}$$

$$\mathfrak{M}, \Gamma \Vdash_{\varphi,\Delta} k : \text{“}A\text{”} \textit{ iff } \mathbf{D}^{\mathfrak{M},\Gamma}_{\varphi,\Delta}(k) \textit{ and } \mathfrak{M}, \mathcal{V}^{\mathfrak{M},\Gamma}_{\varphi,\Delta}(k) \Vdash_{\varphi,\mathcal{V}^{\mathfrak{M},\Gamma}_{\varphi,\Delta}(k)} A \tag{16}$$

In line with Modal Realism [7], we treat the universal quantifier as implicitly ranging over actuality. Therefore, as can be seen in the equation (16), only those assignments under which x succeeds to denote in the context in consideration are required to validate the quantified formula. On the other hand, equations (18) and (19) show how this semantics facilitates entering into an inner context from a relative actuality and reversely transcending back from it.

Definition 8. *A formula A is said to be valid if it is supported by every image Γ of every model $\mathfrak{M}$ under every assignment φ and in terms of every context Δ:* $\Vdash A \textit{ iff } (\forall \mathfrak{M})\,(\forall \Gamma)\,(\forall \varphi)\,(\forall \Delta)\,[\mathfrak{M}, \Gamma \Vdash_{\varphi,\Delta} A]$

As can be appreciated from the definition of the truth function, the principle of bivalence holds with regard to both external and internal negations. However, the bivalence with respect to the internal negation of a formula under a certain context holds if and only if all its terms succeed to denote when considered under that context and the sentence is meaningful, while the bivalence with regard to the external negation of a formula holds regardless of these conditions. Therefore the validity of the principle of bivalence can only be determined locally in the case of internal negations.

3 Conclusions

In this paper we have presented a formal semantics for a logic of context that is inspired by a quasi-pictorial theory of Mental Imagery [6]. The semantics we have elaborated not only addresses how to interpret the reasoning between contexts but also increases the expressivity of previous logics of context by adding some new constructors to the set of logical symbols. Among these are the quotation marks that, like in natural language, enable an agent to use the terms in which another agent expresses herself and the parthood relations, which result very useful when formalizing normalcy assumptions between contexts. On the other hand, we have shown a characterization of the truth function that allows the differentiation between external and internal negations [12], what is necessary in order to adjust the principle of bivalence to the case of meaningless sentences and foreign languages [3]. Besides, this semantics has proved to overcome some unjustified restrictions that were imposed by previous quantificational logics of context [2], like flatness or the use of constant domains among others. This makes our logic more intuitively appropriate for accommodating the concept of context that Guha and McCarthy restated in [5].

References

1. Buvac, S., Buvac, V., Mason, I.A.: Metamathematics of contexts. Fundamenta Informaticae **23**(2/3/4) (1995) 263–301
2. Buvac, S.: Quantificational logic of context. In: Proceedings of the Thirteenth National Conference on Artificial Intelligence. (1996) 600–606
3. Ghidini, C., Giunchiglia, F.: Local models semantics, or contextual reasoning = locality + compatibility. Artificial Intelligence **127**(2) (2001) 221–259
4. Guha, R.V.: Contexts: a formalization and some applications. PhD thesis, Stanford University, California, USA (1992)
5. Guha, R., McCarthy, J.: Varieties of context. In Blackburn, P., Ghidini, C., Turner, R.M., Giunchiglia, F., eds.: Modeling and Using Context: Proceedings of the Fourth International and Interdisciplinary Conference, Context 2003, Berlin, Springer-Verlag (2003) 164–177
6. Kosslyn, S.M.: Mental images and the brain. Cognitive Neuropsychology **22** (2005) 333–347
7. Lewis, D.: On the Plurality of Worlds. Blackwell Publishing (1986)
8. McCarthy, J.: Notes on formalizing contexts. In Bajcsy, R., ed.: Proceedings of the Thirteenth International Joint Conference on Artificial Intelligence, San Mateo, California, Morgan Kaufmann (1993) 555–560
9. McCarthy, J.: Generality in artificial intelligence. In Lifschitz, V., ed.: Formalizing Common Sense: Papers by John McCarthy. Ablex Publishing Corporation, Norwood, New Jersey (1990) 226–236
10. Fitting, M., Mendelshon, R.L.: First Order Modal Logic. Kluwer Academic Publishers, Dordrecht (1998)
11. Simons, P.: Parts: A Study in Ontology. Oxford University Press (2003)
12. Slater, B.H.: Internal and external negations. Mind **88** (1979) 588–591
13. Thomas, N.J.T.: Mental Imagery, Philosophical Issues About. In: Encyclopedia of Cognitive Science. Volume 2. Nature Publishing/Macmillan (2003) 1147–1153

Spatial N-player Dilemmas in Changing Environments

Colm O'Riordan
Dept. of Information Technology, NUI, Galway
Ireland

Dara Curran, Humphrey Sorensen
Dept. of Computer Science, University College Cork
Ireland

September 3, 2007

Abstract

In recent work it has been shown that, given the presence of a community structure in a population of agents, cooperation can be a robust outcome for agents participating in an N-player social dilemma. Through the use of simple imitative learning, cooperation can spread and be the dominant robust behaviour. In this paper, we show that such cooperation can exist in the presence of noise and that persistent small levels of noise can allow the population to adapt suitably to dramatic changes in the environment.

1 Introduction

Questions regarding the emergence and robustness of cooperation arise in a range of domains. One useful approach to answer these questions is through the use of social dilemma games. Commonly adopted social dilemma games include the prisoner's dilemma[1] and its variants; in this paper we adopt a generalised N-player version based on the formalism of Boyd and Richerson [2]. In this game, N players simultaneously interact in a cooperative or non-cooperative manner. All participants receive a benefit but only cooperators are penalised in any way.

In this paper, we explore the emergence of cooperation among agents participating in an N-player social dilemma; agents are arranged spatially and their interactions constrained by a graph topology exhibiting a high level of community structure. We show that with the presence of small levels of noise, the society of agents can adapt to dramatic changes in the environment. We model this radical environmental change by reversing the payoffs associated with the behaviours.

2 Related Work

2.1 N-player prisoner dilemmas

N-player dilemmas are characterised by having many participants, each of whom may choose to cooperate or defect. These choices are made autonomously without any communication between participants. Any benefit or payoff is received by all participants; any cost is borne by the cooperators only. A well-known example is the *Tragedy of the Commons*[5].

Defection represents a dominant strategy, i.e. for any individual, moving from cooperation to defection is beneficial for that player (they still receive a benefit without the cost). However, if all participants adopt this strategy, the resulting scenario is, from a group point of view, sub-optimal and irrational. If any player changes from defection to cooperation, the performance of the society improves, i.e. a society with $i + 1$ cooperators attains a greater payoff than a society with i cooperators. If we consider payoffs for this game, we can see that D dominates C and that total cooperation is better for participants than total defection.

Several evolutionary simulations exist which study the performance of different strategy types playing the N-player game. This work has shown that, without placing specific constraints on the interactions, the number of participants or the strategies involved, the resulting outcome is that of defection[10][14].

2.2 Community structure and N-player social dilemmas

In studying the two-player game, many researchers have explored the effect of placing spatial constraints on the population of interacting agents. These include, among others, experimentation with grid size and topology, graph structure in a choice/refusal framework [11], different learning mechanisms and topologies[8], small world[13] and scale-free graphs.

In more recent work analysing small world and scale-free networks, researchers are often interested in key properties of these graphs. In this paper, we are interested in one key property of a graph: that of *community structure*. This property has been explored in recent work[6]. A graph is said to have a community structure if collections of nodes are joined together in tightly knit groups between which there are only looser connections. This property has been shown to exist in many real-world social networks[9].

In our previous work[3], we demonstrated that cooperation could be robust in a population of self-interested agents participating in an N-player dilemma if a sufficiently strong community structure is present. We showed that with simple learning algorithms where agents learned from neighbours, cooperative communities could exist despite the presence of defectors in the society. Furthermore, we showed that with a second learning rule where agents could periodically check and learn from a larger community, that cooperation could in fact spread throughout the society.

2.3 Changing Environments

Most real world and artificial systems and societies change due to a number of factors—external changes in the environments, agents learning new knowledge, changes in the make up of the population. Several researchers have addressed related issues in previous work: examples include evolutionary models and co-evolutionary models where the population is changing over time, studies in the viscosity of populations[7], changing or reversing the environment [12]. Other researchers have modelled change in the environment by introducing noise into the system whereby agents actions are mis-implemented or mis-interpreted by other agents[4].

3 Model and Experimental Set up

In the simulations described in this paper, agents are located on nodes of a graph. The graph is an undirected weighted graph. The weight associated with any edge between nodes represents the strength of the connection between the two agents located at the nodes. This determines the likelihood of these agents participating together in games. We use a regular graph of degree four, where three of these edges are intra-community(edge weight set to 1.0) and the remaining one is an inter-community edge (edge weight set to 0.1).

Agents in this model can have a strategy of either cooperation (C) or defection (D). Agents interact with their neighbours in a N-player prisoner's dilemma. The payoffs received by the agents are calculated according to the formula proposed by Boyd and Richerson [2], i.e. cooperators receive $(Bi/N)-c$ and defectors receive Bi/N, where B is the social benefit (in this paper, B is set to 5), i is the number of cooperators involved in the game, N is the number of participants and c is another constant representing the cost of cooperation (in this paper, c is set to 3). The values of B and c are chosen to ensure a dilemma.

Each agent participates in several games. The algorithm proceeds as follows: for each agent a in the population, agents are selected from the immediate neighbourhood of agent a to participate in the game. Neighbouring agents are chosen to participate with a probability equal to the edge of the weight between the nodes. An agent's fitness is calculated as the average payoff received in the interactions during a generation.

We adopt a simple update rule whereby an agent may update their strategy to that used by more successful strategies. These neighbours are chosen stochastically; the neighbours are chosen according to the weight of the edge between agent and neighbour. In the first update rule, agents consider other agents who are immediate neighbours. Let $s\_adj(x)$ denote the immediate neighbours of agents x chosen stochastically according to edge weight. The probability of an agent x updating their strategy to be that of a neighbouring agent y is given by: $(w(x,y).f(y))/(\Sigma_{z\in s\_adj(x)}(w(x,z).f(z)))$ where $f(y)$ and $f(z)$ are the fitnesses of an agents y and z, $w(x,y)$ is the weight of the edge between x and y.

We incorporate a second update mechanism. Following several iterations of learning from local neighbours, each community is likely to be in a state of equilibrium—either total cooperation or total defection. An agent that is equally fit as its immediate neighbours may look further afield to identify more successful strategies. The second update rule allows agents to look further afield from their own location and consider the strategies and payoffs received by agents in this larger set. In the second rule, we don't choose the agents in proportion to their edge weight values; we instead consider the complete set of potential agents in the extended neighbourhood. In this way all agents in a community can be influenced by a neighbouring cooperative community[1].

In our experiments we use a population of 800 agents: we allow simulations to run for 1000 generations. We present results averaged over 20 individual runs. In each generation, agents interact with their selected neighbours, update their scores based on these interactions and then learn from their immediate neighbours using the local update rule. Every four generations, agents also look to a larger community and learn from an agent in a larger set of agents. In our experiments, four generations is usually sufficient to allow a local community reach an equilibrium point. The value four is chosen as it is sufficient to allow all agents in a local community to reach an equilibrium. By choosing a larger number, the overall effect would be the same (i.e. cooperation would spread). Choosing a much smaller number (e.g. 1) would cause defection to spread in the population.

We model noise in a simple manner; at every generation there is a probability that an agent will change its strategy. We run sets of experiments with noise levels set to 2%, 3% and 5% respectively. We model dramatic environmental change by reversing the effects of the agents' behaviours. Prior to the dramatic change a certain action (cooperation) is individually dominated but collectively optimal; the other action (defection) is individually dominant but collectively results in a poor outcome.

Following the change, defection is now the collectively optimal action and cooperation is the individually selfish move. In our simulations, this change occurs following the 500th generation.

4 Results

In this experiment, we show that the society can maintain high levels of fitness despite catastrophic change to the environment. Prior to the change, the society evolves to be largely cooperative; full cooperation is not reached due to the levels of noise present. This illustrates that the population is robust to levels of noise. Initially, cooperation quickly falls leaving only cooperative clusters. Following imitation of behaviours from successful cooperative clusters, cooperation subsequently emerges.

Following the change, the fitness collapses quickly (Fig. 1) as the society has previously converged towards a behaviour that is no longer optimal for the new environment. With the presence of some noise, the agents will effectively

[1]This can be viewed as form of group comparison.

explore alternative behaviours; eventually some community will adopt the new collectively optimal behavaiour and the society, through learning, will attain high levels of fitness. With a level of noise equal to 5%, the population quickly attains a level of fitness equal to that prior to the change. For lower levels of noise (2% and 3%), in most scenarios, the society also recovers to a similar level of cooperation. However, the average fitness attained, as depicted in the graph, is somewhat lower to the average before the dramatic change. This is due to some societies not having enough diversity initially in the population and never chancing upon a sub-community of fit agents in the remaining generations.

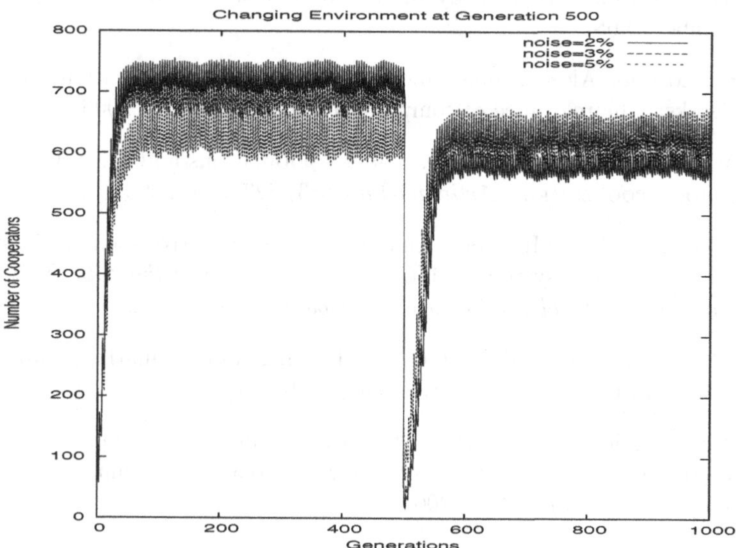

Figure 1: Cooperators in Changing environment

5 Conclusion

In this paper, we modelled dramatic environmental change by reversing the payoffs associated with the possible behaviours. We have shown through experimental simulations, that given the presence of community structure, simple learning update rules, cooperation can continue to exist in given a dramatic environmental change provided there is a low level of noise to maintains diversity the population.

References

[1] Robert Axelrod. *Evolution of Cooperation.* Basic Books, 1985.

[2] Robert Boyd and Peter Richerson. The evolution of reciprocity in sizable groups. *Journal of Theoretical Biology*, 132:337–356, 1988.

[3] C.O'Riordan and H.Sorensen. Stable cooperation in the n-player prisoner's dilemma: the importance of community structure. In *Adaptive Learning Agents and Multi-Agent Systems*, April 2007.

[4] D.Curran, C.O'Riordan, and H.Sorensen. Evolutionary and lifetime learning in varying nk fitness landscapes with changing environments: An analysis of both fitness and diversity. In *AAAI*, 2007.

[5] Garret Hardin. The tragedy of the commons. *Science*, 162:1243–1248, December 1968.

[6] Sergi Lozano, Alex Aranas, and Angel Sanchez. Cooperation on social networks: The relevance of communities. *PACS*, 87(23), 2006.

[7] J A R Marshall and J E Rowe. Viscous populations and their support for reciprocal cooperation. *Artificial Life*, 9(3):327–334, 2003.

[8] M. Moran and C.O'Riordan. Emergence of cooperative societies in structured multi-agent systems. *AICS 05, Proceedings of the 16th Irish Conference on Artificial Intelligence and Cognitive Science*, 2005.

[9] M. E. J. Newman and M. Girvan. Finding and evaluating community structure in networks. *Physics Review E*, 69, 2004.

[10] Colm O' Riordan, Josephine Griffith, John Newell, and Humphrey Sorensen. Co-evolution of strategies for an n-player dilemma. *Congress on Evolutionary Computation*, 2004.

[11] M.D. Smucker, E. Ann Stanley, and D. Ashlock. Analyzing social network structures in the iterated prisoner's dilemma with choice and refusal. Technical report, University of Wisconsin, december 1994.

[12] J. Wu and R. Axelrod. How to cope with noise in the iterated prisoner's dilemma. *Journal of Conflict Resolution*, 39:183–189, March 1994.

[13] Zhi-Xi Wu, Xin-Jian Xu, Yong Chen, and Ying-Hai Wang. Spatial prisoner's dilemma game with volunteering in newman-watts small-world networks. *Physical Review E*, 71:37103, 2005.

[14] X. Yao and P. J. Darwen. An experimental study of n-person iterated prisoner's dilemma games. *Evo Workshops*, pages 90–108, 1994.

Training and Evaluating an E-tutor

Kate Taylor
Centre for Applied Research into Educational Technology (CARET)
University of Cambridge
ksw1000@cam.ac.uk
www.cl.cam.ac.uk/~ksw1000

Abstract

This work generates an ontology for Operating Systems which map the students' lexicon against ours. Their exploration of concepts generates data to train a system that focuses or broadens the interaction with the student to form a conversation. The data we are collecting will also be used to verify the knowledge base design itself by using inductive logic and statistical techniques to find patterns of misunderstanding. The tools allow students to create their own models as well as to ask questions to a Chatbot built on a teacher's model. The students can mark their work against this teacher's model. We start from a pedagogical approach and then evaluate use of our Chatbot to look for causal patterns in the learning material that can be used in future for automatic trouble shooting via a computer initiated dialogue that can discuss the structure of a subject with a student based on that particular student's level of understanding.

1. Introduction

Previous work on our IVC tool [1] for teaching the Verilog hardware definition language looked at generating concept maps that were visible to the user and used to answer simple taxonomic questions. This work takes the concept mapping a stage further for the richer domains of Plant Sciences and Operating Systems.

We have created three simple web-based tools: a chatbot interface to ask questions: the Chatbot; a self test against the ontology language predicates and concepts: Test Your Knowledge (TYK); and a personal map tool using their own language: Draw Your Own (DYO).

Other work [2] where a concept map for Operating Systems is drawn from a student answering questions posed by the system:

> *" shows a positive correlation between the complexity of the map created by the student's responses and the overall grade they finally achieve, weighted by the complexity of the links on the concept map "* [3,p138]

We aim to discover whether this is also true for firstly a concept map that lies behind the answer generation software, and secondly when the student asks questions and then explicitly draws the map themselves. For the latter, they can either draw a completely free form map or check their map against ours. We are also interested in generating a training corpus of how students move from one level of question to another, and these experiments are part of that data collection exercise. We do not assume that this pattern will be the same from subject to subject. We aim to test out the ideas on the Verilog language and Plant Sciences data we already hold, and on operating systems. The Computer Science Operating Systems course has been used as a domain for automated marking systems such as Willow [2] which have already been built and can act as comparisons together with the SA operating system corpus. Learner reflection has been shown to be a vital component of cognitively intensive tasks, such as learning a new programming language. Adaptive systems need to strike a balance between remembering previous interactions, and managing and interpreting the resulting information about the user in a new context. We have started from a standpoint of remembering nothing, relying instead on deducing the focus of the question to place the user in the right area of our concept map when a question is asked. Having located the right area, it is relatively simple to deduce when an illogical question has been asked by measuring the distance between the concepts.

Our dialogue is not controlled by a plan for each learning experience. One of the strengths of our system is that the learning experience is what the user makes of it because they can influence what the system explains to them by the questions that they ask. The majority of answers to questions are a re-presentation of suitably filtered material from the web, but the remainder are text generated from traversing the relations in the ontology [1].

2. Related Work

The Atanaea/Willow family of systems described by Perez-Martin in [2] assess free-text answers as part of an adaptive e-tutor on Operating Systems. The structure of the course is shown as an unlabelled concept map and in various tabular forms. These deliberately overlapping forms help stimulate memory retention. Correlations are calculated between concepts understood and misunderstood.

In linguistic terms, restricting a language to form a *controlled language* is based on the Functional-Lexematic Model (FLM). This has been used in systems such as MARCOCOSTA [3] in which Faber [4] states :

> " *the linguistic description of any specialized concepts should do the following: (1) make category membership explicit; (2) reflect its relations with other concepts within the same category; (3) specify its essential attributes and features* " [4,p138]

Their work on oceanography has generated an ontology with 8000 terms including 200 concepts. Bruza et al in [5] describes how abductive reasoning can help to make new links or short-cuts between concepts. He discusses how storing information against individual words rather than n-grams causes difficulties in reasoning. An n-gram is a sequence of n words. For example, if we used *scheduling* as the basic element, it makes capturing *pre-emptive scheduling* and *scheduling algorithm* difficult. From this insight, we have decided to use the individual concept as the basic component, with some predicates in the knowledge base underlying this to support reasoning: *a particular kind of scheduling algorithm is pre-emptive.* Again following Bruze et al amongst others, we have used shallow parsing techniques to give the ranked list of information flows to be projected onto our lattice and our logic of justification as one of the search methods. We have also made use of their distance measures. This is described with examples in Section 3.

We have followed the style of architecture used by the AQUA [6] question answering system: a process model with a parser, a logical interpreter, a WordNet lexical resource, a failure-analysis system and a question classifier. Our architecture is shown in Figure 1. We focus on the local intranet (the web tutorial) to provide the answers to our questions and for explaining compiler messages. This is described in Section 3.4.

To build the knowledge base, we needed to define the concepts we were to use, using the techniques described above in [3], [4] and [5]. Then we identified the verbs or predicates that we wanted to support and the subset of those that we wanted to use as the ontology language. This subset became the Prolog predicates that formed the knowledge base.

We make use of *synonymy* to reduce the number of predicates in ontology language for internal storage. For example, *stimulates* becomes *causes* and *reduces* becomes *decreases*. This ensures that the external ontology language for human use remains rich. Care is taken to keep within the language of the syllabus and lecture materials. We classify predicates into classes for causality, spatiality and motion to support reasoning. There is interaction between the classes to make frames, for example, *transports* needs to refer to *starts at* and *ends at*. Antonyms, words with opposite meanings are stored to help traverse inverse relationships without explicitly storing both relationships. We store some inversions as well as synonyms, for example, *transports* has the synonym: *carries*, and the inversion: gets, but aim to collect more form the Draw Your Own (DYO) tool. Faber and Tercedor Sanchez's concept of domain in [5] has been mapped to the lecture structure as a first approach, which is again to be reviewed once data from the DYO tool is gathered.

We propose that a student starting to learn a subject might start with a concept question, then focus on particular areas of interest on that subject with a query question and finally would be confident enough to test a hypothesis. Atanea/Willow [2] uses a similar three tier question set to be posed to students: definitions, advantages and disadvantages and yes/no. Alternatively, if the student was confident that they knew a subject, then they would start with a check question. If she is wrong, she will backtrack to a query question or possibly right back to a concept question.

3. Initial Results

Initial results are available for the style of questions from work done in [1] on the Verilog language, Plant Sciences and on the operating system domain. We identified different questioning styles as expected.

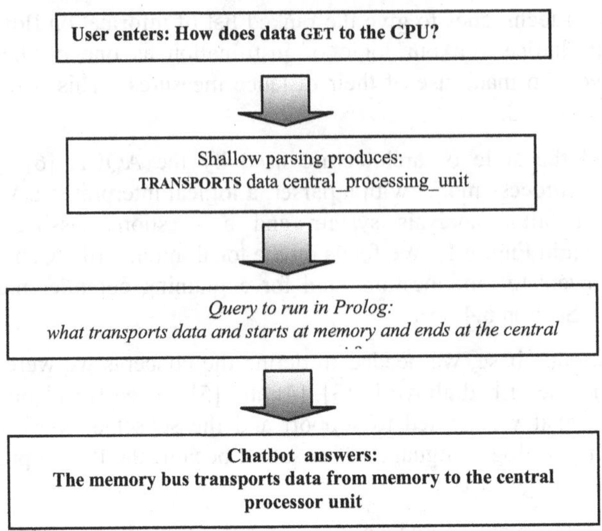

Figure 1 Translating and Responding to a Question

We detected misunderstandings by type checking and from the ontology language itself: having divided up concepts between algorithmic processes and objects, the knowledge base can deduce that *Does round robin have a priority?* is off course because a *priority* is not a property of an *algorithmic process.* This can be reported back as a simple explanation: *No because round robin is a scheduling algorithm and only processes have a priority.*

To complement these deductive abilities, we are in search of a more quantitive approach to be able to train our future e-tutor. First we identify episodes in a student's interaction by a gap in the log more than 120 seconds, or by a jump to a new part of the map with a concept question. Then we look at distances to help identify what error has been made.

Bruza et al in [5] provides three measures of distance. Manhattan distance, Euclidean distance and semantic distance. We do not use Euclidean distance in this paper, but we now consider how to use the other two distance techniques to see how far off subject the student's question is. It could of course be our model that is off course rather than the student's question. Manhattan distance is interpreted as how far apart the two concepts in the question are measured as distance across the lattice, with directly connected concepts scoring 1. Our version of semantic difference is weighted by how often we have moved up and down the taxonomic hierarchy of *is_a_part_of* and *is_a_kind_of* before matching the predicates and concepts used in the question. The question *Does round robin have a priority?* is muddled because a *priority* is not a property of a *scheduling algorithm*. This is reported back as a simple explanation: *No, because round robin is a scheduling algorithm and only process has a priority.*

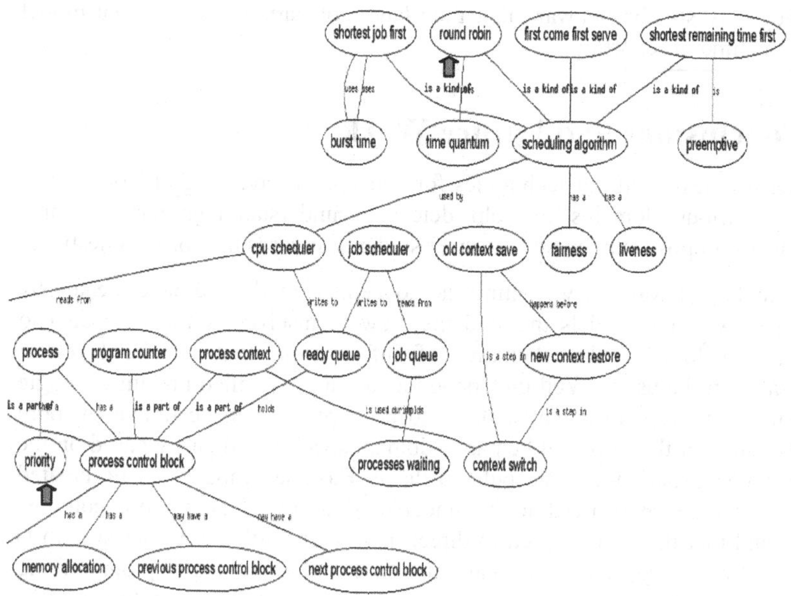

Figure 2 The Partial Concept Map For Scheduling showing the distance between *priority* and *round robin*

Figure 2 shows a part of the Operating Systems concept map derived from notes from [7] used for students reading Computer Science in their final year only. It is annotated with arrows to indicate *round_robin* and *priority* as the start and end points. For errors where the student is in the right area, we use Hamming distance to measure how near the incorrect string *scheduler* is to the one required *scheduling (algorithm)*. The Hamming distance for two strings s and t, H(s, t) is the count of locations in which the two strings have different characters. In our example in Table 1, the overlap is five characters and the Hamming distance is two.

Fact	Hamming Distance	Manhattan Distance	Semantic Distance
First come first served is a kind of scheduling algorithm		1	2
scheduling algorithm is used by a cpu scheduler		1	1
Cpu scheduler is a kind of scheduler	2	1	2
TOTAL		3	5

Table 1 Hamming, Manhattan and Semantic Distances for *Is first come first served a kind of scheduler?*

Collecting qualitative data about what the student's view of the conversation is used to validate what we have detected through these distance measures, though of course they may still be unaware that they have got parts of the concept model wrong at the time of reporting.

4. Conclusions and Future Work

This paper has described our techniques for conceptual modelling and our use of models in various domains to help detect misunderstandings and in some circumstances propose explanations to steer students towards the correct questions.

We have looked at ways of validating the conceptual model we have created by comparing it with the models the students draw themselves. With more data to hand, we can look at the chunking of information, that is, the level of summarisation to be used. Well understood areas can be "rolled up" into a single bubble on the concept map whilst those to be explored can be drawn in more detail. We suspect that this will be partly domain specific and partly based on the user's previous experience. We believe that a Bayesian model can be created based on what concepts need to be understood to understand more complex concepts, and that this can be used to direct the search further. As our system is built on a knowledge base, we can also use inductive logic programming techniques to search for patterns in the students' versions of the conceptual model.

This work is a step along the road to make a tool that can discuss the structure of a subject with a student. It validates the ontology and the style of interaction that a student requires by collecting data to help train the next generation of the system. At present it reacts to what the student asks, but once trained it could also propose concepts to talk about in the same way as a human supervisor will guide a conversation.

References

1. Taylor K. Moore S. Adding Question Answering to an e-tutor for programming languages SGAI 06 Springer Verlag
2. Perez Marin D. R. Adaptive Computer Assisted Assessment of free-text students' answers: an approach to automatically generate students' conceptual models PhD Thesis Universidad Autonoma de Madrid p138, Section 8
3. Vargus-Vera A, Motta E AQUA- Ontology Based Question Answering System MICAI 2004: 468-477
4. Castro M. and Barros E. Controlled Language through The Definitions of Coastal Terms in English CamLing 2007
5. Faber, P. and M.I. Tercedor Sanchez (2001) Codifying conceptual information in descriptive terminology management Meta 46(1) 192 - 204
6. Bruza P., Song D., McArthur R. Abduction in Semantic Space: Towards a Logic of Discovery London Journal of the IGPL Volume 12 No 2 Oxford University Press 104-7
7. Bierman G. Operating Systems Foundations lecture notes 2005 Computer Laboratory, University of Cambridge www.cl.cam.ac.uk.

An Ambient Intelligence Application Integrating Agent and Service-Oriented Technologies

Nikolaos Spanoudakis[a, b] Pavlos Moraitis[b]
[a] Singular Logic S.A.
nspan@singularlogic.eu
www.singularlogic.eu
[b]Paris Descartes University
{nikos, pavlos}@math-info.univ-paris5.fr
www.math-info.univ-paris5.fr

Abstract

This paper presents an agent-based approach into a more general service oriented architecture for addressing the requirements of accessibility content and services in an ambient intelligence context. The developed agent-based information system provides infomobility services for the special requirements of mobility impaired people. Herein, we focus in the task of integrating this multi-agent system in the overall service-oriented architecture. In order to achieve this task we propose a methodology for integrating a FIPA-compliant agent platform with the OSGi service oriented framework.

1. Introduction

Agent technology has been applied to the infomobility services sector in recent years (e.g. the Im@gine IT [6] project). Such services include location-based services like mapping and points of interest search, travel planning and, recently, trip progression monitoring and pushing information and events to the user. A recent research has proposed that elderly and disabled people compose a segment of the population that would profit very much from ambient intelligence (AmI), if the latter was accessible [1]. Furthermore, O'Hare et al. [8] advocate the use of agents as a key enabler in the delivery of ambient intelligence. Thus, in an AmI framework for servicing elderly and disabled (mobility impaired people) the role of agent technology is crucial.

In this paper we present a part of the work proposed in the Integrated Project (IP) "Ambient Intelligence System of Agents for Knowledge-based and Integrated Services for Mobility Impaired users" (ASK-IT, IST-2003-511298), which aims to offer infomobility services to mobility impaired people and support them while on the move. We briefly present the part of the agent-based system that is related to the integration of ambient intelligence in personal travel assistance and focus in showing how we integrate an agent platform compliant to the FIPA standard (Foundation for Intelligent Physical Agents, http://www.fipa.org) with the OSGi

(Open Service Gateway initiative, http://www.osgi.org) service oriented middleware [4].

The rest of the paper is organized as follows: In section 2 we provide a brief presentation of the multi-agent system (MAS) that we conceived for addressing the ASK-IT challenges with regard to ambient intelligence and introduce the need for the integration of the MAS in an overall service oriented architecture (SOA). Following, we firstly present the methodology for integrating the FIPA-compliant agent platform in the OSGi framework in section 3, and then, the integrated architecture for the ASK-IT server and client in section 4. Finally, we conclude in section 5.

2. The Multi-Agent System

The background on relevant agent architectures is the FIPA Personal Travel Assistance [5] standard and the results of the Im@gine IT project [6] that addressed open issues defined by FIPA [5]. The JADE-Leap (Java Agent Development Environment – Lightweight Extensible Agent Platform, http://jade.tilab.com) framework allows for implementing agents on nomad devices like PDAs, laptops and smart phones. Taking all the above into consideration, the proposed ASK-IT architecture is an evolution of the Im@gine IT architecture in two ways:

a. it proposes a server side dynamic coalition formation of specialised agents aiming to serve users with more than one types of impairments (this issue is beyond the scope of this paper and is discussed in [7])
b. it integrates ambient intelligence through the introduction of two new types of agents on the user's device (other than the classical personal assistant type), and,

The family of agents that integrate ambient intelligence includes the following:

- The *Personal Wearable Intelligent Device Agent (PEDA*, acting as a FIPA Mini-Personal Travel Assistant for persons with impairments) that provides the personalized infomobility services to the user
- *Ambient Intelligence Service Agent (AESA)* that configures the environment of the user according to his habits/needs (new type of agent)
- The *Personal Wearable Communication Device Agent (PWDA)* that monitors the user's sensors and provides information either directly to the user or the Personal Wearable Intelligent Device agent in cases of emergency (new type of agent)

In ASK-IT not all cooperating software components are agents, therefore one main challenge of our work was related to the way to connect all the identified modules and agents. Such modules are the *Localization Module* that produces accurate coordinates of the user, the *Navigation Module* that navigates the user to its destination, the *User Interface Module,* the *Domotic Services Module* that allows the user to control and monitor devices in his household (heater, air-condition, etc).

The Open Services Gateway initiative (OSGi) technology provides a service-oriented, component-based environment for developers and offers standardized ways to manage the software lifecycle. It was chosen for integrating all the participating components because of its offering the following possibilities:

a. Firstly, in the same virtual machine, bundles (that is how the OSGi components are named) can be installed, started, stopped, or uninstalled, dynamically on runtime. This feature allows for the best utilization of resources of nomad devices (low computing power).
b. Secondly, a bundle can import but also export java packages when installed. In Java, there is normally a single classpath that contains all the available packages and resources. The OSGi framework caters for controlled linking between different software modules, as they are installed on runtime.
c. Finally, the bundles can locate and invoke services offered by other bundles. This allows for dynamic interoperability between our different components. Services definition is easy and intuitive, as it is based on common Java interfaces definition. Then, these interfaces' implementation classes are started by an OSGi mechanism that undertakes the task of advertising the implemented interfaces in the framework. Then, the OSGi Application Programming Interface (API) can be used for locating and invoking the services.

3. The Integration Methodology

The proposed integration of the FIPA agent platform and OSGi should satisfy the following goals:

- Provide an architecture where agents can simultaneously execute in both the agent platform where they are created and the OSGi architecture integrating the above platform. Any agents that would normally execute in the selected agent platform can also execute normally in the context of the platform's integration in the OSGi architecture.
- Allow the agents to use the OSGi services in an agent instance independent manner. For example, software agents invoke existing web services in a standardized way, having the only prerequisites that the agent has access to the internet and that the service is available. Following this paradigm, the agent should have access to existing OSGi services with the only prerequisites that the agent's platform is integrated with an OSGi platform and the services are available.
- Allow the agents to offer themselves services to the OSGi framework in order to seamlessly integrate with different software modules.

In order to realize the above goals we integrated the agent platform in the OSGi framework and instantiated it as an OSGi service. In Figure 1 the reader can see the operating system on top of which a Java virtual machine executes and the OSGi framework. Different bundles are instantiated, one of which is the agent platform bundle. This approach is more efficient because the OSGi framework offers an environment where any kind of application can execute.

The process for integrating an agent platform into the OSGi SoA framework can be described as follows:

a. Define the ontology that will be common for all bundles and used for defining the services signatures (in the case that all the signatures will use simple Java classes, like Integer and String, then there is no need for an ontology)
b. Define the java interfaces for the services that will be offered by each bundle (all interfaces definitions may import the ontology bundle)
c. Define the different bundles, each implementing the relevant interfaces. All bundles dynamically import the ontology and service descriptions bundles. One of these bundles will be the multi-agent system bundle
d. Select the architecture for directing events from the MAS bundle to the different agents

The final step is relevant to selecting a method for communication between objects and agents. In this case, the multi-agent system bundle instance needs to communicate with the agents. In the JADE-Leap documentation one can find such tools, like in the `SocketProxyAgent` package that defines a JADE agent that can be executed to communicate with remote clients via a plain TCP/IP socket. This choice is especially convenient for nomad device applications, where, due to limited available resources, only basic Java libraries, such as plain TCP/IP sockets, are allowed to execute.

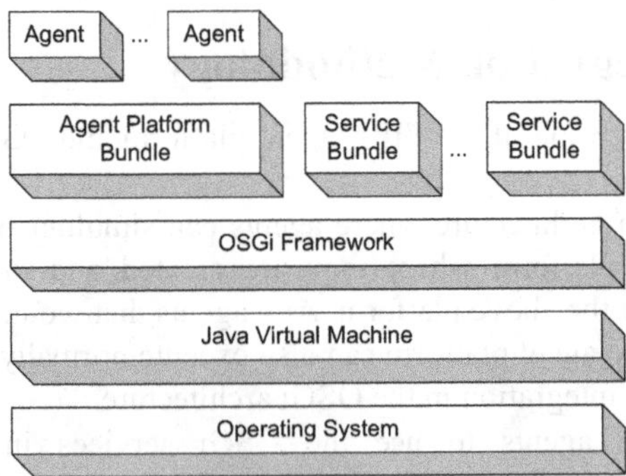

Figure 1: Computing environment structure (five layers)

After a developer has followed this process he can start defining his agents using OSGi services for sensing and acting on his environment, but, also for tracking changes in the environment. Such changes reflect the sudden availability or non-availability of a specific service and OSGi offers the possibility for informing interested bundles about the appearance of specific services.

4. Ambient Intelligence Architecture

In this section we show, as an example, how precisely the OSGi – agent platform integration can provide an efficient solution for the development of ambient intelligence applications, which is our case. Such an application poses a specific limitation on the resources that can be employed on the nomad device but also on the capability for communication with the outside world. The protocol proposed in [2] and the execution of the JADE-Leap agents in split container mode can address these problems. The split execution mode means that the agent platform on the nomad device needs to depend on another agent platform that uses a static IP address somewhere on the internet.

In Figure 2 the reader can see the architecture for our application. The diagram type used is the UML deployment diagram (Unified Modeling Language, http://www.uml.org). The light grey packages show the different identified components, while the dark grey ones depict the open source libraries used, i.e. the knopflerfish OSGi framework (http://www.knopflerfish.org) and the JADE-Leap framework. The domain ontology (*JADE Ontology Beans* component) has been developed using the JADE ontology beans methodology (see [3]). This approach allows for integrating different component manufacturers' modules, some of which could even be application independent. For example, we used as a *Simple Service Bundle* a localization module that was developed by a third party manufacturer and which was distributed as an OSGi bundle. The *Localization, Navigation, Domotics, User Interface* modules were made available to the platform as OSGi bundles.

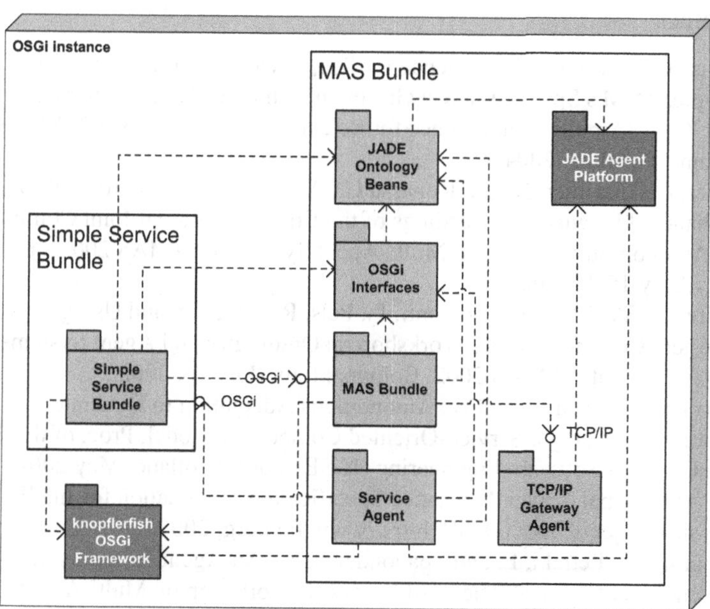

Figure 2: OSGi – agent platform integration architecture on a nomad device

The resulting ambient intelligence system can execute on any nomad device, i.e. it includes the possibility to execute on mobile phones that is the most restricted device type. Figure 2 shows the MAS Bundle and its various components. The *MAS Bundle* component is an implementation class of the MAS Bundle interface (that defines the services that the agents defined in the *Service Agent* component offer) that is included with all other bundles interfaces in the *OSGi Interfaces* component. The *TCP/IP Gateway Agent* gets requests by the *MAS Bundle* instance using TCP/IP plain sockets, communicates with the interested *Service Agent* (e.g. the PEDA or PWDA agent) using ACL messages and replies through the original socket port to the MAS bundle.

The ontology and the OSGi interfaces are in the same bundle with the MAS because the ontology is dependent on the JADE library and the interfaces on the ontology. Also, the JADE architecture does not permit for the JADE files to be installed in a bundle and the agents to be launched by another. Therefore, this architecture demands that all those components be included in the same bundle.

5. Conclusion

In this paper we presented certain aspects of an agent-based system for the personal travel assistance (PTA) domain. We addressed the issue of integrating personal travel assistance applications with ambient intelligence and showed how to integrate an agent platform in a service oriented architecture. We provided a methodology and architectural guidelines that other developers can follow in order to develop their own ambient intelligence, agent-based applications.

References

1. Abascal, J.. Ambient Intelligence for People with Disabilities and Elderly People. ACM's Special Interest Group on Computer-Human Interaction (SIGCHI), Ambient Intelligence for Scientific Discovery (AISD) Workshop, Vienna, April 25, 2004
2. Caire, G., Lhuillier, N. and Rimassa G., A communication protocol for agents on handheld devices. Proceedings of the first International Joint Conference on Autonomous Agents and Multi-Agent Systems (AAMAS 2002), Bologna, Italy, July 15-19, 2002
3. Caire, G., Van Aart, C., Bergenti, F., Pels, R.. Creating and Using Ontologies in Agent Communication. Workshop on Ontologies and Agent Systems (OAS'2002) at AAMAS 2002, Bologna, Italy, July 16, 2002
4. Cervantes, H. and Hall, R.S., Autonomous Adaptation to Dynamic Availability Using a Service-Oriented Component Model. Proc. of the 26th Int. Conf. on Software Engineering (ICSE 2004), Scotland, May 2004.
5. FIPA: Personal Travel Assistance Specification. Foundation for Intelligent Physical Agents, XC00080B, http://www.fipa.org, 2001
6. Moraitis, P., Petraki, E. and Spanoudakis, N., An Agent-Based System for Infomobility Services. The third European Workshop on Multi-Agent Systems (EUMAS2005), Brussels, Belgium, December 7 - 8, 2005
7. Moraitis, P., Spanoudakis N.. Argumentation-based Agent Interaction in an Ambient Intelligence Context. IEEE Intelligent Systems, Special Issue on Argumentation Technology, Nov/Dec '07, 2007 (to appear)
8. O'Hare, G. M. P., O'Grady, M. J., Keegan, S., O'Kane, D., Tynan, R. and Marsh, D.. Intelligent Agile Agents: Active Enablers for Ambient Intelligence. ACM's Special Interest Group on Computer-Human Interaction (SIGCHI), Ambient Intelligence for Scientific Discovery (AISD) Workshop, Vienna, April 25, 2004